New York and Eastern States

Who's Who in America's Restaurants™

1983-84 edition

OTHER EDITIONS OF WHO'S WHO IN AMERICA'S RESTAURANTS

1982 New York and Eastern States
deluxe limited edition

OTHER BOOKS BY SHELDON LANDWEHR

New York's Golden Restaurant Register
New York City and Long Island Country Dining

New York and Eastern States

Who's Who
in America's Restaurants™

1983-84 edition

**Compiled and Edited
by Sheldon Landwehr**

Who's Who in Restaurants, Inc.

1841 Broadway
New York, New York 10023

EDITOR-IN-CHIEF
Sheldon Landwehr

ASSISTANT EDITOR
Konstantinos T. Patukas

ASSOCIATE EDITORS
Bob Henry
Judy Ross
Jesse James Leaf
Doris Lear-Feldman
Barbara de Sherbinin

ILLUSTRATOR
Michael Kaplan

ART DIRECTOR
Gloria Gregurovich

BUSINESS AND MARKETING MANAGER
Arthur J. Silverman

TYPESETTING
Wordsmythe Typographers

First edition

Library of Congress Number:
LC 82-6457944

1983 Hardcover edition
ISBN 0-910297-01-0

1983 Softcover edition
ISBN 0-910297-02-9

ISSN 0735-1801, both 1983 editions

Standard Address Number
SAN 241-4775

Who's Who in Restaurants, Inc.
1841 Broadway, Suite 902
New York, N.Y., 10023
(212) 581-0360

This book is dedicated to Stony
whose unique appreciation of food, and of life,
was an inspiration to all who knew him.
1971-1983

Contents

New York and Eastern States

Who's Who in America's Restaurants™

1983-84 edition

Introduction

The aim of this book is to provide the discriminating individual as well as the business executive with the most up-to-date, comprehensive gastronomical information concerning restaurants in America's most frequented cities and locales throughout the greater Eastern Seaboard: New York City, near-by Long Island, the District of Columbia, Philadelphia, Atlanta, Boston, Miami, and every other major city, urban center, and surburban location up and down the East Coast.

Good food and good service are the principal basis for selection of the dining establishments described herein. Atmosphere, decorations, drinks, music, entertainment, and the status of the patrons are weighed and considered but only as secondary factors in the selection process.

This registry brings to your attention 140 full page restaurant editorial profile features, handsomely illustrated and alphabetically arranged by name in the first part of this volume. As a means of quick reference, each of these restaurant editoral profiles includes all pertinent facts such as city and state, a price guide, and all other specific information after the dark line at the end of each feature.

The second segment contains over 6,000 restaurant listings arranged geographically, making it simple to look for a restaurant in a certain city or area. Each listing includes restaurant name, location, type of cuisine, telephone, days open, private party facilities, credit cards accepted, and the name of the owner.

The third segment is an alphabetized index that lets you quickly locate any particular restaurant by name, be it an editorial profile or geographic listing, as it is here cross-referenced showing the page number on which to find more detailed information.

In compiling a book of this scope, a number of difficulties at once become apparent, and it would be senseless to allege that this register exhausts the subject. There are so many thousands of restaurants on America's East Coast that size alone demands that the majority be omitted. Hopefully, however, very few above-average restaurants have been ignored.

While our primary criteria for inclusion are good food and service, we do, from time to time, deviate from purely epicurean considerations in order to pass on worthwhile tidbits of history and information about certain unique establishments. This means that inclusion and the amount of space devoted to any single restaurant is not necessarily an endorsement of its culinary importance. Any number of fine restaurants have little or no history; some restaurants that are not so hot have a lot.

We have striven to include low-priced, moderately-priced and high-priced restaurants, but it should be noted that this book is not designed for those who are merely seeking adequate food at budget prices; it is for those who are seeking fine *cuisine* and are ready to shell out for it if need be—not excessively, but as calibre dictates. As we have not been influenced by price, we are equally unimpressed by grandeur; some of America's most modest establishments provide some of the most delicious meals.

Though we have struggled for evenhandedness, our remarks and opinions may reveal a few preferences, as we have grown particularly fond of certain restaurants and their considerably efficacious proprietors.

Now here are a few notes, caveats, and tips on using this book: Wines and spirits are a subject in themselves, and since our theme is food, we have avoided mentioning them in the main. Since most restaurants described offer wines and cocktails, we have found it preferable to state where they do not serve alcoholic beverages, rather than where they do.

To protect your billfold against uncomfortable surprises, we have set up the following price scale:

Inexpensive means you can get off for $15 or less, for an average dinner (appetizer, entree, and dessert), exclusive of drinks and tips.

Inexpensive to Moderate means that an average dinner would cost anywhere from $15 to $25 per person, exclusive of drinks and tips.

Moderate means that an average dinner would cost approximately $30 per person, exclusive of cocktails, wines and tips.

Moderate to Expensive means that an average dinner would cost anywhere from $35 to $50 per person, exclusive of drinks and tips.

Expensive means that an average dinner would cost more than $50 per person, exclusive of drinks and tips.

Luncheon costs, except at ultra-swank places, can be figures at about 60% of dinner costs. Where there is a *prix fixe* dinner or luncheon, you know your complete costs upfront.

Bear in mind that the average costs quoted in this book were in effect at the time of publication and are subject to change at any time.

The following is an explanation of the abbreviations used when referring to credit cards:

American Express (AE)
Diners Club (DC)
Carte Blanche (CB)
Mastercard (MC)
Visa (VISA)

Hopefully this restaurant registry will become a well-thumbed addition to your personal library. More than anything else, it represents a diversity of provocative culinary adventures.

So saying, I wish you all *bon appetit*.

SHELDON LANDWEHR
Editor-in-Chief

Restaurant Editorial Profiles

Alphabetized, full-page illustrated
restaurant features

Alfredo the Original of Rome

This is a busy Italian restaurant in the base of the Citicorp Center decorated in modern functionality suited for the high-turnover lunch and dinners. Where the decor is sharp edges, smooth lines, and primary colors, the cuisine is fresh, knowingly prepared, and lushly eye-appealing.

Alfredo the Original of Rome is owned by Guido Bellanca, a gentlemen who has known the acquaintance of *the* Alfredo—inventor of the pasta dish that bears his name. Mr. Bellanca is a consumate businessman, a dapper gourmand who has had the good fortune to turn his avocation into his business by acquiring the rights to use Alfredo's name, hiring the best available restaurant personnel, and overseeing the whole operation from his utilitarian Citicorp offices.

Dinner ranges from a creamy smooth and butter-rich *paglia e fieno* to a hearty *gnocchi al ragu di pomodoro* that is yeasty with potato dough and matched to a simple meat sauce. Veal is offered in all possible incarnations and is, in every case, cooked-to-order, delicately seasoned, and offered in a well-sized serving.

First courses such as the baked clams *Puccini* were among the best. All of Alfredo's pasta comes in a smaller portion for enjoyment as an appetizer and the linguine with red clam sauce was a smorgasbord of clams, basil, red sauce, and pasta topped with clams in the shell and dusted with fresh basil. The fried zucchini was crisp, sweet, and tasted especially fresh, and the famous fettucine was a textbook presentation of harmonious richness sparked with flakes of freshly ground black pepper. The best of the desserts was a *zuppa inglese* dotted with morsels of bittersweet chocolate in a lush yet airy custard that was sprinkled with cinnamon and baker's sugar.

153 East 53 Street
New York, N.Y., 10022
(212) 371-3367

- *Italian Cuisine*
- *Moderately priced*
- *Open 7 days for lunch and dinner*
- *Accepts reservations and major credit cards*
- *Limited, predominantly Italian wine list*

Armando's Seafood Barge

Out on the northern lip of eastern Long Island, on beautiful Peconic Bay is Armando's Seafood Barge. Homespun and rustic, this is a restaurant with a heritage of the sea—it makes its home on the bay's edge, it serves sparkling fresh products of the sea, and it even boasts clams that are literally dug up in its backyard.

Inside are rough-hewn wood and large expanses of window overlooking the boundless bay with its sunlight or moonlight dancing on the water, its sunsets throwing paint across the sky, and sea birds soaring and swooping before your eyes. The interior counterpoint is a sprawling expanse of rustic wood tables unadorned of anything save the condiments one finds in the kitchen at home. The whole mood is one of pleasant wholesomeness.

Host, chef and proprietor Armando J. Cappa is a lively, expansive man, justly proud of his establishment. His vivacious magic is reflected in the pace of his staff, the size of the portions and the honesty of the menu. Big portions are the rule here—at all times and for all categories. The menu is large, but simple—and comprehensive. There is listed practically every seafood item that can be caught, or dug within a stone's throw of the barge.

Appetizers are kept to the bare minimum—there are clams, shrimp and tomato juice—and only two soups, Manhattan and New England clam chowder. While you wonder at the juicy taste of the clams, or roll the clammy, rich tomato Manhattan or creamy New England chowder around your tongue, the kitchen is preparing your entree from scratch.

There are many favorites among the regulars at Armando's. The lobster, of course. You can get a succulent four-pounder steamed to tasty perfection and served with golden drawn butter. The soft shell crabs are most popular: plump and juicy, fork-tender—they keep 'em alive until they're cooked. Then they are coated in a light batter and fried to a nutlike crispness. You might also try to ignore the large shrimp stuffed with crabmeat, simmered in garlic butter and broiled to an aromatic finish, the lightly-breaded calamari or the fresh flounder in wine sauce. But who's to blame when you might chance upon the weakfish, bluefish or trout expertly broiled, or the eels—yes, this might be the day you discover this wonderful food.

For the unabashed landlubber, Armando can whip up a tender and sizzling sirloin or chicken, served with crispy onion rings.

As for desserts, those pies are homemade by Armando's mother. And if you don't have room—take a piece home in a doggie bag, too good to pass by.

Route 25 on Peconic Bay
Southold, L.I., N.Y., 11971
(516) 765-3010

- *Seafood cuisine*
- *Priced moderate*
- *Open 7 days for lunch and dinner May through September*
- *Accepts reservations and all major credit cards*
- *Boat docking facilities available*

Arthur's Eating House

Arthur Horowitz founded a chain of very pragmatic, functional eating places called Junior's, and Arthur's Eating House could be considered the restaurant where Arthur decided to get away from all that and try something completely different. But Arthur knows restaurants, and with his Eating House he has succeeded wonderfully.

The Eating House is large, seating more than 250, and to match the physical size Arthur has made up a menu big enough for everyone to find a personal all-time favorite.

If a dish of stone crabs is one of your favorite appetizers, for instance, Arthur's serves them fresh-off-the-boat with spicy, pungent mustard sauce. Or maybe you prefer to begin a meal with a pasta course. The *canneloni Gianninni* is stuffed with a mixture of beef, sausage, and onions, and it's topped with a hearty tomato sauce and plenty of cheese. Or try the excellent spinach crepes oriental, crepes filled with a blend of fresh spinach, sauteed onions, pimentoes, and eggs, and covered by a rich mustard and curry sauce.

Among the entrees are a nicely broiled sampling of red snapper or salmon, and a broiled, double thick rib veal chop smothered in sauteed mushrooms. The New York cut sirloin for two is expertly carved and served with fresh green peppers, mushrooms, and sauteed onions. The roast duckling comes with a dish of wild rice, some strawberry apple sauce, and a delicately sweet fruit sauce. There's also calf's liver, veal *mercado,* Hungarian beef goulash, prime rib, and a dozen or so fresh shellfish and fish selections to choose from.

The desserts are worth investigating, especially the chocolate Kahlua cake. The wine list, which specializes in California wines, has relatively modest prices.

Arthur has done up his restaurant in an extremely comfortable, pleasant—yet sophisticated—manner; it's someplace on the opposite end of the spectrum from stuffy French "ambience." Huge amber glass lights illuminate the burnt orange and earth tones which dominate the dining rooms, with the result being a relaxing and soothing mood. Sit in the tall, padded booths if privacy is what you want. And wherever you sit you can listen to the pianist playing softly and gaze at one of the many classic examples of contemporary art. Artists such as Rouault, Calder, Stella, and Warhol all have works hanging on Arthur's walls.

Arthur's Eating House is by now a Miami institution—and deservedly so. Excellent food in a pleasant surrounding at a moderate price—it's exactly what a restaurant should be.

1444 Biscayne Boulevard
Miami, Fla., 33137
(305) 371-1444

- *Continental Cuisine/Seafood*
- *Moderately priced*
- *Open Monday through Saturday for lunch; seven days for dinner*
- *All major credit cards and reservations accepted*

Arturo's

This is an establishment with a history written by dedicated restaurateurs—begun more than two decades ago by Arturo Gismandi, and now owned by his sons: chef Guiseppe Gismandi and his brother Vincenzo, the host.

What characterizes Arturo's is a total commitment to control. The buying, cooking, saucing, and serving are carried out by the Gismandi's to exceptionally high standards. Some of their best offerings were invented right here on the premises, sauces are prepared tableside to keep them fresh and hot, even the herbs are homegrown.

Arturo's provides a spacious, attractive environment for its dining. The dining room is woodpaneled and not overly elaborate. There are tables in the bar area which share tenancy with a tank of lobsters—guarantee of freshness for real lovers of this shellfish. Candlelight nestles in hurricane lamps and waiters discreetly scurry in formal roundsmaking.

The cooking here is rich in home-cooked sauces and wine-simmered meats and seafood that goes from the delicate to the hearty. Not to be missed is Arturo's own *torta primavera,* an appetizer that is made from several layers of crepe interspersed with spinach, celery, prosciutto, provolone, roasted peppers, tomato, veal *pate,* egg, mayonnaise and topped with a sauce that ties all the disparate flavors together into a quite amazing whole. Other of the antipasto are likewise bathed in attention. *Zuppa di mussels* is a large plate of plump mussels in an abundantly tasty *marinara* sauce and the fried calamari is a perfection of golden, tender squid surrounded by a special tomato sauce.

Pastas here are all homemade and offer a range of taste for every palate. There is a spicy spaghetti *Gismondi,* flamed with vodka and cooked tableside with smoked salmon, bacon, onion, butter, parsley, heavy cream and cheese. Lighter tastes will go for the smooth-as-silk *fettuccine Alfredo* or the mellow *spaghetti carbonara.*

Space forbids exploring the rest of Arturo's unusual menu, but high on your list should be the plump shrimp *scampi, pollo Romana* and *veal pizzaiola.*

246-04 Jericho Turnpike
Bellerose, L.I., N.Y., 11426
(516) FL2-7418

- *Italian Cuisine*
- *Moderate to expensive*
- *Open 6 days for lunch and dinner; closed Tuesdays*
- *Reservations essential. Accepts all major credit cards*
- *Private party facilities for between 20 and 50 persons*

The Assembly

Although big tender steaks and oversized lobsters are the pride of the House, the menu at The Assembly departs from strict steakhouse style to offer something to please everyone. For many years, this spacious full-service facility has functioned almost as a dining "club" for well-heeled sightseers, local businessmen, and pre-theater diners in the popular Rockefeller Plaza area. Seated in the high-ceilinged salon, decorated in restful Autumnal tones of pumpkin, beige and brown, both regulars and newcomers are served by a professional, mature staff. Tables are widely spaced, between walls of window-pane mirrors and narrow wood-panelling that are hung with framed photographs of celebrity clients.

Appetizers include all the traditionals, from smooth chopped liver and cheese-crusted onion soup to sparkling-fresh briny oysters and clams. A crouton-crunchy Caesar salad prepared tableside is a major Event—although it courts redundancy, considering the House salad of curly red-leaf lettuce and other garden-glories in a creamy garlic dressing that accompanies all entrees.

Even tastier than the usual sirloin, whose beefy flavor attests to a careful aging process, is the same well-marbled and tender cut as a "garlic steak" crusty with aromatic bits of the fresh bulb. The filet mignon is a two-inch-thick pillow running natural juices into the flanking trio of giant mushroom caps. And grand-standing as a crowd-pleaser that banishes the tension of decision-making, a Surf 'N Turf combo pairs a smaller, slightly thinner filet with a meaty lobster tail.

The menu provides the varied clientele with a broad range of Italian, veal, chicken, and seafood selections as well. However, to complete the Steakhouse Experience, one should not overlook the smooth, nutmeggy creamed spinach; the curly, delicately battered onion rings; and the mini-cubes of German-fried potatoes that are crunchy all over.

A rolling dessert cart is a veritable museum of rich favorites: chocolate-candy coated *ganache* cake layered with mousse, vies with marzipan-bedded berries in a cookie-crust, creamy strawberry cheesecake—or simply the fresh berries with a dollop of whipped cream.

An unusually well-selected and considerately-priced wine list appears on the back of the menu— but if you appreciate treasures, ask for the very special Vintage List.

16 West 51st Street
New York, N.Y., 10020
(212) 581-3580

- *Steakhouse, Seafood, American-Italian Specialties*
- *Priced moderate to high*
- *Open Monday through Friday for lunch and dinner; Closed Saturday and Sunday*
- *Private party facilities for 20 to 40*
- *Accepting reservations and all major credit cards*

Attilio's

One of the more engaging Northern Italian restaurants on Long Island is Attilio's. The owners are the chef Attilio Vosilla and his wife, Yolanda, and they are—like their surroundings—without pretense or affectation.

Domiciled in a charming old converted country house (recently expanded to accommodate about 100 persons in two comfortable dining rooms) with walls of aged brick, wood, and paper; bordered by windows and extravagent leaded-glass Gothic type panels, Attilio's has both an atmosphere and a menu exuding polish and *savoir-faire*. Its fresh white linen and candlelit tables are the staging for leisurely enjoyment of a fully homemade meal.

You may start with time-honored appetizers such as proscuitto with fresh melon, or you may delve into unexplored delicacies such as a special dish of thin green noodles tucked with finely chopped smoked salmon and shallots in a fragrant tomato sauce. Or you may warm yourself with one of the satisfying bowls of onion, dumpling, egg drop, or vegetable soup that are daily offered.

Entrees are all made to order and include an array of pasta, fish (fresh daily), chicken, beef and veal dishes—all very well done in Attilio's unique style. Just for example: chicken and sausage peasant style, soothed in brown sauce and mushrooms; veal chop *all'attilio*, lightly breaded, sauteed and served under a mantle of creamy Fontina cheese; sea trout with capers, olives and tomato. Accompaniments, so often a second thought, are here given star billing. The potatoes, seasoned with sage and Jerusalem artichokes, are outstanding. As are the desserts. How does poached pear topped with fresh meringue sound? Or a generous slice of hot apple strudel topped with whipped cream?

In short, Attilio's is as close as you can get for a satisfying and nourishing meal.

59-28 Little Neck Parkway
Little Neck, N.Y., 11363
(212) 224-5715

- *Northern Italian Cuisine*
- *Priced Moderate*
- *Accepts reservations and AE, VISA, MC*
- *Open Monday through Friday for lunch; Monday through Saturday for dinner; Closed Sunday*
- *Jackets recommended*
- *Wine list and private party facilities available*

Au Manoir

This is a long standing French restaurant—inviting, hospitable, charming. It has built its reputation on the comfort and satisfaction of its patrons. The ambiance of a French bistro is attained by its rich wood beams, ceramic tile murals, starched white linen, provincial-style chairs and warm red wool banquettes. Unlike some similar establishments, the waiters here are friendly and most helpful. They will gladly guide you through the large menu which is a billboard of *haute cuisine*, *cuisine regionale* or *bourgeoise*. There are numerous specialties of the day, and not to inquire would to be to miss the choice between it and a delicate bass *beurre blanc*, a moist and flavorsome *fricassee de veau* with a cream cheese sauce or perhaps the *carre d'agneau persille*, the rack of lamb at flavors' edge with parsley and garlic.

There is an unusually large list of appetizers at Au Manoir. A fine *pate maison*, quiche *Lorraine*, smoked ham, herring, *moules au chablis* (mussels gently simmered with chablis and herbs), *escargots*, a delicious *saucisson chaud* (hot salami and potatoes), smoked salmon, and oysters—and this doesn't exhaust the selection!

The dessert choice is equally as mind-boggling. But try not to pass the *mille feuilles*, a fantasy of whipped cream and pastry. Lunch is evey bit as popular as dinner, so reservations might be in order.

---

120 East 56th Street
New York, N.Y., 10022
(212) 753-1447

- *French Cuisine*
- *Priced moderate to high*
- *Open 6 days for lunch and dinner; Closed Sundays and holidays*
- *Accepts reservations and all major credit cards*

Aux Beaux Champs

Aux Beau Champs is the French restaurant of the Four Seasons Hotel in Washington, D.C. It is handsomely furnished, finished with smartly appointed tables, and thickly carpeted in a navy provincial brocade. Tall potted plants provide a lush green contrast to beige velvet upholstery and banquettes.

There are first courses that range from Beluga caviar to *escargots,* wild mushrooms, and pine nuts in red wine sauce. Soups are an equally impressive numbering, from corn bisque dotted with scallops to leek and onion soup flavored with vermouth. The *pates* are all smoothly textured and delicately seasoned. On the day we visited the featured *pates* were fish, rabbit, and *fois gras* in aspic.

The wine list includes a number of fine Californians, as well as almost legendary French Bordeaux and Burgundy labels—alas, too immature for serious consideration, but promise in coming years to provide Aux Beaux Champs with a superior cellar.

Seafood entrees include steamed rockfish with warmed shallot vinaigrette, a selection of grilled fishes, and scallops in an accomplished lobster sauce.

One especially promising entree is three mignonettes of prime meats—beef, lamb, and veal—with an equal number of mustard sauces—tarragon, green peppercorn, and meaux mustard. Another is a loin of venison in juniper and ginger sauce, a dish that shows certain *nouvelle* influences have reached the Aux Beaux Champs kitchens. A lighter meal, better complemented over lunch or with a consomme, is the supreme of chicken champagne made with fresh peppers, peppercorns, and bananas in a delicate cream sauce.

Desserts usually include a choice of two freshly-made sorbets, hazelnuts and almond meringue with lemon cream and pureed strawberries, crepes with orange and curacao for two, or a chestnut and ginger *mousse* in a tulip bisquit.

The menu opens vast new possibilities for dinner, and Aux Beaux Champs provides a suitably refined and hushed atmosphere in which to sample them.

Four Seasons Hotel
2800 Pennsylvania Avenue
Georgetown, Washington, D.C., 20007
(202) 342-0444

- *French Cuisine*
- *Priced expensive*
- *Open Monday through Saturday for breakfast; Monday through Friday for lunch; 7 days for dinner; Sunday brunch; Saturday breakfast til 3:00 PM*
- *Accepts reservations and all major credit cards*
- *Private party facilities available*

Barbetta

However much we enjoy posh dining and the feeling of sumptuous attention we receive at some of the rare fine restaurants today, there is still that longing after the fantasy engendered by motion picture recreations of those few special and elegant restaurants that bejeweled turn-of-the-century New York. We know of Delmonico's and Sherry's only through history. We can never experience the entrances of marble, plush carpeting, crystal chandeliers and curtained walled sumptuousness. These are all gone, pulled down by a city that seemingly refuses to look back.

But there is one opportunity to bridge that long distance between eras. It is Barbetta, dating back to 1906, when Sebastian Maioglio founded this Italian restaurant for the lower and middle income classes that knew what good cooking was all about.

After fifty years of continuous service Sebastian retired and closed his venerable establishment. But those who thought that an era had indeed ended underestimated the Maioglio legacy—both financial and genetic. Old Sebastian had left behind a sizeable estate and ownership to his daughter Laura. She decided to recreate Barbetta in a new image—to build the most elegant Italian restaurant in the city. Laura Maioglio, an art major at Bryn Mawr, succeeded.

Both in its design and cuisine, the theme of Barbetta is Piedmontese. The decor is luxurious. Chairs are upholstered in needle-point and arranged around cocktail tables with privacy all around. The carpeting is plush, and a chandelier that once hung in Victor Emmanual's palace now hangs overhead. Delicate sconces cast soft light on handcarved wood panels on which glitter gold picture frames. This recapture of a lost time is carried out-of-doors to a spacious, stone-walled garden landscaped with lush trees, grape vines, seasonal flowers and a baroque pool and fountain with cherubs straddling dolphins.

The kitchen embraces Piedmontese cuisine, that special corner of Italy in the northwest. And it is one of the very few restaurants in New York, yes the world, that provides meals redolent in fresh white truffles. It is the only restaurant in the city with trufflehounds roaming the woods of the Piemonte.

It would be tiresome to recite adjectives of fine dining and list the creations coming from Barbetta's kitchen. The chicken, pasta, and veal dishes are generally faultless in style and execution, and those formulated with the white truffle are quite unique.

321 West 46 Street
New York, N.Y., 10036
(212) 246-9171

- *Italian Cuisine*
- *Expensive*
- *Reservations advised, necessary for the garden. All major credit cards accepted*
- *Open seven days for lunch and dinner*
- *Private party facilities for between 4 and 300 persons; there are four private party rooms available*

Baron's Cove Inn

Anthony Mazzarella can do a seafood restaurant, this much is now clear. He has two Water Front Crab Houses (in Manhattan and Queens) and he also has the Baron's Cove Inn. But do not mistake them for a chain; by design each location has its own atmosphere and feeling, and each is a separate and distinct restaurant.

But what Anthony has learned in one he has transferred to another, hence they share common knowledge. And one of the first things he learned was that if it's not fresh it doesn't get served. The giant lobster tails are frozen—otherwise they'd get destroyed in transit—but the only thing else in the freezer is ice cream.

The look at Baron's Cove Inn is that of "old style fishhouse." A beamed ceiling, wood trimmed walls adorned with nautical fixtures, an inviting brick fireplace, wooden captain's chairs, the hardwood floor, the old wood bar, and the many hanging plants all combine to give the place a warm and rustic appearance. It's a comfortable and relaxing place to dine.

As already implied, the food at Baron's Cove Inn is seafood. Of course there's a steak, and that peculiarly American offering "Surf and Turf," but ordering those would be like going to a Bavarian beer house and drinking wine—what this place is about is fresh seafood.

The fishes are broiled, sauteed, and fried—take your pick—and whatever way the fish is prepared it's done properly. But there's also raw clams and oysters on the half shell. Shrimp cocktail with a rich, pungent sauce. Lusty deep fried scallops, New Orleans style hot, spicy shrimp—"you peel 'em."

And then there are the house specials. Start with the hot seafood antipasto—a large platter of shrimp stuffed with crabmeat, fried filet of a whitefish, stuffed clams, fried squid, and fried zucchini, all with a light *marinara* sauce on the side. Or go for the fresh lobster, broiled or steamed. And of course there is their own justifiably famous version of *bouillabaisse*—prepared with a whole steamed lobster, clams, shrimp, crab, and mussels on a bed of linguine cooked *al dente*, and again with that *marinara* sauce. It's delicious.

And with all the entrees comes a salad and a nicely cooked vegetable dish, making Baron's Cove Inn a good value as well as a place to get good seafood.

West Water Street,
Sag Harbor, L.I., N.Y., 11963
(516) 725-3332

- *Seafood Cuisine*
- *Priced moderate*
- *Open 7 days for lunch and dinner from April through September; 5 days for lunch and dinner otherwise; Closed Monday and Tuesday*
- *All major credit cards and reservations accepted*
- *Private party facilities for between 25 and 160 persons*

Beatrice Inn

A surviving and thriving breath of the fabled bohemian Greenwich Village, Beatrice Inn still receives artists, writers, and wandering diplomats in a snugly low-ceilinged expanse several steps below street level, where walls of coral stucco are softly illuminated by shaded sconces. Count three distinct areas: a romantic fireplace-alcove; a raised party room with a beamed ceiling and a wall sculpture depicting the Manhattan skyline; and the main room, triply-lined with companionably close-set square and oblong tables immaculately covered with crisp white cloths.

Well populated by local lovers of casual living plus traditional, no-nonsense Italian *cucina,* the 50-year-old facility that started as a speakeasy (the back "escape" door still testifies to insurance against police raids) continues to function as a House Party for the family and loyal fans of bubbly blond Elsie and her staunch husband "Aldo" Cardia. Because her young son and his wife also work on the premises, a concerned member of the family is always on duty here—and the quality reflects such caring supervision. Yet prices are so amazingly gentle that they might have prevailed even in the era of Dante's Beatrice, in whose honor the restaurant was named.

Most full dinners list from $9.50-$13.00 ($16.00 with sirloin steak and lamb chops)—in addition to a complete a la carte roster plus daily specials pinned to the menu on a card. Pay attention, however, to the fleeting delights that come to your mouth only by word of mouth—such as an unlisted perfumey *pesto* that Elsie explains disarmingly: "Why write it down? There's only a little, and when it's gone, it's gone." Be consoled by such honest and robust regular offerings as linguine topped with still-blushingly-rosy, freshly-chopped molluscs in a well-parslied and garlicked sauce, just oily enough to blend all the elements into a coating for the *al-dente* pasta.

An inch-thick sirloin is colorfully caparisoned in a chunky *pizzaiola* of red and green peppers, onions, and mushrooms; such extravagance is balanced by the restraint of greaselessly batter-coated pillows of sweetbreads, moist and texturally fascinating at center. Plump and juicy giant shrimp swim in a pulpy *marinara,* and a cheese blanket bubbles atop casseroles bearing veal scallops. An intriguing and palate-cleansing salad of varied lettuces, artichoke, pimento, tomato, and marinated mushrooms testifies to the contemporary awareness of a House otherwise dedicated to proven culinary traditions. Expect a *ricotta* cheesecake dessert drenched in citrus flavor, with a texture both light and custardy—perfectly counterpointed by intense espresso.

Typically, the House wines by carafe do credit to cuisine and are modestly priced at $8.00—while connoisseurs are accommodated with such oenophilic opportunities as a velvet Gattinara, a fine Barolo, and a rare Amarone—at equally considerate cost. But don't try to alert your savvy friends to Beatrice Inn: if they're the "real stuff," they've known it for years and never bothered to tell you!

285 West 12th Street
New York, N.Y., 10011
(212) 929-6165/243-9826

- *Italian/Continental Cuisine*
- *Moderate prices*
- *Open Monday through Friday for lunch; Monday through Saturday for dinner; closed Sunday*
- *Accepts reservations and all major credit cards*
- *Party facilities for 10 to 50 people*

Ben Benson's Steak House

One of the latest additions to the New York City steakhouse scene is Ben Benson's. And although it recently opened, it's already made a place for itself as a quality steakhouse.

The quickest way for a steakhouse to make that place—in an already crowded field, by the way—is to serve huge chunks of well-aged beef and cook them exactly as the customer requests. Ben Benson's does just that.

The portions are anything but modest here. The sirloins and filets weigh in at about 17 ounces (and the veal chop balances out at about 20 ounces). Ben ages the beef for three weeks before it's served, to make it tender and flavorful, then he cooks it as ordered.

Still, it usually takes more than just a good steak to get people in the door, and Ben also offers excellent appetizers as a lure. When the stone crabs are in season, they're delicious. The crab cocktail is a huge chunk of fresh-off-the-boat crabmeat with a pungent, tangy sauce. The minestrone soup is appropriately rich and hearty, and the mushroom soup is also excellent. The lobster cocktail consists of a fresh, cooked, cold one pound Maine lobster still in its shell with that same pungent sauce. It may be the best appetizer of the lot.

And the entree selection has more than just savory steaks and that mammoth sizzling and juicy veal chop. There's a filet of sole, calf's liver, prime rib, and a whole lemon-peppered chicken, to name a few.

Ben, who says that this is his eighth—and best—restaurant, carries his penchant for largeness from steers to crustaceans: putting the miniscule one pound appetizers aside, any lobster seeking main course employment and tipping the scales at less than four pounds need not apply. And should a Real Lobster Eater walk in, Ben has a few babies coming in at around 13 big ones. Now *that's* a lobster (maybe they'll let you wrestle it before they cook it).

The decor of the restaurant is pleasant enough. Dark wood trim runs around the off-white ceiling and walls, and on the walls and around the bar and dining room hang and sit antiques and examples of early American folk art—many of which Ben secured himself. There are also bronzes and old-fashioned pictures around the place, helping make the restaurant comfortable and attractive.

123 West 52 Street,
New York, N.Y., 10019
(212) 581-8888

- *Steak and Seafood Cuisine*
- *Priced moderate to high*
- *Open seven days for lunch and dinner*
- *Accepts all major credit cards and reservations*
- *Private party facilities available*

Old Original Bookbinder's

The legendary Bookbinder's remains a phenomenon. For sixteen years more than a whole century, this Philadelphia landmark eatery has welcomed savvy local gourmets—as well as every visiting *bon vivant* who knows his territory—to a museum-like complex of historical dining areas. Comfortably-seated in the spacious original salon lined with live lobster tanks or the handsome colonial Hall of Patriots—or the Gunshop Lounge, the old Blacksmith's Shop, the Benjamin Franklin Room or the William Penn Room—guests savor a panorama of American history along with a lengthy roster of fresh fare "from sea to shining sea."

Regal Maine lobsters range from one-pound-plus to four-pound giants, steamed or broiled and crabmeat-stuffed. The kingly crustaceans may also be gently-pampered in a milk stew with celery and tomatoes; sauced with a wine-rich Newburg; or lined up with shrimp and crabmeat on a refreshing cold platter. Meaty stone crab claws from Florida vie in texture and flavor with Maryland's sweetly succulent backfin lumps.

Florida pompano, simply broiled, is prized by many loyal connoisseurs in these precincts—as is the thick swordfish steak, rockfish, and rosy King Salmon—either poached juicy or broiled crispy. And for those who simply cannot make decisions, the obliging management offers their famous Combination: a thirteen-inch platter laden with oysters, fresh fish, scallops, and shrimps—plus salad and french fries to keep it all company. Steaks and *provino* veal are available for the fish-phobic, too.

Whatever their fancy, fans have learned to plan their dining to include one of the House soups: either the tangy Manhattan chowder or the unusual snapper soup, and on Friday nights only Bouillabaisse makes a challenging third choice. Like the rich desserts on display, these soups are so prized that they are sold in presentation packages in the restaurant's gift-shop—a place for browsing either before or after a meal.

A multi-paged wine list tours the vineyards of California, but also includes international selections from France, Italy, Germany, and Portugal—all at most considerate prices.

125 Walnut Street
Philadelphia, Pa., 19106
(215) 925-7027
- *Seafood, Lobsters and Steaks*
- *Moderately priced*
- *Open seven days for lunch and dinner*
- *Reservations and all major credit cards accepted*
- *Private party facilities for between 50 to 250 persons*

Cafe Geiger

The Yorkville section of New York City had at one time a predominantly German population, which spawned many excellent and inexpensive German restaurants. But recently Yorkville has begun to lose that German feel, and with that loss has come the loss of several restaurants. Fortunately, one of the best remains—Cafe Geiger. Cafe Geiger offers good authentic German food at about as reasonable a price as you're likely to find.

From the street the restaurant looks like a genuine *konditorei,* a real German pastry shop. Some sixty or so desserts fill the window, almost obscuring a view of the restaurant, but when you enter you realize that there's much more than dessert here.

The decor is pleasant enough, with the dark, wood-grain paneling being lighted by the illumination of the modern crystal chandeliers and wall sconces. But don't go to Cafe Geiger expecting immaculate table settings and posh plush decor. Go to the Cafe expecting hefty portions of hearty food.

The best dishes are, not surprisingly, the German specialties. The appetizer *oschen maul* consists of marinated beef tongue, sirloin, and sliced onions all mixed together and flavored with a vinaigrette dressing. Their homemade *suelze* (head cheese) gets a topping of the same tasty vinaigrette. Both are delicious.

The *jaegerschnitzel* is a large veal cutlet served in a brown mushroom sauce. The Bavarian *sauerbraten* is a piece of marinated beef, served with potato dumplings and red cabbage. There are of course non-German dishes as well. Broiled salmon is available, as are shrimp sauteed in white wine and garlic. The smoky split pea soup with plenty of ham chunks is particularly savory.

The Cafe does not distinguish between a lunch menu and a dinner menu, and once breakfast is over the entire selection, save for a few specialities, is available until closing, making it possible to have a large, delicious meal in the middle of the day or late at night, if that's your desire.

And for dessert, well, that window full of calories is not just for looks. From apple strudel to *weiner waffel* it's all here. And, nicely enough, you can go to the window and check them out before you eat one.

All in all, Cafe Geiger is one of the best restaurant buys in New York.

---

206 East 86 Street
New York, N.Y., 10028
(212) RE4-4428

- *German Cuisine*
- *Priced inexpensive*
- *Open seven days for lunch and dinner*
- *No credit cards*
- *Reservations accepted*
- *Private party facilities for between 2 and persons*

Captain Nemo's

Some six years ago, Captain Nemo started as a neighborhood hole-in-the-wall offering downpriced seafoods to local residents in an artsy, tunnel-like submarine-styled room that would ideally have suited Jules Verne's undersea hero. Popular response and the sudden surge of seafood appetites soon mandated a metamorphosis into a startling new elegance: all that remains of the original subterranean craft is the wall of brass-buttoned oblong portholes and the curved metal overhead beams. Romantically candelit tables are overhung with sprays of greenery bejewelled by pinpoint Christmas-lights—all reflected in cleverly-placed mirrors.

A cozy, three-table cocktail area adjoins the long bar up-front, in view of the open kitchen and the bubbling lobster-tank that guarantees only fresh live crustaceans. A large part of Captain Nemo's rapid rise to recognition is, in fact, due to these creatures—who supply the popular "Homarus Americanus" dinner: incredibly priced at just $14.95, it starts with plump steamer clams or mussels in herbed fish broth, or a thick home-made chowder; goes on to a self-selected (if you wish) one and one-quarter pound Maine lobster—either broiled or tenderly steamed; includes potato or saffron rice plus salad; and brings a *lagniappe* of a glass of white wine.

Obviously, despite the upgraded atmosphere, tariffs remain down-to-earth on a menu that would be distinguished for variety and originality at any price. Consider sizzling steel platters serving up such deep-sea denizens as scrod, sole, snapper, or bass, with your own choice of such imaginative sauce-ery as *a la Grecque,* Amandine, Nemo's special garlic-butter, or onion-garlic *Duxelles.*

Or have your finny friend simply broiled, poached, or fried with the expertise of a kitchen devoted to preserving the natural flavors and textures of each fish. Similarly, shrimps may be scampi-ed, curried, stuffed with crabmeat dressing, or included in the elegantly cognac-cream-sauced *Fruits de la Mer* casserole among juicy chunks of lobster, crablegs, and clams. Another bubbly casserole brings crabmeat in a sherry-spiked cheddar melt, or baby *langoustines* in curry cream. A lovely demonstration of the complexity demanded of a platter based on "simple" ingredients is the fresh flounder filet lightly stuffed with vegetables and oysters.

Desserts are typically seductive Westside delicacies with home-baked richness: perhaps a chocolate *roulade* banded with Amaretto-laced whipped cream, a dense, nutty cinnamon-apple cake, or a lavishly-fruited Hungarian plum strip.

137 West 72 Street
New York, N.Y., 10023
(212) 595-5600

1131 Lexington Avenue
New York, N.Y., 10021
(212) 988-6756

- *Seafood Cuisine*
- *Priced inexpensive to moderate*
- *Open 7 days for Lunch and Dinner*
- *Accepting all major credit cards and reservations*

City Tavern

If you should be dining at City Tavern and start to imagine yourself back in the times of the Revolutionary War, listening to a young man named Thomas Jefferson speak of life, liberty, and the pursuit of happiness, it won't be because owner Michael Nilon hasn't tried to put you in that frame of mind. Located in East Philadelphia, City Tavern is a re-creation of the original tavern that stood on the same plot of land—and that establishment began serving roast duckling and English trifle in 1783.

The five rooms which make up the tavern try to give the customer five slightly different versions of life at the birth of a nation. Each has been authentically and beautifully restored, and while one re-creates the formal tone that surrounded balls and receptions held at the time, another tries to bring back the feeling of a room where merchants discussed the business of the day. There are also smaller rooms which are reserved for private parties, and they're pleasant and pretty places to dine.

The waiters and waitresses at City Tavern wear costumes from the Revolutionary War era. What's more, they attend weekly classes given by the Park Service on the history of the original tavern. You're encouraged to join in the show—ask them whatever you like about the tavern where George Washington probably slept and they'll do their best to answer you.

The food also tries to bring back the feeling of Revolutionary times, with the hearty, solid fare being a mixture of locally available beef, fowl, and fish. At dinner you can choose from prime rib, rack of lamb, roast duck, or baked crab, to name a few of the selections; at lunch the offerings include meat pies, and sandwiches, and their special "salamagundy," the 18th century version of a chef's salad.

City Tavern is an enjoyable restaurant. The settings, food, and service combine to take you back to a different era and help you forget whatever difficulties you may be having in the present one.

Second St. near Walnut
Philadelphia, Pa., 19106
(215) 923-6059

- *American Cuisine*
- *Priced Moderate*
- *Open seven days for lunch and dinner; Closed Mondays in January, February, and March*
- *AE, MC, Visa and Reservations accepted*
- *Private party facilities available*

The Coach and Six Restaurant

When a restaurant has a mural over the bar of 450 of its regular patrons and there are probably several thousand people clamoring to get in the mural—even after an official waiting list of 100—and when a restaurant has over 3,000 house accounts, it's safe to say that the restaurant is a local institution serving excellent food at a moderate price in a friendly atmosphere. So it is with The Coach and Six in Atlanta.

Beverlee Soloff-Shere is the owner, and maybe the most spectacular feat she accomplishes is to keep the quality high in a restaurant which has done essentially the same thing for 20 years—and to keep the place away from complacency while it's being so successful. She does it by attention to all the details of the operation, both big and small.

Large crowds back up in the bar, the patrons either waiting for a friend or a table or simply socializing. These are regulars who come to the Coach and Six for the expertly aged, butchered and prepared beef, and for the club-like atmosphere. Those who want to dine will probably have the justifiably famous black bean soup and some form of beef, be it prime rib, steak *au poivre,* club steak, steak *Angelo* (a filet with sauteed mushrooms, onions, and green peppers), or filet tips *en brochette.*

People are treated as if they're old friends, even when it's their first time. As soon as you sink down into one of the big, padded, bright-red, booth-type banquettes you receive a bowl of *crudites*—with zucchini, celery, carrots, cauliflower, cherry tomatoes, and black and green olives—a bowl of seven kinds of home-made bread, and a plate of hot appetizers (spinach pastries and melted cheese toast). The service is a combination of being friendly but not patronizing and frank but not insulting. ("You don't want the shrimp cocktail—have the black bean soup.")

But there's more to eat than just black bean soup and beef, even if they are the most popular dishes. For appetizers, there's smoked salmon, cherrystone clams, blue point oysters, steaming onion soup, or prosciutto and melon.

The fish and seafood entrees include rainbow trout *almondine,* broiled grouper, a 2- to 4-pound live Maine lobster, and sauteed bay scallops.

Meats other than beef include the expertly broiled triple loin lamb chops, calf's liver, a double veal loin chop, and veal *francais, parmigiana,* and Florentine.

For dessert, just as you should have the black bean soup to start, you should have the chocolate *mousse.* But there's also a cheesecake, chocolate velvet, and their daily specials.

1776 Peachtree Street
Atlanta, Ga., 30309
(404) 872-6666

- *Steak and Seafood Cuisine*
- *Priced moderate to high*
- *Open seven days for lunch and dinner*
- *Reservations necessary. Accepts all major credit cards*

Coach House

This is one of the exceptional restaurants in New York, having earned four stars from critics who laud the Coach House in terms such as "extraordinarily high quality," "perfectionism," and "a genuine original."

Credit for such accolades goes to Leon Lianides, who founded and has operated his restaurant at the same Greenwich Village location for more than three decades. His distinguished bearing and beaming face make him one of the more genial hosts in Manhattan. His guests frequently include the famous, and always the cosmopolitan, but he is ubiquitously on hand to greet and oversee with discretion and proficiency.

Lianides' domain is a real coach house, built 140 years ago for the Wanamaker estates. It has the look of a country inn, with its fresh floral bouquets, warm brick and red-trimmed walls, English oil paintings, and a finely-crafted wrought-iron stairway leading to a small dining balcony that used to be the hayloft.

The house classic is a dark, velvety black bean soup, its savor infused with Madeira. But how can you pass up the city's best mushroom *a la Grecque* (with light oil and lemon juice, oregano and dill), *escargots* sauteed with croutons and garlic butter, or an inspired quiche?

And what enjoyment awaits as you first bite into a succulent rack of lamb, delicate and juicy, or the mignonettes of veal *a la Champagne* made with glazed chestnuts, mushrooms, and baby onions. Other triumphs include the roast ribs or beef, duck, fresh striped bass in white wine, and an immortal rendering of soft shell crabs. For accompaniments, the Coach House tempts you with hot, buttered cornsticks, crusty Italian bread, or Greek salad on request.

Desserts are all prepared in the kitchen, from the freshly baked pecan pie, to the house chocolate cake, bread pudding, *dacquoise* (crunchy hazelnut meringue and mocha butter cream), or fresh fruit. The wine list is large and personally chosen by Mr. Lianides.

110 Waverly Place
New York, N.Y., 10011
(212) 777-0303

- *American Cuisine*
- *Prices are prix-fixe average $30*
- *Reservations necessary*
- *Accepts major credit cards*
- *No private party facilities*

The Common Good

This is the place to eat American-Continental—the service is good, the prices are reasonable, the quality grumble-proof. To take the chill off a cold night try the *flagiole* (if it happens to be the soup that night), this aromatic thick pasta broth is filled with vegetables in a rich tomatoey base; or try the chunky/spicy chili in a heavy glass mug crowned with onions. Mushrooms LaSalle—delicate with the fragrance of sherry, shallots, and lemon—is an elegant way to perk up your appetite for the recommended tender slices of marinated sirioin in the Yankee steak sandwich. The barbequed and spiced thick Texas ribs served with house fries, crisp coleslaw, and sourdough bread, is also recommended. Chicken Orientale is a *melange* of tastes—being deep-fried in beer batter, dusted with sesame seeds, and coated with an unusual sauce blending orange marmalade and horseradish.

Fish is consistently fresh; the Louisiana shrimp fry is lightly breaded and non-oily, moist yet crunchy to the bite. The profusion of shellfish, garlic and tomatoes in the Ciappino stew is laced with the sparkling combination of white wine and anisette. Add to this a julienne of colorful vegetables and an assortment of breads, and you have a satisfying meal. Catch of the day, fresh from Fulton Market, is moist and pleasing to the eye and palate. The pasta galore is a different dish daily, such as the green tortellini—these small pockets of dough are bathed in a savory meat sauce and served with house salad and bread.

For dessert lovers there's *coupe marron* rich with chestnuts in vanilla syrup ladled over a smooth ice cream crowned with a mound of freshly-whipped cream, or a buttery-crusted chocolate walnut pie covered in dark chocolate. For the hot fudge sundae *aficianado:* a great ball of vanilla ice cream smothered with an extraordinarily rich steaming fudge and topped with a profusion of whipped cream.

The premises offer a theatrical, split-level setting with ceiling spotlights showcasing exotic long-stemmed flowers nestled in delicate bud vases on each table, and further reflected in the mirrored walls and columns. A profusion of plants partitions the levels of the dining room from each other and from the diminutive bar, and tiny lights strung about the dining room cast a soft, face-flattering glow. A pianist renders old time favorites as patrons cluster around the piano bar or enjoy a satisfying meal.

304 East 48 Street
New York, N.Y., 10017
(212) 935-9840

- *American/Continental Cuisine*
- *Priced inexpensive to moderate*
- *Open Monday through Friday for lunch; 7 days for dinner; Sunday brunch*
- *Accepts reservations and AE only*
- *Private party facilities for up to 250 people*

Company

Company treats diners in a setting of splendor scarcely hinted by the modest Third Avenue facade. For over ten years, the present piano-lounge-bar-area up front functioned as a colonial-styled snackery—but with the recent recruiting of a serious young chef from the ranks of the Nouvelle Young Turks and the burgeoning of a spacious rear salon, the complex has developed into an elegant expanse: black ceilings networked with track-mounted spotlights are enclosed by all-mirror walls that reflect sensuously curved cinnamon banquettes and elaborate seasonal florals seemingly extending into eternity. A youthful staff takes evident pride in reciting a roster of the evening's specials to magnify a printed menu that already presents an embarrassment of riches in both imaginative *nouvelle* creations and adaptations of classic cuisine. They may be proud, too, of a considerateness that lists single orders of delicacies usually restricted to twosomes as such Caesar salad and rack of lamb (here gilded with a sauce *choron*).

More tender touches include a basket of warmed breads: both sesame-studded pumpernickel and a crusty country loaf—and the exemplary candor of a waitress scrupulously specifying that a garnish is "wild rice mixed with white," rather than passing it off as the costly all-wild stuff. In any case, a remarkable molded mound of potato cubes sauteed with bacon and onion crisps outpoints any sort of rice—and a chunky herbed *ratatouille* is an altogether appropriate adjunct to any of the hearty House entrees, from prime rib with horseradish cream to a steak *au poivre* crunchy with both green and black whole peppercorns in a pungent but creamy sauce.

Woo a delicate palate with an airy puff-pastry appetizer suspending a cloud of succulent crabmeat in golden, parsley-flecked butter sauce. Or elect an assertively seasoned foursome of moist yet densely textured seafood-sausage rounds afloat on a pool of lobster-sauce well-flavored with carapace. Pastas—sauced either in traditional Alfredo or *nouvelle primavera* styles—are offered as half-portion appetizers or full entrees. An ingenious duckling entree is memorable as a presentation-platter defining the best of both worlds, *nouvelle* and traditional: spokelike slices of rare duck breast *maigret* radiate from a focus of twin crisp-skinned joints—all surrounded by a rich, melba-type raspberry sauce.

It requires a special menu card to list the goblets of multi-liquered coffees crowned with whipped-cream, the myriad of rich desserts, and the sophisticated after-dinner drinks favored by fans who have learned to linger in these gracious, glamorous precincts, where every diner is indeed cherished "company."

365 Third Avenue
New York, N.Y., 10016
(212) 532-5222

- *French/Italian Cuisine*
- *Priced moderately*
- *Open Monday through Friday for lunch; 7 nights for dinner; Sunday brunch*
- *Reservations and all major credit cards accepted*
- *Private party facilities for between 25 and 60 persons*

Copacabana

In the days before Mary Poppins taught us to say, "Supercalifragilisticexpialidocious," the buzz-word for something in splendid shape was "Copasetic,"—and the term may just have been based on the way the Copacabana conducts their incomparable catering operation. Whether you're of the age group that counted on the endearingly nicknamed "Copa" for supper-club glamor with leggy showgirls—or of the generation that looks forward to occasional disco evenings here—you'll discover something old and something new at this legendary locale that has evolved into our city's unique, centrally-located, all-purpose catering facility.

The upstairs room is still a Disneyland, canopied with the oversized *papier-mache* fruits and veggies that adorned Carmen Miranda's headgear; mind you, these are the originals—nostaligia pieces restored at great pains and expense to delight the fans. They are reflected in the mirrored walls that surround burgundy-upholstered lounge seating. A savvy local clientele uses this room for pressure-free weekday lunches served by a polished European staff—but this is the only "restaurant" meal offered by the New Copa.

All the rest is Party Time, in a mind-boggling variety of styles. Festivities may begin with butler-passed *hors d'oeuvres* in the upstairs area, then progress to either a sit-down feast or a mammoth buffet downstairs—where the red-carpeted expanse accommodates tiers of pink-linened tables, a plush dais-stage, and a polished wooden dance floor. Using one or both of these areas, Director Peter Dorn (the man to see for making arrangements) can play perfect Host to parties ranging from 75 to 1,000; to disco-dancing sweet-sixteens or dignified Golden Weddings (or to both age groups at the same party, simply by assigning different musical groups to each of the rooms); to Bar Mitzvahs, weddings, christenings, and corporate celebrations. This last is his super-specialty, as attested by an album of thank-you's from IBM, Price-Waterhouse, People Magazine, and that one-woman institution Liz Smith (whose traditional January party is a Copa regular-event).

The popularity of these precincts is easily explained. Consider the enthusiastic, European-trained young staff; an ambitious dutch Chef who turns out such appetizers as whole oranges stuffed with duckling or green-and-white *tortellini*—to be followed by rack of lamb or veal cordon bleu—or snapper and pompano as fish choices; a record library supplying music styles from Big Bands to disco; and a management willing and able to secure names-entertainment, a *sushi* chef, or an on-the-scene French crepe chef if the client so desires. If you know of any other facility in New York that can fulfill your fondest fantasy with all these features—we'd like to know about it.

10 East 60 Street
New York, N.Y., 10022
(212) PL 5-6010

- *Continental-American Cuisine*
- *Moderate prices*
- *Open Monday through Saturday for lunch only; Closed Sundays*
- *Accepting AE, CB, DC, MC, VISA*
- *Private parties 7 days, for 75 to 1000*

Copper Beech Inn

The ancient wide-spreading massive copper beech tree shades a stately old mansion, whose Country French Cuisine has been voted a four star rating (Mobil Restaurant Guide), plus #1 restaurant three years in a row (Connecticut Magazine). Paul and Louise Ebeltoft, owners since 1981, have worked with the skilled and dedicated staff to upgrade an already first-rate dining experience. The foyer welcomes you with a working fireplace and the four dining rooms have a comfortable elegance and charm. The sparkling crystal, china, sterling silver table appointments, and the fresh vibrant flowers complement the Queen Ann-Chippendale furnishing, giving one the feeling of dining in a private home agleam with brass chandeliers, fine panelings, old prints, and antiques.

The chef has talent for creating with imagination combinations such as poached oysters wrapped in spinach leaves, flavored with lemon butter, garnished with caviar and diced pimientos; a *pate* of chicken with a lobster mousse center, served with a sauce of red currants, port wine, orange rind and ginger; or snails simmered in brandy and white wine, enveloped and baked in a puff pastry with pine nuts and garlic butter, and served with a lemon-flavored brown sauce.

The inn's famous pale pink lobster bisque is thick with chunks of lobster and rich with sherry, while the chilled cream of white bean soup is satiny and mellow.

Dining by romantic candlelight—then choosing from at least nineteen entrees such as sauteed medallions of veal stuffed with freshly shucked bluepoint oysters, served with lemon butter sauce and spinach noodles; tender young rabbit marinated in burgundy and herbs, braised in rich brown sauce with sliced mushrooms and bacon lardons; beef Wellington in a Madeira sauce made with truffles; or elegant sauteed veal sweetbreads with champagne sauce served in a brioche will give one great satisfaction.

Dessert choices are many, all freshly made at the inn. For chocoholics, there's rich Viennese chocolate torte, filled apricot marmalade, covered with semi-sweet chocolate, and served with whipped cream; or chocolate mocha cheesecake flavored with Kahlua. There's refreshing assorted sorbets served with a wild raspberry sauce or a ramekin of blackberries served with carmelized brown sugar and whipped cream flavored with Grand Marnier.

Main Street
Ivoryton, Conn., 06442
(203) 767-0330
- *Country French Cuisine*
- *Priced moderate to expensive*
- *Open 6 days for lunch and dinner; Closed Mondays*
- *Accepts reservations and AE, DC, MC, VISA*
- *Private party facilities for between 6 and 100 persons*

Danker's

In the heart of the theatre district, the restaurant is an especially popular place with amiable show-biz celebrities, theatre-goers, journalists, and businessmen. Danker's has been around for years and continues to offer the delightful ambience and meritable cuisine that were the keystones in establishing its well-deserved popularity.

The interior, including the second floor (used for over-flow crowds as well as private parties) is strictly masculine. Walls are natural stucco with wood trim (the early-American tavern-look), lined with theatrical posters and pictures of theatre personalities.

What attracts customers is not only the beef and seafood but the personality of the owner, Richard Danker, a genial, young host who has been the sole proprietor of this restaurant for the past six years, and has not only maintained the standards previously set but enhanced the operation by being alert to improvements.

The menu contains a stalwart list of eating suggestions, but an order of roast prime ribs of beef will solve the problem of choice. The extra-heavy cut is tender and tasty. There are also blue ribbon sirloins and filet mignons prepared on the flamepit—oversized steaks, weighing about a pound after broiling. Alaskan crab and jumbo shrimp sauteed in lashings of creamy butter are hard to resist, but then so are the barbecued spareribs marinated Western style, or the cool, crisp Louisiana shrimp salad (a blend of steamed shrimp, celery, and mayonnaise garnished with tomato wedge and hard boiled egg).

If you can still manage, there are desserts such as the carrot cake, rich cheesecake (plain or with fruit), or apple crumb pie. There's also a reasonable assortment of wines, and it flows fast, because it's sensibly priced. Two locations:

1209 E Street, NW
Washington, D.C., 20004
(202) 628-2330

The Jim Thorpe Foundation
ARTBA Building
525 School Street, SW
Washington, D.C., 20024
(202) 554-2902

- *American Steak House*
- *Price moderate*
- *Open 6 days for lunch, dinner, and after-theatre supper; closed Sunday*
- *Reservations advised. All major credit cards*
- *Private party facilities for between 20 and 150 persons*

Danny's

Danny and Beatrice Dickman have had Danny's for 21 years, and in that time they've established a justifiable reputation of owning and running an excellent restaurant.

Danny's has a feel of Colonial elegance. The walls are a mixture of mirrors and wood panels, and the seating is a mixture of wood and leather booths, tables and chairs. The overall dim lighting is enhanced by illumination from attractive wall sconces and chandeliers.

The menu at Danny's is one of enormous variety, being a mixture of French, Italian, and distinctly American offerings. Let's say you want oysters—do you choose the oyster stew, oysters on the half shell, oysters Rockefeller, or oysters Bernard? And Danny's is not primarily a seafood restaurant.

Non-oyster appetizers include the house *pate,* clams *italienne,* shrimp *cote d'azur,* eggplant parmesean, and Beluga caviar. The soups are cream of mushroom, *vichyssoise,* French onion, and crab soup—which is a thick, hearty broth filled with fresh vegetables and chunks of crab meat.

The meat entrees include veal *francaise,* veal Stronganoff, or veal with mushrooms and white wine topped by a brown sauce. Beef is handled in a *tournedos tranche Rossini* manner (three pieces of filet topped with liver *pate,* mushrooms, truffles, and a *perigourdine* sauce), or as beef Stronganoff, a filet with *bernaise* or Maderia sauce, chateaubriand, steak Diane, beef Wellington, sirloin steak with mushrooms and a *bordelaise* sauce, or prime rib. There's also roast duck with an orange sauce and a saddle of lamb with a mint sauce.

If seafood is what you want, choose from *coquille St. Jacques cote d'azur,* dover sole *menuiere,* dover sole *Caprice* (sole with sauteed banana and hollandaise sauce), crab cakes, sauteed crab lumps, the broiled fish of the day, lobster thermidor, Maine lobster stuffed with crab lumps, or boiled or broiled Maine lobster. Quite a selection of entrees.

Danny and Beatrice believe that dessert is as important as the rest of the bill-of-fare, and they've given desserts a seperate menu to prove it. The choices are extensive, ranging all the way from vanilla ice cream to flaming desserts, chocolate *souffle,* and baked Alaska.

1201 North Charles Street
Baltimore, Md., 21201
(301) 539-1393

- *French, Steak and Seafood Cuisine*
- *Priced moderate*
- *Open Monday through Friday for lunch; Monday through Saturday for dinnner; Closed Sunday*
- *All major credit cards and reservations accepted*

Domenico

Ristorante Domenico—largely due to present management—has grown into a really good Italian dining establishment. Its stylish interior of stucco, soft contemporary lighting, well-placed tables, and stained glass murals is quite engaging, airy, and unaffected.

The bill-of-fare has plenty of selections among the pastas, veals, seafoods, steaks, chops, and poultry. Start with the macaroni, perhaps a small varied assortment. Linguine with white clam sauce is light and aromatic with rafts of clams, home-made *canelloni* are seasoned with a flourish, and one is properly torn whether to try the fettucini *carbonara* or the spaghetti *al dente* thoroughly laced with shrimp sauce. Scampi as an opener is also well-handled, the shrimp prepared butterfly-style in a fragrant, savory *farce*.

Entrees include a succulent pair of tenderly broiled veal chops, an elaborate veal cutlet (lightly breaded, fried in olive oil, brushed with tomato sauce and mozzerella cheese, and baked), a hearty platter of pork chops spicy with vinegar and peppers, and chicken *cacciatora* woven with genrous amounts of prosciutto and mushrooms, its tomato sauce infused with rich flavorings. Main dishes like these are brightened with sides of fresh vegetables such as peas and carrots, stringbeans *marinara,* fried zucchini and the like. Among the salads, sliced tomato and Bermuda onion is excellent, thickly sliced and accented with the dressing of your choice.

On the short, Ristorante Domenico is a satisfying blend of comfortable surroundings and agreeable food at moderate prices.

---

120 East 40 Street
New York, N.Y., 10016
(212) 682-0310

- *Northern Italian Cuisine*
- *Priced moderate to high*
- *Open Monday through Friday for lunch; Monday through Saturday for dinner; Closed Sunday*
- *Reservations and all major credit cards accepted*
- *Private party facilities for 10 through 150 persons*

Don Ciccio Pescatore

(now Rossini's)

A promising start has been made at the new Don Ciccio Pescatore by the founder Vincenzo Rossini, who previously established the noted Rossini's on the same site in 1979.

The look of the place is comfortably attractive, with its three intimate dining rooms and big separate bar done up warmly in natural woods and stucco, decorated with hanging plants and a couple of mammoth fish tanks stocked with mammoth gold-type fish.

Imagination and artistry have combined to produce some unusual *plats.* These qualities are evident in the seafood salad, its marinated red cabbage and celery blended with hunks of lobster, shrimp, squid and dressed in a tasty garlic and lemon sauce; in the *spiedino all fiadone* (delicately fried bread layered with melted cheese and Italian ham, brushed with anchovy paste) and in the *paglia e fieno all chitarra,* which is homemade green and white noodles in a lavish tomato and onion sauce. Pasta examples, in general, are good. For more formal gorging, the most satisfactory main course includes the *vitello illuminati,* a delicacy consisting of veal garnished with prosciutto, moist mozzarella cheese and slices of avocado, and the *scapece alla vastese,* which is striped bass cooked in wine and capers. Sausage and peppers is always on the menu, as is the fresh halibut served broiled or marinara style.

Salad you can have with the entree or between entree and dessert; it's a pleasant serving of cool, crisp greens imported from Trieste to which is added fresh endive and a classic dressing, not remarkably subtle but good.

360 Atlantic Avenue
Freeport, L.I., N.Y., 11520
(516) 868-2207

- *Italian Cuisine*
- *Moderately priced*
- *Open 7 nights for dinner*
- *Reservations and all major credit cards accepted*
- *Private party facilities for between 30 and 100 persons*
- *A la carte items served with salad and vegetable*
- *Guitar entertainment weekends*

Downing Square

Walking into Downing Square transports you back to an era of substance—in architecture and in cuisine. The dining room is huge, a story and a half high, and clothed in rich, dark wood-paneling supporting portraits of the twelve most influential British Prime Ministers. The dining hall comes replete with imposing chandeliers, large banquettes, sturdy well-placed tables flanked by roomy leather and brass-trimmed chairs.

One expects abundance of provender here, and there is no surprise at the servings of food and drink. At the start, the appetizers are so generously laid, that one fears fading out at mid-meal—until a sample is taken of the full, fresh taste of the chopped chicken liver with Bermuda onion garnish, or the crusty baked clams, or the aromatic crock of onion soup.

These polished off with hungry efficiency, one can dig into the choice of meat or fish ahead. This is basically a steak place, and the kitchen will grant every wish from a chopped sirloin to chateaubriand. There is prime T-Bone and sirloin, mixed grill and filet mignon. Prime ribs come with rib bone in or English cut. For variety, there is calf's liver and medallions of veal, shish-kebab, veal cutlet, chicken, scampi, filet of sole and much more. Side dishes include potato pancakes, large and fluffy and perfect to draw in the beef juices that might otherwise go to waste.

Desserts can also pique the palate, from pies to ice cream to creamy cheesecake. Service in this large place is professional and you never feel lost or unminded.

500 Lexington Avenue
New York, N.Y., 10017
(212) 826-9730

- *English Steakhouse*
- *Priced moderate to high*
- *Open 7 days for lunch and dinner*
- *Reservations necessary. All major credit cards accepted*
- *Private party facilities for between 10 and 150 persons*
- *Jackets preferred*

El Rincon De Espana

El Rincon de Espana not only gives New Yorkers a chance to try authentic Spanish food, but the restaurant gives New Yorkers two locations to get the food. One branch is in the Wall Street area and the smaller branch is in Greenwich Village.

Both locations have a relaxed, casual atmosphere. The intimate quarters in Greenwich Village sport attractive wood trim and Spanish paintings on stucco walls. Behind the bar sits an imposing stone wall. The Wall Street operation is a shade more dramatic and much more spacious.

The menu at both locations is the same, and it features several versions of the classic Spanish dish *paella*. You can have the seafood *paella* without the addition of lobster and chicken, with one added, or with both.

Another speciality is the octopus. The marinated devilfish has none of the chewiness usually associated with octopus and it's accompanied by a delicious, tangy sauce. Another excellent seafood dish is *gambos al ajillo*, succulent shrimp expertly cooked and flavored with a spicy, pungent garlic sauce. Like most of the dishes at El Rincon de Espana, an excellent *risotto* is served alongside.

There are some dozen other seafood dishes to choose from, ranging from a broiled stiped bass to *mejillones diablo* (mussels in a tangy hot sauce).

The restaurant also offers several versions of veal, beef, pork, and chicken. One veal dish is *medallones de ternera con salsa de lemon.* In it tender medallions of veal get smothered by a rich, slightly creamy lemon sauce that has a full lemon flavor.

Dessert offerings consist of vanilla and caramel custards, guava jelly with cheese, and cheesecake. For openers try the mussels *a la Carlo* simmered in a hot, peppery garlic and tomato sauce.

The location on Beaver Street has another plus: it offers Spanish entertainment nightly. On weekdays a guitarist performs modern and classical Spanish songs, and on weekends a complete *Flamenco* shows joins the guitarist.

Two locations:
82 Beaver Street   *226 Thompson Street*
New York, NY   *New York, NY*
(212) 344-5228   *(212) 371-7777*

- *Spanish Cuisine*
- *Moderately priced*
- *Beaver Street: Open Monday through Saturday for lunch and dinner; Closed Sunday*
- *Thompson Street: Open 7 days for dinner; Sunday only for lunch*
- *All major credit cards and reservations accepted*

Flavio's

Flavio's has been around for almost 25 years, and they're still turning out excellent Italian and French food. Flavio and Angie De Filippo still own it, but they've brought in their son and daughter-in-law to help out: Oreste (Pete) does the cooking and Carol is the host. And, nicely enough, Flavio's still makes its own delicious breadsticks and breads.

The predominant color at Flavio's is brick-red, with the brick arches and walls being trimmed with wood and adorned with paintings. The tables are well-spaced and covered with white and red tablecloths.

The offerings at Flavio's encompass the standard Northern Italian and French cuisines as well as a few more adventurous dishes. You can begin your meal with cooked cold shrimp in Flavio's own tomato-based sauce or with an *antipasto* of salami, capocolla, prosciutto, and assorted cheeses—or try an exciting *escargot chablisienne*, which is wine-marinated snails filled with parsley and garlic butter and sprinkled with a parmesean cheese/bread crumb mixture.

Their soups include *zuppa di nozze* (chicken broth with small meat balls, whipped eggs, and grated Romano cheese), and *potage aux champignon* (an old-fashioned French mushroom soup with a chicken stock base and flavored with pepper and nutmeg).

The selection of entrees is very large. For example, there are eleven veal dishes alone, and they range from two different treatments of *saltimbocca* (stuffed veal scaloppini) to *osso bucco* (veal shanks) to veal *marsala* to two varieties of veal tripe. Chicken is handled several ways as well—boneless breasts can have a wine sauce, a Grand Marnier sauce, or a tomato, mushroom, and wine sauce—or you can have your chicken stuffed with prosciutto and mozzarella and smothered in a sherry sauce. Or you can opt for the classic chicken *cacciatore*.

Beef receives a variety of treatments as well, whether it be steak Diane (a brandy sauce), *filet de boeuf chasseur* (a prosciutto and mushroom-wine sauce), beef *con peperoni e pomidori* (pieces of beef sauteed in butter with a tomato-pepper sauce), the *chateaubriand* for two, or a simple broiled tender filet or sirloin.

The fish and seafood selection includes broiled rainbow trout, fried shrimp or oysters, poached flounder, stuffed flounder, dry cod cooked in tomato sauce, and broiled lobster.

And no restaurant would call itself even half Italian if it didn't serve pasta. Flavio's offers *lasagna*, *manicotti*, *canelloni*, *spaghetti carbonara*, *tagliatelle*, *ravioli*, *rigatoni*, and *linguini* with clam sauce. *Buon appetito* and *bon appetit*.

---

212 Warren Avenue
Apollo, Pa., 15613
(412) 478-2961

- *French and Italian Cuisine*
- *Prices are moderate to high*
- *Open Tuesday through Sunday for dinner only; Closed Monday*
- *Accepts reservations and all major credit cards*

Fonda La Paloma

Mexican food, after completely conquering the West Coast and Southwestern United States, is finishing its revolution in the East. Unfortunately, its fiercely loyal following had precious few first rate restaurants to cater to its needs. But for sheer romanticism, and for the satisfaction of that craving for finely flavored food, Fonda La Paloma (even the name sounds like rhythmically strumming guitars) fills the bill.

The restaurant takes up a full three stories in a converted townhouse (the top floor is used for private parties) and is a bit of old Mexico up North. The atmosphere is warm and hospitable, with colorfully attired musicians strolling amongst the patrons singing the softly romantic music of Mexico.

Lunch and dinner menus feature a full range of Mexican dishes for the neophyte or professional Mexican nut (once you are hooked, you are hooked bad). The staples are here in their glory: A nicely peppered tortilla topped with melted cheese, *tostados* with beef or chicken and, of course, tacos. You may also delve further—to the *Puerto Adovado* (pork with a sauce that raises it above the ordinary), *carne Maya* (Mayan-style pot roast), or a number of

combination platters that let you sample a world of goodies at once like the *chihuahua* (stuffed pepper, taco, enchilada, *carne asada,* rice and refried beans—not for a chihuahua appetite!).

House specialties included *camarones a la Fonda* (shrimp sauteed in wine and fine spices), *chiles rellenos* (beef or cheese stuffed peppers) and the combination platters that brim with food. A full complement of Spanish Riojas are available and recommended, as are the special drinks—*margaritas,* a great *pina colada* and *cafe con piquette* (Mexican coffee infused with a Benedictine and brandy).

256 East 49 Street
New York, N.Y., 10017
(212) 421-5495

- *Mexican Cuisine*
- *Priced moderate*
- *Open Monday through Friday for lunch; 7 nights for dinner*
- *Reservations are necessary. Accepts all major credit cards*
- *Strolling musicians nightly*

Forlini's

Pointedly poised on the international borderline where Chinatown and Little Italy meet, Forlini's is concealed behind heavy oak doors that open into a two-room crimson and gilt environment. Here, super-spacious, ultra-high-backed tufted banquettes sit beneath brass chandeliers, surrounded by panelled walls hung with bright oil paintings in scrolled baroque frames. An ambitious wine book listing most Italian vintages plus representative labels further accommodates with a choice among California and imported Italian wines by-the-glass; such consideration facilitates tasting delicate seafood appetizers with an appropriate white wine, and complementing heartier entrees with the robust reds of the nebbiolo grape. (Note three different Spannas and several reputable Barolos, as well as a clutch of Chiantis.)

An embossed leather menu also offers a pride of preferences, including a multi-course Gourmet Dinner for two comprised of select House specialties. The *prix-fixe* feast ranges from hot seafood antipasto and pasta; to a mixed entree of seafood, chicken, and veal served with fried zucchini; plus dessert with coffee and anisette or amaretto—all priced at $45.00.

Blazing your own trail, however, also has charms. Consider the House special *tortellini con la cua* ("with tails"): giant, tear-shaped dumplings stuffed with ricotta-spinach souflee, in a gossamer cream sauce kissed with nutmet and sparked with prosciutto. The hot antipasto is an overflowing platter of pairs of lightly oregano-crumbed clams, mussels, shrimp, stuffed mushrooms, artichoke hearts, and thin-sliced scallops of sauteed eggplant. The dinner salad accompanying each entree is a melange of juicy ruby tomato wedges, sliced onion, watercress and varied lettuces, tossed at table by a uniformed waiter. Then there's a veal chop *val dostana:* albaster *plume de veau* ribboned with rosy prosciutto and mellow melted mozzerella—all laved in rich wine sauce floating fat freshly-sliced mushrooms. Or indulge in a kingly *fra diavolo* feast of lobster, mussels, clams and shrimp, with a side of *al dente* linguine to be lavished with the pulpy, peppery, herbacious tomato sauce.

For dessert, the Forlini cheesecake is a diplomatic blend of New York cream cheese and Italian ricotta—a clever combination of rich texture with light consistency. Contemporary chic is served by the currently fashionable *tartufo* of mixed ice creams with citron in a chocolate-candy shell. A gracious host offers anisette with potent, foamy espresso.

93 Baxter Street
New York, N.Y., 10013
(212) 349-6779

- *Italian Cuisine*
- *Moderately priced*
- *Open seven days for Lunch and Dinner. Closed Easter, Christmas, first two weeks of August*
- *Reservations and all major credit cards accepted*

The Four Seasons

Nestled at the base of the Seagram's Building, The Four Seasons was every bit as spectacularly innovative as the whisky-colored office building that forms its crown when the two opened their doors in 1959. Both the Seagram's and the restaurant have proved their worth and remain today landmarks of creative farsightedness.

The restaurant was designed as a dining experience—the palatial interior is strung with shimmering metal draperies, a garden of green plants, a splendiferous marble pool capped by a soaring majestic ceiling. The bar is separate both in decor and menu. Definitely masculine in style, dark French-rosewood panels the walls, black upholstery covers the furnishings, and gleaming brass rod sculptures hang from the ceiling.

The name comes from the original conception of a seasonally changing restaurant, with foods, plants and accessories altered with the weather. This treatment, still honored today, is reflected in an eclectic menu drawing on many cuisines and periods of history for inspiration.

The menu is huge, and gets even bigger when it unfolds into one of the largest wine lists in town. A nice touch, and one that should be emulated by others, is the presenting of dishes in English with the main ingredient in capital letters. This helps home in on a menu that measures nearly two feet high and contains such imaginative creations as *gratin* of crayfish tails and *chanterelles*, lobster fricassee with shallots and bourbon, and crisped shrimp filled with mustard fruits. The Four Seasons also has more than an ample number of straight up favorites like skillet steak smothered in onions, broiled calf's liver, and cold roast duck.

There is a separate menu for the Grill Room at The Four Seasons, a very attractive and stylish bar on two levels. The food comes out of the same kitchen, is slightly cheaper, and centers on the simple, masculine, and grilled.

There are enough menus to start a collection—separate lunch and dinner menus for both the barroom and main dining room, after-theater menus, theater dinners at fixed prices, etc.

99 East 52 Street
New York, N.Y., 10022
(212) 754-9494

- *Continental Cuisine*
- *Priced expensive*
- *Prix-fixe pre-theatre dinner for $28.00*
- *Open 6 days for lunch and dinner; closed Sunday*
- *Reservations strongly advised, except for dinner at the bar. Accepts all major credit cards*
- *Private party facilities for between 10 and 150 people*

Gage & Tollner

New York's most venerable eating establishment, Gage & Tollner opened its doors in 1879 and hasn't let up since. It is a place that has captured the past—practically all of the original decor remains intact, and the menu still features the same variety of foods and style of cooking that has kept it famous for more than a century. Food is cooked over anthracite coal, as it has been through the invention of electricity, frozen food, and microwave ovens.

The eating house was first opened by Charles M. Gage at 302 Fulton Street, a few doors down the block from its present location. He was joined five years later by Eugene Tollner, and five years after that the restaurant was moved to its present location. Here, the owners, distrustful of that new fangled electricity, installed the dual gas-electricity lighting fixtures that still function today. They work so well, in fact, that their utility during two New York blackouts made the newspapers.

Ownership of Gage & Tollner has changed hands only twice, the first time in 1911 to friends of the owners, and again in 1919, this time to the Dewey family, where it has remained ever since. As part of the deal, Mr. Tollner was kept on as a life-long member of the staff to maintain continuity.

This desire to maintain a feeling of family at Gage & Tollner extends to the staff. The waiters wear insignia on the sleeves denoting length of service. At one time, the head waiter had been with G&T 61 years.

Gage & Tollner looks, inside and out, almost exactly as it did a century ago, and has been named to landmark status twice—once for its facade, and again for its interior. All original and irreplaceable are the cherry woodwork on the walls, the burgundy velvet tapestry between the tier-type mirrors, the *lincrusta* plaster around the mirror arches and the bar. The oak and marble bar dates back to the original opening in 1879. Even the tables are those that seated guests when they first entered 372 Fulton Street in 1889, and the woolen carpet is custom loomed to the original pattern and colors.

You can get the freshest of seafood here, but G&T is famous for its native dishes. Chief among them (and the menu is enormous) is crabmeat Virginia, broiled soft clam bellies, and clams casino, which arrive on a bed of hot rock salt.

G&T also offers a multi-selection of steaks,

chops, mutton, lamb, and kidneys; also chicken dishes and omelettes, to cater to every whim. appetite, and budget. You may even pick and choose among several salad dishes including a wonderful plate of fried tomatoes.

The Deweys are decended from Lake Erie winemakers, so it is no surprise to find a good-sized American-dominated wine list and more than a dozen choices of beer and ale.

372 Fulton Street
Brooklyn, N.Y., 11201
(212) 875-5181

- *American Cuisine*
- *Priced moderate*
- *Open Monday through Friday for lunch; Monday through Saturday for dinner; Closed Sunday*
- *Private party facilities for 20 to 180 persons*
- *Special $15.50 prix-fixe menu daily until 7:00 PM*

The Ginger Man

One of the nice things about the new wave of restaurants and restaurateur is the desire to turn out an honest meal in honest surroundings. Among the many new restaurants hovering around Lincoln Center, none is more successful at meeting the needs of its clientele than The Ginger Man. It is a genuinely friendly and courteous place, and this goes even in the hours of great busy-ness when the main dining room, secondary rooms and glass-enclosed sidewalk cafe are filled with eager talkers and eaters.

As with most of the new wave, the menu concentrates on a few favorites, expertly prepared. Your entrance is saluted with crisp, fresh rolls and sweet butter, a rarity in restaurants of any ilk. Just a few soups and hot and cold appetizers are offered, but those that are can be first-rate. The steamed mussels bathed with white wine and shallots are a warming intro, and for a real change try the crisp baked potato skins topped with sour cream. There is also a house *pate,* tasty fettuccini with a tomato and *pesto* sauce, and shrimp cocktail, cold and satisfying.

The entrees are time-tested dishes like filet of sole, moist and flavorful with its lemon butter dressing, a snappy shrimp scampi, duckling with fresh peaches or steak tartare.

Some subtle delights are the paillard of chicken, grilled with garlic and *pancetta,* calf's liver with onions, leeks, and chives—and terriyaki steak, for a twist on an old standby.

Lighter eaters can indulge in crispy fresh salads (recommended especially is the endive, arugula and walnut combination), sandwiches and burgers, and a long list of omelettes (not the least of which contain caviar, eggplant and tomato, smoked salmon, fine herbs, etc.).

And after the meal and some good conversation, The Ginger Man is the perfect place to linger over espresso and their homemade almond nut roll whose velvet richness, scent, color, texture, and taste is one of life's great joys.

51 West 64 Street
New York, N.Y., 10023
(212) 399-2358

- *American/Continental Cuisine*
- *Priced moderate to expensive*
- *Open seven days for lunch and dinner*
- *Reservations and all major credit cards accepted*

Greene Street

Supper club, jazz spot, restaurant, art gallery, architectural marvel, local hangout—just what is Greene Street? Well, it's all of the above and more. The most immediately striking aspect of the place is its design and decor. Owner Tony Goldman acquired a large, five-story building in Manhattan's Soho area and he first planned to sell each floor as living/work spaces for artists. But no sooner had he signed the lease than he saw the building's potential to be a unique restaurant.

The kitchen and dining room take up the bottom two floors of Goldman's building—most of the ceiling/floor dividing the two levels has been taken out, leaving just a balcony running around the huge room. Against the back wall, soaring two stories high is an arresting multi-colored mural by artist Francoise Shein. The other walls are raw brick; they surround tiered dining areas on which Goldman has scattered tables and chairs. The balcony not only houses coves and nooks ideal for drinks and intimate coversation, but also the Greene Street Space Gallery, an art gallery featuring the works of local Soho artists.

As if all that weren't enough, Goldman has planted a raft of towering palms, which serve not only as decoration but also as a living wall separating the bar from the dining room.

The restaurant is so spacious that theatre instruments have been used to light part of it—and that's doubly convenient since Greene Street offers nightly entertainment. The acts range from single performers to groups that usually perform pop or jazz music. Greene Street also has its own play-reading series, where new plays and performance pieces receive their first public debut. What's more, local radio personality Les Davis hosts his nightly jazz show from Greene Street.

Accompanying the unique setting and multitude of artistic happenings is a large selection of quality comestibles. Chef Lawrence Vito has a menu that while having a *nouvelle* slant does not go wild with experimentation. The hearty wild mushroom soup, for instance, is a rich, full-bodied marvel teeming with chunks of wild mushrooms and chicken quenelles. The octopus appetizer consists of a caviar-topped julienne of white radishes encircled by tender pieces of soy vinegar-marinated octopus. The ballantine of duck has a delicately spiced truffle sauce. Other appetizers include duck liver and lobster-striped bass terrines.

The extensive list of entrees offers a complete range of dishes. The expertly-cooked filet of Norwegian salmon gets topped with a dill-scented *hollandaise* sauce. The tender veal chop comes smothered in a port, cream, and green peppercorn sauce and accompanied by braised endive and *spaetzel*. Among the other entrees are poached turbot, baked pork chops, and a rare breast of duck.

101 Greene Street
New York, N.Y., 10012
(212) 925-2415

- *American nouvelle cuisine*
- *Priced expensive*
- *Open 7 nights for dinner only; Sunday brunch*
- *Accepts all major credit cards and reservations suggested*
- *Private party facilities available*

Gurney's Inn

Take an ocean cruise without leaving your chair, from the Admiral's, Captain's, Commodore's, or Skipper's dining room at Gurney's Inn. A highly rated resort-spa, Gurney's gourmet restaurant caters to residents and a steady stream of passing trade.

The glass enclosed dining rooms overlook a spectacular view of the majestic Atlantic Ocean, fueling your appetite for such seafood delicacies as shrimp *monochina,* broiled Peconic Bay scallops, baked oysters, grilled thick swordfish steak, or a cold salad plate of avocado with king crab meat and green herb mayonnaise. Your tastebuds will also be a soft touch for the fresh fish catch, right off the boat.

The friendly waitresses at lunch, as well as the waiters at dinner, give prompt attentive service. The staff may suggest the beautifully done buffet lunch containing at least seven savory dishes such as bubbling beef stew chunky with vegetables, crisp

pizza, and steamship roast beef—rare and juicy. Amongst the other choices are *al dente* pasta of the day, fresh ham, Virginia ham, smoked nova salmon, roast swordfish or whitefish.

Enjoy your lunch under ship's wheel chandeliers, seated at the polished wooden tables with small pots of flowering plants, or dine leisurely at dinner by flattering candlelight on fine starched linens.

The rich New England clam chowder is filled with good size pieces of clams and potatoes, while the white *gazpacho* soup is a filling adventure of flavors or, for a change of pace, go Italian with sweet roasted style peppers and anchovies complementing each other. Any of these might be a prelude to veal *Francaise,* done the classic way in egg batter with tangy lemon and butter—a regular favorite and highly recommended. Pasta devotees will love it sauteed with a heady combination of fresh tomatoes, pungent garlic, broccoli, and olive oil—and the palliard of beef is admirably prepared with rosemary and lemon giving it a certain vibrancy.

If you are too satiated to indulge yourself in dessert don't despair, you can still taste tempting desserts at home by visiting the Gurney's Inn Bake Shop. All breads, cakes, pies, and desserts are prepared fresh daily on the premises. An admirable prize to take home can surely be found here.

When that important day, wedding, anniversary, bar mitzvah, company dinner, or important conference comes up, Gurney's Inn will festively arrange it for you with their catering service for up to 300 people.

Old Montauk Highway
Montauk, L.I., N.Y., 11954
(516) 688-2345 -or- (212) 895-6400

- *French, Italian, American, Continental, Steak, Seafood Cuisine*
- *Moderately priced*
- *Open 7 days*
- *Reservations necessary. Most major credit cards accepted*
- *Private facilities for from 2 to 300 persons*

Hampshire House

The Hampshire House is housed in one of the grand mansions on Beacon Hill, overlooking the Public Garden in Boston. Built in 1911, the Baker Library and ballroom warmly paneled in oak with sparkling crystal chandeliers, snowy linens and comfortable leatherette chairs, retain an elegance of an era gone by. They are ideal for weddings, fund raising, board meetings, press conferences, private parties and celebrations. Additional rooms suitable for small gatherings (10 to 50) are handily situated on the third floor.

If you are in a casual mood, try the Bull and Finch Pub. It was the inspiration for the TV series "Cheers" and is known for the best Bloody Mary's, large tasty burgers, and the best Margaritas in Boston. A friendly comfortable place, it's where the sharp young professionals gather to socialize. It's a truly neighborhood pub with hefty sandwiches, omelettes and hot spicy homemade chili.

When you prefer a turn-of-the-century elegance with top-notch service and excellent Continental cuisine, dine in the Hampshire House for lunch daily, dinner nightly—and brunch on weekends.

A generous *melange* of dried fruits and nuts, sauteed vegetables and bread crumbs are the surprise ingredients stuffed inside the moist, boneless breast of chicken that is slowly baked in the oven and glazed with an orange-honey sauce. For the fish *aficionado*: the scallops *Soltner* filled with tender white scallops and rosy pink baby shrimp, sauteed in fresh creamery butter with julienned carrots and leeks, and finished with a sauce of white wine, cream, and fish *veloute*. The justly famous filet of Boston Scrod is lightly dusted with bread crumbs and broiled in white wine and butter, while you have your choice of the King Salmon poached in court *bouillion* or broiled with butter.

The duckling is roasted to a crisp burnished brown, served with an Amaretto sauce and finished with sesame seeds and toasted almonds. For the steak lover, steak *au poivre* is enveloped in a rich velvety sauce of cognac, cream and *demi-glace,* done to a turn and served with green salad vinaigrette, vegetable of the day and fresh French bread. For lighter fare: a fresh and different quiche every day, served with a green salad—or mussels *mariniere*

poached in white wine with a fish *veloute,* shallots and garlic. At lunch you can choose from man-size sandwiches, crepes, soups, omelettes, scallops, mussels, and quiches.

To cleanse your palate at the end of your meal, try the light Haagen Dazs Cassis sorbet, or forget the calories and try the old-fashioned Rum Cake, or *creme carmel,* served with a dollop of fresh cream. There is a good wine list; also beers, and sensational coffees, teas, and drinks.

84 Beacon Street
Boston, Mass., 02108
(617) 227-9600

- *Continental Cuisine*
- *Priced moderate to high*
- *Open seven days for lunch and dinner; Weekend brunch*
- *Accepts reservations and all major credit cards*
- *Private party facilities for between 20 and 250 persons*

Harbor Terrace

For a panoramic view of Boston Harbor, Long Wharf, and Logan Airport, on any of three terraced levels come and dine in the semi-circular Harbor Terrace dining room. Shades of rich red, beige, and gray color the room, with the colors repeated in the comfortable banquettes facing the windows covered with snow white lace curtains that let you enjoy the view while filtering the strong morning sun. The recessed uppermost level is defined by coramendel screens, with traditional Chinese motifs carved in lacquer, while the soft face-flattering indirect lighting is cleverly concealed in a starburst pattern in the ceiling. An added plus is outdoor terrace dining when the weather turns warm—and fireworks over the harbor on the 4th of July or New Year's Eve can be enjoyed from your table.

Breakfast runs the gamut from fresh squeezed juice, cereals, eggs, to an assortment of breakfast breads made and baked daily in the kitchen, to Benedict twins—each different—one english muffin topped with Canadian-style bacon the other with sauteed mushrooms, both with a poached egg and hollandaise.

Lunch ranges from appetizers such as oysters, clams, shrimp, or crisp fresh vegetables with a smooth peppercream dip. You can choose combinations of hearty healthy salads such as chicken Oriental salad (lightly marinated meaty chunks of chicken in a peanut dressing with fresh pasta, all over spinach leaves) or the Chef's Salad, that not only has a julienne of roast turkey breast, ham and various cheeses, but also sports zucchini and sprouts as well as a choice of dressing.

For a treat, try the sophisticated fettuccine with chicken livers, or *tempura* shrimp, light and golden and sparked with the delicious flavor of a honey-mustard sauce presented on the side, or the beautiful pale-pink chilled poached salmon uniquely topped with a delicately seasoned cucumber dill sauce.

The early bird dinners served till 6:30 PM are high on taste, low in price, and attract a faithful clientele. The specials of the day always feature a fresh catch of the day, "The Evening Roast," and the "Chef's Choice of Veals." Another good way to start is the plump, juicy *escargot bourguignon* or chef's *pate*.

Outstanding entrees include chicken in champagne sauce, Cioppino (California-style *bouillabaise* swimming with fresh seafood), lamb Long Wharf (young and tender), or fruits *de mer* (lobster, shrimp and scallops vibrant with a parsley sauce over fettuccine).

If you don't mind courting addiction, for dessert try the "Rumbooze," a rich and creamy ice cream and a chocolate cup filled with liquer, combine them or eat them separately. For the chocoholic, there's the sinfully rich "Double Devil," a huge chewy brownie topped with Haagen-Dazs ice cream, steaming-thick hot fudge, fresh whipped cream and chocolate sprinkles.

296 State Street
Boston, Mass., 02109
(617) 227-0800

- *Continental Cuisine*
- *Priced moderate to high*
- *Open 7 days for breakfast, lunch, and dinner; also Sunday Champagne brunch*
- *Accepts reservations and all major credit cards*
- *Private party facilities available*

Hisae's

Originator of a unique culinary style that combines the exotic flavors of Eastern cookery with sophisticated international accents, Hisae Vilca created a fashion in food. So widely was her formidable formula duplicated by dozens of disciples, that anyone unaware of her history might conclude that the several Hisae locations around town are merely followers of the trend—whereas, in fact, they were the first. Hisae's East 58 Street premises are perhaps most luxurious: the spacious entry sports murals of *Belle Epoque* society and etched glass panels. In the expansive dining salon, walls are covered with shirred mauve fabric mounted with oversized mirrors in purple frames of carved laurel wreaths. Diners recline against tufted banquettes of eggplant velvet, or similarly upholstered thronelike chairs, softly illuminated by recessed spotlights set into the high, mauve-enamelled ceiling.

The major distinction of Hisae's style is a creative commitment to adventures on the vegetable and seafood frontiers. It is easy enough to elect vegetables without tears when they have been transformed by macrobiotic magic into such center-stage stars as an appetizer of cold eggplant cubes in a sesame-sprinkled *miso* dressing; seasonal asparagus baptized in bleu cheese; or mushrooms sauteed in wine sauce. Either alabaster rounds of tender calamari or sturdy shields of gamey-flavored *scungilli* in pungent vinaigrette laced with translucent slices of pickled onion, listed among the appetizers, are apportioned to serve adequately as a luncheon entree—or as a starter for at least two people. The same fine hand also turns out a daily pasta—perhaps green shells tossed with peas and mushrooms in a very light cream sauce.

The popular *bouillabaisse,* abrim with lobster, shrimp, scallops, mussels, and chunks of fish, is distinguished from ordinary versions by an abundance of whole tomatoes and cubed vegetables. Chief among Hisae's gastronomic graces, however, is her Oriental touch: Golden-browned baby scallops are sauteed with snowpeas, sprouts, and scallions; sea bass is glorified with ginger-sprinkled black bean sauce; and a moist, thick slab of delicately poached salmon is showered with mushrooms and scattered with dill. All entrees are accompanied by a fascinatingly chewy brown rice, studded with raisins and walnuts—wonderful by itself and an excellent sop for the final drops of Hisae's exotic sauces.

The infamously irresistible dessert table compounds such home-baked temptations as dense but sugarless chocolate cake, authentically crunchy *linzer torte,* and apple-walnut crumb-cake with clouds of freshly whipped cream. An international wine list offers fine labels from France, Italy, Germany, Spain, and California at gentle prices. Service is deft, solicitous, and highly professional.

---

45 East 58 Street
New York, N.Y., 10022
(212) 753-6555

12 West 72 Street
New York, N.Y., 10023
(212) 787-5656

- *Gourmet Natural Cuisine*
- *Prices are moderate*
- *Open 7 days for lunch and dinner*
- *Reservations and AE, DC, VISA accepted*
- *Private party facilities for between 50 and 500 persons*

Hoexter's Market

Hoexter's Market was a success from the moment it opened its doors in late 1977. It had not aged five months before the New York Times awarded it two stars, and it was way before that that the jaded upper East Siders began flocking to enjoy the surroundings and food.

Interior design is modern and dramatic. Natural brick walls set off cut mirrors and the romantically dim theatrical lighting. A fine, old bar is a perfect foil to the dining area, in taupe and white linen. Above it all, the original tin ceiling recalls an earlier day and has been gratefully saved.

Dedicated restaurant goers develop a sixth sense about a place just from the bread basket. At Hoexter's, you are served one of the most tantalizing in town—warm and crusty Italian white and whole wheat breads, and pumpernickel rolls filled with raisins that, when topped with the fresh, sweet butter, threaten to become a meal in itself.

Appetizers here are a special treat—as novel as they are delicious. There is a lightly smoked and sliced chicken breast that comes with a horseradish cream sauce, *escargot* in cream with mushrooms, garlic and tomato, and *escalope* of fish sauteed with basil and cucumber. This doesn't exhaust the possibilities, but you get the idea.

Quality and originality are carried through to the entree selection which, except for the fresh fish of the day, is all meat and poultry. Classic treatments are to be found here—filet mignon in a *bearnaise* sauce, steak tartare, rosy-red with a fine assortment of condiments, the market steak in slabs for two or more. But more adventurous flights are undertaken. There is a unique rendition of duck in cassis sauce and topped with raspberries and kiwi fruit, there is a filet teased with three peppercorn and coriander sauce, or a juicy stuffed veal chop sauteed with fresh herbs that bring out new flavors.

Confections here are all homemade and far from cliche. There is a triple rich chocolate fudge cake that will be explosive to chocoholics. And the now-famous white chocolate *mousse* cake under a layer of fresh, ripe strawberries and chocolate topping. Palates can also be refreshed with a choice of four assorted sorbets or fresh berries of the season and *zabaglione* sauce.

1442 Third Avenue (81 Street)
New York, N.Y., 10028
(212) 472-9322

- *American Cuisine*
- *Priced moderate to expensive*
- *Open 7 days for dinner only*
- *Reservations necessary. All major credit cards*
- *Private party facilities for between 30 and 75 persons*

Hoffmann House

It's the same Hoffmann House as ever—a couple of dining rooms supporting carved wooden paneling from a 19th century German schooner, giving the place a *Gemütlich* 1923 look which, if absorbent, must by now be saturated with sighs of satisfaction over the Hoffmann House provender and quaffstuffs. A long, wooden bar runs down one side of the main floor dining room, and tables and chairs fan out from it. Ceiling fans turn overhead, contributing to the atmosphere, and the German-International cuisine is prepared in bountiful portions by the present owner-chef, William Hyland.

Among the appetizers, the *tages suppe* (soup of the day) is often the black bean. A light, delicate broth holds a mixture of black beans and pieces of chicken, and it's a delicious, well-seasoned *potage*.

Another excellent appetizer is the *ochsenmaul-salat*—thinly sliced marinated tongue on a bed of crisp romaine lettuce garnished with slices of sweet red peppers. Other appetizers include baked oysters with parmesean cheese and lemon, a cream-based crab, corn, and roasted red pepper soup, and steak tartare.

The *haus salat* (house salad) also deserves mentioning. Seedless and skinless cucumber slices and cherry tomatoes get mixed with crisp greens and a delicious vinaigrette.

The list of entrees is a blend of traditional German dishes and some special creations of chef Hyland. The *hasenrucken*, for instance, is a braised saddle of rabbit served with a fresh rosemary, lemon, and red wine sauce. The *schweinbraten mit kummel* is thick sliced pork loin served in a caraway, sour cream, and reduced pork stock. Game lovers will enjoy the *rehrucken aut Hoffmann art*, sauteed venison in a tangy sauce of ginger, gin, and green peppercorns. There are also the more traditional dishes, such as *weinerschnitzel, rheinischer sauerbraten,* and *schnitzel a la Holstein.*

Among the toothsome desserts is a German apple pancake (filled with a hot apple, raisin, and almond mixture and covered with whipped cream) and their award-winning *sacher torte,* a very rich, very moist, very chocolaty example of that layered delight.

Hoffmann House is an outstanding restaurant, a place where first-rate food, attentive service, and comfortable surroundings all make a visit quite enjoyable.

1214 Sansom Street
Philadelphia, Pa., 19107
(215) 925-8778

- *German Cuisine*
- *Moderate to high prices*
- *Open Tuesday through Friday for lunch; Tuesday through Saturday for dinner; Closed Sunday and Monday*
- *All major credit cards accepted*
- *Reservations recommended*
- *Private party facilities for between 20 and 45 persons*

Horn of Plenty

This is a multi-levelled establishment cool with plants, and greenery, and warm with a hospitable staff. The whole big repertoire of American food is the fare at this combination restaurant, lounge with entertainment, and unofficial headquarters of Southern expatriates at large in the city.

You can begin with soups like chicken gumbo brimming with okra, vegetables, and chicken, or a thick, aromatic creamed asparagus soup. Appetizers range from fiery-hot devilled crabmeat mixed with celery, bell peppers, and eggplant, to a smoothly-textured and delectable Cajun crab. Main courses are changed regularly with new surprises cropping up daily. One day may see pan-fried chicken coddled in a rich brown gravy while another brings stuffed center-cut pork chops with cornbread dressing and apple sauce. You can be sure there will be spare ribs spiked with fragrant and spicy hot sauce, Louisianna shrimp *creole,* or pan-fried calf's liver with crisp bacon or onion. Surf N' Turf shares the menu with pork chitlins and, in an International cuisine departure from thorough Americana, Indian chicken curry and beef Stroganoff made a welcome and surprising cameo appearances.

The South is famous for accompaniments served during the meal, and the Horn has plenty—black-eyed peas, candied yams with a dash of cinnamon, collard greens, corn-on-the-cob, baked potato, and rice. Warm-from-the-oven cornbread is a constant, too.

All of the pies, cakes, and cobblers are baked on the premises. The cobblers are unique, deep casseroles of fruit baked to a down-home finish, served warm and brimming with fresh fruit. A fat slice of chocolate Grand Marnier layer cake or a thick wedge of Mississippi mud pie are two velvety-smooth endings that assure a big finish.

This restaurant also features modern jazz and cabaret vocalists in its upstairs Music Room nightly from 9:00 PM. Adjacent is a sleek and spacious bar where you can listen to the entertainment and nibble complimentary barbequed snacks.

91 Charles Street
New York, N.Y., 10013
(212) 242-0636

- *Southern/International Cuisine*
- *Priced moderate*
- *Open 7 days for dinner only*
- *Reservations and all major credit cards accepted*
- *Entertainment nightly except Monday*

Jean-Pierre Restaurant

Jean Michel Farret was born in a village in the Champagne region of France. He began his colorful, multinational career in restaurants at the hotel Plaza-Athenee in Paris, and from there it was on to five exclusive establishments in Dublin, New York, Mexico, Bermuda, and, finally, to Washington, D.C. In Washington he ran Rive Gauche before opening his own place, Jean-Pierre Restaurant. But peripatetic Jean Michel's travels had a point: he learned from each restaurant he worked in, and he determined exactly what he felt a restaurant should be and do. Jean-Pierre Restaurant is the culmination of all his experience.

It's an elegant French place, where nicely illuminated oil paintings line the attractive beige walls. Banquettes and French provincial chairs of a deeper cream color surround tables which are covered by linens and appointed with silver and crystal. The room is broken up by handsome mirrored dividers.

People come to a restaurant to do more than just sit in a pretty room, however, and at Jean-Pierre Restaurant customers get food equal to the surroundings.

One of the tempting appetizers is the *coquille St. Jacques,* and like most of the dishes here, the presentation of the food is worth admiring before you begin eating. The scallops and their velvety cream sauce are accompanied by a beautiful arrangement of carrots, broccoli, and mushroom caps filled with creamed spinach, all of it tantalizingly set on a blue-white plate. Other appetizers include smoked salmon, frog legs, mussels, and shrimp. A periodic offering is a dish of sauteed wild mushrooms in a creamy sauce with shallots. The soup of the day is sometimes a savory mushroom soup that uses a squab broth as a base.

Among the entrees one of the most eye-catching and mouth-watering is the salmon *en croute*, where a rich, buttery pastry shell envelopes an expertly cooked salmon filet. The chateaubriand is topped with a provocative roquefort sauce, and again the presentation is beautiful. There's also a beef filet with a red wine and shallot sauce, and a medallion of veal with a lemon sauce. The tenderloin of lamb arrives cooked as ordered, juicy and tender, alongside creamy scalloped potatoes served *au gratin*.

Jean-Pierre Restaurant makes all its own desserts, foremost among them being the raspberry *souffle*, a light, delicate, sumptuous creation.

1835 K Street NW
Washington, D.C., 20006
(202) 466-2022

- *French Cuisine*
- *Priced expensive*
- *Open Monday through Saturday for lunch and dinner; closed Sunday*
- *All major credit cards accepted*
- *Reservations required*

Kalyva

If you can't afford an airline ticket to Greece this year, Kalyva is the closest thing to being in the islands. In the Greek style, it is unimposing on the outside, but once passed you enter a world of honest gutsy eating. The kitchen is open and up-front, as is butcher-shop counter displaying fresh fish, meat and vegetables, as well as a live lobster tank. Freshness here is gospel, and what the customers don't eat up, the help does.

Kalyva is a neighborhood place, and this being the Greek section of Astoria (the largest outside of the Aegean) you know they play to a critical audience. You can lose yourself in the travel fantasy. Half the menu here is in Greek, and much of the help only speak that language (not to worry—a call to one of the other waiters or waitresses in time of language difficulty will bring help).

The place is comfortable—you're here to eat, not look. Two dining rooms, one with murals of the old country, the other in a marine motif will set the wanderlust astirring.

Owner Mike Moraitis is head of this family-run operation, and he provides an unusually broad and varied menu that encompasses not only the expected lamb dishes, but a very generous assortment of beef, pork, poultry, and especially seafood—shrimp, lobster, crab, octopus, and more. And what is perhaps best of all, prices here are so reasonable, looking down the menu you have the feeling that somebody gave you one a decade-old by mistake.

This is the restaurant to explore new tastes in. Such unlikely foods as charbroiled octopus turn out to be tasty little morsels; fried lamb's liver and sweetbreads an unexpected find; and even such old favorites as simple broiled snapper and mullets take on a different taste here.

"Kalyva" means hut in Greek, owner Mike's reflection of the Greek style of understatement. This hut houses not only the best cooking in the area, but the most contented customers.

36-15 Ditmars Boulevard
Astoria, N.Y., 11105
(212) 932-9229

- *Greek Cuisine*
- *Priced inexpensive*
- *Open 7 days for lunch and dinner*
- *Reservations accepted on weekends only;*
  No credit cards
- *Private party facilities for between 30 and 40 people*

Kamehachi

This venerable name, famous in Tokyo for its high culinary standards, has come to the United States with branches in New York and Chicago. The menu is complete, varied, and goes from the familiar to the adventurously exotic.

Housed in quarters that focus almost entirely on the food, there is no self-conscious emulation of mythical Japanese tea rooms or private homes, but a spacious and serene establishment with large, leather-covered booths of glossy-red enamel and wood-trimmed walls. There is a separate sushi bar for less formal and individual dining that might be a fine idea for other restaurants to copy.

But one comes here for the unusual—and it is here in plenty. Name after exotic name graces the menu—in English, Japanese, and description. But let us start with the familiar. There is shrimp, fish, and vegetable *tempura* with a soft, light egg batter hiding delicately cooked green pepper, onions, eggplants, mushrooms, tender shrimp, and fish. The *sukiyaki*, tender beef and green vegetables is one of the best. This is also the place to go if you are a lover of *teriyaki*—Kamehachi makes its own sauce and it is delicious on beef, chicken, and salmon.

Sushi devotees will find the authentic stuff here. It is served with vinegared rice, marinated cucumbers, pickled ginger and shredded white radish with raw fish delicacies as sliced salmon, tuna, red snapper, sea urchin, eel, octopus, salmon roe, and crab. There is a little sushi chart and you may order whatever kind of seafood you like.

Kamehachi has an unusually wide range of appetizers. They are justly proud of their *yamakake*, raw tuna over a pungent sauce and topped with the ubiquitous mash of white yams that lends a mild counterpoint. You might also explore the recesses of Japanese cuisine with the *tarako* (baked cod roe), *yudofu* (boiled bean cake), *yakitori* (chicken shish kebob), *yakinasu* (baked eggplant), *ikamomijiae* (squid with cod roe), and many, many others.

Also to be experienced are the exotic twists given the *tonkatsu*—deep-fried tenderloin pork, *negimayaki*—sliced beef with vegetables, and *kani-nabe*—crabmeat with vegetables. And for simple pleasures, try the *ocha-zuke*—bowls of rice with seaweed, salmon, cod roe, shrimp or tuna, or the noodles in soup.

14 East 47 Street
New York, N.Y., 10017
(212) 765-4737

- *Japanese cuisine*
- *Priced inexpensive to moderate*
- *Open 6 days for lunch and dinner; Closed Sunday*
- *Accepts reservations and all major credit cards*
- *Private party facilities for between 10 and 80*

Jack Kaplan's at West 47 Street

Nothing is more New York than the foods fondly known as "deli"—and nobody does them better than Jack Kaplan's, strategically situated on the borderline between the Broadway bustle and the jewelry/diamond district. Jack himself, and Manager Mel Nudelman—both sporting their trademark scarlet suspenders—play hearty hosts to bigtime buyers, browsing tourists, and theatergoers who arrive panting for pastrami, craving corned beef, and longing for *latkas*. Typical deli-decor starts with a window exhibit of hanging salamis and jars of sours, but the three dining areas are unusually sleek and comfortable: cherry cerise-upholstered nooks stand against wood-grain panelled walls; down the center runs a lineup of spotlessly shiny blondwood tables. Another civilized comfort: in addition to the mandatory celery tonic and cream soda, beers and wines are available.

At the heart of every great deli is a menu abundant to the point of confusion: choosing among the *blintzes,* the hearty soups, the cured meats, the potato pancakes, the smoked fish—and more—is almost enough to ruin an appetite. Jack's answer to the dilemma is the "Noshtalgia Platter" for two: *kasha varnishkes; derma* as smooth and rich as grandma's; chicken fricassee; crisp-skinned potato pancakes well seasoned with onion and spices; and stuffed cabbage rolls filled with moist meat sparked by raisins—with globules of silky sweet-sour sauce clinging to the leaves. For a special sensation, don't fail to add an order of the remarkable House knish: over an inch thickness of freshly-mashed potato—both fluffy in texture and laced with some nuggets for contrast, plus the crunch of raw onion—encased in a greaseless crust as delicate as a coat of batter.

Smoked whitefish, sturgeon and nova are offered on bagels, as individual salads, or on another of the mammoth House assorted platters. "Mammoth" is simply the way it's done around here: all the sandwiches—either simple tongue, turkey or pastrami, or the mind-boggling combos of varied meats and cheeses—are built from a full seven ounces of meat. And like any deli worth its brine, Jack's place boasts great sour pickles and pickled tomatoes—as well as a basket of onion rolls, pumpernickel, and rye breads that are delivered fresh three times daily. These necessities supplement steaming bowls of chicken in the pot, boiled beef,

and the Kaplan Family Goulash—and round out the chicken cacciatore, sauteed steak and onions, or Hungarian deli omelette entrees on the amazingly-priced $7.95 full pre-theatre dinner.

Finally—there's really fresh fresh fruit salad that always includes berries in season and never stoops to any artificial additives. Only the brave and the skinny dare to devour such devilish-rich desserts as triple-fudge-frosted chocolate cake; nutty, moist, multi-layered carrot cake; and a memorable chocolate-chip creamcheese cake, dotted with chocolate bits throughout and based on a candy shell that forms during the baking from the melting chips. With such provocative pastries one is grateful for the good, rich coffee generously poured by a motherly waitress.

71 West 47 Street
New York, N.Y., 10036
(212) 391-2333

- *New York Jewish Deli*
- *Inexpensive*
- *Open Monday through Friday from 7 am til 7 pm; Saturday from 9 am til 4 pm; Closed Sunday*
- *Accepting all major credit cards*
- *Private party facility for up to 70*

Keewah Yen

W hen you're new in town, the safest way to select a restaurant is to find one that's popular with the locals. Well if you walked into Keewah Yen in New York during a weekday lunch hour, you'd guess it might be the hottest and best joint in town.

Located in the middle of the skyscraper-filled darkness that has become Midtown Manhattan, Keewah Yen, with good reason, has become a favorite restaurant among the business people of New York. They're tired of the steak/fish menus of most restaurants in the area, and the sophisticated Chinese decor and cuisine is a welcome change.

The place is handsome. Chinese antiques and original works of Chinese art and calligraphy decorate the walls, and beautiful Chinese wooden room dividers separate the four dining areas. Works of jade and ivory dot the rooms, adding to the beautiful look. The elegance even extends to the table settings, where the china is actually from China.

Whatever you do at Keewah Yen, don't skip over the appetizers. At cocktail time there may be up to a dozen of them, most of which are delicious. The stuffed crab claws, wrapped in a crisp coating, are especially good, as is the *dim sum*, which actually may be one of the best examples of *dim sum* in New York.

The emphasis is on Cantonese food at Keewah

Yen, which means most of the flavors are subtle and graceful (as opposed to the fiery hotness of much Szechuan cooking). The veal with snow peas is a thoroughly excellent combination of buttery veal and crisp snow peas—don't pass it up. The *Gon Shiu* mignon is a beef dish that has an interesting peppery sweetness to it.

If chicken is what you want, try the pine seed chicken—chicken sauteed with pine nuts, diced water chestnuts, and bamboo shoots, and given a nice sampling of fresh ginger.

One nice aspect of Keewah Yen is the very knowledgeable staff. If you should have trouble deciding which dishes to choose, they will gladly recommend some and describe them for you.

And should you not want Cantonese food, Keewah Yen also has several Szechuan and Hunan dishes.

---

50 West 56 Street
New York, N.Y., 10019
(212) 246-0770

- *Chinese Cuisine*
- *Priced moderate*
- *Open Monday through Friday for lunch; 7 days for dinner*
- *Reservations accepted*
  AE, VISA, DC accepted

King's Landing

It's doubtful that kings ever landed here, but certainly a great many other people, and especially goods did: In the 19th century the building housing this very popular fine French restaurant was part of a busy Potomac River (near Washington, D.C.) warehouse and ship-loading complex. But despite the more or less Colonial motif used in the decoration, it would be difficult to surmise the building's past from looking at it today.

Today it's a restaurant, and in all the different dining rooms the look and feel is very relaxed and comfortable. The main dining room upstairs is called the "King's Loft." It's a stylish room, where a seemingly endlessly long bar, a beautiful fireplace, and a copperleaf waterfall all lend an imposing presence yet also balance each other. The downstairs dining room, with brick walls and a paneled ceiling, has a similarly warm and friendly feeling.

Also worth noting is the smaller upstairs dining room which can be reserved for private parties. Recently it has become somewhat of a popular rendezvous for movers and shakers in and out of politics who want to eat well while they're moving and shaking.

And eat well you do. The accent here is French, but they also serve a lot of what, if the name didn't have *le* or *les* in front of it, you'd call "American Seafood." As an example there's the *saumon frais grille,* which is an expertly grilled filet of Nova Scotia salmon. The portion is large and the fish is tender, moist, and tasty. There's also the *filet de sole au crabmeat,* which is a nicely cooked sole filet topped with juicy crabmeat.

When fresh mussels are available chef Jacques Duplaa, who hails from Toulouse, in France, gently steams them and serves them in a light, delicate white wine and cream sauce—they're delicious.

The *St. Germain* soup is also a winner. It's very rich and creamy and has an almost breathtaking aroma. In the fall pumpkin soup is a frequent visitor; it's a thick, richly-textured soup with a pungent pumpkin scent.

Besides the many seafood entrees—there's also pompano with tomatoes and anchovies, poached turbot, and rock fish in a tomato, fennel, and wine sauce, to name a few of the fish dishes—King's Landing also offers a complete range of meat dishes, most done in a French style.

There is a full selection of desserts—but the house speciality is *vacherin,* a universal favorite consisting of chocolate chip and vanilla ice cream, almonds, meringue, and whipped cream.

King's Landing is a justifiable favorite in Alexandria.

121 South Union Street
Alexandria, Va., 22314
(703) 836-7010

- *French Cuisine and Seafood*
- *Priced moderate to high*
- *Open seven days for lunch and dinner*
- *All major credit cards. Reservations recommended*
- *Private party facilities available*

La Belle Epoque

During *la belle epoque* in *la belle France* (around the turn of the century), the beautiful people of Parisian society met and dined at Maxim's, either before or after, or before and after, going to the opera. The restaurant La Belle Epoque may not be Maxim's, but it's doing its best to fulfill the same function in Dade County that Maxim's fulfilled in Paris.

Chef and owner Denis Rety hails from Brittany, in France, but he's spent his last 18 years in Florida and his last six years at La Belle Epoque. His dedication to the restaurant is such that he is still the head chef and he teaches all the chefs below him how he wants things done; he also does all the preparation work himself for most of the dishes.

His perseverance pays off, especially when it comes to dishes *en croute* (wrapped in pastry). The beef Wellington, for instance, is almost a work of art with the beef inside the pastry being perfectly tender and juicy. Denis also serves a salmon filet topped with crabmeat and wrapped in pastry, and the salmon is perfectly cooked, too. The accompanying cream sauce complements the dish expertly. And if chicken is what you want, there's a breast of chicken wrapped in pastry and filled with mushrooms, ham, and cream sauce *(poulet Josephine en croute).* For an appetizer there's the *escargot bourguignons en croute,* snails wrapped in pastry with garlic butter, and the fragrant snails have an almost silky texture. Clearly, Denis can do *en croute.*

But there's much more at La Belle Epoque. Appetizers cover the gamut, a few of them being smoked trout, clams casino, prosciutto and melon, and crabmeat and mushrooms in a light cream sauce wrapped in a crepe.

Denis serves over a dozen fish and seafood dishes, some of them being frogs legs *provencal,* dover sole *meuniere, bouillabaisse,* broiled snapper, broiled Maine lobster, and a poached salmon with hollandaise.

The meat dishes include *boeuf bourguignon,* veal Oscar, steak *au poivre,* rack of lamb, steamed pheasant stuffed with goose liver and truffles, filet *bernaise,* duck *a l'orange,* and a boneless half chicken with prosciutto, cheese, and a light cream sauce.

And the setting for all this food is very attractive. The glass wall that closes off the large patio can be covered with rich, elegant drapes, so, depending on the weather and the day, one can look onto a beautiful patio or not. The dining room is richly appointed with fine linen, silver, and crystal, and the feeling the room gives off is of quiet, harmonious elegance.

1045 95th Street
Bay Harbor Isles, Fla., 33154
(305) 865-6011

- *French Cuisine*
- *Priced moderate to high*
- *Open seven days for dinner only*
- *Reservations recommended and all major credit cards accepted*
- *Private party facilities for between 20 and 65 persons*

La Camargue

Camargue is an island in the Rhone delta in southeast France, and chef/owner Marcel Brosette has picked up where the original owner left off and made La Camargue reflect that part of France in both cuisine and decor.

The restaurant, reminiscent of a rustic French inn, has brick walls, beamed ceilings, a fireplace, and an overall French "country" feeling. But rustic is not to say unrefined, and there's an understated elegance present, too, with starched pink linen and soft lighting testifying to it.

For your first course at La Camargue choose from a large sampling of appetizers. If *pates* are your pleasure, try the tangy, coarse country *pate (terrine de campagne)*, or the smooth, delicate goose liver *pate (parfait de foies volaille)*. The *avocat estoril* is an avocado, shrimp, and hearts of palm salad, with a rich French dressing and fresh mushrooms. There's also smoked Scottish salmon, cold fresh lobster,

escargot, pike *mousse,* and clams with lemon, butter, and bacon.

La Camargue's soups are excellent, and they range from the classically done onion soup to their own *soupe de poisson*, a smooth, rich salmon-colored fish soup into which they stir a fragrant garlic-pepper paste just before serving.

Their ample list of entrees has several excellent dishes. The calf's liver *(foie de veau sauce diable)* is perfectly cooked, and the sauce complements it wonderfully. The vegetables served alongside are fresh and crisp. Periodically La Camargue serves a scallops and fettucinni dish. The sinfully rich sauce that blends well with the scallops makes this entree a delight.

Marcel offers several other fish dishes, among which is a juicy, succulent *peche du jour en papillotte*. The *peche du jour* is usually red snapper, and it's wrapped in parchment, thus cooking in its own juices. There's also a grilled filet of swordfish, a filet of sole served with mussels and shrimp, and fresh lobster served with a light curry sauce.

But don't overlook the meats, including roast pheasant, sweetbreads with spinach and cream sauce, rack of lamb, and *boeuf au poivre*.

There's also a plentiful selection of freshly-made desserts to finish off either lunch or dinner.

La Camargue is that type of restaurant that is unfortunately becoming increasingly scarce: a place serving delicious French food in a very comfortable atmosphere at moderate prices. *Felicitations,* Marcel!

1119 Walnut Street
Philadelphia, Pa., 19106
(215) 922-3148

- *French Country Cuisine*
- *Priced moderate*
- *Open Monday through Friday for lunch; Monday through Saturday for dinner; Closed Sunday*
- *AE, VISA, and reservations accepted*

La Caravelle

One of the handful of four-star *haute cuisine* restaurants in New York, La Caravelle is famous for its classic cuisine, ambiance and service. Decor is unmistakably Parisan, with park scenes dominating the walls, plush banquettes, softly tinted walls, and draperies setting a mellow counterpoint to the vibrant menu and bustling staff.

Visiting La Caravelle is always an experience, whether it is by—or to view—hungry celebrities and leaders of enterprise, or to celebrate a special occasion. Any choice will bring forth a performance from the kitchen because the restaurant specializes in immpeccably chosen food in complex sauces. The kitchen is closely supervised by owners Robert Meyzen and Roger Fessaguet, who applied what they learned as *maitres d'hotel* under the legendary Henry Soule at Le Pavillion—a formidable teacher. But that was more than two decades ago, and the two have led La Caravelle into its own legendary niche in gastronomic history.

33 West 55 Street
New York, N.Y., 10019
(212) JU6-4252

- *French Cuisine*
- *Priced expensive.*
- *Open 6 days for lunch and dinner; closed Sunday.*
- *Reservations necessary. AE, DC, MC, VISA accepted*
- *Prix-fixe lunch for $21.75; Dinner is a la carte*
- *No private party facilities*

La Cascade

La Cascade is one of the more appropriately named restaurants around, since *la cascade* means "the waterfall," and the restaurant is dominated by one wall that is entirely a cascading sheet of water. And since the entire wall opposite the waterfall is a mirror, and it completely reflects the waterfall, *une cascade* is the dominant visual image at La Cascade no matter where you sit.

The effect of all this water, be it a reflection or the real thing, is that the restaurant feels very soothing and relaxing. And when you add the small palm trees, the rows of flowers, the beautiful rattan chairs, the nicely-spaced tables, the recessed lighting, the gold banquettes, and the fine linen, crystal, or syliver appointments, the end result is an exceptionally tranquil place to dine.

The food at La Cascade is French *nouvelle,* and in this case the *nouvelle* is a subtle little twist given to classic French dishes. Instead of *coquille St. Jacques,* for instance, Le Cascade serves *le feuillet de St. Jacques au beurre blanc*, where the tasty bay scallops and their rich sauce are encased in a delicious pastry shell. There's also a savory pike quenelle that has a perfectly seasoned sauce. The Norwegian smoked salmon is perfectly garnished, and other appetizers include a goose liver *pate in a brioche*, and smoked trout.

The list of entrees is not extensive, but it is varied. The dover sole *meuniere* is nicely prepared and accompanied by cooked potatoes and green beans, and veal mignonettes are also expertly prepared and presented. Other entrees include a breast of duck with berries, chicken with morels, and a rack of lamb—to name but a few.

Desserts are a strong suit at La Cascade, the offerings being those of the famed bakery Delices La Cote Basque. This noteworthy bakery is part of La Cascade restaurant and provides pastries and baked goods for your take home pleasure, as well as for other Manhattan restaurants and cafes. There are tarts, mousses, mousse cakes, and even ice cream concoctions, and all are guaranteed to satisfy even the most picky dessert eater.

Le Cascade also has a small operation directly above the restaurant proper, off to one side of the lobby of the Olympic Tower, called Le Cafe. Le Cafe serves breakfast, sandwiches, light entrees, and more of those delicious pastries throughout the day.

---

645 Fifth Avenue
New York, N.Y., 10022
(212) 935-2220

- *French nouvelle cuisine*
- *Priced moderate to high*
- *Open Monday-Friday for lunch and dinner; Closed Saturday and Sunday. Le Cafe: Monday-Friday 8:00 AM through 10:30 PM; Saturday 9:00 AM through 8:00 PM; Closed Sunday*
- *Reservations and all major credit cards accepted*

La Cote Basque

In the landscape of fine French restaurants, La Cote Basque stands as a beacon, both gastronomically and historically. In dining here, you have the opportunity to experience an establishment so thoroughly sound and accomplished that it ranks as one of the best French restaurants in the country. There is also the unique opportunity to become part of gourmet history, for La Cote Basque stands on the site of the original Le Pavillion, founded in 1941 by the now legendary Henry Soule, whose flawless cuisine made it the standard for luxury restaurants throughout the country. Many years later, Mr. Soule moved Le Pavillion and in its place created La Cote Basque as a sort of second generation descendant—less classic and expensive, but just as transcendant.

The restaurant was operated by Mr. Soule, and then by an associate until 1980, when it was purchased by Jean Jacques Rachou. Mr. Rachou, a chef of modest, gentle ways, had already gained notice and praise as owner of Le Lavandou (located at 134 East 61 Street), an establishment known as much for its warmth and friendliness as for its wholly dependable cuisine.

Mr. Rachou's stamp of ability and authority are everywhere evident at La Cote Basque. The dining room is subdued and unostentatious, highlighted with murals of Basque harbor and countryside. The walls are ivory, trimmed in dark wood and flank plush red banquettes, chairs, and tables set with stunning Villeroy & Bosch china and glistening stemware. This is a place to admire, but not to be in awe of. A place to relax while observing what a totally successful restaurant should be.

As recognition in any profession demands a trademark, Mr. Rachou's is elaborate serving and garnishing of the food, prepared to its quintessence. He can, in short, flawlessly produce anything in the *haute cuisine* repertoire, and it is a useless exercise to attempt to steer the diner around his menu. There is nothing to avoid—all is special

Perhaps one might be addressed to the transcendant. The tonic preparation of the *pates* and *terrines* that have magic in their blend and taste. Or the breathtaking—the *soupe de pecheur* that comes dense with shrimp, scallops, chunks of lobster and julienne strips of fresh vegetables, all burnished with a pink garlic-and-cayenne flavored sauce *rouille*. One critic called it "celestial." Otherworldly, too, is Rachou's rendering of chicken breast stuffed with quail *mousse,* sumptuous medallions of veal in a sauce spiked with savory black truffles, duck served with contrasting sauces, and no less than perfection is the Dover sole surrounded with oysters, scallops, and crayfish in a sauce *Nantua.*

La Cote Basque is a thoroughly balanced establishment—from flawless cuisine to atmosphere to service. It takes its place in its hallowed location as a landmark.

5 East 55 Street
New York, N.Y., 10022
(212) 688-6525

- *French cuisine*
- *Priced expensive*
- *Open 6 days for $24.00 prix-fixe lunch and $40.00 prix-fixe dinner; closed Sunday*
- *No private parties*

La Coupole

In a city with hundreds of French restaurants, you'd think all bases would be covered. But restaurateurs Jean de Noyer and Jean Manuel Rozan found that there was one type of restaurant New York City lacked: an authentic French *brasserie*. They saw that New York needed a place where one could go from noon until early in the morning to get a full range of dishes, from onion soup to steak *au poivre*, all of which would have a distinctly French flair and taste. They knew it had to be casual yet chic, and that it had to appeal to the so-called beautiful people. So they opened La Coupole.

There's also a La Coupole in Paris, you see (it's on the famed Left Bank, on Boulevard Montparnasse, and Gertrude Stein's lost generation of Ernest Hemingway, F. Scott Fitzgerald, and friends used to find each other there for coffee and drinks). Well, de Noyer and Rozan cloned that Parisian La Coupole—this one is almost identical, art deco down to the flatware and the Limoges china. What's more, it's a legal copy—they got permission from the French owners.

And like the one in Paris, this La Coupole is impressive. It's a large, high-ceilinged room room punctuated by massive wood-covered pillars and illuminated by Art-Deco light fixtures. Burgundy banquettes divide the room, and wooden chairs upholstered in the same burgundy sit next to attractively appointed tables. Some two thirds of the way up the walls, the heavy dark wood stops and a pristine white look takes over—making the room seem even more spacious and airy.

Another attraction at La Coupole is the people who go there. Even though it recently opened, it has already established itself as a haunt for the celebrated and beautiful people de Noyer and Rozan wanted.

La Coupole serves an authentic *brasserie* menu, offering all types of salads, soups, appetizers, sandwiches, heavy and light entrees, and desserts. Among the standout soups is a hearty lentil *potage,* thick and tasty. The *L'Americaine* is a savory dish of plump, firm shrimp surrounding a mound of angler fish in a smooth, rich cream sauce. They also dispense a mouth-watering *cassoulet*, which is served in a piping hot baking crock and brimful with white beans and chunks of tender meat.

Among the desserts the foremost may be the *bombe pralinee*, an ice cream cake layered with nut pralinee.

2 Park Avenue
New York, N.Y., 10016
(212) 696-0100

- *French Brasserie Cuisine*
- *Priced moderate to high*
- *Open seven days for lunch and dinner*
- *All major credit cards*
- *Reservations recommended.*

La Folie

When La Folie opened its doors in the spring of 1977, it stunned even the most sophisticated with its decorative concept. What they saw was a futuristic creation of the late Frederick P. Victor and David Barrett—rare Russian green malachite pillars, pink Norwegian and Italian marble, green velvet banquettes cleaving to mirrored walls, specially designed stained glass panels and restrooms done in clear plexiglass. The stupendous bar stands in ladies' and men's mannequin feet, dressed up with shoes and socks. Original paintings by Cassigneul and a four-foot bronze sculpture of Charlie Chaplin by Georges Charpentier finish off an interior as startling as any stage setting.

And this is a setting aimed at those who enjoy the good life, for La Folie enjoys a high reputation for classic and *nouvelle* cuisine. The menus, created by owner-chef Bernard Norget are structured on a fixed price basis and exhibit an utter sophistication.

Preparation of the entrees is carried through perfectly: the rack of lamb is tender, pink and juicy; veal dishes are delicate and succulent; the lobster thermidor is tender and savory; and *tournedos* spiked with Perigord knows few equals.

The desserts are a fitting finale in this showplace on the Eastside. Do not pass the classic *souffle au Grand Mariner* or *La Tulipe de L'Ardeche*—a free-form crunchy pastry lathered with softened homemade ice cream, blended with liqueurs and chestnuts.

One further innovation in this startling establishment is La Folie's Caviar Bar. It is a unique presentation of every manner of the delicacy, from precious Beluga to American brands, plus a distinguished assemblage of imported vodka.

21 East 61 Street
New York, N.Y., 10021
(212) 765-1400

- *French Cuisine*
- *Priced expensive*
- *Open Monday through Friday for both a la carte and $22.50 prix-fixe pre-theater dinner from 6:00 PM till 7:30 PM; Monday through Saturday for a la carte or $37.50 four course prix-fixe dinner 7:30 till 10:30 10:30 PM; Monday through Saturday for $22.50 post-theater prix-fixe dinner; closed Sunday*
- *Reservations suggested. Accepts all major credit cards*
- *Private party facility for 25 to 30 persons during open hours; 70 to 150 persons for private Saturday lunch or Sunday lunch and/or dinner parties*

La Fontaine

La Fontaine is barely over a year old, yet it's already established itself as an exquisite French restaurant. Pierre and Christine de Vautravers transformed what was the Post and Paddock into an elegant yet friendly place to dine. Pierre was born in France and although he spent many years living in South America he has retained his love for France and his passion for French food, a fact his restaurant clearly demonstrates.

One way Pierre helped to ensure an authentic French cuisine at La Fontaine was to hire a Parisian chef, Denis Saunier. Thirty-two year old Denis hasn't been in this country too long—his English is still weak—but his training is completely French. Much of the rest of the kitchen staff is also from Paris.

Pierre has sumptuously decorated La Fontaine. Underneath a stunning carved wood ceiling, red crushed velvet drapes cut across dark blue walls. A carpet of the same dark blue hue extends from wall to wall, and the chairs are upholstered with dark blue crushed velvet. Fresh red roses sit atop salmon-pink linen tablecloths alongside tapered candles in elegant hurricane lamps. Strategically placed spotlights help to complete the elegant, romantic atmosphere.

La Fontaine's menu is studded with many classic French dishes. Among the appetizers there are the *pates,* for example, chicken and game *pate,* and a duck *pate.* There's also *escargot,* a salmon *mousse,* poached oysters, and caviar. Among the soups are onion soup, *vichyssoise,* and lobster bisque. Pierre's vegetable soup is a beautifully textured, lightly creamy change of pace. The salads include crisp hearts of palm, endives, Caesar, and a green salad with a French vinaigrette.

Just about anything you'd think La Fontaine ought to serve, it serves—from the frogs legs *provencale,* to the dover sole *meuniere* with capers and lemon sauce, to the chicken with tarragon, to the veal *francaise*—just to name a sampling of the entrees. Pierre has his *nouvelle*-style specialties as well. Lobster is topped with a fish *mousee,* wrapped in puff pastry, and served with a champagne and lobster sauce. A juicy, tender rack of lamb is accompanied by perfectly cooked vegetables and a delicate sauce. There's also filet of venison, roast pigeon, and a pheasant casserole.

Besides an ice cream made from his grandmother's recipe, Pierre offers *crepes Suzette,* a selection of French cheeses, and chocolate *mousse* for dessert—as well as a trolley of nightly specialities.

9650 East Bay Harbor
Bay Harbor Isles, Fla., 33154
(305) 866-8706

- *French cuisine*
- *Priced moderate to high*
- *Open seven days for dinner only*
- *Reservations recommended, and all major credit cards accepted*

La Goulue

La Goulue is one of those restaurants that seems to be perfectly situated: in the middle of Manhattan's very posh and very expensive Upper East Side. It's a polished, stylish restaurant serving a contingent of polished, stylish people.

The old-fashioned dark wood walls are broken up only by large inset mirrors and windows that have lace-like white curtains over them. A new, dark tin ceiling extends high overhead and a wooden floor stretches beneath. Dark leather banquettes line the room, and around it antique crystal sconces cast a pretty light. To complete the look of understated elegance, a fresh tulip in a glass vase rests on the white linen of each table and the waiters wear long white butcher aprons over black pants and jackets.

La Goulue does not offer a great number of dishes, but they do offer a nice variety: veal, lamb, duck, beef, chicken, and fish are all served, each in a different manner. The duck, for instance, is served with chestnuts, while the medallions of veal have a morel sauce. There's also *pave d'agneau aux herbes,* bass Goulue, and *entrecote au poivre.*

The list of appetizers is also limited, but again diverse, offering mushrooms *a la Greque, escargot bourguignonne,* smoked salmon, a beautifully presented prosciutto and melon, duck *pate,* and celery remoulade.

Dessert is nicely handled, again with a small but varied selection, ranging from the classic *creme caramel* and chocolate *mousse* to an excellent *bombe praline.*

La Goulue is also a popular spot for lunch, and the menu is very similiar to the dinner menu. More salads are served—a *nicoise* and a chef's salad, for instance—and there are also omelettes, an excellent filet of sole with a Nantua sauce, calf's liver, and a very popular cheese *souffle.* The *souffle* comes piping hot out of the oven, still in its brown baking dish, all fluffy and golden brown, seemingly more air than cheese.

La Goulue is an expensive, classy, very French restaurant with a large group of regular customers.

---

28 East 70th St.
New York, N.Y., 10021
(212) 988-8169

- *French Cuisine*
- *Priced expensive*
- *Open Monday through Saturday for lunch and dinner; Closed Sunday*
- *All major credit cards*
- *Reservations recommended*

La Grenouille

3 EAST 52°

One of the more extraordinary restaurants in New York, La Grenouille is an example matched by few other establishments. It was founded in 1972 by Charles Masson, who joined the ranks of *maitre d'hotel* under Le Pavillion's Henri Soule who set off on their own to create other oases of *haute cuisine* in the mold of the master. It was a tragic twist that Masson lived only three years after fulfilling his dream, but fortune smiled on us all as his wife Gisele, and son Charles took over the restaurant and kept it at the level it was left at by Charles senior.

La Grenouille is the headquarters of New York's beautiful people. Its trademark, fresh floral bouquets in artistic arrangements, run to $75,000 a year alone.

The menu is purposefully kept limited and is generally flawless. There can be nothing recommended without grave injustice to any other, and this includes appetizers and desserts.

3 East 52 Street
New York, N.Y., 10022
(212) 752-1495

- *French Cuisine*
- *Priced expensive*
- *Open 6 days for lunch and dinner; closed Sundays*
- *Prix-fixe lunch for $28.00; Prix-fixe dinner for $46.75*
- *Reservations necessary. AE and DE accepted*
- *No private parties*

La Petite Marmite

After a tough day haranguing the General Assembly, more than one country's Ambassador to the United Nations has been known to zip over to the nearby La Petite Marmite to unwind over a fine French dinner. It's a classy, stylish, comfortable restaurant that may be a little pricy for some but that nonetheless delivers excellent French food with just a dash of *nouvelle cuisine.*

Jacky Ruette, who's owned La Petite Marmite since 1968, had a chef leave him a few years ago, and he invited chef Pascal Derringer to be his partner and take care of the cooking. (Pascal was formerly head chef at La Gauloise in New York City.) Pascal accepted, and now La Petite Marmite has the classic partnership of chef and host running the restaurant.

The place is formal, yet also comfortable. The high ceiling, the soft lighting, the well-spaced tables, and the accomodating staff give it a very pleasant feeling.

Of the appetizers, *la bouchee Joinville* (crawfish in a Nantua sauce held in puff pastry) is one of the best. The salad of green beans and shallots is also excellent *(les haricots verts aux echalottes),* as is the white Chilean asparagus in a zesty vinaigrette.

Among the eighteen or so entrees (there are specialities every night), some are strictly classical while others have a touch of *nouvelle* about them (the subtly flavored whitefish brill with a sauce Nantua and a mushroom puree, for example). The sauteed salmon Florentine served on a bed of spinach is excellent as are the breast of duck with a green peppercorn sauce and the veal chop with a calvados and cream sauce. Other entrees include a rack of lamb and *ris de veau Forestiere* (sweetbreads with a Forestiere sauce).

Among the deserts, perhaps the frozen Grand Marnier *souffle* is the stand-out. Fresh berries, when they're in season, are always good, and there's the nightly specials that roam the dining room on the handsome dessert cart.

**5 Mitchell Place
(East of 49 Street and First Avenue)
New York, N.Y., 10017
(212) 826-1084**

- *French Cuisine, with a touch of Nouvelle*
- *Priced expensive*
- *All major credit cards accepted*
- *Reservations necessary*
- *Open Monday through Friday for lunch; Monday through Saturday for dinner; Closed Sunday*
- *Available private party facilities*

La Recolte

In the deeply-carpeted, crystal-lit, muted beige environment of La Recolte, the table-setting tells the story: on a white-linen surface arrayed like an alter to gastronomy, among the octogonal silver service plates, graceful stemware and heavy flatware, is a dimpled shallow "tablespoon" designed for critical sauce-tasting. Obviously, the kitchen is committed to delivering a culinary experience rather than merely frivolous feeding. The spoon demands immediate exercise upon arrival of the day's complimentary *hors d'oeuvre:* usually an inventive morsel of suavely sauced seafood such as turbot in dilled butter or lobster *perigourdine.*

The *nouvelle* hallmark dish of "warm" salad is nowhere more winningly executed than in this domain of youthful Chef Patric Pinon, a protege of Paul Bocuse. His rendition of pinkly tender slices of duck, garlanded with chanterelle mushrooms, speckled with costly truffle-bits, and generously mounded upon varied lettuces, is an offering worthy of any Temple of Gastronomy. Equally exciting, a luxurious lobster salad showered with a julienne of papaya, creates a byplay of colors, textures, and flavors atop a collage of bright watercress and purple cabbage leaves. Even *escargots* escape from the ordinary into a spectacular display of nine ceramic cuplets, cushioned with fennel *mousse* and topped with garlicky croutons to complement the plump snails. Crab bisque, too, is remarkable for an unusually rich infusion of carapace flavor.

Bread plates are scrupulously changed between courses by deft young acolytes in cutaway jackets, whose careful observance of all the elegant formalities barely contains their obvious enthusiasm over the remarkable entrees that they reveal from under silver lids. Surrounded by a colorful vegetable palette of spinach *mousse* dotted with caviar, carved green and yellow squash, and crunchy snowpea pods, emerges a moist and picture-perfect pink salmon scallop sided with sauce *choron.* Veal *mignons* sauteed with asparagus, ginger-sparked crisp Dover sole, rare duck breast with precious globules of marrow, and gently poached turbot with tiny leeks reposing in a puff-pastry shell are also offered.

Such lavish displays should provide ample preparation for a dessert cart that offers four varied fruit sorbets in deep silver tubs; a high, light chocolate-*mousse* layered cake; butter-crusted tarts of fruits or almond paste or—from the kitchen— warm casseroles of orange slices topped with souffleed sabayon, or ice-cream-topped pineapple rounds in peppered(!) fruit sauce.

---

110 East 49 Street
New York, N.Y., 10017
(212) 421-4389

- *French Cuisine*
- *Priced expensive*
- *Open Monday through Friday for lunch; Monday through Saturday for dinner; closed Sunday*
- *Accepting reservations and all major credit cards*
- *Party facilities for up to 20 persons dining from pre-arranged menu*

La Strada East

A facade of graceful arches supported by fluted columns provides a suitable prelude to the interior of La Strada East: rooms that are a symphony in scarlet. Walls are covered with burgundy-striped cut velvet, the floor with deep crimson carpeting, and everyone cuddles into the cushiony curves of sweeping lipstick-red banquettes. Even the stucco ceiling is bright red, creating a contrast to elaborate, a petal-shaped crystal chandeliers. The largest of these, shaped to suggest palm fronds, overhangs a deliciously decadent dessert display, set beside a cart mounted with copper chafing dishes. This showy serving station is much-manned by a formally tuxedoed staff—always absolutely correct but never stuffy or pretentious. Their friendly concern and enthusiastic recommendations of the day's specialties are taken seriously by a clientele of relaxed but well-heeled habitues.

Most of the regular crowd are neighborhood people and old fans of the proprietor from the days when he operated a spot in the theater district; one overhears them chatting about the prestige restaurants at which they've been dining during the week—but they seem at their happiest just where they are at the moment.

Their loyalty and pleasure are no surprise to anyone who has been served a hot *antipasto Luigi:* from the copper warming pan come succulent morsels of shrimp, clam and sweet lobster meat—so gently sauteed in white wine and scattered with oregano crumbs that the briny juices blend with the spices to create a delicate yet intense flavor. Sometimes there's a *pesto,* so freshly made that it seems to float along the palate, emanating a subtle perfume rather than assertive flavor.

Yet the menu boasts an equally admirable robust repertoire. Perhaps the most celebrated House specialty, among all the tableside-showy pastas, the seafoods and the scalloppines, is the absolutely unique invention of the Host/Owner that he calls the "Tennis Racquet." More a feat of alimentary architecture than of athletics, here is a dish to daunt even McEnroe: a thick white veal chop is cut lengthwise, creating an inner pocket to be plumped with melted cheese laced with a confetti of prosciutto and specks of fragrant basil. The construction is enrobed in golden batter then overlaid with a slice of eggplant, prosciutto, and more melted cheese—the whole finally baptised in a sauce of herbed crushed tomato.

A lusty, garlicky steak *pizzaiola* balances such delicate offerings as chicken breasts *Gellis,* sauteed with artichokes, bass *Livornese* garnished with olives and capers, and spinach-bedded veal scallops *Saltimbocca.*

If you must, give up eating all week to do it, but nevertheless make a point of sampling the chocolate *mousse* cake—a chiffon-textured yet seductively intense chocolate cloud set in a fragile glazed puff-pastry shell. Rich, thick hot *zabaglione,* whipped up in full view in a copper pan is also exemplary. Usually, there are seasonal fresh berries to go with it—or to enjoy alone.

---

274 Third Avenue
New York, N.Y., 10010
(212) 473-3760

- *Italian Cuisine*
- *Priced moderate to high*
- *Open for lunch and dinner 7 days*
- *Reservations and all credit cards accepted*
- *Private party facilities for between 12 and 40 persons*

La Truffe

Simply put, La Truffe is one of the best French restaurants in Philadelphia. Opened almost 20 years ago with a distinct French Country Cuisine slant to its menu, La Truffe today presents a blend of classic French *haute* and *nouvelle cuisines*. Throughout its evolution, though, La Truffe has always succeeded in presenting that rare occurrence: an exquisite atmosphere in a refined setting, with food and service to match.

Jeannine Mermet and her husband Leslie Smith are the proprietors. Jeannine takes care of the decor which, from the composed, attractive bar seen upon entering to the white linens draping the tables set in exquisite silver, tapered candles, and fresh flowers in cut-crystal holders, can be summed up by La Truffe's keyword: Elegance.

Leslie began his restaurant career in England and then decided to bring his skill and dedication across the Atlantic. He's intelligent enough not to try any *nouvelle cuisine* experimentation simply for that cuisine or that experimentation's sake. Therefore, the food at La Truffe is a blend of the proven traditional and the traditional with delicious variation. An example: Not only do you have a crock of sweet-butter alongside your crusty bread,

you also have a crock of delicately flavorsome fish butter.

As befits a fine restaurant, each dish is served with strict attention to what it looks like as well as what it tastes like, which makes dining at La Truffe a visually satisfying experience as well as a gustatory one.

The appetizers include *le consomme de petoncles aux petits legumes* (wonderfully-seasoned vegetable consomme), and nicely-prepared shrimp or mussels in a light cream sauce. There's also Beluga caviar for those who want to splurge, as well as duck terrine and smoked fish with La Truffe's special sauce.

The wide range of entrees includes crayfish in cream sauce with shallots and chives *(les crevettes d'Espagne a la creme d'escalotes et ciboulette)*, Maine lobster stuffed with caviar *(le homard du Maine au caviar Dore)*, a savory mussel stew *(le ragout de moules au basilie)*, and a filet of sole fragrant with saffron *(L'escalope de saumon au pistil de safran)*. Among the meats there's chicken in tarragon *(les eminces de poulet a l'estragon)*, strips of duck in peppercorn sauce *(les aiguilettes de canard aux deux poivres)*, lamb cutlets with thyme *(les coteletes d'agneau au jus de thym)*, and filet of beef in red wine sauce *(le mignon de boeuf au vin rouge)*. And don't be put off by the lack of English on the menu, one of the waiters will be more than happy to translate.

The extraordinary wine list deserves mention: it features French and California labels that range from the good to the legendary. Desserts at La Truffe are changed daily, which gives you another excellent excuse to return to this restaurant.

10 South Front Street
Philadelphia, Pa., 19106
(215) 627-8630

- *French/Nouvelle Cuisine*
- *Priced expensive*
- *Open Monday through Friday for lunch; Monday through Saturday for dinner; Closed Sunday*
- *All major credit cards accepted; Reservations suggested*
- *Private party facilities for between 10 and 50 persons*

L'Auberge du Cochon Rouge

Once a functioning farmhouse, this restaurant offers classic French fare with just a *soupcon* of *nouvelle cuisine* and with a fairly large dash of French country inn atmosphere. The feeling of rusticity begins on the grounds of the restaurant where a cat periodically stalks with the resident flock of geese. Once inside, the two fireplaces, the Victorian-styled cocktail lounge, and the authentic farmhouse decor help increase the feeling. If you'd like a little more formal and elegant setting for your meal, one of the dining rooms has been done up quite poshly.

L'Auberge du Cochon Rouge is run by chef-proprietor Etienne Merle who is renowned for his French kitchen and his lively Friday night lobster festivals (the clawed crustacean gets six different preparations). It is country stuff this on an excellent level and much of the cooking is deeply traditional. Smoked mackerel is nicely presented, accompanied by a cherry tomato, a wedge of lemon, and a spinach leaf. Etienne likes *pates* and he offers three in his restaurant as appetizers: *pate forestiere*, *terrine Louis Joereau*, and *pate de canard*. There's also *escargot de bourguignonne,* and, for that seafood lover in you, a seafood Newburg crepe and an avocado stuffed with crabmeat, which, like the smoked mackerel, is also adorned with a cherry tomato, a wedge of lemon, and spinach leaf.

Among the soups, the cold cream of spinach soup is especially good. It's thick, rich, and delicious. There's also the chef's special soup called, logically enough, *soupe d'Etienne*, and the ubiquitous and classic onion soup.

The entree selection leans heavily towards meats. Beef is served as a filet done either *poivre vert* or *Rossini* (green peppercorn sauce or madeira sauce), or a chatebriand *periguordine* for two. Lamb is served either as a rack of lamb for two or as *jarret d'agneau Berrichone*. Duck can be either *confit de canard aux marrons* or *aiguillette de canard a l'orange*. There's also roast game hen and veal sweetbreads.

Non meat-eaters can go for either a *coquilles St. Jacques*, bass *a la Dinardaise*, or salmon *au beurre rouge*. Locals and out-of-towners brave the worst weather to enjoy a dish of veal Oscar; and there is much to be said for Mr. Merle's Sunday brunch.

1152 Danby Road
Ithaca, N.Y., 14850
(607) 273-3464

- *French Cuisine*
- *Priced moderate to high*
- *Open 7 days for dinner only; Sunday brunch*
- *Reservations and all major credit cards are accepted*
- *Private party facilities for between 2 and 38 persons*

Laurent

Restaurant Laurent is one of the venerable eating establishments in New York. Now entering its forth decade of culinary achievement, Laurent offers *haute cuisine* of another era.

Surroundings are dignified and stately with a heavy patina of dignity. Molded wood-paneled walls are hung with oil paintings and flanked with banquettes with smartly appointed tables and chairs. Softly lighted crystal chandeliers, starched with white linen, sprays of fresh flowers, and a smart clientele set the pace for distinguished dining.

The menu changes daily with the seasonal offerings of New York's meat and vegetable markets, so it would be difficult to give unwavering choices. The specialties of the house are the etheral and rare Beluga caviar, *saumon fume, crepes Laurent, escargots, tournedos,* and a few others that are printed on the menu. The rest are handwritten in a Gaulic hand.

If you begin with the *crepe,* you might be rewarded with lobster and crab wrapped in a light pancake, and topped with a sauce touched with curry. Another specialty, *langoustines Laurent* with garlic, is succulent and delicate. The duck with cherries is a transcendent combination of deboned and sliced bird sided with candied sweet potato and a pastry cup filled with cherry sauce heavy with whole bing cherries.

Desserts are rich and full, and begin with a tray of cookies just for taste. Laurent is famous for its *souffles,* but you should order them at meal's beginning to insure they will be ready at the end.

Laurent is also known for its wine cellar, one of the last great cellars in New York, or the country for that matter. They actually have three cellars, one for every day with about 1,100 bottles, the *Grand Cave* which houses up to 22,000 bottles, and the *Vieille Cave,* entered through a trap door and housing 10,000 aging wines. When business permits, they will allow you to visit the cellars. If you just care to drink, there are two lists, one short and digestible, the other, a book that offers the very modest to the most expensive.

111 East 56 Street
New York, N.Y., 10022
(212) 753-2729

- *French Cuisine*
- *Priced expensive*
- *Open 7 days for lunch and dinner*
- *Reservations necessary. Accepts AE, DC, and CB*
- *Private party facilities for between 10 and 100 persons*

La Veranda

La Veranda is all wrought iron and crystal against an ivory and red backdrop. The tables sport fresh flowers, the ceiling a sky-blue mural, and the menu a host of choices.

Can't decide what to eat? Just ask Tito or Luigi, the co-owner-hosts who'll gladly recommend a lively meal full of Italian zest and with a touch of French culture. They might suggest the hot, mixed seafood plate: an assortment of tender bay scallops, mussels, squid, octopus and fish in a light, well-flavored *marinara* sauce, or another seafood catch such as the *scampi Veranda* set in an interesting garlic-Chablis sauce.

The unexpected surprises extend far from things of the sea. Under the chef's hands, the cliche of veal *parmigiana* takes on new taste, and the tender and succulent veal chops are a satisfying choice in their tangy *marinara*.

And more surprises come out of the kitchen. Diced, boneless, and skinless chicken is delivered with a white wine sauce flavored with sauteed herbs, and the loin of veal *Dore* becomes a lusty saute of minced prosciutto, headcheese and eggplant served in a wine and cream sauce.

Desserts are refreshingly offered both plain and fancy. A nice touch is the complimentary bowl of ripe fruit and a basket of mixed nuts as a palate freshener.

---

60 East 54 Street
New York, N.Y., 10022
(212) 758-5560

- *Italian Cuisine*
- *Priced moderate*
- *Open Monday through Friday for lunch;
  7 days for dinner*
- *Reservations and all major credit cards accepted*
- *Private party facilities available for between 100 and 200 persons*

La Viola

This Northern Italian/French/Continental restaurant deserves special affection. Designed for expansiveness, it is pleasant, refined, and serves abundant portions. La Viola's distinctive decor is punctuated with plush and roomy banquettes, and a spacious lounge and bar set apart from the rest of the dining area.

Here, nothing is carried to the *nth* degree, but everything is as it should be. The welcome and service you get is sincerely congenial without being irritatingly excessive; people you see here, if not glittering, are wellbred; the food doesn't call for a gastronomical pilgrimage, but is reminiscent of the kind served in the great houses of European grandmothers.

Noteworthy meals include such dishes as the *scampi alla Lino* (named after La Viola's owner); capon *estragon;* soft shell crabs, in season; and the crispy Long Island duckling *flambe.* Nor can you resist the glow of the hot pastas, steamy and bracing.

Many dishes at La Viola are prepared with the extra added attraction of a tableside show. The Caesar salad and green and white *tortellini* are two of the wonders that take shape before your eyes.

There are little touches that mean a lot here. Canapes are served with before-dinner drinks, and cookies after the meal. Desserts are a nice surprise, with offerings such as homemade nut roll, pineapple *mousse* and a kiwi and blueberry tart made with custard in a puff pastry. A must!

Generous drinks are administered regularly, and there's a good selection of wines to complement your dinner.

---

571 Chestnut Street
Cedarhurst, L.I., N.Y., 11516
(516) 569-6020

- *Northern Italian/French/Continental Cuisine*
- *Priced moderate to expensive*
- *Open 6 days for dinner only; closed Monday*
- *Accepts reservations and AE, DC credit cards*
- *Private party facilities for between 10 and 125 persons*

Le Chambord

Once you've been chosen as Connecticut's best French restaurant three years in a row, the struggle would seem to be to fight off complacency and to maintain the same high quality of food that earned you that title. But what if, by consensus, you'd been chosen as Connecticut's best restaurant for the last *six* years? At Le Chambord, the recipient of such acclaim, owners Oscar Basler, who runs the dining room, and chef Robert Pouget do it simply by caring about every detail of their restaurant.

Le Chambord is an elegant restaurant. Attractive oil paintings and beige trellises adorn the cream colored walls of the three dining rooms. Almond-colored linens cover the tables, and on them, at every table, sit fresh baskets of blooming plants. Soundproofed ceilings and thick carpets keep the rooms quiet and intimate.

Robert was trained in France, and his offerings are classic French—with a few seldom seen dishes as well. One of the latter is *moules Biarritz*, where mussels are cooked on the half shell with garlic and butter. Other appetizers include a light and fluffy *quiche lorraine*, clams casino, and prosciutto and melon.

As expected at a restaurant of this caliber, there is no "best" entree; they all receive careful attention. Grilled meats come cooked as ordered, and there are over a dozen regular entrees as well as the daily specials covering the complete range of French cooking from frog legs *Provencale*, to steak *au poivre*. And the accompanying vegetables receive careful consideration, too, be they crispy cooked zucchini, equally well done carrots, or imported mushrooms.

Among the many desserts the light, rich velvet cake deserves mention, but there's also chocolate mousse, a Grand Marnier souffle, crepes Souzette, and many others.

And there's one more reason why Le Chambord has received such acclaim—the faultless food is not inexpensive, but it's value received all the way. You'll need a reservation at both dinner and lunch.

1572 Post Road East
Westport, Conn., 06880
(203) 255-2654

- *French Cuisine*
- *Priced moderate to high; prix fix dinners available as well as a la carte*
- *Open Tuesday through Friday, for lunch; Tuesday through Saturday for dinner; Closed Sunday and Monday*
- *Reservations required; all major credit cards*
- *Private party facilities for between 10 and 50 persons*

Le Champignon

Founded some 15 years ago, Le Champignon is an inviting French restaurant in John Wanamaker's former 1875 townhouse on West 56th Street. Divided into two floors, the establishment presents different facades for dining. Downstairs exhibits the casual charm of subdued lighting, cafe-like tables, black patent leather banquettes and padded cane chairs. A bric-a-brac design scheme of varied statuary, brocade, and napery are all unified in their representation of "Le Champignon"—French for "The Mushroom."

Upstairs, however, the townhouse's original 19th century origins are shown in the high-ceilinged rooms spanned by polished mahogany beams, the mahogany parquet panelling extending partway up the walls, and tasteful wallpaper in a black-and-white floral design with matching drapes. The restaurant has 11 working fireplaces and tables are well-spaced throughout, featuring crisp white linen tablecloths placed diagonally over deep red ones,

padded straight-backed upholstered chairs, heavy silverware, and a single candle flickering in what looks like an antique brass-and-crystal holder. The softly burning fireplace and candles create a warm and subdued atmosphere. Characteristic of owner/hostess Jacqueline Paine, the scene is one of restrained grace.

It should come as no surprise that many of Le Champignon's menu offerings are prepared with mushrooms. The specialty of the house, *les champignons farcis sauce madere,* is an appetizer of *pate*-filled mushrooms bathed in a rich savory madeira wine sauce, nestled under a handsome glass bell covering. Other good appetizers include a delicate liver *pate,* marinated mussels, and *champignon a la Grecque.*

All sorts of entrees are changed daily but the fish is consistently exceptional. Sauteed filet of sole, for example, is a beautiful piece of firm yet delicate sole in a warm, golden, lemon-butter sauce. All of Le Champignon's dinner selections arrive handsomely arrayed on a pre-warmed plate—a nice touch— and the service staff is courteous and unobtrusive. Other entrees include a tender steak *au poivre,* beef *bourguignonne,* and veal sweetbreads with wild mushrooms. There is a *table d'hote* four-course pre-theater dinner for $11.50 and the wines are predominantly French and all well-chosen. Steaming freshly brewed coffee is certainly worth mentioning but perhaps the most fitting end to a meal here would be one of the light and creamery-rich pastries from the gleaming and fully-stocked cart.

35 West 56 Street
New York, N.Y., 10019
(212) 245-6335

- *French Cuisine*
- *Priced moderate to high*
- *Open 6 days for lunch, pre-theater dinner, and dinner; closed Sunday*
- *Accepting reservations and all major credit cards*
- *Private party facilities are available*

Le Chantilly

This is more than just another elegant, plush French restaurant, with picturesque murals and sparkling crystal chandliers. As far as we are concerned, chef Roland Chenus' version of classic French cuisine and Paul Dessibourg's direction of the dining room has elevated Le Chantilly to the pinnacle of New York's French establishments.

The bill-of-fare introduces diners to an assortment of dishes more often than not exquisite to the palate. A vegetable quiche, with it's souffle-like custard filling rich with distinctive celery flavor, might start the meal, or a light beginning could also be smoked salmon—a generous portion, a pale blushrose, not too salty, smooth textured, nicely garnished, and flavor-sparked with capers and sweet onions.

Terrines such as the light and delicate sweetbreads, woven with threadlike strands of orange rind, and the spicy, herbed terrine of truffled duck also show the kitchen's talent to advantage.

For the seafood lover there's glistening fresh little necks, cherrystone, or chunky pink and white crabmeat cocktail.

Pheasant is likely to be beautifully cooked and presented—brought to you on a service tray with a woven potato basket. The captain skillfully cuts it tableside and it's savored with golden potato puffs, wild rice, goose liver *pate* laced with a rich natural gravy and truffle sauce. The chef's talent is clearly evident also in the fork-tender kidneys, rosyred, rare

at the heart, lavishly bathed in a pork, cream, and Armagnac sauce perfumed with a whisper of mustard. The plump twin quenelles had a lovely light texture with a melting moistness topped by a sauce that couldn't have been more brightly flavorful.

For a serious dessert *aficionado* the souffles are more shadow than substance and better than at any other place, while the pastries, buttery and rich with the fruits huge and fresh, make the choice almost impossible—or you can consider a platter of outstanding ripe cheeses and the wine selection will give you much pleasure.

Lunch time is brisk and lively with expert service and dinner leisurely, quiet, and intimate. As an added feature, they will make to order whatever your request even if it's not on the menu.

Until you have tried Le Chantilly, you will never realize that you have not known all the good things of life after all.

106 East 57 Street
New York, N.Y., 10022
(212) 751-2931

- *French Cuisine*
- *Prix-fixe luncheon is $29.50 and prix-fixe dinner $36.75*
- *Open 6 days for lunch and dinner; Closed Sunday*
- *Reservations are accepted as are all major credit cards*
- *Private party facilities for between 12 and 20 persons*

Le Cygne

A fine French restaurant recently redesigned when it moved to its new quarters. Happily, the qualities that made "The Swan" a first-class eating establishment have been carried over.

And what made Le Cygne a mecca for native and tourist alike was the ambiance of urbanity, efficiency of service and cuisine that blends *haute* with *bourgeoise*.

In other words, it is a class restaurant without being intimidating, skilled without prissiness, sophisticated without condescension.

Strong points abound here, from the wonderful soups *(try the billi bi),* through some truly unique appetizers, to the selected entrees of veal, poultry, lamb, and fish. Le Cygne is especially noted for its *poularde au champagne, paillard* of beef, kidneys and Grand Marnier mousse.

55 East 54 Street
New York, N.Y., 10022
(212) 759-5941

- *French Cuisine*
- *Priced expensive*
- *Open Monday through Friday for lunch; Monday through Saturday for dinner; Closed Sunday*
- *Reservations necessary. Accepts all major credit cards*
- *Private party facilities for between 12 and 24 persons*

Le Jardin

It is small and rather private, more of a home rather than a commercial establishment, a place where you can lose yourself in conversation with your companions. It is in a townhouse in the city on a quiet block. There is a small bar, for that is one of life's pleasures. The dining area is snug, with soft banquettes lining a room of quiet decoration, and it opens out into an enclosed city garden, softly lit to emulate a comfortable spring day. The food is sensitively and harmoniously prepared by an owner-chef who daily stakes his reputation and prestige on personally pleasing his customers.

In short, Le Jardin is the product of one man, George Magerus, who has constructed a world of taste and serene enrichment of place and meal. Some examples of his hand are a hot asparagus *mousse* in a delicately herbed cream sauce, or a unique seafood sausage stuffed with shrimps, mussels and scallops. Soups here are star performers in their own right; there is *consomme* with duck quenelles and an etheral cream of mushroom and truffles.

The main courses are a stylish array—from rabbit stew blended with mushrooms, bacon, and onions in a red wine sauce to a sparkling fresh grilled bass fortified with a mustard and *Hollandaise* sauce. There is medallion of veal in cream and (surprise!) roquefort, and a *cassoulet* brought to table in a steaming hot crock of beans, sausage and lamb.

Desserts add another dimension, whether the simple pleasures of fresh fruit and cream or a cultivated white chocolate *mousse*. And all of this can be complemented with a wine from a carefully chosen wine list of French and California labels.

248 East 49 Street
New York, N.Y., 10017
(212) 355-1810

- *French Cuisine*
- *Priced moderately*
- *Open 6 days for lunch and dinner; closed Sundays*
- *Accepts reservations and all major credit cards*
- *Private party facilities for between 4 and 45 persons*

Le Lavandou

Proprietor-chef Jean Jacques Rachou has built a solid reputation for Le Lavandou on the finest of ingredients, precise—almost fussy—preparation, and excellent service. Add to this elegant surroundings and a rational fixed price policy and you have the reasons for continuing popularity that keeps the reservations book full days in advance.

Mr. Ranchou, also proprietor-chef of the famed La Cote Basque, has devised a menu that combines both classic *haute cuisine* and *nouvelle.* The result is a selection of depth, ambition, and interest. Choosing here starts from a lengthy list of hot and cold *hors d'oeuvres* and soups, continues through sumptuous seafood, meat, and poultry courses, and ends in desserts full of sorbets, souffles, bombes, and fruits.

Le Lavandou's large menu is heavy with delights that change with availability. Not to be missed are the quenelles of pike in a sauce aromatic with Pernod or the *terrine de crab cressonnette,* which is not to discourage any of the other excellent entrees.

134 East 61 Street
New York, N.Y., 10021
(212) 838-7987

- *French Cuisine*
- *Priced expensive*
- *Open Monday through Saturday for $18.00 prix-fixe lunch and $30.00 prix-fixe dinner; Closed Sunday*
- *Reservations necessary. Accepts all major credit cards*
- *No private parties*
- *Wine list*

Lello

While Italian restaurants abound in New York, and are favorites of the lustful eating crowd, there are not too many Northern Italian establishments—those specializing in the most refined taste of butter and cream sauces rather than the tomato-based, and of the fresh, ribbon pasta, rather than the dried, tube variety preferred in the South.

Proprietor Lello Arpaia, as any good restaurateur, has strongly stamped his personality and imbued his ability onto his establishment. He is a joy to talk with and to observe going about the business of his business. He is sophisticated with the added touch of a sense of humor. He is fastidious and immaculate, so you know what his kitchen looks like. His hair is dark, his face like a seraph's, his skin like a baby's, his smile frank and contagious. Can such a man serve inferior fare?

Of course not. Nor in inferior surroundings. Lello, like the man, is sophisticated. Dark mirrors catch and reflect enormous sprays of silk flower arrangements, gentle lighting from crystal chandeliers, elegant pictures, brown velvet walls and beige, suede-like banquettes.

The food is done with a creative, classical turn. Soups, antipasto and pasta dishes are exceptionally good. Such seemingly simple dishes as *tortellini in brodo* and *fettucine Alfredo* are mentioned here only because Lello shows to what heights these dishes can be taken. Like the fettucine, other Northern Italian pasta with cream sauce accompaniment are a delight.

Which is not to say there are no complicated exercises here. The pasta *cartoccio* is a veritable extravaganza with slender pasta enriched with chunks of lobster, shrimp, and baby peas succulently sauteed in a bag.

This is a cuisine that does real justice to dessert. The luxuriant *zabaglione* is considered perhaps the best in the city. It is made in front of the diner, the egg yokes whipped over a flame with marsala and sugar, and served hot over dewy strawberries, raspberries, or whatever fruit is chosen. There are other wonders here—thick chocolate *mousse* roll and a fresh assortment of fruits in season. Fragrant cups of *cappuccino* with spices help you slowly back to earth.

65 East 54 Street
New York, N.Y., 10022
(212) 751-1555

- *Northern Italian Cuisine*
- *Priced expensive*
- *Open Monday through Friday for lunch; Monday through Saturday for dinner; closed Sundays*
- *Reservations necessary. Accepts all major credit cards*
- *Private party facilities for between 20 and 100 persons*

Le Plaisir

This is a comfortable, yet elegant representative of polished *nouvelle cuisine* in the United States. In internal design and menu construction there is the open discipline of breeding laced with casual charm that characterizes owner Pierre Jourdan.

Le Plaisir is a small establishment seating only 46 people. The warmth and intimacy is carried forth in its fabric wall coverings of deep coral which frame a rotating collection of original art, glowing recessed lighting, tables dressed in white linen flanked by cane-backed arm chairs. The conversation matches the atmosphere, subdued, relaxed, and contented.

Dining *nouvelle cuisine* is always an adventure in a place boasting a chef with an instinct for the successfully eclectic. Le Plaisir, although a relatively young establishment, has already made a reputation for itself for its excellent appetizers. A specialty of the house is the *foie de canard saute aux raisins,* duck liver sauteed with raisins, presented on a bed of gently wilted lettuce and transformed by a mellow sherry vinegar. Other appetizers of note are the lobster salad pointed up with basil and dill, the unusual crayfish flan with its delicately flavored crayfish sauce, *gravlax a la Francaise*—cured salmon with dill and green peppercorns artfully arranged on the plate with tomatoes and cucumber strips and the *tourte de gibier a plume,* a flavorsome game bird *pate* secure in pastry shell and warmed with Madeira sauce.

The fish and seafood main courses spark with originality. The tender poached lobster is elevated with a tomato cream sauce, served with seasoned rice and artfully placed on its serving plate. The sliced salmon comes glazed with mustard and the filet of stripped bass is wrapped in a lettuce leaf and ennobled with a *Sauternes* sauce.

The meat courses are especially prized here. The house specialty, breast of squab in a delicate green peppercorn sauce, is not to be missed. But neither are the *noisettes* of lamb proud in their own juices, the sliced loin of veal in a sprightly lemon sauce, or the shell steak with the surprise of honey shallots.

There is a cheese assortment here for a traditional end of meal finish, or one might delve into the pleasures of the bitter-chocolate-and-meringue cake (the owner's favorite) and the assortment of homemade pastries, tarts, and cakes.

There is a fine wine list to complement the meal, with generous advice freely offered on the somewhat unusual dishes prepared here.

969 Lexington Avenue
New York, N.Y., 10021
(212) 734-9430

- *French Cuisine*
- *Priced expensive*
- *Open for dinner only; Closed Sundays and one month in summer*
- *Reservations recommended. Accepts all major credit cards*
- *Private party facilities for 90 only; smaller parties pay cost of 90*

Le Restaurant

A few estimable pioneers have sought to bring the heights of the *haute cuisine* kitchen to the narrow strip of land that is known as New York's Long Island. Of the three or four that qualify as world-class restaurants is the newly christened Le Restaurant.

This is an enterprise of dedication, as all successful restaurants inevitably must be. It is the life ambition of owner John Diassinos who lavishes his attention and care with a persistent devotion. He had brought to his establishment as chief chef Guy Gauthier, a man of fine credentials who learned his craft in the kitchens of France, Belgium, England, Spain, and New York.

Setting for these men of taste is the gold coast, the North Shore of Long Island in the town of Glen Cove. They have taken a large country house built in 1788 and tastefully remodeled it to hold both the best of the past and the benefits of the new. You will dine in an atmosphere that holds history from the time of our Revolution—it retains its original hand-hewn beams and slate flooring—while conversing over large tables formally set in pink linen over lace and surrounded by an elegant French-Colonial decor. There is a main dining room with three other cozy little rooms that give a special cultivated air to the place, emphasized by a service of relaxed urbanity open to the diner's needs.

This ambiance of subtle yet elegant *elan* is carried over into Chef Gauthier's accomplishments. Especially recommended are the two fish terrine *pates, escargots bourguignonne,* smoked trout and salmon and *coquille St. Jacques.* The *moules poulette* is a steamy crock of mussels removed from their shells and cradled in a rich and fragrant cream sauce. A memorable alternative is the velvetly smooth lobster bisque, formally served from a tureen.

Chef Gauthier amply shows the depth of his repertoire by exhibiting such sumptious entrees as trout stuffed with shrimps and mushrooms, French bay scallops that are broiled to perfection, rack of lamb, and a snapping fresh snapper whose flavor is interestingly combined with lobster sauce. And there are more surprises—calf's liver dressed with raisins and a tantalizing raspberry vinegar sauce, rock cornish game hen with grapes and bass with shallots and wine.

Cedar Swamp Road
Glen Cove, Long Island, N.Y., 11542
(516) 671-2890

- *French Cuisine*
- *Priced expensive*
- *Open for Lunch Tuesday through Thursday only; Dinner Tuesday through Sunday; Closed Monday*
- *Accepts reservations and all major credit cards*
- *Private party facilities for between 20 and 175 persons*

Le Soir

Michael and Janina Kaziewicz own Le Soir (he runs the kitchen while she runs the dining room). Michael grew up in France and received his culinary training in Paris, and his menu offers a fairly traditional range of dishes—which isn't to imply that he doesn't cover all the bases.

For example, two of his appetizers are *coquille St. Jacques* and *escargots de Bourgogne*, two time-honored and also, unfortunately, often time-worn dishes. However, Michael's scallops are firm and delicate and the smooth, rich cream sauce is an ideal accompaniment. His *escargot* are also expertly cooked in an appropriately aromatic and savory garlic and butter sauce.

One of his more distinguished entrees is the rack of lamb: a tender and succulent rack beautifully presented alongside mushrooms and crisp fresh vegetables. The sweetbreads come with a calvados and mushroom cream sauce, and they're also outstanding. When salmon is in season, Michael prepares it one of several ways that change nightly at his whim.

There's more on the menu, of course, including several *pates* and onion soup as appetizers, and a selection of entrees that includes filet mignon *bordelaise*, filet of sole *meuniere*, and veal *francaise*, to name a few.

All the desserts are made at the restaurant, and the floating island deserves special mention. The island floats in a bowl of cream with a crystalized caramel topping—it's a must for dessert lovers.

Janina has given the dining room a country feeling. The pale stucco walls are tastefully trimmed in wood and given a dash of color by several stained glass windows. Hanging plants add a nice touch, and recessed pink lighting casts a romantic glow over the room.

All in all, Le Soir is one of the exceptional values in French dining.

O ne simple yet telling testimony to the excellence of Le Soir is the consistent need for a reservation—and the restaurant isn't located in the middle of New York City with a half a million people a short cab hop away. It's out in eastern Long Island, but the patrons of Le Soir know they've found a good thing and they continue to pack the place.

Le Soir's popularity is due to a very rare combination: exquisite French food, moderate prices, and a very relaxed atmosphere. This is *haute cuisine Francaise* with a friendly attitude instead of that pretentious "ambience" (say om-bee-awnce) and without the sky-high prices that sometimes require that you ask your accountant if you can afford to eat out. And the food is as good as you're likely to find.

---

825 Montauk Highway
Bayport, L.I., N.Y., 11705
(516) 472-9090

- *French Cuisine*
- *Priced moderate*
- *Open Tuesday through Sunday for dinner only; Closed Monday*
- *Reservations required and AE & VISA accepted*

Le Vert-Galant

Le Vert-Galant is a long-established, highly fashionable French restaurant that has built a fine reputation among gastronomics—but so charming and affable are owners Maurice Hemery and his wife, Marilyn, that his establishment retains the feel of the most congenial of the fine restaurants in France. It is efficient, but relaxed, a place that inspires admiration, but doesn't intimidate. Maurice does not encourage discriminatory treatment of his guests. There arc no "good" and "bad" tables. The waiters are helpful and pleasant—no "attitudes" permitted here. Surroundings are distinguished and cultivated, but not self-consciously plush or tinselly. It is, in short, a meticulously designed restaurant, from the decor to the cuisine.

In a context where every dish brought out of the kitchen is made with a light, sure touch, there are some dishes which have come to be associated with Le Vert-Galant. One is a sumptuously perfumed onion soup that comes delicately textured and crusted over with a sardo cheese. Another special treat are the homemade *pates,* unusual for their full flavor.

Le Vert-Galant's treatment of many main course favorites is also noteworthy. The rack of lamb, served for two, is carved at tableside by a captain, working at speed to capture the savor of the juices. The chops are small and succulent, pink at the heart, crisply brown outside and ennobled with garlic. The *canard a l'orange* is sizzling hot, deboned, and with a savory side dish of wild rice. Other leaps of taste can be found in the *tournedos* with an impressive *bernaise* sauce and Maurice's own *cote de veau farcie* (stuffed veal chops).

The restaurant is spacious, with a 17th-century Parisian atmosphere. A roomy lounge and bar, set apart, feature nightly musical entertainments.

109 West 46 Street
New York, N.Y., 10036
(212) 382-0022

- *French Cuisine*
- *Priced moderate to expensive*
- *Open Monday through Friday for lunch; Monday through Saturday for dinner; closed Sunday*
- *Reservations advised. Accepting all major credit cards*
- *All meals are prix-fixe ranging from $12.00 to $16.00 for lunch; $16.00 to $23.00 for dinner*
- *Private party facilities available for between 10 and 75 persons*
- *Piano entertainment nightly from 7:00 pm except Monday*

Lutece

The unvarying recipient of superlatives, Lutece is on everybody's list of the two best restaurants in the United States (it is the other one that is subject to violent argument). Quite simply, Andre Soltner and his talented staff have created a cathedral of epicurian achievement. Based in the classic tradition, Soltner nevertheless is a genius at innovation and exploiting seasonal and even daily changes in the availability of raw materials.

Lutece's charming townhouse retains the feel of a private home—especially the two comfortable and relaxed dining rooms on the second floor. The main dining area is housed in an enclosed garden where patrons who can tear their attention from the food may enjoy the softly filtered sunlight of an afternoon.

It is a decidedly unrealistic expectation to encompass the dimension of Lutece's menu with mere written words. Nor will it do to pick and choose among the constantly changing creations that come out of that tiny kitchen. One can only suggest that visitors to Lutece leave it to Chef Soltner or the waiter-captain to lead you through your meal. Or, for a memorable feast, attempt the menu *degustation*, a *tour de force* of some 11 courses of earthly delights.

249 East 50 Street
New York, N.Y., 10022
(212) 752-2225

- *French Cuisine*
- *Priced expensive*
- *Open Tuesday through Friday for $24.00 prix-fixe lunch; Monday through Saturday for a la carte dinner; Closed Sunday*
- *Reservations necessary. AE, CB and DC only*
- *Private party facility for between 16 and 22 persons*

Mahoney's Hillside Restaurant

Mahoney's is a prize example of a steak, chop, and seafood restaurant that remains popular and crowded because it offers good food in comfortable surroundings at reasonable prices—not a bad goal for any restaurant.

Like the food, the decor is simple and to the point—and very pleasing. And although the lively bar gets noisy at times, the high-backed wooden booths do a good job of keeping the racket out of the separate dining room. Sea-related trappings adorn the walls, giving the place color and life. Present are buoys and fish nets, of course, and a model of a three-masted schooner—but there's also a back-lit, stained glass picture of an airborne sailfish leaping out of the ocean with "Mahoney's" arched over it.

Most of the food is straightforward stuff—broiled steaks of fish or beef, battered and deep-fried seafood and a variety of daily specials. Perhaps primary among the fried seafood is Mahoney's fried clam strips: crisp, golden brown mollusks fried expertly. You can also get scallops and shrimp, or a combination plate of all three. For those who want a sampling of tastes there's also the Fisherman's Catch, containing fried oysters, broiled scrod, and flounder.

The usual forms of steaks and chops are offered, and the meat comes in large portions and is cooked as ordered. The premier chicken dish is chicken *cordon bleu*, a boneless breast stuffed with ham, gruyere, and mozzarella cheese.

To begin your dinner, try the tasty baked clams *orreganta* or the shrimp cocktail with a pungent and rich sauce. Fried zucchini is also excellent. Or you can skip the appetizer and head straight for the lavish salad bar, which runs along one wall of the dining room and offers—besides the normal salad material—tender, plump mussels and shrimps.

If, by any miracle, you still have room for dessert, try the mud pie, a blend of chocolate ice cream, fresh whipped cream, and coffee topped with a bitter-sweet chocolate icing.

If you go there for lunch, try one of the large burger platters. The bleu, onion, and bacon-cheese burgers are all excellent, as are the corned beef, pastrami, and Reuben sandwiches.

26 Hillside Avenue
Williston Park, L.I., N.Y., 11596
(516) 746-9643

- *Steak and Seafood Cuisine*
- *Priced moderate*
- *Open seven days for lunch and dinner*
- *Accepts all major credit cards and reservations*

McSorley's Old Ale House

McSorley's is more a state of mind than a place. It is an institution as closely connected with the history of our country as our public monuments or yellowed documents laid in the archives. It is living history that dates back to 1854 when John McSorley was persuaded to lay down his blacksmith tools and open an ale house to help slake the thirst of the 69th Regiment across the street. The 69th was Custer's regiment and McSorley was their full-time smith and part-time ale-brewer before he took over an old forge house, bought a beer pump from an even older ale house in the village called Greenwich (which got it off an old clipper ship) and went into a business that hasn't closed since.

Lincoln drank here—when he wasn't attending Bible readings in the back room or chewing on a three-pound slab of steak made the way he liked (with a slice of onion in the middle) cooked over an open fire. Well, the fireplace is still there and so is the "Bible house" sign and old Abe's signature left on a liquor license for the place.

But that's only the tip of an archival iceberg. McSorley's is a living museum where the ghosts of customers past still cling to a mosaic of prints, photos, memorabilia and ephemera that cover the walls and stagger the inquisitive. There are snapshots of Teddy Roosevelt and old paintings and souvenirs of a long-dead Derby winner. There are the boots worn by JFK'S grandfather who, in the 1870's, hung them on the ceiling where they've been ever since.

There is a continuity of life as well. Descendants of old McSorley's black cat still prowl underfoot—watching the place for their ancestor's master (or is it the master himself, as some believe?).

They come to McSorley's as they have for 130 years—in prohibition or not—for the ale. It is unquestionably the best in the city. Two kinds, light and dark—for McSorley believed that that is all any man requires. Yes, man. Until 1970, McSorley's was for men only. Forced to integrate, the owners, descendants of the original proprietor, sold out rather than serve feminine lips. As luck would have it, they passed the sacred keys to one Matthew Maher, a son of Killarney with a born love of the place. He guards its legacy with a passion.

But back to the ale. It flows at the rate of a keg every 20 minutes, and is still made from the original recipe in Philadelphia, trucked up several times a week.

The food is straightforward and honest. For lunch, chef Hector (an alumnus of The Palace, no less) is given *carte blanche* to create at will. For several dollars less than they would spend further up or downtown, businessmen flock to McSorley's for the hot plate special, which could be roast beef or corned beef and cabbage. And there's always chili or a cheese plate, so good with the ale. Heaven. So much so, that New York's Mayor Koch is a regular.

The regular menu after lunch: Sandwiches—ham, liverwurst, American cheese, turkey, or a combo; the cheese plate (cheddar, liederkranz and American) and ale. That's it. You can stuff yourself and still have change for a fin. McSorley's—a state of being.

15 East 7 Street
New York, N.Y., 10003
(212) 473-8800

- *Ale House*
- *Inexpensive*
- *Open 7 days for lunch; Sandwiches and cheese plates til closing*
- *No reservations or credit cards*
- *No private parties*

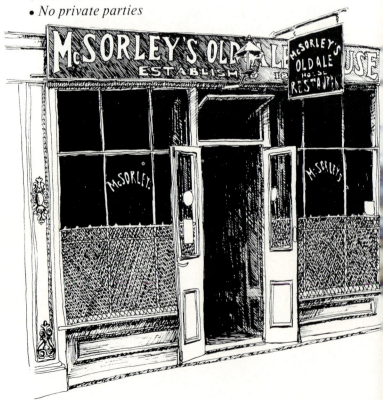

Montego Bay

Maybe it's the romance of the name itself even before you enter, but the whole feel of Montego Bay seems right from the first. The interior is casual and secure, with beamed ceilings, stucco and barnwood walls, wooden tables, banquettes and brick tile flooring. The mood is private because Montego Bay is not a large place—no noisy mobs here to intrude. There is a substantial, relaxed feeling about that, which is carried over to the food, which is served homemade, good and in bountiful portions.

But this is better than home, because you don't have to do the dishes, and the menu is varied to suit every mood and degree of hunger. There are seafood platters, hearty beef dishes and sandwiches, all straightforwardly, but seriously, prepared with a side of vegetable, potato and salad. And for those who crave variety, there are different specialties that change daily, depending on what the chef can get fresh in season.

Some examples of the flexibility of the kitchen— one typical day had specialties consisting of a healthy helping of *scungilli* (conches embedded with pickled red and green peppers, carrots and olives, lightly cooked in garlic and oil); and there was pasta *al dente,* well stocked with fresh North Shore clams, white clam sauce and a sprinkling of parsley.

Some old favorites are always at hand, and well handled—Alaska king crab legs, sliced steak on garlic bread, scallops and shrimp are a perpetual treat. For more casual dining (or for the kids), Montego Bay thoughtfully offers an assortment of sandwiches and burgers, plus a selection of salads that are simple, yet purposefully seasoned. Add some bread and wine, and you have a satisfying light meal for all occasions.

300 Central Avenue
Bethpage, L.I., N.Y., 11714
(516) 822-6783

- *American/Continental Cuisine*
- *Priced inexpensive*
- *Open seven days for lunch and dinner*
- *Reservations and all major credit cards accepted*

Monte's Venetian Room

They drive in from all around town to enjoy the cuisine and conviviality of Monte's Venetian Room, the famous Brooklyn bistro that has been owned and operated by the Monte family since 1906. The bright white stucco frontage comes as a sudden surprise on this drab neighborhood side-street—and the interior startles still more: pastel murals of Venetian canals circle above tufted red banquettes; tropical fish preen themselves in an aquarium behind the bar; and a mammoth brass espresso machine sprouting an impressive multiplicity of spigots dominates the rear wall. Although the room is casual, and generally crowded, the conversational buzz rarely interferes with private pleasures, and as many tables accommodate hand-holding twosomes as they do hearty groups of shirt-sleeved trenchermen. Waiters who have been with the Montes 18 to 20 years know just what dishes to suggest—although one should always consult the multi-paged menu painstakingly hand-printed by Manager Frank Caputo. By choice or recommendation, a platter of crumb-crisped fried zucchini, greaseless outside and sweetly juicy within, is a favorite accompaniment to cocktails.

Some specialties worth waiting for are the House baked shrimp: pounded into mini-cutlets, coated in garlicked and herbed breadcrumbs, the fleshy morsels are gently butter-sauteed and succulent. Paper-thin slices of eggplant *Romana* are rolled around a ricotta cheese center, then blanketed in a melted mozzerella and tomato sauce that creates a creamy dividend when it blends with the oozing ricotta. The long list of pastas includes a trendy *primavera,* a classic *carbonara,* and fresh ultra-thin angel's hair pasta ennobled by a white clam sauce in the lightest of briny broths. A Caesar salad of cold, crisp romaine leaves, assertively coated with anchovy and other spices is crunchy with croutons obviously made in-house from their own crusty bread.

Nuggets of chicken *scarpariello* and scallops of veal *sorrentina* layered with prosciutto, cheese, and a shower of sliced mushrooms in dark wine sauce, may both be garnished with stalks of fresh buttery asparagus or lightly crumb-fried broccoli branches. With strong espresso, presented in a sugar-rimmed glass set into a silver holder (beside the Anisette bottle, of course) one somehow finds space to sample the unusual Italian cheese cake: a moist, pudding-like sweet.

Note that the obliging management not only supplies valet parking in the adjoining lot—but the menu invites guests to request that the parking attendant pre-heat their car when the weather is nasty.

---

451 Carroll Street
Brooklyn, N.Y., 11215
(212) 264-8984

- *Italian Cuisine*
- *Priced moderately*
- *Open 7 days for lunch and dinner*
- *Reservations are suggested. Only Visa accepted*
- *Private Party Facilities for groups up to 55*

Mormando

I t's always nice to "discover" a restaurant, especially one that serves surprisingly good food at decent prices in a pleasant atmosphere. Even though Mormando has been around for a while, for some reason it didn't get talked about or noticed as much as it deserved. One of the highlights is the chef, who may be the best kept secret in New York. Chef Anton Varga grew up in Hungary, and 25 years ago he came to the United States. In 1974 he took over as chef at Mormando, and he continues to turn out excellent food.

The menu is a nice sampling of Continental cuisine, that combination of French and Italian food that ranges from light, rich *coquille St. Jaques* to a delicate steak tartare to a hearty chicken *Bolognese.*

On the Italian side of Mormando's Continental menu, the linguini with a white clam sauce is meritable. The sauce over the *al dente* noodles has the proper garlicky tangyness—and also has plenty of clams. The veal in the veal *parmigiana* is excellent, a big, thick cutlet expertly cooked. Likewise the veal chop—big, juicy, served sizzling hot with a delicate sauce.

There's a wide range of appetizers, soups, and salads—again covering both sides of the Italian/French border. The *escargot Bourguignnone* are served piping hot, and the clams casino are pungent and tasty. The tomato and onion salad is delicious in its simplicity—sliced, juicy tomatoes get mixed up with ribbons of onions and a lovely creamy Italian dressing.

There are several meat dishes, including chateaubriand, calf's liver, and a broiled half chicken. Seafood is present, too, including broiled bay scallops and filet of sole almondine.

Mormando is a fairly big place; the three dining rooms seat close to 200 people. The rooms are all elegantly done—the tables have fresh flowers and white linen on them, and candles burn in attractive glass containers. The recessed lighting casts a complimentary light on the framed etchings that decorate the walls. Plush carpets help keep the noise level down, ensuring a pleasant intimacy. And a long row of beautiful plants lines the large window facing a bustling part of Lexington Avenue. The entire look is relaxed and comfortable.

541 Lexington Avenue
New York, N.Y., 10022
(212) 935-9570

- *French/Italian Cuisine*
- *Priced moderate to high*
- *Open 7 days for breakfast, lunch, and dinner*
- *Accepts reservations and all major credit cards*
- *Private party facilities available*

Mr. Lee's

You are too late to chalk this up as a personal find, but not too late to join other knowledgeable New Yorkers, who travel here for outstanding cooking. Tucked in an out-of-the-way corner, Mr. Lee's is a unique blend of identities that merge to create a remarkable French/Continental cuisine.

The clientele includes many affluent looking types—media people, celebrities, business execs and manufacturers. This means you'll be with folks with lots of panache, or at least lot of bucks (your first look at the menu immediately reassures you, if that is the right word, that you're not going to get off lightly).

The variety of images and influences that make up Mr. Lee's is exhilarating. Proprietor Mr. Gim Lee is a Chinese gentleman of sophistication and education. His Japanese wife Ruth serves as chef. The menu is French/Continental with Chinese and even Japanese highlights. The table help is American—in tuxedo or long dress. The outside is not much, but the interior has a smartly designed and comfortable atmosphere that recreates a garden with its brick and white plaster walls, stained-glass skylights and profusion of plants.

Dishes here run through a remarkable range of styles. You may order assorted crepes, done with a deft hand, as well as other old favorites such as mushrooms stuffed with ground breast of capon (bathed in *bearnaise* and Champagne sauce), *bouillabaise,* broiled salmon in scampi sauce, lobster cardinal and onion soup. But here on the same menu is shrimp in lobster sauce, veal *piccata,* chicken Kiev, beef Stroganoff, veal *Cordon Bleu,* Hungarian pork chops slowly simmered in sour cream, paprika, and spices, and an outstanding banana bass—a sauteed filet graced with a ripe banana, heightened by the flavor of banana fruit brandy which is flambeed.

Desserts Mr. Lee's has but, to our taste, the most extraordinary is the double rich chocolate *mousse.*

In short, take Mr. Lee's for what it is and enjoy the refined but expensive pleasures it has to offer. The entire experience is one of enormous cultivation and grace—a reflection of involved owner-management.

---

337 Third Avenue (25 Street)
New York, N.Y., 10011
(212) MU9-6373

- *French/Continental Cuisine*
- *Priced expensive*
- *Lunch is served Monday through Friday; dinner Monday through Saturday; Closed Sunday and the month of August*
- *Reservations necessary. Accepts all major credit cards*

My Pi

The wonderful thing about food (and, by extension, restaurants) is the infinity of different ways essentially the same ingredients can be prepared. This is no surprise.

But sometimes there are surprises. My Pi sells mostly pizza. But it is pizza, really, in name only. If that (admit it) luscious peasant invention is ever permitted to be upgraded to the heights of *haute cuisine,* then the My Pi recipe should be so designated. This is not the pancake-flat pizza pie that has become as American as apple pie, but a deep-dish, quiche-like variant that was invented by a Chicago businessman whose hobby was food. The dough is not rolled out and stretched, but allowed to rise three times. It is then generously topped with great heaps of Pennsylvania mushrooms, onions, olives, garlic, anchovy and green peppers, and brushed with a thick, pungent tomato sauce. The result is a meal that is appreciably more substantial than your everyday pizza.

Nor is the restaurant your everyday pizza parlor. The design is casual and full of individualism (they happily admit it was not professionally preplanned—and good for them) with warm cedar walls, a friendly fireplace, stained glass windows and lamps, roomy butcherblock tables and carefully chosen background music on some fairly sophisticated audio equipment.

Nor does My Pi limit itself to pizza any longer. Among the new additions to the menu are a char-broiled beefburger presented on black bread and served with meaty, juicy tomato slices; *fedelini* pasta imported from Italy, cooked to order, and served Alfredo-style; hearty homemade chili; double-crusted *souffle* of spinach, brocolli, and mozzarella cheese constructed over My Pi triple-risen pizza dough and topped with dabs of tomato sauce and parmasan cheese. Also new are My Pi's mini-pizza—smaller custom-made versions of their famed deep-dish pies. A wine list has also been recently added. It presents a selection of Italian and California wines that will embarrass neither you in the ordering nor My Pi's cuisine in the drinking. Desserts are a splashy close to your meal. Don't miss the brandy freeze, matched only by the billowy hot fudge sundae.

333 Sunrise Highway
Massapequa, L.I., N.Y., 11758
(516) 541-4401

Mid-Island Plaza
Hickville, L.I., N.Y.
(516) 681-8710

- *Italian/American Cuisine*
- *Priced inexpensive*
- *Open seven days for lunch and dinner*
- *No reservations or credit cards accepted*

New York Steak House

The beef is splendid, so rely on a base of beef and Burgundy rounded off by some slick desserts if you want to side-step the more elaborate specialties such as the 3- to 5-pound lobster, stone crabs, bar-b-que Canadian back ribs, roasted chicken, shrimp scampi, red snapper almondine, and beef Stroganoff. Either way you will feed very well.

Surroundings are casual, but attractively understated—designed to appeal to the male of the species with chalk boards replacing menus, walls supporting rafts of caricatures (steady customers) and celebrities' photos (also steady customers), a rambling bar set apart from the dining rooms, and pleasant piano entertainment.

Though the place has few frills, the service must be counted among them. The welcome is hospitable, and waiters in butcher's aprons are quick on their feet and concerned with what you order. Friendliness seems almost a reflex action.

Here prime, tender red beef is presented in an array of interesting and reliable manners. And what could be more appealing than a steak for two, broiled and prepared illustriously as *Chateaubriand* backed by a tempting bottle of robust wine. Ah, what beauty lies in the basics!

If seafood is more in your line, owner Marty Sussman hasn't forgotten about you. Succulent, moist, buttery, and tender lobsters are flown in daily from New England. These marvels may be ordered by the pound and even the five-pound beauties are light and delicate. But do not jump into this crustacean before savoring a giant bowl of clam chowder accompanied by a big basket of large flaky crackers and a chunk of sweet butter.

In addition to the menu, all dinners include an enormously diversified fresh crunchy salad complemented with assorted dressings, a choice of baked potato, steak fries, or the newly-added crisp potato skins.

Fresh New Zealand strawberries and chocolate chip cheesecake are the exceptional desserts here. It should be noted that the price paid for such pleasures is dear, but it's value for money all the way.

19115 Collins Avenue
Miami Beach, Fla., 33160
(305) 932-7676

- *Steak House Cuisine*
- *Priced expensive*
- *Open 7 days for lunch and dinner*
- *Reservations suggested; All major credit cards accepted*

Old Tubby House

Over a hundred years ago the Tubby family built a large house in what is now Roslyn Village on Long Island. The gracious 19th century colonial household is now the home of a notable Continental restaurant, named, respectfully enough, Ye Old Tubby House. The owner and experienced restaurateur Len de Pas has created an establishment the Tubby family would be glad to have carrying on their name.

Ye Old Tubby House's Continental cuisine is especially appropriate insofar as the chef received his training in Switzerland, a country that in parts is more French or Italian than Swiss. And the menu has what you'd expect—a sampling of pasta, veal, beef, chicken, and fish dishes.

In addition, however, there's a selection of huge, half-pound hamburgers with various toppings, several kinds of omelettes, and a "diet center" that offers more than a dozen low-calorie dishes. And these diet meals aren't just scoops of cottage cheese alongside a lettuce leaf: lobster tails, chicken breasts, filets of sole, shrimp, and vegetables are all prepared imaginatively yet without the rich, mega-calorie sauces that might discourage some diners.

The appetizers run the gamut from *escargot bourguignonne* and delicate *pates* to mussels *marinara* and baked brie cheese. There are also a hearts of palm salad vinaigrette and several clam offerings.

Among the many salads, the avocado and shrimp salad is among the best; slices of avocado, tomato, radish, and pieces of carrot get placed on a bed of lettuce and topped with shrimp and a tangy vinaigrette. Or you can go for a Caesar, Greek, or *Nicoise* salad—or any of a half dozen others.

The pasta dishes include an angel hair noodle creation, where the wavy strands get covered by a delectable shrimp sauce nicely enlivened with a smattering of appropriate spices. The *panna* sauce smothering the *tortellini* is properly rich and creamy, too.

Ye Old Tubby House proclaims that its specialities are the rack of lamb and the expertly-broiled chateaubriand, but don't overlook the cooked-as-ordered veal chop, the delicate poached salmon with a *hollandaise* sauce, or the *tornados Rossini*.

Ye Old Tubby House has two dining rooms and

each offers a distinct mood and feeling. The casual downstairs has a very friendly atmosphere—attractive beaded curtains and wood beams separate the dining areas, making the room seem to be all nooks and corners. The upstairs room is more formal; it's an elegant, stylish room with white linens on the tables and a quiet, relaxed tone to it.

And should you need a little late-night excitement, Old Tubby House has a small disco downstairs catering to the dusk-to-dawn crowd.

1401 Old Northern Boulevard
Roslyn Village, L.I., N.Y., 11576
(516) 621-7888

- *Continental Cuisine*
- *Moderate to high prices*
- *Lunch Monday through Friday; dinner 7 days; Sunday brunch*
- *Accepts all major credit cards; Reservations required upstairs, suggested downstairs*

Oliver's

This is the kind of warm, friendly place that people like to drop into for a drink if only to keep in touch with the place. And owner Michael Wharton likes it that way—he even keeps a picture of his kids in full view. How many restaurant or pub owners do you know who do that? And there is good, honest fare here at prices you have to look twice at to make sure you are seeing right.

An American/British-inspired menu runs the gamut from chili to lobster bisque, from eggs *a la Russe* to burger *a la Francaise.* Of the highest quality, you can exult in the simple delights of a bacon cheeseburger, or go wild with the Russian burger which comes with caviar and sour cream. Dieting? There's crackling fresh salads, including the apex of salad evolution, the Artful Dodger, which combines smoked breast of chicken, swiss cheese and walnuts on a bed of romaine and iceberg, garnished with cherry tomatoes, cucumber and hard-boiled eggs. Want something even heftier? There is a good choice of fresh broiled fish, roast chicken, and some excellent varieties of steak and prime ribs.

The dessert bill of fare is equally no-nonsense—try the English trifle or the homemade pecan pie. Add some mugs of cold foamy beer or wine and you'll find yourself leaving Oliver's figuring, with a smile, when you can next return.

---

141 East 57 Street
New York, N.Y., 10022
(212) 753-9180

- *American/British Cuisine*
- *Priced inexpensive*
- *Open 7 days for lunch and dinner*
- *Accepts reservations and all major credit cards*
- *Private party facilities for between 20 and 80 people*

Orsini's

Orsini's is one of New York's most fashionable restaurants where you can observe the celebrities, the rich and the beautiful, while you enjoy sparkling Italian food. Thirty years at the same spot, it is still on the list of hot "in" places in the Big Apple. It has grown from a small bar and downstairs dining room, to include a large upstairs room set out in stylish pink—walls, tables, napkins.

Breaking from people watching, reading over the large menu poses the problem of an embarrassment of riches. Appetizers imbue one with great expectations. Try the *crostini alla Romana,* baked mozzarella highlighted with a butter sauce with anchovies and capers. Another winner is the *rollatine di Melanzane,* which consists of eggplant rolled around ricotta cheese and topped with a delicate fresh tomato sauce. The minestrone soup brims with the goodness of fresh vegetables.

There are many surprises hidden in the pastas. Favorites are the *penne alla vodka* and *rigatoni alla baronessa.* The former, cooked tableside, is pasta cooked in vodka, flamed, and with a touch of cream and fresh tomato. The rigatoni is a hearty pasta basking in a sauce of tomatoes, mushroom, and chicken livers. Also recommended is the *tortellini alla panna*—dumplings filled with chicken, butter, and cream sauce, and *ghe crespelle alla Fiorentina*—delicate crepes filled with spinach, prosciutto, and bechamel.

Seafood lovers can bask in what is called *la pescatora.* It serves two and teams clams, lobster, shrimp, mussles, and squid in a fresh spicy tomato sauce. Less ambitious eaters can chose the many scampi creations, calamari made with peas, wine, and garlic, or *spignola in brodetto*—fillets of fresh striped bass, clams, and mussels in wine sauce.

Veal is the favorite at Orisini's, and there are many varieties—from the simple *piccata al limone,* made in a lemon and butter sauce, to *scaloppine San Remo,* which is egg-dipped veal sauteed with artichokes and peas. Chicken dishes are well represented here, as in the *pollo all Orsini,* scaloppine of chicken breasts in a wine sauce with fresh baby artichokes.

For dessert, you can get the famous Roman ice cream *tartufo,* Italian cheesecake, *zuppa Ingelese,* or chocolate *mousse* tarte. And San Giustino wine, made in the vinyard owned by Orsini, is an exclusive here.

41 West 56 Street
New York, N.Y., 10019
(212) 757-1698

- *Italian Cuisine*
- *Priced expensive*
- *Open 6 days for lunch and dinner; Closed Sundays and major holidays*
- *Reservations are required. Accepts all major credit cards*
- *Private party facilities for between 30 and 70 persons*

Oscar's Salt of the Sea

A landmark on upper Third Avenue for 36 years, Oscar's Salt of the Sea was sorely missed during a brief closing last year while ownership was transferred from erstwhile omnipresent owner, black-shirted Oscar Karp, to the hands of longtime restaurateur Tom Lazarakis and his partner Nicholas Panas. They have wisely kept intact the most treasured traditions of this sleekly Scandinavian-styled seafood sanctum. Only the motherly waitresses have been replaced by eager youthful waiters. The rest remains familiar—from the gleaming glass and panelled interior with its clean geometric lines and no-nonsense polished wood tables, to the vast and moderately priced menu offering only daily-fresh fish and seafoods in so many permutations and combinations that the variety seems inexhaustible.

For instance: any one of some dozen fish may be broiled, fried, steamed, creole-sauced, almond-sauteed, or steamed with veggies and branches of fresh dill (a $2 surcharge). Add to the finny-folk a full roster of shellfish and crustaceans—curried, creole-ed, and crabmeat-stuffed—plus such occasional "specials" as an Italian-accented *marinara* of shellfish with linguine, or a Greek-inspired "Duo of Sole filets," one stuffed with crabmeat the other with feta-sparked spinach, and you understand why crowds line up in the spacious bar-entry, expectantly scanning the blackboards that list the day's "catch."

Full dinners, starting with clams, oysters, or chowder, including creamy cole slaw or salad, plus potato and coffee, tally just $10.95-$14.95—and that's for top-quality, briny-fresh sea-fare exclusively. It's the formula on which Oscar's first built its reputation—and the new management shows no sign of letting it lapse.

A crabmeat cocktail consists of abundantly apportioned delicately flavorful backfin lumps—none of the watery frozen stuff. An original version of oysters Rockefeller presents deep-shelled giants beneath a mountain of feta-sparked spinach, finished with a dollop of smooth bechamel; listed as an appetizer, the platter is sufficiently plentiful and rich to serve as a whole meal, with each of the six specimens like a Greek spinach pie concealing a juicy oyster "prize" at the bottom!

A heaping mound of king crab legs is steamed to the juicy peak of perfection—as is an inch-thick salmon steak mantled in fronds of dill that also perfume *al dente* chunks of carrot and strips of celery and onion that create crunch to contrast with the moist fish flesh—at the bottom collects a flavorful soup worthy of spooning to the last drop. The rich dessert syndrome here demands a special card listing an intensely fudgey chocolate cheesecake, lime-chiffon pie, chocolate layer cake and pecan pie—as well as such down-home comforts as rice pudding or a gorgeously grenadine-glazed baked apple.

To complement such fare, there's a decent house Soave by the carafe ($8.50), a varied listing of white wines ranging from an elegant $26.00 *Pouilly Fuisse* to a popular $10.50 *Verdiccho* along with both domestic and imported beers.

1155 Third Avenue
New York, N.Y., 10021
(212) 879-1199

- *Seafood Cuisine*
- *Priced moderately*
- *Open 7 days for lunch and dinner*
- *Accepts reservations and AE, MC, VISA*

Palm

After more than 50 years, this venerable establishment shows no sign of losing its considerable energy, its hordes of satisfied customers, its tons of extraordinary food rolling out of its super large kitchens. Kitchens in plural because the Palm, after half a century, has spawned an offspring in Washington, D.C., Los Angeles, Houston, Chicago, Miami, and Easthampton, Long Island. And all owned by the offspring of the original owners.

The Palm is an original, a gustatory juggernaut which was first opened in 1926 by two Italian immigrants, Pio Bozzi and John Ganzi. It remains much the same today as it was then: a loud, masculine, sawdust-covered place with tin ceilings, globe lighting and walls filled with cartoon art that characterizes the famous names of the past in sports, journalism, and the world at large. This harks back to the days when the Palm was a hangout for the two-fisted journalists who published in what was, in the 20's and 30's, a newspaper center in New York. It is still a favorite of the old newspaper crowd—being near the Daily News Building—but the ranks have been cultivated by the international set, the well-to-do, tourists, and New Yorkers who know where it's at.

The menu boasts none of the effete fad foods so common nowadays, but hardy meat, Italian, and seafood dishes of absolutely gargantuan size. One of the endearing quirks of the Palm is that there is no menu. You will have to ask the waiter to reel off the day's offerings and prod him when he starts to wind down. You will surely hear of the steaks, the filet and sirloin for which the Palm is justly famous. Humongous slabs of beef, charcoaled to a perfection you will rarely encounter anywhere else. You might also hear of the broiled chicken, roast beef, pork chops, and lamb chops. If you persist, and the waiter is not too distracted by his work, you may also learn of the Palm's Italian specialties—its veal dishes, and its pasta.

Pressing on, you will get to the seafood—monster-sized lobsters that take nearly an hour to devour, fragrant scallops, scampi. There are desserts, too, if you (recommended) split an entree, and served of course in superhuman proportion.

If you love good food, served in proportions unknown and even unheard of today, the Palm and its sister restaurant across the street, Palm Too, should be on your special list.

---

837 Second Avenue ***840 Second Avenue***
New York, N.Y., 10017 ***New York, N.Y., 10017***
(212) MU7-2953 ***(212) MU7-5198***

- *Steakhouse Cuisine*
- *Priced expensive*
- *Open 6 days for lunch and dinner; Closed Sunday*
- *Reservations accepted at lunch only. Accepts all major credit cards*

Pie In The Sky

What if you don't want a full, big meal in an expensive, fancy restaurant but you still want to get gourmet food? Or what if you want to get gourmet food you can bring back to the office, the house, or to a picnic in the park? If you're in Manhattan consider stopping into Pie In The Sky. Pie In The Sky consistently puts up delectable *pates,* soups, salads, hot and cold sandwiches, hot and cold light entrees, as well as a raft of pies and desserts—and all of it can be taken out or eaten on the premises. But be forewarned: the premises aren't huge, and the popularity of this mother-and-daughter-run operation makes for crowded mealtimes.

Lynne Bien and her daughter Deborah Bien Jensen make all the gourmet *charcuterie* offerings daily, including *pates* and *croissants.* As well as their delicious salads, sandwiches, *terrines,* and such, they have recently introduced a wide range of hot entrees. Some of these include a light and fluffy quiche, a traditional English Cornish pastie (a turnover filled with beef, onion, and potato), roast Cornish game hen, and several notable chicken dishes. Vegetable lovers will like the hot vegetable dish with melted Monterey Jack cheese coating a mixture of steamed seasonal vegetables.

The sandwiches at Pie In The Sky are served on a croissant, and the combination of chicken salad and cheese, or tuna salad—or whatever you choose—and the light, rich croissant is delicious.

Among the vegetable salads, the salad of crisp green string beans laced with slivers of Bermuda onion and sprinkled with a delicate vinaigrette, and the cucumber slices in sour cream dressing are savorous. Two curry dishes, curried chicken salad and curried rice with currants and raisins, have light and mild overtones.

And the desserts, well, they submit close to a dozen pies and a half dozen cakes—and that's not counting the numerous types of toothsome scones, bisquits, muffins, and the like.

Should you want to eat their offerings on the spot, you'll find the small dining room a very pleasant place: Wood tables and chairs sit amid painted brick walls on which an art display changes every few months.

173 Third Avenue
New York, N.Y., 10003
(212) 228-2760 or (212) 228-2791

- *American Gourmet take-out and eat-in*
- *Moderately priced*
- *Open 7 days for lunch and dinner*
- *No credit cards; No reservations*

Ponte's

Ponte's nests two blocks south of Canal near West Street and not far from the West Side Highway. It was in 1967 that the Ponte brothers—Joseph, Angelo, Frank, and Anthony—decided to indulge their knowledge of good food and open a dining establishment far from the beaten path. Their original restaurant of one dining room has been expanded to three rooms holding some 320 guests, and there is never a problem filling the seats. The feeling is club-like. Downstairs is a fancy reception room, and upstairs are the wood-paneled dining rooms jeweled in glittering ceilings, colorful oil paintings, and sparkling table settings. There is comfort and privacy here, with unusually large tables with generous space between. Service is professional—polite and attentive. There is a chalkboard menu that is wheeled to the table, but the regulars consult with the Captain or Maitre d' to find the perfect combination to suit moods, climate, and temperature. The final touch is given by strolling musicians who good-naturedly entertain the satisfied diner.

Ponte's offers a wide range of elevated Italian cooking. Even so unassuming a dish as green and red peppers comes out cool and light with the accompaniment of anchovies, black and green olives, capers, and mozzarella. The homemade cannollini is a pillow of meat and spinach-stuffed crepe topped with a tasty fresh tomato sauce. We can get more complex with the duckling au Grand Marnier, deeply flavored with the orange liquor and crisp on the palate. Veal is excellent here—it is known for its *piccata.* And the parmagiana has added proscuitto for richness. And don't miss, on one of your visits, the Hungary Lobster, a huge silver platter of succulent lobster prepared at whim by the chef who combines his ingredients as the muses dictate and sautes large pieces of lobster, shrimp, meaty clam in olive oil, until they blend into an intoxicating, golden-redish combination that assaults the senses.

The dessert trolley is wheeled laden with cheesecake, Italian pastries, and a refreshing fresh fruit mix that is a perfect *finito.*

37 Desbrosses Street
New York, N.Y., 10013
(212) 226-4621-2-3

- *Italian Cuisine*
- *Priced expensive*
- *Open 6 days for lunch and dinner; Closed Sundays*
- *Reservations suggested. All major credit cards accepted*
- *Private party facilities for between 25 and 110 persons*

Portoroz

Under a twinkling mica-studded ceiling of midnight blue stucco, and surrounded by chunky fieldstone walls dressed up with mirror panels and lantern-sconces, Portoroz salutes the Adriatic seaside, where Yugoslavia's Dalmatian coast and the calf of Italy's "boot" share the secrets of seafoods and other Italian-inspired delicacies sparked with Slavic flair. Tuxedoed waiters, red carpeting, candlelight, and fresh flowers further support the sophistication of a retreat distinguished by neighborhood-chic and global gastronomy. Appropriately, a wine-book lists some unusual and worthwhile Yugoslavian wines as well as Italian and French labels.

Any Italian chef might be proud of an *al dente* linguine crowned with resilient rounds of squid in a full-bodied tomato sauce accented by whole basil leaves. A panoply of pastas also includes the classic *carbonara, Alfredo, Bolognese,* and both red and white clam sauces.

A complete listing of favorite Italian chicken, veal, and seafood dishes is augmented by such Slavic specialties as Macedonian style stuffed cabbage, sausage smothered in a savory pepper and onion melange, and the signature Middle-Eastern shish-kebab. Both coastlines claim credit for *teletina Marco Polo,* twin roulades of tender veal enclosing prosciutto and melted mozzerella, showered with mushroom-wine sauce. A nightly roster of fresh fish might include snapper, swordfish, and tuna-steak—the latter either broiled or glorified with a *marechaire* sauce floating mussels and clams cooked with such admirable restraint that the natural briny juices spurt to blend with the dominant herbs.

Dessert and coffee honors are harmoniously distributed among a flaky, nutty, honeyed *baklava* and a sponge-layered *zuppa inglese,* soaked in liqueurs, bound with custard and studded with citron plus chocolate chips—and to balance the bouffe choose thick Turkish coffee, potent espresso, foamy cappucino—or Coffee Portoroz: a diplomatic entente of espresso laced with slivovitz and brandy, then crowned with whipped-cream.

340 Lexington Avenue
New York, N.Y., 10016
(212) 687-8195

- *Italian Cuisine*
- *Priced moderate*
- *Open Monday through Friday for lunch and dinner; Closed Saturday and Sunday*
- *Reservations and all major credit cards accepted*

Primavera

A European-styled and inordinately handsome restaurant, Primavera is filled with oil paintings, antique mirrors reflecting walls of natural brick and fine paneling, bentwood cane chairs, and a miniature marble topped bar. Service is adept and personable and the food is good to glowing, the selection varied and beautifully presented, and the very busy dining room is well organized.

An unusual house speciality is *capratto ala Romano* (succulent baby goat, oven-roasted with the spice of rosemary). It's like lamb, tender and sweet with a slightly game tang. Not at all fatty, it's accompanied by crisply roasted burnished, moist potatoes. An appetizer to begin with can be *carpaccio alla Toscana,* thinly sliced rosy pink, tender raw beef glistening with excellent olive oil, served with a highly complementary *pesto* sauce presented prettily in a hollowed out lemon. A rich choice is the *spiedino alla Romana,* mozzarella with bread, deep fried to a golden brown on a skewer, in a light egg batter, served piping hot with a caper and anchovy sauce. The fragrantly light tomato, basil, onion sauce inspires the delicious moon-shaped pasta stuffed with veal, chicken and prosciutto in *agnolotti ala Romano.* It's a hearty trencherman's portion. As is the *antipasto Primavera* filled with a refreshing assortment of firm zucchini stuffed with meat, seafood salad, artichoke hearts, roasted peppers, anchovies, and other selections. The huge broiled to your order veal chop is fully seasoned, very pink, juicy, and tender. Plenty of fresh lightly cooked clams with just the right touches of garlic, make the *al dente* linguine with white clam sauce a winner along with *spaghetti degli Innamorte,* which combines mushrooms, zucchini and other vegetables in a creamy rick pink sauce.

All the pastry is freshly homemade and at the end of the meal, a lovely touch, a colorful plate of fruit is served on ice. A very caring atmosphere.

The wine list leans towards the Italian with some French wines available. Meals at Primavera are very popular, so reserve well ahead.

1570 First Avenue
New York, N.Y., 10028
(212) 861-8608

- *Classic Italian Cuisine*
- *Priced moderate to high*
- *Open 7 days for dinner only*
- *Accepts reservations and most major credit cards*

Pronto

Like the city of Rome, Pronto is a place of many moods and vast popularity—undoubtedly for that very reason. The experience depends on where you are seated in this dual-levelled expanse, everywhere decorated in dazzling white, with accents of brass banisters, gleaming mirrors and such witty whimsies as a mural-collage composed entirely of various pasta-shapes. The bar is extremely popular as an after-work watering spot for nearby Madison Avenue types.

Happily, the bar action is well separated by a narrow corridor from the dining salon itself. Here, each white-linen-draped table sits under an individual hanging lamp that has been cleverly swathed in a square of silk to produce the most flattering light possible. To the rear of the room, an eye-level brick oven is utilized during the day for practical demonstrations that produce the crisp rolls served at table. A third area—with its own separate entrance—is the very popular "kitchen" where the varied pastas of the House are rolled, cut, and hung to dry in full view, behind a glass enclosure.

Throughout this cuisinary complex, the identical menu applies. Obviously, freshly-made, succulently-sauced pastas are the hands-down specialty—with particular emphasis on eggy fettucine with a *frutti di mare* seafood sauce; a creamy *alla Pronto* creation sparked with julienned ham and chicken; and the inventive *carbonara di pesce* luxuriously laced with smoked salmon and red caviar. For a light palate-cleanser, the Pronto salad is an ingenious variation on spinach-salad: here, hard-boiled egg and bacon bits are lavished on leaves of spicy arugola for a vivid taste sensation.

Entrees include all your North-Italian favorites, from a *zuppa di pesce* and garlic-buttered scampi to the full roster of veal scalloppines. Note that *scalloppine Pronto* successfully weds a slice of eggplant with white veal rounds; and a chicken *gismonda* bedded on spinach also deserves attention.

In true European fashion, a sophisticated selection of well-ripened national cheeses is offered to precede or to stand for dessert; blue-veined Gorgonzola, sharp Provolone, and mellow Bel Paese might almost deflect attention from the sweet seductions on the list, so be warned: in addition to the citron-studded, chocolate-candy wrapped ice-cream *tartufo,* the House chocolate cake is a memorable structure of chocolate-sponge layers bound with chocolate mousse and frosted with icing.

The wine-list, while not eye-opening, is considerately priced and well-selected, with Italian labels naturally the best bets. Espresso and cappuccino are both expertly concocted and served with traditional flair by a white-jacketed staff.

30 East 60 Street
New York, N.Y., 10022
(212) 421-8151

- *North Italian Cuisine*
- *Moderately Priced*
- *Open Monday through Saturday for lunch; 7 days for dinner*
- *Accepts reservations and all major credit cards*
- *Private party facilities for a minimum of 20 people*

Pyrenees

The rugged mountain chain of the Pyrenees separates the Iberian peninsula from the rest of Europe, forming the boundary between France and Spain. The Pyrenees Restaurant, however, is a place that brings together the cuisines of France and Spain, the result being a Basque-ish combination where the French classic *soupe al'oignon gratinee* is offered alongside the Spanish classic *paella al la Valenciana.*

As you enter Pyrenees you descend a staircase to the dining room, and right away you feel the Mediterranean aura the restaurant gives off. The walls of brick intermixed with stone and stucco, the brass and wood trappings, the rustic sconces and the beautiful chandelier which give the dining room a soft amber light all combine to make Pyrenees a handsome and comfortable place to eat.

Fran and Tony Sanchez not only own Pyrenees, they also directly control it and ensure the quality of the food and service—Tony runs the kitchen and Fran runs the dining room. Tony picked up some of his skills from the famed chef Michelle Bordo, but he's brought his own brand of creative cooking to Pyrenees.

For example, Tony serves octopus as an appetizer occasionally. He serves the tender devilfish in an olive oil, white wine, and butter sauce. Or, for those seeking more traditional fare, there's a serving of excellent smoked salmon, accompanied by tomatoes and onions. Or you can try the clams casino, the mushroom caps stuffed with snails, the *mussels costa brava* (mussels in a tomato and wine sauce), or the *soupe a la Mariscada* (a zesty Spanish seafood soup).

Pyrenees offers a large selection of fish dishes, and to illustrate the dual nationality of the restaurant, right beneath the French classic *coquille St. Jacques* (scallops and shrimp in a brandy and cream sauce) on the menu sits the Spanish dish *cioppino,* a tangy, hearty fish and shellfish soup/casserole. Pyrenees also serves red snapper (stuffed with crabmeat), flounder, lobster tails also stuffed with crabmeat, and shrimp (either sauteed with garlic and wine or stuffed with crabmeat). At one dinner grouper was the fish of the day, and it was perfectly cooked.

Pyrenees also offers a wide array of meat dishes—everything from roast duckling in an orange sauce to a combination of roast pork and clams in a tomato

and wine sauce (or you can try veal and clams in the same sauce). There's also rack of lamb, a New York steak with *bordelaise* sauce, or a chicken breast stuffed with apples and raisins and smothered in a brandy and mushroom sauce.

Fran not only runs the dining room, she somehow finds time to make all the desserts, too. Hence the selection varies according to Fran's mood and whichever special ingredients might be in season. Almost always available are her cheesecake, her rum pie, and her chocolate *mousse,* and they're delicious.

627 South 2nd Street
Philadelphia, Pa., 19147
(215) 925-9117

- *French and Spanish Cuisine*
- *Priced moderate*
- *Open 7 days for dinner only*
- *Reservations and all major credit cards are accepted*

Raga

Virtually a magic-carpet tour of the culture and cuisine of India, the spacious and opulent *Raga* immediately engulfs the guest in the authentic, sinuous music of sitar and tabla—provided during the dinner hour—as well as in the haunting fragrance of saffron and spices permeating the air. The room is divided into cozy corners by columns and by rows of couch-seating across the center. Apart from the multi-colored woven carpet, all else is in restfully muted, warm brown tones.

Among appetizers, oysters Bombay, delicately handled with minced onion and the tang of ginger, repose in an oversized scallop shell; and a baked ramekin of spicy shredded crab *goa* mingled with onion and tomato are best teamed with whipped-yogurt *raita*—here stuffed with crunchy cucumber bits and diced tomato. Excellent Indian breads include whole wheat *aloo paratha* stuffed with potato, golden *puri,* and substantial *keema nan* speckled with seasoned lamb granules.

Lobster Malabar simmered with ginger is another of the rare house specialties—as is the *goan* fish curry prepared with freshly-ground coconut.

All the Tandoori specialties emerge from the intensity of the clay ovens well-seared on the outside to retain all the inner moistness until the juices spurt at the first bite.

The unique vegetarian cookery of India is well-represented by silky, smoky *baingan bhurta,* aromatic saffron rices, and the traditional lentil *dal.*

In addition to the usual *kulfi,* a pistachio-stuffed iced confection hauntingly flavored with saffron and cardamon, this establishment also offers real creamy ice cream in such appropriately exotic flavors as mango, rose, and chocolate-cinnamon.

---

57 West 48 Street
New York, N.Y., 10020
(212) 757-3450

- *Indian Cuisine*
- *Moderately priced*
- *Open 7 days for dinner; Monday through Friday for lunch*
- *Reservations and all major credit cards accepted*

Raimondo's

For samplings of the best of Northern Italian specialties, no Florida dining spot outclasses Raimondo's. Usually when one finds an owner-chef combination, good food is almost assured. Then one encounters Raimondo's and experiences nourishment taken into the dimension of artistry. And it is this uncompromising creativity that sets Raimondo's apart.

Established 18 years, its present location does not overpower the diner with ominous surroundings. Raimondo's wife Jule deserves credit for tasteful orchestration of the three casually rustic dining rooms serving 150 people. They are well-organized with selected paintings decorating the walls. Waiters scurry around attentively, and the over-all expertise of the management results in that impression of leisured assurance which inspires confidence in even the most diffident diner.

An evening at Raimondo's is an evening of discovering new dimensions in taste. Here, a soup is a soup is a special surprise. One mellow spoonful of the vibrant mussels in a broth of white wine and cream and you are hooked. The flavor-charged potato-leek soup is another fine example of the chef's flair. Attempt any of the antipasti—artichoke stuffed with crabmeat and bathed in *Mornay* sauce, baked oysters *cavalier,* or be special with the canape of Beluga caviar OPEC priced by the ounce! And don't overlook the imaginative concoctions of *al dente farinacci* such as the richly smooth and supple fettucine or the *canneloni Excelsior,* a crepe divinely stuffed with the complex combination of veal, spinach, and cheese—dripping with a savory sauce.

Entrees are extensive for this caliber establishment, where each dish is individually prepared—*veal Dante in cartoccio* (veal stuffed with ham, cheese, peas, herbs, rolled and delicately breaded with *crissiene* and almonds and served in a bag); a sumptious *zuppa di pesce* (poached blend of lobster, fish, clams, mussels in a winy tomato *farce* redolent of shallots and herbs); and breast of chicken stuffed with veal *mousse,* mushrooms, and

cheese. If, perchance nothing on the bill-of-fare tempts, Raimondo's will create a dish personally for you. In other words, Raimondo's will rise to any occasion. This level of excellence in the kitchen is Raimondo's grip on the Florida dining circuit.

4612 Le Jeune Road
Coral Gables, Fla., 33146
(305) 666-9919

- *Northern Italian Cuisine*
- *Priced expensive*
- *Open 7 days for dinner only*
- *Reservations suggested; all major credit cards accepted*

Rainbows

Simply put, an Art-Deco restaurant where the glitter and fun is matched by good food. The dominant colors are the red and beige of the chairs and walls and the deep blue of the wall-to-wall carpeting, and the dominant image is reflection, since there seem to be mirrors just about everywhere. It all makes for a splashy and flashy modern look which is at once both fun and pleasant. Fresh flowers on the tables, the many suspended plants, and the subdued recess lighting add to the charm.

And if you like stone crabs don't pass them up here. They're beautifully presented—decorated by carrot ribbons and sprouts on a bed of lettuce—and they have two dipping sauces, drawn butter and a zesty mustard number. Their speciality appetizer is called "shrimp of the stars," and while they won't divulge precisely what they do to the shrimp, it's clear they're battered, stuffed, and fried—and delicious. Other appertizers include cherrystone clams, Nova Scotia salmon, prosciutto and melon, *escargots en croute, fettucini Alfredo,* and an artichoke heart stuffed with marinated shrimp.

They serve the ubiquitous French onion soup, and they always offer another soup. Often it's a fine example of cream of mushroom, a very smooth, creamy broth with pieces of mushroom scattered throughout. Their salads deserve mentioning; they're aesthetically presented with nifty dressings.

Fish is well represented on their large menu. You can pick your swimming lobster out of a tank, for instance. Or you can try their speciality *"Rainbow Trout Supreme:"* Rainbow as in the restaurant and in the fish. There's also their catch of the day, fried Gulf shrimp, Alaskan king crab, and South African lobster tails.

Veal dishes include *Oscar* (crabmeat and asparagus on top), *Veronique* (mushrooms and grapes on top), and *Francais* (battered, buttered, and sauteed). There's also prime rib, a filet smothered in mushrooms, filet with *bernaise* sauce, *tournedos Rossini,* lamb chops, *coq au vin,* and roast duck.

Among the array of desserts are chocolate

mousse, cheesecake, *crepes Suzette,* and, of course, rainbow sherbet.

Rainbows has entertainment every night but Monday, and it ranges from bands to trios to comedians. This gives the place a cabaret feeling at times, and since the kitchen stays open until 5 a.m., it makes for a nice place to enjoy late supper.

6600 SW 57 Avenue
South Miami, Fla., 33143
(305) 666-4641

- *Continental Cuisine*
- *Priced moderate to high*
- *Open Monday through Fridy for lunch; Tuesday through Sunday for dinner; a late supper till 5:00 a.m.*
- *All major credit cards and reservations accepted*
- *Private party facilities for between 25 and 250 persons*

Rene Pujol

The spirit and flavor of a cozy French provincial inn greet you as you enter Rene Pujol. Rustic, dark, rough-hewn wooden ceiling beams highlight the light stucco walls hung with copper utensils, pottery, and scenic murals, while a small brick fireplace in the second dining room beckons you with it's warmth on chilly days.

Some memorable fresh appetizers are the fruits of the sea. For garlic lovers: *escargots* plump, juicy, and bubbling hot in a lusty garlicky sauce or *coquilles St. Jacques* dramatically served in a shell, brimming with scallops, shrimp, mushrooms, and lobster. Also good is the delicate cloud of fish *mousse* vibrant with a rich brown sauce. All the appetizers are exceptionally pleasing. For lobster lovers there's the chef's special salad with chunks of pink and white lobster nestled on a bed of crisp lettuce colorfully surrounded by a julienne of carrots and zucchini in a vinagrette.

A vichyssoise, thick, creamy, robust with seasoning and potato, or a fully flavored, custardy quiche lorraine, or sturdy thickly textured *pate,* with just the right accent of herbs, brings to mind the French countryside.

Beautifully prepared and presented entrees are supplemented daily by specials such as Dover sole, sauteed to a flavorful fragrant finish, then speedily and skillfully deboned, tableside. An interesting melange is the elegant boneless breast of chicken, chock-full of lobster and mushrooms, bathed in a distinctive Mornay sauce, served with a fresh vegetable, spinach, and a wild rice ring mold. Majestic, meaty, and juicy, the veal roast (country style) is attractively presented with potatoes, fresh vegetables, and spinach, that add to its overall success. A hearty dish, cassis duck, roasted to a crisp non-fatty finish, is deboned, cut, and served with berries, spinach, and a nutty wild rice. It's moist, flavorful, and satisfying.

Dessert offerings are special at Rene Pujol. Freshly baked in-house, the pastries alone are worth a trip. The light flaky crust of the strawberry tart is filled with ripe, full-flavored plump juicy glazed berries, anchored in a rich custard, the Grand

Marnier cake is a rainbow of colors, served with an excellent rasberry sauce, and decorated with paper-thin slices of orange. The traditional chocolate *mousse,* and a cooling *creme caramel* or *crepes suzettes* are also a treat and make dessert selection a feast for the eyes as well as the palate.

The meal ends on a triumphant note with a beautifully decorated courtesy tray of assorted freshly baked cookies interposed with glazed oranges. The wine cellar has a fine selection of French wines and a smaller selection of American wines.

Established for 12 years, Rene Pujol has a loyal clientele, is extremely busy before the theatre, but allows for a very relaxing dinner experience.

321 West 51 Street
New York, N.Y., 10019
(212) 246-3023

- *Classical French Cuisine*
- *Table d'hote lunch and dinner ($14.50 for lunch; $18.00 to $22.00 for dinner)*
- *Reservations and all major credit cards accepted*
- *Private parties from 10 to 50 persons*

Rive Gauche

Sometimes when a well-established, popular, and excellent restaurant changes location the move somehow damages the delicate and precise balance that made the place so good in the first place. Fortunately, Rive Gauche's move from the corner of Wisconsin and M Streets in Georgetown, Washington, D.C., to the Georgetown Inn did not harm it at all; Rive Gauche—D.C.'s oldest French restaurant—is still an elegant and exceptional place to dine.

In 1980 chef Michel J.F. Laudier bought out his partners and took control of the restaurant, which he and his wife now run. In so doing, Michel let Rive Gauche reflect more of his upbringing in the Normandy part of France. (From Normandy, Michel went to Paris, where he refined his culinary skills, and then he came to Rive Gauche, much to the delight of restaurant go-ers in the Washington area.)

Rive Gauche stresses the appearance and the feel of dining there as much as it stresses the quality of the food. As an example, many dishes are *flambeed* at the table, adding a fun theatrical air to the restaurant. An instance of this theatricality: the occassional speciality, Red Snapper for two.

The waiter brings out the entire cooked snapper in a cradle on a silver platter. He douses it with Pernod and sets it aflame. Then while it is still burning, he cuts off the head and tail, bones it and skins it, and just as the flames die down he sets two large, perfect filets on your plates and scoops the delicious shallot and white wine sauce over them.

The menu offers more simply served dishes as well, of course, and overall it's a study in classical French cooking. The appetizers range from smoked salmon to *escargots Bourguignonne*—and covering all the bases in between. There are delicious soups and salads, including a sumptuous lobster bisque and superb Caesar salad.

The large selection of entrees hits upon all types of French dishes. Some of the specialities include *la cote de boeuf Rive Gauche* (for two), *les coquilles St. Jacques a la Vapeur*, and *la cote de veau sautee aux morilles*.

The decor also deserves mentioning. Dominating one dining room is a huge crystal chandelier, with two smaller chandeliers alongside it. The soft pink lighting complements the large burgundy banquettes and the red leather chairs nicely. While one room is a little less formal than the other, both are plush, elegant, comfortable places to dine.

Besides lunch and dinner, Rive Gauche also serves breakfast, and it's a popular spot for business men to have breakfast meetings.

1312 Wisconsin Avenue NW
Washington, D.C., 20007
(202) 333-6440

- *French Cuisine*
- *Priced expensive*
- *Open seven days for lunch and dinner; Breakfast Monday through Saturday; prix-fix Sunday brunch*
- *All major credit cards and reservations accepted*
- *Private party facilities available for between 20 and 120*

Rose And Thistle

There's more to the name "Rose and Thistle" than just botany. The term stands for the sometimes friendly, sometimes fiercely combatative rivalry between England (the rose) and Scotland (the thistle). The two lands share a border and much history, yet there always has been, and still remains, a strong sense of independence and difference between them.

Now what does all this have to do with a restaurant? Well, in a way the name sums up what the restaurant wants to do: it wants to have the feel of a pub you might find in Great Britain, and it wants to have a menu that, while offering many English dishes, includes the cooking of Scotland, Wales, and Ireland. Happily, the restaurant accomplishes its objective—it serves good hearty food in a very relaxed pub-ish atmosphere. (And it doesn't cost you an arm and a leg, either.)

The Rose and Thistle is a converted house, which is probably part of the reason the place has such a cozy, comfortable feeling about it. After you pass through the rustic-looking bar area, you enter the first of the dining rooms. (Considerately, one of the dining rooms is for non-smokers only.) Attractive wooden booths and tables are pleasantly spaced. Old-fashioned posters and pictures decorate the wall, contributing to the English tavern feel.

The Rose and Thistle has three menus—for lunch, dinner, and their "late nite dinner"—but they all offer similiar, if not the same, dishes. The soups and salads are the same, and they're what you'd expect in a tavern: French onion soup, a hearty seafood chowder, a spinach salad, and a chef's salad, to name a few. During lunch some of the items are marked "express," which means that you'll get it within ten minutes of ordering. Thick, juicy burgers are served all the time, as are several excellent sandwiches.

The dinner menu offers some more complicated dishes. Trafalgar shrimp gives you jumbo shrimp nicely sauteed in wine, butter, lemon, and garlic. Chicken Galway Bay is a boneless breast battered and sauteed in dry vermouth, scallions, and mushrooms. There's also a stuffed sole dish, broiled lobster, scallops, a nice sirloin steak, and shrimp in a Brittany sauce.

In short, you get good food at a good price in a very pleasing setting. Well done, lads.

---

47 New Street
Huntington Village, L.I., N.Y., 11743
(516) 421-1444

- *English, Scottish, Welsh, and Irish Cuisine*
- *Priced moderately*
- *Open 7 days for lunch and dinner*
- *Reservations and all major credit cards accepted*
- *Private party facilities for up to 90 persons*

Ruggero's

Proving that class and skill will always tell, Ruggero's has come back from a disastrous fire stronger than ever. Its series of dining rooms have been redecorated with taste and wisdom. Walls are tailored with pale tan tweed fabric and trimmed with mahogany wood panels. One wall is commanded by a fieldstone fireplace framed in a heavy wooden mantel and adorned with a charming clock. Underfoot, a burgundy carpet adds to the restfulness and comfortable family feel, while chairs and tables designed for people bring the dining experience here very close to home. This despite the elegance of tuxedoed waiters who are, nonetheless, friendly, attentive, and considerate.

The very full menu here concentrates on Italian cuisine and a mixture of the simple and grand. Portions are very large, and an appetite to match will be amply satisfied. An example is the hot antipasto offering *mozzarella in carozza* (sandwiched in egg-dipped bread and fried), stuffed red peppers, whole baked clams, stuffed mushrooms, shrimp and eggplant. Quite a way to begin a meal. Other well-prepared starters include stuffed artichokes, eggplant *rollatine, spiedini alla Romana* or *pasta primavera,* a specially ordered dish made with fresh vegetables in season.

The waiters will be happy to recommend one of the many dishes and specialties of the house, and it might even be mandatory—what with the diner faced with an array of mouthwatering choices of veal, chicken, pork, pasta, and steak. Most assuredly, one of the tips will be veal, for Ruggero's has built a reputation in its preparation. Television viewers are familiar with the veal *cartocci* spotlighted on a local news program. But you will find *scaloppine* here as well, not to say *parmigiana, milanese* and *sorrentino.* For Ruggero's has a kitchen steeped in the tradition of fine Italian cooking—as witness the homemade manicotti, cannelloni and ravioli (visit and taste it as it should be made).

There is so much more to brag about here that it is a chore to attempt to choose. The steak, chops, and veal dishes alone would make a reputation, and that is to fail to mention the fish and shellfish so fresh that you pick your lobster live from a tank.

Desserts here can be a tableside show should you decide on a *tortoni* and fruits, crowned with lemon liqueur and cognac, constructed at your side.

A strolling guitarist sets just the right mood for no-nonsense Italian eating.

194 Grand Street
New York, N.Y., 10013
(212) 925-1340

- *Italian Cuisine*
- *Priced moderate*
- *Open 7 days for lunch and dinner*
- *Accepts reservations and AE, MC, VISA only*
- *Private party facilities for 20 to 100 persons*

Billy Shaw's Saffron

Billy Shaw's Saffron is the place to go if you're looking for that nice blend of classical and traditional dishes intermixed with some adventurous American *nouvelle* numbers.

The look at Billy Shaw's Saffron is a neat and serene one; the four dining rooms are decorated in plum, lavender, and purple, sporting attractive latticework ceilings. In one of the rooms sits an enclosed garden with skylight. On the tables rest handsome silverware and vases holding fresh flowers.

But back to the eclectic menu, which can be typified in the way they handle duck: They get their ducks from the nearby duck farms and then offer eight different methods of preparation ranging from the classic orange sauce to sauces of green peppercorns, brandied bing cherries, and peaches in cassis, to name a few. There's also a nicely traditional scallopine of veal served either *piccata* or *marsala*. There's also a veal chop "Saffron," where the chop is breaded, sauteed and then topped with pieces of tomato marinated in a piquant vinaigrette.

Among the appetizers, consider Saffron's version of angels on horseback—oysters wrapped in bacon *en brochette*—or the shrimps barbecued in their shells New Orleans style.

The delicacies on the dessert table invite inspection before ordering, and make sure you look over the Grand Marnier chocolate mousse and the *tartufo di Roma*.

When too many restaurants seem too much alike, Billy Shaw's Saffron is a refreshing place to eat with a unique menu and a pleasant, relaxed atmosphere.

---

730 West Broadway
Woodmere, L.I., N.Y., 11578
(516) 295-0200

- *American cuisine, some nouvelle and some not*
- *Priced moderate*
- *Open Tuesday through Sunday for lunch and dinner; Closed Monday*
- *Accepts all major credit cards and reservations*
- *Private party facilities for between 25 and 120 persons*

Sardi's

If people from out of town were asked to name just one New York restaurant, it might very well be Sardi's. And if they were asked to name just one restaurant that caters to the theatre crowd, it probably *would* be Sardi's. Sardi's has gone beyond just being a restaurant—it's become an institution.

Even though Broadway suffers through occasional poor seasons, and the price of tickets keeps climbing to outrageous new heights, and million dollar shows close in one night, Sardi's seems unfazed. The thousand or so caricatures of famous Broadway stars still line the walls. Actors still lunch with their agents there. Many an actor still skips in after a performance to have a drink or a snack. And celebrity watchers still flock there to catch glimpse of someone famous. Come what may, Sardi's is still going to be Sardi's.

Part of Sardi's appeal to the theatre crowd is its proximity to the theatre district—it's right in the middle of it and therefore a very convenient place to go before or after a show. And since the staff knows you're going to a show, and because they're used to it, they'll get you out in time for the curtain. That may not sound like much, but few things are more frustrating than trying to bolt down your coffee and get your check so you can get to your $40 seats—while your waiter lingers in the kitchen. This won't happen at Sardi's.

And Sardi's is a polite place to go. If you take Aunt Mabel in after a show, hoping to let her see a Broadway star in the flesh, the management won't be appalled and stick you in the corner. They'll plunk her down right in the middle of the action, making Aunt Mabel very happy.

Sardi's is also an attractive place to go—attractive because it's comfortable and stylish without being pretentious and stuffy. Red leather is the dominant motif, covering the numerous banquettes and chairs. And should you want to hit the new "in" place for the young, up-and-coming Broadway talent, try the upstairs bar and dining room, once a veritable social Siberia but thawing out lately.

When you order, go for everybody's favorite at Sardi's—the *cannelloni au gratin.* And if you're not up for the pasta, try Sardi's barbequed ribs, lamb chops, oven-roasted beef, veal *parmagiana,* smoked trout, or the crabmeat *a la Sardi's.* There are sandwiches for lunch, too. The best of them are the chicken breast with mayonnaise, crabmeat salad sandwiches, burgers, and pastrami. Desserts are a veritable smorgasbord featuring treats like homemade pound cake, strawberries with *zabaglione,* frozen and liqueured sundaes, rice pudding, and parfaits.

234 West 44 Street
New York, N.Y., 10036
(212) 221-8440

- *Continental Cuisine*
- *Priced moderate to high*
- *Open Monday through Saturday for lunch; 7 days for dinner; Sunday brunch*
- *All major credit cards accepted*
- *Reservations recommended*
- *Private party facilities*

Sea Fare of the Aegean

The standards here are, to pick up on the Greek theme, herculean; the attention to detail exhaustive. The setting is spacious, beautiful and spotless. The decorations consist of paintings and ancient art treasures taken from important collections of Greek and Roman artifacts.

The menu is the equal of the surroundings. It is, in fact, unique—an eight-page book illustrated in two colors with art treasures and scenes of ancient and modern Greece. A menu of this size is needed to accommodate a selection of fish and seafood that is breathtaking in its scope. At one count, there are 124 choices of appetizers, soups and stews, fish specialties—scallops, shrimp, crab and lobster—poultry, salads, desserts, cheeses and beverages (not including alcoholic which would add some 20 more).

It is obviously a human impossibility to attempt a description or an evaluation of an offering of this magnitude. One can simply say that it is the general opinion that execution is almost unfailingly flawless. Broiled foods come properly cooked throughout and frying is greaseless, with a thin golden crust on the outside, the inside moist. Cold foods—the salads, oysters, and clams—are fresh and flavorful.

For just the slightest direction you may be pointed to the house specialties. Shrimp Santorini are jumbo sized and dressed with grilled tomato and a creamy slice of feta cheese. Poached red snapper is in thick *avgolemono* sauce. But to go further is a useless exercise—the bass dishes are above-average whether Santorini or Aegean style—or in the styles of Scorpios, Skopelos, Andros, Crete, Syros, or Rodos. A veritable gastronomic tour of the islands.

There are 15 different ways to end a meal at Sea Fare with desserts such as *baklava,* that honey-thick pastry of the Middle East, and various Aegean style fruits and puddings. That is, if you can pass up the custard, strawberry shortcake, parfaits, sherbet, apple pie or ice cream.

25 West 56 Street
New York, N.Y., 10019
(212) 581-0540

- *Seafood Cuisine*
- *Priced Expensive*
- *Open seven days for lunch and dinner*
- *Accepts reservations and all major credit cards*
- *No private parties*

Seascapes

There are so few first-rate seafood restaurants—those with the knowledge, concern, and level of refinement to match their Continental colleagues—that it is a pleasure to include this new member on the scene. Seascapes is the creation of owner-host Attila Danku, who has brought to bear the experience of nearly a decade at the indominable Four Seasons. Creation is the right word; Mr. Danku has had an intimate hand in every aspect of Seascapes—even to making with his own hand the bar and some wood fixtures around the place. Walking in from the hub of the world, Forty-Second Street, you enter a small bar which is located totally apart from the dining room and overlooks the continuing drama of the street. Further in, a serene world of salmon-colored walls, recessed lighting, comfortable banquettes, tables, and lush carpeting are framed by natural wood doors made by the owner.

The menu offers a goodly array of fin, claw, and shell, of course, and there is enough grilled meat to satisfy any carnivore diehard. In addition, homemade pasta is a secret offering—not listed on the menu, but amply available in many succulent forms. Ask for the linguine with seafood and you will be rewarded with a fragrant dish of an abundance of lobster, crab, mussels, shrimp, clams, and scallops in a light tomato sauce. And there is seafood in a changing repertoire of preparation. There are fried shrimp in mustard sauce, crab cakes, fresh flounder, halibut, yellow perch, scrod, bass, swordfish, shrimp, and *chipolatas.*

Desserts here are all made in house, an accomplishment beyond the mere telling when you consider the selection includes Napoleon, cheesecake, chocolate *torte, mousse,* fresh fruit tart, and apple pie.

202 East 42 Street
New York, N.Y., 10017
(212) 370-0098

- *Continental/Seafood Cuisine*
- *Priced moderate*
- *Open 7 days for lunch and dinner; Special $9.95 prix-fixe dinner daily*
- *Reservations recommended and all major credit cards accepted*
- *Private party facilities for between 25 and 75 persons*

Shun Lee Palace

Shun Lee Palace is one New York's splashiest, jazziest, chic-est, and (if you go wild with a raft of specialities) most expensive Chinese restaurants. Fortunately, it's also one of the best.

Presiding over the squadron of chefs that turn out Shun Lee Palace's food is Micheal Tong, and over the years he has established a reputation as one of New York's most talanted and original Chinese chefs. (A private banquet he threw at the restaurant some years ago is still mentioned periodically.) His originality is evident in some of the wonderful dishes unique to Shun Lee Palace.

Chief among the specialities may be "Beggar's Chicken." Given a day's notice, the staff will turn out a chicken the likes of which you probably haven't seen before. The chicken is stuffed with vegetables and pork and seasoned with an unrevealed blend of spices. Then it's wrapped in lotus leaves, encased in clay soil, and baked at a very high temperature for four hours, getting basted frequently with what they call "rose petal liquer." The result is succulent and thoroughly enjoyable.

The extensive menu does not limit itself to the cooking of any one region of China, but offers Catonese, Szechuan, and Hunan dishes instead— some fiery hot while others have a very delicate, subtle flavor. The kitchen will alter the spiciness of any dish according to your wishes.

Among the appetizers spicy yang chow chicken soong (pieces of chicken, carrots, celery, pine nuts, and scallions in a unique tasting hot sauce), hacked chicken (sliced white chicken in a spicy sesame sauce, served cold), and corn soup—a light flavorful soup that, once tasted, makes most others pale in comparison.

The Peking Duck is a delicious speciality. It's carved at your table, with the golden brown skin being sliced before the tender meat. It's served with Chinese *crepes* and a tangy *hoisin* sauce.

The two poshly done rooms offer a study in contrast. The back room is a loud, active—almost tumultuous—place with excitement and action being the keynotes. The front room, though, is a subdued and quiet area that has secluded booths and a raised section with comfortable banquettes.

Shun Lee Palace—flashy, splashy, and excellent.

155 East 55th St.
New York, N.Y., 10022
(212) 371-8844

- *Chinese Cuisine*
- *Priced moderate to high*
- *Open seven days for lunch and dinner*
- *Reservations recommended and AE, DC, CB accepted*

Shun Lee West

Shun Lee Palace had established itself a one of New York's premiere Chinese restaurants, and the owners wanted to bring the same high level of food, service, and decor to an area which they felt lacked a top-flight Chinese restaurant: the West Side of Manhattan, near Lincoln Center. So they opened Shun Lee West ("Shun Lee" means "good luck") and, simply put, the area now has its top-flight restaurant.

Michael Tong and the others also own Shun Lee Dynasty and Hunam, and they've avoided the trap of having one basic restaurant with several different branches. Each restaurant has its own look, feel, and menu. Being near Lincoln Center, Shun Lee West naturally caters to the before and after theatre crowd (and the before and after opera, dance, and music crowds, for that matter). If you arrive at Shun Lee West before 6:30 p.m. you'll have time to enjoy a sumptuous Chinese feast and still make one of Lincoln Center's 8:00 curtains.

After the performance, and also on weekends, Shun Lee West offers a special Chinese treat: a *dim sum* menu. *Dim Sum*, loosely translated, means "to lightly touch the heart," and a *dim sum* meal is one where you choose your food from passing waiters carrying trays of delicious looking dishes. When you finish eating a waiter counts your empty serving plates and calculates your bill. *Dim Sum* dishes usually include spare ribs, spring rolls, fried shrimp balls, fried dumplings, stuffed green peppers, stuffed bean curd, and other similiar offerings.

Shun Lee West also offers a complete menu of Hunan, Szechuan, and Cantonese dishes. There's Peking Duck, of course, and a delicious crispy sea bass Hunan style—a whole fish which looks as if it were swimming in a sea of sauce carrying an exotic creature made of minced red and green chilies, ginger, and scallions on its back. There's also varying treatments of prawns, shrimp, beef, lamb, pork, and veal, as well as several excellent noodle dishes. Some dishes are quite spicy, while others are more delicate, and the spiciness of all dishes can be altered to fit your taste.

The decor of Shun Lee West is no less posh than the glittery elegance of Shun Lee Palace. Comfortable banquettes line a well-lit room that's broken up only by a row of mirrored columns. The nice gray walls are decorated with beautiful examples of Chinese art.

Shun Lee West—an equal younger brother to the prestigious Shun Lee Palace.

43 West 65th Street
New York, N.Y. 10023
(212) 595-8895

- *Chinese Cuisine*
- *Priced moderate to high*
- *Open Monday through Friday for lunch; Dim sum lunch Saturday and Sunday; Dinner 7 days; Dim sum dinner from 10 PM-midnight 7 days.*
- *AE, DC, CB accepted and reservations recommended*

Siva's

The food at Siva's is that of Northern India, and while the menu draws on one geographic region for its inspiration, the selection of dishes is by no means limited. A *tandoor*—a special clay oven using charcoal—sits in the the glass-enclosed kitchen, and from it come many of the distinct offerings. And to further ensure the food's distinctness, the staff at Siva's custom-blends their own spices. They won't tell exactly how much of which particular spices they use, of course, but you can safely bet that at least one of your courses will be flavored with some combination of saffron, cardamom, coriander, allspice, cumin, cloves, and fenugreek (the seeds of the clover-like fenugreek plant).

The tandoori specialities are a varied lot. To begin, try one of the several kinds of *roti* (breads), which you can dip into one of the many chutneys. Also from the clay oven comes chicken marinated in yogurt and one of the exotic spice mixtures. Or maybe you'd like the chicken without the yogurt and with just the spices. Or try the roasted lamb, beef, or prawns, each cooked in the *tandoor* and each with its own distinctive blend of spices.

If clay ovens don't do much for you, go for any of the poached or sauteed fish dishes (fish with a coconut and spice mixture, or prawns in a puree of fresh green herbs, blended with fresh mint and sauteed onions), or any of the *basmati* rice specialties (aromatic, long-grained *basmati* rice cooked with spices, fruit, nuts, cheese, vegetables, or meats).

For the herbivore, Siva's offers a large selection of meatless dishes, ranging from a spinach, cheese, and spice combination or roasted eggplant with tomatoes to lentil-burgers or a feta-cheese-based casserole.

Accompanying the food is a pleasing, soothing ambience, which is created by owner Amar Bhalla's attention to detail. On the saffron-tinted linen tablecloths sit vases of fresh flowers and softly glowing tapered candles. Around the room wicker lamps give off a quiet, mild light. On the upper level of the restaurant are comfortably over-stuffed, four-poster mahogany booths, and throughout the

restaurant emphasis is on gentle almond and straw colors. The keyword here: pleasantness.

So combine virtuoso food with the tranquil atmosphere and you have a very fine place to go for exotic Indian cuisine.

---

34 South Front Street
Philadelphia, Pa., 19106
(215) 925-2700

- *Northern Indian Cuisine*
- *Priced moderate*
- *Open Tuesday through Friday for lunch; Tuesday through Sunday for dinner; Sunday brunch; closed Monday*
- *All major credit cards and reservation accepted*

Stella del Mare

A finely appointed and well thought out establishment that specializes in Northern Italian cooking with the emphasis on seafood. It is divided into a bar and lounge downstairs and delightful dining room upstairs augmented by a recessed glass-ceilinged garden area. The lighting is soft and relaxing with the nice touch of overhead spotlights picking up the colors of a fresh long-stemmed rose on each table. The whole feeling is one of service to the customer—tables are large, well-spaced, and appointed in warm beige and white, the walls are natural-brick with marble-like panelling.

The cooking is satisfying and without cliche. The sauces are creative, the pasta all homemade, the fish fussily fresh, the meat prime. There is a very good choice of appetizer. The chef shows his worth in as simple a creation as the mussels with a gentle, yet complex *mariniere* sauce that combines white wine,

garlic, parsley and fresh tomato. The *scampi oreganata o pescatore* is butterfly shrimp sauteed in a highly seasoned brown sauce that infuses quite an excellent flavor.

Other appealing openers are the *avocado ripieno*, a peeled avocado whose soft, bland meat is enlivened by a shrimp and crab stuffing; *antipasto caldo*, clams *casino*, shrimp, mussels and filled mushrooms; and *vongole cassino o posillipo*, finely textured clams cooked in white wine and tomato sauce.

Pasta lovers will find a wonderful *linguine alle vongole o marechiaro* which is a garlic-laced white clam sauce dressed at table, *capellini primavera*, fettuccine, and gnocchi made from fresh potato dough.

Fish is the strong point here, of course, and it is one of the best such houses in the city. Be on the alert for the Mako shark. It is not always in season, but when it is make it a point to order this very simply made but exquisitely textured and flavorful fish. And the portion is immense. Other satisfying selections include bay scallops that are cooked "to your pleasure," a rare opportunity to direct the chef; stuffed whole flounder; calamari that is soft and unique in taste; snapper, bass and more, including live lobster.

Unrepentant meat eaters have a selection from filet mignon through sirloin steak, double veal chop, rack of lamb garni , and a hefty chateaubriand with sauce *Bernaise*.

Desserts are a delightful surprise for their elegance. You can pick from the Venetian wagon, savor fresh fruits, or marvel at the *crepes flambe*. Espresso and cappuccino are served as the perfect ending.

346 Lexington Avenue
New York, N.Y., 10016
(212) 687-4425

- *Seafood/Northern Italian Cuisine*
- *Priced moderate*
- *Open 6 days for lunch and dinner; Closed Sundays*
- *Accepts reservations, AE and MC only*
- *Private party facilities for between 15 and 45*

Streb's South

Imparting both a dress-up and casual flavor, Streb's quartet of dining rooms are quartered within a warm and elegant brick building. The table settings are attractive, and despite a full house there's room to wield one's elbows as well as one's tongue. The menu awaiting you at Streb's defies the diner to arrive at a request beyond the far reaching selections available. Diverse food groupings are reflected with humor and respect. For 18 years now owner, Peter Eaffaldano has served crowds of diners appealing to both their palate and their purse. Through volume and a continuing quest for improvement, he has been able to maintain freshness in everything he serves.

Classified as about halfway between New England cuisine and an American steak and lobster house, Streb's has something for everyone. For the hearty, there are over a pound of robust ribs, sauce-dabbed and hickory smoked, served with a big basket of homebaked marble bread. For the delicate palate, there are tender, tasty morsels of veal *marsala*. Appetizers are tastefully presented and mainly delicious to taste: *escargot* with mushroom caps bobbing and garlic sauce dripping. Stone crabs excel and are available only in season to insure freshness—no sticking shells to indicate freezing here. Like a horn-of-plenty brimming over you'll find your dinner including an all-you-can-eat salad bar, assorted relishes, soup, fresh vegetable or potatoes, loaves of bread fresh daily and made on the premises are accompanied by lashings of butter.

Should prime ribs be your choice of entree, limit your complimentary intake as you have a trencherman's portion of beef ahead of you. Allow for even more room if ordering an end cut with the bone-in. Streb's special oven allows perfect cooking even of the ends, providing the diner with red, succulent meat beautifully crusted.

The dessert roster includes homebaked cheesecake, key lime pie made with true key limes only and strawberry pie—difficult to snub no matter how heartily you've eaten. Accompany these sweets with hot, mellow espresso or cappuchino made personally for your table.

Streb's South in Boca Raton recently opened a branch called Streb's III, 10 miles north of its Boca location on Federal Highway. Although the menus vary, the management is striving to equal the quality, service and dependability.

Strebs South:
1450 North Federal Highway
Boca Raton, Fla., 33432
(305) 395-9496

Streb's III:
2320 South Federal Highway
Boynton Beach, Fla., 33435
(305) 734-3033

- *American/Steakhouse Cuisine*
- *Priced moderately*
- *Open Monday through Friday for lunch; 7 days for dinner*
- *Reservations accepted and all major credit cards*

Suggar's

It's not too often that a place serving good food has a disco in it. Conversely, it's not too often that a place having a disco serves good food. Well, at Suggar's both are true: You can sup on stuffed eggplant and jumbo shrimp *parmigiana* and then work off all those calories on the dance floor—grooving to the latest tunes as engineered by one of the expert disc jockeys.

Suggar's is big and very popular: the look is brash, exciting, and fun, and the creditable food is moderately priced.

The design of Suggar's is multi-levelled with large potted plants adding to the look, further dividing the rooms and levels, and enhancing the overall contemporary feeling. Most of the modern appearance, however, comes from the plentitude of jazzy and snazzy neon lights and signs—giving the place even more energy and spirit. The floors are an attractive mix of shining, polished hardwood and stylish, lush carpeting.

The food is distinctly American, which means besides the excellent burgers, fluffy omelettes, and substantial sandwiches, there's a smattering of dishes with varying national origins—as well as the time-honored entrees such as lobster tails and a thick, cooked-to-order sirloin.

An appetizer with Italian inspiration, for example, is the *fettucini primavera* with vegetables and shrimp. The *al dente* pasta is covered with a well-flavored cream sauce into which crisp, fresh vegetables and plump shrimp are added. Another dish with an Italian slant is the veal *marsala,* where chunks of un-pounded veal are smothered in a good, strong, mushroom-filled brown sauce. Suggar's also offers an array of vegetarian salads, so those who don't eat meat or fish won't feel left out.

One testimony to the popularity of the food at Suggar's (the chef is Kevin Newman) is the large catering business the kitchen does.

1137 Broadway
Hewlett, L.I., N.Y., 11557
(516) 374-1212
- *American Cuisine*
- *Priced moderate*
- *Open Tuesday through Sunday for lunch and dinner; Closed Monday*
- *Reservations and AE only accepted*
- *Private party facilities for between 20 and 150 persons*
- *Disc Jockey spins dance records nightly*

Szechuan Taste

There are those who feel that to get the best Chinese food in New York City you have to go to Chinatown. But once there, which of the many restaurants do you choose? You won't go wrong if you opt for Szechuan Taste in Chatham Square, where, if you wish, you can sit in a glass-enclosed sidewalk patio section and look out on the constant activity that is Chinatown.

As its name implies, the emphasis here is on the cooking of the Szechuan region of China, and many of Chef Lau's dishes have that noted Szechuan fire and zip. But good spicy cooking has more than just hotness to it, and what makes this restaurant special is the richness and complexity of even Chef Lau's tangiest creations.

As an example consider Lau's version of hot and sour soup (called here "hot and pungent soup"). Suspended in the savory broth are pieces of beef, pork, bean curd, bamboo shoots, scallions, and mushrooms. While the soup is appropriately sharp and piquant, as well as being spicy, the flavors aren't overpowering—beneath all the zing and gusto lies a luscious complexity that makes the soup a pleasure to eat.

If you want something equally fulfilling but less spicy, try the admirable assorted flavor soup, some of the flavors being chicken, ham, shrimp, Chinese cabbage, and a hearty chicken stock. This is a satisfying deeply-flavored soup that's an excellent way to begin a meal.

At Szechuan Taste you can appease that proclivity for the unusual by tasting the cold shreds of jellyfish, which consist of tasty pieces of jellyfish that have a mild garlic background to them.

It's best at Szechuan Taste to eschew the more standard selections and go for the specialities of the house. Once such specialty is *young-shun* beef, which consists of slices of beef, green onions, mushrooms, and green peppers in Chef Lau's secret brown sauce. *Young-shun* beef is a bit milder than many of his offerings, but no less mouth-watering. The shrimp in Imperial Shrimp are large and plump, served in a pungent peanut sauce.

Among the noodle dishes, the noodles with sesame paste comes either hot or cold, but always with plenty of the sesame flavoring. Perhaps one "must" at Szechuan Taste is the noodles with meat sauce, which has a delicate, almost exotic taste.

The restaurant's decor is pleasant and friendly. A partition of a Chinese design, flanked by many hanging plants, separates the sidewalk cafe section from the rest of the downstairs dining room. Upstairs is another dining room, and there's also a space for private parties.

23 Chatham Square
New York, N.Y., 10038
(212) 267-0672
- *Chinese Cuisine*
- *Moderate prices*
- *Open seven days for lunch and dinner*
- *All major credit cards accepted; Reservations a good idea*

Talk of the Town

T alk of the Town just may be the talk of this town—Manhasset, New York. If the outstanding nourishment doesn't do it, the decor certainly will.

And what decor—the type of decor that would get immediate applause if it were put on a stage. The overall appearance is, well, what the 21st century might look like. One dining room has two walls of windows and a ceiling that is at least one-third skylight. Turrets protrude from the ceiling as well. Pillars covered with mirrors and plum-colored and black velvet break up the room, and around the room sit custom-made over-stuffed chairs covered with the same plum-colored velvet. Crystal and wood trappings dot the room, along with immaculately-appointed tables set with beautiful

tapered candles and bouquets of flowers.

The menu may define what the term "American-Continental" means—it's a mixture of offerings, some of which have a distinctly French background, others a distinctly Italian background, others a distinctly American background, and there are even a few distinctly "multinational" dishes. Four quick examples: breast of chicken *francaise*, veal chop Florentine, reef and beef (the sister of surf and turf), and filet mignon kebab.

Begin your meal with one of the international appetizers, coconut fried shrimp—crustaceans thickly battered, fried, and served with a smooth, zesty Indian curry sauce—or try the seafood salad, a combination of calamari, scallops, crabmeat, and shrimp marinated in oil, lemon, and herbs. If *gazpacho* is what you're after, their *andaluz* version is appropriately rich and spicy. There's also smoked trout, a spinach salad, and mushrooms *a la greque,* to name a few other dinner openers.

The Talk of the Town offers a rare treat done beautifully—a baby rack of lamb *Persillee* for one— with a fresh mint sauce and tomato *Provencale.* The chicken *a la Talk of the Town* is also a winner. It's a rolled boneless breast stuffed with assorted cheeses and almonds, sauteed, and served with a rich sour cream sauce. There's another international offering, *Jaegerschnitzel,* a huge, nicely-breaded cutlet cooked with mushrooms, onions, bacon, and green peppers. Fish fanciers might go for the expertly broiled red snapper.

Dessert doesn't get slighted. Besides their rightly famous Black Forest cherry cake, there's also a large selection of pastries on their dessert cart.

1115 Northern Boulevard
Manhasset, L.I., N.Y., 11030
(516) 627-5415
- *American Continental Cuisine*
- *Priced moderate to high*
- *Open Monday through Friday for lunch; seven days for dinner*
- *All major credit cards and reservations accepted*
- *Private party facilities for between 50 to 200 persons*

Tandoor

Bright orange awnings beckon you into tasting some of the finest northern Indian cooking in Washington, D.C. As you enter Tandoor, the red walls with polished brass lanterns accent the beautiful large batik draped along the wall. The pungent aroma of freshly ground spices mingling with the scent of dishes being served, makes the mouth water and the nose tingle with anticipation.

Tandoor is named for the clay pot oven which can be seen behind a glass wall, in which poultry, fish, and meats are skewered and suspended over charcoal, emerging burnished and steaming, the breads puffed and crisp.

The friendly owner, Jack Katyal, and his informed staff will help guide you through the intricacies of the exotic menu. You may surmise that you're in for a generously portioned gastronomical adventure—you will not be disappointed, because the dishes range from creamy with yogurt, cheesed, or lightly curried to hot with curry and spices.

Tandoor specialties are rightfully highlighted and among them an interesting mixed grill of two moist filets of fish, plump pink shrimp, scented tender lamb and juicy browned chicken, or a filet of lamb marinated for 24 hours in fresh herbs and spices, then gently cooked to rosy perfection. Both are served with rice pilaf, pickle, and pappadum.

To spice up your tastebuds, try starting with the minced lamb balls very hot, spicy and juicy to the bite, or fresh shrimp subtly seasoned and batter-fried to a golden goodness. Try the surprisingly light pastry tricorns filled with mildly spiced beef or well seasoned potatoes and green peas. For the soup lovers, an ample bowl of mulligatawny soup filled with vegetables and rich chicken broth, or lentil soup spiced and served with lemon will more than suffice.

The 13 choices of breads are outstanding, from the plain to the very over-stuffed. Some are filled with minced meat, others with yogurt, boiled potatoes, red pepper and burnt cumin seeds, to some deep-fried or bursting with fresh tomatoes, onions and cucumbers.

The desserts are well done and intensely sweet,

but an Indian tea, *Punjabi,* flavored with cardamom and fennel is an exotic, pleasurable way to finish the evening; or if you prefer, Indian beer or cocktails are available.

3315 M Street NW
Georgetown, Washington, D.C., 20007
(202) 333-3376

- *Indian Cuisine*
- *Moderately priced*
- *Open seven days for lunch and dinner; Brunch served Saturday and Sunday*
- *Major credit cards accepted*
- *Reservations recommended*
- *Private party facilities available*

Tandoor

The Tandoor gets its name from the clay pot oven used to dry bake meats, poultry, fish and breads. It is a fascinatingly simple way to cook, and the restaurant has thoughtfully encased its tandoor chef in a glass-fronted room for interested patrons to watch. And it is nice to see the foods emerge, browned and steaming, the breads peeled off the sides crispy and bubbled.

This sparse manner of cooking, combined with combinations of spiced sauces, is the strength and specialty of the Tandoor, and it is the premier exponent of this cuisine in the city.

The restaurant is splendiferously decorated in the Indian manner—hand-carved teakwood arches, bright red banquettes, impressive artworks. Service is friendly and helpful to those just discovering Indian cooking. The menu is replete with definitions and explanations of the exotic but tantalizingly named dishes that await.

The menu here is quite varied, and especially noted for its first course selections which, with the possible exception of the French, are the most complex of appetizers. Excellent are the chicken *pakora*, delicately spiced deep fried chicken fritters and the *alu chaat*, potatoes and salad diced and marinated in a tangy sauce rich in coriander. The Indian cuisine is particularly rich in its

accompaniments. The mulligatawny soup is a robust infusion of vegetables and rich-thickened chicken stock that holds its own between courses. Breads are superb here, from the simple nan, baked in the tandoor before your eyes, to the stuffed breads: special *nan* (stuffed with nuts, almonds, eggs and herbs), also *paratha* (whole wheat bread stuffed with mildly spiced potatoes) and *keema nan* (stuffed with minced lamb).

The main courses are numerous, and are uniformly good. The tandoor chicken sizzles on a bed of onions. Also try the *seekh kebobs*, chopped meat flavored with onions and herbs and skewer roasted in the tandoor. One of the joys of Indian cuisine is the things they do with vegetables. A choice of their many creations is a surprising trip to pleasures not experienced with all-vegetable meals.

40 East 49 Street
New York, N.Y., 10017
(212) 752-3334

- *Indian Cuisine*
- *Priced moderately*
- *Open seven days for lunch and dinner*
- *Reservations recommended. All major credit cards accepted*

Teddy's

In the 1920's the space housing what is now this excellent Italian restaurant was the home of a roarin', flappin' speakeasy. With the repeal of Prohibition in 1933 the speakeasy became a German bar and grill. Then in 1945 Sal Cucinotta opened Teddy's, which, until it closed about three years ago, was a very "in" haunt for celebrities and would-be celebrities. Now Richard Borsia has opened a new Teddy's, and it's one of the better restaurants in New York's emerging Tribeca area.

There are only a few items on the menu which aren't distinctly Italian, and the large selection includes almost every Italian favorite you can think of, from *assortito antipasti* to *zabaglione.* And you can count on them being very well prepared.

Among the appetizers, for instance, is the stuffed mushrooms. Mushroom caps are filled with a bread crumb and crabmeat mixture, put on a bed of rich tomato sauce and topped with melted cheese. They're delicious. Other choices include baked clams, melon and prosciutto, and smoked salmon.

The *fettucini ala prosciutto* is a frequent pasta special. A smooth cream sauce dotted with chunks of prosciutto tops nicely *al dente* cooked noodles. Other pasta dishes include linguine with clam sauce (red and white), angel hair pasta with a *primavera* sauce, and *tortellini ala Bolognese.*

The more than two dozen entrees offer a wide range of dishes. Filets of sole are broiled, or served *meuniere,* almondine, or *Savoia.* Bass and snapper are broiled. There's also scampi, stuffed shrimp, and other seafood dishes.

Among the preparations of veal are *marsala, Francaise, parmigiana,* and *piccata.* There are also several chicken and beef offerings. A special of the house is lamb chops *Arrabiata,* broiled lamb chops covered with a delicious mixture of pimentos, peppers, mushrooms, and artichoke hearts.

The look of Teddy's is plush and comfortable. Porcelain chandeliers and sconces gracefully light the gilt-edged paintings that adorn the walls. The tables are covered with white linen, decorated with fresh flowers, and nicely spaced amid the

comfortable booths and banquettes. A balcony overlooks the main dining room and adds additional room for tables.

219 West Broadway
New York, N.Y., 10013
(212) 226-8131

- *Italian Cuisine*
- *Priced moderate to high*
- *Open Monday through Friday for lunch; Monday through Saturday for Dinner; Closed Sunday*
- *All major credit cards and reservations accepted*
- *Private party facilities for between 10 and 100 persons*

Ted Liu's

Hidden in a courtyard in downtown Washington, D.C., Ted Lui's restaurant, specializing in Szechuan and Hunan cuisine, is a work of art—serene, harmonious, breathtaking in its decor and design.

This unusual two-story Chinese restaurant's walls are not painted with fiery dragons; instead pale blue quilted cotton hugs the walls, acting as a buffer keeping conversation levels to a soft murmur. Seated on the teal blue banquettes your eye focuses first on the embroidered silk kimonos caught between sheets of glass that hang as colorful room dividers. If you prefer to dine basking in the sunlight, sweep up the grand staircase to the second level, where the glass walls bring the outdoors in.

The luncheon menu is modest in length and price but not in taste. There's fried wontons, spring rolls, spare ribs, and shrimp toast. Spicy hot and sour soup, chock-full of vegetables and pork, just peppery enough to let the flavor shine through. Rich and creamy chicken and corn soup, or light wonton soup in a clear broth, filled with plump dumplings.

The dinner menu has six pages to choose from, with a half-dozen soups and fourteen appetizers from cold and spicy *bon bon* chicken—tender and white, tingling on the tongue—to smoked fish Chinese-style, perfumed in a special sauce. The fried bean curd skin is a contrast in texture, with its light crisp skin filled to bursting with finely minced pork and crunchy water chestnuts. The shrimp toast, crisply golden outside, is rich with shrimp, tender and moist within. An unusual feature on the dinner menu is the elegant and complicated Peking duck—which usually requires 24 hours advance notice—but here offered on the regular menu. For the steak lover there's New York steak Chinese style: marinated in a barbecue-type sauce, then sauteed with fresh snow peas, mushrooms, and water chestnuts. Lobster chicken is steeped with spices and herbs and coated with water chestnuts puree; it becomes a spicy contrast to the mild, sweet white lobster meat and crisp vegetables. Spicy crispy whole fish is a painting come to life—a whole fish crispy and golden, dotted with green peppers, black mushrooms, and water chestnuts crowned with a tomatoey hot sauce.

Saturday or Sunday brunch offers some of the best Eastern *dim sum.* There's a mind-boggling forty-four dishes to choose from: crisp turnip crepes, soups, cold appetizers, and gourmet specials. The aromatic spices lend a fragrant scent to the dishes. End the meal flawlessly with the "steamed eight precious layer cakes," this potpourri of fruits and nuts steamed till the fruit is plump and delicate is not overly sweet.

1120 20th Street NW (Between M and L Streets)
Washington, D.C., 20036
(202) 223-5160

- *Szechuan and Hunan Cuisine*
- *Moderate*
- *Open Monday through Friday for lunch; 7 days for dinner; Saturday and Sunday brunch*
- *Accepts reservations for parties of four or more. AE, MC, VISA only*
- *Private party facilities for groups up to 50*

The 37th Street Hideaway

For two decades, the Hideaway has been wooing lovers of both romance and food with its unique surroundings, attentive management and good cuisine at reasonable prices. It is located in an elegant townhouse that is both off the frenetic restaurant circuit, yet close to all that matters in midtown—shopping, theater and the Garden.

The restaurant occupies a fine, old townhouse, once the residence of actor John Drew, one of a long line of famous thespians that reigned on stages in New York and around the world decades before the Civil War and continuing in an unbroken chain to the early days of the present century. Drew's townhouse reflects the genteel refinements of an earlier day, combined with solid craftsmanship no longer to be seen, unless you can chance a visit here. The original rooms and architectural appointments remain intact. The walls are panelled mahogany, an impossible luxury today. A huge marble fireplace stands working today as it has for a century and solid mahogany corinthian columns extend from mantel to ceiling.

To the romance of history is added the romance of dance music, a fixture here for as long as the place has been open, soft lighting and candlelight reflecting from the mirrored wall.

The cuisine is Italian-Continental, with many native favorites offered, especially seafood. Good, substantial cooking with a la carte or price fixed dinners at more than reasonable prices. Chef's specialties are an ethereal shrimp scampi, sea food marichiare, veal chop peperoni, medallion of beef marsala and shrimps and scallops fra diavolo. Which is not at all to discount a very full menu of grilled beef, lamb, chicken, pasta, seafood, and accompaniments.

---

32 West 37 Street
New York, N.Y., 10018
(212) 947-8940

- *Italian/Continental Cuisine*
- *Moderately priced*
- *Open Monday through Friday for lunch; Monday through Sunday for dinner; Closed Sunday*
- *There is also a featured $18.50 prix-fixe dinner*
- *Private party facilities for between 20 and 60 persons*

The Three Bears Restaurant

Over two centuries ago travellers going between New York City and Boston would stop at a tavern in Westport, Connecticut for rest and food. That tavern was called The Three Bears Tavern—so named, they say, because the Italian architect that designed the original building had fallen in love with the story of Goldilocks when he first learned English—and portions of that very first building are still in use today. After Prohibition, with "Tavern" having the wrong connotations, the name was changed to The Three Bears Restaurant.

The present owner, Stephen C. Vazzano, bought the restaurant in 1965 and in 1967 he enlarged it to its present commodious state. (The three dining rooms seat a total of 225 people.) He also brought in his museum-quality collection of glassware, which is on view in the lobby. It's a stunning array of etched, cut, and hand-blown works of glass, and it's worth looking at carefully.

The Three Bears Restaurant has a large, distinctly American menu for both lunch and dinner. The lunch list encompasses snacks, sandwiches, and large complete meals; there are soups, salads, beef Stroganoff, deep fried shrimp, broiled filet mignon or New York steak, chicken and tuna salad, and much more.

The appetizers at dinner also cover a wide range of tastes, ranging from tomato juice to *escargot champignons,* which is a dish of large, plump snails in firm, tasty mushroom caps in a garlic sauce. Or there's fried mozzarella, mozzarella dipped in a parmesan cheese/egg batter and breaded and fried. The cheese comes out crisp on the outside and runny on the inside, and it's delicious. There's also chicken liver *pate,* clams (on the half shell or casino), soups, and an excellent salad. And don't pass up the delicious garlic bread.

The list of entrees is no less extensive. You can have broiled chicken, duckling, lamb chops, filet or New York steak, prime rib, or pork chops. If fish is what you're after choose from baked crab, broiled rainbow trout or filet of sole, fried bay scallops or fantail shrimp, and rainbow trout or filet of sole *almondine.* They also serve an expertly cooked calf's liver with bacon, veal *marsala,* and veal *francais.*

The look of The Three Bears Restaurant will add to the enjoyment of your meal. It's an elegant, rustic appearance and feeling, with huge, hand-hewn beams all around and a glossy wide wood-paneled floor beneath you. Many authentic antiques enliven the dining rooms, and genuine Tiffany chandeliers give off a pleasing light.

333 Wilton Rd. (Rte 33)
Westport, Conn., 06880
(203) 227-7219

- *American Cuisine*
- *Priced moderate*
- *Open Tuesday through Sunday for lunch and dinner; Closed Monday*
- *Reservations and all major credit cards accepted*
- *Private party facilities for between 8 and 110 persons*

Tino's

Tino's is the headquarters for classic Italian cooking and a thoroughly professional attitude that extends from the kitchen to the cleanup crew.

But the heart and soul of the matter rests in the presence and recherche of dapper owner Tino Scarpa, who is all concentration, informed and ubiquitous in his control of things.

Most meals are prepared with classic simplicity that brings out the best of first-quality foods. But there is also respect paid to specialized gustatory creations, some of which are unique to Tino's. These include a pureed broccoli over linguine invention, a Parisian rendition of soft shell crabs, *osso buco*—veal shank with cheese-treated rice elevated by exotic spices— *misto di pesce allo scoglio* heavy with assorted seafood, and a fragrant boneless breast of chicken that comes gently simmered in *bechamel* sauce and wine.

There are other main courses that have reached the level of obsessions with some diners here. The chicken *alla Tino Scarpa* teams boneless cuts of chicken, mushrooms and artichokes in a wine sauce, the broiled flounder comes moist and pearly, stuffed with shrimps and crabmeat; and *mignonette peperonata* is a tender filet mignon with peppers brushed with a spiced tomato sauce.

There are remarkable vegetable side dishes here, too, that change with the season—as they should. And the dessert menu holds classic splendors such as homemade cheesecake, rum cake, cappuccino chocolate *mousse* and *zabaglione*.

Let us not leave Tino's without a salute to its marvelous provincial surroundings—with hanging potted plants on aged brick walls warmed through sun-drenched skylights.

---

235 East 58 Street
New York, N.Y., 10022
(212) 751-0311

- *Italian Cuisine*
- *Priced expensive*
- *Open Monday through Friday for lunch;*
  7 days for dinner
- *Reservations advised. Accepts all major credit cards*
- *Private room for between 12 and 30 people*
- *Jackets suggested*

Tio Pepe

To get to Spain from New York City you have to cross the Atlantic, and to get to Mexico from New York you have to cross almost a dozen states. But to get the food of Spain and the food of Mexico you don't even have to leave town, and you don't even need to change restaurants (if you're in the right one). While not too many restaurants in New York serve either Mexican or Spanish food, Tio Pepe serves both.

Though Mexico was once a colony of Spain and much of Mexican cuisine does have its roots in the cuisine of Spain, the cooking of the two countries is nonetheless separate and distinct. Tio Pepe's examples of both types of cooking will let you compare the similarities and differences yourself.

Depending on where you sit, the restaurant will have a different type of look and feel. There's a

glass-enclosed section that borders the sidewalk; here you can gaze out at the street and watch the world go by. An inside dining room has a tile floor and rustic feel, with the stucco walls being decorated by pleasant green flocking. And eating in the back dining room, with its dozens of hanging plants, is almost like eating in a garden.

Tio Pepe offers several classic Spanish dishes. There are three different kinds of *paella,* for example *(paella Valenciana, paella Valenciana* with lobster, and *paella Marinera con Langosta).* There's also a delicious *Mariscada* in green sauce, which is a nicely presented seafood stew consisting of shrimp, clams, mussles, and lobster. The *chorizo* (Spanish sausage) appetizer is chunks of the sausage crisply fried and served in a beautiful copper casserole.

Tio Pepe offers other types of Spanish food as well. There's gazpacho, of course, as well as the classic *arroz con pollo* (chicken and rice). There's also a broiled sirloin steak, and veal with onion and peppers or in a mushroom and wine sauce, as well as several seafood offerings.

The Mexican dishes at Tio Pepe cover the range of everything you'd expect. There are *tacos, enchiladas, tamales, tostadas, rellenos,* and *burritos,* and they're all prepared excellently. For appetizers Tio Pepe offers, among others, *nachos* and *guacamole.*

The desserts include *flan al caramelo* (carmel custard), *natilla espanola* (cream custard), and cheese cake.

And to top things off, along with their reasonable prices Tio Pepe has nightly entertainment.

---

168 West Fourth Street
New York, N.Y., 10014
(212) 242-9338

- *Spanish and Mexican Cuisine*
- *Priced inexpensive to moderate*
- *Open seven days for lunch and dinner; Sunday brunch*
- *Private party facilities for between 10 and 75 persons*
- *Entertainment nightly*

Tony's

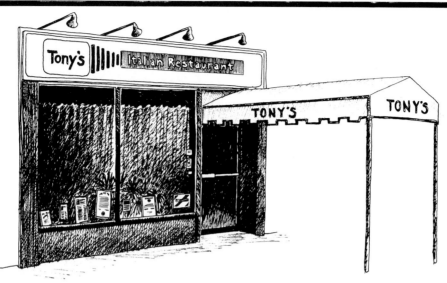

What do you do when you want a good meal but you don't want to cook—but you also don't want to go out to a fancy restaurant and pay fancy restaurant prices just to get something good to eat? You go to Tony's.

From the outside, surrounded by stores on a crowded street, Tony's doesn't look such a much. But inside you'll find a cozy dining room, tastefully appointed with well-lit paintings, mirrors, and pressed cork walls. Owner Frank Lumaj is also the host, and it's clear he wants you to dine pleasantly and comfortably.

The food at Tony's is Northern Italian, and the menu offers all the most popular Italian specialties. Among the appetizers, for example, is what Frank calls *scampi alla Tony*. The dish consists of large shrimp nicely broiled and topped with a delicately seasoned tomato sauce. Or there's the calamari salad, with tender pieces of squid bathed in a tangy, garlicky vinaigrette dressing. Or you can opt for the classics: prosciutto and sweet melon or mussels *marinara*..

An Italian menu wouldn't be complete without offering *minestrone* or *tortellini in brodo,* and both of these soups are savory at Tony's. Tony's even branches out to serve French onion soup. Not exactly Italian, but the full, rich flavor will have you unworried.

If you want a pasta course, you'll find one you'll like—the list reads like a classic Italian cookbook: *Fettucini Alfredo* (fettucini in a parmesan and romano, cream, and butter sauce), *tortellini alla panna* (a cream sauce), *spaghetti alla carbonara, spaghetti bolognese, lasagna, cannelloni, ravioli,* baked *ziti,* and *gnocchi.* All the pasta is fresh daily and prepared knowledgeably; these are some fine examples of Italian cookery.

The entrees cover the gamut of Northern Italian and Neopolitan dishes from broiled veal chops to lobster tail *fra diavola.* A specialty is the striped bass *livornese,* which is fresh striped bass served with a sauce of capers, onions, sliced peppers, garlic, and olives in white wine. The veal *sorrentino* is also commendable, being slices of veal topped with prosciutto, eggplant, cheese, and light brown sauce. There's also an excellent veal *piccata,* with garlic in the lemon and butter sauce, and several other veal offerings. Chicken gets treated right at Tony's, too—it's served *parmigiana, cacciatore, bolognese,* and *francese.*

Or be a little more adventurous and try the frog legs *provencale.* But whatever you try, you won't be disappointed. Tony's serves good food in a comfortable setting at reasonable prices—*va bene!*

33-12 Ditmars Boulevard
Astoria, Queens, N.Y., 11105
(212) 278-1505

- *Northern Italian Cuisine*
- *Priced moderately*
- *Open Tuesday through Friday for lunch; Tuesday through Sunday for dinner; Closed Monday*
- *AE, MC, VISA accepted*
- *A small place—make reservations*

Trudie Ball's Empress

Washington politics may change every four years, but the Empress Restaurant—established 16 years at the same location, is a back-bone of the community, moderately priced, well appointed, and organized, with nicely presented, tasty old style Szechuan/Mandarin cuisine.

Out of the ordinary dishes like tiger lobster, beggar-style chicken and braised shark's fin, must be ordered in advance, but the house special of Peking duck, which Empress Restaurant popularized in Washington, is a regular on the menu. There's the choice of three sauces to glaze the moist fresh fish filet, mushroom sauce, scallion and wine sauce, or hot spicy ginger sauce that heightens the sweet light flavor of the fish. Some fiery dishes to savor are sliced beef with orange flavor, tenderly scented with garlic and ginger, fresh lobster Szechuan with hot sauce, Hunan-style lamb, whole fish with hot bean sauce, duck meat with hot pepper, and shrimp with hot garlic sauce. Excellent and authentic with these dishes is *Hakutsura* sake, or *Shaoshing* rice wine. Also featured are cocktails, white and red wines, and champagne.

For the vegetable lover, there's the bright fresh crunch of Chinese vegetables in Buddist delight, the garlicky hot Szechuan eggplant, or the interesting taste of fresh watercress saute. The traditional hot and sour soup is hearty and thick with vegetables, and the noodles are made fresh on the premises.

Corporations, politicians, international businesses, and family celebrations are all accommodated in the third floor banquet room that seats 150. The main kitchen is located on the second level, which is popular with Chinese clientele. The first floor is an attractive formal, square dining room with soft cream colored walls, offsetting large glassed Chinese paintings, colorful carved Chinese patterned ceiling, and crisp white table linens covered with a sparkle of glass and highlighted with fresh carnations.

There's a full house at lunch, but you can always enjoy a leisurely dinner.

1018 Vermont Avenue NW
Washington, D.C., 20005
(202) 737-2324

- *Chinese Cuisine (Mandarin/Szechuan)*
- *Priced moderately*
- *Open seven days for lunch and dinner*
- *Accepts reservations and all major credit cards*
  There's also an Empress in Philadelphia, P.A. See
  page 129

Trudie Ball's Empress

Mandarin/Szechuan banquets of up to 25 people each are a definite plus at Trudie Ball's Empress, an offshoot of the Empress in Washington, D.C. (see page 128). The all-encompassing menu varies from light fare to sophisticated entrees. showing the chef's influence with spices and herbs.

Established four years ago, an attractive contemporary polished wooden bar greets you as you enter, with huge iron baker's rack cleverly used for bottles and glistening glassware.

Walk gracefully through the moongate into a spacious earthtone dining room. Tan, brown, mustard colored booths and banquettes line the walls, highlighted by some interesting examples of Chinese art. Wall-to-Wall carpet muffles the sounds of conversation and movement of the blond wood chairs round the tables, dressed in white starched cloths and a clear glass overlay. Ceiling fans moving lazily and soft recessed lighting complete the picture.

A couple of appetizers to tempt your tastebuds are the six meat pastries which, made to order, take 20 to 30 minutes. Pastry is carefully wrapped round a dense, herbed, smooth textured meat filling offered with chopped scallions and a tasty sauce. Fried shrimp balls are golden, crunchy, but burstingly moist inside with the taste of the sea, and there are also several tempting appetizers that are made to share amongst 2 to 6 people. Shredded pork and preserved vegetable soup has the richness of stew, while sliced chicken mushroom soup with sizzling rice is a contrast in textures.

Perfumed with tingling spices and brown sauce, Szechuan string beans mixed with minced pork and scallions are crisply irresistible. Chinese mushrooms, slivers of bamboo shoots and *al dente* snow peas each make a colorful counterpoint to a meal.

A spicy new entree, phoenix and dragon delight, marries lobster and chicken in a unique blending of flavors, while Peking style shrimp with snow peas has an elegant, mild pink sauce covering plump, delicate shrimp and bright-green crisp snow peas. The hot-sauced lamb and marinated beef were vibrant with flavor and forktender.

The choice of dessert can be as simple as *lichee,* fruit platter, ice cream or as rich as eight fruits rice pudding. Chinese candied bananas, or sweet rice cake.

1711 Walnut Street
Philadelphia, Pa., 19103
(215) 665-0390

- *Chinese Cuisine (Mandarin/Szechuan)*
- *Priced moderate to expensive*
- *Open seven nights, six days; Closed for luncheon Sunday*
- *Accepts reservations and all major credit cards*
- *Private party facilities for up to 28 people*

Tucano at Club A

Within the Brazilian wonderland of oversize glass lighting fixtures shaped like apples, bananas, oranges, and pineapples, mirrored smoked glass ceilings, velvet banquettes, a curved back wall conveying a jungle, and the barbaric splendor or contemporary Brazilian paintings found at Tucano (adjoining the exclusive private Club A), you can order anything from classic French dishes to elements of stylized *nouvelle cuisine.*

You can count on fresh ingredients at Tucano, so you would do especially well to order *terrine* and *mousse* dishes, *pates* and seafoods. Some of the outstanding appetizers range from simple, lightly smoked, rosy salmon, to a jeweled mold of vegetables and veal in aspic, to a still life of salmon *mousse* with pistachio nuts imparting a subtle flavor, garnished with mayonnaise and tomato carved in the form of a flower. Two pleasantly new and different salads are crisp greens mixed lightly with tender, warm boneless bits of frogs' legs, and raw mushrooms tossed with julienne slices of *foie gras* and slim *haricot verts.* Soups such as rich lobster bisque, tangy cream of sorrel and lettuce or smooth cream of mussel, makes that choice difficult. An attractively presented entree is *tresse de sole freres Troisgros,* in which red, ripe tomatoes are diced and sauteed in cream, then covered with fresh, firm, strips of Dover sole interwoven amongst rosy pink (tomato) and green (spinach) broad noodles. Other specialties that satisfy are fresh duck with elegant raspberry sauce and tender medallions of veal in a morelle-and-champagne sauce. The kitchen, under the watchful eyes of chef Gerard

Reuther, is also adept at embellishing cuts of beef, veal, duck, and seafood, with flavorful sauces and the fresh vegetables that change with the seasons.

Desserts are extravagantly varied and one of the best is the *tulip de sorbets,* a deep tulip-shaped butter cookie, filled with scoops of fresh fruit sherbet and slices of ripe fruit; coffee is served piping hot. The wine list is an impressive display, though very expensive.

Tucano is the result of the joint efforts and talents of nightclub owner Ricardo Amaral and restaurateur Jean-Claude Pujol. In Club A, Amaral and Pujol provide a private room featuring cocktails, wines and dancing, and directly adjacent to the Club is the Bar Des Theatres, a small bistro that offers food and conversation for a less formal evening and affords dancers a place to step aside for a late night bite.

Tucano serves prix-fixe luncheons for $19.50 and dinners for $34.75.

333 East 60 Street
New York, N.Y., 10022
(212) 308-2333

- *French Cuisine*
- *Priced expensive*
- *Open Monday through Friday for lunch; Monday through Saturday for dinner; Closed Sunday*
- *Accepts all major credit cards and reservations strongly recommended*
- *Private party facilities for between 20 and 40 people*

"21"

For more than a half century, the rich, famous and important have entered the narrow foyer of the world-famous "21" Club to be catered to, watched and served at their highly visible tables.

Yes, the stories are true that "21" was a speakeasy during the dull dry days of the thirties, but even then it had class. New York had voted not to legally enforce the Volstead act, and a handful of federal agents were left to clean up the 32,000 "speaks" in town. In January of 1930, Jack and Charlie's "21" Club opened on a block of well-known speaks, and from the first it was a hit among the elite of business, society, and politics. This insured its invulnerability from fed probing (aside from one small raid), and set it on its booming business and destiny as feeding trough for the beautiful people.

"21" is a place to be seen. Sure, the food's good, and more than expensive enough. It is known for its game, the steaks are fine and the drinks faultless.

But it is the daily floor show that people watch while gladly paying 13 bucks for a burger. This is where Gerald Ford and Richard Nixon push their forks, where Sinatra and Nelson Doubleday sup, where the ghosts of Bogie and Flynn and Steinbeck and Benchley hover and lend their names to various tables. Fame does have its rewards.

---

21 West 52 Street
New York, N.Y., 10019
(212) 582-7200

- *American/Continental Cuisine*
- *Priced expensive*
- *Open 6 days for lunch and dinner; Closed Sunday (Closed weekends during June, July, and August)*
- *Reservations mandatory. All major credit cards accepted*
- *Private party facilities for between 20 and 120 persons*

Union Oyster House

You can't argue with the success of a restaurant in continuous service for over 150 years. The Union Oyster House, Boston's oldest restaurant, had Daniel Webster as a favored client—downing freshly shucked oysters, six plates at a time.

Although time has stood still (the stalls and oyster bar are original and in their original positions, the hand hewn beams, wide woodplank flooring, and walls are original, too) there's now air conditioning, newer wooden booths and tables topped with fresh flowers and bowls of oysterettes, bentwood chairs and new lantern lighting. The casual atmosphere is family-oriented, and very friendly with lots of steady clientele and a hefty tourist trade. The second and third floors are used mainly for dining, while the top level has a long polished bar with a salad bar adjunct. Through the windows downstairs you can look out on Boston from the oyster bar where Daniel Webster sat.

A distinctively unusual appetizer which appeals to the eye as well as the palate is the Union Oyster House sampler for two, featuring their special Union oysters, baked stuffed cherrystones, clams casino, oysters Rockefeller, and shrimp scampi, all on a bed

of rice pilaf studded with peas, mushrooms, and red peppers. The Union Oyster House is a treasure house of most any type of mouth-watering seafood—caught fresh practically at the door. The fish is moist and laced with just the right amount of seasoning and herbs. The fish chowder is a wonderfully creamy soup loaded with fish and chunks of potatoes. The clam chowder is filled with clams and comes with excellent homebaked corn bread for sopping up every last drop of soup. There's also chunky pink lobster stew, a tasty oyster stew, or cherrystone stew to choose from.

Lobsters are the centerpiece at the best dinners here and they come broiled, baked, stuffed, or as Lazy Man's Lobster—sauteed meaty chunks seasoned with sherry, lightly sprinkled with buttered bread crumbs, and served *en casserole*. Lobster Thermidor is also worth a look-see—the meat of the lobster is combined with fresh mushrooms, crisp green peppers, and red pimento, blended in a rich sherry and wine sauce, glazed with parmesan cheese, and baked in its own shell. It's a masterful creation. Lobster Newburg is served with rice pilaf, and a lucious seafood platter (no lobster in that one) is large enough for a trencherman and chock-full of pearly scallops, breaded shrimp, flaky fish filet, oysters, and crab legs, and served with a delicate seafood sauce that doesn't mask the flavor of the fish.

If you prefer red meat, there is broiled filet mignon or New York strip sirloin *bernaise,* pork chops with applesauce, spring lamb chops with mint jelly, or braised sirloin tips with mushrooms.

Desserts are made on the premises and include a rich Grasshopper pie laced with mint, fresh whipped cream, and a layer of chocolate cake. The mocha almond layer cake teases the tastebuds with its subtle flavor and moistness, but the baker suggests apple pandowdy, flavorful and thick with apples. Dessert wines, cordials, and liquers bring a happy conclusion to a robust meal.

41 Union Street
Boston, Mass., 02109
(617) 227-2750

- *American Cuisine*
- *Priced moderately*
- *Open 7 days for lunch and dinner*
- *Reservations and all major credit cards accepted*

Vienna '79

Vienna '79 is one of those rare restaurants where dinner is often a faultless experience. The service is friendly yet completely professional and the restaurant possesses an understated elegance—polished, snug, and sophisticated. Pale gray brick walls are lined with tasteful original oils that contrast favorably with darker gray furnishings; track lighting throws a soft glow over well-spaced tables dressed in crisp white linen and set with fresh roses and flickering candles; and the cuisine is exquisite.

Co-owner Peter Grunauer and his partners Karl Zartler and Wolf Kraine have worked with chef Thomas Frelich to create a unique type of cooking— one that can best be described as *nouvelle* Viennese. Viennese cuisine is generally considered anything but *nouvelle,* and it is a testimony to the chef's and partners' skill and dedication that they could fashion a marriage of the light, delicate *nouvelle* techniques and philosophies with the traditional, often hearty fare that is Viennese food.

But marry them they have, and the result is a cuisine that has a wide scope of tantalizing tastes and dishes—ranging from conventional *wiener schnitzel* that's golden and completely greaseless and *wiener backhuhn* (a grease-free flattened, boneless breast that elevates fried chicken to a new height) to the creative *tournedos* of beef with a gooseliver and truffle sauce.

The imagination and skill of the restaurant can be seen in any of the excellent salads, among them a marvelous combination of marinated beef, sliced green pepper, and onion slivers. There's also an equally succulent shrimp salad—a mix of jumbo shrimp marinated in oil and vinegar, egg, tomato, white asparagus tips, and radish slices.

Other appetizers include a kaiser roll filled with a snail, garlic, shallots, and parsley combination that's laced with cream, and freshly house-made head cheese garnished with chopped onions and a tasty vinaigrette.

Vienna '79 serves more than a dozen entrees, and it's hard to go wrong. The veal goulash is spiced with pepper and paprika and accompanied by tiny curlycue dumplings to absorb the gravy. The boiled beef comes with a chive and apple-horseradish sauce. The lamb chops, after marinating in olive oil spiced with oregano and caraway, get lightly sauteed.

Whatever you do, save room for a lavish climax. The illustrious *salzburger nockerl* is made of little souffles floating in *creme Anglaise. Palatschinken* consists of crepes stuffed with a chestnut puree and covered with a kirsch-flavored bittersweet chocolate sauce and whipped cream. And of course there are several other truly remarkable desserts.

320 East 79 Street
New York, N.Y., 10021
(212) 734-4700

- *Nouvelle Viennese Cuisine*
- *Priced expensive*
- *Open 7 days for dinner only*
- *Reservations required; All major credit cards accepted*

Villa Francesca

The old world atmosphere, the singing waiters, the steady family clientele, and the pleasant greeting you get as you enter Francesca's with its warm brick walls, embossed metal ceilings, softly glowing hanging globes, bentwood chairs, and sparkling crystal, combine to make you feel comfortably at home.

As you walk in, the satiny old wooden bar to your left sparkles with glassware and an extensive assortment of wines, beers, and liqueurs. An old wooden ice box stands near the bar as a conversation piece and storage cabinet. In the center of the room, looking like a still life painting full of colors and textures, is the dessert table, its contents all made fresh on the premises.

Italian flags hang over the bar, and fresh garlic and hot peppers hang in the brick archways along with wall sconces and oil paintings. Downstairs the Catacomb Room with potted plants, wine casks on the wall, and beamed ceiling has a more cozy and intimate atmosphere.

A gusty appetizer is *mozzarella carozza,* made with rich spicy red *marinara* sauce; it is delicately laced with a white wine and lemon sauce and finished with anchovy butter. For a stick-to-the-ribs soup try the *pasta fagioli,* a flavorful broth filled with beans and pasta. The vegetable dishes of either broccoli or mushroom saute are done in a spicy bouquet of garlic, oil, and parsley; they perfume the palate.

Some pasta dishes of considerable merit in taste and presentation are *spaghetti a la carrettiere* and *spaghetti a la disperato*—these are taste tempting treats.

There are at least 28 entrees of veal, chicken, or seafood to choose from and the chef's talent is clearly evident in the special touches added. Some of the beautifully prepared veal courses are a sparkling intermingling of tastes. *Veal scallopini marsala* is subtle and delicate; eggplant *parmagiana* is deeply satisfying, shrimp *cacciatore* is brightly flavorful, and the full boneless breast of chicken *pescatore,* is stuffed with shrimp seasoned with bread crumbs and mozzarella cheese.

For a dessert experience order the *cannoli.* The waitress will bring the crisp fresh shell to your table and fill it with fresh cream from a pastry bag. The taste is exquisite and you can enjoy it or cheesecake *a la patcharin* or old fashioned shortcake with fresh berries and whipped cream with espresso, capuccino, mocha, tea or Italian soda.

150 Richmond Street
Boston, Mass., 02109
(617) 367-2948

- *Italian Cuisine*
- *Priced moderate*
- *Open 7 days for dinner only*
- *Reservations and AE, DC, CB accepted*

Villa Maria

No one would ever believe that this humble-appearing pizza and take-out place houses some rather remarkable Italian preparations at prices from another (and long past) era. It nevertheless does just that.

Unassuming as the decor is—it is a family place after all—owner Luigi Di Nucci and his wife Nancy have put before us an elaborate menu with choice enough to impress a connoisseur. Think of it—spaghetti with a choice of ten sauces, more than a dozen macaroni specialties, pizza, heros, fifteen veal dishes, steaks, sausages, chicken and seafood from lobster to calamari. And the pricing will leave you wondering what they know that other restaurateurs don't.

Just as a pointer, Luigi's specialties are the veal *sorrentino,* sea food *marinara* and linguine with shrimp sauce. There is a very well stocked bar, and wines are available.

746 North Broadway
Massapequa, L.I., N.Y., 11758
(516) 798-9035

- *Italian Cuisine*
- *Priced inexpensive to moderate*
- *Open Tuesday through Friday for lunch;*
  7 nights for dinner
- *Accepts reservations and all major credit cards*

Villa Mosconi

Villa Mosconi is the kind of restaurant you go to for consistently good, authentic Italian fare served in a comfortable and orderly atmosphere. The kind of place that offers no unpleasant surprises, no nerve-wracking service problems, no off dishes you try to avoid. In short, it is what you dine out for.

The restaurant is family-run and headed up by Mr. Mosconi, originally from Bologna, Italy. He handles the kitchen with an authoritative but benign hand, is serious about his cooking, and very careful about his culinary standards. This should be a requisite for all eating establishments. It is a personal involvement that one has in one's own home, and it is this home-like attention to detail that makes Villa Mosconi a place with an exceedingly high rate of regulars.

The large old-fashioned menu puts an emphasis on *farinacei,* made here daily by a particularly talented pasta chef (also from Bologna), with lots of cooked-to-order macaroni and spaghetti dishes to state its case.

A leading pasta item, *tortellini,* is a delicious, creative dish that any of the city's more affluent Italian places might gladly serve. In it you'll find five different cheeses harmoniously-blended, spiced with nutmeg, and elegantly wrapped in handrolled pasta shells. Another specialty, *paglia e fieno,* is slightly more austere, but pleasing nonetheless: simply green and white noodles commingled with fresh peas and diced onions in a fresh cream and butter sauce.

Another Mosconi triumph is the *costoletta alla Milanese,* a flattened piece of veal with the bone-in, lightly breaded, and served succulent yet greaseless. The veal kidney prepared with wine and mushrooms is another superior presentation you won't find in many other places around town. Mr. Mosconi has a deft hand with vegetables and salads as well. He does a sauteed zucchini that is pronouncedly garlicky yet also buttery, and there's a certain refinement about the cool fresh arugula salad.

In sum, Villa Mosconi is one of those neighborhood restaurants whose well-run, graceful, and competent management has made it a favorite far beyond its precincts.

69 MacDougal Street
New York, N.Y., 10012
(212) 673-0390

- *Italian Cuisine*
- *Priced moderately*
- *Open 6 days for lunch and dinner; Closed Sunday*
- *Reservations suggested; all major credit cards accepted*

Washington Street Cafe

New York is a city of constantly changing neighborhoods, and one of the new chic, still-emerging neighborhoods is Tribeca. (No romantically named part of town here: "Tribeca" means TRIangle BElow CAnal Street; the area is Manhattan's south-western tip and used to be mainly industrial.) Restaurants are still in the process of blooming in Tribeca, and one of the more recent, more creditable sprouts is the Washington Street Cafe.

As befits a district consisting primarily of lofts and inhabited (theoretically) chiefly by artists, the dress of the patrons and the atmosphere of the restaurant are at once casual and hip. It has a small outdoor dining area that's dominated by a long mahogany bench, chairs, and matching tables. More mahogany awaits you inside in the form of a tremendous custom-made bar, which holds the forty or more wines this restaurant and wine bar serves—plus one of New York's first Cruvinet Wine Machines. This machine allows wines to be kept under ideal conditions by regulating temperatures for both red and white wines. In the dining room proper peach-buff painted brick walls sport photography exhibitions by noted artists—and these photos are for sale—which are nicely lit by excellent track lighting. Ceiling fans and abundant exotic flower arrangements further enliven this handsome restaurant.

The menu isn't large, but it is varied, covering a wide range of food and offering some unique dishes. There's a spicy, ice-cold gazpacho—which can be ordered laced with a shot of similarly ice-cold Stolichnaya vodka. Or try the green fettucine, cooked *al dente,* sprinkled with pieces of prosciutto and covered with melted roquefort cheese and a luscious cream sauce. Or maybe you'd prefer the seafood salad, a gentle combination of shrimps, scallops, squid, and hearts of palm—or the spicy sausage selection with choice of mustards.

The more standard, but no less palatable fare includes a salad of smoked mozzarella, tomatoes, and dried tomatoes—or a rich, fluffy quiche.

Among the entrees are the cheese and vegetable *lasagne*—which comes in a thick tomato sauce—a poached salmon filet, a sauteed filet of sole that's served with mixed vegetables and cut potatoes in their jackets, and a buoyant shrimp and scallop curry with spinach and sweet peppers. The filet mignon is tender and juicy and accompanied by a savorous *bernaise* sauce; the veal *marsala* is equally good.

The dessert list includes an apple pie in a thin crust, key lime pie, or—a chocolate lovers delight—a double *mousse* cake made of white and dark chocolate dotted with pistachios. And should you want a dessert wine to go with your cake, the knowledgeable staff will gladly help you pick one out.

422 Washington Street
New York, N.Y., 10013
(212) 925-5119

- *American/Continental Cuisine (for lack of a more precise term)*
- *Priced moderately*
- *Open Tuesday through Saturday for dinner only; Closed Sunday and Monday*
- *Reservations necessary; All major credit cards accepted*

Water Front Crab House

For some reason, the best of the seafood houses are those that retain the salty, gutsy tang of the ocean air in their decor and ambience. Maybe it has to do with a feeling for the ocean's products, a respect for it that shows through in the preparation.

Anthony Mazzarella is a seafood restaurant owner who knows his seafood and knows his business. So much so that he has been able to open three robust establishments and make successes of each. There is one located in Sag Harbor, Long Island, one in Manhattan, and there remains the flagship, the Water Front Crab House in Long Island City, Queens. This is a zesty, crowded, sprawling place that exudes good nature and good food, plain and simple. Tony has kept his original place in the tradition of the old fish houses—rustic walls of brick and stucco are framed in seasoned wood and hung with sea nets, fish, wine barrels, and even a full-sized row boat suspended from the ceiling.

Needless to say, the fish is fresh—except for the necessity of shipping frozen stone crabs and lobster tails (two-pounders that remain juicy and flavor-packed from start to finish). The secret—a dab of butter and judicious broiling. Period.

There are other simple pleasures, broiled filet of sole and jumbo shrimp, but that is to overlook some of the most tempting creations of brook and ocean. Water Front serves up hot seafood *antipasto*—a large platter of shrimps stuffed with crabmeat, fried fish filets, stuffed clams, calamari, and fried zucchini, all covered with a light, flavorsome *marinara* sauce.

You must also try the *bouillabaisse,* uniquely prepared with whole steamed lobster, clams, shrimp, crabs, and mussels on a bed of linguine prepared *al dente* and topped with pungent *marinara* sauce. By the way, there is a savory selection of pasta centered around linguine with crab, clam, and shrimp sauces.

A visit to the Water Front is to get close to the sea, and close to its culinary heritage. An offshoot on a somewhat smaller scale called Water Front Crab House Too is located in Manhattan at 325 Bowery. It's basically the same as the original. Call (212) 254-0050 for reservations there.

Waterfront Crab House
2-03 Borden Avenue
Long Island City, Queens, N.Y., 11130
(212) 729-4862

- *Seafood Cuisine*
- *Priced moderate*
- *Open 7 days for lunch and dinner, but no lunch on Monday*

Waterfront Crab House Too
325 Bowery
New York, N.Y., 10003
(212) 254-0050

- *Seafood Cuisine*
- *Priced moderate*
- *Open 7 days for lunch and dinner*

Wee Tappee Inn

This small, landmark house sets the scene for French-Italian cooking. Proprietor Peter Casuscelli has found the right combination of location, design, and menu to afford the visitor a relaxed, congenial evening of satisfying dining. Copper utensils hang on barnwood walls, long, graceful candles rest in glass holders, flowers appear everywhere, and a rustic fireplace exudes warmth.

There is a fine menu, with some especially impressive choices. Appetizers may include *crevettes* cocktail, *avocado Felicia,* mussels in wine sauce or possibly *clams St. Tropez,* among others. Entrees are varied—from house specialties like veal chop Florentine, a huge 3½-pound lobster for two, duckling with fresh raspberry and orange sauce, to the simple and rich *fettucine Alfredo,* or beef brochette in its unadorned elegance.

Desserts are an end in themselves—with the *cerises jubilees,* bananas *flambee* with ice cream, apple crepe *Francaise* and *dolci al caretto* heading the list.

---

1 Intervale Avenue
Roslyn Estates, L.I., N.Y., 11576
(516) MA1-9600/2200

- *Northern Italian/French Cuisine*
- *Priced moderately*
- *Open Monday through Friday for lunch; Monday through Saturday for dinner. Closed Sundays except for private parties*
- *Accepts reservations and all major credit cards*

Windows on the World

Windows is really three restaurants and two bars that, with the private Hudson River Suites and Ballroom, take up the two floors of the second tallest building in the world. The main dining room, called simply The Restaurant, flows across the north and east sides of the 107th floor. The scale is dramatic, yet the feeling remains intimate because The Restaurant is built on several terraces. This also means that every table has a clear view of the city's skyline—and of 50 miles beyond.

The cuisine is International in scope, but American in flavor. Specialties include rack of young lamb James Beard; rainbow trout stuffed and baked in phyllo; and fricassee of lobster and sweetbreads.

Centering The Restaurant is the Grand Buffet Table where pastries are arrayed on its brass expanse at dinner, and where a buffet is set out for Saturday lunch and all day Sunday.

The Hor's d'Oeuvrerie, which embraces the City Lights Bar, is a multi-function area with the great appeal of needing no reservations. Daily, there are myriad small delicacies prepared by International chefs in native dress. In the afternoon, a traditional tea with sandwiches and pastries is offered. Music begins in later afternoon and continues to the wee hours. A Sunday brunch is served with dishes representative of the world's cuisines.

The Cellar in the Sky is a small, romantic dining room within the larger restaurant. It is the working wine cellar for the entire complex, the bottles serving as a spectacular setting for dining, both to look at and to drink. The single, seven-course menu is designed around wines and is limited to 35 diners each night. A classical guitarist plays throughout the night. The feeling is one of an intimate house party in a vineyard cave, enclosed by thousands of colorful bottles of wine and lit by dappled lights that reflect the wines' colors onto the marble floor.

107th Floor
World Trade Center
New York, N.Y., 10048
(212) 938-1111

- *International/American Cuisine*
- *Priced moderate to expensive*
- *Open 7 days for lunch and dinner*
- *Reservations for The Restaurant and for the Cellar in the Sky. Reservations not accepted for the Hors d'Oeuvrerie except for Sunday brunch*
- *All major credit cards are accepted*
- *Ties and jackets required in The Restauant, jackets in the Hors d'Oeuvrerie, denims not permitted*
- *Private party facilities available*

Wine Press

The Wine Press is a personal salute from radio personality Sally Jessy Raphael to the members of the wine/food establishment who have been her fellow travelers over the past decade. Many remain fans of the ebullient blonde who hostesses proceedings on occasional weeknights and always on Saturdays at her very own, whimsically appointed wine-bar-cum-restaurant.

Polished plank floors, low vaulted stucco ceilings hung with native basketry, and tables covered in Provencal prints echoed by the window-drapes, recreate the image of a French wine-cellar—while napkin-lined wooden fruit baskets serve up warm loaves of bread, and flickering candles are set in stem goblets. Along with these "Sally's" of inspired whimsy: the beat of a live piano at dinner hour and until very late—expect the unexpected from Sally Jessy's larder.

Indeed, it would be easy just to dine with a good bottle from the extensive wine-book—but that would be to miss the essential point of the place. Elsewhere, one selects food—then looks for a complementary wine. Here, one does well to query one of the youthful waiters as to which fine wines have been opened and made available by-the-glass for this evening; then choose foods to go with the wines you fancy. And do make it wines in the plural: where else are you so cordially urged to sample three or four varied vintages in the course of a single meal?

Appetizers are sufficiently hearty and interesting to carry some sophisticated labels. Smoked trout with a ramekin of lingonberry-spiked horseradish-cream is a lovely counterpoint to some fine white wine; while a full-bodied red complements a round of Black Forest mushroom caps steeped in Marsala. A fruit and cheese platter is geared to please addicted samplers—but if a real meal is in order, the thick and pungent steak *au poivre* or the rich spinach pasta laced with scallops and shrimp are typically satisfying entrees. Fresh fish, lamb chops and veal specialties round out a menu of sophisticted Manhattan favorites.

Desserts are intensely chocolate or bright with seasonal fruits; the atmosphere is as casually "in-group" as may be imagined.

1160 First Avenue
New York, N.Y., 10021
(212) 688-4490

- *French Country Cuisine*
- *Priced moderate*
- *Open seven nights for dinner only*
- *Reservations and all major credit cards accepted*
- *Private party facilities available*

Yangtze River

Chinese restaurants seem to pop up all over New York City and, in the rush to try the newest spots, that good neighborhood place often gets neglected. The regulars who frequent Yangtze River, however, continue to bypass experimentation in favor of returning to a restaurant they know serves dependably good Chinese food.

Part of Yangtze River's appeal is its central location. Situated on 57th Street in Manhattan, it's close to Carnegie Hall, Lincoln Center, the Broadway theaters, the best shops, and the midtown business district.

But most of Yangtze River's appeal is due to the tasty food served in a casual, friendly atmosphere at very reasonable prices. The restaurant is bright and bustling with a block-long bar that's frequently packed. The decor is simple and attractive—the restful color scheme is punctuated by Chinese prints and wooden plaques with brass Chinese characters.

Now when comparing the food of different Chinese restaurants it must be said that since the the same dish—beef with oyster sauce, for instance—is often made with slight variations at each restaurant comparison becomes difficult. Thus, there's a need for a standard, one dish that will test the mettle of every restaurant equally. Now, just as vanilla is the flavor to taste when comparing ice cream parlors, hot and sour soup is the criterion in Chinese restaurants; it's a Chinese staple which most places serve. Well, Yangtze River serves *terrific* hot and sour soup. It's appropriately spicy and also rich and hearty—the bowl brims with vegetables and pieces of lean pork.

For appetizers try the fried or boiled dumplings, the shrimp toast, the fried shrimp balls, and the baby spare ribs. When it comes to entrees, give short shrift to the commonplace and go for the house specialties. The sizzling seafood dish is a combination of lobster, shrimp, scallops, and special rice. The crispy whole yellow fish gets bathed in a fragrant hot sauce.

One of their lobster creations features tender lobster pieces put back in the shell and garnished with baby corn, vegetables, and red peppers done in a rich garlic sauce.

But what if the extensive menu—which stresses Cantonese, Polynesian, and Mandarin dishes—leaves you confused? Just ask Mike Shih, who runs the place, for help. Mike or one of his staff will give you friendly and thorough descriptions of the dishes, and they'll offer suggestions as to which you'll like.

250 West 57 Street
New York, N.Y., 10019
(212) 246-3659

- *Chinese Cuisine*
- *Inexpensively priced*
- *Open 7 days for lunch and dinner*
- *Reservations and all major credit cards accepted*

Geographical Listings

Over 6,000 restaurants arranged alphabetically
within specific geographical areas up
and down the Eastern Seaboard

CONNECTICUT

AVON

AVON OLD FARMS INN.... Rte. 44, Avon, Conn., 06001. (203) 667-2818. Cuisine: American. Open 6 days for lunch and dinner; Closed Monday. No credit cards.

CHEZ SERGE.... Avon Park North, Avon, Conn., 06001. (203) 678-0175. Cuisine: French. Credit cards: All major.

J. COPPERFIELD, LTD.....225 West Main St., Avon, Conn., 06001. (203) 678-0170. Cuisine: American. Open 7 days for lunch and dinner; Sunday brunch. Credit cards: AE, MC, VISA. Reservations: Accepted.

BERLIN

HAWTHORNE INN....2387 Wilbur Cross Hwy., Berlin, Conn., 06037. (203) 828-3571. Cuisine: American Credit cards: AE, MC, VISA.

BETHEL

OLIVER'S.... Rte. 6, Bethel, Conn., 06801. (203) 744-1343. Cuisine: American. Open 6 days for lunch and dinner. Credit cards: AE, MC, VISA.

SAN MIGUEL....8 P.T. Barnum Square, Bethel, Conn., 06801. (203) 748-2396. Cuisine: Mexican. Open Tuesday through Sunday for dinner only; Closed Monday. No credit cards.

BETHLEHEM

PAINTED PONY....32 Main St., Bethlehem, Conn., 06751. (203) 266-7477. Cuisine: Steaks/Chops/American. Open 7 days for breakfast, lunch, and dinner. Credit cards: AE, MC, VISA. Reservations: Necessary. Entertainment: Live entertainment nightly.

BLOOMFIELD

HU KE LAU.... Mountain Ave., Bloomfield, Conn., 06002. (203) 243-2921. Cuisine: Chinese/Polynesian. Open 7 days for lunch and dinner. Credit cards: AE, MC, VISA. Reservations: Suggested. Entertainment: Live entertainment nightly.

BOLTON

FIANO'S...275 Boston Tpke., Bolton, Conn., 06040. (203) 643-2342. Cuisine: Italian. Open 7 days for dinner only. Credit cards: All major. Reservations: Accepted.

BRANFORD

CONNOLLY'S....686 West Main St., Branford, Conn., 06405. (203) 481-7284. Cuisine : American. Open Monday through Friday for lunch; 7 days for dinner. Credit cards: AE, MC, VISA.

CHEZ BACH....1070 Main St., Branford, Conn., 06405. (203) 488-8779. Cuisine: Vietnamese. Open Tuesday through Sunday for lunch and dinner; Closed Monday. Credit cards: AE, MC, VISA. Reservations: Accepted.

CHOWDER POT III....560 East Main St., Branford, Conn., 06405. (203) 481-2670. Open 7 days for lunch and dinner. Credit cards: AE, MC, VISA.

DOWNEAST....420 East Main St., Branford, Conn., 06405. (203) 488-0500. Cuisine: Continental. Open Monday through Friday for lunch; 7 days for dinner; Sunday brunch. Credit cards: MC, VISA. Reservations: Accepted. Entertainment: Live entertainment nightly. Proper attire required.

OKI JAPANESE STEAK HOUSE....869 West Main St., Branford, Conn., 06405. (203) 481-2301. Cuisine: Japanese. Open 7 days for dinner only. Credit cards: AE, MC, VISA. Reservations: Suggested.

SU CAS...400 East Main St., Branford, Conn., 06405. (203) 481-5001. Cuisine: Mexican. Open Tuesday through Sunday for lunch and dinner; Closed Monday. Credit cards: MC, VISA. Reservations: Accepted.

TANDOMS....120 North Main St., Branford, Conn., 06405. (203) 481-5539. Cuisine: French/Italian. Open 7 days for lunch and dinner; Sunday brunch. Credit cards: AE, MC, VISA. Reservations: Accepted. Entertainment: Live entertainment nightly.

BRIDGEPORT

BLOODROOT....85 Feriss St., Bridgeport, Conn., 06605. (203) 576-9168. Cuisine: Vegetarian. Open daily for lunch and dinner; Sunday brunch. No credit cards. Private party facilities: Available.

FERRYBOAT JUNCTION.... Stratford Ave. Pier, Bridgeport, Conn., 06604. (203) 367-4195. Cuisine: American. Open 6 days for lunch and dinner; Closed Monday. Credit cards: AE, DC, MC, VISA. Private party facilities: Available. Reservations: Accepted. Entertainment: Live entertainment nightly.

OCEAN SEA GRILL....1328 Main St., Bridgeport, Conn., 06604. (203) 336-2132. Cuisine: Seafood. Owner: Robert Rolleri. Open 6 days for lunch and dinner; Closed Sunday; Credit cards: All major. Annual sales: $500,000 to $1 million. Total employment: 36.

POMPOUS BULL....2068 East Main St., Bridgeport, Conn., 06610. Cuisine: Steak/Seafood. Open Monday through Friday for lunch; 7 days for dinner. Credit cards: CB, DC, MC, VISA. Reservations: Accepted.

BROOKFIELD

CANDLEWOOD INN.... Candlewood Rd., Brookfield, Conn., 06804. (203) 775-1281. Cuisine: American. Open 7 days for lunch and dinner; Sunday brunch. Credit cards: AE, DC, MC, VISA. Reservations suggested.

CHRISTOPHER'S.... Rte. 7, Brookfield, Conn., 06804. (203) 775-4409. Cuisine: American. Open 7 days for lunch and dinner. Credit cards: All major. Reservations: Suggested.

GATSBY'S....257 Federal Rd., Brookfield, Conn., 06804. (203) 775-1141. Cuisine: Continental. Open Wednesday through Monday for lunch and dinner; Closed Tuesday. Reservations: Suggested. Entertainment: Live entertainment nightly. Proper attire required.

THE HEARTH.... Rte. 7, Brookfield, Conn., 06804. (203) 775-3360. Cuisine: American/Seafood. Credit cards: AE, MC, DC.

SHIP'S WHEEL.... Rte. 7, Brookfield, Conn., 06804. (203) 775-4597. Cuisine: Seafood. Open 7 days for lunch and dinner. Credit cards: AE, DC, MC, VISA. Reservations: Accepted. Entertainment: Live entertainment nightly.

BROOKLYN

C.J. MULLANEY'S.... Rte. 6, Brooklyn, Conn., 06234. (203) 774-9644. Cuisine: American. Open Monday through Friday for lunch; 7 days for dinner; Sunday brunch. Credit cards: All major. Reservations: Suggested. Entertainment: Live entertainment nightly.

GOLDEN LAMB BUTTERY.... Bush Hill Rd., Brooklyn, Conn., 06234. (203) 774-4423. Open Tuesday, Wednesday, and Thursday only for lunch; Friday and Saturday only for dinner; Closed Sunday and Monday. No credit cards. Reservations: A must. Entertainment: Live entertainment available. Proper attire required.

BURLINGTON

BURLINGTON INN.... Rte. 4, Burlington, Conn., 06013. (203) 673-4544. Cuisine: Continental. Open daily for lunch and dinner. Credit cards: AE, DC, MC, VISA. Reservations: Accepted. Entertainment: Live entertainment nightly.

BYRAM

AMERIGO'S....2 South Water St., Byram, Conn., 06830 (203) 531-9890. Cuisine: Italian. Open 7 days for lunch and dinner. Credit cards: MC, VISA. Reservations: Suggested.

CANTON

ICHABOD'S....144 Albany Tpke., Route 44, Canton, Conn., 06019. (203) 693-0740. Cuisine: American. Open 7 days for lunch and dinner. Credit cards: AE, MC, VISA.

MARGARITAVILLE....144 Albany Tpke., Canton, Conn., 06019. (203) 693-8237. Cuisine: Mexican. Open 7 days for dinner only. Credit cards: AE, MC, VISA.

CENTERBROOK

INE BOUCHE.... Main St., Centerbrook, Conn., 06049. (203) 767-1277. Cuisine: French. Open Tuesday through Saturday for dinner only; Closed Sunday and Monday. Credit cards: MC, VISA. Reservations: Suggested. Proper attire required.

CHESHIRE

PAVILLION....1721 Mill Dale Rd., Cheshire, Conn., 06410. (203) 272-3584. Cuisine: Italian/American. Credit cards: AE, DC, MC, VISA.

RESTAURANT DU VILLAGE.... Main St., Cheshire, Conn., 06410. (203) 526-5058. Cuisine: French. Open Tuesday through Sunday for lunch; 7 days for dinner. Credit cards: MC, VISA. Reservations: Accepted. Proper attire required.

VICTORIAN HOUSE....22 Le Maple Ave., Cheshire, Conn., 06410. (203) 272-5743. Cuisine: American. Open 7 days for lunch and dinner. Credit cards: AE, MC, VISA.

CHESTER

CHART HOUSE.... West Main St., Chester, Conn., 06412. (203) 526-9898. Cuisine: Continental. Credit cards: AE, DC, MC, VISA.

CLINTON

TOP OF THE DOCK.... Cedar Isle Marina, Clinton, Conn., 06413. (203) 669-7808. Cuisine: Seafood. Open 7 days for lunch and dinner. Credit cards: AE, MC, VISA. Reservations: Accepted. Entertainment: Live entertainment nightly.

CORNWALL BRIDGE

CORNWALL INN.... Rte. 7, Cornwall Bridge, Conn., 06754. (203) 672-6884. Cuisine: American. Open Tuesday through Sunday for lunch and dinner. Credit cards: All major. Reservations: Necessary.

COS COB

CLAM BOX RESTAURANT....453 East Putnam Ave., Cos Cob, Conn., 06807. (203) 869-2900. Cuisine: Seafood. Owner: Anna and Arthur Gross. Open 7 days. Private party facilities: Up to 150. Annual sales: $1 million to $3 million. Total employment: 135. Corporate name: Clam Box Inc.

FONDA LA PALOMA....531 Boston Post Rd., Cos Cob, Conn., 06807. (203) 661-9395. Cuisine: Mexican. Open Monday through Saturday for lunch and dinner; Closed Sunday. Credit cards: All major. Reservations: Suggested. Entertainment: Live entertainment nightly. Proper attire required.

JARDINE'S RESTAURANT....3 River Rd., Cos Cob, Conn., 06807. (203) 661-0204. Cuisine: Continental. Open 7 days. Credit cards: AE, MC, VISA. Private party facilities: 20 to 120. Total employment: 55. Corporate name: Combine of Fairfield, Inc.

TUMBLEDOWN DICK'S....85 Post Rd., Cos Cob, Conn., 06807. (203) 869-1820. Cuisine: American. Open 7 days for lunch and dinner. Credit cards: All major. Reservations: Accepted.

DANBURY

BELLA ITALIA RESTAURANT....2 Padanaram Rd., Danbury, Conn., 06810. (203) 743-3828. Cuisine: Continental. Owner: Angello Galano. Credit cards: AE, MC, VISA. Annual sales: $500,000 to $1 million. Total employment: 25.

CHUCK'S STEAK HOUSE....20 Seger St., Danbury, Conn., 06810. (203) 655-2254. Cuisine: Steak/Seafood/ American. Open 7 days for lunch and dinner. Credit cards: AE, DC, MC, VISA.

1848 HOUSE....Newton Rd., Danbury, Conn., 06810. (203) 744-0918. Cuisine: German. Open Tuesday through Saturday for lunch and dinner; Closed Sunday and Monday. Credit cards: AE, MC, VISA. Reservations: Accepted. Proper attire required.

EL DORADO....152 West St., Danbury, Conn., 06810. (203) 743-6375. Cuisine: Italian. Open Tuesday through Sunday for dinner only; Closed Monday. Credit cards: AE, MC, VISA. Reservations: Accepted.

FAIRFIELD'S....The Danbury Hilton, 18 Old Ridgebury Rd., Danbury, Conn., 06810. (203) 749-0600. Cuisine: Continental. Open Monday through Friday for lunch; Monday through Saturday for dinner; Closed Sunday. Credit cards: AE, CB, MC, VISA. Reservations: Accepted.

MAGNIFICO'S....58 Main St., Danbury, Conn., 06810. (203) 748-1118. Cuisine: Italian. Open Monday through Saturday for lunch and dinner. Credit cards: AE, DC, MC, VISA.

THE PLANKHOUSE....103 Newtown Rd., Danbury, Conn., 06810. (203) 744-5674. Cuisine: Steaks. Open 7 days for lunch and dinner. Credit cards: AE, MC, VISA. Reservations: Accepted. Entertainment: Live entertainment nightly.

SESAME SEED....68 West Wooster St., Danbury, Conn., 06810. (203) 743-9850. Cuisine: Middle Eastern. Open 7 days for lunch and dinner. No credit cards.

DARIEN

CHUCK'S STEAK HOUSE....1340 Post Rd., Darien, Conn., 06820. (203) 655-2254. Cuisine: American. Open 7 days for lunch and dinner. Credit cards: AE, MC, VISA. Entertainment: Live entertainment nightly.

HARPER'S....319 Post Rd., Darien, Conn., 06820. (203) 655-7481. Cuisine: American. Open 7 days for lunch and dinner; Sunday brunch. Credit cards: AE, MC, VISA. Reservations: Suggested. Entertainment: Live entertainment nightly.

HEINKEL'S....972 Post Rd., Darien, Conn., 06820. (203) 655-1020. Cuisine: Continental. Open 7 days for lunch and dinner; Sunday brunch. Credit cards: AE, MC, VISA. Reservations: Accepted. Proper attire required.

THE PLANKHOUSE....111 Old King's Hwy., Darien, Conn., 06820. (203) 655-8286. Cuisine: Steaks. Open 7 days for lunch and dinner. Credit cards: AE, MC, VISA. Reservations: Accepted. Entertainment: Live entertainment nightly.

LOCK, STOCK & BARREL....Good Wines Shopping Center, Darien, Conn., 06820. (203) 655-8869. Cuisine: Italian. Credit cards: All major.

RED COACH GRILL....154 Post Rd., on Rte. 1, Darien, Conn., 06820. (203) 655-9794. Cuisine: American. Open 7 days for lunch and dinner. Credit cards: All major. Private party facilities: Up to 150. Annual sales: $1 million to $3 million. Total employment: 55. Corporate name: Imperial Group Ltd.

RORY'S....416 Post Rd., Darien, Conn., 06820. (203) 655-9453. Cuisine: American. Open 7 days for lunch and dinner; Sunday brunch. Credit cards: AE, MC, VISA.

TWIN FACES EAST....2748 Post Rd. East, Darien, Conn., 06820. (203) 348-8080. Cuisine: Continental. Open Monday through Saturday for lunch and dinner; Closed Sunday. Credit cards: All major. Reservations: Accepted. Entertainment: Live entertainment nightly. Proper attire required.

VICTORIA STATION....54 Post Rd., Darien, Conn., 06820. (203) 655-7604. Cuisine: American. Open 7 days for lunch and dinner. Credit cards: All major. Reservatons: Suggested.

DERBY

CONNIE'S CUCINA....208 Main St., Derby, Conn., 06418. (203) 734-9659. Cuisine: Italian. Open for breakfast and lunch 7 days weekly; Dinner on Friday only. No credit cards.

EAST HADDAM

GELSTON HOUSE....Goodspeed Landing, East Haddam, Conn., 06423. (203) 873-9300. Cuisine: Continental. Open 7 days for lunch and dinner. Credit cards: AE, DC, MC, VISA. Reservations: Accepted.

TEA CADDY....3 Main St., East Haddam, Conn., 06423. (203) 873-8371. Cuisine: English. Open Tuesday through Saturday for lunch only; Closed Sunday and Monday. No credit cards. Reservations: Accepted.

EAST HARTFORD

THE HORSELESS CARRIAGE....411 Connecticut Blvd., East Hartford, Conn., 06108. (203) 289-2737. Cuisine: Italian. Open 7 days for lunch and dinner. Credit cards: AE, MC, VISA. Reservations: Accepted. Entertainment: Live entertainment nightly.

MARCO POLO....1250 Burnside Ave., East Hartford, Conn., 06108. (203) 289-2704. Cuisine: Italian. Open 6 days for lunch and dinner; Closed Monday. Credit cards: AE, DC, MC, VISA.

REUBEN'S RESTAURANT....350 Roberts St., East Hartford, Conn., 06108. (203) 528-0767. Cuisine: American. Open 7 days for lunch and dinner. Credit cards: AE, MC, VISA. Reservations: Recommended. Entertainment: Live entertainment nightly.

RUSTLER'S INN....500 Main St., East Hartford, Conn., 06118. (203) 569-3117. Cuisine: Steak/Seafood. Open 7 days for lunch and dinner. Credit cards: AE, DC, MC, VISA. Reservations: Accepted.

EAST HAVEN

CAP'N NICK'S....Hemingway Ave., East Haven, Conn., 06512. (203) 469-4397. Cuisine: American. Open 7 days for lunch and dinner. Credit cards: All major.

CHUCK'S STEAK HOUSE....369 Main St., East Haven, Conn., 06512. (203) 934-5300. Cuisine: Steak/ Seafood/American. Open 7 days for lunch and dinner. Credit cards: AE, DC, MC, VISA.

EAST LYME

BLACK WHALE....Rte. 156, East Lyme, Conn., 06333. (203) 739-7382. Cuisine: Italian. Open 6 days for lunch and dinner; Closed Tuesday. Credit cards: AE, MC, VISA. Reservations: Accepted. Entertainment: Live entertainment nightly.

THE CHOPPING BLOCK....Rte. 161, East Lyme, Conn., 06333. (203) 739-5515. Cuisine: American. Open 7 nights for dinner. Credit cards: MC, VISA. Private party facilities: Up to 60. Annual sales: $500,000 to $1 million. Total employment: 30. Corporate Name: Chopping Block Restaurant, Inc.

EAST NORWALK

ABRUZZI KITCHEN....195 Liberty Sq., East Norwalk, Conn., 06855. (203) 838-6776. Cuisine: Italian. Open 7 days for lunch and dinner. Credit cards: MC, VISA.

SKIPPER'S....Beach Rd., East Norwalk, Conn., 06854. (203) 838-2211. Cuisine: Steak/Seafood. Credit cards: AE, DC, VISA, MC.

ELLINGTON

VALLEY FISH MARKET....80 West Rd., Ellington, Conn., 06029. (203) 872-9659. Cuisine: Seafood. Open Tuesday through Saturday for lunch and dinner; Closed Sunday and Monday. No credit cards. Bring your own wine or beer.

ENFIELD

THE MOUNTAIN LAUREL....701 Enfield St., (Rte. 5), Enfield, Conn., 06082. (203) 745-4687; 734-4969. Cuisine: American/Seafood. Owner: Leon S. Simons and Dennis Sabettini. Open Tuesday through Sunday. Credit cards; AE, DC, MC, VISA. Private party facilities: 16 to 250. Annual sales: $1 million to $3 million. Total employment: 30 to 60. Corporate name: Mountain Laurel Restaurant, Inc.

ESSEX

GRISWOLD INN....46 Main St., Essex, Conn., 06426. (203) 767-0991. Cuisine: American. Open 7 days for lunch and dinner. Credit cards: AE, DC, MC, VISA. Private party facilities: 10 to 70. Annual sales: $1 million to $3 million. Corporate name: Griswold Inn, Inc.

THE GULL....Pratt St., Essex, Conn., 06426. (203) 767-767-0916. Cuisine: Continental. Credit cards: AE, MC, VISA.

TUMBLEDOWN'S CAFE....29 Main St., Essex, Conn., 06426. (203) 767-0233. Open daily for lunch and dinner. Credit cards: AE, MC, VISA.

FAIRFIELD

ANGUS RESTAURANT...2133 Black Rock Tpke., Fairfield, Conn., 06430. (203) 366-5902. Cuisine: American. Open 7 days for lunch and dinner. Credit cards: All major. Entertainment: Available.

BREAKAWAY....2316 Post Rd., Fairfield, Conn., 06430. (203) 255-0026. Cuisine: American. Credit cards: None.

DOGWOODS....2070 Boston Post Rd., Fairfield, Conn., 06430. (203) 255-2683. Cuisine: American. Open 7 days for lunch and dinner; Sunday brunch. Credit cards: AE, DC, MC, VISA.

FERN'S....52 Sanford St., Fairfield, Conn., 06430. (203) 259-3304. Cuisine: Continental. Credit cards: AE, MC, VISA. Reservations: Accepted.

FREDERICKSBURG....1201 Kings Hwy., Fairfield, Conn., 06430. (203) 333-1201. Cuisine: Continental. Open Monday through Saturday for lunch and dinner; Closed Sunday. Credit cards: All major. Private party facilities: Available. Reservations: Suggested. Entertainment: Live entertainment nightly. Proper attire required.

RUSTIC GROTTO....417 Post Rd., Fairfield, Conn., 06430. (203) 255-2624. Cuisine: Italian. Open 7 days for lunch and dinner. Credit cards: AE, MC, VISA. Reservations: Accepted. Entertainment: Live entertainment nightly.

THE SCENARIO....1418 Post Rd., Fairfield, Conn., 06430. (203) 255-2641. Cuisine: American. Open 7 days for lunch and dinner. Credit cards: All major. Reservations: Accepted. Entertainment: Live entertainment nightly.

VALENTINE'S RESTAURANT....881 Post Rd., Fairfield, Conn., 06430. (203) 255-4190. Cuisine: American. Open Monday through Saturday for lunch and dinner; Closed Sunday. Credit cards: MC, VISA. Reservations: Accepted.

WILLOWBY'S....226 Kings Hwy. East, Fairfield, Conn., 06430. (203) 576-9124. Cuisine: American/Continental. Owner: Joseph S. Sepot. Open 7 days for lunch and dinner. Credit cards: AE, DC, MC, VISA. Private party facilities: Up to 125. Annual Sales: $1 million to $3 million. Total employment: 65.

FARMINGTON

AUBERGE DE PARIS...1593 Farmington Ave., Route 4, Farmington, Conn., 06032. (203) 673-5405. Cuisine: French. Open Tuesday through Friday for lunch; Tuesday through Saturday for dinner; Closed Sunday. Credit cards: AE, MC, VISA. Reservations: Suggested.

THE BLACK OLIVE....Rte. 10, Farmington, Conn., 06032. (203) 677-7600. Cuisine: Italian. Open Monday through Friday for lunch; 7 days for dinner. Credit cards: AE, MC, VISA. Reservations: Accepted.

BUCKBOARD....220 Farmington Ave., Farmington, Conn., 06032. (203) 677-1589. Cuisine: American. Open Monday through Saturday for dinner only. Credit cards: AE, DC. Reservations: Accepted. Proper attire suggested.

CHUCK'S STEAK HOUSE....588 Farmington Ave., Farmington, Conn., 06032. (203) 677-7677. Cuisine: Steak/Seafood/American. Open 7 days for lunch and dinner. Credit cards: AE, DC, MC, VISA.

COPPER KETTLE....1305 Farmington Ave., Farmington, Conn., 06032. (203) 677-0301. Cuisine: American. Open for breakfast, lunch, and dinner 7 days. Reservations: Accepted.

MAGIC PAN RESTAURANT....322 Westfarms Mall, Farmington, Conn., 06032. (203) 561-3200. Cuisine: Continental. Open 7 days for lunch and dinner; Sunday brunch. Credit cards: AE, MC, VISA Reservations: Accepted.

THE READING ROOM....Mill Lane, Farmington, Conn., 06032. (203) 677-7997. Cuisine: "Eclectic." Open 7 days for lunch and dinner. Credit cards: MC, VISA.

THE SILO....330 Main St., Farmington, Conn., 06032. (203) 677-0149. Cuisine: Continental. Open Monday through Saturday for lunch and dinner; Closed Sunday. Credit cards: AE, DC, MC, VISA. Reservations: Accepted. Entertainment: Live entertainment nightly.

GAYLORDSVILLE

FOX & FOX....Rte. 7, Gaylordsville, Conn., 06755. (203) 354-6025. Cuisine: Continental. Open Wednesday through Friday for lunch and dinner; Sunday brunch; Closed Tuesday. Credit cards: AE, MC, VISA. Reservations: Suggested.

GLASTONBURY

THE BLACKSMITH'S TAVERN....2300 Main St., Glastonbury, Conn., 06033. (203) 659-0366. Cuisine: Continental. Open 7 days for lunch and dinner. Credit cards: All major.

GORDIE'S PLACE....141 New London Tpke., Glastonbury, Conn., 06033. (203) 659-2656. Cuisine: American. Open 7 days for lunch and dinner; Sunday brunch. Credit cards: AE, MC, VISA. Reservations: Suggested. Entertainment: Live entertainment nightly.

MARKETPLACE RESTAURANT....39 New London Tpke. Extension, Glastonbury, Conn., 06033. (203) 633-3832. Cuisine: Continental. Credit cards: AE, MC, VISA.

RAFFA'S....2815 Main St., Glastonbury, Conn., 06033. (203) 659-1355. Cuisine: Italian. Open 7 days for lunch and dinner; Sunday brunch. Credit cards: AE, MC, VISA. Reservations: Suggested. Entertainment: Live entertainment nightly.

TAI-PAN....2858 Main St., Glastonbury, Conn., 06033. (203) 633-2470. Cuisine: Oriental. Open Tuesday through Sunday for lunch and dinner; Closed Monday. Credit cards: AE, MC, VISA. Reservations: Accepted.

GLENVILLE

MORGAN....256 Glenville Rd., Glenville, Conn. 06830. (203) 531-5100. Cuisine: American. Credit cards: All major.

GREENWICH

BOODLE'S....21 Field Point Rd., Greenwich, Conn., 06830. (203) 661-3553. Cuisine: American. Open daily for lunch and dinner; Sunday brunch. Credit cards: AE, MC, VISA.

CAFE BAGATELLE....18 North Putnam Ave., Greenwich, Conn., 06830. (203) 869-8383. Cuisine: French. Credit cards: All major.

CHOPPING BLOCK....366 Greenwich Ave., Greenwich, Conn., 06830. (203) 869-1700. Cuisine: American. Open Monday through Saturday for lunch and dinner; Closed Sunday. Credit cards: MC, VISA. Reservations: Suggested.

CINQUANTE-CINQ....55 Arch St., Greenwich, Conn., 06830. (203) 869-5641. Cuisine: French. Open 6 days for lunch and dinner; Closed Sunday. Credit cards: AE, MC, VISA.

DEMO'S....44 Oldfield Pt. Rd., Greenwich, Conn., 06830. (203) 869-6767. Cuisine: Italian. Credit cards: AE, VISA.

GARBO'S....579 West Putnam Ave., Greenwich, Conn., 06830. (203) 661-3630. Cuisine: American. Open 7 days for lunch; Tuesday through Sunday for dinner. Credit cards: AE, MC, VISA. Reservations: Accepted. Entertainment: Live entertainment nightly.

GASLIGHT....1309 Post Rd., Greenwich, Conn., 06830. (203) 637-2214. Cuisine: French. Credit cards: All major.

GREENSTREET RESTAURANT....253 Greenwich Ave., Greenwich, Conn., 06830. (203) 661-4459. Cuisine: Continental. Owner: Arthur Johannsen, John DeLucia, & Carl Magnotta. Open 7 days. Credit cards: All major. Private party facilities: 10 to 35 persons. Annual sales: $500,000 to $1 million. Total employment: 40. Corporate name: CAJAC, Inc.

GRYPHON CAFE....130 East Putnam Ave., Greenwich, Conn., 06830. (203) 661-2483. Open 7 days for lunch and dinner. Credit cards: AE, MC, VISA. Reservations: Accepted.

JONATHAN'S OTHER BROTHER....34 East Putnam Ave., Greenwich, Conn., 06830. (203) 661-3491. Cuisine: American. Credit cards: All major.

KAGETSU....28 West Putnam Rd., Greenwich, Conn., 06830. (203) 622-9264. Cuisine: Japanese. Credit cards: All major.

LA GRANGE AT THE HOMESTEAD INN....420 Field Point Rd., Greenwich, Conn., 06830. (203) 869-7500. Cuisine: French. Owner: Lessie Davison and Nancy Smith. Open Monday to Friday for lunch; 7 days for dinner. Credit cards: All major. Total employment: 50.

LEWIS STREET CHOWDER HOUSE....61 Lewis St., Greenwich, Conn., 06830. (203) 622-9827. Cuisine: Seafood. Open Monday through Saturday for lunch and dinner; Closed Sunday. No credit cards. Reservations: Accepted.

LOTUS EAST....64 Greenwich Ave., Greenwich, Conn., 06830. (203) 661-4156. Cuisine: Chinese. Open 7 days for lunch and dinner. Credit cards: AE, MC, VISA.

LUCA'S STEAK HOUSE....35 Church St., Greenwich, Conn., 06830. (203) 869-4403. Cuisine: American. Open 7 days for lunch and dinner. Credit cards: All major.

MANERO'S....559 Steamboat Rd., Greenwich, Conn., 06830. (203) 869-0049. Cuisine: American. Credit cards: All major.

MAYA OF JAPAN....4 Lewis Ct., Greenwich, Conn., 06830. (203) 869-4322. Cuisine: Japanese. Credit cards: All major.

NICKLEBY'S....409 Greenwich Ave., Greenwich, Conn., 06830. (203) 622-0799. Cuisine: American. Open 7 days for lunch and dinner; Sunday brunch. Credit cards: AE, MC, VISA.

PEPINO'S....19 Glenville St., Greenwich, Conn., 06830. (203) 531-9660. Cuisine: Italian. Open 7 days for lunch and dinner. Credit cards: AE, MC, VISA. Reservations: Suggested. Entertainment: Live entertainment nightly.

PORTOFINO....16 West Putnam Ave., Greenwich, Conn., 06830. (203) 869-8383. Cuisine: Italian. Open Monday through Friday for lunch; 7 days for dinner; Sunday brunch. Credit cards: AE, MC, VISA. Reservations: Accepted.

SHOWBOAT INN—THE PATIO....Steamboat Rd., Greenwich, Conn., 06830. (203) 661-9800. Cuisine: Seafood. Credit cards: All major.

SZECHUAN TASTE....137 West Putnam Ave., Greenwich, Conn., 06830. (203) 661-3300. Cuisine: Chinese. Open 7 days for lunch and dinner. Credit cards: AE, DC, MC, VISA. Reservations: Accepted.

VERSAILLES....Greenwich Ave., Greenwich, Conn., 06830. (203) 661-6634. Cuisine: French. Open 7 days for breakfast, lunch, and dinner. No credit cards.

GROTON

BOOTLEGGER....359 Thames St., Groton, Conn., 06340. (203) 448-1617. Cuisine: American. Open 7 days for lunch and dinner. Credit cards: AE, MC, VISA. Entertainment: Live entertainment nightly.

GUILFORD

THE CENTURY HOUSE....2455 Boston Post Rd., Guilford, Conn., 06437. (203) 453-2216. Cuisine: French. Open Tuesday through Sunday for lunch and dinner; Sunday brunch; Closed Monday. Credit cards: All major. Reservations: Suggested. Entertainment: Live entertainment nightly. Proper attire required.

CHELLO OYSTER HOUSE....Boston Post Rd., Guilford, Conn., 06437. (203) 453-2670. Cuisine: Seafood. Open 6 days for lunch and dinner; Closed Tuesday. Credit cards: AE, CB, MC, VISA. Reservations: Suggested.

SACHEM COUNTRY HOUSE....Goose Lane, Guilford, Conn., 06437. (203) 453-5261. Cuisine: Country French. Owner: Noorollah Khorsondi. Open 6 days for lunch and dinner; Closed Monday. Credit cards: AE, DC, MC, VISA. Annual sales: $250,000 to $500,000. Total employment: 26.

HAMDEN

J.J. STARTS....4137 Whitney Ave., Hamden, Conn., 06514. (203) 281-1669. Cuisine: American. Open 7 days for dinner only. Credit cards: All major. Reservations: Recommended. Entertainment: Live entertainment nightly.

SANFORD BARN....135 Sanford St., Hamden, Conn., 06514. (203) 288-3309. Cuisine: American. Open 7 days for lunch and dinner; Sunday brunch. Credit cards: AE, MC, VISA. Reservations: Accepted.

VALENTINO'S....2987 Whitney Ave., Hamden, Conn., 06514. (203) 288-7707. Open Tuesday through Sunday for lunch and dinner; Closed Monday. Credit cards: AE, DC, MC, VISA. Reservations: Recommended.

HARTFORD

ADAJIAN'S RESTAURANT....297 Asylum Ave., Hartford, Conn., 06103. (203) 534-5181. Cuisine: Armenian. Open Monday through Saturday for lunch and dinner; Closed Sunday. Credit cards: AE, DC, MC. Reservations: Accepted. Entertainment: Live Armenian entertainment nightly.

BOMBAY CUISINE....481 Wethersfield Ave., Hartford, Conn., 06114. (203) 522-2797. Cuisine: Indian. Open Tuesday through Sunday for dinner only; Closed Monday. Credit cards: MC, VISA. Reservations: Accepted.

THE BROWNSTONE....124 Asylum St., Hartford, Conn., 06103. (203) 525-1171. Cuisine: American. Open 7 days for lunch and dinner; Sunday brunch. Credit cards: All major. Reservations: Suggested.

BROWN THOMPSON & CO.....942 Main St., Hartford, Conn., 06103. (203) 525-1600. Cuisine: International. Open 7 days for lunch and dinner; Sunday brunch. Credit cards: AE, MC, VISA. Entertainment: Live entertainment nightly.

CAPRICCIO'S....626 Franklin Ave., Hartford, Conn., 06114. (203) 246-4122. Cuisine: Italian. Open 7 days for lunch and dinner. Credit cards: AE, MC, VISA.

CARBONE'S RISTORANTE....588 Franklin Ave., Hartford, Conn., 06114. (203) 249-9646. Cuisine: Italian. Owner: C.A. Carbone. Closed Sunday. Credit cards: AE, MC, VISA.

CASA PORTUGUESA....1999 Park St., Hartford, Conn., 06106. (203) 233-6954. Cuisine: Portugese. Open 6 days for lunch and dinner; Closed Monday. Credit cards: MC, VISA. Reservations: Accepted.

CLUB 60....60 Washington St., Hartford, Conn., 06106. (203) 527-6060. Cuisine: American. Open 6 days for lunch and dinner; Closed Sunday. Credit cards: AE, MC, VISA.

CONNECTICUT ROOM....G. Fox & Co., 960 Main St., Hartford, Conn., 06103. (203) 241-3446. Cuisine: American. Open 7 days for lunch and dinner. No credit cards.

FETTERHOFF'S....181 Ann St., Hartford, Conn., 06103. (203) 525-3336. Cuisine: American. Open 7 days for lunch and dinner. Credit cards: AE, MC.

GAETANO'S....1 Civic Center Plaza, Hartford, Conn., 06101. (203) 249-1629. Cuisine: Continental. Open 6 days for lunch and dinner; Closed Sunday. Credit cards: AE, MC, VISA. Reservations: Required. Entertainment: Live entertainment nightly. Proper attire required.

GIONFRIDDO'S....283 Asylum St., Hartford, Conn., 06103. (203) 247-0032. Cuisine: Italian. Open 7 days for lunch and dinner. Credit cards: All major. Reservations: Accepted.

GREAT TRAIN ROBBERY CAFE....50 Union Pl., Hartford, Conn., 06103. (203) 247-7717. Cuisine: American. Open Monday through Saturday for lunch and dinner. Credit cards: AE, MC, VISA.

GREENHOUSE CAFE....Hotel Sonesta, 5 Constitution Plaza, Hartford, Conn., 06103. (203) 278-2000. Cuisine: American. Open 7 days for breakfast, lunch, and dinner; Sunday brunch. Credit cards: AE, MC, VISA.

THE HEARTHSTONE....678 Maple Ave., Hartford, Conn., 06114. (203) 246-8814. Cuisine: Continental. Credit cards: AE, MC, VISA.

HONISS' OYSTER HOUSE COMPANY....44 State St., Hartford, Conn., 06103. (203) 522-4177. Cuisine: Seafood. Credit cards: All major.

HO'S MANDOO RESTAURANT....498 Farmington Ave., Hartford, Conn., 06105. (203) 232-0842. Open Tuesday through Sunday for lunch and dinner; Closed Monday. Credit cards; MC, VISA. Reservations: Accepted.

HUBBARD'S PARK....26 Trumbull St., Hartford, Conn., 06103. (203) 728-0315. Cuisine: French. Open Monday through Friday for lunch; 7 days for dinner; Sunday brunch. Credit cards: All major. Entertainment: Live entertainment nightly.

IL CAPRICCIO....626 Franklin Ave., Hartford, Conn., 06114. (203) 246-4122. Open 6 days for lunch and dinner; Closed Sunday. Credit cards: AE, MC, VISA. Reservations: Accepted. Entertainment: Live entertainment nightly.

JONATHAN'S....Wadsworth Athenum, 600 Main St., Hartford, Conn., 06103. (203) 278-2670. Cuisine: American. Open Tuesday through Friday for lunch; Sunday brunch; Closed Saturday and Monday. No credit cards. Reservations: Suggested.

J.P. OF HARTFORD....15 Asylum St., Hartford, Conn., 06103. (203) 247-8144. Cuisine: American. Open 6 days for lunch and dinner; Closed Sunday. Credit cards: AE, MC, VISA. Reservations: Accepted. Entertainment: Live entertainment nightly.

LANGSTON'S....116 Ann St., Hartford, Conn., 06103. (203) 527-6990. Open 6 days for lunch and dinner; Closed Sunday. Credit cards: All major. Entertainment: Live entertainment nightly.

LAST NATIONAL BANK RESTAURANT....752 Main St., Hartford, Conn., 06103. (203) A HOLD UP. Cuisine: Continental/American. Owner: Ferg Jansen, Jr. Open 7 days. Credit cards: All major. Private party facilities: 6 to 60. Annual sales: $1 million to $3 million. Total employment: 65. Corporate name: LCR Inc.

MARBLE PILLAR....22 Central Row, Hartford, Conn., 06103. (203) 247-4549. Cuisine: German. Open Monday through Saturday for lunch and dinner; Closed Sunday. Credit cards: MC, VISA. Reservations: Accepted.

PARMA....271 Sheldon St., Hartford, Conn., 06106. (203) 556-9407. Cuisine: Italian. Open Monday through Saturday for lunch and dinner; Closed Sunday. Reservations: Required.

PIPPIE'S....628 Wethersfield Ave., Hartford, Conn., 06114. (203) 246-4448. Cuisine: Italian. Open 7 days for lunch and dinner. Credit cards: All major. Reservations: Accepted. Entertainment: Live entertainment nightly.

RIB ROOM....Hotel Sonesta, 5 Constitution Plaza, Hartford, Conn., 06103. (203) 278-2000. Cuisine: American. Open 7 days for lunch and dinner. Credit cards: All major.

RISING SUN RESTAURANT....1 Civic Center Plaza, Hartford, Conn., 06101. (203) JAPAN—00. Cuisine: Japanese. Open 7 days for lunch and dinner. Credit cards: All major.

SHENANIGAN'S....1 Gold St., Hartford, Conn., 06103. (203) 522-4117. Open 7 days for breakfast, lunch, and dinner; Closed Saturday for lunch; Sunday brunch. Credit cards; All major. Reservations: Suggested. Entertainment: Live entertainment nightly.

SIGNATURE....1 Civic Center Plaza, Hartford, Conn., 06103. (203) 249-1629. Cuisine: Continental. Credit cards: All major.

THE SISSON TAVERN....86 Sisson Ave., Hartford, Conn., 06103. (203) 233-5156. Cuisine: Italian. Open 7 days for lunch and dinner. Credit cards: MC, VISA. Reservations: Accepted.

SONG HAYS....87-93 Asylum St., Hartford, Conn., 06103. (203) 525-6388. Cuisine: Chinese. Open 7 days for lunch and dinner. Credit cards: AE, DC, MC. Reservations: Accepted.

36 LEWIS STREET....36 Lewis St., Hartford, Conn., 06103. (203) 247-2300. Cuisine: American. Open 6 days for lunch and dinner; Closed Sunday. Credit cards: AE, MC, VISA. Entertainment: Live entertainment nightly.

HIGGANUM

GLOCKENSPIEL....Rte. 81, Higganum, Conn., 06441. (203) 345-4697. Cuisine: German. Open Tuesday through Sunday for lunch and dinner; Closed Monday. Credit cards: MC, VISA. Reservations: Accepted.

IVORYTON

COPPER BEECH INN....Main St., Ivoryton, Conn., 06442. (203) 767-0330. Remote country stuff offering warm lights at dusk, five inviting sleeping rooms furnished with charm, attractive dining rooms decorated with lovely antiques, and owners Paul and Louise Ebeltoft who like nothing better than producing country cooking for hungry travellers. Their menu includes such fare as poached oysters in spinach leaves, pate of chicken with a lobster *mousse* center, thick pale lobster bisque, and beef Wellington in a *madeira* sauce with truffles. Open Tuesday through Sunday for lunch and dinner; Closed Monday. Moderate to high prices. Reservations: Suggested. Credit cards: All major. Private party facilities: 6 to 100. Annual sales: $1 million to $3 million. Total employment: 60. Corporate name: Copper Beach Inn, Inc.

KENT

BULL'S BRIDGE INN....Rte. 7, Kent, Conn., 06757. (203) 927-3263. Cuisine: Continental. Open 7 days for lunch and dinner; Sunday brunch. Credit cards: AE, MC, VISA. Reservations: Accepted. Entertainment: Live entertainment nightly.

FIFE 'N' DRUM....Rte. 7, Kent, Conn., 06757. (203) 927-3509. Cuisine: Continental. Open Wednesday through Monday for lunch and dinner; Sunday brunch; Closed Tuesday. Credit cards: All major. Reservations: Accepted. Entertainment: Live entertainment nightly. Proper attire required.

LAKEVILLE

ANTHONY'S VINEYARD....Interlaken Rd., Lakeville, Conn., 06039. (203) 435-9878. Cuisine: Continental. Credit cards: AE, MC, VISA.

INTERLAKEN INN....Rte. 112, Lakeville, Conn. 06039. (203) 435-9878. Cuisine: American/Continental.

LYME

OLD LYME INN....85 Lyme St., Lyme, Conn., 06333. (203) 434-2600. Cuisine: French. Open 6 days for lunch and dinner; Closed Mondays. Credit cards: All major.

MADISON

CAFE LAFAYETTE....725 Boston Post Rd., Madison, Conn., 06443. (203) 245-2380. Cuisine: French. Open Monday through Saturday for lunch and dinner; Closed Sunday. Credit cards: AE, DC, MC VISA. Reservations: Accepted. Entertainment: Live entertainment nightly.

FRIENDS & COMPANY....11 Boston Post Rd., Madison, Conn., 06443. (203) 245-0462. Cuisine: Continental. Open 7 days for lunch and dinner; Sunday brunch. Credit cards: AE, MC, VISA.

WOODLAWN....438 Boston Post Rd., Madison, Conn. 06443. (203) 245-2616. Cuisine: Continental.

MANCHESTER

CAVEY'S....45 East Center St., Manchester, Conn., 06040. (203) 643-2751. Cuisine: French. Open Tuesday through Saturday for dinner only; Closed Sunday and Monday. Credit cards: All major. Reservations: Suggested. Proper attire required.

THE ISLANDER RESTAURANT....179 Tolland Tpke., Manchester, Conn., 06040. (203) 643-9529. Cuisine: Polynesian/American. Open 7 days for lunch and dinner. Credit cards: AE, MC, VISA. Reservations: Accepted.

WILLIE'S STEAK HOUSE....444 Center St., Manchester, Conn., 06040. (203) 649-5271. Cuisine: American. Open 6 days for lunch and dinner; Closed Sunday. Credit cards: All major. Reservations: Accepted.

MANSFIELD

MANSFIELD DEPOT....Middle Tpke., Route 44A, Mansfield Depot, Conn., 06251. (203) 429-3663. Cuisine: Continental. Open Tuesday through Sunday for lunch and dinner. Credit cards: AE, MC, VISA. Reservations: Accepted.

MERIDEN

CHATEAU BIANCA....2003 Berlin Tpke., Meriden, Conn., 06450. (203) 235-0515. Cuisine: Continental. Open 7 days for lunch and dinner. Credit cards: AE, DC, MC, VISA. Reservations: Accepted. Entertainment: Live entertainment nightly. Proper attire required.

VERDOLINI'S RESTAURANT....126 Hanover Ave., Meriden, Conn., 06450. (203) 235-5317. Cuisine: Italian. Open 6 days for lunch and dinner; Closed Mondays. No credit cards.

MIDDLEFIELD

GREEN FIELDS....Lyman Orchards Country, Rtes. 147 & 157, Middlefield, Conn., 06455. Cuisine: American Open 7 days for lunch; Tuesday through Saturday for dinner; Sunday brunch. Credit cards: MC, VISA. Reservations: Accepted.

MIDDLETOWN

ALFREDO'S RIVERSIDE....141 Bridge St., Middletown, Conn., 06457. (203) 346-6714. Cuisine: Italian. Open 7 days for lunch and dinner. Credit cards: AE, MC, VISA. Reservations: Accepted.

LA BOCA....526 Main St., Middletown, Conn., 06457. (203) 346-4492. Cuisine: Mexican. Open Thursday, Friday, and Saturday for lunch; 7 days for dinner. Credit cards: MC, VISA.

MACANDREWS....3 Columbus Plz., Middletown, Conn., 06457. (203) 346-6655. Cuisine: American. Open 7 days for lunch and dinner: Sunday brunch. Credit cards: MC, VISA. Reservations: Recommended.

PEKING HOUSE....200 Main St., Middletown, Conn., 06457. (203) 344-1122. Cuisine: Chinese. Open 7 days for lunch and dinner. Credit cards: AE, MC, VISA. Reservations: Accepted.

TOWN FARMS INN....Silver St., Middletown, Conn., 06457. (203) 347-7438. Cuisine: Continental. Credit cards: AE, MC, VISA.

MILFORD

THE GATHERING....989 Boston Post Rd., Milford, Conn., 06460. (203) 878-6537. Cuisine: American. Credit cards: AE, MC, VISA.

LA CANTINA....248 New Haven Ave., Milford, Conn., 06460. (203) 877-1170. Cuisine: Italian. Open 7 days for lunch and dinner. Credit cards: AE, MC, VISA. Reservations: Accepted.

SCRIBNER'S....31 Village Rd., Milford, Conn., 06460. (203) 878-7019. Cuisine: Seafood. Open Monday through Friday for lunch; 7 days for dinner. Credit cards: MC, VISA. Reservations: Accepted.

SHIP'S WHEEL....471 New Haven Ave., Milford, Conn., 06460. (203) 877-1461. Cuisine: Seafood. Open 7 days for lunch and dinner. Credit cards: AE, DC, MC, VISA. Reservations: Accepted. Entertainment: Live entertainment nightly.

STEAK & ALE....1360 Boston Post Rd., Milford, Conn., 06460. (203) 878-0691. Cuisine: American. Open 7 days for lunch and dinner. Credit cards: All major. Reservations: Accepted. Entertainment: Live entertainment nightly.

MORRIS

DEER ISLAND GATE....Rte. 209, Morris, Conn., 06763. (203) 567-0913. Open Wednesday through Sunday for dinner; Sunday brunch; Closed Monday and Tuesday. Credit cards: MC, VISA. Reservations: Accepted.

MYSTIC

BINNACLE....Whaler's Inn, 20 East Main St., Mystic, Conn., 06355. (203) 536-2135. Cuisine: American. Open 7 days for breakfast, lunch, and dinner. Credit cards: All major. Entertainment: Live entertainment nightly.

CHUCK'S STEAK HOUSE....12 Water St., Mystic, Conn., 06355. (203) 536-4589. Cuisine: Steak/Seafood/American. Open 7 days for lunch and dinner. Credit cards: AE, DC, MC, VISA.

FLOOD TIDE....Rte. 1, Mystic, Conn., 06355. (203) 536-9604. Cuisine: Continental. Credit cards: MC, VISA.

FLYING BRIDGE....Whaler's Inn, 20 East Main St., Mystic, Conn., 06355. (203) 536-1506. Cuisine: Seafood. Open 7 days for lunch and dinner. Credit cards: All major.

J.P. DANIEL'S....Main St., Mystic, Conn., 06355. (203) 536-3664. Cuisine: Continental. Open 7 days for lunch and dinner. Credit cards: AE, MC, VISA. Reservations: Suggested. Entertainment: Live entertainment nightly.

MYSTIC OYSTER HOUSE....Rte. 27, Mystic, Conn., 06355. (203) 572-0085. Cuisine: Seafood. Open 7 days for lunch and dinner. Credit cards: AE, MC, VISA.

SAILOR ED'S....Rte. 1, Mystic, Conn., 06355. (203) 572-0085. Cuisine: Seafood. Open 6 days for lunch and dinner; Closed Monday. Credit cards: All major.

SEAMEN'S INNE....Greenmanville Ave., Mystic, Conn., 06355. (203) 536-9649. Cuisine: Seafood. Open 7 days for lunch and dinner. Credit cards: All major. Private party facilities: 20 to 500 people. Annual sales: $1 million to $3 million. Total employment: 150. Corporate name: Mystic Seaport Museum.

STEAMBOAT CAFE....73 Steamboat Wharf, Mystic, Conn., 06355. (203) 536-1975. Cuisine: Seafood. Open 7 days for lunch and dinner; Sunday brunch. Credit cards: MC, VISA. Reservations: Suggested.

NEW BRITAIN

PEKING HOUSE....488 Slater Rd., New Britain, Conn., 06101. (203) 735-5100. Cuisine: Chinese. Open 7 days for lunch and dinner. Credit Cards: AE, MC, VISA. Reservations: Accepted.

NEW CANAAN

BROCK'S....111 Cherry St., New Canaan, Conn., 06840. Cuisine: American. Open daily for lunch and dinner. Credit cards: AE, MC, VISA.

FAT TUESDAY....105 Elm St., New Canaan, Conn., 06840. (203) 972-0445. Cuisine: Continental. Credit Cards: All major.

GATES....10 Forest St., New Canaan, Conn., 06840. (203) 966-8666. Cuisine: Continental. Open 7 days for lunch and dinner; Sunday brunch. Credit cards: AE, MC. VISA. Entertainment: Live entertainment nighly.

HUCKLEBERRY'S....43 Grove St., New Canaan, Conn., 06840. (203) 972-1709. Cuisine: American. Open 7 days for lunch and dinner; Sunday brunch. Credit cards: AE, MC, VISA

ROGER SHERMAN INN....195 Oenoke Ridge, New Canaan, Conn. 06840. (203) 966-4541. Cuisine: Continental. Credit cards: All major.

NEW HAVEN

ANNIE'S FIREHOUSE RESTAURANT....19 Edwards St., New Haven, Conn. 06511. (203) 865-4200. Cuisine: American. This reconverted firehouse is open daily for lunch and dinner. No credit cards.

BACKSTREET....368 Orange St., New Haven, Conn., 06511. (203) 776-5116. Cuisine: American. Open 7 days for lunch and dinner; Sunday brunch. Credit cards: AE, MC, VISA. Reservations: Accepted. Entertainment: Live entertainment nightly.

BASEL'S....933 State St., New Haven, Conn., 06511. (203) 624-9361. Cuisine: Greek. Open 6 days for lunch and dinner; Closed Monday. Credit cards: All major.

BLESSINGS....45 Howe St., New Haven, Conn., 06511. (203) 624-3557. Cuisine: Chinese. Open Monday through Saturday. Credit cards: AE only.

BOURBON STREET....883 Whalley Ave., New Haven, Conn., 06515. (203) 389-6200. Cuisine: American. Open 7 days for lunch and dinner; Sunday brunch. Credit cards: AE, MC, VISA. Reservations: Suggested. Entertainment: Live entertainment nightly.

CARRANO'S....100 Wooster St., New Haven, Conn., 06511. (203) 624-5289. Cuisine: Italian. Open Tuesday through Sunday for lunch and dinner; Closed Monday. Credit cards: AE, MC, VISA. Reservations: Accepted.

CASA MARRA....321 East St., New Haven, Conn., 06511. (203) 777-5148. Cuisine: Italian. Open 7 days for lunch and dinner. Credit cards: AE, DC,MC, VISA. Reservations: Suggested. Entertainment: Live entertainment nightly.

CHART HOUSE....100 South Water St., New Haven, Conn. 06511. (203) 787-3466. Cuisine: American. Open 7 days for dinner; Sunday brunch. Credit cards: AE, DC, MC, VISA.

DELMONACO'S....232 Wooster St., New Haven, Conn., 06511. (203) 865-1109. Cuisine: Italian. Open 6 days for lunch and dinner; Closed Tuesday. Credit cards: AE, DC, MC, VISA. Reservations: Necessary. Proper attire required.

FITZWILLY'S....338 Elm St., New Haven, Conn., 06511. (203) 624-9438. Cuisine: American. Open daily for lunch and dinner; Sunday brunch. Credit cards: AE, MC, VISA.

500 BLAKE STREET....500 Blake St., New Haven, Conn., 06851. (203) 387-0500. Cuisine: Italian. Open 7 days for lunch and dinner; Sunday brunch. No credit cards. Reservations: Accepted. Entertainment: Piano bar daily.

GEPPI'S....113 Grand Ave., New Haven, Conn., 06516. (203) 776-0100. Cuisine: Italian. Open Tuesday through Saturday for lunch and dinner; Closed Sunday and Monday. Credit cards: AE, MC, VISA. Reservations: Accepted. Entertainment: Live entertainment nightly.

LEON'S....321 Washington Ave., New Haven, Conn., 06518. (203) 789-9049. Cuisine: Northern Italian. Open Tuesday through Friday for lunch; Saturday and Sunday only for dinner; Closed Monday. Credit cards: All major. Reservations: Limited reservations. Proper attire required.

PAOLO'S RESTAURANT....150 Chapel St., New Haven, Conn., 06513. (203) 787-5099. Cuisine: Italian. Open Monday through Saturday for lunch and dinner; Closed Sunday. Credit cards: AE, MC, VISA. Reservations: Accepted. Proper attire required.

PEEPER'S....230 George St., New Haven, Conn., 06510. (203) 776-9227. Cuisine: American. Open 6 days for lunch and dinner; Closed Sunday. Credit cards: AE, MC, VISA.

PEKING GOURMET....500 New Haven Ave., New Haven, Conn., 06525. (203) 735-5100. Cuisine: Chinese. Open 7 days for lunch and dinner. Credit cards: AE, MC, VISA. Reservations: Accepted.

POCO LOCO....8 Whalley Ave., New Haven, Conn., 06511. (203) 789-9328. Cuisine: Mexican. Open 7 days for dinner only. Credit cards: All major. Reservations: Accepted.

ROTISSERIE NORMANDIE....Colony Inn, 1157 Chapel St., New Haven, Conn., 06511. (203) 776-4814. Cuisine: French. Open 7 days for lunch and dinner. Credit cards: All major. Reservations: Accepted. Entertainment: Live entertainment nightly. Proper attire required.

SHERMAN'S TAVERNE....1032 Chapel St., New Haven, Conn., 06850. (203) 777-2524. Cuisine: Continental. Open Monday through Saturday for lunch and dinner; Closed Sunday. Credit cards: All major. Reservations: Accepted. Entertainment: Live entertainment nightly.

TEDOSIO'S....101 Whitney Ave., New Haven, Conn., 06510. (203) 288-0402. Cuisine: Italian. Open Monday though Friday for lunch; Monday through Saturday for dinner; Closed Sunday. Credit cards: All major. Reservations: Accepted. Entertainment: Live entertainment nightly.

VENICE RESTAURANT....808 Dixwell Ave., New Haven, Conn., 06511. (203) 865-0271. Cuisine: Italian. Open 7 days for lunch and dinner. No credit cards.

WEST OF ELEVEN....1104 Chapel St., New Haven, Conn., 06510. (203) 787-9004. Cuisine: American. Open 7 days for lunch and dinner. Credit cards: All major.

NEW LONDON

CHUCK'S STEAK HOUSE....250 Pequot Ave., New London, Conn., 06355. (203) 443-1323. Cuisine: Steak/Seafood/American. Open 7 days for lunch and dinner. Credit cards: AE, DC, MC, VISA.

GONDOLIER....92 Huntington St., New London, Conn., 06320. (203) 447-1781. Cuisine: Italian. Open 7 days for dinner only. Credit cards: AE, MC, VISA.

SHIP'S WHEEL....182 Captain's Walk, New London, Conn., 06320. (203) 442-9433. Cuisine: Seafood. Credit cards: All major.

YE OLDE TAVERN....345 Bank St., New London, Conn., 06320. (203) 442-0353. Open Monday through Saturday for dinner only; Closed Sunday. Credit cards: All major. Reservations: Accepted.

NEW MILFORD

BOOTH HOUSE....New Milford, Conn., 06776. (203) 354-354-1128. Cuisine: French. Open 6 days for lunch and dinner; Closed Monday. Credit cards: AE, MC, VISA.

THE BUCKBOARD RESTAURANT.... 300 Kent Rd., Rte. 7, New Milford, Conn., 06776. (203) 354-4840. Cuisine: Continental. Open 7 days for lunch and dinner. Credit cards: MC, VISA.

COACH 'N SEVEN....Rte. 7, New Milford, Conn., 06776. (203) 354-9303. Cuisine: American. Credit cards: AE, MC, VISA.

FIN & CLAW....Rte. 7, New Milford, Conn., 06776. (203) 355-2122. Cuisine: Seafood. Open 7 days for lunch and dinner. Credit cards: MC, VISA.

THE IRON KETTLE....Rte. 7, New Milford, Conn., 06776. (203) 354-1809. Cuisine: American/French. Open 6 days for lunch and dinner; Closed Tuesdays. Credit cards: AE, MC, VISA. Reservations: Accepted.

JOEY'S....188 Danbury Rd., New Milford, Conn., 06776. (203) 354-2255. Cuisine: Italian. Open Tuesday through Saturday for lunch and dinner. Credit cards: MC, VISA. Reservations: Accepted.

RUDY'S....122 Litchfield Rd., New Milford, Conn., 06776. (203) 354-7727. Cuisine: Swiss. Open Tuesday through Sunday for dinner only; Closed Monday. No credit cards. Reservations: Suggested

NEW PRESTON

BIRCHES INN....West Shore Rd., New Preston, Conn., 06777. (203) 868-0229. Cuisine: Continental. Open 7 days for lunch and dinner; Sunday brunch. Credit cards: MC, VISA. Reservations: Accepted. Entertainment: Live entertainment nightly.

BOULDERS....Rte. 45, New Preston, Conn., 06777. (203) 868-7918. Cuisine: Continental. Credit cards: MC, VISA.

HOPKINS INN....Hopkins Rd., New Preston, Conn., 06777. (203) 868-7295. Cuisine: Continental. Owner: Franz and Beth Schober. Open 6 days for lunch and dinner; Closed Monday; Closed January 2 to April 2. Credit cards: None. Annual sales: $250,000 to $500,000. Total employment: 30.

INN AT LAKE WARAMAUG....New Preston, Conn., 06777. (203) 868-2168. Cuisine: American. Open 7 days for lunch and dinner; Sunday Brunch. Credit cards: AE, MC, VISA. Reservations: Suggested. Entertainment: Live entertainment nightly. Proper attire required.

LE BON COIN....Rte. 202, New Preston, Conn., 06777. Cuisine: French. Owner: J.J. and Clement Herman. Open Wednesday through Sunday for lunch and dinner; Closed Monday and Tuesday. Credit cards: MC, VISA. Private party facilities: Up to 35. Annual sales: $250,000 to $500,000. Total employment: 12. Corporate name: Le Bon Coin, Inc.

NEWTOWN

HAWLEY MANOR INN....19 Main St., Newtown, Conn., 06470. (203) 426-4456. Cuisine: Continental. Open Monday through Saturday for lunch and dinner; Sunday brunch. AE, MC, VISA. Reservations: Accepted. Entertainment: Live entertainment nightly.

NEWTOWN INN....160 South Main St., Newtown, Conn. 06470. (203) 426-2325. Cuisine: Continental. Credit Cards: All major.

NIANTIC

CONNECTICUT YANKEE....Box 479, Niantic, Conn. 06357. (203) 739-5483. Cuisine: American. Credit cards: All major.

FATONE BROTHERS RISTORANTE....156 West Main St., Niantic, Conn., 06357. (203) 739-8141. Cuisine: Italian. Open 7 days for lunch and dinner. Credit cards: MC, VISA.

NOANK

ABBOTT'S LOBSTER IN THE ROUGH....Pearl St., Noank, Conn., 06340. (203) 536-7719. Cuisine: Seafood. Open 7 days weekly from May 1 to October 1 for lunch and dinner. Credit cards: AE, MC, VISA.

YANKEE FISHERMAN....Groton Long Point Rd., Noank, Conn., 06340. (203) 536-1717. Cuisine: Seafood/Continental. Owner: James and Eleanor Woviotis. Open 6 days for lunch and dinner; Closed Monday. Credit cards: AE, DC, MC, VISA. Private party facilities: Up to 30. Annual sales: $500,000 to $1 million. Total employment: 35.

NORFOLK

BLACKBERRY RIVER INN....Rte. 44, Norfolk, Conn., 06058. (203) 542-5100. Cuisine: Nouvelle French. Open Wednesday through Sunday for lunch and dinner; Open seasonally, call for times. Credit cards: MC, VISA. Annual sales: $250,000 to $500,000. Total employment: 14. Corporate name: Harland Associates, Inc.

MOUNTAIN VIEW INN....Rte. 272, Norfolk, Conn., 06058. (203) 542-5595. Cuisine: Continental. Open Tuesday, Friday, Saturday, and Sunday only. Credit cards: MC, VISA. Reservations: Required.

NORTHFORD

MILLPOND TAVERNE.... Rte. 17, Middleton Ave., Northford, Conn., 06472. (203) 484-9316. Cuisine: American. Open 6 days for lunch and dinner; Closed Monday. No credit cards.

NORWALK

ADAM'S INN.... General Putnam Inn, 1 Park St., Norwalk, Conn., 06851. (203) 847-2468. Cuisine: American. Open 7 days for lunch and dinner. Credit cards: All major.

ANAND OF INDIA....20 North Ave., Norwalk, Conn., 06851. (203) 847-3181. Cuisine: Indian. Open 6 days for lunch and dinner; Closed Monday. Credit cards: AE, DC, MC, VISA. Reservations: Accepted.

EL ACAPULCO....233 Main St. (Rte. 7), Norwalk,, Conn., 06851. (203) 846-3557. Cuisine: Mexican. Open 6 days for lunch and dinner; Closed Monday. Credit cards: MC, VISA. Reservations: Accepted. Entertainment: Live entertainment on Friday and Saturday.

HUGO'S AGAIN....70 North Main St., Norwalk, Conn., 06851. (203) 838-1776. Cuisine: Continental. Open 7 days for lunch and dinner. Credit cards: AE, MC, VISA. Reservations: Accepted. Entertainment: Live entertainment nightly.

HUNAN U.S. 1....80 Connecticut Ave., Norwalk, Conn., 06850. (203) 838-91111. Cuisine: Chinese. Open 7 days for lunch and dinner. Credit cards: AE, MC, VISA.

THE LIGHTHOUSE RESTAURANT.... Post Rd., Norwalk, Conn., 06856. (203) 846-3266. Cuisine: Seafood. Open 7 days for lunch and dinner; Sunday brunch. Credit cards: MC, VISA. Reservations: Accepted. Entertainment: Live entertainment nightly.

MY PI....280 Connecticut Ave., Norwalk, Conn., 06854. (203) 838-2331. Cuisine: Italian. Open 7 days for lunch and dinner. Credit cards: MC, VISA.

PARSLEY....531 Westport Ave., Norwalk, Conn., 06851. (203) 846-1657. Cuisine: American. Open Monday through Saturday for lunch and dinner. Closed Sunday. Credit cards: AE, DC, MC, VISA.

PASTA PLUS....690 Connecticut Ave., Norwalk, Conn., 06902. (203) 866-7444. Cuisine: Italian. Open 7 days for lunch and dinner. Credit cards: MC, VISA. Reservations: Suggested.

SILVERMINE TAVERN.... Silvermine Ave., Norwalk, Conn., 06800. (203) 847-4558. Cuisine: American. Owner: Francis C. Whitman, Pres. Closed Tuesdays. Credit cards: All major. Private party facilities: Up to 140. Annual sales: $1 million to $3 million. Total employment: 75 to 100. Corporate name: The Whitman Co., Inc.

UNCLE JOE'S....17 Bartlett Ave., Norwalk, Conn., 06850. (203) 847-4876. Cuisine: Italian. Open Monday through Saturday for lunch and dinner; Closed Sunday. No credit cards.

OLD GREENWICH

CAFE DU BEC FIN....199 Sound Beach Ave., Old Greenwich, Conn., 06870. (203) 637-4447. Cuisine: French. Open Tuesday through Friday for Lunch; Monday through Saturday for dinner; Closed Sunday. Credit cards: MC, VISA. Reservations: Accepted. Proper attire required.

LOU SINGER'S STEAKHOUSE....192 Post Rd., Old Greenwich, Conn. 06870. (203) 637-3522. Cuisine: American. Credit Cards: All major.

TRACKS....148 Sound Beach Ave., Old Greenwich, Conn., 06870. (203) 637-3604. Cuisine: Continental. Open 7 days for lunch and dinner; Sunday brunch. Credit cards: AE, DC, MC, VISA. Reservations: Accepted.

OLD LYME

BEE & THISTLE INN....100 Lyme St., Old Lyme, Conn., 06371. (203) 434-1667. Cuisine: American/Continental. Open for breakfast, lunch, and dinner; Sunday brunch. Credit cards: AE, DC, MC, VISA. Reservations: Suggested.

OLD MYSTIC

YESTERDAY'S MANNER.... Rte. 184, Old Mystic, Conn., 06372. (203) 536-1228. Cuisine: American. Open Tuesday through Sunday for dinner only; Closed Monday. Credit cards: All major. Reservations: Suggested.

OLD SAYBROOK

CUCKOO'S NEST....1712 Boston Post Rd., Old Saybrook, Conn., 06475. (203) 399-9060. Cuisine: Mexican. Open 7 days for lunch and dinner. Credit cards: MC, VISA. Entertainment: Live entertainment nightly.

DOCK 'N DINE AT SAYBROOK POINT.... Rte. 154, Saybrook Point, Old Saybrook, Conn., 06475. Cuisine: Seafood. Open 7 days for lunch and dinner. Credit cards: All major. Reservations: Accepted. Entertainment: Live entertainment nightly.

SAYBROOK FISH HOUSE....99 Essex Rd., Old Saybrook, Conn. 06475. (203) 388-4836. Open 7 days for lunch and dinner. No credit cards.

WHITEHOUSE....1686 Boston Post Rd., Old Saybrook, Conn., 06475. (203) 399-6291. Cuisine: Continental. Open Tuesday through Sunday for lunch and dinner; Closed Monday. Credit cards: All major. Reservations: Accepted.

WILLY J'S....142 Ferry Rd., Old Saybrook, Conn., 06475. (203) 388-1441. Cuisine: French. Open Monday through Saturday for lunch; 7 days for dinner. Credit cards: All major.

ORANGE

THE PLANKHOUSE....439 Boston Post Rd., Orange, Conn., 06477. (203) 795-4784. Cuisine: Steak/Seafood. Open 7 days for lunch and dinner; Sunday brunch. Credit cards: AE, MC, VISA. Reservations: Suggested. Entertainment: Live entertainment nightly.

PUTNAM

CHUCK'S STEAK HOUSE.... Grove St., Putnam, Conn., 06260. (203) 928-3900. Cuisine: Steak/Seafood/American. Open 7 days for lunch and dinner. Credit cards: AE, DC, MC, VISA.

MY KITCHEN....1 Canal St., Putnam, Conn., 06260. (203) 928-3663. Cuisine: American. Open Monday through Saturday for lunch and dinner. Credit cards: MC, VISA. Reservations: Accepted.

REDDING RIDGE

SPINNING WHEEL.... Rte. 58, Redding Ridge, Conn., 06876. (203) 938-2511. Cuisine: American. Open Tuesday through Sunday for lunch and dinner; Sunday brunch. Closed Monday. Credit cards: AE, DC, MC, VISA. Reservations: Suggested. Proper attire suggested. Entertainment: Live entertainment; Outdoor jazz on Sundays.

RIDGEFIELD

CONNOLLY'S....896 Ethan Allen Hwy. (Rte. 7), Ridgefield, Conn., 06877. (203) 438-9355. Cuisine: American. Open 7 days for lunch and dinner; Sunday brunch. Credit cards: AE, MC, VISA.

THE ELMS INN....500 Main St., Ridgefield, Conn., 06877. (203) 438-2541. Cuisine: Continental. Credit cards: All major.

INN AT RIDGEFIELD....20 West Lane, Ridgefield, Conn., 06877. (203) 438-8282. Cuisine: French/Continental. Owner: Henry H. Prieger. Open Tuesday through Sunday for lunch and dinner; Closed Monday. Credit cards: All major. Private party facilities: Up to 85. Reservations: Suggested. Entertainment: Live entertainment nightly. Annual sales: $1 million to $3 million. Total employment: 30.

LUIGI'S.... Rte. 7, Ridgefield, Conn., 06877. (203) 544-8739. Cuisine: Italian. Open Monday through Friday for lunch; 7 days for dinner. Credit cards: AE, MC, VISA. Reservations: Accepted.

STONEHENGE.... Rte. 7, Ridgefield, Conn., 06877. (203) 438-6511. Cuisine: Continental. Credit cards: All major.

TOUCHSTONE'S....470 Main St., Ridgefield, Conn., 06877. (203) 438-4367. Cuisine: American. Open 7 days for lunch and dinner. Credit cards: MC, VISA.

RIVERSIDE

GREENWICH GREEN....1114 Post Rd., Riverside, Conn., 06878. (203) 637-3691. Cuisine: Chinese. Credit cards: All major.

HUNAN GARDEN....1114 Post Rd., Riverside, Conn., 06878. (203) 637-8773. Cuisine: Chinese. Open 7 days for lunch and dinner. Credit cards: AE, MC, VISA. Reservations: Accepted.

RIVERTON

CATNIP MOUSE.... Rte. 20, Riverton, Conn., 06065. (203) 379-3745. Cuisine: American. Open Tuesday through Saturday for lunch only; Closed Monday. No credit cards. Reservations: Accepted. Bring your own wine.

OLD RIVERTON INN.... Rte. 20, Riverton, Conn., 06065. (203) 379-8678. Cuisine: American. Open 6 days for lunch and dinner; Closed Monday. Credit cards: AE, MC, VISA. Reservations: Accepted.

ROCKY HILL

CHUCK'S STEAK HOUSE....2199 Silas Deane Hwy., Rocky Hill, Conn., 06067. Cuisine: Steak/Seafood/American. Open 7 days for lunch and dinner. Credit cards: AE, DC, MC, VISA.

HU KE LAU.... Townline Rd., Rocky Hill, Conn., 06067. (203) 563-2335. Cuisine: Chinese/Polynesian. Open 7 days for lunch and dinner. Credit cards: AE, MC, VISA. Reservations: Accepted. Entertainment: Live entertainment nightly.

SMUGGLER'S INN....1360 Silas Deane Hwy., Rocky Hill, Conn., 06067. (203) 563-6517. Cuisine Steak/Seafood. Open 7 days for lunch and dinner. Credit cards: AE, MC, VISA. Entertainment: Live entertainment nightly. Proper attire required.

ROWAYTON

HIGGINS RESTAURANT AND GROGGERY....148 Rowayton Ave., Rowayton, Conn., 06853. (203) 853-6062. Cuisine: Seafood. Open 7 days for lunch and dinner. Credit cards: MC, VISA. Reservations: Accepted.

SALISBURY

RAGAMONT INN....Main St., Salisbury, Conn., 06068. (203) 435-2372. Cuisine: Swiss/German. Owner: Rolf Schenkel. Open May to November; Closed Monday. Credit cards: None. Total employment: 14.

UNDERMOUNTAIN INN....Undermountain Rd., Salisbury, Conn., 06068. (203) 435-0242. Cuisine: Continental/American.

WHITE HART INN....Rte. 44, Salisbury, Conn., 06068. (203) 435-2511. Cuisine: Chinese. Open 7 days for breakfast, lunch, and dinner; Sunday brunch. Credit cards: AE, DC, MC, VISA. Reservations: Suggested.

SIMMSBURY

FIDDLER'S EATING AND DRINKING EMPORIUM....10 Wilcox St., Simmsbury, Conn., 06070. (203) 651-3526. Cuisine: American. Open 7 days for lunch and dinner. Credit cards: AE, MC, VISA. Reservations: Necessary. Entertainment: Live entertainment nightly.

SOMERS

SOMERS INN....585 Main St., Somers, Conn., 06071. (203) 749-2256. Cuisine: American. Open 6 days for lunch and dinner; Closed Monday. Credit cards: MC, VISA. Reservations: Required.

SOUTHBURY

BAZAAR....Poverty Rd., Southbury, Conn., 06488. (203) 246-6969. Cuisine: Steak/Seafood. Open 7 days for lunch and dinner; Sunday brunch; Closed for dinner on Sunday. Credit cards: AE, MC, VISA. Reservations: Accepted.

COUNTRY TAVERN....418D Heritage Village, Southbury, Conn., 06488. (203) 264-6771. Cuisine: Continental. Open 6 days for lunch and dinner; Closed Monday. Credit cards: All major. Reservations: Accepted. Entertainment: Live entertainment nightly. Proper attire required.

SOUTH GLASTONBURY

PARSON'S DAUGHTER....Rte. 17, South Glastonbury, Conn., 06033. (203) 633-8698. Cuisine: Continental. Open Tuesday through Sunday for lunch and dinner; Sunday brunch; Closed Monday. Credit cards: AE, CB, MC, VISA. Reservations: Suggested. Proper attire required.

SOUTH NORWALK

50 WATER STREET....50 Water St., South Norwalk, Conn., 06856. (203) 838-9044. Cuisine: American. Open 7 days for lunch and dinner. Credit cards: AE, MC, VISA. Reservations: Accepted. Entertainment: Live entertainment nightly.

THE GOOD EARTH....15 North Main St., South Norwalk, Conn. 06851. (203) 838-7714. Cuisine: Chinese. Open 7 days for lunch and dinner. Reservations: Accepted.

THE PIER....144 Water St., South Norwalk, Conn., 06854. (203) 838-8200. Cuisine: Seafood. Open 7 days for lunch and dinner. Credit cards: AE, DC, MC, VISA. Entertainment: Live entertainment nightly.

SOUTH WOODSTOCK

BALD HILL RESTAURANT....Rtes. 169 & 171, South Woodstock, Conn., 06267. (203) 974-2240. Cuisine: French. Open Tuesday through Friday for lunch; Tuesday through Sunday for dinner; Sunday brunch; Closed Monday. Credit cards: AE, MC, VISA. Reservations: Suggested.

STAFFORD SPRINGS

CHEZ PIERRE....179 West Main St., Stafford Springs, Conn., 06076. (203) 684-5826. Cuisine: French. Owner: Peirre E. Courrieu. Open Wednesday through Sunday during the winter; Monday through Saturday during the summer. Credit cards: All major. Annual sales: $250,000 to $500,000. Total employment: 9. Corporate name: Chez Pierre Restaurant, Inc.

STAMFORD

THE BRASS RAIL....99 Stillwater Ave., Stamford, Conn., 06902. (203) 324-5523. Cuisine: Italian. Open 6 days for lunch and dinner; Closed Tuesday. Credit cards: MC, VISA. Reservations: Accepted.

THE COUNTRY TAVERN....2635 Long Ridge Rd., Stamford, Conn., 06977. (203) 322-5316. Cuisine: American. Credit cards: All major.

ETTORUCCI'S RESTAURANT....559 Newfield Ave., Stamford, Conn., 06905. (203) 348-4616. Cuisine: Italian. Owner: Joseph DiNozzi, Marion DiNozzi, Vincent Sulpizi. Open Monday through Friday for lunch; Monday through Saturday for dinner; Closed Sunday. Private party facilities: 30 to 50. Annual sales: $500,000 to $1 million. Total employment: 30.

GIOVANNI'S STEAK HOUSE....1297 Long Ridge Rd., Stamford, Conn., 06977. (203) 322-8870. Cuisine: American.

LA BRETAGNE....2545 Summer St., Stamford, Conn., 06905. (203) 324-9539. Cuisine: French. Open Monday through Saturday for lunch and dinner; Closed Sunday. Credit cards: All major. Reservations: Accepted.

LEMON TREE CAFE....600 Summer St., Stamford, Conn., 06977 (203) 327-5330. Cuisine: American. Credit cards: All major

PELLICCI'S....98 Stillwater, Stamford, Conn., 06902. (203) 323-2542. Cuisine: Italian. Open Tuesday through Sunday for lunch and dinner. Credit cards: All major. Reservations: Accepted.

PLATIA....920 Hope St., Stamford, Conn., 06075. (203) 324-4822. Cuisine: Greek. Credit cards: MC, VISA.

RUGATINO'S....1308 East Main St., Stamford, Conn., 06902. (203) 327-4490. Cuisine: Italian. Open Monday through Saturday for lunch and dinner; Closed Sunday. Credit cards: AE, MC, VISA. Reservations: Suggested.

SHŌGUN....206 Richmond Hill Ave., Stamford, Conn., 06902. (203) 438-8355. Cuisine: Japanese. Open Monday through Friday for lunch; 7 days for dinner. Credit cards: All major. Reservations: Accepted.

STERLING OCEAN HOUSE....1329 Newfield Ave., Stamford, Conn., 06903. (203) 322-0244. Cuisine: Seafood. Open 7 days for lunch and dinner; Sunday brunch. Credit cards: All major. Reservations: Accepted. Entertainment: Live entertainment nightly.

STONINGTON

HARBORVIEW....60 Water St., Stonington, Conn., 06378. (203) 535-2720. Cuisine: French. Open 7 days for lunch and dinner. Credit cards: AE, DC, MC, VISA. Reservations: Suggested. Entertainment: Live entertainment nightly.

STORRS

ALTNAVEIGH....957 Storrs Rd., Storrs, Conn. 06268. (203) 429-4490. Cuisine: American. Open 7 days for lunch and dinner; Sunday brunch. Credit cards: MC, VISA. Reservations: Accepted. Entertainment: Live entertainment nightly.

STRATFORD

BLUE GOOSE....326 Ferry Rd., Stratford, Conn., 06497. (203) 375-9168. Cuisine: American. Open 7 days for lunch and dinner; Sunday brunch. Credit cards: AE, DC, MC, VISA.

FAGAN'S....946 Ferry Blvd., Stratford, Conn., 06497. (203) 378-6560. Cuisine: American. Open Monday through Saturday for lunch and dinner; Closed Sunday. Credit cards: All major. Reservations: Accepted.

TOMIKOS....520 Sniffen Lane, Stratford, Conn., 06497. (203) 375-3986. Cuisine: Japanese. Open Monday and Friday only for lunch; 6 days for dinner; Closed Tuesday. Credit cards: MC, VISA. Reservations: Accepted.

THOMASTON

LE CHALET....Rte. 8, Thomaston, Conn., 06787. (203) 283-5835. Cuisine: French. Open 6 days for lunch and dinner; Closed Monday. Credit cards: MC, VISA. Reservations: Accepted. Entertainment: Live entertainment nightly. Proper attire required.

TORRINGTON

VENETIAN RESTAURANT....52 East Main St., Torrington, Conn., 06790. (203) 489-9892. Cuisine: Italian. Open 6 days for lunch and dinner; Closed Tuesday. Credit cards: MC, VISA. Reservations: Accepted.

YANKEE PEDLAR INN....93 Main St., Jct. Rtes. 8 & 25, Torrington, Conn., 06790. (203) 489-9226. Cuisine: American/Continental. Owner: Arthur & Gerlad Rubens, Innkeepers. Open 7 days for breakfast, lunch, and dinner. Credit cards: All major. Private party facilities: Up to 125. Annual sales: $500,000 to $1 million. Total employment: 50.

WALLINGFORD

TEA & SPICE COMPANY....707 North Colony Rd., Wallingford, Conn., 06492. (203) 574-5810. Cuisine: American. Open 7 days for lunch and dinner; Sunday brunch. Credit cards: MC, VISA. Reservations: Accepted.

YANKEE SILVERSMITH INN....1033 North Colony Rd., Wallingford, Conn., 06492. (203) 269-8771. Cuisine: American. Open 7 days for lunch and dinner; Closed December 24, 25, and 26. Credit cards: All major.

WASHINGTON

MAYFLOWER INN....Rte. 47, Washington, Conn., 06793. (203) 868-0515. Cuisine: American. Open Wednesday through Sunday for lunch and dinner; Sunday brunch; Closed Monday and Tuesday. Credit cards: AE, MC, VISA. Reservtions: Accepted.

WATERBURY

EDDIE BACCO'S RESTAURANT...550 Chase Ave., Waterbury, Conn., 06704. (203) 775-1173. Cuisine: Italian. Open 6 days for lunch and dinner; Closed Monday. Credit cards: MC, VISA.

LOMBARDI'S RESTAURANT....1449 South Main St., Waterbury, Conn., 06706. (203) 575-9441. Cuisine: Italian. Open 7 days for lunch and dinner. Credit cards: AE, MC, VISA.

NO FISH TODAY....457 Main St., Waterbury, Conn., 06720. (203) 574-4483. Cuisine: Seafood. Open 6 days for lunch and dinner; Closed Sunday. Credit cards: MC, VISA. Reservations: Accepted.

1249 WEST....1249 Main St., Waterbury, Conn., 06720. (203) 756-4609. Cuisine: Italian. Open Tuesday through Sunday for lunch and dinner; Closed Monday. Credit cards: AE, MC, VISA. Reservations: Accepted.

WATERFORD

POOR RICHARD'S....49 Boston Post Rd., Waterford, Conn., 06385. (203) 443-1813. Cuisine: Continental. Open 7 days for lunch and dinner; Sunday brunch. Credit cards: AE, MC, VISA. Reservations: Accepted. Entertainment: Live entertainment nightly.

WESTBROOK

ANDERSON'S ANGUS CORRAL....Boston Post Rd., Westbrook, Conn., 06498. (203) 669-2109. Open 7 days for lunch and dinner. Credit cards. AE, MC, VISA. Reservations: Accepted. Entertainment: Singing Waiters.

WESTBURY

CARRIAGE HOUSE RESTAURANT....1200 Post Rd., Westbury, Conn., 06706. (203) 227-4171. Cuisine: Creole. Open 7 days for lunch and dinner. Credit cards: AE, MC, VISA.

WEST CORNWALL

THE DECK....Rte. 128, West Cornwall, Conn., 06796. (203) 672-6765. Cuisine: Continental. Credit cards: AE, MC, VISA.

WEST HARTFORD

BROCK'S....1245 New Britain Ave., West Hartford, Conn., 06111. (203) 561-3434. Cuisine: American. Open 7 days for lunch and dinner; Sunday brunch. Credit cards: AE, MC, VISA. Reservations: Accepted. Entertainment: Live entertainment nightly.

EDELWEISS....980 Farmington Ave., West Hartford, Conn., 06107. (203) 236-3096. Cuisine: American. Open Monday through Saturday for lunch and dinner; Closed Sunday; Late supper also. Credit cards: AE, MC, VISA. Reservations: Accepted.

FIORELLO'S....904 Farmington Ave., West Hartford, Conn., 06119. (203) 233-5556. Cuisine: Italian. Credit cards: All major.

HU KE LAU....New Britain Ave., West Hartford, Conn. 06106. (203) 521-1370. Cuisine: Chinese/Polynesian. Open 7 days for lunch and dinner. Credit cards: AE, MC, VISA. Reservations: Accepted. Entertainment: Live entertainment nightly.

JOSHUA TREE....445 South Main St., West Hartford, Conn., 06103. (203) 521-8664. Cuisine: American. Open daily for lunch and dinner. Credit cards: AE, MC, VISA. Reservations: Accepted. Entertainment: Live entertainment nightly.

THE SEAFARER....631 South Quaker Lane, West Hartford, Conn., 06110. (203) 233-3675. Cuisine: Seafood. Open 7 days for lunch and dinner. Credit cards: AE, MC, VISA.

VAL'S....992 Farmington Ave., West Hartford, Conn., 06107. (203) 523-4233. Cuisine: American. Open 6 days for lunch and dinner; Closed Sunday. No credit cards. No liquor.

WEST HAVEN

GOOD FORTUNE....Post Plaza, 1045 Orange Ave., West Haven, Conn., 06516. (203) 934-8050. Cuisine: Chinese. Credit cards: AE, MC. Reservations: Accepted.

HARBOUR MIST....6 Rock Street, West Haven, Conn., 06516. (203) 933-4666. Cuisine: Seafood. Open 7 days for lunch and dinner. Credit cards: All major. Reservations: Accepted. Entertainment: Live entertainment nightly.

PEKING GARDEN....220 Captain Thomas Blvd., West Haven, Conn., 06516. (203) 934-7536. Cuisine: Chinese. Credit cards: AE, DC, MC, VISA. Open 7 days for lunch and dinner.

RED COACH GRILL....354 Sawmill Rd., West Haven, Conn., 06516. (203) 932-2235. Cuisine: American. Open daily for lunch and dinner. Credit cards: All major. Reservations: Accepted.

WESTON

COBB'S MILL INN....Weston Rd., Weston, Conn., 06883. (203) 847-4558. Cuisine: American. Credit cards: All major.

WESTPORT

ALLEN'S CLAM & LOBSTER HOUSE....191 Hillts Pt. Rd., Westport, Conn., 06880 (203) 226-4411. Cuisine: Seafood. Credit Cards: AE.

THE ARROW....60 Charles St., Westport, Conn., 06880. (203) 227-4731. Cuisine: Italian. Owner: Frank Nistico. Open 7 days for lunch and dinner. Credit cards: All major. Annual sales: $1 million to $3 million. Total employment: 100.

BACKSTAGE....25 Powers Court, Westport, Conn., 06880. (203) 226-6959. Cuisine: Continental. Open Monday through Saturday for dinner only; Closed Sunday. Credit cards: AE, MC, VISA. Reservations: Accepted. Entertainment: Dancing from 9:00 PM.

BON APPETIT....47 Riverside Ave., Westport, Conn., 06880. (203) 226-0575. Cuisine: French. Open Tuesday through Saturday for lunch only; Closed Sunday and Monday. No credit cards. Reservations: Suggested.

CAFE DE LA PLAGE RESTAURANT....233 Hillspoint Rd., Westport, Conn., 06880. (203) 227-7208. Cuisine: Continental/Seafood. Owner: Daniel G. Lorenzetti. Open Tuesday through Friday for lunch; Tuesday through Sunday for dinner; Sunday brunch; Closed Monday. Credit cards: All major. Private party facilities: Up to 80. Annual sales: $250,000 to $500,000 Total employment 15.

THE CHAMBERS....272 Post Rd., Westport, Conn., 06880. (203) 226-7060. Cuisine: Continental. Open 7 days for lunch and dinner. Credit cards: All major

CHEZ PIERRE....142 Main St., Westport, Conn., 06880. (203) 227-5295. Cuisine: French. Open Monday through Saturday for lunch and dinner; Closed Sunday. Credit cards: All major. Reservations: Accepted. Proper attire required.

CHUCK'S STEAK HOUSE....20 Segar St., Westport, Conn., 06880. (203) 729-5555. Cuisine: American. Open 7 days for lunch and dinner. Credit cards: AE, MC, VISA. Entertainment: Live entertainment nightly.

CONNOLLY'S....221 Post Rd. West, Westport, Conn., 06880. (203) 226-5591. Cuisine: American. Open 7 days for lunch and dinner; Sunday brunch. Credit cards: AE, MC, VISA.

DAMEON....32 Railroad Pl., Westport, Conn., 06880. (203) 226-6580. Cuisine: Continental. Open 7 days for lunch and dinner. Credit cards: AE, DC, MC, VISA. Reservations: Suggested. Entertainment: Live entertainment nightly.

DEROSA'S....577 Riverside Ave., Westport, Conn., 06880. (203) 227-7596. Cuisine: Italian. Open 7 days for lunch and dinner. Credit cards: AE, MC, VISA. Reservations: Accepted.

GREENINGS....376 Post Rd. East, Westport, Conn., 06880. (203) 227-3767. Cuisine: Continental. Open Monday through Saturday for lunch and dinner; Closed Sunday. Credit cards: AE, MC,. Reservations: Accepted.

HUNAN GARDEN II....8 Sherwood Sq., Westport, Conn., 06880. (203) 226-8012. Cuisine: Chinese. Credit cards: AE, MC, VISA. Open 7 days for lunch and dinner. Reservations: Accepted.

INN AT LONGSHORE....260 Compo Rd. South, Westport, Conn., 06880. (203) 226-3316. Cuisine: Contiental. Open 7 days for lunch and dinner; Sunday brunch. Credit cards: All major. Reservations: Suggested. Entertainment: Live entertainment nightly.

LA NORMANDIE....1300 Post Rd. East, Westport, Conn., 06880 (203) 255-3485. Cuisine: French. Credit cards: AE, MC, VISA.

LE CHAMBORD....1572 Post Rd. East, Westport, Conn., 06880. (203) 255-2654. By acclamation, Connecticut's best French restaurant. Exquisite food in elegant surroundings at good value—what more do you want? Oscar Basler, who runs the dining room, and chef Robert Pouget own Le Chambord and have kept it on top for six years—flying in fresh ingredients to do so when necessary. Everything here is consistently good—here's a partial listing of what they serve: mussels *Biarritz*, quiche *lorraine*, clams casino, sole *meuniere*, chicken with wild mushrooms, and rack of lamb. They also offer *prix-fixe* dinners. Open Tuesday through Friday for lunch; Tuesday through Saturday for dinner; Closed Sunday and Monday. Priced moderate to high. Reservations are required for both lunch and dinner. Major credit cards are accepted. Private party facilities for between 10 and 50 persons. Annual sales: $1 million to $3 million. Total employment: 35. Corporate name: Fernan, Inc.

LEONG'S PALACE....1495 Post Rd. East, Westport, Conn., 06880. (203) 255-6156. Cuisine: Chinese. Open 7 days for lunch and dinner. Credit cards: All major. Reservations: Accepted.

LOAVES AND FISHES....456 Main Ave., Westport, Conn., 06880. (203) 846-0022. Cuisine: Seafood. Open 7 days for lunch and dinner. Credit cards: AE, MC, VISA. Reservations: Accepted.

MANERO'S OF WESTPORT....540 Riverside Ave., Westport, Conn., 06880. (203) 227-1500. Cuisine: American. Open 7 days for lunch and dinner. Credit cards: All major. Reservations: Accepted.

MANSION CLAM HOUSE....541 Riverside Ave., Westport, Conn., 06880. (203) 227-9661. Cuisine: Seafood. Open 7 days for dinner only. Credit cards: AE, MC, VISA.

MARIO'S....36 Railroad Pl., Westport, Conn., 06880. (203) 226-0308. Cuisine: American. Open 7 days for lunch and dinner. Credit cards: AE, MC, VISA. Reservations: Accepted.

MATTHEW'S....188 Post Rd. East, Westport, Conn., 06880. (203) 226-3008. Open 7 days for lunch and dinner. Credit cards: AE, MC, VISA. Reservations: Accepted. Entertainment: Live entertainment nightly.

THE MOORING....299 Riverside Ave., Westport, Conn., 06880. (203) 227-0757. Cuisine: Seafood. Open 7 days for lunch and dinner; Sunday brunch. Credit cards: AE, MC, VISA. Reservations: Accepted. Entertainment: Live entertainment nightly.

PANCHO VILLA'S....35 Main St., Westport, Conn., 06880. (203) 226-0211. Cuisine: Mexican. Open 7 days for lunch and dinner; Sunday brunch. Credit cards: All major. Reservations: Suggested. Entertainment: Live entertainment nightly.

PEARL'S....36 Riverside Ave., Westport, Conn., 06880. (203) 226-6003. Cuisine: American. Open Tuesday through Sunday for lunch and dinner. No credit cards.

PEKING INN....7 Main St., Westport, Conn., 06498. (203) 226-8157. Cuisine: Szechuan and Hunan Chinese. Open 7 days for lunch and dinner. Credit cards: All major.

PEPPERMILL STEAKHOUSE....1700 East State St., Westport, Conn., 06880. (203) 259-8155. Cuisine: Steaks. Open 7 days for lunch and dinner only. Credit cards: AE, DC, MC, VISA.

RED BARN....292 Wilton Rd., Westport, Conn., 06880. (203) 226-1079. Cuisine: American. Credit cards: All major.

ROCCO'S....1330 Post Rd., Westport, Conn., 06880. (203) 255-1017. Cuisine: Italian. Open Monday through Saturday for lunch and dinner; Closed Sunday. Credit cards: AE, MC, VISA. Reservations: Accepted.

SAKURA....680 Post Rd. East, Westport, Conn., 06880. (203) 222-0802. Cuisine: Japanese. Open Monday through Friday for lunch; 7 days for dinner. Credit cards: AE, MC, VISA. Reservations: Accepted.

SEASCAPE....580 Riverside Ave., Westport, Conn., 06880. (203) 227-8810. Cuisine: Seafood. Open Tuesday through Sunday for lunch and dinner. Sunday brunch; Closed Monday. Credit cards: AE, MC, VISA. Reservations: Accepted. Entertainment: Live entertainment nightly.

SHIPS....44 Post Rd. East, Westport, Conn., 06880. (203) 227-0790. Cuisine: American. Open 7 days for lunch and dinner. Credit cards: MC, VISA. Reservations: Accepted.

SILVERMOON CAFE....3 Bay St., Westport, Conn., 06880. (203) 222-1740. Cuisine: American. Open Tuesday through Saturday for breakfast, lunch, and dinner. Credit cards: AE, MC, VISA.

SOUP'S ON....111 Main St., Westport, Conn., 06880. (203) 227-2227. Cuisine: American. Open Monday through Saturday for lunch and dinner. No credit cards.

SZECHUAN WESTPORT....2702 Post Rd., Westport, Conn., 06880. (203) 226-7060. Cuisine: Chinese. Open 7 days for lunch and dinner. Credit cards: AE, MC, VISA. Reservations: Accepted. Entertainment: Live entertainment nightly.

TANGLEWOODS....833 Post Rd. East, Westport, Conn., 06880. (203) 226-2880. Cuisine: American. Open 7 days for lunch and dinner; Sunday brunch. Credit cards: AE, MC, VISA. Entertainment: Live entertainment nightly.

THE THREE BEARS RESTAURANT....333 Wilton Rd. (Rte. 33). Wesport, Conn., 06880. (203) 227-7219. American food in a restaurant of which at least parts date back over two centuries, when it was opened as The Three Bears Tavern. The current regime has been in power almost twenty years and they're turning out excellent food. The dining rooms are dominated by huge hand-hewn beams and a glossy wide-planked wood floor—the look is elegant rusticity. Specialties include: Fresh filet of sole with crabmeat stuffing and Newberg sauce, baked or boiled Maine lobster, broiled loin lamb chops, broiled half spring chicken, calf's liver with bacon, and veal *Marsala*. Owner: Stephone C. Vazzano. Predominantly American cuisine. Open Tuesday through Sunday for lunch and dinner; Closed Monday. Moderately priced. Reservations and all major credit cards accepted. Private party facilities for between 8 and 110 persons.

VIVA ZAPATA....530 Riverside Ave., Westport, Conn., 06880. (203) 227-9880. Cuisine: Mexican. Credit cards: All major.

WETHERSFIELD

SAM PAN....1115 Silas Deane Ave., Wethersfield, Conn., 06109. (203) 563-0691. Cuisine: Chinese. Open 7 days for lunch and dinner; Sunday brunch. Credit cards: AE, MC, VISA. Reservations: Accepted.

WILLIAMANTIC

THE CLARKS....32 North St., Williamantic, Conn., 06226. (203) 423-1631. Cuisine: American. Open 7 days for lunch and dinner. Credit cards: All major. Reservations: Accepted. Entertainment: Live entertainment nightly.

WILTON

OLD SCHOOL HOUSE....30 Cannon Rd., Cannon Crossing, Wilton, Conn., 06897. (203) 834-0066. Cuisine: American. Open Tuesday through Sunday for lunch and dinner; Sunday brunch; Closed Monday. No credit cards. Reservations: Suggested. Bring your own wine.

WINDSOR

TAVERN GOURMET....450 Bloomfield Ave., Windsor, Conn., 06095. (203) 688-5221. Cuisine: Continental. Open Monday through Saturday for dinner only; Closed Sunday. Credit cards: All major. Reservations: Accepted. Proper Attire required.

WINDSOR HOUSE ON THE GREEN....219 Broad St., Windsor, Conn., 06095. (203) 688-3673. Cuisine: American. Open 7 days for lunch and dinner; Sunday brunch. Credit cards: AE, MC, VISA. Reservations: Suggested. Entertainment: Live entertainment nightly.

WOODBURY

CURTIS HOUSE....Main St., Woodbury, Conn., 06798. (203) 263-2101. Cuisine: American. Open daily for lunch and dinner. Credit cards: MC, VISA.

YALESVILLE

BRITANNIA SPOON....296 Church St., Yalesville, Conn., 06492. (203) 265-6199. Cuisine: American. Open 7 days for lunch and dinner; Sunday brunch. Credit cards: AE, MC, VISA. Reservations: Accepted. Entertainment: Live entertainment nightly.

DELAWARE

REHOBETH

AVENUE....32 Rehobeth Ave., Rehobeth, Del., 19971. (302) 227-2770. Cuisine: Seafood, Steaks, and American. Owner: Kenneth Simpler. Open 7 days for breakfast, lunch and dinner Easter to October; closed Monday and Tuesday otherwise. Credit cards: VISA, MC. Private party facilities: 200+. Annual sales: $1 million to $3 million. Total employment: 50+.

OLDE DINNER BELL INN....Second and Christian Sts., Rehobeth, Del., 19971. (302) 227-2561. Cuisine: American. Owner: Carrie J. Deibler. Open April to October; Closed Tuesdays, except July & August. Credit cards: All major. Private party facilities: Up to 250. Annual sales: $500,000 to $1 million. Total employment: 100.

REHOBETH BEACH

KELLEY'S....112 Rehobeth Ave., Rehobeth, Del., 19971. (302) 227-7655. Cuisine: Seafood and Ribs. Owners: Tom and Donna Stone. Open 7 days for lunch and dinner. Credit cards: VISA. MC. Private party facilities: Up to 250. Annual sales: $250,000 to $500,000. Total employment: 50.

FLORIDA

BAL HARBOUR

COCONUTS....9449 Collins Ave., Surfside/Bal Halbour, Fla., 33154. (305) 865-3551. Cuisine: Continental. Open 7 days for dinner only. Credit cards: Call for cards. Reservations: Accepted. Entertainment: Live entertainment nightly in "Coconuts Lounge."

TIBERIO....9700 Collins Ave., Bal Harbor, Fla., 33154. (305) 861-6161. or 1-800-TIBERIO. Cuisine: Italian. Owner: Giulio Santillo. Open 7 days for lunch and dinner. Credit cards: All major. Private party facilities: 10 to 70. Annual sales: Over $3 million. Total employment: 38. Corporate name: Tiberio, Inc.

BAY HARBOR ISLAND

LA BELLE EPOCH....1045 95th St., Bay Harbor Island, Fla., 33150. (305) 865-6011. French food cooked by a French chef in an elegant French setting—a meeting place for the rich, the famous, and the discerning (alas, in that order). There is a fundamental simplicity in the subtly finished articles which emerge from this kitchen which takes the cooking out of the general top-flight restaurant class into that of the grand private kitchen. Specialties include: filet of sole *Bretonne*, Maine lobster broiled with a *buerre blanc* sauce, beef *bourguinon*, and several fine veal dishes. Owner: Denis Rety. Open 7 days for dinner. Priced moderate to high. Accepting credit cards and reservations. Corporate name: La Belle Epoque, Inc.

BOCA RATON

THE ABBEY ROAD....5798 North Federal Hwy., Boca Raton, Fla., 33432. (305) 997-6900. Cuisine: Steak/Seafood. Owner: Robert C. Scofield, Alan Andrzejewski, Sam H. Schernekau. Charles Faremouth, and Wellington Bonsecours. Open 7 days for dinner; Sunday brunch. Credit cards : AE, MC, VISA. Private party facilities: 10 to 25. Annual sales: Over $3 million (3 restaurants). Corporate name: Abbey Road Enterprises.

AUBERGE LE GRILLON....6900 North Federal Hwy., Boca Raton, Fla., 33431. (305) 997-6888. Cuisine: French. Owner: Harm Meijer & Malcolm R. Miller. Open 7 days for dinner. Credit cards: MC, VISA. Private party facilities: 15 to 25. Annual sales: $250,000 to $500,000. Total employment: 10. Corporate name: Auberge Le Grillon, Inc.

CAPTAIN'S CABIN....6298 North Federal Hwy., Boca Raton, Fla., 33431. (305) 392-6314. Cuisine: American. Open daily for lunch and dinner. Credit cards: AE, MC, VISA.

CHEZ MARCEL....21212 St. Andrew's Blvd., Boca Raton, Fla., 33434. (305) 391-6676. Cuisine: French. Open daily for dinner only. Credit cards: AE, MC, VISA.

CORK 'N CLEAVER....2300 Executive Center Dr. NW, Boca Raton, Fla., 33432. (305) 944-1255. Cuisine: American. Open daily for lunch and dinner. Credit cards: AE, MC, VISA.

EBB TIDE....5910 North Federal Hwy., Boca Raton, Fla., 33431. (305) 997-6600. Cuisine: American. Open daily for dinner only. Credit cards: MC, AE, VISA.

FIREHOUSE....6751 North Federal Hwy., Boca Raton, Fla., 33431. (305) 368-6006. Cuisine: American. Open daily for dinner only. Credit cards: MC, VISA.

GEPETTO'S TALE OF THE WHALE....3400 North Federal Hwy., Boca Raton, Fla., 33431. (305) 392-3400. Cuisine: American. Open daily for dinner only. Credit cards: MC, VISA.

GIORGIO'S....200 West Camino Real, Boca Raton, Fla., 33432. (305) 368-3292. Cuisine: Italian. Open 7 days for dinner only. Credit cards: MC, VISA.

JASONS....1499 West Palmetto Park Rd., Boca Raton, Fla., 33432. (305) 368-3404. Cuisine: Continental. Ope 6 days for lunch and dinner; Closed Sunday. Credit cards: All major.

JOE MUER SEAFOOD....6450 North Federal Hwy., Boca Raton, Fla., 33432. (305) 997-6688. Cuisine: Seafood. Owner: William, Thomas, and Joe Muer. Open 7 days; closed Monday from May to December. Credit cards: AE, MC, VISA. Annual sales: $1 million to $3 million. Total employment: 70. Corporate name: Muer's Oyster House, Inc.

LA SOUPIERE....515 NE 20th St., Boca Raton, Fla., 33431. (305) 395-5553. Cuisine: French. Open 7 days for lunch and dinner. Credit cards: AE, MC, VISA.

LA VIEILLE MAISON....770 East Palmetto Park Rd., Boca Raton, Fla., 33432. (305) 391-6701. Cuisine: French. Open 7 days for dinner only. Credit cards: All major. "Mobil 5-star rating."

L'HEXAGONE....1600 North Federal Hwy., Boca Raton, Fla., 33432. (305) 391-7200. Cuisine: French. Open daily for dinner only. Credit cards: MC, VISA.

NATALE'S PORTS OF CALL....145 Golfview Dr., Boca Raton, Fla., 33432. (305) 368-0903. Cuisine: Italian. Open daily for lunch and dinner. Credit cards: AE, MC, VISA.

NIGHT TRAIN....2200 West Glade Rd., Boca Raton, Fla., 33431. (305) 395-8700. Cuisine: American. Open Thursday through Saturday for dinner only. Credit cards: MC, VISA.

OXLEY'S....6300 Clint Moore Rd., Boca Raton, Fla., 33434. (305) 944-1883. Cuisine: American. Open daily for lunch and dinner. Credit cards: AE, VISA.

RIZZO'S....5990 North Federal Hwy., Boca Raton, Fla., 33431. (305) 997-8080. Cuisine: Italian. Open daily for lunch and dinner. Credit cards: AE, DC, MC, VISA.

STREB'S SOUTH RESTAURANT....1450 North Federal Hwy., Boca Raton, Fla., 33432. (305) 395-9496. This has become an old standby, one of the harbors of good eating amidst the assorted forgetable non-wonderspots of Florida's Gold Coast. A bouncy, cheerful place, it can be classified as about halfway between New England cuisine and an American steak-and-lobster house. Specialties include: New York sirloin, Maine Lobster, swordfish steak, and Alaskan king crab. Owner: Robert J.McCombs, Peter A. Eaffaldano. Open 7 days. Moderately priced. Reservations are accepted. Credit Cards: AE, MC, VISA. Private party facilities: 25 to 75. Annual sales: $1 million to $3 million. Total employment: 140. Corporate name: Streb's South, Inc.

TOP OF THE BRIDGE RESTAURANT & SUPPER CLUB....999 East Camino Real, Boca Raton, Fla., 33432. (305) 368-9500. Cuisine: Continental. Open October through June; Closed Mondays. Credit cards: AE, MC, VISA. Private party facilities: Up to 250. Annual sales: $500,000 to $1 million. Total employment: 100. Corporate name: Boca Real Corp.

VILLA VENEZIA....4135 North Federal Hwy., Boca Raton, Fla., 33431. (305) 392-5396. Cuisine: Italian. Open daily for lunch and dinner. Credit cards: MC, VISA.

BOYNTON BEACH

BERNARD'S....1730 North Federal Hwy., Boynton Beach, Fla., 33435. (305) 737-2236. Cuisine: Continental. Open daily for lunch and dinner. Credit cards: AE, MC, VISA.

GENTLEMAN JIM'S....2404 South Federal Hwy., Boynton Beach, Fla., 33435. (305) 734-2244. Cuisine: Continental. Open 7 days for lunch and dinner. Credit cards: All major.

STREBS III....2320 South Federal Hwy., Boynton Beach, Fla., 33435. (305) 272-2772. Cuisine: Continental. Owner: Peter A. Eaffaldano, Robert J. McCombs. Open 7 days for lunch and dinner. Credit cards: All major. Annual sales: $500,000 to $1 million.

VINTAGE....715 South Federal Hwy., Boynton Beach, Fla., 33435. (305) 732-1900. Cuisine: Continental. Open daily for lunch and dinner. Credit cards: AE, MC, VISA.

CLEARWATER

BAUMGARDNER'S....924 McMullen-Booth Rd., Clearwater, Fla., 33519. (813) 726-3312. Cuisine: Continental/American. Open for dinner Tuesday through Sunday; Open for lunch Sunday and seasonal; Closed Monday from May to December. Credit cards: All major. Private party facilities: Up to 250. Annual sales: $500,000 to $1 million. Total employment: 40. Corporate name: Kapok Tree Inns Corporation.

BENTLEY'S....2516 North McMullen-Booth Rd., Clearwater, Fla., 33519. (813) 797-1177. Cuisine: Continental. Open 7 days for lunch and dinner. Credit cards: All major. Reservations: Accepted. Proper attire requred.

CALICO JACK'S ON-THE-BEACH....430 South Gulfview Blvd., Clearwater, Fla., 33515. (813) 443-5714. Cuisine: Continental. Open for breakfast, lunch, and dinner daily; Sunday brunch. Credit cards: All major

CASA JUANITA MEXICAN RESTAURANT....2284 Gulf-to-Bay Blvd., Clearwater, Fla., 33515. (813) 446-4191. Cuisine: Mexican. Open Monday through Friday for lunch; Monday through Saturday for dinner; Closed Sunday. Credit cards: AE, DC, MC, VISA. Reservations: Accepted. Entertainment: Live entertainment Thursday through Sunday.

CHI CHIS....2630 Gulf-to-Bay Blvd., Clearwater, Fla., 33519. (813) 752-5581. Cuisine: Mexican. Open 7 days for lunch and dinner. Credit cards: AE, DC, MC, VISA.

DAVIDSON'S....2560 U.S. Hwy. 19 North, Clearwater, Fla., 33515. (813) 796-8806. Cuisine: Continental. Open 7 days for dinner only. Credit cards: AE, MC, VISA. Reservations: Accepted.

HELLMAN'S BEACHCOMBER....447 Mandalay Ave., Clearwater, Fla., 33515. (813) 442-4144. Cuisine: Seafood. Credit cards: AE, DC, MC, VISA.

THE KAPOK TREE INN....923 McMullen-Booth Rd., Clearwater, Fla., 33519. (813) 726-4734. Cuisine: American. Owner: June E. Baumgartner. Open 7 days for lunch and dinner. Credit cards: All major. Private party facilities: Up to 1000. Annual sales: Over $3 million. Total employment: 125. Corporate name: Kapok Tree Inns Corporation.

OTTAVIO'S PALACE....45 North Fort Harrison Ave., Clearwater, Fla., 33515. (813) 442-6659. Cuisine: Italian/Continental. Open 6 days for dinner only; Closed Sunday. Credit cards: MC, VISA.

PANDA....1201 Cleveland St., Clearwater, Fla., 33515. (813) 447-3830. Cuisine: Northern Chinese. Open Monday through Saturday for lunch; 7 days for dinner. Credit cards: MC, VISA.

PEKING PALACE....1608 Gulf-to-Bay Blvd., Clearwater, Fla., 33515. (813) 471-4414. Cuisine: Mandarin, Szechuan, Hunan, and Cantonese Chinese. Open Monday through Friday for lunch; Monday through Saturday for dinner; Sunday dinner from noon. Credit cards: AE, MC, VISA. Reservations: Suggested.

PELICAN....470 Mandalay Ave., Clearwater, Fla., 33515. (813) 442-3151. Cuisine: International. Open 7 days for lunch and dinner. Credit cards: AE, DC, MC, VISA. Reservations: Recommended.

SIPLE'S GARDEN SEAT....1234 Druid Rd., Clearwater, Fla., 33516. (813) 442-9681. Cuisine: American. Owner: Richard Siple. Open 7 days for lunch and dinner; Sunday brunch. Credit cards: All major. Annual sales: $1 million to $3 million. Total employment: 80.

SWANSON'S....2325 Ulmerton Rd., Clearwater, Fla., 33520. (813) 576-4371. Cuisine: "Homemade European." Open Monday through Friday for lunch; Monday through Saturday for dinner; Closed Sunday. Credit cards: AE, MC, VISA. Reservations: Suggested.

TALK OF THE TOWN....1260 U.S. Hwy. 19, Clearwater, Fla., 33515. (813) 535-1934. Cuisine: Steak/Seafood. Open 7 days for lunch and dinner. Credit cards: AE, MC, VISA.

TIO PEPE....2930 Gulf-To-Bay Blvd., Clearwater, Fla., 33519. (813) 725-3082. Cuisine: Spanish. Owner: Jose Rodrigez. Credit cards: MC, VISA.

CLEARWATER BEACH

GIDEOS....435 Mandalay Ave., Clearwater Beach, Fla., 33515. (813) 443-3169. Cuisine: Sicilian. Open 7 days for lunch and dinner. Credit cards: VISA only.

COCONUT GROVE

ANGELA'S CAFE....3484 Main Hwy., Coconut Grove, Fla., 33133. (305) 444-1735. Cuisine: Italian/French. Open 7 days for lunch and dinner. Credit cards: AE, MC, VISA.

BUCCIONE'S....2833 Bird Ave., Coconut Grove, Fla., 33133. (305) 444-4222. Cuisine: Italian. Open 6 days for dinner only; Closed Monday. Credit cards: All major.

CAFE EUROPA....3157 Commodore Plz., Coconut Grove, Fla., 33133. (305) 448-5723. Cuisine: French. Days closed: Open 7 days. Credit cards: AE,MC,VISA.

GINGER MAN....3390 Mary St., Coconut Grove, Fla., 33133. (305) 448-9919. Open daily for lunch and dinner; Sunday brunch. Credit cards: All major. Entertainment: Live jazz quartet nightly.

HORATIO'S....2649 Bayshore Dr., Coconut Grove, Fla., 33133. (305) 856-2500. Cuisine: American/Seafood. Open Monday through for dinner only. Credit cards: All major. Reservations: Accepted.

JP'S AT DINNER KEY....3360 Pan American Dr., Coconut Grove, Fla., 33133. (305) 858-7510. Cuisine: Continental. Open 7 days. Credit cards: AE, DC, MC, VISA.

KALEIDOSCOPE....3112 Commodore Plz., Coconut Grove, Fla., 33133. (305) 466-5010. Cuisine Continental. Open 7 days. Credit cards: AE, MC, VISA. AE, MC, VISA.

MAGIC PAN....Mayfair, 3390 Mary St., Coconut Grove, Fla., 33133, (305) 448-8420. Cuisine: Crepes. Open 7 days. Credit cards: AE, MC, VISA.

MAIN LOBSTER....3480 Main Hwy., Coconut Grove, Fla., 33133. (305) 446-4335. Cuisine: Seafood. Open nightly for dinner only. Credit cards: AE, MC, VISA.

MONTY TRAINER'S BAYSHORE....2560 South Bayshore Dr., Coconut Grove, Fla., 33133. (305) 858-1431. Cuisine: Seafood. Open Monday through Friday for lunch; 7 days for dinner; Saturday and Sunday for breakfast. Credit cards: All major. Entertainment: Calypso/Jazz bands alternate.

PRONTO RISTORANTE....3390 Mary St., Coconut Grove, Fla., 33133. (305) 446-3798. Cuisine: Italian. Open daily for lunch and dinner. Credit cards: AE, DC, MC, VISA.

TAURUS STEAK HOUSE....3450 Main Hwy., Coconut Grove, Fla., 33101. (305) 448-0633. Open Monday through Friday for dinner; 7 days for dinner. Credit cards: All major. Entertainment: "Mellow rock combo" on Friday and Saturday.

VILLAGE INN....3131 Commodore Plz., Coconut Grove, Fla. 33133. (305) 445-8721. Cuisine: American. Days closed: Open 7 days. Credit cards: All major.

CORAL GABLES

THE ALLEY....3875 Shipping Ave., Coral Gables, Fla., 33146. (305) 448-4880. Cuisine: American. Days closed: Sunday. Credit cards: AE, DC, MC, VISA.

BILTMORE....1201 Anastasia Ave. (in the Metropolitan Museum bldg.), Coral Gables, Fla., 33134. (305) 447-1556. Cuisine: American. Days closed: Monday. Credit cards: All major.

THE BISTRO....2611 Ponce de Leon Blvd., Coral Gables, Fla., 33134. (305) 442-9671. Cuisine: Continental. Open 7 days. Credit cards: CB, DC, MC, VISA.

CHARADE....2900 Ponce de Leon Blvd., Coral Gables, Fla., 33134. (305) 448-6077. Cuisine: Continental. Open Monday through Friday for lunch; 7 days for dinner; Sunday brunch. Credit cards: AE, MC, VISA.

CHEZ MAURICE....382 Miracle Mile, Coral Gables, Fla., 33134. (305) 448-8984. Cuisine: French. Open Monday through Saturday for lunch and dinner. Credit cards: CB, MC, VISA.

CHEZ VENDOME....David William Hotel, 700 Biltmore Way, Coral Gables, Fla., 33134. (305) 443-4646. Cuisine: French. Open Monday through Saturday for lunch; 7 days for dinner. Credit cards: All major.

CHRISTY'S....3101 Ponce de Leon Blvd., Coral Gables, Fla., 33134. (305) 446-1400. Cuisine: Steakhouse. Open Monday through Friday for lunch; 7 days for dinner; Sunday brunch. Credit cards: All major.

EL CID....11 NW Le Jeune Rd., Coral Gables, Fla., 33126. (305) 541-3514. Cuisine: Spanish. Open 7 days for lunch and dinner. Credit cards: All major. Reservations: Accepted.

THE FRENCH CONNECTION....219 Palermo Ave., Coral Gables, Fla., 33134. (305) 442-9374. Cuisine: French. Open Monday through Friday for lunch; 7 days for dinner. Credit cards: All major.

GREENSTREETS....2051 SW 42 Ave., Coral Gables, Fla., 33134. (305) 445-2131. Cuisine: American. Open daily for dinner only. Credit cards: AE, DC, MC, VISA.

HOUSE OF INDIA....22 Merrick Way, Coral Gables, Fla., 33134. (305) 444-2348. Cuisine: Indian. Open Monday through Saturday for lunch; 7 days for dinner. Credit cards: All major. Sitar music.

K.C. CAGNEY'S....2121 Ponce de Leon Blvd., Coral Gables, Fla., 33134. (305) 442-1997. Cuisine: American. Open 7 days for lunch and dinner. No credit cards.

LE FESTIVAL....2120 Salzedo St., Coral Gables, Fla., 33134. (305) 442-8545. Cuisine: French. Owner: Jean-Paul Robin & Jacques Bauclean. Open Monday through Friday for lunch; Monday through Saturday for dinner; Closed Sunday. Credit cards: AE, MC, VISA. Annual Sales: $500,000 to $1 million. Total employment: 25. Corporate name: Le Festival, Inc.

LE MANOIR....2534 Ponce de Leon Blvd., Coral Gables, Fla., 33134. (305) 442-1990. Cuisine: French. Open Monday through Friday for lunch; Monday through Saturday for dinner; Closed Sunday. Credit cards: All major.

MELODY INN....108 Aragon Ave., Coral Gables, Fla., 33134. (305) 448-0022. Cuisine: Swiss and French. Open 7 days. Credit cards: major. Owner: Hans Burri.

PAINTED BIRD....65 Merrick Way, Coral Gables, Fla., 33134. (305) 445-1200. Cuisine: Continental. Days closed: Sunday. Credit cards: All major.

PICKFORD'S....394 Giralda Ave., Coral Gables, Fla., 33134. (305) 443-4376. Cuisine: American. Open Monday through Friday for lunch; Wednesday through Sunday for dinner. Credit cards: AE, DC, MC, VISA.

RAIMONDO'S RESTAURANT....4612 Le Jeune Road, Coral Gables, Fla., 331346. (305) 666-9919. One of Miami's most distinguished Northern-Italian restaurants in a charming, casual setting. Run by owner-chef Raimondo and his wife Jule, and worth a special pilgrimage. A vein of old family traditional cooking characterizes the cuisine. Fastidious attention to smallest details. Grist for gourmets: *canneloni Excelsior* (a crepe stuffed with veal, spinach and cheese), and *zuppa di pesce* (seafood in a rich broth that is unforgettable). An endless choice of outstanding wines may be had and cocktails are expertly bartendered. Owner: Raimondo and Jule Laudisio. Open 7 days for dinner only. Price: Expensive. Reservations: Suggested. Credit cards: AE, DC. Annual sales: $500,000 to $1 million. Total employment: 25. Corporate name: Ray-Jule, Inc.

RALPH'S AMERICAN CAFE....148 Giralda Ave., Coral Gables, Fla., 33134. (305) 446-9551. Cuisine: American. Open Monday through Friday for lunch; Monday through Saturday for dinner; Closed Sunday. No credit cards.

RESTAURANT ST. MICHEL....2135 Ponce de Leon Blvd., Coral Gables, Fla., 33134. (305) 446-6572. Cuisine: French. Open 7 days. Credit cards: All major.

ROUND TABLE....1320 South Dixie Hwy., Coral Gables, Fla., 33198. (305) 665-6505. Cuisine: American. Open 7 days for lunch and dinner. Credit cards: All major.

700 CLUB....700 Biltmore Way, Coral Gables, Fla., 33134. (305) 445-7821. Cuisine: Continental. Open Monday through Friday for lunch; 7 days for dinner. Credit cards: All major. "Located in the David William Hotel penthouse."

SPIRAL RESTAURANT....1630 Ponce de Leon Blvd., Coral Gables, Fla., 33134. (305) 446-1591. Cuisine: Natural foods. Owner: Jerry Goldschein. Open Monday through Friday for lunch; 7 days for dinner. Credit cards: MC, VISA. Annual Sales: $250,000 to $500,000. Total employment: 20. Corporate name: J&A Restaurant Corporation.

TASTE OF INDIA....1930 Ponce de Leon Blvd., Coral Gables, Fla., 33134. (305) 445-0595. Cuisine: Indian. Open Monday through Friday for lunch; 7 days for dinner. Credit cards: Call for cards. Reservations: Suggested.

TIGER'S....303 Aragon Ave., Coral Gables, Fla., 33134. (305) 446-9839. Cuisine: American. Open 6 days for breakfast, lunch, and dinner; Closed Sunday. Credit cards: No credit cards. No alcohlic beverages.

TONY ROMA'S....6601 South Dixie Hwy., Coral Gables, Fla., 32905. (305) 667-4806. Cuisine: American. Open 7 days for lunch and dinner. Credit cards: MC, VISA.

VINTON'S....116 Alhambra Circle, Coral Gables, Fla., 33134. (305) 445-2511. Cuisine: Continental. Open Monday through Friday for lunch; Monday through Saturday for dinner; Closed Sunday. Credit cards: AE, DC, MC, VISA. "Special gourmet dining every Monday night."

WHIFFENPOOF....2728 Ponce de Leon Blvd., Coral Gables, Fla., 33134. (305) 445-6603. Cuisine: French. Open Tuesday through Friday for lunch; Tuesday through Saturday for dinner; Closed Sunday and Monday. Credit cards: AE, DC, MC, VISA.

ZACHERY'S....3848 Shipping Ave., Coral Gables, Fla., 33146. (305) 447-1004. Cuisine: American. Open daily for lunch and dinner. Credit cards: AE, MC, VISA. Entertainment: Disc jockey nightly.

CORAL PARK

FUNG WONG OF CHICAGO....9796 SW 8th St., Coral Park, Fla., 33174. (305) 226-8032. Cuisine: Mandarin & Cantonese Chinese. Credit cards: Call for cards. Open 7 days.

DANIA

CLUBHOUSE RESTAURANT....(at Dania Jai-Lai), 301 East Dania Beach Blvd., Dania, Fla., 33004. (305) 945-4345. Open Monday through Thursday for "Early Bird" dinner special; 7 days for regular dinner. Credit cards: Call for cards. Reservations: Requested.

LA CREPE DE BRETAGNE....1434 North Federal Hwy., Dania, Fla., 33004. (305) 927-4100. Cuisine: Crepes. Days closed: Sunday. Credit cards: AE, MC, VISA.

LE CORDON BLEU....1201 North Federal Hwy., Dania, Fla., 33004. (305) 922-3519. Cuisine: French. Open 7 days for dinner and pre-theater dinner; Closed from end of May to Thanksgiving. Credit cards: AE, DC, MC, VISA. Reservations: Suggested.

NEVER ON SUNDAY/CHEZ TON TON....129 North Federal Hwy., Dania, Fla., 33004. (305) 921-5557. Cuisine: Continental. Days closed: Sunday. Credit cards: All major.

TOBLER'S SWISS RESTAURANT....1605 North Federal Hwy., Dania, Fla., 33004. (305) 922-1819. Cuisine: Swiss. Open Monday through Friday for lunch; 7 days for dinner. Credit cards: AE, CB, MC, VISA.

DAVIE

HO-TOI....8270 Griffin Rd., Davie, Fla., 33314. (305) 434-4897. Cuisine: Chinese. Open daily for dinner. Credit cards: MC, VISA.

DAYTONA BEACH

CHEZ BRUCHEZ....304 Seabreeze Blvd., Daytona Beach, Fla., 32018. (904) 252-6656. Cuisine: French. Credit cards: All major.

KAY'S COACH HOUSE....734 Main St., Daytona Beach, Fla., 32018. (904) 253-1944. Cuisine: Continental. Credit cards: AE, DC, MC, VISA.

DEERFIELD BEACH

BROOK'S....500 South Federal Hwy., Deerfield Beach, Fla., 33441. (305) 427-9302. Cuisine: French/Continental. Open 7 days. Credit cards: MC, VISA.

THE CAPTAIN'S TABLE.... Cove Yacht Basin, Deerfield Beach, Fla., 33441. (305) 427-4000. Cuisine: American. Owner: Bert T. Laaks. Open 7 days. Credit cards: AE, MC, VISA. Private party facilities: 35 to 200. Annual sales: Over $3 million. Total employment: 150. Corporate name: National Food Services, Inc.

CARAFIELLO'S....949 South Federal Hwy., Deerfield Beach, Fla., 33441. (305) 421-2481. Cuisine: Italian. Open daily for lunch and dinner. Credit cards: MC, VISA.

THE COVE.... Hillsboro Blvd. and Intracoastal Waterway, Deerfield Beach, Fla., 33441. (305) 421-9272. Cuisine: American. Open daily for lunch and dinner. Credit cards: MC, VISA.

HENRY'S....201 SE 15th Terrace, Deerfield Beach, Fla., 33441. (305) 426-4166. Cuisine: American. Open daily for lunch and dinner. Credit cards: AE, MC, VISA.

THE LOBSTER TRAP....2020 NE Second St., Deerfield Beach, Fla., 33441. (305) 426-0035. Cuisine: Seafood. Open daily for dinner only. Credit cards: MC, VISA.

SEAFOOD SHANTY....1025 East Hillsboro Blvd., Deerfield Beach, Fla., 33441. (305) 428-9607. Cuisine: Seafood. Open daily for dinner only. Credit cards: MC, VISA.

THE RIVERVIEW ROULETTE.... East Riverview Rd., Deerfield Beach, Fla., 33441. (305) 428-3468. Cuisine: Regional plus Western Beef. Open 7 days. Credit cards: All major.

DELRAY BEACH

COCHRAN'S....307 East Atlantic Ave., Delray Beach, Fla., 33444. (305) 278-7666. Cuisine: American. Open daily for lunch and dinner. Credit cards: AE, MC, VISA.

PAOLETTI'S....815 North Federal Hwy., Delray Beach, Fla., 33444. (305) 272-2988. Cuisine: Italian. Open daily for lunch and dinner. Credit cards: MC, VISA.

PATIO DELRAY....714 East Atlantic Ave., Delray Beach, Fla., 33444. (305) 276-7126. Cuisine: American. Open daily for lunch and dinner. Credit cards: AE, MC, VISA.

VITTORIO....25 SE Sixth Ave., Delray Beach, Fla., 33444. (305) 278-5525. Cuisine: Italian. Open daily for dinner only. Credit cards: Call for cards.

DUNEDIN

BON APPETIT....148 Marina Plz., Dunedin, Fla., 33528. (813) 733-2151. Cuisine: Continental. Credit cards: MC, VISA.

LE COTE D'AZUR FRENCH RESTAURANT....1143 Main St., Dunedin, Fla., 33528. (813) 734-2620. Cuisine: French. Owner: Emile and Beatrice Sebban. Open 7 days. Credit cards: All major. Private party facilities: 90. Annual sales: $250,000 to $500,000. Total employment: 8.

FORT LAUDERDALE

AKI-SAN....1015 SE 17th St., Fort Lauderdale, Fla., 33316. (305) 522-0257. Cuisine: Japanese. Open daily for lunch and dinner. Credit cards: AE, MC, VISA.

ALASKAN KING....91 NE 44th St., Fort Lauderdale, Fla., 33334. (305) 776-1616. Cuisine: Seafood. Open daily for dinner only. Credit cards: MC, VISA.

AMBRY....3016 East Commercial Blvd., Fort Lauderdale, Fla., 33308. (305) 771-7342. cuisine: Steakhouse. Open daily for lunch and dinner. Credit cards: AE, MC, VISA.

AMERICO'S....2222 North Ocean Blvd., Fort Lauderdale, Fla., 33305. (305) 563-4351. Cuisine: Italian. Open daily from 5:00 PM. Credit cards: All major. Reservations: Accepted.

BENIHANA OF TOKYO....4343 West Tradewinds Ave., Ft. Lauderdale, Fla., 33308 (305) 776-0111. Cuisine: Japanese. Open 7 days. Credit cards: AE, MC, VISA.

BOBBY RUBINO'S PLACE FOR RIBS....4100 North Fedral Hwy., Fort Lauderdale, Fla., 33308. (305) 561-5305. Cuisine: American (Ribs). Open 7 days for lunch and dinner. Credit cards: AE, MC, VISA.

BOBBY RUBINO'S PLACE FOR RIBS....1450 17th St. Causeway, Fort Lauderdale, Fla., 33316. (305) 522-3006. Cuisine: American (Ribs). Open 7 days for lunch and dinner. Credit cards: AE, MC, VISA.

BOMBAY INDIAN....199 East Oakand Park Blvd., Fort Lauderdale, Fla., 33334. (305) 561-9165. Open 7 days for dinner only. Credit cards: AE, DC, MC, VISA.

BRAUHAUS....1701 East Sunrise Blvd., Fort Lauderdale, Fla., 33304. (305) 764-4104. Cuisine: German. Owner: Michael and Maria Steinberger and Peter Schubert. Open Tuesday through Sunday. Credit cards: AE, MC, VISA. Private party facilities: Up to 75. Annual sales: $500,000 to $1 million. Total employment: 30. Corporate name: Theresa Investments, Inc.

BRICKYARD....1608 East Commercial Blvd., Fort Lauderdale, Fla., 33308. (305) 761-5305. Cuisine: American. Open daily for lunch and dinner. Credit cards: AE, MC, VISA. Entertainment: Live dinner shows nightly.

BUBBA'S JAZZ RESTAURANT....1624 East Sunrise Blvd., Fort Lauderdale, Fla., 33304. (305) 764-2388. Cuisine: American. Open 6 days for lunch and dinner; Closed Monday. Credit cards: All major.

BUSHWACKER....2428 East Commercial Blvd., Fort Lauderdale, Fla., 33308. (305) 772-2850. Cuisine: American. Open 7 days. Credit cards: AE, MC, VISA.

CAFE DE GENEVE....1519 South Andrews Ave., Fort Lauderdale, Fla., 33301. (305) 522-8928. Cuisine: Swiss. Open daily for lunch and dinner. Credit cards: All major.

CAFE DU BEAUJOLAIS....3134 NE Ninth St., Fort Lauderdale, Fla., 33334. (305) 566-1416. Cuisine: French. Days closed: Sunday. Credit cards: All major.

CAFE MARTINIQUE....2851 North Federal Hwy., Fort Lauderdale, Fla., 33306. (305) 566-6108. Cuisine: Continental. Open 7 days. Credit cards: AE, MC, VISA.

CAPTAIN PERRY'S SEA CHEST....2750 Giffin Rd., Fort Lauderdale, Fla., 33312. (305) 987-1971. Cuisine: Seafood. Open daily for dinner only. Credit cards: AE, MC, VISA.

CARLOS AND PEPE'S....1302 SE 17th St., Fort Lauderdale, Fla., 33316. (305) 467-8335. Cuisine: Mexican. Open daily for lunch and dinner. Credit cards: AE, MC, VISA.

CASA DE LUCA....4331 Ocean Dr., Fort Lauderdale, Fla., 33308. (305) 491-1100. Cuisine: Italian. Open daily for dinner only. Credit cards: MC, VISA.

CASA VECCHIA....209 North Birch Rd., Fort Lauderdale, Fla., 33304. (305) 463-7575. Cuisine: Italian. Open daily for dinner only. Credit cards: AE, VISA.

THE CAVES RESTAURANT....2205 North Federal Hwy., Ft. Lauderdale, Fla., 33305. (305) 561-4622. Cuisine: Continental. Owner: Saul & Jackie Hochman. Open 7 days. Credit cards: AE, MC, VISA. Private party facilities: Up to 12. Annual sales: $500,000 to $1 million. Total employment: 40. Corporate name: The Caves Restaurant, Inc.

CHI CHI'S....6500 North Federal Hwy., Fort Lauderdale, Fla., 33308. (305) 771-4622. Open 7 days for lunch and dinner. Credit cards: AE, DC, MC, VISA.

CHRISTINE LEE'S NORTHGATE....6191 Rock Island Rd., Fort Lauderdale, Fla., 33319. (305) 726-0430. Cuisine: Chinese. Open daily for dinner only. Credit cards: AE, DC, MC, VISA. "Probably the best in Broward."

CHUCK'S STEAK HOUSE....1207 SE 17th St., Fort Lauderdale, Fla., 33316. (305) 764-3333. Cuisine: Steak/Seafood/American. Open Monday through Friday for lunch; 7 days for dinner. Credit cards: AE, DC, MC, VISA. Reservations: Accepted. Entertainment: Live entertainment nightly from 9:00 PM.

CLAUDIA'S....2980 North Federal Hwy., Fort Lauderdale, Fla., 33306. (305) 563-1840. Cuisine: Continental. Closed Monday and Sunday. Credit cards: AE.

CRAB POT....4361 North Dixie Hwy., Fort Lauderdale, Fla., 33334. (305) 563-7938. Cuisine: Seafood. Open daily for dinner only. Credit cards: MC, VISA.

CRAB SHANTY....2960 North Federal Hwy., Ford Lauderdale, Fla., 33306. (305) 564-4522. Cuisine: Seafood. Open for lunch and dinner. Credit cards: AE, MC, VISA.

DANTE'S....2871 North Federal Hwy., Fort Lauderdale, Fla., 33306. (305) 564-6666. Cuisine: Continental. Days closed: Open 7 days. Credit cards: AE, MC, VISA.

DON ARTURO....1198 Riverland Rd., Fort Lauderdale, Fla., 33312. (305) 584-7966. Cuisine: Spanish/Cuban. Open daily for lunch and dinner. Credit cards: None.

THE DOWN UNDER....3000 East Oakland Park Blvd., Ft. Lauderdale, Fla., 33306. (305) 563-4123. Cuisine: Continental. Days closed: Open 7 days. Credit cards: All major.

EDUARDO'S....2400 East Las Olas, Fort Lauderdale, Fla., 33301. (305) 467-2400. Cuisine: Continental. Open 7 days. Credit cards: All major.

ERNIE'S....1843 South Federal Hwy., Fort Lauderdale, Fla., 33316. (305) 523-8636. Cuisine: American. Open daily for lunch, dinner, and late supper. Credit cards: Call for cards.

15TH STREET FISHERIES....1900 SE 15th St., Fort Lauderdale, Fla., 33316. (305) 763-2777. Cuisine: Seafood. Open daily for dinner; Sunday lunch. Credit cards: AE, MC, VISA.

THE FISHERMAN....3880 North Federal Hwy., Fort Lauderdale, Fla., 33308. (305) 566-1695. Cuisine: Seafood. Open daily for dinner only. Credit cards: AE, MC, VISA.

FORBIDDEN CITY....3060 West Oakland Park Blvd., Fort Lauderdale, Fla., 33311. (305) 485-7777. Cuisine: Chinese. Open daily for lunch and dinner. Credit cards: AE, MC, VISA.

FRANKIE'S....3333 NE 32nd Ave., Fort Lauderdale, Fla., 33309. (305) 566-7853. Cuisine: Continental. Open 7 days. Credit cards: All major.

FRENCH QUARTER....2195 SE Eighth Ave., Fort Lauderdale, Fla., 33301. (305) 463-8000. Cuisine: French. Open daily for dinner only. Credit cards: AE, MC, VISA.

THE GARDEN GREEN....620 East Las Olas Blvd., Fort Lauderdale, Fla., 33312. (305) 467-0671. Cuisine: American. Open daily for lunch and dinner. Credit cards: AE, MC, VISA.

GIBBY'S STEAKS & SEAFOOD....2900 Northeast 12 Ter., Fort Lauderdale, Fla., 33334. (305) 565-2929. Cuisine: Continental/Steak/Seafood. Owner: Donald, Eric and Steven Hersh. Open 7 days for lunch and dinner. Credit cards: All major. Private party facilities: 50 to 200. Annual sales: Over $3 million. Total employment: 140. Corporate name: Herco Holding Co.

THE GOLD RUSH....1630 East Oakland Park Blvd., Fort Lauderdale, Fla., 33334. (304) 566-1880. Cuisine: Steak/Seafood. Open 7 days for lunch and dinner. Credit cards: All major.

GOLDEN SPIKE.... Casey Jones Tavern, 6000 North Federal Hwy., Fort Lauderdale, Fla., 33308. (305) 491-6000. Cuisine: Steak/Seafood/American. Open Monday through Friday for lunch; 7 days for dinner; Sunday brunch. Credit cards: AE, MC, VISA.

HARRISON'S ON THE WATER....3000 NE 32nd Ave., Fort Lauderdale, Fla., 33309. (305) 566-9667. Cuisine: Continental. Days closed: Open 7 days. Credit cards: MC, VISA.

HELMAN'S BRAUHAUS....1701 East Sunrise Blvd., Fort Lauderdale, Fla., 33304. (305) 764-4103. Cuisine: Bavarian. Open Monday through Friday for lunch; 7 days for dinner. Credit cards: All major. Entertainment: Nightly Wednesday through Sunday.

HENRY'S CHINA HOUSE....2600 South Federal Hwy., Fort Lauderdale, Fla., 33316. (305) 763-3333. Cuisine: Mandarin, Cantonese, and Szechuan Chinese. Open Monday through Friday for lunch; 7 days for dinner; Late supper 7 days. Credit cards: All major.

HOULIHAN'S OLD PLACE.... Broward Mall, Fort Lauderdale, Fla., 33310. (305) 473-5444. Cuisine: American. Open daily for lunch and dinner. Credit cards: AE, MC, VISA.

IL GIARDINO....609 East Las Olas Blvd., Ft. Lauderdale, Fla., 33301, (305) 763-3733. Cuisine: Italian. Open 7 days. Credit cards: AE, DC, MC, VISA.

IRELAND'S INN....2220 North Atlantic Blvd., Fort Lauderdale, Fla., 33305. (305) 564-2331. Cuisine: Continental. Open 7 days. Credit cards: All major.

JIMMY'S PRIME RIBS....1200 North Federal Hwy., Fort Lauderdale, Fla., 33304. (305) 564-9944. Open 7 days for lunch and dinner. Credit cards: Call for cards. Entertainment: Live entertainment nightly.

KONA KAI....17th St. Causeway, Fort Lauderdale, Fla., 33310. (305) 463-4000. Cuisine: Polynesian/Chinese. Open daily for dinner only. Credit cards: All major.

LA BONNE AUBERGE....4300 North Federal Hwy., Fort Lauderdale, Fla., 33308 . (305) 491-5522. Cuisine: French. Open 7 days. Credit cards: AE, DC, MC, VISA.

LA BONNE CREPE....815 East Las Olas Blvd., Fort Lauderdale, Fla., 33301. (305) 761-1515. Cuisine: French. Open 6 days for lunch and dinner; Closed Sunday. Credit cards: MC, VISA.

LA FERMA....1601 East Sunrise Blvd., Fort Lauderdale, Fla., 33304. (305) 764-0987. Cuisine: French. Days closed: Monday. Credit cards: AE, MC, VISA.

LA PERLA....1818 East Sunrise Blvd., Fort Lauderdale, Fla., 33304. (305) 765-1950. Cuisine: Italian. Open daily for dinner only. Credit cards: MC, VISA.

LA RESERVE....3115 NE 32nd Ave., Fort Lauderdale, Fla., 33309. (305) 563-6644. Cuisine: French. Open 7 days. Credit cards: AE, DC, MC, VISA.

LA REZZA....1506 East Commercial Blvd., Fort Lauderdale, Fla., 33334. (305) 491-1983. Cuisine: Italian. Open daily for dinner only. Credit cards: AE, MC, VISA.

LARRY'S CLAM HOUSE....5770 North Federal Hwy., Fort Lauderdale, Fla., 33308. (305) 776-6170. Cuisine: Seafood. Open daily for lunch and dinner. Credit cards: MC, VISA.

LE CAFE DE PARIS....715 East Las Olas Blvd., Fort Lauderdale, Fla., 33301. (305) 467-2900. Cuisine: French. Open Monday through Saturday for lunch; 7 days for dinner. Credit cards: AE, MC, VISA. Entertainment: Strolling musicians nightly. "Visit 'The French Quarter' raw bar."

LE CAFE DU BEAUJOLAIS....3134 Northeast 9 St., Fort Lauderdale, Fla., 33304. (305) 566-1416. Cuisine: French. Owner: Leon Teboul. Open 7 days. Credit cards: All major. Private party facilities: 4 to 45. Annual sales: $500,000 to $1 million. Corporate name: Le Cafe du Beaujolais, Inc.

LE DOME.... Top of Four Seasons, 333 Sunset Dr., Fort Lauderdale, Fla., 33301. (305) 463-3303. Cuisine: Continental. Days closed: Monday. Credit cards: AE, DC, MC, VISA.

THE LEFT BANK RESTAURANT....214 SE Sixth Ave., Fort Lauderdale, Fla., 33301. (305) 462-5376. Cuisine: French. Owner: Jean-Pierre Bremier. Open 7 days. Credit cards: All major. Private party facilities: 10 to 35. Annual sales: $500,000 to $1 million. Total employment: 21. Corporate name: Jean-Pierre, Inc.

LESTER'S....U.S. Route 1 (½-block South of Sears Town), Fort Lauderdale, Fla., 33310. (305) 763-9748. Cuisine: Supreme "custom-built" sandwiches. Call for times and credit cards.

LES TROIS MOUSQUETAIRES....2447 East Sunrise Blvd., Fort Lauderdale, Fla., 33304. (305) 564-7513. Cuisine: French. Credit cards: AE, DC, MC, VISA.

L'ILE-DE-FRANCE....3025 North Ocean Blvd., Fort Lauderdale, Fla., 33308. (305) 565-9006. Cuisine: French. Days closed: Sundays, May-October. Credit cards: MC, VISA.

LUIGI'S....563 West Oakland Park Blvd., Fort Lauderdale, Fla., 33311. (305) 561-3322. Cuisine: Italian. Open daily for dinner only. Credit cards: MC, VISA.

MAI-KAI....3599 North Federal Hwy., Fort Lauderdale, Fla., 33308. (305) 563-3272. Cuisine: Polynesian. Open 7 days for dinner only. Credit cards: Call for cards. Reservations: Suggested. Entertainment: Polynesian musical shows with dancing nightly, 7:30 PM, 10:30 PM, and Midnight. Drink and dinner specials different daily.

MA POMME....6451 North Federal Hwy., Fort Lauderdale, Fla., 33308. (305) 771-4353. Cuisine: Continental. Open daily for dinner only. Credit cards: All major.

MARIE'S....714 SE 17th St., Fort Lauderdale, Fla., 33316. (305) 462-6886. Cuisine: German. Open daily for dinner only. No credit cards.

MICHAEL'S BACKYARD....233 SE Fifth Ave., Fort Lauderdale, Fla., 33301. (305) 463-4627. Cuisine: Continental. Days closed: Sundays and holidays. Credit cards: AE, MC, VISA.

MR. LAFF'S....1135 North Federal Hwy., Fort Lauderdale, Fla., 33304. (305) 561-3400. Cuisine: American. Open daily for lunch and dinner. Credit cards: AE, MC, VISA.

NADA'S....3433 Giffin Rd., Fort Lauderdale, Fla., 33312. (305) 981-5343. Cuisine: Eastern European. Open Wednesday through Sunday for dinner only; Closed Monday and Tuesday. Credit cards: Call for cards.

NATURE'S OVEN....1635 North Federal Hwy., Fort Lauderdale, Fla., 33305. (305) 563-5899. Cuisine: Natural. Open 7 days. Credit cards: None.

NEW RIVER STOREHOUSE....2175 State Rd. 84, Fort Lauderdale, Fla., 33310. (305) 791-8010. Cuisine: American/Prime Rib. Open 7 days for dinner only. Credit cards: AE, DC, MC, VISA.

OCEAN'S BOUNTY....5400 North Federal Hwy., Fort Lauderdale, Fla., 33308. (305) 771-9070. Cuisine: Seafood. Open daily for lunch and dinner; Sunday brunch. Credit cards: AE, CB, DC, VISA.

THE ORANGERIE....230 Las Olas Blvd., Fort Lauderdale, Fla., 33301. (305) 520-0000. Cuisine: American. Days closed: Sunday. Credit cards: All major.

PASQUALE'S....2535 North Federal Hwy., Fort Lauderdale, Fla., 33305. (305) 561-3322. Cuisine: Italian. Open daily for dinner only. Credit cards: AE, DC, MC, VISA.

PATRICIA MURPHY'S CANDLELIGHT RESTAURANT....A1A at the Bahia Mar Yachting Cntr., Fort Lauderdale, Fla., 33310. (305) 467-1413. Cuisine: American. Open daily for lunch and dinner. Credit cards: All major. Table d'hote menu. "Come by boat or by car."

THE PLUM ROOM....3001 East Oakland Pk. Blvd., Fort Lauderdale, Fla., 33306. (305) 561-4400. Cuisine: Continental. Days closed: Sunday. Credit cards: AE, MC, VISA.

PORTAGE....1717 Eisenhower Blvd., Fort Lauderdale, Fla., 33316. (305) 467-6600. Cuisine: Continental. Open 7 days. Credit cards: AE, MC, VISA.

PORT OF CALL....701 SE 17th St., Fort Lauderdale, Fla., 33316. (305) 761-1116. Cuisine: Seafood. Open daily for lunch and dinner. Credit cards: AE, MC, VISA.

PORTOFINO RESTAURANT....4140 North Federal Hwy., Fort Lauderdale, Fla., 33308. (305) 566-5700. Cuisine: Continental. Owner: Rocco Costantino. Open 7 days. Credit cards: All major. Private party facilities: 10 to 70. Corporate name: Roste Corp.

RAINDANCER....3031 East Commercial Blvd., Fort Lauderdale, Fla., 33308. (305) 772-0337. Cuisine: Steakhouse. Open daily for dinner only. Credit cards: AE, MC, VISA.

RATHSKELLER....5727 North Federal Hwy., Fort Lauderdale, Fla., 33308. (305) 491-2500. Cuisine: German. Open daily for lunch and dinner. Credit cards: All major.

THE RED DERBY....3100 North Federal Hwy., Fort Lauderdale, Fla., 33306. Cuisine: Steak. Open 7 days for dinner only. Credit cards: All major. Reservations: Accepted. Happy hour from 5:00 PM to 6:30 PM, bar drinks only $1.00.

THE REEF....2700 South Andrews Ave., Fort Lauderdale, Fla., 33316. (305) 525-3435. Cuisine: American/Seafood. Open daily for lunch and dinner. Credit cards: AE, DC, MC.

RISTORANTE GIAN CARLO....408 South Andrews Ave., Fort Lauderdale, Fla., 33301. (305) 463-1924. Cuisine: Italian. Days closed: Sunday. Credit cards: AE, MC, VISA.

RISTORANTE ZI'TERESA....928 NE 20th Ave., Fort Lauderdale, Fla., 33304. (305) 462-2666. Cuisine: Italian. Open 7 days. Credit cards: All major.

RUNWAY 84....330 State Rd. 84, Fort Lauderdale, Fla., 33310. (305) 467-8484. Cuisine: Continental. Open Monday through Saturday for lunch and dinner; Closed Sunday. Credit cards: AE, MC, VISA.

RUSTIC INN CRABHOUSE....4331 Ravenswood Rd., Fort Lauderdale, Fla., 33313. (305) 584-1637. Cuisine: Seafood. Open Monday through Saturday for lunch; 7 days for dinner. Credit cards: AE, DC, MC, VISA. Private party facilities: Up to 200.

SEA GRILL....1619 NE Fourth Ave., Fort Lauderdale, Fla., 33301. (305) 763-8922. Cuisine: Seafood. Open daily for lunch and dinner. Credit cards: AE, MC, VISA.

SEA SHANTY....3841 Griffin Rd., Fort Lauderdale, Fla., 33312. (305) 962-1921. Cuisine: Seafood. Open daily for dinner only. Credit cards: AE, MC, VISA.

SEA VIEW....801 Seabreeze Blvd., Fort Lauderdale, Fla., 33316. (305) 764-2233. Cuisine: Steak/Seafood. Open 7 days for dinner only. Credit cards: All major.

SEA WATCH....6002 North Ocean Blvd., Fort Lauderdale, Fla., 33308. (305) 781-2200. Cuisine: Seafood. Open daily for dinner only. Credit cards: AE only.

SPAGHETTI FACTORY....3151 West Oakland Park Blvd., Fort Lauderdale, Fla., 33311. (305) 739-5411. Cuisine: Italian/Steak/Seafood. Open 7 days for dinner only. Credit cards: All major. Reservations: Accepted.

STAN'S UPSTAIRS....3300 East Commercial Blvd., Fort Lauderdale, Fla., 33316. (305) 772-3700. Cuisine: American. Open Wednesday through Sunday for dinner only; Closed Monday and Tuesday. Credit cards: AE, MC, VISA. Entertainment: Dancing overlooking the water.

STARBOARDSIDE RESTAURANT.... Sheraton Yankee Clipper Hotel, 1140 Seabreeze Blvd., Fort Lauderdale, Fla., 33316. (305) 524-5551. Cuisine: Continental. Open 7 days. Credit cards: All major.

STOUFFER'S ANACAPRI INN....1901 North Federal Hwy., Fort Lauderdale, Fla., 33305. (305) 563-1111. Cuisine: Continental/American. Open 7 days for breakfast, lunch, and dinner. Credit cards: All major.

STOUFFER'S LAUDERDALE SURF HOTEL....440 Seabreeze Ave., Fort Lauderdale, Fla., 33316. (305) 462-5555. Cuisine: Continental/American/Seafood. Open 7 days for lunch and dinner; Sunday brunch. Credit cards: AE, DC, MC, VISA. Reservations: Suggested. Entertainment: Live lounge entertainment nightly.

SWISS CHALET....321 West Sunrise Blvd., Fort Lauderdale, Fla., 33311. (305) 764-1004. Cuisine: Continental. Open 7 days: Closed Mondays during summer. Credit cards: All major. Owner Albert Meier.

THOR'S....2419 East Commercial Blvd., Fort Lauderdale, Fla., 33308. (305) 771-3733. Open 6 days for lunch and dinner; Closed Monday. Credit cards: AE, MC, VISA.

TINA'S SPAGHETTI HOUSE AND RESTAURANT...2110 South Federal Hwy., Fort Lauderdale, Fla., 33316. (305) 522-9443. Cuisine: Italian. Open 7 days. Credit cards: AE, DC, VISA.

TOP OF THE SURF...440 Seabreeze Ave., Fort Lauderdale, Fla., 33316. (305) 462-5555. Cuisine: American. Days closed: Monday. Credit cards: AE, DC, MC, VISA.

TROPICAL ACRES....2500 Griffin Rd., Fort Lauderdale, Fla., 33312. (305) 989-2500 or (305) 761-1744. Open daily for dinner only. Credit cards: All major.

TROPICANA....2670 East Sunrise Blvd., Fort Lauderdale, Fla., 33313. (305) 731-3060. Cuisine: Italian. Open daily for lunch and dinner. Credit cards: AE: MC, VISA.

VERDI'S....5521 West Oakland Park Blvd., Fort Lauderdale, Fla., 33313. (305) 731-3060. Cuisine: Italian. Open daily for lunch and dinner. Credit cards: AE, MC, VISA.

VINCENT'S ON THE WATER....3445 Griffin Rd., Fort Lauderdale, Fla., 33312. (305) 961-5030. Cuisine: Seafood. Open daily for dinner only. Credit cards: MC, VISA.

THE WHARF....1 Commercial Blvd., Fort Lauderdale, Fla., 33309. (305) 776-0001. Cuisine: Seafood. Open daily for dinner only. Credit cards: AE only. "Florida's most expensive seafood restaurant."

WILLIAMSON'S....1401 South Federal Hwy., Fort Lauderdale, Fla., 33316. (305) 523-1443. Cuisine: Continental/American. Open Wednesday through Sunday for dinner only; Closed Monday and Tuesday. Credit cards: MC, VISA.

THE WINE CELLAR....2651 North Federal Hwy., Fort Lauderdale, Fla., 33306. (305) 565-9021. Cuisine: Continental. Open daily for lunch and dinner. Credit cards: MC, VISA. Reservations: Suggested.

WOLFIE'S....2501 East Sunrise Blvd., Fort Lauderdale, Fla., (305) 566-7476. Cuisine: Delicatessen. Open daily. Credit cards: VISA only.

YESTERDAY'S....301 East Oakland Park Blvd., Fort Lauderdale, Fla., 33334. (305) 561-4400. Cuisine: American. Open 7 days for dinner only. Credit cards: AE, MC, VISA. Entertainment: Live entertainment nightly from 9:00 PM.

FORT MYERS

THE SHALLOWS....5833 Winkler Rd., Fort Myers, Fla., 33900. (813) 481-4644. Credit cards: AE, DC, MC, VISA.

HALLANDALE

BOBBY RUBINO'S PLACE FOR RIBS....4520 West Hallandale Beach Blvd., Hallandale, Fla., 33009. (305) 987-5500. Cuisine: American (Ribs). Open 7 days for lunch and dinner. Credit cards: AE, MC, VISA.

MANERO'S....2600 East Hallandale Beach Blvd., Hallandale, Fla., 33009. (305) 456-1000. Cuisine: American. Open 7 days. Credit cards: AE, MC, VISA.

YACHT CLUB RESTAURANT....1975 South Ocean Dr., Hallandale, Fla., 33009. (305) 458-7350. Cuisine: Traditional Jewish-style. Open daily from 8 AM to 9:30 PM. Credit cards: AE, MC, VISA.

HIALEAH

EL SEGUNDO VIAJANTE....2846 Palm Ave., Hialeah, Fla., 33500. (305) 888-5465. Cuisine: Latin. Credit cards: All major.

LA PAPILLON CAFE....1104 West Okeechobee Rd., Hialeah, Fla., 33010. (305) 883-8565. Cuisine: Continental and Creole. Days closed: Monday. Credit cards: MC, VISA.

MY FRIENDS....865 West 490th St., Hialeah, Fla., 33012. (305) 823-4353. Cuisine: Continental. Open Monday through Friday for lunch; Monday through Saturday for dinner; Closed Sunday. Credit cards: Call for cards.

HOLLYWOOD

BAVARIAN VILLAGE RESTAURANT AND COCKTAIL LOUNGE....1401 North Federal Hwy., Hollywood, Fla., 33020. (305) 922-7321. Cuisine: Bavarian German. Open Monday through Friday for lunch; 7 days for dinner; Sunday dinner from noon. Credit cards: AE, CB, DC, VISA. Reservations: Suggested. Entertainment: Strolling accordian player nightly.

BEVERLY HILLS CAFE....4000 North 46th Ave., Hollywood, Fla., 33021. (305) 963-5220. Cuisine: American. Open 6 days for lunch and dinner; Closed Sunday. Credit cards: MC, VISA.

CELEBRITY ROOM....3515 South Ocean Dr., Hollywood, Fla., 33019. (305) 457-8111. Cuisine: Continental. Open daily for dinner only. Credit cards: All major.

GEPETTO'S TALE OF THE WHALE....1828 Harrison St., Hollywood, Fla., 33020. (305) 920-9009. Cuisine: American. Open daily for dinner only. Credit cards: MC, VISA.

GOLD COAST....606 North Ocean Dr., Hollywood, Fla., 33019. (305) 923-4000. Cusine: American. Open daily for dinner only. Credit cards: AE, MC, VISA.

HEMINGWAY'S....219 North 21st Ave., Hollywood, Fla., 33020. (305) 923-0500. Cuisine: American. Open daily for dinner and late supper. Credit cards: All major. Entertainment: Live band nightly; piano player before 9:30 PM nightly. "Bustling New York ambiance."

LE DAUPHIN....1824 Harrison Ave., Hollywood, Fla., 33020. (305) 929-3581. Cuisine: Continental. Open daily for dinner only. Credit cards: AE, MC, VISA.

NATURAL EATS....4907 Sheraton St., Hollywood, Fla., 33025. (305) 981-0555. Cuisine: Natural. Days closed: Sunday. Credit cards: None.

NEW ENGLAND OYSTER HOUSE....4401 Hollywood Blvd., Hollywood, Fla., 33021. (305) 961-5251. Cuisine: Seafood. Open 7 days for lunch and dinner. Credit cards: AE, MC, VISA.

OLD SPAIN....2333 Hollywood Blvd., Hollywood, Fla., 33020. (305) 944-2298, Dade; (305) 921-8485, Broward. Cuisine: Contiental. Open 7 days. Credit cards: All major.

SEA INN....906 East Hallandale Beach Blvd., Hollywood, Fla., 33032. (305) 454-8900. Cuisine: American. Open daily for lunch and dinner. Credit cards: All major.

TIFFANY GARDENS RESTAURANT....1716 Harrison St., Hollywood, Fla., 33020. (305) 921-7377. Cuisine: Italian/American. Owner: Michael Romanelli and Dominick Romanelli. Open Monday to Friday for lunch; 7 days for dinner. Credit cards: All major. Private party facilities: 10 to 400. Annual sales: $250,000 to $500,000. Total employment: 20. Corporate name: Tiffany Gardens Restaurant, Inc.

TOP OF THE HOME....1720 Harrison St., Hollywood, Fla., 33020. (305) 949-3549. Cuisine: Continental/International. Open 7 days for dinner only. Credit cards: All major. Entertainment: Dancing nightly. "Dining and dancing with a panoramic view of the city and ocean."

WAN'S MANDARIN HOUSE....3331 Sheridan St., Hollywood, Fla., 33021. (305) 963-6777. Cuisine: Chinese. Open daily for lunch and dinner. Credit cards: All major.

ZINKLER'S BAVARIAN VILLAGE....1401 North Federal Hwy., Hollywood, Fla., 33020. (305) 922-7321. Cuisine: German. Open daily for lunch and dinner. Credit cards: All major.

HOLLYWOOD-BY-THE-SEA

DIPLOMAT....3515 South Ocean Dr., Hollywood-by-the-Sea, Fla., 33019. (305) 949-2442. Cuisine: American. Open 7 days. Credit cards: All major.

HOMESTEAD

MOREY'S MARKET....8727 South Dixie Hwy., Homestead, Fla., 33039. (305) 661-3100. Cuisine: American. Open 7 days. Credit cards: AE, MC, VISA.

PAPPAGALLO....16999 South Dixie Hwy., Homestead, Fla., 33039. (305) 253-5300. Cuisine: Italian. Open 7 days. Credit cards: MC, VISA.

QUINTESSENCE....15801 South Dixie Hwy., Homestead, Fla., 33039. (305) 233-6151.Cuisine: Continental. Open 7 days. Credit cards: AE, MC, VISA.

INDIAN SHORES

LE POMPANO....19325 Gulf Blvd., Indian Shores, Fla., 32960. (813) 596-0333. Cuisine: French/Continental. Owner: Michel Denis. Open 7 days for lunch and dinner. Credit cards: All major. Private party facilities: 50 to 200. Annual sales: $500,000 to $1 million. Total employment: 50. Corporate name: Le Pompano, Inc.

SCANDIA....19829 Gulf Blvd., Indian Shores, Fla., 32960. (813) 595-4928. Cuisine: Scandanavian/American. Open for breakfast, lunch, and dinner daily. Credit cards: All major. Reservations: Suggested.

ISLAMORADA

CORAL GRILL.... Mile Marker 83.5, Islamorada, Fla., 33036. (305) 664-4803. Cuisine: American. Days closed: Monday, April through December, also month of September. Credit cards: MC, VISA.

ERIK'S FLOATING RESTAURANT.... Mile Marker 85.5, Islamorada, Fla., 33036. (305) 664-9141. Cuisine: Continental. Days closed: Tuesday. Credit cards: DC, MC, VISA.

S. WELLINGTON'S.... At the Holiday Isle Resort, Mile Marker 84.5, Islamorada, Fla., 33036. (305) 664-2321. Cuisine: American. Open 7 days. Credit cards: AE, MC, VISA.

JACKSONVILLE

GREEN DERBY....578 Riverside Ave., Jacksonville, Fla., 32202. (904) 356-7691. Cuisine: American. Credit cards: AE, MC, VISA.

STRICKLAND'S TOWN HOUSE....3510 Philips Hwy., Jacksonville, Fla., 32207. (904) 396-1682. Cuisine: Seafood/Steak. Credit cards: All major.

VICTORIA STATION....7579 Arlington Exp., Jacksonville, Fla., 32211. (904) 725-3977. Cuisine: American. Credit cards: AE, MC, VISA.

KEY BISCAYNE

ENGLISH PUB/JAMAICA INN....320 Crandon Blvd., Key Biscayne, Fla., 33149. (305) 361-5481. Inn cuisine: Prime Rib and Roast Duck; Pub cuisine: American. Pub open 7 days for lunch and dinner; Inn open for dinner only; Raw Bar open for dinner only. Credit cards: All major. "Choose between elegant and casual dining."

RIB ROOM.... Sonesta Beach Hotel, 350 Ocean Dr., Key Biscayne, Fla., 33149. (305) 361-2021. Cuisine: American. Open 7 days. Credit cards: AE, DC, MC, VISA.

ROGER'S ON THE GREEN.... At Key Biscayne Golf Course, 4444 Crandon Blvd., Key Biscayne, Fla., 33149. (305) 361-9460. Cuisine: Continental. Open 7 days. Credit cards: All major.

THE SANDBAR....301 Ocean Dr., Key Biscayne, Fla., 33149. (305) 361-1049. Cuisine: Seafood. Open daily for lunch and dinner; Saturday and Sunday for breakfast. Credit cards: AE, MC, VISA.

SEA SHANTY....13575 Biscayne, Blvd., Key Biscayne, Fla., 33149. (305) 945-8170. Cuisine: Seafood. Open Monday through Friday for lunch; 7 days for dinner. Credit cards: MC, VISA.

STEFANO'S....24 Crandon Blvd., Key Biscayne, Fla., 33149. (305) 361-7007. Cuisine: Northern Italian. Open daily for lunch and dinner. Credit cards: All major. Entertainment: Vocalist/combo Monday through Saturday; Calypso Sunday.

SUNDAY'S ON THE BAY.... Crandon Marina, Key Biscayne, Fla., 33149. (305) 361-6777. Cuisine: Seafood. Open 7 days for lunch and dinner; Weekend breakfast; Sunday brunch. Credit cards: Call for credit cards. Reservations: Required. Raw Bar & BBQ on outside terrace.

TWO DRAGONS.... Sonesta Beach Hotel, 350 Ocean Dr., Key Biscayne, Fla., 33149. (305) 361-2021. Cuisine: Chinese and Japanese. Open daily for dinner only. Credit cards: All major. Two restaurants under one name.

KEY WEST

A & B LOBSTER HOUSE....700 Front St., Key West, Fla., 33040. (305) 294-2536. Cuisine: Seafood. Open Monday through Saturday for dinner only; Closed Sunday. Credit cards: MC, VISA. Overlooking Key West harbor and shrimp fleet.

CHEZ EMILE....423 Front St., Key West, Fla., 33040. (305) 294-6252. Cuisine: Continental. Days closed: Monday. Credit cards: AE, DC, MC, VISA.

CHEZ NANCY....3420 North Roosevelt Blvd., Key West, Fla., 33040. (305) 294-5541. Cuisine: French. Credit cards: AE, DC, MC, VISA.

CLAIRE....900 Duval St., Key West, Fla., 33040. (305) 296-5558. Cuisine: American and Thai. Open 7 days. Credit cards: AE, DC, MC, VISA.

HENRY'S.... Marriott's Casa Marina Resort, Reynolds St., Key West, Fla., 33040. (305) 296-3535. Cuisine: Continental. Open 7 days. Credit cards: All major.

LA CREPERIE....124 Duval St., Key West, Fla., 33040. (305) 294-7677. Cuisine: Crepes. Open 7 days. Credit cards: AE, DC, MC, VISA.

LA TERRAZA DE MARTI....1125 Duval St., Key West, Fla., 33040. (305) 294-0344. Cuisine: French/Chinese. Owner: Lawrence Formica, Prop. Open 7 days for lunch and dinner; No dinner on Sunday. Credit cards: All major. Annual sales: $1 million to $3 million. Total employment: 40.

MARTHA'S....1801 South Roosevelt Blvd., Key West, Fla., 33040. (305) 294-3466. Cuisine: Steak/Lobster. Open daily for dinner only. Credit cards: AE, MC, VISA. Entertainment: Piano nightly.

PIER HOUSE.... One Duval St., Key West, Fla., 33040. (305) 294-9541. Cuisine: American. Open 7 days. Credit cards: All major.

PORT OF CALL....431 Front St., Key West, Fla., 33040. (305) 294-6707. Cuisine: Continental. Days closed: Tuesday. Credit cards: AE, MC, VISA.

THE QUEEN'S TABLE.... Santa Maria Hotel, 1401 Simonton Street, Key West, Fla., 33040. (305) 296-5678. Cuisine: American. Open 7 days for lunch and dinner. Credit cards: All major.

ROOFTOP CAFE....310 Front St., Key West, Fla., 33040. (305) 294-2042. Cuisine: American. Open 7 days. Credit cards: AE, MC, VISA.

THE SANDS.... Simonton St. on the Atlantic, Key West, Fla., 33040. (305) 294-6669. Cuisine: American. Open 7 days. Credit cards: AE, MC, VISA.

LAKE BUENA VISTA

ALFREDO THE ORIGINAL OF ROME....EPCOT center, Lake Buena Vista, Fla., 32830. (305) 827-8430. A functional, cherry Italian establishment in Disney's new EPCOT center, Alfredo the Original of Rome retains the charm of the New York original. The staff is bubbly, the food is splendid, the table turnover high, and the prices comfortable. Try the fettucine Alfredo and sample where the whole show began. Other specialties include: Veal *picatta*, chicken *cacciatore*, and *linguine al pesto*. Owner: Guido Bellanca. Open 7 days for lunch and dinner. Moderately priced. Reservations: Accepted. Credit cards: AE, MC, VISA. Corporate name: Alfredo the Original of Rome (Fla.), Inc.

LAKE WORTH

THE ABBEY ROAD....7306 Lake Worth Road, Lake Worth, Fla., 33463. (305) 967-4852. Cuisine: Continental. Open 7 days for lunch and dinner. Credit cards: AE, MC, VISA.

PANCHO VILLA....4621 Lake Worth Road, Lake Worth, Fla., 33463. (305) 964-1112. Cuisine: Mexican. Open daily for lunch and dinner. No credit cards.

SQUIRE RESTAURANT AND LOUNGE....7859 Lake Worth Rd., Lake Worth, Fla., 33463. (305) 968-5000. Cuisine: Continental. Open 7 days. Credit cards: All major.

LANTANA

ANCHOR INN....2810 Hypoluyo Rd., Lantana, Fla., 33462. (305) 965-4794. Cuisine: Seafood. Open daily for dinner only. Credit cards: MC, VISA.

LARGO

HUNAN GARDEN....1355 East Bay Dr., Largo, Fla., 33541. (813) 581-4848. Cuisine: Chinese. Open daily for lunch and dinner. Credit cards: AE, DC, MC, VISA. "The steamed dumplings are outstanding."

LIGHTHOUSE POINT

THE ABBEY ROAD....4460 North Federal Hwy., Lighthouse Point, Fla., 33064. (305) 781-1740. Cuisine: Continental. Open 7 days for lunch and dinner. Credit cards: AE, MC, VISA.

CAP'S PLACE.... Cap's Dock, Lighthouse Point, Fla., 33064. (305) 941-0418. Cuisine: Seafood. Open daily for dinner only. Credit cards: MC, VISA.

FIN & CLAW RESTAURANT....2502 North Federal Hwy., Lighthouse Point, Fla., 33064. (305) 782-1060. Cuisine: Seafood. Owner: Joseph Gerres. Open: Tuesday through Sunday. Credit cards: All major. Private party facilities: Up to 40. Annual sales: $500,000 to $1 million. Total employment: 25. Corporate name: Fin & Claw Restaurant, Inc.

GENTLEMAN JIM'S....2031 NE 36th St., Lighthouse Point, Fla., 33064. (305) 946-1231. Cuisine: Continental. Open 7 days for lunch and dinner. Credit cards: All major.

LE BISTRO....4626 North Federal Hwy., Lighthouse Point, Fla., 33064. (305) 946-9240. Cuisine: French. Open daily for lunch and dinner. Credit cards: AE, DC, MC.

SEAFOOD WORLD....4602 North Federal Hwy., Lighthouse Point, Fla., 33064. (305) 942-0742. Cuisine: Seafood. Open daily for lunch and dinner. No credit cards.

LONGBOAT KEY

THE FIELD'S BUCCANEER INN....595 Dream Island Rd., Longboat Key, Fla., 33548. (813) 383-1101; 383-4357. Cuisine: American. Owner: Herbert P. Field. Open 7 days for lunch and dinner. Credit cards: All major. Private party facilities. 26 to 100. Annual sales: $1 million to $3 million. Total employment: 50. Corporate name: Buccaneer Inn Corp.

L'AUBERGE DU BON VIVANT....7003 Gulf of Mexico Drive, Longboat Key, Fla., 33548. (813) 383-2421. Cuisine: French. Owner: Micheal & Judy Zouhor & Francis & Madeleine Hatton. Credit cards: All major. Annual sales: $500,000 to $1 million. Total employment: 20. Corporate name: L'Auberge du Bon Vivant, Inc.

MADEIRA BEACH

LE ST. TROPEZ....14975 Gulf Blvd.,, Madeira Beach, Fla., 33708. (813) 397-4620. Cuisine: French. Open Monday through Saturday for dinner only; Closed Sunday. Credit cards: All major. Reservations : Necessary.

MARGATE

NORRIS "CATFISH" RESTAURANT....4701 Coconut Creek Pkwy., Margate, Fla., 33063. (305) 972-9827. Cuisine: American. Open 7 days for dinner only. No credit cards.

MIAMI

THE ACAPULCO....727 NW 27th Ave., Miami, Fla., 33127. (305) 642-6961. Cuisine: Mexican. Call for hours and credit cards. Reservations: Accepted.

THE AFFAIRE....6027 Biscayne Blvd., Miami, Fla., 33138. (305) 754-6929. Cuisine: International. Owner: R. Gerezz, W. Saric. Open 6 days for lunch and dinner; Closed Monday. Credit cards: AE, MC, VISA. Private party facilities: Up to 70. Annual sales: $250,000 to $500,000. Corporate name: The Affaire, Inc.

ALEXANDRE'S....1601 Biscayne Blvd., Miami, Fla., 33132. (305) 358-9111. Cuisine: Continental. Open daily for buffet lunch, continental dinner; Wednesday dinner buffet. Credit cards: AE, DC, MC, VISA. Entertainment: Latin music 6 nights weekly; disco Friday and Saturday.

ARTHUR'S EATING HOUSE....**1444 Biscayne Blvd., Miami, Fla., 33132. (305) 371-1444. A Miami institution, and deservedly so, not only because of the unique artwork on the walls, but for a huge meal of delicious food. Terrific fresh stone crabs with a mustard sauce. Excellent *canneloni Giannini* and spinach crepes Oriental. They broil the always-fresh fish expertly, and they do all right by steaks and chops, too. But don't overlook the veal *mercado*, the calf's liver, the roast duckling, or any of the fresh shellfish, either. Owner: Arthur Horowitz. Open Monday through Saturday for lunch; 7 days for dinner. Prices moderate to high. Accepting reservations and all major credit cards. Private party facilities are available.**

BAGATELLE....115 Duval St., Miami, Fla., 32951. (305) 294-7195. Cuisine: Bahamian. Open 7 days for lunch and dinner; Sunday brunch. Credit cards: AE, DC, MC, VISA.

BEVERLY HILLS CAFE....7321 Miami Lakes Dr., Miami, Fla., 33162. (305) 558-8201. Cuisine: American. Open 6 days for lunch and dinner; Closed Sunday. Credit cards: MC, VISA.

BODEGA....9801 South Dixie Hwy., Miami, Fla., 33156. (305) 667-2574. Cuisine: American. Open 7 days for lunch and dinner. Credit cards: AE, MC, VISA.

BRASSERIE DE PARIS....250 NE 3rd St., Everglades Hotel, Miami, Fla., 33101. (305) 374-0122. Cuisine: French. Open 7 days. Credit cards: All major.

BROTHERS TWO....13515 South Dixie Hwy., Miami, Fla., 33176. (305) 253-8200. Cuisine: American. Open Monday through Saturday for lunch; 7 days for dinner. Credit cards: AE, MC, VISA. Entertainment: Live entertainment Tuesday through Saturday.

CAFE LE BLANC JARDIN....1401 Biscayne Blvd., Miami, Fla., 33132. (305) 374-2876. Cuisine: Continental. Days closed: Sunday. Credit cards: AE, DC, MC, VISA.

THE CALIFORNIA CLUB....750 California Dr., Miami, Fla., 33179. (305) 651-5100. Cuisine: Continental. Open daily for lunch and dinner. Credit cards: All major. "A private membership club."

CARINO'S....10760 Biscayne Blvd., Miami, Fla., 33161. (305) 893-3971. Cuisine: Italian. Open 7 days for dinner; Sunday dinner from 2:00 PM. Credit cards: All major.

CENTRO VASCO....2235 SW 8th St., Miami, Fla., 33135. (305) 643-9096. Cuisine: Spanish/Basque. Owner: Joan Saizarbitoria. Open 7 days for lunch and dinner. Credit cards: All major. Private party facilities: 20 to 150. Annual sales: $1 million to $3 million. Total employment: 50.

CHALET GOURMET....1470 NW Le Jeune Rd., Miami Fla., 33134. (305) 871-4944. Cuisine: American. Credit cards: All major.

CHARDA....13885 Biscayne Blvd., Miami, Fla., 33181. (305) 940-1095. Cuisine: Hungarian. Open 7 days for dinner only. Credit cards: Call for cards. Reservations: Suggested.

CHINA MAID....9280 Bird Rd., Miami, Fla., 33165. (305) 226-0331. Cuisine: Cantonese Chinese. Open 6 days for dinner only; Closed Tuesday. Call for credit cards. Reservations: Accepted.

COCK AND BULL....Biscayne Blvd. at 29th St., Miami, Fla., 33132. (305) 893-9990. Cuisine: Steak/Seafood. Open 7 days for dinner only. Credit cards: All major. Entertainment: Dancing from 8 PM nightly.

COMME CHEZ SOI....235 NW 37th Ave., Miami, Fla., 33127. (305) 649-4999. Cuisine: Belgian/French. Open 6 days for lunch and dinner; Closed Monday. Credit cards: AE, MC, VISA.

COURTYARD INN....2451 Brickell Ave., Miami, Fla., 33129. (305) 858-5770. Cuisine: American. Open Monday through Friday for lunch; 7 days for dinner; Weekend brunch. Credit cards: All major.

THE CRABHOUSE....1551 79th Street Causeway, Miami, Fla., 33141. (305) 868-7085. Cuisine: Seafood. Owner: E.R. Scharps, Pres. Open 7 days. Credit cards: AE, MC, VISA. Annual sales: Over $3 million. Total employment: 85. Corporate name: The Crabhouse, Inc.

CROWN AND SCEPTRE....3941 NW 22nd St., Miami, Fla., 33142. (305) 871-1700. Cuisine: American. Open Monday through Saturday for dinner only. Credit cards: All major. Entertainment: Disco nightly.

CSARDA HUNGARIAN RESTAURANT....13885 Biscayne Blvd., Miami, Fla., 33181. (305) 940-1095. Cuisine: Hungarian. Open Tuesday through Sunday for dinner only; Closed Monday. Credit cards: All major. Entertainment: Live gypsy music.

CYE'S RIVERGATE....444 Brickell Ave., Miami, Fla., 33131. (305) 358-9100. Cuisine: Continental/American. Owner: Cye Mandel. Open Monday through Saturday. Credit cards: All major. Private party facilities: 20 to 60. Annual sales: $1 million to $3 million. Total employment: 90. Corporate name: Rivergate Restaurant Corp.

DAPHNE'S RESTAURANT AND LOUNGE....3900 NW 21st St., Miami, Fla., 33142. (305) 871-3200. Cuisine: Continental. Owner: Sherwood Weiser & Donald Lefton. Open 7 days for lunch and dinner. Credit cards: All major. Private party facilities: Up to 40. Annual sales: $1 million to $3 million. Total employment: 75. Corporate name: The Contenetal Companies, Inc.

DA VALENTINO....131 SE Third Ave., Miami, Fla., 33131. (305) 358-1395. Cuisine: Italian. Days closed: Saturday, Sunday. Credit cards: All major.

THE DEPOT....5830 South Dixie Hwy., Miami, Fla., 33143. (305) 665-6261. Cuisine: Continental/American. Open 7 days. Credit cards: All major. Private party facilities: 8 to 60. Total employment: 35 to 40. Corporate name: Specialty Taverns of American, Inc.

DOCKSIDE TERRACE....Miamarina, Miami, Fla., 33132. (305) 358-6419. Cuisine: American/Continental. Open 7 days for lunch and dinner. Credit cards: Call for cards. Reservations: Suggested.

DON JULIO'S RESTAURANT....139 NE 20th St., Miami, Fla., 33137. (305) 573-8412. Cuisine: Mexican/International. Call for days and times. Credit cards: AE, DC. Reservations: Accepted.

DOWNSTAIRS/UPSTAIRS....17450 Biscayne Blvd., Miami, Fla., 33160. (305) 949-9753. Cuisine: American. Open daily for dinner and late supper. Credit cards: AE, DC, MC, VISA. Entertainment: Two jazz/rock bands nightly from 10:00 PM.

DURTY NELLIE'S CRABHOUSE....18101 SW 98th Ct., Miami, Fla., 33157. (305) 253-1868. Cuisine: Seafood. Open nightly for dinner only. Credit cards: AE, MC, VISA.

EAST COAST FISHERIES....360 West Flagler St., Miami, Fla., 33130. (305) 373-5514. Cuisine: Seafood. Open 7 days. Credit cards: Call for cards.

EL ARRIERO ARGENTINO....261 East Flagler St., Miami, Fla., 33131. (305) 377-9112, (305) 358-0177, or (305) 374-5651. Cuisine: Argentine. Days closed: Sunday. Credit cards: All major.

EL BODEGON CASTILLA....2499 SW 8th St., Miami, Fla., 33135. (305) 649-0863. Cuisine: Spanish. Open 7 days for lunch and dinner. Credit cards: AE, MC, VISA. Reservations: Accepted.

EL CID....117 Le Jeune Rd., Miami, Fla., 33126. (305) 541-3514. Cuisine: Continental. Open 7 days. Credit cards: All major.

EL FLORIDITA....145 East Flagler St., Miami, Fla., 33131. (305) 358-1556. Cuisine: Spanish/Cuban. Open Monday through Saturday for lunch and dinner; Closed Sunday. Credit cards: All major. Reservations: Accepted.

EL TERNERO, THE STEAK HOUSE....9553 South Dixie Hwy., Dadeland Plz., Miami, Fla., 33156. (305) 661-4742. Cuisine: Steak. Owner: Marco, Maria and Sara Bermudez, Maria Kelly, Horacio and Amalia Guzman. Open 7 days. Credit cards: All major. Private party facilities: 20 to 60. Annual sales: $250,000 to $500,000. Total employment: 15. Corporate name: Commercial Food & Service of Fla., Inc.

EMBERS....22 St. off Collins Ave., Miami, Fla., 33139. (305) 538-4345. Cuisine: American. Open 7 days. Credit cards: All major.

FLAMENCO....991 NE 79th St., Miami, Fla., 33138. (305) 751-8631. Cuisine: Spanish/Mexican. Open 6 days for dinner; No dinner Tuesday. Credit cards: AE, DC, MC, VISA. Entertainment: Two floor shows with dinner; 9:30 PM and 11:30 PM.

FOLLIES INTERNATIONAL....3301 West Okeechobee Rd., Miami, Fla., 33101. (305) 557-2221. Cuisine: Continental. Open 7 days for lunch and dinner. Credit cards: All major. Entertainment: Las Vegas revues nightly.

FOLLIES INTERNATIONAL....21440 Biscayne Blvd., Miami, Fla., 33180. (305) 932-1487. Cuisine: Continental. Open 7 days for lunch and dinner. Credit cards: All major. Entertainment: Las Vegas-style revues.

FOOD AMONG THE FLOWERS....21 NE 36th St., Miami, Fla., 33137. (305) 920-7076 Broward, or, (305) 576-0000 Dade. Cuisine: Continental. Open 7 days. Credit cards: All major.

GAMBIT'S....1201 NW 42nd Ave., Miami, Fla., 33126. (305) 649-5000. Cuisine: American. Open Monday through Friday for lunch; daily for dinner. Credit cards: All major. Entertainment: Disco Monday through Saturday from 9:00 PM.

GATTI'S....147 West Ave., Miami, Fla., 33139. (305) 673-1717. Cuisine: Northern Italian. Open 6 days for dinner; Closed Monday; Closed mid-May through October. Credit cards: AE, DC, MC, VISA.

GENTLEMAN JIM'S....12502 North Kendall Dr., Miami, Fla., 33186. (305) 271-5287. Cuisine: Continental. Open 7 days for lunch and dinner. Credit cards: All major.

THE GOOD ARTHURS....790 NE 79th St., Miami, Fla., 33138. (305) 756-0631. Cuisine: Continental. Days closed: Monday. Credit cards: AE, MC, VISA. Owner: Arthur Hamm.

GORDON'S 7 SEAS....1700 79th St. Causeway, Miami, Fla., 33141. (305) 868-6542. Cuisine: Seafood. Open Monday through Friday for lunch; 7 days for dinner. Credit cards: All major.

GRANNY FEELGOOD'S RESTAURANT & HEALTH FOODS....121 SE Second Ave., Miami, Fla., 33131. (305) 358-6233. Cuisine: Natural. Days closed: Sunday. Credit cards: CB, MC, VISA.

GREAT ESCAPE....1127 NE 163 St., Miami, Fla., 33162. (305) 949-2135. Cuisine: American. Open Monday through Saturday for lunch; 7 days for dinner. Credit cards: All major.

GULFSTREAM....1601 Biscayne Blvd., Jordan Marsh Omni, Miami, Fla., 33139. (305) 377-1911. Cuisine: American. Open 7 days for lunch and dinner. Credit cards: AE, DC.

GULFSTREAM....Dadeland Mall Jordan Marsh, North Kendall Dr., Miami, Fla., 33156. (305) 666-6565. Cuisine: American. Open 7 days for lunch and dinner. Credit cards: AE, DC.

HITCHING POST....445 East Okeechobee Rd., Miami, Fla., 33472. (305) 887-6012. Cuisine: American (Barbeque). Owner: Michael Trachter. Open 6 days for lunch and dinner; Closed Monday. No credit cards. Annual sales: $500,000 to $1 million. Total employment: 16.

HOLLEMAN'S RESTAURANT AND LOUNGE....On the Circle in Miami Springs, 1 Curtiss Pkwy., Miami, Fla. 33166. (305) 888-8097. Cuisine: American. Open 7 days. Credit cards: AE, DC, MC, VISA.

HORATIO'S....2649 Bayshore Dr., Miami, Fla., 33133. (305) 858-2500. Cuisine: Continental. Credit cards: All major.

HY-VONG....3458 SW 8th St., Miami, Fla., 33135. (305) 447-9760. Cuisine: Vietnamese. Open Tuesday through Sunday for lunch and dinner; Closed Monday. No credit cards.

JUANITO'S CENTRO VASCO....2235 SW 8th St., Miami, Fla., 33135. (305) 643-9606. Cuisine: Spanish. Owner: Juan Saizarbitoria. Open daily for lunch and dinner. Credit cards: All major. Private party facilities: 20 to 150. Annual sales: $1 million to $3 million. Total employment: 58. Corporate name: Motrico, Inc.

K.C. CAGNEY'S....5813 Ponce de Leon Blvd., Miami, Fla., 33146. (305) 661-7091. Cuisine: American. Open 7 days for lunch and dinner. No credit cards.

KELLY'S SEAFOOD HOUSE....17550 Collins Ave., Miami, Fla., 33160. (305) 931-7145. Cuisine: Seafood/Steak. Open 7 days for dinner only. Credit cards: All major. Reservations: Accepted.

KING ARTHUR'S COURT....500 Deer Run, Miami, Fla., 33166. (305) 871-6000. Cuisine: American. Days closed: Monday. Credit cards: All major.

KING'S WHARF....1201 NW Le Jeune Rd., Miami Fla., 33126. (305) 649-5000. Cuisine: American. Open daily for lunch and dinner; Sunday brunch. Credit cards: All major. Entertainment: Piano bar nightly in Windjammer lounge.

LA CARAVELLE....555 NE 15th St., (at the Plaza Venetia), Miami, Fla., 33132. (305) 374-3211. Cuisine: French. Open daily for lunch and dinner. Credit cards: AE, MC, VISA. Entertainment: Live entertainment nightly in lounge.

LA PALOMA....223 NE 16th St., Miami, Fla., 33139. (305) 358-2125. Cuisine: Continental. Open 7 days. Credit cards: AE, MC, VISA.

LAS TASCA....2741 West Flagler St., Miami, Fla., 33135. (305) 642-3762. Cuisine: Spanish. Open Tuesday through Sunday for lunch and dinner; Closed Monday. Credit cards: AE, CB, MC, VISA.

LE CHATEAU....801 South Bayshore Dr., Miami, Fla., 33131. (305) 377-1966, (800) 327-5708. Cuisine: French County. Credit cards: All major. Annual sales: $500,000 to $1 million. Total employment: 20.

LE MINERVA....265 NE 2nd St., Miami, Fla., 33132. (305) 374-9420. Cuisine: Spanish/Mexican. Open daily for lunch and dinner. No credit cards.

LEONARDO'S....2655 Biscayne Blvd., Miami, Fla., 33137. (305) 573-4212. Cuisine: Italian. Open 7 days. Credit cards: All major.

LES FOLLIES....11806 Biscayne Blvd., Miami, Fla., 33181. (305) 893-7632. Cuisine: Spanish/Mexican. Open nightly for dinner from 7:30 PM. Credit cards: All major. Entertainment: Three nightly entertainment shows, 9:30 PM, 11:30 PM, and 1:30 AM. Cover charge.

LES VIOLINS....1751 Biscayne Blvd., Miami, Fla., 33132. (305) 371-8668. Cuisine: Spanish/Mexican. Open 7 nights weekly for dinner. Credit cards: AE, DC, MC, VISA. Entertainment: Sister-club to **Flamenco** with two shows nightly, 9:30 PM and 11:30 PM. Cover charge & minimum.

LINDY'S CAFE....Omni International, 1601 Biscayne Blvd., Miami, Fla., 33132. (305) 358-8700. Cuisine: Jewish-American. Open 9:00 AM to 9:00 PM daily. Credit cards: Call for cards.

THE LUCKY DUCK/THE LAME DUCK....17868 Biscayne Blvd., Miami, Fla., 33132. (305) 931-1922. Cuisine: "Gourmet/Continental." Open 7 days for lunch, dinner, late supper. Credit cards: Call for cards. Reservations: Accepted. Entertainment: Piano bar & singer.

MADRID....2475 Douglas Rd., Miami, Fla., 33145. (305) 446-2250. Cuisine: Spanish. Owner: Juan Lata. Open 6 days for lunch and dinner; Closed Sunday. Credit cards: All major. Annual sales: $500,000 to $1 million. Total employment: 20.

MAISON....Omni International Hotel, 1601 Biscayne Blvd., Miami, Fla., 33132. (305) 374-0000. Cuisine: French. Days closed: Sunday. Credit cards: major.

MALAGA RESTAURANT....740 SW Eighth St., Miami, Fla., 33130. (305) 858-4224. Cuisine: Latin. Credit cards: All major.

MANSENE'S....291 NW 37th Ave., Miami, Fla., 33125. (305) 649-4111. Cuisine: Italian. Days closed: Sunday. Credit cards: AE, MC, VISA.

MASTHEAD....801 South Bayshore Dr., Miami, Fla., 33131. (305) 377-1966. Cuisine: American. Open daily for lunch and dinner; Sunday brunch. Credit cards: All major.

MENAGE....2333 Brickell Ave., (in the Brickell Bay Club), Miami, Fla., 33129. (305) 856-5331. Cuisine: Continental/American. Open Monday through Friday for lunch; Monday through Saturday for dinner; Sunday brunch; Sunday "Gourmet Dining" from 8:00 PM. Credit cards: All major. "Sunday prix-fixe gourmet dinner for $16.95."

MIAMI RIVER RAW BAR....422 SW Second Ave., Miami, Fla., 33130. (305) 374-4381. Cuisine: Seafood. Open daily for lunch and dinner. Credit cards: MC, VISA.

MIDDLE EAST RESTAURANT....1764 SW 3rd Ave., Miami, Fla., 33129. (305) 446-5334. Cuisine: Arabic. Owner: Ibrahim Kawa. Open 7 days for lunch and dinner. Credit cards: All major. Private party facilities: 10 to 150. Annual sales: $250,000 to $500,000. Total employment: 18. Corporate name: Jerusalem Star Corp.

MIKE GORDON'S SEAFOOD RESTAURANT....1201 NE 79th St., Miami, Fla., 33138. (305) 751-4429. Cuisine: Seafood. Open Tuesday through Sunday for lunch and dinner. Credit cards: AE,DC,MC,VISA.

NEW YORK, NEW YORK....8867 SW 107th Ave., Miami, Fla., 33176. (305) 595-8300. Cuisine: American. Open daily for breakfast, lunch, and dinner. Credit cards: MC, VISA.

NEW YORK STEAK HOUSE....19115 Collins Ave., Miami, Fla., 33160. (305) 932-7276. Best in the area! The beef is splendid, so reckon on a base of beef and Burgundy rounded off by some slick desserts if you want to side-step the more elaborate specialties such as the 3- to 5-pound lobsters, stone crabs, bar-b-que Canadian back ribs, roasted chicken, shrimp scampi, red snapper almondine, and beef Stroganoff. Either way you will feed very well. Owner: Martin Sussman. Open 7 days for lunch and dinner. Priced expensive. Reservations are accepted. Credit cards: All major. Annual sales: $1 million to $3 million. Total employment: 50.

NICK AND ARTHUR'S....1601 79th St. Causeway, Miami, Fla., 33141. (305) 864-2200. Cuisine: American. Open daily for dinner only. Credit cards: All major.

94th AERO SQUADRON....1395 NW 57th Ave., Miami, Fla., 33126. (305) 261-4220. Cuisine: Continental. Open 7 days. Credit cards: All major.

ON STAGE.... Decorators Row, 39th St. and NE Second Ave., Miami, Fla., 33140. (305) 576-8677. Cuisine: Continental. Open 7 days. Credit cards: AE, MC, VISA.

PALM....3131 Collins Ave., Miami, Fla., 33140. (305) 868-7256. Same food, same crowds, same crush over cocktails and dinner as the Manhattan restaurant that started it all. Same caricatures on the wall, same clutter, same great steaks. Different city. That's all. Owner: Bruce Bozzi, Walter Ganzi. Open Monday through Friday for lunch; Monday through Saturday for dinner; Closed Sunday. Priced moderate to high. Reservations: A good idea to book a table. Credit cards: All major. Corporate name: Just One More Restaurant, Inc.—Palm Restaurant, Inc.

PANZONI'S....1794 NE Fourth Ave., Miami, Fla., 33132. (305) 374-6060. Cuisine: Italian. Open 7 days. Credit cards: All major.

PICCADILLY HEARTH....35 NE 40th St., Miami, Fla., 33137. (305) 576-1818. Cuisine: Continental. Days closed: Sunday. Credit cards: AE, DC, MC, VISA.

PLACE FOR STEAK....1335 79th St., Miami, Fla., 33141. (305) 758-5581. Cuisine: American. Open 7 days for dinner. Credit cards: All major. Entertainment: Rock/jazz combo nightly.

PRINCE HAMLET....8301 Biscayne Blvd., Miami, Fla., 33138. (305) 754-4400. Cuisine: Scandinavian. Credit cards: AE.

PUMPERNIK'S....11415 South Dixie Hwy., Miami, Fla., 33156. (305) 235-2424. Cuisine: Deli specials. Open 7 days from 7:00 AM to midnight. Credit cards: AE, MC, VISA. No alcoholic beverages.

PUMPERNIK'S....12599 Biscayne Blvd., Miami, Fla., 33181. (305) 891-1255. Cuisine: Deli specials. Open 7:00 AM to midnight 7 days weekly. Credit cards: AE, MC, VISA.

REFLECTIONS AT MIAMARINA.... Off Biscayne Blvd. & NE 5th St., Miami, Fla., 33161. (305) 371-6433. Cuisine: Continental. Open Monday through Friday for lunch; Monday through Saturday for dinner; Closed Sunday. Credit cards: All major. Reservations: Suggested. Free valet parking.

RODEO STEAKHOUSE....2521 Biscayne Blvd., Miami, Fla., 33137. (305) 576-8688. Cuisine: South American "Churrascaria Gaucho". Open 6 days for lunch and dinner; Closed Sunday. Credit cards: Call for cards. Reservations: Suggested. Entertainment: Live Brazillian music nightly.

ROUND TABLE....1800 NE 124th St., Miami, Fla., 33181. (305) 893-5600. Cuisine: American. Open 7 days for lunch and dinner. Credit cards: All major.

SEEDA THAI....5930 South Dixie Hwy., Miami, Fla., 33143. (305) 661-8314. Cuisine: Thai. Days closed: Open 7 days. Credit cards: AE, DC, MC, VISA.

SORRENTO RESTAURANT & LOUNGE....3059 SW 8th St., Miami, Fla., 33135. (305) 643-3111-2. Cuisine: Italian Owner: Vincent Amanzio. Closed Tuesday; Open Monday, Wednesday, Thursday, and Friday for lunch; Wednesday through Monday for dinner. Credit cards: All major. Private party facilities: 20 to 100. Annual sales: $500,000 to $1 million. Total employment: 32. Corporate name: Sorrento Restaurant & Lounge, Inc.

THE STUDIO....2340 SW 32nd Ave., Miami, Fla., 33145. (305) 445-5371. Cuisine: American. Open Tuesday through Sunday for dinner only; Closed Monday. Credit cards: All major. No reservations.

SUN INN....2235 Biscayne Blvd., Miami, Fla., 33137. (305) 573-5351. Cuisine: Chinese (Szechuan). Owner: Wor Wing Liu & Sie-Fung Tang. Open 7 days for lunch and dinner. Credit cards: AE, MC, VISA. Private party facilities: 10 to 35. Annual sales: $250,000 to $500,000. Total employment: 20. Corporate name: Sun Inn Chinese Restaurant, Inc.

SWISS CHATEAU....2471 SW 32nd Ave., Miami, Fla., 33145. (305) 445-6103. Cuisine: Continental. Open 7 days. Credit cards: major.

THE TERRACE....1601 Biscayne Blvd., Miami, Fla., 33132. (305) 374-0000. Cuisine: American. Open Monday through Saturday for lunch; 7 days for dinner; Sunday brunch. Credit cards: All major.

THAI HOUSE RESTAURANT....715 East 9th St., Miami, Fla., 33139. (305) 887-0561. Cuisine: Thai. Open Monday through Saturday for lunch; 7 days for dinner. Credit cards: DC, MC, VISA. Reservations: Suggested.

TIEN KUE INN....2860 Coral Way, Miami, Fla., 33129. (305) 444-2717. Cuisine: Chinese. Open 7 days for lunch and dinner. Credit cards: All major.

TIGER TIGER TEAHOUSE....2235 Biscayne Blvd., Miami, Fla., 33137. (305) 573-2689. Cuisine: Chinese. Credit cards: AE.

TIN LIZZIE....12500 Biscayne Blvd., Miami, Fla., 33181. (305) 893-1177. Cuisine: American. Open Monday through Saturday for lunch; 7 days for dinner; Late supper nightly. Credit cards: AE, DC, MC, VISA.

TIN SING HOUSE....14059 North Kendall Dr., Miami, Fla., 33186. (305) 385-4585. Cuisine: Chinese. Open 7 day for lunch and dinner. Credit cards: Call for cards.

THE TOP OF THE COLUMBUS....312 NE First St., Columbus Hotel, Miami, Fla., 33139. (305) 373-4411 Cuisine: Continental. Open 7 days. Credit cards: All major.

TOP OF THE TURF.... Holiday Inn at Calder, 21485 NW 27th Ave., Miami, Fla., 33192. (305) 621-5801. Cuisine: American. Open daily for lunch and dinner. Credit cards: Call for cards. Reservations: Accepted. Entertainment: Music and dancing in "Winner's Circle" lounge nightly.

TONI'S CASA NAPOLI....12350 NE 6th Ave., Miami, Fla., 33161. (305) 893-6071. Cuisine: Italian. Open Monday through Saturday for three seatings of dinner; Closed Sunday. Credit cards: AE, DC, MC, VISA.

TONY ROMA'S....2665 SW 37th Ave., Miami, Fla., 33133. (305) 443-6626. Cuisine: American. Open 7 days for lunch and dinner. Credit cards: MC, VISA.

TONY ROMA'S....15700 Biscayne Blvd., Miami, Fla., 33160. (305) 949-2214. Cuisine: American. Open 7 days for lunch and dinner. Credit cards: MC, VISA.

TRATTORIA PIZZERIA....1630 Biscayne Blvd., Miami, Fla., 33132. (305) 358-161. Cuisine: Italian. Open 7 days. Credit cards: none.

TUTTLES.... Charter Club, 600 NE 36th St., Miami, Fla., 33137. (305) 576-7676. Cuisine: Continental. Credit cards: All major. Open 6 days for dinner only; Closed Sunday. Entertainment: Friday and Saturday disco.

VALENTI'S....9101 South Dixie Hwy, Miami, Fla., 33156. (305) 667-0421. Cuisine: Italian. Owner: Charles J. Valenti, Jr. Open 7 days for dinner. Credit cards: All major. Private party facilities: 10 to 100. Annual sales: $1 million to $3 million. Total employment: 37. Corporate name: Valenti's South, Inc.

VERSAILLES....3555 SW 8th St., Miami, Fla., 33135. (305) 445-7614. Cuisine: Spanish/Mexican. Open 7 days for breakfast, lunch, dinner, and late supper. Credit cards: All major.

VICTORIA STATION....1480 North Miami Gardens Dr., Miami, Fla., 33179. (305) 940-2296. Cuisine: American. Open 7 days for lunch and dinner. Credit cards: AE, MC, VISA.

VICTORIA STATION....6301 NW 36th St., Miami, Fla., 33166. (305) 871-1563. Cuisine: American. Open 7 days for lunch and dinner. Credit cards: AE, MC, VISA.

VIZCAYA....2436 SW 8th St., Miami, Fla., 33135. (305) 642-2452. Cuisine: Spanish/Mexican. Open daily for lunch and dinner. Credit cards: All major.

WAH SHING....9503 South Dixie Hwy., Miami, Fla., 33156. (305) 666-9879. Cuisine: Cantonese Chinese. Open 7 days for lunch and dinner. Credit cards: MC, VISA.

WONG'S SHANGHAI....12420 Biscayne Blvd., Miami, Fla., 33181. (305) 891-4313. Cuisine: Chinese. Open 7 days for lunch and dinner. Credit cards: Call for cards.

MIAMI BEACH

BAL MASQUE SUPPER CLUB.... Sheraton Bal Harbour, 9701 Collins Ave., Miami Beach, Fla., 33154. (305) 865-7511. Cuisine: Continental. Open 7 days. Credit cards: All major.

BENIHANA OF TOKYO....1665 79th St. Cswy., Miami Beach, Fla., 33141. (305) 866-2768. Cuisine: Japanese. Open 7 days. Credit cards: AE, MC, VISA.

BOGEY'S WATERFRONT....10880 Collins Ave., Miami Beach, Fla., 33139. (305) 945-6766. Cuisine: American. Open 7 days for lunch and dinner. Credit cards: AE, DC, MC, VISA. Located on the docks at Baker's Haulover.

CAFE CHAUVERON....9561 East Bay Harbour Dr., Miami Beach, Fla., 33139. (305) 866-8779. Cuisine: French. Call for hours. Credit cards: All major. Notable wine cellar.

CARINO'S....10760 Biscayne Blvd., Miami Beach, Fla., 33161. (305) 893-3971. Cuisine: Italian. Open 7 days Credit cards: All major.

CASA SANTINO....10999 Biscayne Blvd., Miami Beach, Fla., 33161. (305) 895-1440. Cuisine: Italian. Days closed: Mondays, May-October. Credit cards: AE, DC, MC, VISA.

CHRISTINE LEE'S GASLIGHT....18401 Collins Ave., Miami Beach, Fla., 33139. (305) 931-7700. Cuisine: Szechuan Chinese. Open 7 days for dinner only. Credit cards: All major.

EBERHARDT'S "HOUSE OF STEAK"....940 71st St., Miami Beach, Fla., 33139. (305) 866-6006. Cuisine: Steak/Viennese. Open 6 days for dinner only; Closed Monday. Credit cards: Call for cards.

ENRICO AND PAGLIERI....18288 Collins Ave., Miami Beach, Fla., 33139. (305) 932-0247. Cuisine: Italian. Open 7 days for dinner only. Credit cards: AE, DC, MC, VISA.

FONTAINEBLEAU HILTON....4441 Collins Ave., Miami Beach, Fla., 33140. (305) 538-2000. Cuisine: Continental. Open 7 days. Credit cards: All major.

THE FORGE....432 Arthur Godfrey Rd., Miami Beach, Fla., 33139. (305) 538-8533. Cuisine: American. Open 7 days for dinner only. Credit cards: All major. Entertainment: Disco in bar daily from 2:00 PM.

GATTI'S....1427 West Ave., Miami Beach, Fla., 33139. (305) 673-1717. Cuisine: Northern Itaian. Days closed: Mondays, mid-May to October. Credit cards: AE, DC, MC, VISA.

HARBOUR HOUSE....10275 Collins Ave., Miami Beach, Fla., 33139. (305) 864-2251. Cuisine: American. Open Monday through Saturday for lunch; 7 days for dinner. Credit cards: All major.

HENRI'S.... Konover Hotel, 5445 Collins Ave., Miami Beach, Fla., 33139. (305) 865-1500. Cuisine: Continental "gourmet." Open Tuesday through Sunday for dinner only; Closed Monday. Credit cards: All major.

HOUSE OF INDIA....534 Arthur Godfrey Rd., Miami Beach, Fla., 33139. (305) 531-1511. Cuisine: Indian. Open Monday through Saturday for lunch; 7 days for dinner. Credit cards: All major. Sitar music.

INSIDE....1009 Kane Concourse, Miami Beach, Fla., 33139. (305) 864-2049. Cuisine: American. Open Monday through Saturday for lunch and dinner; Closed Sunday. Credit cards: AE, MC, VISA.

JOE'S STONE CRAB...227 Biscayne Blvd., Miami Beach, Fla., 33139. (305) 673-0365. Cuisine: Seafood. Open Monday through Friday for lunch; 7 days for dinner; Closed May through October. Credit cards: AE, DC, MC, VISA. No reservations.

LA COQUILLE....16526 NE 6th Ave., Miami Beach, Fla., 33162. (305) 940-6950. Cuisine: French. Days closed: Sunday and Monday. Credit cards: MC, VISA.

LALIQUE....9701 Collins Ave., Miami Beach, Fla., 33139. (305) 865-7511. Cuisine: Continental. Open for dinner nightly. Credit cards: All major. "Three menus: The Land, The Sea, The Air."

LE PARISIEN....474 Arthur Godfrey Rd., Miami Beach, Fla., 33140. (305) 534-2770. Cuisine: French. Days closed: Sunday. Credit cards: All major.

L'HOSTELLERIE D'ARGETEUIL....9650 East Bay Harbor Dr.,Miami Beach, Fla., 33139. (305) 866-8706. Cuisine: French. Open 6 days for dinner only; Closed Sunday. Credit cards: All major.

THE MAIN GALLERY....4441 Collins Ave., Miami Beach, Fla., 33139. (305) 538-2000. Cuisine: Continental. Open 7 nights weekly for dinner. Credit cards: All major. Reservations: Suggested. Entertainment: Live entertainment nightly. Located at the Fountainbleau Hilton.

MARCELLA'S MY KITCHEN....13886 West Dixie Hwy., Miami Beach, Fla., 33161. (305) 891-8220. Cuisine: Italian. Credit cards: All major.

MASA-SAN....19355 NW Second Ave., Miami Beach, Fla., 33169. (305) 651-7782. Cuisine: Japanese. Days closed: Open 7 days. Credit cards: AE, MC, VISA.

MITCH'S STEAK RANCH....7419 Collins Ave., Miami Beach, Fla., 33139. (305) 865-7922. Cuisine: American. Open daily for dinner. Credit cards: AE, MC, VISA.

PAPPAGALLO....11500 Biscayne Blvd., Miami Beach, Fla., 33161. (305) 895-3730. Cuisine: Northern Italian. Days closed: Sunday. Credit cards: AE, DC, MC, VISA.

PASTA NOSH....13943 Biscayne Blvd., Miami Beach, Fla., 33181. (305) 944-1026. Cuisine: Italian. Days closed: Monday. Credit cards: MC, VISA.

PICCIOLO'S....136 Collins Ave., Miami Beach, Fla., 33139. (305) 673-1267. Cuisine: Italian. Open 7 days for dinner only. Credit cards: All major. "Enormous menu listing practically every Italian dish ever created."

PIETRO'S....1233 Lincoln Rd., Miami Beach, Fla., 33139. (305) 673-8722. Cuisine: Italian. Open Wednesday through Sunday for dinner only; Closed Monday and Tuesday. Credit cards: AE, MC, VISA.

THE PORCH....4525 Collins Ave., Miami Beach, Fla., 33139. (305) 531-0000. Cuisine: American. Open daily for dinner only. Credit cards: All major.

PUMPERNIK'S....6800 Collins Ave., Miami Beach, Fla., 33139. (305) 866-0246. Cuisine: Deli specials. Open 7 days from 7:00 AM to midnight. Credit cards: AE, MC, VISA. No alcoholic beverages.

RASCAL HOUSE RESTAURANT....17190 Collins Ave., Miami Beach, Fla., 33160. (305) 947-4581. Cuisine: American/Delicatessen. Owner: Wolfie Cohen. Open 7 days. Credit cards: None. Annual sales: Over $3 million. Total employment: 250.

SANREMO....4300 Collins Ave., Miami Beach, Fla., 33138. (305) 531-4159-6. Cuisine: Northern Italian. Call for days and times. Credit cards: Call for cards: Reservations: Strongly suggested.

SAUCY CREPE.... In Bal Harbour Shops, 9700 Collins Ave., Miami Beach, Fla., 33139. (305) 868-1200. Cuisine: Crepes. Days closed: Sunday. Credit cards: AE, MC, VISA.

STAMPTERS....5875 Collins Ave., Miami Beach, Fla., 33139. (305) 865-8645. Cuisine: Continental/International. Open Monday through Saturday for dinner only; Closed Sunday. Credit cards: All major. "Jackets and reservations required."

STARLIGHT ROOF....4833 Collins Ave., in the Doral-On-The-Ocean, Miami Beach, Fla., 33140. (305) 532-3600. Cuisine: Continental. Days closed: Monday. Credit cards: All major.

TIBERIO....9700 Collins Ave., Miami Beach, Fla., 33139. (305) 861-6161. Cuisine: Northern Italian. Open Monday through Friday for lunch; 7 days for dinner. Credit cards: All major.

TONY ST. THOMAS.... In Seacost Towers North, 5225 Collins Ave., Miami Beach, Fla., 33140. (305) 864-0381. Cuisine: Natural. Days closed: Monday, Tuesday. Credit cards: AE, MC, VISA.

TOUR D'ARGENT....9955 Collins Ave., Miami Beach, Fla., 33139. (305) 865-8611. Cuisine: Continental/French. Open daily for dinner only. Credit cards: All major. In the Beau Rivage Hotel.

THE UNICORN....16454 NE Sixth Ave., Miami Beach, Fla., 33162. (305) 944-5595. Cuisine: Natural. Closed Sunday. Credit cards: None.

MIAMI SPRINGS

THE GARDEN....17 Westward Dr., Miami Springs, Fla., 33166. (305) 887-9238. Cuisine: Natural. Open 7 days. Credit cards: All major.

NORTH BAY VILLAGE

THE PLACE FOR STEAK....1335 79th St., North Bay Village, Fla., 33141. (305) 758-5581. Cuisine: Steak/American. Owner: Hy Uchitel. Open 7 days for lunch and dinner. Credit cards: All major. Private party facilities: 25 to 200. Annual sales: $1 million to $3 million. Corporate name: H.J.U. Sales & Investments, Inc.

NORTH MIAMI

PRIME STEAK HOUSE....11190 Biscayne Blvd., North Miami, Fla., 33181. (305) 893-4989. Cuisine: Prime Steaks. Open 7 days for dinner only. Credit cards: Call for cards. Reservations: Accepted.

NORTH MIAMI BEACH

BANGKOK CUISINE....16295 Biscayne Blvd., North Miami Beach, Fla., 33160. (305) 948-6859. Cuisine: Thai. Open Monday through Friday for lunch; 7 days for dinner from 4:00 PM. Credit cards: Call for cards. Reservations: Suggested.

THE BEVERLY HILLS CAFE....17850 West Dixie Hwy., North Miami Beach, Fla., 33160. (305) 935-3660. Cuisine: Continental. Owner: Mark and Sharon Richman, David Paull, Ken Friedman, John Shuler. Open Monday through Saturday. Credit cards: AE, MC, VISA. Private party facilities: 100. Annual sales: $500,000 to $1 million. Total employment: 35. Corporate name: Beverly Hills Cafe III, Inc.

PLUM BLOSSOM....18101 Biscayne Blvd., North Miami Beach, Fla., 33162. (305) 932-0177. Cuisine: Chinese. Owner's names: Joe Franchi and Ken·Roth. Credit cards. All major. Annual sales: $1,500,000. Total employment: 35.

THE TOAST OF THE TOWN....13675 Biscayne Blvd., North Miami Beach, 33181. (305) 947-1514. Cuisine: American. Owner Toby S. Spector. Open every day til 6:00 AM. Credit cards: All major. Annual sales: $1 million to $3 million. Total employment: 41. Corporate name: Toby's Toast of the Town Restaurant, Inc.

NORTH PALM BEACH

ASHLEY'S....1162 US 1, Oakbrook Sq., North Palm Beach, Fla., 33408. (305) 626-3222. Cuisine: Continental. Days closed: Sunday. Credit cards: AE, MC, VISA.

THE FLAME RESTAURANT.... Rte. 1, North Palm Beach, Fla. 33408. (305) 626-6200. Credit cards: AE, MC, VISA.

NORTH REDDINGTON BEACH

WINECELLAR RESTAURANT....17307 Gulf Blvd., North Reddington Beach, Fla., 33708. (813) 393-3491. Cuisine: Continental. Owner: Ted Sonnenscein, Peter Schukert, Karl Klumpp. Closed Monday. Credit cards: All major. Private party facilities: 15 to 300. Annual sales: $500,000 to $1 million. Total employment: 75. Corporate name: Winecellar Restaurant, Inc.

NORTH ST. PETERSBURG

CAMPANELLAS ITALIAN RISTORANTE....5051 66th St., North St. Petersburg, Fla., 33709. (813) 541-7541. Cuisine: Italian. Owner: Raffaele and Rita Campanella. Open Tuesday through Sunday. Credit cards: All major. Annual sales: $250,000 to $500,000. Total employment: 44.

OAKLAND PARK

ANTONIO CAMPAGNE'S SPAGHETTI FACTORY....3151 West Oakland Park Blvd., Oakland Park, Fla., 33311. (305) 739-5411. Cuisine: Continental/Steak/Seafood. Owner: Allan B. Dawson. Open 7 days for dinner. Credit cards: AE, MC, VISA. Private party facilities: 30 to 175. Annual sales: $250,000 to $500,000. Total employment: 6 to 17. Corporate name: Antonio's Food Service, Inc.

TEXAN STEAK HOUSE....4050 NE Fifth Ave., Oakland Park, Fla., 33334. (305) 566-6260. Cuisine: Mexican. Open daily for lunch and dinner. Credit cards: AE, VISA.

OCALA

O'NEAL BROTHERS I....24 SE Broadway, Ocala, Fla., 32678. (904) 351-8555. An inviting cafe-restaurant decorated in clean lines and primary colors. This slick Florida continental restaurant is run by the same folks that run O'Neals's Baloon in Manhattan—and the same charm and exuberence are also present here. The staff is friendly and the food is notably fresh, well-prepared, and satisfying. Specialties range through roast beef, continental veal entrees, fresh pastas, and a wide selection of area seafood. Desserts are changed daily and there are featured Irish and French coffees. Owner: Michael O'Neal, Patrick O'Neal, Ture Tufvesson. Open 7 days for lunch and dinner. Priced moderately. Reservations: Accepted. Credit cards: All major. Annual sales: $500,000 to $1 million. Total employment: 50. Corporate name: I, Inc.

OCEAN RIDGE

BUSCH'S SEAFOOD RESTAURANT....5855 North Ocean Blvd., Ocean Ridge, Fla., 33160. (305) 732-8470. Cuisine: Seafood. Days closed: Monday. Credit cards: AE, MC VISA. Owner: The Lambrakis family.

ORLANDO

LILI MARLENE'S AVIATORS PUB & RESTAURANT....129 West Church St., Orlando, Fla., 32801. (305) 422-2434. Cuisine: American. Credit cards: AE, MC, VISA. Total employment: 55.

PALM BEACH

ANGELIQUE....237 Worth Ave., Palm Beach, Fla., 33480. (305) 655-0950. Cuisine: French. Open daily for breakfast, lunch, and dinner. Credit cards: VISA only.

CAFE L'EUROPE.... Esplande, Worth Ave., Palm Beach, Fla., 33480. (305) 655-4020. Cuisine: French. Open daily for lunch and dinner. Credit cards: AE, MC, VISA.

CAPRICCIO.... Royal Poinciana Plz., Palm Beach, Fla., 33480. (205) 659-5955. Cuisine: Italian. Open daily for lunch and dinner. Credit cards: AE, MC, VISA.

CHARLEY'S CRAB....465 South Ocean Blvd., Palm Beach, Fla., 33480. (305) 659-1500. Cusine: Seafood. Open daily for dinner only. Credit cards: AE, MC, VISA.

DOHERTY'S....288 South Ocean Blvd., Palm Beach, Fla., 33480. (305) 695-7196. Cuisine: American. Open daily for breakfast, lunch, and dinner. Credit cards: AE, MC, VISA. No reservations.

LE MONEGASQUE....2505 South Ocean Blvd., Palm Beach, Fla., 33480. (305) 585-0071. Cuisine: French. Owner: Ann & Also G. Rinerot. Open Tuesday to Sunday for dinner; Closed Monday. Credit cards: AE. Private party facilities: 50 to 80. Annual sales: $250,000 to $500,000. Corporate name: Le Monegasque, Inc.

PETITE MARMITE....315 Worth Ave., Palm Beach, Fla., 33480. (305) 655-0550. Cuisine: French. Open daily for lunch and dinner. Credit cards: All major.

TA-BOO RESTAURANT....221 Worth Ave., Palm Beach, Fla., 33480. (305) 655-5562. Cuisine: Continental/American. Owner: John & Paul Lambrakis. Open 7 days in winter; closed Sunday in summer. Credit cards: AE, MC, VISA. Private party facilities: Up to 80. Annual sales: $1 million to $3 million. Total employment: 75. Corporate name: TA-BOO of Palm Beach, Inc.

PALM BEACH GARDENS

THE ABBEY ROAD....10800 North Military Tr., Palm Beach Gardens, Fla., 33410. (305) 622-2101. Cuisine: Steak/Seafood. Owner: Robert C. Scofield, Alan Andrzejewski, Charles Falmouth, Sam H. Scherenkau, and Wellington Bonsecours. Open Monday through Friday for lunch; 7 days for dinner. Credit cards: AE, MC, VISA. Private party facilities 10 to 25. Annual sales: Over $3 million (three restaurants). Total employment: Approximately 200 (three restaurants). Corporate name: Abbey Road Enterprises. Entertainment: Live entertainment nightly except Monday.

LA CAPANNINA....10971 North Military Tr., Palm Beach Gardens, Fla., 33480 (305) 395-9333. Cuisine: Italian. Open daily for lunch and dinner. Credit cards: AE, MC, VISA.

PINELLAS PARK

CAMPANELLA'S....6665 Park Blvd., Pinellas Park, Fla., 33310. (813) 546-3101. Cuisine: Italian. Owner's name: Ralph and Rita Campanella. Credit cards: MC, VISA.

PLANTATION

DAN DOWD'S....601 South State Rd. 7, Plantation, Fla., 33310. (305) 584-7770. Cuisine: American. Open daily for lunch and dinner. Credit cards: AE, MC, VISA.

LAI-LAI....1804 North University Dr., Plantation, Fla., 33322. (305) 473-5534. Cuisine: Chinese. Open daily for lunch and dinner. Credit cards: AE, VISA.

MOTHER RHINE....5219 West Broward Blvd., Plantation, Fla., 33317. (305) 581-1422. Cuisine: German. Open daily for lunch and dinner. Credit cards: All major.

TAKEYAMA....6920 Cypress Rd., Plantation, Fla., 33317. (305) 792-0350. Cuisine: Japanese. Open daily for lunch and dinner. Credit cards: MC, VISA.

TONY ROMA'S PLACE....460 NW 40th Ave. (441), Plantation, Fla., 33309. (305) 587-2998. Cuisine: American. Open daily for lunch and dinner. Credit cards: Call for cards.

PLANTATION KEY

MARKER 88.... Mile Marker 88, Plantation Key, Fla., 33324. (305) 582-5503 or (305) 852-9315. Cuisine: Seafood. Open Tuesday through Sunday for dinner only; Closed Monday. Credit cards: AE, DC, MC, VISA.

POMPANO BEACH

BOBBY RUBINO'S PLACE FOR RIBS....2501 Federal Hwy., Pompano Beach, Fla., 33064. (305) 781-7550. Cuisine: American (Ribs). Open 7 days for lunch and dinner. Credit cards: AE, MC, VISA.

CAPTAIN'S COVE....700 South Federal Hwy., Pompano Beach, Fla., 33062. (305) 943-9100. Cuisine: Steak/Seafood. Open 7 days for dinner only. Credit cards: AE, MC, VISA. Reservations: Accepted.

DIANA....3325 East Atlantic Blvd., Pompano Beach, Fla., 33062. (305) 941-7960. Cuisine: American. Open daily for breakfast, lunch, and dinner. No credit cards.

FLAMING PIT....1150 North Federal Hwy., Pompano Beach, Fla., 33064. (305) 943-3484. Cuisine: American. Open daily for lunch and dinner. Credit cards: MC, VISA.

THE FRENCH PLACE....360 East McNab Rd., Pompano Beach, Fla., 33060. (305) 785-1920. Cuisine: French. Open daily for lunch and dinner. Credit cards: MC, VISA.

HARRIS IMPERIAL HOUSE.... North Ocean Dr., Atlantic Blvd., Pompano Beach, Fla., 33063. (305) 941-2200. Cuisine: American/Chinese. Open daily for lunch and dinner. Credit cards: AE, CB, MC. Reservations: Accepted.

HIDDEN HARBOR....1500 North Federal Hwy., Pompano Beach, Fla., 33062. (305) 781-1500. Cuisine: Seafood. Open 5 days for dinner only; Closed Monday and Tuesday. Credit cards: MC, VISA. "Weekly dynamic Sunday brunch."

ITALIAN VILLA....2190 North Federal Hwy., Pompano Beach, Fla., 33062. (305) 942-5510. Cuisine: Italian. Open daily for dinner only from 5:00 PM. Credit cards: AE, CB, VISA. Reservations: Accepted.

LA VERANDA....2121 East Atlantic Blvd., Pompano Beach, Fla., 33062. (305) 943-7390. Cuisine: Italian. Open daily for dinner only. Credit cards: Call for cards.

LE MORVAN....600 North Federal Hwy., Pompano Beach, Fla., 33062. (305) 943-5980. Cuisine: French. Open 6 days for dinner only. Credit cards: AE, MC, VISA. Reservations: Accepted.

MARANDOLA'S....1201 South Federal Hwy., Pompano Beach, Fla., 33062. (305) 943-9560. Cuisine: Italian. Open daily for dinner only. Credit cards: AE, MC, VISA.

MR. FISHBONE'S....200 East McNab Rd., Pompano Beach, Fla., 33060. (305) 785-7040. Cuisine: Seafood. Open daily for dinner only. Credit cards: AE, MC, VISA.

VESUVIO....420 North Federal Hwy., Pompano Beach, Fla., 33062. (305) 941-1594. Cuisine: Italian. Open daily for dinner only. Credit cards: AE, MC, VISA.

VILLA D'ESTE....1624 East Atlantic Blvd., Pompano Beach, Fla., 33060. (305) 943-9726. Cuisine: Italian. Open daily for lunch and dinner. Credit cards: MC, VISA.

RAINTREE

RAINTREE....181 North University Dr., Raintree, Fla., 33324. (305) 473-2303. Cuisine: American. Open daily for lunch and dinner. Credit cards: AE, MC. VISA.

REDINGTON BEACH

LOBSTER POT....17814 Gulf Blvd., Redington Beach, Fla., 33708. (813) 391-8592. Cuisine: Seafood. Open Monday through Saturday for dinner only; Closed Sunday. Credit cards: AE, MC, VISA. Reservations: Requested. Entertainment: Live classical music.

ST. PETERSBURG

ARIGATO JAPANESE STEAK HOUSE....3600 36th St. North, St. Petersburg, Fla., 33713. (813) 343-5200. Cuisine: Japanese. Open 7 days for dinner only. Credit cards: AE, DC, MC, VISA. Reservations: Accepted.

BILL NAGY'S....10400 Gandy Blvd., St. Petersburg, Fla., 33702. (813) 577-1565. Cuisine: Continental/Czech. Credit cards: AE, MC, VISA.

FISHERMAN'S INN....9595 4th St. North, St. Petersburg, Fla., 33702. (813) 576-4252. Cuisine: Seafood. Owner: William L. Phillips, Sr. Open 7 days for lunch and dinner. Credit cards: All major. Private party facilities: Up to 150. Annual sales: $1 million to $3 million. Total employment: 105. Corporate name: Fisherman's Inn Inc.

ISLAND CLUB OF THE ISLA DEL SOL....6000 Sun Blvd., St. Petersburg, Fla., 33715. (813) 867-3121. Cuisine: French/Continental. Open Monday through Saturday for lunch and dinner; Closed Sunday. Credit cards: All major. Reservations: Suggested. Entertainment: Live entertainment nightly.

LE CAFE PLAZA....1 Plaza Pl. NE, #209, St. Petersburg, Fla., 33701. (813) 823-8888. Cuisine: Continental. Open Monday through Saturday for breakfast, lunch, and dinner; Closed Sunday. Credit cards: MC, VISA.

NINETY-FOURTH AERO SQUADRON....Roosevelt Blvd. (behind St. Petersburg-Clearwater Airport), St. Petersburg, Fla., 33702. (813) 536-0400. Cuisine: "Featuring Roast Duck and Prime Rib." Open Monday through Saturday for lunch; 7 days for dinner; Sunday dinner from 3:00 PM. Credit cards: All major. Entertainment: World War I guns and sandbags adorn this imaginative dining room.

PEPIN'S....4125 Fourth St. North, St. Petersburg, Fla., 33703. (813) 821-3773. Cuisine: Spanish. Credit cards: AE, MC, VISA.

ROLLANDE ET PIERRE....2221 Fourth St. North, St. Petersburg, Fla., 33704. (813) 822-4602. Cuisine: French. Credit cards: All major.

TED PETERS SMOKED FISH....1350 Pasadena Ave., St. Petersburg, Fla., 33707. (813) 381-7931. Cuisine: Seafood. Open 6 days for lunch and dinner; Closed Tuesday. No credit cards. Annual sales: $500,000 to $1 million. Total employment: 25. Corporate name: Ted Peters Smoked Fish, Inc.

TEN BEACH DRIVE....10 Beach Dr. NE, St. Petersburg, Fla., 33701. (813) 894-6398. Cuisine: American. Credit cards: MC, VISA.

ST. PETERSBURG BEACH

KING CHARLES AT THE DON CESAR....3400 Gulf Blvd., St. Petersburg Beach, Fla., 33706. (813) 360-1881. Cuisine: Continental. Open 7 days for dinner only; Sunday brunch. Credit cards: All major. Reservations: Suggested.

WATERSHIP DOWN....10 Corey Ave., St. Petersburg Beach, Fla., 33706. (813) 367-4588. Cuisine: Seafood/Continental/American. Open Monday through Friday for lunch; 7 days for dinner. Credit cards: AE, MC, VISA. Entertainment: Live entertainment nightly. Reservations: Suggested.

SARASOTA

THE BUCCANEER....595 Dream Island Rd., Sarasota, Fla., 33500. (813) 383-1101. Cuisine: Seafood/Steak. Credit cards: All major.

CAFE L'EUROPE....431 Harding Circle, Sarasota, Fla., 33577. (813) 388-4415. Cuisine: Continental. Credit cards: All major.

COLUMBIA, GEM OF SPANISH RESTAURANTS....St. Armands Circle, Sarasota, Fla., 33578. (813) 388-3987. Cuisine: Spanish. Owner: Cesar, Adela, Casey and Richard Gonzmart. Open 7 days. Credit cards: All major. Private party facilities: 8 to 45. Annual sales: $1 million to $3 million. Total employment: 75. Corporate name: Columbia Restaurant of Sarasota, Inc.

L'AUBERGE DU BON VIVANT....7003 Gulf of Mexico Dr., Sarasota, Fla., 33581. (813) 383-2481. Cuisine: French. Credit cards: AE, MC, VISA.

MARINA JACK....Marina Plz., Sarasota, Fla., 33577. (813) 365-4232. Cuisine: Seafood. Owner: J.W. Graham. Open 7 days for lunch and dinner. No credit cards. Private party facilities: Available. Annual sales: Over $3 million. Total employment: 100. Corporate name: Marina Jack, Inc.

SOUTH MIAMI

CAFE MENDOCINO....5950 Sunset Dr., South Miami, Fla. 33143. (305) 666-7911. Cuisine: Natural. Open 7 days. Credit cards: AE, MC, VISA.

NEON LEON'S....5859 SW 73rd St., South Miami, Fla., 33143. (305) 665-0511. Cuisine: American. Days closed: Sunday. Credit cards: All major.

RAINBOWS....6600 SW 57th Ave., South Miami, Fla., 33143. (305) 666-4641. An art deco restaurant with a stunning red, blue, and mirrored look. When the entertainment is performing there's a genuine nightclub atmosphere of glitter and glamour. Specialties include: Stone crabs, "shrimp of the stars," clams oreganato, filet mignon *aux champignons, tournedos Rossini,* chicken *diablo,* veal Oscar, Alaskan king crab legs, *cotes d'agneau,* crepes *suzette,* bananas *flambe,* rainbow sherbert. Owner: Steve Dachs, Michelina Mell. Continental cuisine. Moderately priced. Reservations and major credit cards accepted. Private party facilities for between 25 and 250 persons. Total employment: 45.

TIGER TIGER TEAHOUSE....5716 South Dixie Hwy., South Miami, Fla., 33143. (305) 665-5660 or 665-5675. Cuisine: Mandarin and Szechuan. Open 7 days. Credit cards: AE, MC, VISA.

SOUTHWEST DADE

CIAO....10176 South Dixie Hwy., Southwest Dade, Fla., 33156. (305) 667-4676. Cuisine: Italian. Open 7 days for lunch and dinner. Credit cards: AE, MC, VISA.

TGI FRIDAY'S....8888 SW 136th St., Southwest Dade, Fla., 33176. (305) 225-1480. Cuisine: American. Open 7 days. Credit cards: All major.

SUNRISE

MR. GUMPS....2075 North University Dr., Sunrise, Fla., 33324. (305) 741-7714. Cuisine: American. Open 7 days. Credit cards: AE, MC, VISA.

SEA SHANTY....7529 West Oakland Park Blvd., Sunrise, Fla., 33319. (305) 741-8055. Cuisine: Seafood. Open daily for dinner only. Credit cards: AE, MC, VISA.

TAMARAC

STEAK AND ALE....West Commerical Blvd., Tamarac, Fla., 33319. (305) 722-3090. Cuisine: American. Open daily for dinner only. Credit cards: AE only.

TRIGG'S....5718 North University Dr., Tamarac, Fla., 33321. (305) 722-7110. Cuisine: American. Open daily for lunch and dinner. Credit cards: AE, MC, VISA.

TAMPA

ADRIAN'S....4644 West Kennedy Blvd., Tampa, Fla., 33609. (813) 879-3708. Cuisine: American. Open 6 days for lunch and dinner; Closed Sunday. AE, MC. VISA.

BAY HARBOR INN....7700 Courtney Campbell Cswy., Tampa, Fla., 33607. (813) 886-0562. Cuisine: Continental. Credit cards: AE, CB, MC, VISA.

BERN'S STEAK HOUSE....1208 South Howard Ave., Tampa, Fla., 33606. (813) 251-2421. Cuisine: Steak. Owner: Bern Laxer. Open 7 days for dinner. Credit cards: All major.

BOBBY'S SEAFOOD AND SPIRITS....13254 North Dale Mabry Hwy., Tampa, Fla., 33618. (813) 963-2900. Cuisine: Creole/Seafood. Open 7 days for lunch and dinner. Credit cards: MC, VISA.

BONG HWANG CHINESE RESTAURANT....3336 Henderson Blvd., Tampa, Fla., 33609 (813) 876-3881. Cuisine: Chinese. Open Monday through Friday for lunch; Monday through Saturday for dinner; Closed Sunday. Credit cards: MC, VISA.

CAFE DE PARIS....4430 West Kennedy, Tampa, Fla., 33609. (813) 876-5422. Cuisine: French. Credit cards: All major.

CAFE GENEVA....713 North Franklin St., Tampa, Fla., 33602. (813) 223-6446. Cuisine: Swiss. Open Monday through Friday for lunch only. Credit cards: MC, VISA.

CAFE PEPE....2006 West Kennedy Blvd., Tampa, Fla., 33606. (813) 253-6501. Cuisine: Spanish. Credit cards: AE, MC, DC, VISA.

CAFE SEVILLA....3602 North Armenia, Tampa, Fla., 33607 (813) 876-5429. Cuisine: Spanish. Credit cards: All major.

CAFE TONI....10200 North 30th St., Tampa, Fla., 33612. (813) 253-6501. Cuisine: Italian/Spanish. Open Monday through Saturday for dinner; Saturday afternoon brunch; Closed Sunday. Credit cards: MC, VISA.

CAPONE'S PIZZA....1010 North Westshore Blvd., Tampa, Fla., 33607. (813) 977-0022. Cuisine: Chicago-style pizza. Open 7 days. Credit cards: AE, MC, VISA.

CHATEAU PARISIEN, FRENCH GOURMET RESTAURANT... 7672 Courtney Cswy., Tampa, Fla., 33607. (813) 884-3040. Cuisine: French. Owner: Rick Diaz. Open Monday through Saturday. Credit cards: All major. Annual sales: $500,000 to $1 million. Corporate name: Bahama Inn, Inc.

CHAVEZ AT THE ROYAL....2109 Bayshore Blvd., Tampa, Fla., 33606. (813) 251-6186. Cuisine: Continental. Owner: Helen Chavez. Closed Sundays. Credit cards: AE, MC, VISA. Annual sales: $500,000 to $1 million. Total employment: 15. Corporate name: Chavez Back of the Bay, Inc.

CHINATOWN MONGOLIAN BARBEQUE....13248 North Dale Mabry Hwy., Tampa, Fla., 33618. (813) 961-9489. Cuisine: Mongolian Barbeque. Hours change seasonally; call for times. Credit cards: AE, MC, VISA.

CHINATOWN MONGOLIAN BARBEQUE....2373 East Fowler Ave., Tampa, Fla., 33612. (813) 977-2510. Cuisine: Mongolian Barbeque. Hours change seasonally; call for times. Credit cards: AE, MC, VISA.

CHINESE PAVILLION....232 North Dale Mabry Hwy., Tampa, Fla., 33609. (813) 870-2266. Cuisine: Chinese. Credit cards: AE, DC, MC, VISA.

CHUCK'S STEAK HOUSE....11911 North Dale Mabry Hwy., Tampa, Fla., 33618. (813) 962-2226. Cuisine: American. Open Monday through Friday for lunch; 7 days for dinner; Cocktails nightly. Credit cards: AE, MC, VISA.

COURTYARD....6734 South Westshore Blvd., Tampa, Fla., 33616. (813) 837-4700. Cuisine: Continental. Credit cards: All major

CRAWDADDY'S....2500 Rocky Point Dr., Tampa, Fla., 33607. (813) 885-5151. Cuisine: Continental. Open 7 days for lunch and dinner. Credit cards: AE, DC, MC, VISA.

THE EMBASSY....2801 Busch Blvd., Tampa, Fla., 33612. (813) 933-2885. Cuisine: Seafood/Steak/Italian. Open 7 days for dinner only. Credit cards: All major. Reservations: Accepted.

FLAGSHIP....1200 North Westshore Blvd., Tampa, Fla., 33607. (813) 879-1750. Cuisine: Steak/Seafood. Open 7 days for dinner only. Credit cards: All major. Reservations: Accepted. Entertainment: Live entertainment Friday, Saturday, and Sunday.

GREEK TAVERNA....13180 North Dale Mabry Hwy., Tampa, Fla., 33618. (813) 961-1270. Cuisine: Greek. Open 7 days for lunch and dinner. Credit cards: MC, VISA. Entertainment: "Monthly entertainment."

HORATIO HEAVEN....3342 South Westshore Blvd., Tampa, Fla., 33609. (813) 837-1270. Cuisine: Continental/Italian. Open 7 days for lunch and dinner; Sunday brunch. Credit cards: AE, MC, VISA.

JIMMY MAC'S....113 South Armenia Ave., Tampa, Fla., 33609. (813) 879-0591. Cuisine: American. Owner: James L. McNorrill, Jr., Trevor Smith, and Ford Smith. Open 6 days for lunch and dinner; Closed Sundays. Credit cards: AE, MC, VISA. Private party facilities: Up to 200. Annual sales: $500,000 to $1 million. Total employment: 38. Corporate name: Jimmy Mac's, Inc.

KASTAN'S....1001 North Westshore Blvd., Tampa, Fla., 33607. (813) 876-9611. Cuisine: International. Owner: N. Goget. Open 7 days. Credit cards: All major. Private party facilities: Up to 600. Annual sales: Over $3 million. Total employment: 350. Corporate name: Marriott, Inc. (Tampa).

LA CAVE....405 South Howard Ave., Tampa, Fla., 33606. (813) 257-1001. Cuisine: French. Credit cards: CB, DC, MC. VISA.

LAURO'S RISTORANTE....4010 Waters Ave., Tampa, Fla., 33614. (813) 884-4366. Cuisine: Italian. Open Monday through Friday for lunch; Monday through Saturday for dinner; Closed Sunday. Credit cards: AE, MC, VISA. Reservations: Suggested.

LE MEDITERRANEE....5000 North Dale Mabry Blvd., Tampa, Fla., 33614. (813)876-6924. Cuisine: French. Open Tuesday through Sunday for dinner only; Closed Monday. Credit cards: AE, MC, VISA.

LE "PETITE FLEUR"....3401 Cypress St., Tampa, Fla., 33607. (813) 879-1993. Cuisine: Continental/French. Credit cards: AE, DC, MC, VISA.

LICATA'S STEAK HOUSE....312 Tampa St., Tampa, Fla., 33602. (813) 229-6596. Cuisine: Steak. Open Monday through Friday for lunch; 7 days for dinner. Credit cards: AE, CB, DC, MC. Reservations: Suggested.

LORELLO'S....3717 Cypress St., Tampa, Fla., 33607. (813) 872-7708. Cuisine: Northern Italian. Open Tuesday through Friday for lunch; Tuesday through Sunday for dinner; Closed Monday. Credit cards: AE, DC, MC, VISA. Entertainment: Daily fashion show starting at noon.

LORENZO'S....3615 West Humphrey St., Tampa, Fla., 33614. (813) 932-6641. Cuisine: Italian. Open 7 days for dinner only. Credit cards: AE, MC, VISA. Reservations: Suggested.

MALIO'S....301 South Dale Mabry Hwy., Tampa, Fla., 33609. (813) 879-3233. Cuisine: Steak/Seafood. Open Monday through Friday for lunch; Monday through Saturday for dinner; Closed Sunday. Credit cards: All major. Reservations: Suggested.

MARCELLO'S RESTAURANT....4814 West Laurel St., Tampa, Fla., 33607. (813) 870-3398. Cuisine: Italian. Open Monday through Friday for lunch; Monday through Saturday for dinner; Closed Sunday. Credit cards: AE, MC, VISA. Reservations: Accepted.

MARIA'S....3671 South Westshore Blvd., Tampa, Fla., 33609. (813) 839-1296. Cuisine: Italian. Open Monday for lunch only; Tuesday through Saturday for lunch and dinner; Sunday for dinner from 1:00 PM. Credit cards: DC, MC. VISA.

MELTING POT....13170 North Dale Mabry, Village Center, Tampa, Fla., 33618. (813) 962-6936. Cuisine: Fondue. Credit cards: MC, VISA.

MILLER'S SEA FOOD CENTER....2315 West Linebaugh, Tampa, Fla. 33612. (813) 935-4793. Cuisine: Seafood. Credit cards: AE, MC, VISA.

MIRABELLA'S....327 North Dale Mabry Hwy., Tampa, Fla., 33607. (813) 876-2844. Cuisine: Seafood. Open 7 days for lunch and dinner. Credit cards: AE, DC, MC, VISA.

MONTE CARLO....3940 West Cypress, Tampa, Fla., 33607. (813) 879-6245. Credit cards: All major.

MULLLET INN....6415 Courtney Campbell Cswy., Tampa, Fla., 33607. (813) 884-6461. Cuisine: Seafood/American. Open 7 days for lunch and dinner. Credit cards: AE, DC, MC, VISA.

NATURAL KITCHEN....4100 West J.F. Kennedy Blvd., Tampa, Fla., 33609. (813) 870-1385. Cuisine: "Wholesome American cooking." Open Monday through Saturday for lunch and dinner; Closed Sunday. No credit cards.

PEKING CHINESE RESTAURANT....2310 North Dale Mabry Hwy., Tampa, Fla., 33607. (813) 870- 0921. Cuisine: Mandarin Chinese. Open Monday for dinner. Credit cards: All major. Reservations: Suggested.

PETITE FLEUR INTERNATIONAL RESTAURANT....3401 Cypress St., Tampa, Fla., 33607. (813) 870-1993. Cuisine: French/Continental. Owner: Jara and Jana Novotny. Open Tuesday through Saturday for dinner. Credit cards: All major. Annual sales: $250,000 to $500,000. Total employment: 8. Corporate name: European Foods, Inc.

ROUGH RIDERS RESTAURANT....1901 13th St., Tampa, Fla., 336-5. (813) 248-2756. Cuisine: American/Steak/Seafood. Owner: Michael Shea, Harris Mullen and Lee Davis. Open 7 days. Credit cards: AE, MC, VISA. Private party facilities: 6 to 42. Annual sales: $500,000 to $1 million. Total employment: 45. Corporate name: San Juan Hill Enterprises.

SAMPAN...3614 West J.F. Kennedy Blvd., Tampa, Fla., 33609. (813) 876-9977 or (813) 877-0455. Cuisine: Chinese. Open Monday through Friday for lunch; Monday through Saturday for dinner; Closed Sunday. Credit cards: MC, VISA. Reservations: Accepted. Entertainment: Live Entertainment Tuesday through Saturday.

SEABREEZE RESTAURANT....3409 22nd St., Tampa, Fla., 33604. (813) 247-2103. Cuisine: Seafood. Open 6 days for lunch and dinner; Closed Monday. Credit cards: AE, DC, MC, VISA. "On the bay since 1929."

SEA WOLF....4115 East Busch Blvd., Tampa, Fla., 33617. (813) 985-3112. Cuisine: Seafood. Credit cards: All major.

SELENA'S....1623 Snow Ave., Tampa, Fla., 33606. (813) 251-2116. Cuisine: "New Orleans-style." Open Monday through Friday for lunch; 7 days for dinner. Credit cards: All major. Reservations: Necessary. Entertainment: Nightly in the "Third Edition Lounge."

SPANISH PARK....3517 East 7th Ave., Tampa, Fla., 33605. (813) 248-6138. Cuisine: Spanish. Open Monday through Saturday for lunch and dinner; Closed Sunday. Credit cards: All major. Reservations: Suggested.

STEAKS, YOU AND I....328 West Brandon Blvd., Tampa, Fla., 33603. (813) 685-2166. Cuisine: Steak. Open 7 days for dinner only. Credit cards: AE, MC, VISA. Reservations: Recommended.

TEA ROOM....815 South Rome Ave., Tampa, Fla., 33606. (813) 251-8783. Cuisine: Continental. Open Monday through Friday for lunch only. Credit cards: MC, VISA. Reservations: Unnecessary.

TERIYAKI PARIS....11120 North 30th St., Tampa, Fla., 33612. (813) 977-7021. Cuisine: "Fast food curry and teriyaki." Open 7 days for lunch and dinner.

TOWNE HOUSE RESTAURANT....902 East Brandon Blvd., Tampa, Fla., 33603. (813) 689-0485. Cuisine: American. Open 7 days for dinner. Reservations: Accepted. Credit cards: AE, DC, MC, VISA.

VALLE'S....1712 North Dale Mabry Hwy., Tampa, Fla., 33607. (813) 877-5763. Cuisine: Steak/Seafood. Open 7 days for lunch and dinner. Credit cards: All major. Reservations: Accepted.

VERANDAH....5220 West J.F. Kennedy Blvd., Tampa, Fla., 33604. (813) 876-0168. Cuisine: French/ Continental. Open Monday through Friday for lunch; 7 days for dinner. Credit cards: All major. Reservations: Suggested.

VERONIQUE....4812 East Busch Blvd., Tampa, Fla., 33617. (813) 988-5739 or (813) 253-2128. Cuisine: French. Owner: Veronique Corbett. Open 5 days for dinner; Closed Sunday and Monday. Credit cards: MC, VISA. Private party facilities: Up to 30. Total employment: 6. Corporate name: Veronique Corbett, Inc.

VICTORIA STATION....2903 North Dale Mabry Hwy., Tampa, Fla., 33607. (813) 879-9800. Cuisine: Steak/Seafood/American. Open Monday through Friday for lunch; 7 days for dinner. Credit cards: AE, DC, MC, VISA.

TARPON SPRINGS

LOUIS PAPPAS....10 West Dodecanese Blvd., Tarpon Springs, Fla., 33500. (813) 937-5101. Cuisine: Greek. Michael L. Pappas, Pres. Open 7 days for lunch and dinner. Credit cards: All major. Private party facilities: 250. Annual sales: Over $3 million. Total employment: 290. Corporate name: Louis Pappas Riverside Restaurant, Inc.

THONOTOSASSA

DOM'S RUSTIC LODGE....421 Mistletoe, Thonotosassa, Fla., 33592. (813) 986-1550. Cuisine: Steak/Seafood. Open Tuesday through Saturday for lunch and dinner; Closed Sunday and Monday. Credit cards: DC, MC, VISA. Reservations: Accepted.

TREASURE ISLAND

LENNY DEE'S KING'S INN....10551 Gulf Blvd., Treasure Island, Fla., 33740. (813) 360-3660. Cuisine: American. Owner: Lenny Dee. Open Tuesday through Saturday for dinner only; Closed Sunday and Monday. Credit cards: AE, MC, VISA. Private party facilities: Up to 325. Annual sales: $500,000 to $1 million. Total employment: 35.

VENICE

WEDGEWOOD FAMILY DINING....100 West Tampa Ave., Venice, Fla., 33595. (813) 488-4017. Cuisine: American. Owner: Norman Reninger. Open 7 days for lunch and dinner. Credit cards: MC, VISA. Private party facilities: Up to 150. Annual sales: $500,000 to $1 million. Total employment: 60. Corporate Name: N&J Enterprises, Inc.

WEST PALM BEACH

THE ABBEY ROAD....1100 North Congress Ave., West Palm Beach, Fla., 33409. (305) 683-4600. Cuisine: Continental. Open 7 days for lunch and dinner. Credit cards: AE, MC, VISA.

CLEMATIS STREET CAFE....531½ Clematis St., West Palm Beach, Fla., 33401. (305) 833-4703. Cuisine: American. Open daily for lunch only. No credit cards.

FREDERIC'S....1930 North Dixie Hwy., West Palm Beach, Fla., 33407. (305) 833-3777. Cuisine: American. Open daily for dinner only. Credit cards: AE, MC, VISA.

WILTON MANORS

OLD FLORIDA SEAFOOD HOUSE....1414 NE 26th St., Wilton Manors, Fla., 33334. (305) 566-1044. Cuisine: Seafood. Open daily for lunch and dinner. Credit cards: AE, MC, VISA. Available raw bar.

SIAM CURRY HOUSE....2010 Wilton Dr., Wilton Manors, Fla., 33334. (305) 564-3411. Cuisine: Thai. Open Monday through Friday for lunch; 7 days for dinner. Credit cards: MC, VISA.

SIR NICHOLAS INN....23rd Rd. & 6th Ave., Wilton Manors, Fla., 33334. (305) 564-4901. Cuisine: Polish. Open 6 days for dinner only; Closed Monday. Credit cards: All major. Reservations: Suggested.

GEORGIA

ALBANY

DAVIS BROS. SUBURBAN RESTAURANT....101 North Slappery Dr., Albany, Ga., 31701. (912) 432-1120. Cuisine: American. Credit cards: All major.

ATLANTA

THE ABBEY....163 Ponce de Leon Ave., Atlanta, Ga., 30308. (404) 876-8831. Cuisine: Continental. Owner: William F. Swearingen. Open 7 days. Credit cards: All major. Private party facilities: Up to 350. Annual sales: Over $3 million. Total employment: 150. Corporate name: The Abbey, Inc.

ANARKALI....2115 North Decatur Rd., Atlanta, Ga., 30312. (404) 321-0251. Cuisine: Indian. Owner: Abu Faruque. Open for lunch Monday to Friday; Open for dinner Monday to Saturday. Credit cards: All major. Annual sales: Less than $250,000. Total employment: 6

BERNARD'S....1193 Collier Rd. NW, Atlanta, Ga., 30318. (404) 352-2778. Cuisine: French. Credit cards: AE, VISA.

BUGATTI.... Marietta & International Blvd., Omni International Hotel, Atlanta, Ga., 30335. (404) 659-0000. Cuisine: Italian. Open 7 days for breakfast, lunch and dinner. Credit cards: All major. Private party facilities: Up to 25. Annual sales: $500,000 to $1 million.

CLUB ATLANTIS.... Hyatt Regency, Atlanta, Ga., 30301. (404) 577-1234. Cuisine: Continental. Credit cards: All major.

COACH AND SIX RESTAURANT...1776 Peachtree St., Atlanta, Ga., 30309. (404) 872-6666. A well-established Atlanta institution. Everything in the place is polished, including the cooking. Beverlee Soloff-Shere runs the house and not unreasonably, does a roaring trade. There are many who insist that it is the greatest restaurant in town and we agree. First-timers are instructed to have the black bean soup and the chocolate mousse, and in-between they can choose any of a dozen entrees from broiled fish, live Maine lobster, and delicious triple loin lamb chops, excellent calf's liver, or by scallops or a double veal chop. Open 7 days for lunch and dinner. Private party facilities are available. Reservations and major credit cards are accepted.

DANTE'S DOWN THE HATCH....3380 Peachtree Rd. NE, Atlanta, Ga., 30326. (404) 266-1600. Cuisine: Swiss. Open 7 days for lunch and dinner. Credit cards: All major. Private party facilities: 12 to 420. Annual sales: $1 million to $3 million. Total employment: 55. Corporate name: Stepperson, Inc.

D.B. KAPLAN.... Lenox Square, Atlanta, Ga., 30306. (404) 266-1111. Cuisine: Delicatessen. Credit cards: None.

THE FRENCH RESTAURANT.... Marietta & International Blvd., Omni International Hotel, Atlanta, Ga., 30303. (404) 659-0000. Cuisine: French. Credit cards: All major.

GENE & GABE'S....1578 Piedmont Ave. NE, Atlanta, Ga., 30324. (404) 874-6145. Cuisine: Northern Italian. Owner: Gene Dale. Open 7 days for dinner. Credit cards: All major. Private party facilities: Up to 180. Annual sales: $1 million to $3 million. Total employment: 25.

GRAND CHINA....2975 Peachtree Rd., Buckhead, Atlanta, Ga., 30305. (404) 231-8690. Cuisine: Chinese. Owner's name: Che Chee. Credit cards: AE, DC, MC, VISA.

HAL'S....375 Pharr Road, Atlanta, Ga., 30305. (404) 262-2811. Cuisine: Hungarian/Mid-European. Owner: Ronald George Cohn. Closed Sunday and Monday. Credit cards: All major. Private party facilities: Up to 50. Corporate name: Harold Charles, Ltd.

HAROLD'S....171 McDonough Blvd. SE, Atlanta, Ga., 30315. (404) 627-9268. Cuisine: Barbecue. Credit cards: None.

HUGO'S.... Hyatt Regency, Atlanta, Ga., 30301. (404) 577-1234. Cuisine: Continental. Credit cards: All major

JOE DALE'S CAJUN HOUSE....3209 Maple Dr. NE, Atlanta, Ga., 30308. (404) 261-2741. Cuisine: Creole. Credit cards: All major.

JOSEPH'S....3129 Piedmont Rd. NE, Atlanta, Ga., 30305. (404) 261-3232. Cuisine: Country French. Owner's names: Ronald E. and Theodora J. Story. Credit cards: All major

LA GROTTA-RESTAURANT ITALIANO....2637 Peachtree Rd. NE, Atlanta, Ga., 30305. (404) 231-1368. Cuisine: Italian. Owners: Sergio Favalli & Antonio Pecondon. Closed Sunday and Monday. Credit cards: All major. Annual sales: $500,000 to $1 million. Total employment: 27. Corporate name: La Grotta, Inc.

MARY MAC'S TEA ROOM....224 Ponce de Leon, Atlanta, Ga., 30308. (404) 875-4337. Cuisine: Southern Regional/American. Owner: Margaret K. Lupo. Open for breakfast, lunch, and dinner Monday through Friday; Closed Saturday and Sunday. No credit cards. Private party facilities: 100 to 300. Annual sales: $1 million to $3 million. Total employment: 93. Corporate name: Mary Mac's Ltd.

MCKINNON'S LOUISIANE....2100 Cheshire Bridge Rd. NE, Atlanta, Ga., 30324. (404) 325-4141. Cuisine: Creole. Credit cards: AE, MC, VISA.

MIDNIGHT SUN....225 Peachtree Rd. NE, Atlanta, Ga., 30303. (404) 577-5050. Cuisine: European. Open 7 days for dinner. Open for lunch Monday to Friday. Credit cards: All major. Private party facilities available.

NICOLAI'S ROOF.... Atlanta Hilton, 255 Courtland St. NW, Atlanta, Ga., 30308. (404) 659-2000. Cuisine: French. Credit cards: All major.

PANO'S AND PAUL'S RESTAURANT....1232 West Paces Ferry Road, Atlanta, Ga., 30339. (404) 261-3662. Cuisine: Continental/American. Owners: I. Pano Karatassos & Paul A. Albrecht. Open Monday through Saturday for lunch and dinner; Closed Sunday. Annual sales: $1 million to $3 million. Total employment: 65. Corporate name: Papa, Inc.

PETITE AUBERGE....2935 North Druid Hills Rd. NE, Atlanta, Ga., 30329 (404) 634-6268. Cuisine: French. Closed Sunday. Open for lunch Monday to Friday; Open for dinner Monday to Saturday. Credit cards: All major. Private party facilities: Up to 150. Annual sales: $500,000 to $1 million. Corporate name: Petite Auberge, Inc.

PEWTER MUG....38 Auburn Ave. NE, Atlanta, Ga., 30303. (404) 577-6161. Cuisine: American. Credit cards: AE, MC, VISA.

PITTYPAT'S PORCH....25 International Blvd., Atlanta, Ga., 30303. (404) 525-8228. Cuisine: Southern. Credit cards: All major.

RUE DE PARIS....315 East Paces Ferry Rd., Buckhead, Atlanta, Ga., 30339. (404) 261-9600. Cuisine: French. Owner: Yves Durand. Credit cards: AE, DC, MC, VISA. Private party facilities available. Annual sales: $500,000 to $1 million. Total employment: 25.

SIDNEY'S "JUST SOUTH"....4225 Rosewell Road, Atlanta, Ga., 30342. (404) 256-2339. Cuisine: Continental. Owner: Sidney Glazer. Open Monday through Friday for lunch; 7 days for dinner. Credit cards: All major . Annual sales: $500,000 to $1 million. Total employment: 27. Corporate name: Just South, Inc.

THOMAS'....3442 Stewart Ave., Atlanta, Ga., 30354. (404) 768-4101. Cuisine: Southern. Credit cards: AE, MC, VISA.

AUGUSTA

THE GREEN JACKET RESTAURANT....2563 Washington Ave., Augusta Ga., 30904. (404) 733-2271. Cuisine: Seafood/Steaks. Open Monday through Friday for lunch; 7 days for dinner. Owner: Robert M. Sinclair. Credit cards: All major. Private party facilities: 3 rooms; 20 to 100 people. Annual sales: $1 million to $3 million. Total employment: 80.

TOWN TAVERN....15 Seventh St., Augusta, Ga., 30902. (404) 724-2461. Cuisine: American. Credit cards: All major.

COLUMBUS

GOETCHIUS HOUSE....405 Broadway, Columbus, Ga., 31901. (404) 324-4863. Cuisine: Continental. Owner: Werner Bludau. Open Monday through Friday for lunch; 7 days for dinner. Credit cards: All major. Private party facilities: Up to 200. Annual sales: $500,000 to $1 million. Total employment: 45.

MACON

CAG'S RESTAURANT....4330 Forsyth Rd., Macon, Ga., 31210. (912) 477-3171. Cuisine: Italian/American. Credit cards: AE, DC, MC, VISA.

SAVANNAH

THE CHART HOUSE....202 West Bay St., Savannah, Ga., 31401. (912) 234-6686. Cuisine: Steak/Seafood. Open 7 days for dinner. Credit cards: All major. Private party facilities: Up to 125. Annual sales: $1 million to $3 million. Total employment: 75. Corporate name: Chart House Enterprises.

JOHNNY HARRIS....1651 East Victory Dr., Savannah, Ga., 31404. (912) 354-7810. Cuisine: Southern. Credit cards: AE, CB, MC, VISA.

PIRATE'S HOUSE....20 East Broad St., Savannah, Ga., 31401. (912) 233-5757. Cuisine: Southern & Regional. Owner: Herb S. Traub. Open 7 days for lunch & dinner. Credit cards: All major. Private party facilities: Up to 250. Annual sales: Over $3 million. Total employment: 250.

THUNDERBOLDT

TASSEY'S PIER....3122 River Dr., Thunderboldt, Ga., 30000. (912) 354-2973. Cuisine: Seafood. Credit cards: AE, DC, MC, VISA.

MAINE

AUGUSTA

GUIDO'S WINE CELLAR....333A Water St., Augusta, Me., 04330. (207) 622-4725. Cuisine: Continental and Italian. Open 6 days for lunch and dinner; Closed Sundays. Credit cards: All major. Private party facilities: Up to 150. Annual sales: $250,000 to $500,000. Total employment: 15. Corporate name: Santarelli Enterprises, Inc.

BAILEY ISLAND

LAND'S END....Bailey Island, Me., 04003. (207) 833-2313. Cuisine: Steak/Seafood/Italian. Open 7 days for dinner seasonally (June through Sept.). Credit cards: AE, MC, VISA.

MACKERAL COVE RESTAURANT....Mackeral Cove Rd., Bailey Island, Me., 04003. (207) 833-6656. Cuisine: Seafood. Open 7 days for breakfast, lunch, and dinner seasonally (May to Oct.). Credit cards: All major. Private party facilities: Available.

ROCK OVENS....Rte. 24, Bailey Island, Me., 04003. (207) 833-6911. Cuisine: Steak/Seafood. Open 7 days for lunch and dinner seasonally (mid-May to mid-Oct.). No credit cards.

BANGOR

THE HELM....193 Broad St., Bangor, Me., 04401. (207) 947-4356. Cuisine: American. Credit cards: MC, VISA.

HILTON LE CHATEAU RESTAURANT....308 Godfrey Blvd., Bangor, Me., 04401. (207) 947-6721. Open 7 days for breakfast, lunch, and dinner; Sunday brunch. Credit cards: All major. Reservations: Suggested.

MILLER'S RED LION....427 Main St., Bangor, Me., 04401. (207) 945-5663. Cuisine: American. Credit cards: AE, DC, MC, VISA.

MURPHY'S STEAK HOUSE....797 Wilson St., Bangor, Me., 04401. (207) 989-1474. Cuisine: Steakhouse. Owner: William F. Murphy. Open 7 days for dinner only. Credit cards: AE, MC, VISA. Annual sales: $1 million to $3 million. Total employment: 82.

PILOT'S GRILL....1528 Hammond St., Bangor, Me., 04401. (207) 942-6325. Cuisine: Steak/Seafood. Credit cards: AE, DC, MC, VISA.

WEST MARKET SQUARE....Wheelwright Block, Bangor, Me., 04401. (207) 942-2717. Cuisine: American/Continental. Open 7 days for lunch and dinner. Entertainment: Live entertainment nightly. *"West Market Down-Under features buffet lunches and happy hour daily."*

BAR HARBOR

THE BRICK OVEN....21 Cottage St., Bar Harbor, Me., 04609. (207) 288-3708. Cuisine: Continental. Credit cards: AE, DC, MC, VISA.

DUFFY'S QUARTERDECK....1 Main St., Bar Harbor, Me., 04609. (207) 288-5292. Cuisine: French. Credit cards: MC, VISA.

GOLDEN ANCHOR INN....West St., Bar Harbor, Me., 04653. (207) 288-5033. Cuisine: Seafood. Open for breakfast, lunch, and dinner 7 days year-round. Credit cards: AE, MC, VISA.

LORENZO CREAMER'S LOBSTER POUND....Granite Point, Bar Harbor, Me., 04609. (207) 288-5033. Cuisine: Seafood. Credit cards: AE, DC, MC, VISA.

TESTA'S....53 Main St., Bar Harbor, Me., 04609. (207) 288-3327. Cuisine: Italian. Credit cards: MC, VISA.

TRIPP'S....45 Main St., Bar Harbor, Me., 04609. (207) 288-5001. Cuisine: Seafood. Credit cards: AE, MC, VISA, DC.

VAGABONDS....17 Main St., Bar Harbor, Me., 04609. (207) 288-5618. Cuisine: Continental/Seafood. Open January to October with seasonal hours. Credit cards: MC, VISA. Reservations: Recommended.

BATH

J.R. MAXWELL & CO.....122 Front St., Bath, Me., 04530. (207) 443-4461. Cuisine: Beef & Seafood. Open 7 days for lunch and dinner year-round. Credit cards: All major. Reservations: Recommended. Entertainment: Live entertainment nightly.

WIFE OF BATH....97 Commercial St., Bath, Me., 04530. (207) 433-3036. Cuisine: "Gourmet American." Open 7 days for lunch and dinner; Sunday brunch. Credit cards: MC, VISA. Reservations: Recommended.

BETHEL

McKEEN'S RESTAURANT & LOUNGE.... Sunday River Ski Area Access Rd., Bethel, Me., 04217. Cuisine: American/Italian. Open 6 days for lunch and dinner year-round; Closed Monday. No credit cards.

BLUE HILL

FIREPOND....Main St., Blue Hill, Me., 04614. (207) 374-2135. Cuisine: French/Seafood. Credit cards: MC, VISA.

BOOTHBAY HARBOR

BROWN BROS. WHARF....Atlantic Ave., Boothbay Harbor, Me., 04538. (207) 633-5440. Cuisine: Seafood. Credit cards: AE, MC, VISA.

EBB TIDE....67 Commercial St., Boothbay Harbor, Me., 04538. (207) 633-5692. Cuisine: American. Open 7 days for breakfast, lunch and dinner. No credit cards. "The best of food at the most reasonable of prices."

GILCHRIST'S EAST....61 Commercial St., Boothbay Harbor, Me., 04538. (207) 633-5692. Cuisine: Seafood/Italian. Open 7 days for dinner only seasonally (June 12 to September 6). Credit cards: AE, MC, VISA. Reservations Accepted.

GREENHOUSE RESTAURANT....Lakeview Rd., Boothbay Harbor, Me., 04538. (207) 633-5381. Cuisine: Continental/Seafood. Open for breakfast and dinner only seasonally (April 1 to December 31). Credit cards: MC, VISA. Reservations: Recommended.

THISTLE INN....53 Oak St., Boothbay Harbor, Me., 04538. (207) 633-3541. Cuisine: French/Scottish. Open 7 days for lunch and dinner. Credit cards: AE, MC, VISA. Reservations: Accepted.

TUGBOAT INN....100 Commercial St., Boothbay Harbor, Me., 04538. (207) 633-4434. Cuisine: Steak/Seafood. Open 7 days for lunch and dinner. Credit cards: AE, MC, VISA. "Inn is actual tugboat docked in Boothbay Harbor Marina."

BREWER

WHITE ELEPHANT....508 Wilson St., Brewer, Me., 04412. (207) 989-3824. Cuisine: Seafood/Steak. Credit cards: MC, VISA.

PEPINO'S MEXICAN RESTAURANT....515 South Main St., Brewer, Me., 04412. (207) 989-1330. Open 7 days for lunch and dinner. No credit cards.

BRIDGTON

SWITZER STUBLI DINING ROOM....Ridge Rd., Bridgton, Me., 04009. (207) 647-2522. Cuisine: Swiss. Credit cards: DC.

BRUNSWICK

THE BOWDOIN STEAK HOUSE....115 Maine St., Brunswick, Me., 04011. (207) 725-2314. Cuisine: Steak/Seafood. Open 6 days for lunch and dinner; Closed Mondays. Owner: Jonathan R. Ewing & Michelle Morris. Credit cards: AE, MC, VISA. Annual sales: $500,000 to $1 million. Total employment: 30.

THE GOLDEN FAN....Chinese Holiday Inn, Cook's Corner, Brunswick, Me., 04011. (207) 729-5554. Cuisine: Szechuan and Peking Chinese. Open 7 days for breakfast, lunch, and dinner. Credit cards: AE, MC, VISA.

22 LINCOLN RESTAURANT/THE SIDE DOOR LOUNGE....22 Lincoln St., Brunswick, Me., 04011. (207) 725-5893. Cuisine: "Innovative." Open 7 days for dinner; Sunday brunch. Credit cards: MC, VISA. Reservations: Suggested.

CAMDEN

AUBEGIN RESTAURANT AND INN....6 Belmont Ave., Camden, Me., 04843. (207) 236-8053. Cuisine: French Nouvelle. Open Tuesday through Sunday for dinner only; Closed Monday. No credit cards. Reservations: A must.

THE BINNACLE AND COMPASS....69 Elm St., Camden, Me., 04843. (207) 236-4823. Cuisine: Continental/Seafood. Open 7 days for lunch and dinner; Sunday brunch. Credit cards: MC, VISA. Reservations: Accepted. Cocktail lounge.

BOOK TEA NOOK.... The Owl and The Turtle Bookshop's Tearoom, Public Landing, Camden, Me., 04843. (207) 236-4769. Cuisine: American. Open seasonally for breakfast, lunch, and afternoon tea; Monday, Tuesday, Thursday, Friday, and Saturday for full servings; Wednesday and Sunday for afternoon tea only. Credit cards: MC, VISA (lunch only). "Offering fine foods, a unique harbor view, and a relaxing atmosphere."

CAMDEN HARBOUR INN....83 Bay View St., Camden, Me., 04843. (207) 236-4200. Cuisine: Regional American. Open 7 days for dinner; Sunday brunch. Credit cards: MC, VISA. Reservations: Suggested. Entertainment: Live entertainment nightly in the Thirsty Whale Tavern.

PETER OTT'S TAVERN & STEAKHOUSE....16 Bay View St., Camden, Me., 04843. (207) 236-4032. Cuisine: Steak/Seafood. Open 7 days for dinner only from April to December. Credit cards: MC, VISA.

THE WHITEHALL INN....52 High St., Camden, Me., 04843. (207) 236-3391. Cuisine: Continental/Seafood. Open 7 days for breakfast and dinner only, seasonal from mid-June to October 12. Credit cards: AE, MC, VISA. Reservations: Accepted. $50.00 minimum on credit cards.

CAPE PORPOISE

SPICER'S GALLEY.... Pier Rd., Cape Porpoise, Me., 04014. (207) 967-2745. Cuisine: Seafood/Steak.

CASTINE

THE PENTAGOET INN.... Main St., Castine, Me., 04421. (207) 326-8616. Cuisine: "Good Down East cooking." Open May to November for dinner; one seating at 7:00 PM only. Credit cards: All major. Reservations: Imperative.

DAMARISCOTTA

THE CHEECHAKO.... Box 177, Lewis Pt., Damariscotta, Me., 04543. (207) 563-3536. Cuisine: Seafood. Open 6 days for lunch and dinner; Closed Mondays. Credit cards: AE, MC, VISA. Private party facilities: Up to 250. Annual sales: $250,000 to $500,000. Total employment: 35+. Corporate name: The Cheechako, Inc.

DENNYSVILLE

LINCOLN HOUSE COUNTRY INN.... Rtes. 1 & 86, Dennysville, Me., 04628. (207) 726-3953. Cuisine: Regional American. Open Tuesday through Saturday June 1 to October for dinner only; Closed Sunday and Monday. Credit cards: MC, VISA. Reservations: Essential. "Two entrees each evening from a selection of home-cooked meals." Lodging and breakfast also available.

DOVER-FOXCRAFT

BLETHEN HOUSE....37 East Main St., Dover-Foxcroft, Me., 04426. (207) 564-2841. Cuisine: Seafood. Credit cards: MC, VISA.

EAST NEWPORT

LOG CABIN DINER.... Rte. 2, East Newport, Me., 04933. (207) 368-4444. Cuisine: Steak/Seafood. Open mid-April to mid-October 7 days for lunch and dinner. No credit cards.

EASTPORT

CANNERY WHARF RESTAURANTS...."At the Ferry Landing," Eastport, Me., 04631. (207) 853-4800. Cuisine: Steak/Seafood. Open mid-June to mid-September 7 days for lunch and dinner. Credit cards: AE, MC, VISA. Reservations: Accepted. Consists of The Clam Kibben, for lunch, The Cannery, for dinner, and The Pickling Shed, for cocktails.

THE NEW FRIENDLY RESTAURANT.... Rte. 1, Eastport, Me., 04631. (207) 853-6610. Cuisine: American. Open April through October daily for lunch and dinner. No credit cards.

ELLSWORTH

JASPER'S RESTAURANT & MOTEL.... Rte. 1, Ellsworth, Me., 04605. (207) 667-5318. Cuisine: Steak/Seafood. Open 7 days for breakfast, lunch, and dinner. Credit cards: AE, MC, VISA.

FALMOUTH

THE GALLEY.... Foreside Rd., Falmouth, Me., 04105. (207) 781-4262. Cuisine: Seafood. Owner: Merle Hallett. Open 7 days for lunch and dinner. Credit cards: All major. Private party facilities: Up to 40. Total employment: 75.

GARDINER

PAPA'S PASTA....263 Water St., Gardiner, Me., 04345. (207) 582-5786. Cuisine: Italian. Open Monday through Saturday for lunch and dinner; Closed Sunday. Credit cards: MC, VISA. Open year-round.

GORHAM

GORHAM STATION....29 Elm St., Gorham, Me., 04038. (207) 839-3354. Cuisine: Steak/Seafood. Open Monday through Friday for lunch; 7 days for dinner; Sunday dinner served from Noon. Credit cards: AE, MC, VISA. "Restored 1800s railroad station."

GUILFORD

WAGON WHEEL RESTAURANT.... Rte. 15, Guilford, Me., 04443. (207) 876-3712. Cuisine: Steak/Seafood. Open 7 days for lunch and dinner. No credit cards.

HANCOCK

CARDINAL LOBSTER POOL & SNACK BAR.... Rte. 1, Hancock, Me., 04640. (207) 422-3954. Cuisine: Seafood. Open mid-May to late-September 7 days for lunch and dinner. No credit cards. Scenic view.

LE DOMAINE.... Rte. 1, Hancock, Me., 04640. (207) 422-3395. Cuisine: French. Credit cards: AE, MC, VISA.

JEFFERSON

DAMARISCOTTA LAKE FARM.... Rtes. 32 & 126, Jefferson, Me., 04348. (207) 549-7953. Cuisine: Steak/Seafood. Open 6 days for dinner in July and August; weekends only in the off season. No credit cards. Reservations: Necessary. Scenic view.

KENNEBUNK

THE KENNEBUNK INN....45 Main St., Kennebunk, Me., 04043. (207) 985-3351. Cuisine: International. Open 6 days for lunch and dinner; Closed Sunday. Credit cards: All major. Reservations: Suggested. Restored inn dating from 1799.

THE UNICORN & LION.... Box 57, Rte. 1, Kennebunk, Me., 04043. (207) 985-2985. Cuisine: French/Continental. Credit cards: AE, MC, VISA. Owner: George L. Wiltshire. Open 7 days for lunch and dinner. Credit cards: AE, MC, VISA. Total employment: 25.

KENNEBUNKPORT

THE BREAKWATER RESTAURANT AND INN.... Ocean Ave., Kennebunkport, Me., 04046. (207) 967-3118. Cuisine: American. Open 7 days for dinner May 5 to October 23. Credit cards: MC, VISA. Reservations: Suggested.

CAPE ARUNDEL INN.... Ocean Ave., Kennebunkport, Me., 04046. (207) 967-2125. Cuisine: Continental/American/Seafood. Open June to mid-October 7 days for breakfast, lunch, and dinner. Credit cards: MC, VISA. Reservations: Accepted.

THE KENNEBUNKPORT INN.... Dock Sq., Kennebunk, Me., 04046. (207) 967-2621. Cuisine: Seafood/Continental. Open April to October 7 days for breakfast and dinner only. Credit cards: All major. Reservations: Accepted.

THE LOBSTER CLAW....425 Ocean Ave., Kennebunkport, Me., 04046. (207) 967-2562. Cuisine: Seafood/Steak. Open mid-April to mid-October 7 days for lunch and dinner. No credit cards. Reservations: Accepted.

THE OLD GRIST MILL.... Mill La., Kennebunkport, Me., 04046. (207) 967-4781. Cuisine: American. Open 6 days for lunch and dinner; Closed Mondays. Owner: David F. Lombard. Credit cards: All major. Private party facilities: Up to 200. Annual sales: $250,000 to $500,000. Total employment: 35.

SHAWMUT INN.... Turbats Creek Rd., Kennebunkport, Me., 04046. (207) 967-3931. Cuisine: Steak/Seafood. Open May to October 7 days for dinner. Credit cards: AE, MC, VISA. Reservations: Accepted.

VILLAGE COVE INN.... South Main St., Kennebunkport, Me., 04046. (207) 967-3993. Cuisine: "Regional cuisine." Open seasonally, Tuesday through Sunday for dinner, Sunday brunch, closed Mondays during peak season; Thursday through Sunday for dinner only during the winter. Credit cards: AE, MC, VISA. Reservations: Accepted.

WHITE BARN INN.... Beach St., Kennebunkport, Me., 04046. (207) 967-2321. Cuisine: French/American. Credit cards: MC, VISA.

KINGFIELD

ONE STANLEY AVENUE.... Stanley Ave., Kingfield, Me., 04947. (207) 265-5541. Cuisine: Continental. Open 6 days for dinner; Closed Mondays. Owners: Daniel & Susan Davis. Credit cards: MC, VISA. Private party facilities: Up to 40. Annual sales: Less than $250,000. Total employment: 7.

KITTERY

VALLE'S STEAK HOUSE.... Kittery, Me., 03904. (207) 439-0010. Cuisine: Seafood/Steak. Credit cards: AE, DC, MC, VISA.

LEWISTON

STECKINO'S....106 Middle St., Lewiston, Me., 04240. (207) 784-4151. Cuisine: Italian/American. Credit cards: AE, MC, VISA.

LINCOLN

THE TIMER HOUSE....1 Fleming St., Lincoln, Me., 04457. (207) 794-3007. Cuisine: American/Seafood/Pasta. Open 7 days for breakfast, lunch, and dinner. No credit cards.

LINCOLNVILLE

LOBSTER POUND....Lincolnville, Me., 04849. (207) 789-5550. Cuisine: Seafood. Credit cards: AE, MC, VISA.

MACHIAS

HELEN'S....32 Main St., Machias, Me., 04654. (207) 256-6505. Cuisine: American. Credit cards: MC, VISA.

MANSET

SEAWALL DINING ROOM....Seawall Rd., Manset, Me., 04656 (207) 244-3020. Cuisine: American. Open 7 days for lunch and dinner year-round. Credit cards: AE, MC, VISA. Reservations: Recommended in summer.

NEW HARBOR

GOSNOLD ARMS....Rte. 32, New Harbor, Me., 04554. (207) 677-3727. Cuisine: Steak/Seafood. Open June 24 through September 7, 7 days for breakfast and dinner; Sunday brunch. Credit cards: MC, VISA.

NORTH ANSON

LUANNE'S RESTAURANT & BAKERY....Elm St., North Anson, Me., 04958. (207) 635-2466. Cuisine: "New England fare." Open 7 days for breakfast, lunch, and dinner. Credit cards: MC, VISA.

NORTHEAST HARBOR

THE MAST AND RUDDER....Huntington Rd., Northeast Harbor, Me., 04662. (207) 276-5857. Cuisine: Continental and "Down East." Open year-round 7 days for breakfast, lunch, and dinner. Credit cards: AE, MC, VISA.

NORTH EDGECOMB

McLELLAN'S....Rte. 1, North Edgecomb, Me., 04556. (207) 882-6000. Cuisine: Seafood/American. Open 7 days for breakfast, lunch, and dinner from March through November. No credit cards.

NORTH WINDHAM

BARNHOUSE TAVERN....Rtes. 35, 302, & 115, North Windham, Me., 04062. (207) 892-6000. Cuisine: Steak/Seafood. Open 7 days for lunch and dinner; Sunday brunch. Credit cards: MC, VISA. "Distinguished fare presented in a rustic barn of the 1800s."

OGUNQUIT

BARBARA DEAN'S....Shore Rd., Ogunquit, Me., 03907. (207) 646-2241. Cuisine: Steak/Seafood. Open May to October for dinner at varying days and times; call them first. Credit cards: AE, MC, VISA. Reservations: Suggested.

BARNACLE BILLY'S....Perkins Cove, Ogunquit, Me., 03907. (207) 646-5575. Cuisine: Seafood/America. Credit cards: AE, MC, VISA.

THE CLIFF HOUSE....off Shore Rd., Ogunquit, Me., 03907. (207) 646-5124. Cuisine: Seafood/American. Open May to October for breakfast and dinner. Credit cards: AE, MC, VISA. Reservations: Suggested. Entertainment: Live entertainment nightly.

GYPSY SWEETHEARTS....18 Shore Rd., Ogunquit, Me., 03907. (207) 646-7021. Cuisine: Seafood. Open May to October for breakfast and dinner. Credit cards: AE, MC, VISA. Reservations: Accepted. Upstairs cocktail lounge.

THE LAURA W. TANNER HOUSE....1 Pine Hills Rd., Ogunquit, Me., 03907. (207) 646-5400. Cuisine: Continental/American. Open May 20 through October 11 for dinner; Sunday brunch. Credit cards: AE, MC, VISA. Reservations: Accepted. Entertainment: Piano bar.

OGUNQUIT LOBSTER POUND....Rte. 1, Ogunquit, Me., 03907. (207) 646-2516. Cuisine: Seafood. Credit cards: MC, VISA.

OLD VILLAGE INN....30 Main St., Ogunquit, Me., 03907. (207) 646-7088. Cuisine: Continental/Seafood. Credit cards: MC, VISA.

TAVERN AT CLAY HILL FARM....Agamenticus Rd., Ogunquit, Me., 03907. (207) 646-2272. Cuisine: Seafood/American. Credit cards: AE, MC, VISA.

WHISTLING OYSTER....Perkins Cove, Ogunquit, Me., 03907. (207) 646-9521. Cuisine: Continental/American Nouvelle. Owner: Alan Parilla. Open for lunch and dinner; call for days closed. Credit cards: AE, MC, VISA. Private party facilities: Up to 70. Corporate name: The Whistling Oyster, Inc.

PORTLAND

THE ART GALLERY....121 Center St., Portland, Me., 04101. (207) 772-2866. Cuisine: Continental. Credit cards: AE, MC, VISA.

THE BAKER'S TABLE....434 Fore St., Portland, Me., 04101. (207) 775-0303. Cuisine: International. Open 7 days for lunch and dinner year-round. Credit cards: DC, MC, VISA. Reservations: Recommended.

BOONE'S....6 Custom House Wharf, Portland, Me., 04104. (207) 774-5725. Cuisine: Seafood/Steak. Credit cards: AE, DC, MC, VISA.

DI MILLO'S ON THE WATERFRONT....121 Commercial St., Portland, Me., 04111. (207) 772-2216. Cuisine: Seafood. Owner: Antonio DiMillo, Pres. Open 7 days for lunch and dinner. Credit cards: All major. Private party facilities: 25 to 200. Annual sales: $1 million to $3 million. Total employment: 68.

DOCKFORE....336 Fore St., Portland, Me., 04101. (207) 772-8619. Cuisine: Regional American. Open 7 days for lunch and dinner; hours vary seasonally. Credit cards: MC, VISA.

ESPOSITO'S....1335 Congress St., Portland, Me., 04102. (207) 772-9167. Cuisine: Italian. Open 7 days for lunch and dinner. No credit cards.

THE GREAT LOST BEAR-DINING & DRINKING....540 Forest Ave., Portland, Me., 04102. (207) 772-0300. Cuisine: Steak/Seafood/American. Open 7 days year-round for lunch and dinner. Credit cards: All major. Reservations: Accepted. "Voted Portland's best restaurant in *Portland Chronical* reader's poll."

HORSEFEATHERS....193 Middle St., Top of Old Port, Portland, Me., 04101. (207) 773-3501. Open Monday through Saturday for lunch and dinner; Closed Sunday. Credit cards: MC, VISA. "Sustenance, merriment, and cheer."

HU SHANG 2 RESTAURANT & LOUNGE....7-13 Brown St., Portland, Me., 04101. (207) 774-0800. Cuisine: Hunan, Szechuan, Mandarin, and Shanghai Chinese. Open Monday through Saturday for lunch; 7 days for dinner; Sunday dinner from 3:30 PM. No credit cards.

PORT GALLEY....29 Exchange St., Portland, Me., 04101. (207) 772-8744. Cuisine: "Maine seafood." Open Monday through Saturday year-round for lunch and dinner. Credit cards: All major.

THE ROMA....769 Congress St., Portland, Me., 04102. (207) 773-9873. Cuisine: Italian. Credit cards: AE, MC, VISA.

ROCKLAND

BAY POINT RESTAURANT....Samoset Resort, Warrenton St., Rockland, Me., 04841. (207) 594-2511. Cuisine: New England/Continental. Open year-round for breakfast, lunch, and dinner. Credit cards: All major. Reservations: Accepted.

ROCKPORT

THE HELM....Rockport, Me., 04856. (207) 236-4337. Cuisine: French/Seafood.

SACO

CASCADE INN....Rte. 1, Saco, Me., 04072. (207) 283-3271. Cuisine: Seafood/American. Owner: Theodore Truman. Closed Jan, Feb, Mar. Credit cards: AE, MC, VISA. Private party facilities: Up to 400. Annual sales: $1 million to $3 million. Total employment: 50 to 100 (seasonal). Corporate name: Cascade Inn, Inc.

HUOT'S SEAFOOD RESTAURANT....Camp Ellis Beach, Saco, Me., 04072. (207) 282-1642. Cuisine: Seafood/Steak. Open 7 days for lunch and dinner from April through September. Credit cards: All major.

SANFORD

OK CHA'S EGG ROLL HOUSE....290 Main St., Sanford, Me., 04073. (207) 324-7024. Cuisine: Oriental, Szechuan, and Bul Ko Kee. Open Tuesday through Saturday for lunch; Tuesday through Sunday for dinner; Sunday diner from 3:00 PM. No credit cards.

SCARBOROUGH

MARSHVIEW....Portland Rd., Scarborough, Me., 04074. (207) 883-3401. Cuisine: Seafood/Steak. Credit cards: AE, DC, MC, VISA.

SEARSPORT

THE LOBSTER SHACK....Trundy Rd., Searsport, Me., 04874. (207) 743-2851. Cuisine: Seafood. Open May 7 to mid-October for lunch and dinner 7 days weekly. No credit cards. "It's truly a Maine experience."

NICKERSON TAVERN....Rte. 1, Searsport, Me., 04874. (207) 548-2220. Cuisine: French. Open Monday through Friday for lunch in July and August only; Year-round 7 days for dinner. Credit cards: MC, VISA. Reservations: Accepted.

YARDARM RESTAURANT....Rte. 1, Searsport, Me., 04874. (207) 548-2404. Cuisine: Steak/Seafood. Open 7 days June to mid-October for breakfast and dinner. Credit cards: All major. Reservations: Suggested.

SKOWHEGAN

WHITTEMORE'S....171 Madison Ave., Skowhegan, Me., 04976. (207) 474-9864. Cuisine: Steak/Seafood. Owner: Norman H. Smith, Mgr. Open 7 days for breakfast, lunch, and dinner. Credit cards: MC, VISA. Private party facilities: Up to 75. Total employment: 32. Corporate name: JAK'S, Inc., D/B/A Whittemore Restaurant.

SOUTH PARIS

MAURICE....113 Main St., South Paris, Me., 04281. (207) 743-2387. Cuisine: French. Open 6 days for dinner; Sunday brunch; Closed Mondays. Owner: John L. Tisdale. Credit cards: All major. Annual sales: $250,000, to $500,000. Total employment: 15.

SOUTHPORT

LAWNMEER INN.... Southport, Me., 04569. (207) 633-2544. Cuisine: American/Seafood. Credit cards: AE, MC, VISA.

SOUTH PORTLAND

CAP'N NEWICK'S LOBSTER HOUSE....740 Broadway, South Portland, Me., 04106. (207) 799-3090. Cuisine: Steak/Seafood. Open year-round 7 days for lunch and dinner. No credit cards. Reservations: Accepted.

JOHN MARTIN'S MERRY MANOR INN....700 Main St., South Portland, Me., 04106. (207) 755-5642. Cuisine: Seafood/Steak. Credit cards: All major.

SOUTHWEST HARBOR

GALLEY WEST.... Main St. at Lawlor La., Southwest Harbor, Me., 04679. (207) 244-5071. Cuisine: "Native seafood"/Steaks/Italian. Open 7 days year-round for lunch and dinner. Credit cards: MC, VISA.

THE HAPPY CRAB RESTAURANT.... Rte. 102, Southwest Harbor, Me., 04679. (207) 244-5131. Cuisine: Seafood. Open 7 days year-round for breakfast, lunch, and dinner. Credit cards: MC, VISA. Reservations: Accepted.

LONG'S DOWNEAST CLAMBAKES.... Rte. 102, Southwest Harbor, Me., 04679. (207) 244-5255. Cuisine: Seafood. Open May through September 7 days for dinner only. Credit cards: MC, VISA. Reservations: Accepted.

STRATTON

COUNTRY MILE.... Box 236, Rte. 27, Stratton, Me., 04982. (207) 247-2131. Cuisine: Continental. Credit cards: MC, VISA.

VINALHAVEN

THE HAVEN.... Main St., Vinalhaven, Me., 04863. (207) 863-4969. Cuisine: International/Seafood. Open year-round; call for winter times; Open Tuesday through Saturday for breakfast and lunch; 7 days for dinner. No credit cards.

WATERFORD

KEDARBURN INN.... Rte. 35, Waterford, Me., 04888. (207) 583-6182. Cuisine: American. Open year-round Monday through Friday for breakfast; Saturday and Sunday for brunch. Call for menu changes and credit cards.

WATERVILLE

JOHN MARTIN'S MANOR....54 College Ave., Waterville, Me. 04901. (207) 873-5676. Cuisine: Seafood/Steak. Open 7 days for lunch and dinner. Credit cards: AE, MC, VISA. Private party facilities: Up to 400. Annual sales: $1 million to $3 million. Total employment: 75. Corporate name: John Martin Enterprises.

SILENT WOMAN.... Kennedy Memorial Dr., Waterville, Me., 04901. (207) 873-4522. Cuisine: American.

WELLS

HENRI'S.... Post Rd., Wells, Me., 04090. (207) 646-3988. Cuisine: Continental/Seafood. Owner: Henry A. Smattmann. Open 7 days for lunch and dinner; Closed 15 October to 15 April. Credit cards: MC, VISA. Private party facilities: Up to 300. Annual sales: $500,000 to $1 million. Total employment: 75. Corporate name: Henri's Restaurant, Inc.

NE'R BEACH CLAMBAKE & LOBSTER POUND.... Rte. 1, Wells, Me., 04090. (207) 646-2636. Cuisine: Seafood. Open mid-May to mid-October 7 days for lunch and dinner. Credit cards: MC, VISA. Reservations: Unnecessary.

SLEEPYTOWN RESTAURANT.... Rte. 1, Wells, Me., 04090. (207) 646-3785. Cuisine: American/Seafood. Open mid-May to mid-October 7 days for lunch and dinner. Credit cards: AE, MC, VISA. Reservations: Accepted.

WINTHROP

BRANDING IRON RESTAURANT.... Box 357, Winthrop, Me., 04364. (207) 377-2271. Cuisine: Steak/Seafood. Owners: Lionel Anctil & Ronald Bilodeau. Open 7 days for lunch and dinner. Credit cards: MC, VISA. Private party facilities: Up to 275. Annual sales: $500,000 to $1 million. Total employment: 53. Corporate name: ABM, Inc., D/B/A Branding Iron.

STEER HOUSE.... Box 357, Winthrop, Me., 04364. (207) 377-2271. Cuisine: Steak/Seafood. Credit cards: AE, MC, VISA.

WISCASSET

ARLENE'S RESTAURANT & TAKE-OUT, INC.... Rte. 1, Wiscasset, Me., 04578. (207) 882-5012. Cuisine: Seafood. Open year-round 7 days weekly for lunch and dinner. No credit cards. No reservations: "The Best Damn Fried Clams in Maine."

LE GARAGE.... Water St., Wiscasset, Me., 04578. (207) 882-5409. Cuisine: American. Credit cards: DC, MC, VISA.

WOOLWICH

MONTSWEAG FARM.... Rte. 1 Woolwich, Me., 04579. (207) 443-6563. Cuisine: Steak/Seafood. Open year-round for lunch and dinner. Credit cards: AE, MC, VISA. Reservations: Not accepted for weekend evenings.

YARMOUTH

HOMEWOOD INN.... Drinkwater Point, Yarmouth, Me., 04096. (207) 846-3351. Cuisine: Regional American. Open mid-June to mid-October. Tuesday through Sunday for dinner; breakfast also. Credit cards: AE, MC, VISA. Reservations: Necessary.

YORK

DOCKSIDE DINING ROOM... Harris Island Rd., York, Me., 03909. (207) 363-4800. Cuisine: Continental. Credit cards: MC, VISA.

YORK BEACH

NUBBLE LIGHT DINING ROOM.... Nubble Rd., York Beach, Me., 03910. (207) 363-4054. Cuisine: Seafood. Credit cards: MC, VISA.

YORK HARBOR

BILL FOSTER'S DOWNEAST LOBSTER & CLAMBAKE.... Rte. 1A, York Harbor, Me., 03911. (207) 363-3255. Cuisine: Regional seafood/American. Open June 30 through Labor Day, Wednesday through Sunday for dinner only; Open Sunday only for dinner in September. Credit cards: MC, VISA. Reservations: Suggested.

STAGE NECK INN.... Rte. 1A, York Harbor, Me., 03911. (207) 363-3850. Cuisine: Regional American/Continental. Three meals a day 7 days a week, mid-April to mid-November. Credit cards: MC, VISA.

MARYLAND

ANNAPOLIS

BUSCH'S CHESAPEAKE INN....321 Revell Hwy., Annapolis, Md., 21401. (301) 757-1717, 974-0454, 261-2034. Cuisine: Steak/Seafood. Owner: Robert R. Busch. Open 7 days. Credit cards: All major. Private party facilities 25 to 75 persons. Annual sales: $1 million to $3 million. Total employment: 105. Corporate name: R & J Busch, Inc.

WHITEHALL INN.... On 50 & 301, Annapolis, Md. 21401. (301) 757-3737. Cuisine: Seafood. Credit cards: All major.

BAHO

PIMLICO HOTEL....5301 Park Heights Ave., Baho, Md., 21215. (301) 664-8014. Cuisine: Continental and Chinese. Owner: Alfred Davis and Leonard Kaplan. Open 7 days . Credit cards: AE, MC, VISA. Private party facilities: 8 to 90. Annual sales: $1 million to $3 million. Total employment: 183. Corporate name: Nalee, Inc.

BALTIMORE

ATTMAN'S....1019 East Lombard St., East Baltimore, Md., 21202. (301) 563-2666. Cuisine: Delicatessan. Owner: Seymour Attman. Open 7 days from 8:00 AM to 7:00 PM; Closed Jewish religious holidays. No credit cards. Annual sales: $1 million to $3 million. Total employment: 15.

BRENTWOOD INN....6700 Brentwood Ave., Baltimore, Md., 21222. (301) 285-0520. Cuisine: American. Credit cards: All major.

CAFE DE PARIS....413 North Charles St., Baltimore, Md., 21201. (301) 685-1211. Cuisine: Mediterranean. Credit cards: MC, VISA.

CAFE DES ARTISTES....9 Hopkins Plz., Baltimore, Md., 21201. (301) 837-6600. Cuisine: French. Credit cards: AE, MC, AE.

CAPRICCIO....242 South High St., Baltimore, Md., 21202. (301) 685-2710. Cuisine: Italian. Credit cards: AE, DC, MC, VISA.

CASA GIANNERINI....6826 Harford Rd., Baltimore, Md., 21234. (301) 254-1060. Cuisine: Italian. Owners: Michael J. Giannerini, Mary C. Giannerini, Laura L. Clark. Open 7 days. Credit cards: AE, MC, VISA. Private party facilities: 3 to 75. Annual sales: $500,000 to $1 million. Total employment: 35. Corporate name: Giannerini, Inc.

THE CHESAPEAKE....1701 North Charles St., Baltimore, Md., 21201. (301) 837-7711. Cuisine: Seafood. Credit cards: AE, CB, DC, MC, VISA.

CHIAPPARELLI'S....237 South High St., Baltimore, Md., 21202. (301) 837-0309. Cuisine: Italian. Owner: Buddy Chiapparelli. Open 7 days for lunch and dinner. Credit cards: All major. Private party facilities: Up to 75. Total employment: 65.

COUNTRY FARE INN....100 Painters Mill Rd., Baltimore, Md., 21233. (301) 363-3131. Cuisine: French. Owner: Stuart A. Teper. Open 7 days for dinner; Monday through Friday for lunch. Credit cards: MC, VISA. Private party facilities: 15 to 250. Annual sales: $1 million to $3 million. Total employment: 75.

DANNY'S....1201 North Charles St., Baltimore, Md., 21201. (301) 539-1393. One of Baltimore's most popular restaurants, with a menu that encompasses classic French dishes, steaks, and seafood dishes, all the way from *tournedos Rossini* to crab cakes, and vanilla ice cream to crepes suzette. Danny's also provides a delightful atmosphere of permanence and stability, and is in demand for special celebrations. Specialties include: Crab crepes, veal Stroganoff, eggs Benedict, Maine Lobster, and fresh fish of the day stuffed with crab lumps. Owner: Danny Dickman and Beatrice E. Dickman. Cuisine: French/Steak/Seafood/American. Open Monday through Saturday for dinner; Closed Sunday. Reservations and all major credit cards are accepted. Private party facilities can be accommodated.

HAUSSNER'S....3244 Eastern Ave., Baltimore, Md., 21224. (301) 327-8365. Cuisine: German. Owner: L. Frances W. Haussner. Open Tuesday through Saturday for lunch and dinner; Closed Sunday and Monday. Credit cards: MC, VISA. Private party facilities: 2 private rooms for up to 130. Annual sales: Over $3 million. Total employment: 210.

HERSH'S ORCHARD INN....1528 East Joppa Rd., Baltimore, Md., 21204. (301) 823-0384. Cuisine: Continental/American. Owner: Hersh Pachino. Open 7 days for lunch and dinner. Credit cards: AE, MC, VISA. Private party facilities: 10 to 100. Annual sales: $1 million to $3 million. Total employment: 80. Corporate name: Hersh's Orchard Inn, Inc.

HOLLANDER'S....14 East 25th St., Baltimore, Md., 21218. (301) 467-1662. Cuisine: American. Credit cards: All major.

IKAROS....4805 Eastern Ave., Baltimore, Md., 21224. (301) 633-9825. Cuisine: Greek. Credit cards: None.

IMPERIAL PALACE....3541 Brenbrook Dr., Baltimore, Md., 21233. (301) 922-3300. Cuisine: Chinese. Credit cards: AE, MC, VISA.

JAI HIND INDIAN RESTAURANT....5511 York Rd., Baltimore, Md., 21212. (301) 323-8440. Cuisine: Indian. Owner: Narindar Pal Singh Suri. Open 6 days for lunch and dinner; Closed Monday. Credit cards: All major. Private party facilities: 40 to 80. Annual sales: $250,000 to $500,000. Total employment: 10. Corporate name: Suri Enterprises, Inc.

JIMMY WU'S NEW CHINA INN....2426-2434 North Charles St., Baltimore, Md., 21218. (301) 235-8744. Cuisine: Chinese/American. Owner: Jimmy Wu. Open 7 days. Credit cards: AE, MC, VISA. Private party facilities: 8 to 40. Annual sales: $250,000 to $500,000. Total employment: 18.

THE MADRID RESTAURANT.... North Charles at 33rd, Baltimore, Md., 21218. (301) 243-3668. Cuisine: Spanish/Continental. Owner: Jose A. Gutierrez. Open 7 days. Credit cards: AE, MC, VISA. Private party facilities: 20 to 80. Annual sales: $250,000 to $500,000. Total employment: 10. Corporate name: Lila, Inc.

MARCONI'S....106 West Saratoga St., Baltimore, Md., 21201. (301) 752-9286. Cuisine: Continental/American. Credit cards: None.

OBRYCKI'S OLDE CRAB HOUSE....1729 East Pratt St., Baltimore, Md., 21202. (301) 732-6399. Cuisine: Seafood. Credit cards: None.

PRIME RIB....1101 North Calvert St., Baltimore, Md., 21202. (301) 539-1804. Cuisine: American. Credit cards: All major.

SHANES'S....1924 York Rd., Timonium, Baltimore, Md., 21204. (301) 252-4100. Cuisine: Continental. Credit cards: AE, MC, VISA.

SPANISH MESON....1717 Eastern Ave., Baltimore, Md., 21231. (301) 327-9340. Cuisine: Spanish. Owner: Jose Luaces. Credit cards: AE, MC, VISA. Annual sales: $250,000 to $500,000. Total employment: 10. Corporate name: La Cost del Sol. Inc.

TIO PEPE....10 East Franklin St., Baltimore, Md., 21202. (301) 539-4675. Cuisine: Continental. Credit cards: AE, MC, VISA.

TORREMOLINOS....101 West Monument St., Baltimore, Md., 21201. (301) 752-9305. Cuisine: Spanish. Credit cards: AE, MC.

BETHESDA

CHINA GARDEN....4711 Montgomery La., Bethesda, Md., 20814. (301) 657-4665. Cuisine: Cantonese. Owner: Pak Ken Lee. Open 7 days for lunch and dinner. Credit cards: AE, MC, VISA. Private party facilities: Up to 80. Annual sales: $500,000 to $1 million. Total employment: 23.

DIPLOMAT....7345 Wisconsin Ave., Bethesda, Md., 20814. (301) 657-3058. Cuisine: Eastern (Greek). Open Monday through Friday for lunch; 7 days for dinner. Credit cards: AE, CB, MC, VISA. Reservations: Suggested for parties over five.

FRASCATI....4806 Rugby Ave., Bethesda, Md., 20814. (301) 652-9514. Cuisine: Italian. Open Tuesday through Friday for lunch; Tuesday through Sunday for dinner; Closed Monday. Credit cards: AE, DC, MC, VISA. Reservations: Accepted. Beer and wine only.

LA MICHE....7905 Norfolk Ave., Bethesda, Md., 20814. (301) 986-0707. Cuisine: French. Open 7 days for lunch and dinner; Closed Monday. Credit cards: MC, VISA. Reservations: Suggested for dinner.

O'DONNELL'S SEA GRILL....8301 Wisconsin Ave., Bethesda, Md., 20814. (301) 656-6200. Cuisine: Seafood. Credit cards: All major.

PINES OF ROME....4709 Hampden La., Bethesda, Md., 20814. (301) 657-8775. Cuisine: Italian. Open 7 days for lunch and dinner. Credit cards: All major. No reservations. Beer and wine only.

CUMBERLAND

BISTRO....37 North Centre, Cumberland, Md., 21502. (301) 774-8462. Cuisine: Continental. Credit cards: All major.

CHEVY CHASE

RICH'S PLACE....5520 Wisconsin Ave., Chevy Chase, Md., 20815. (301) 656-7600. Cuisine: Continental. Owner: Seymour Rich and Donald Rich. Credit cards: All major. Private party facilities: 15 to 150. Annual sales: $500,000 to $1 million. Total employment: 60. Corporate name: Norman's Inc.

EASTON

TIDEWATER INN.... Dover & Harrison Sts., Easton, Md., 21601. (301) 822-1300. Cuisine: Steaks/Seafood. Owner: Anton J. Hoevenaars. Open 7 days for breakfast, lunch and dinner. Credit cards: All major. Private party facilities: Up to 300. Annual sales: Over $3 million. Total employment: Up to 125.

FROSTBURG

AU PETIT PARIS.... Paisley Ct., Frostburg, Md., 21532. (301) 689-8946. Cuisine: French. Credit cards: All major.

GRANTSVILLE

PENN ALPS.... Rte. 40 & Casselman River Bridge, Grantsville, Md., 21536. (301) 895-5985. Cuisine: Dutch. Owner: John Wengard. Open 6 days for breakfast, lunch, and dinner; Closed Sunday. Credit cards: MC, VISA. Private party facilities: Up to 85. Annual sales: $500,000 to $1 million.

HAGERSTOWN

RED HORSE STEAK HOUSE....1800 Dual Hwy., Hagerstown, Md., 21740. (301) 733-3788. Cuisine: Steak/Seafood. Owner: R.C. Jefferies, Mgr. Open 7 days for dinner; Monday through Friday for lunch. Credit cards: All major. Private party facilities: Up to 60. Annual sales: $250,000 to $500,000. Total employment: 32. Corporate name: Red Horse, Inc.

HYATTSVILLE

CASA BAEZ....6551 Riggs Rd., Hyattsville, Md., 20782. (301) 422-7766. Cuisine: Latin American. Open Tuesday through Sunday for lunch and dinner; Closed Monday. No credit cards. No reservations. No alcoholic beverages.

LEDO....2420 University Blvd. East, Hyattsville, Md., 20783. (301) 422-8622. Cuisine: Italian. Open 7 days for breakfast, lunch and dinner. No credit cards. No reservations.

LA VALE

PEKING PALACE....1209 National Hwy., La Vale, Md., 21502. (301) 729-1400. Cuisine: Chinese. Credit cards: MC, VISA.

OCEAN CITY

THE GARDEN....145 St. & Coastal Hwy., Ocean City, Md., 21842. (301) 524-4121. Cuisine: Continental. Credit cards: MC, VISA.

PHILIPS CRAB HOUSE....2004 Philadelphia Ave., Ocean City, Md., 21842. (301) 289-6821. Cuisine: Seafood.

PHOENIX

PEERCE'S PLANTATION....Dulaney Valley Rd., Phoenix, Md., 21131. (301) 252-3100. Cuisine: French. Credit cards: AE, MC, VISA.

POTOMAC

OLD ANGLER'S INN....10801 MacArthur Blvd., Potomac, Md., 20854. (301) 365-2425. Cuisine: Continental. Open seasonally; September through May on Saturday and Sunday only for lunch; 6 days for dinner; Closed Monday; May through September on Tuesday through Sunday for lunch; 6 days for dinner; Closed Monday. Credit cards: All major. Reservations: Suggested. Free parking.

REISTERTOWN

FIORI....Rte. 140, Reistertown, Md., 21136. (301) 833-6300. Cuisine: Italian. Owner: Donald P. Wright. Open 7 days for dinner; Monday through Friday for lunch. Credit cards: MC, VISA. Annual sales: $250,000 to $500,000. Total employment: 80. Corporate name: Fiori Restaurant, Inc.

ROCKVILLE

AMALFI....12307 Wilkins Ave., Rockville, Md., 20852. (301) 770-7888. Cuisine: Italian. Open Tuesday through Friday for lunch; Tuesday through Sunday for dinner; Closed Monday. Credit cards: AE, MC, VISA. Reservations: Accepted for parties over six only. Beer and wine only. Free parking.

LA RUCHE OF WHITE FLINT....White Flint Mall, Rockville, Md., 20850. (703) 468-1155. Cuisine: French. Open Monday through Saturday for lunch and dinner; Closed Sunday. Credit cards: MC, VISA. No reservations.

O'BRIEN'S PIT BARBEQUE....1314 Gude Dr., Rockville, Md., 20850. (301) 340-8596. Cuisine: American/ Southern. Open daily for lunch and dinner. No credit cards. No reservations. Free parking.

PINE AND BAMBOO....5541 Nicholson La., Rockville, Md., 20852. (301) 468-0011. Cuisine: Chinese. Open 7 days for lunch and dinner. Credit cards: MC, VISA. Reservations: Accepted for parties over five only. Free parking.

SZECHUAN AND HUNAN....1776 East Jefferson St., Rockville, Md., 20852. (301) 770-5020. Cuisine: Chinese. Open Monday through Saturday for lunch; 7 days for dinner. Credit cards: MC, VISA. Reservations: Accepted for parties of four or more only. Free parking.

SZECHUAN GARDEN....7945 Tuckerman Lane, Rockville, Md., 20854. (301) 299-3525. Cuisine: Chinese. Open Monday through Saturday for lunch; 7 days for dinner. Credit cards: AE, DC, MC, VISA. Reservations: Suggested.

SILVER SPRING

CHESAPEAKE CRAB HOUSE....8214 Piney Branch Rd., Silver Spring, Md., 20910. (703) 589-9868. Cuisine: Seafood. Open 7 days for lunch and dinner. Credit cards: MC, VISA. No reservations.

CRISFIELD....8012 Georgia Ave., Silver Spring, Md., 20910. (301) 589-1306. Cuisine: Seafood. Open 6 days for lunch and dinner; Closed Monday. No credit cards. No reservations. Beer and wine only.

MRS. K'S TOLL HOUSE....9201 Colesville Rd., Silver Spring, Md., 20910. (301) 589-3500. Credit cards: AE, MC, VISA.

SAKURA PALACE....7926 Georgia Ave., Silver Spring, Md., 20910. (301) 587-7070. Cuisine: Japanese. Open Tuesday through Sunday for dinner only; Closed Monday. Credit cards: AE, MC, VISA. Reservations: Suggested.

SUITLAND

LA SCALA....4915 Silver Hill Rd., Suitland, Md., 20746. (301) 568-3400. Cuisine: Italian. Open Monday through Friday for lunch; 7 days for dinner. Credit cards: MC, VISA. Reservations: Accepted for parties over six only.

WHEATON

SIAM INN....11407 Amherst Ave., Wheaton, Md., 20850. (301) 942-0075. Cuisine: Thai. Open Monday, Tuesday, Thursday, and Friday for lunch; 7 days for dinner. Credit cards: MC, VISA. Reservations: Suggested. Beer and wine only.

TUNG BOR....11154 Georgia Ave., Wheaton, Md., 20902. (301) 933-3687. Cuisine: Chinese. Open 6 days for lunch and dinner; Closed Monday. Credit cards: MC, VISA. Private party facilities: Up to 100. Annual sales: $500,000 to $1 million. Total employment: 20 Corporate name: Tung Bor, Inc.

MASSACHUSETTS

AMHERST

PLUMBLEY'S OFF THE COMMON....30 Boltwood Walk, Amherst, Mass., 01002. (617) 253-9586. Cuisine: American. Owner: Edward Stuart, Gen. Mgr. Open 7 days for lunch and dinner. Credit cards: AE, MC, VISA. Private party facilities: Up to 100. Annual sales: $1 million to $3 million. Total employment: 85.

ANDOVER

ANDOVER INN....Chapel Ave., Andover, Mass., 01810. (617) 475-5903. Cuisine: Continental. Owner: Henry Broekoff. Open 7 days for breakfast, lunch, and dinner; Closed Sunday lunch. Credit cards: All major. Private party facilities: Up to 140. Total employment: 80.

VALLE'S STEAK HOUSE....New River Rd., Andover, Mass., 01810. (617) 458-0151. Cuisine: Steakhouse. Credit cards: AE, DC, MC, VISA.

BERNARDSTON

MUCHMORE'S RESTAURANT....Huckle Hill, Bernardston, Mass., 01337. (413) 648-9107. Cuisine: American. Owner: Andrew St. Hilaire. Open 7 days. Private party facilities: 20 to 200. Annual sales: $500,000 to $1 million. Total employment: 30. Corporate name: Louco, Inc.

BEVERLY

THE COMMODORE....45 Enon St., Beverly, Mass., 01915. (617) 922-5590. Cuisine: Seafood/Steak. Credit cards: All major.

BOSTON

AKU AKU....390 Commonwealth Ave., Boston, Mass., 02215. (617) 536-0420. Cuisine: Polynesian. Open 7 days for lunch and dinner. Credit cards: AE, DC, MC.

AL SABLONE'S VEAL N' VINTAGE....107 Porter St., East Boston, Mass., 02128. (617) 567-8140. Cuisine: Italian/American. Owner: Al Sablone. Open 6 days. Credit cards: AE, MC, VISA. Annual sales: $500,000 to $1 million. Total employment: 30. Corporate name: Sablone's Veal N' Vintage, Inc.

ANTHONY'S PIER 4....140 Northern Ave., Boston, Mass., 02210. (617) 423-6363. Cuisine: Seafood. Credit cards: All major.

THE BAY TOWER ROOM....60 State St., Boston, Mass., 02109. (607) 723-1666. Cuisine: Continental. Owner: James Bennett, Pres.; Clifton Zwirner, V.P., Gen. Mgr. Open Monday through Saturday. Credit cards: All major. Private party facilities: 10 to 100. Annual sales: Over $3 million. Total employment: 140. Corporate name: Bay Tower Restaurant, Inc.

BRIGHAM'S OF CHINATOWN....11 Tyler St., Boston, Mass., 02111. (617) 338-9280. Cuisine: Ice cream and sandwiches. Days closed: Open 7 days. Credit cards: None.

CAFE BUDAPEST....90 Exeter St., Copley Sq., Boston, Mass., 02116. (617) 734-3388. Cuisine: Hungarian. Credit cards: All major.

CAFE FLORIAN....85 Newbury St., Boston, Mass., 02116. (617) 247-7603. Cuisine: Continental. Open 7 days. Credit cards: None.

CAFE L'ANANAS....281a Newbury St., Back Bay, Boston, Mass., 02115. (617) 353-0176. Cuisine: Continental. Credit cards: AE, MC, VISA.

CAFE MARLIAVE....10 Bosworth St., Boston, Mass., 02108. (617) 423-6340. Cuisine: Italian/American. Days closed: Sundays. Credit cards: AE, MC.

CAFE PROMENADE....The Colonnade Hotel, 120 Huntington Ave., Boston, Mass., 02116. (617) 261-261-2800. Cuisine: Informal Continental. Open 7 days. Credit cards: AE, CB, DC, MC. VISA.

CAFFE PARADISO II....255 Hanover St., Boston, Mass., 02113. (617) 523-8872. Cuisine: Northern Italian. Days closed: Tuesdays. Credit cards: None.

C'EST SI BON RESTAURANT....17 Arlington St., Boston, Mass., 02116. (617) 266-8421. Cuisine: Continental. Days closed: Sundays and Mondays. Credit cards: AE, MC, V.

CHADWICK PARK....184 High St., Boston, Mass., 02110. (617) 542-0841. Cuisine: American. Open 7 days. Credit cards: AE, DC, MC, VISA.

THE CHARLES ON BEACON HILL....75 Chestnut St., Boston, Mass., 02108. (617) 523-4477. Cuisine: Northern Italian. Owner: Nathan S. Grifkin. Credit cards: All major. Private party facilities available for 7. Total employment: 18. Corporate name: Carna, Inc.

CHARLIE'S EATING & DRINKING SALOON....344 Newbury St., Boston, Mass., 02115. (617) 266-3000. Cuisine: American. Open 7 days for lunch and dinner. Credit cards: AE, CB, DC, MC.

CHARLES STREET WHARF....145 Charles St., Boston, Mass., 02114. (617) 523-8896. Cuisine: Seafood. Days closed: Sundays. Credit cards: None.

CHART HOUSE....60 Long Wharf, Boston, Mass., 02110. (617) 227-1576. Cuisine: American. Credit cards: AE, DC, MC, VISA.

COPLEY'S....Copley Plaza Hotel, Copley Sq., Boston, Mass., 02116. (617) 267-5300. Cuisine: Steakhouse. Credit cards: All major.

CRICKET'S....South Market Bldg., Faneuil Hall Marketplace, Boston, Mass., 02109. (617) 227-3434. Cuisine: Continental. Open 7 days. Credit cards: AE, MC.

CROSSROADS....495 Beacon St., Boston, Mass., 02215. (617) 262-7371. Cuisine: Pizza and Chicken Kabobs. Open 7 days. Credit cards: MC, VISA.

D'AMORE'S....76 Salem St., Boston, Mass., 02113. (617) 523-8820. Cuisine: Italian. Open 7 days. Credit cards: None.

DANTE'S....23 Joy St., Boston, Mass., 02114. (617) 523-9229. Cuisine: Italian. Closed days: Mondays. Credit cards: None.

DAVIO'S RESTAURANT....269 Newbury St., Boston, Mass., 02116. (617) 262-4810. Cuisine: Italian. Owner: Christopher David Enterprises. Open Monday through Saturday for lunch; 7 days for dinner. Credit cards: All major. Private party facilities: 10 to 25. Annual sales: $500,000 to $1 million. Total employment: 20. Corporate name: David Christopher Enterprises, Inc.

DELMONICO'S....710 Boylston St., Boston, Mass., 02116. (617) 536-2200. Cuisine: Continental. Days closed: Sundays. Credit cards: AE, CB, DC, MC, VISA.

DINI'S SEA GRILL....94 Tremont St., Boston, Mass., 02108. (617) 227-0380. Cuisine: Seafood. Open 7 days. Credit cards: AE, MC, VISA.

DUBARRY FRENCH RESTAURANT....159 Newbury St., Boston, Mass., 02116. (617) 262-2445. Cuisine: French. Open 7 days. Credit cards: AE, CB, DC, MC, VISA.

DURGIN PARK....30 North Market St., Boston, Mass., 02109. (617) 227-2038. Cuisine: American. No credit cards. Open 7 days for lunch and dinner.

EL PHOENIX RESTAURANT....1430 Commonwealth Ave., Boston, Mass., 02134. (617) 566-8590. Cuisine: Mexican. Open 7 days. Credit cards: None.

FELICIA'S RESTAURANT....145 Richmond St., Boston, Mass., 02109. (617) 523-9885. Cuisine: Italian. Owner: Felicia Solimine. Open 7 days for dinner. Credit cards: AE, CB, DC. Private party facilities: 15 to 30. Annual sales: $250,000 to $500,000. Total employment: 15.

THE 57 RESTAURANT....200 Stuart St., Boston, Mass., 02116. (617) 423-5700. Cuisine: American. Open 7 days. Credit cards: AE, CB, DC, MC, VISA.

FLORENCE'S....190 North St., Boston, Mass., 02109. (617) 523-4480. Cuisine: Sicilian. Open 7 days. Credit cards: No credit.

FLOURCHILD'S....42 Charles St., Boston, Mass., 02114. (617) 523-9768. Cuisine: Informal gourmet sandwiches and whole-wheat pizza. Open 7 days. Credit cards: None.

FRANCESCA'S & VILLA FRANCESCA....147 and 150 Richmond St., Boston, Mass., 02109. (617) 523-8826. Cuisine: Italian. Owner's name: Bill Ramauro. Credit cards: AE, DC.

GALLAGHER....55 Congress St., Boston, Mass., 02109. (617) 523-6080. Cuisine: French/American. Owner: Mark E. Gallagher III. Open 7 days a week. Credit cards: All major. Private party facilities: 10 to 80. Annual sales: $1 million to $3 million. Total employment: 85. Corporate name: Gallagher, Inc.

GREAT AMERICAN LOBSTER....200 Faneuil Hall Marketplace, Boston, Mass., 02109. (617) 742-1829. Cuisine: Seafood. Owner: Richard D. Carr. Open 7 days for breakfast, lunch, and dinner. No credit cards. Annual sales: $500,000 to $1 million. Total employment: 20. Corporate name: Market Lobster Co., Inc.

GREAT GATSBY'S....79 Providence St. or 300 Boylston St., Boston, Mass., 02116. (617) 526-2626. Cuisine: American & Continental. Open 7 days. Credit cards: None.

THE GROUND ROUND.... Prudential Center, Boston, Mass., 02199. (617) 247-0500. Cuisine: American. Open 7 days for lunch and dinner. No credit cards.

THE HAMPSHIRE HOUSE....84 Beacon St., Boston, Mass., 02108. (617) 967-9600. An old-fashioned, solid, reliable establishment housed in one of the grand mansions on Beacon Hill. Pleasant cooking, good service and a setting overlooking the Public Garden in Boston. The chef makes memorable broiled scallops—by no means such a simple thing as many folk imagine! The roast duckling, calves liver and veal dishes are well done too, and the fish is of admirable quality. Owner: Thomas A. Kershaw. Open 7 days for lunch and dinner. Saturday and Sunday brunch. Credit cards: All major. Private party facilities: 20 to 250. Annual sales: $1 million to $3 million. Total employment: 50. Corporate name: Hampshire House, Inc.

HARBOR TERRACE.... Boston Marriot Hotel, Long WHarf, 296 State St., Boston, Mass., 02109. (617) 227-0800. Quartered in the large, new grand Marriot's Long Wharf Hotel, Harbor Terrace is a deluxe well-run establishment. The food is fairly international but, in our opinion, the plainer rather than the richer dishes are superior. This is essentially a house that, at its best, exemplifies the shattering truth that the hardest dishes to cook and serve to perfection are often the most simple. Specialties include: Cioppino seafood stew, chef's veal of the day, and lamb long wharf. Owner: Marriot Hotel Corporation. Open 7 days for lunch and dinner. Credit cards: All major. Corporate name: Marriot Corporation.

HARVARD GARDENS....310-320 Cambridge St., Boston, Mass., 02114. (617) 523-2727. Cuisine: Informal American Days closed: Sundays. Credit cards: None.

HAVAH-NAGILA ISRAELI RESTAURANT....280 Cambridge St., Boston, Mass., 02134. (617) 523-9838. Cuisine: Israeli/Middle Eastern. Open 7 days for lunch and dinner. No credit cards.

HERMITAGE RESTAURANT....955 Boylston St., Boston, Mass., 02115. (617) 267-3652. Cuisine: Russian/International. Owner: Rafael A. Pons and Larry J. Kirkpatrick. Open for lunch Tuesday through Friday *and* Sunday; Open for dinner Tuesday through Saturday. Credit cards: All major. Private party facilities: 50 to 300. Annual sales: $250,000 to $500,000. Total employment: 15. Corporate name: Slavia, Inc.

THE HOUNDSTOOTH....150 Boylston St., Boston, Mass., 02116. (617) 482-0722. Cuisine: Continental. Owner: Dominic Gorio. Open Tuesday to Friday for lunch; Monday to Saturday dinner. Credit cards: AE, DC, CB. Annual sales: $500,000 to $1 million. Total employment: 30. Corporate name: Outside-In Inc.

HO YUEN TING RESTAURANT....13A Hudson St., Boston, Mass., 02111. (617) 426-2316. Cuisine: Chinese/Seafood. Owner: Kwok Mui. Closed Wednesday. Credit cards: None. Annual sales: $250,000 to $500,000.

IMPERIAL TEA HOUSE....70-72 Beach St., Boston, Mass. 02111. (617) 426-8543. Cuisine: Chinese. Owner: Frank K. Wong. Open 7 days. Credit cards: All major. Private party facilities: 40 to 200. Annual sales: $1 million to $3 million. Total employment: 29. Corporate name: Imperial Tea House, Inc.

KEN'S AT COPLEY....549-553 Boylston St., Copley Sq., Boston, Mass., 02116. (617) 266-6106. Cuisine: Delicatessen. Credit cards: None.

KING WAH....25-29 Beach St., Chinatown, Boston, Mass., 02129. (617) 426-2705. Cuisine: Chinese. Credit cards: AE, MC.

LECHNER'S GOURMET RESTAURANT....21 Broad St., Boston, Mass., 02109. (617) 523-1016. Cuisine: German/Continental. Credit cards: AE, DC, MC, VISA.

LEGAL SEA FOODS.... Boston Park Plaza Hotel, 34 Columbus Ave., Boston, Mass., (617) 426-4444. Cuisine: Seafood. Owner: D.H. Revah, Comptroller.

LEGAL SEA FOODS....27 Columbus Ave., Statter Office Bldg., Boston, Mass., (617) 426-5566. Cuisine: Seafood. Owner: D.H. Revah, Comptroller

THE LIBRARY.... The Copley Plaza Hotel, Copley Sq., Boston, Mass., 02116. (617) 267-5300. Cuisine: Cocktails. Days closed: Sundays. Credit cards: AE, CB, DC, MC, V.

LOCKE-OBER....3 Winter Pl., Boston, Mass., 02108. (617) 542-1340. Cuisine: Continental/Seafood. Credit cards: AE, MC, VISA.

MICHAEL'S WATERFRONT RESTAURANT....85 Atlantic Ave., Boston, Mass., 02110. (617) 367-6425 or 367-6176. Cuisine: Continental/Steak/Seafood. Owners: Michael Gillen and Jim O'Brien. Open 7 days. Credit cards: AE, MC, VISA. Private party facilities: 15 to 150. Annual sale: $1 million to $3 million. Total employment: 65. Corporate name: Gilsinko of Mass.

NO-NAME RESTAURANT....15½ Fish Pier, Boston, Mass., 02210. (617) 338-7539. Cuisine: Seafood. Credit cards: None.

THE RITZ DINING ROOM....15 Arlington St., Back Bay, Boston, Mass., 02116. (617) 536-5700. Cuisine: French. Owner: John P. Cantin. Credit cards: AE, MC, VISA.

UNION OYSTER HOUSE....41 Union St., Boston, Mass., 02108. (617) 227-2750. This choice piece of Americana beautifully preserved has been in continuous service for over 150 years. It is a treasure house of most any type of mouth-watering seafood, caught fresh practically at the door. Countless fans claim there's no place like it for oysters and clams in all the ways these bivalves can be served. Other seafood offerings include lobster in its manifold forms, shrimps, scallops, and crab legs. Management is also proud of its steaks and chops. Moistenments expertly bartended. Owner: Joseph A. Milano, Mary Ann Milano. Open 7 days for lunch and dinner. Moderately priced. Reservations are encouraged. Credit cards: All major. Corporate name: Union Oyster House, Inc.

VILLA FRANCESCA....150 Richmond St., Boston, Mass., 02109. (617) 367-2948. Very popular, attractive, and dedicated to introducing Boston palates to the delights of subtly seasoned provender *a la Italiano*. Watch the "regulars" make their slow, relentless approach to their favorite seats. They know what lies ahead with the dishes brought lovingly from the kitchen. Specialties include: Veal *ponte vecchio*, fish *guglielmo*, chicken *pescatore*. Owner: Bill Ranawro. Open 7 days for lunch and dinner. Moderately priced. Reservations are suggested. Credit cards: AE, CB, DC. Private party facilities: Available. Annual sales: $500,000 to $1 million. Total employment: 28. Corporate name: Villa Francesca, Inc.

ZACHARY'S.... The Colonnade Hotel, 120 Huntington Ave., Boston, Mass., 02116. (617) 261-2800. Cuisine: Continental. Days closed: Sundays. Credit cards: AE, CB, DC, MC, VISA.

BRAINTREE

CHARLEY'S EATING & DRINKING SALOON.... South Shore Plz., Braintree, Mass., 02184. (617) 848-0200. Cuisine: American. Open 7 days for lunch and dinner. Credit cards: AE, CB, DC, MC.

BREWSTER

CHILLINGSWORTH.... Rte. 6A, Brewster, Mass., 02631. (617) 896-3640. Cuisine: French. Owner: Robert Pitt Rabin. Call for times. Credit cards: All major. Private party facilities: Up to 75. Annual sales: $250,000 to $500,000. Total employment: 42.

BROOKLINE

BO SHING....284 Washington St., Brookline, Mass., 02146. (617) 734-1870. Cuisine: Chinese. Open 7 days. Credit cards: MC, VISA.

CAPUCINO'S RESTAURANT....1370 Beacon St., Brookline, Mass., 02146. (617) 731-4848. Cuisine: Italian. Owner: Richard S. Keesan. Open 7 days for lunch and dinner. Credit cards: AE, DC, MC, VISA. Private party facilities: 15 to 65. Annual sales: $1 million to $3 million. Total employment: 50. Corporate name: Capucino's, Inc.

CHARDAS....1306 Beacon St., Brookline, Mass., 02146. (617) 232-4050. Cuisine: Hungarian and International. Open 7 days. Credit cards: AE, MC, VISA.

CHEZ RAINER....85 Washington St., Brookline, Mass., 02146. (617) 566-9161. Cuisine: French. Days closed: Sunday and August. Credit cards: MC.

THE COLORADO PUBLIC LIBRARY.... Hearthstone Plz., Brookline, Mass., 02100. (617) 734-6772. Cuisine: Steak/Seafood. Open 7 days for dinner only. Credit cards: AE, MC, VISA. Private party facilities: Up to 60. Annual sales: $1 million to $3 million. Total employment: 55. Corporate name: Barnsider Management Corporation.

COMMON STOCK....48 Boylston St., Brookline, Mass., 02146. (617) 566-9750. Cuisine: Vegetarian. Days closed: Monday. Credit cards: None.

GOLDEN TEMPLE RESTAURANT & LOUNGE....1651 Beacon St., Brookline, Mass., 02146. (617) 277-9722. Cuisine: Chinese. Open 7 days. Credit cards: None.

HAVAH-NAGILA ISRAELI RESTAURANT....1653 Beacon St., Brookline, Mass., 02168. (617) 277-3433. Cuisine: Israeli/Middle Eastern. Open 7 days for lunch and dinner. No credit cards.

JAFF'S....299 Harvard St., Brookline, Mass., 02146. (617) 738-5635. Cuisine: Steak/Seafood. Owner: Charles Jaffe, Pres. Open 7 days. Credit cards: All major. Private party facilities: 15 to 70. Annual sales: $1 million to $3 million. Total employment: 80. Corporate name: Premier II Corp.

BUZZARDS BAY

THE WINDJAMMER....3131 Cranberry Hwy., Buzzards Bay, Mass., 02532. (617) 759-7262. Cuisine: Seafood. Credit cards: AE, MC, VISA.

CAMBRIDGE

AKU AKU....149 Alewife Brook Pkwy., Cambridge, Mass., 02140. (617) 491-5377. Cuisine: Polynesian. Open 7 days for lunch and dinner. Credit cards: AE, DC, MC.

HARVEST....44 Brattle St., Harvard Sq., Cambridge, Mass., 02138. (617) 492-1115. Cuisine: Continental. Owner: Benjamin Thompson. Open 7 days for lunch and dinner. Credit cards: All major. Private party facilities: Up to 20. Annual sales: $1 million to $3 million. Total employment: 100.

LEGAL SEA FOODS....5 Cambridge Cntr., Kendall Sq., Cambridge, Mass., (617) 864-3400. Cuisine: Seafood. Owner: D.H. Revah, Comptroller.

MODERN TIMES CAFE....134 Hampshire St., Cambridge, Mass., 02139. (617) 354-8371. Cuisine: American. Owner: Benjamin E. Jeffries. Open 6 days for lunch and dinner; Closed Sundays. No credit cards. Annual sales: $250,000 to $500,000. Total employment: 15. Corporate name: Modern Times Cafe, Inc.

PANACHE RESTAURANT....798 Main St., Cambridge, Mass., 02134. (617) 492-9500. Cuisine: French. Owner: Bruce Frankel. Open Tuesday through Saturday for dinner. Lunch Thursday and Friday only. Credit cards: All major. Annual sales: $250,000 to $500,000. Corporate name: Panache Restaurant, Inc.

THE RIB ROOM.... Hotel Sonesta, 5 Cambridge Pkwy., Cambridge, Mass., 02142. (617) 491-3600. Cuisine: Continental. Owner: Sonesta International Hotels, Roger Sonabend, Pres. and Chmn. Open 7 days. Credit cards: All major. Private party facilities: 5 to 25. Annual sales: $500,000 to $1 million. Total employment: 30. Corporate name: Sonesta International Hotels.

THE VOYAGERS....45½ Mt. Auburn St., Harvard Sq., Cambridge, Mass., 02138. (617) 354-1718. Cuisine: Continental. Owner: Gary V. Heller. Open 6 days for dinner only; Closed Monday. Credit cards: AE, MC, VISA. Private party facilities: Small parties only. Annual sales: $250,00 to $500,00. Total employment: 15.

CHARLEMONT

PLANTATION HOUSE.... East Hawley Rd., Charlemont, Mass., 01339. (413) 339-8371. Cuisine: American/Continental. Owner's name: Philip and Paul Dibenedetto. Credit cards: DC.

CHARLESTON

THE FRONT PAGE EATING AND DRINKING, INC.... The Bunker Hill Mall, Charleston, Mass., 02129. (617) 242-5010. Cuisine: American. Owner: John F. Carroll, Sr., John F. Carroll, Jr., Open 7 days for lunch and dinner. Credit cards: All major. Annual sales: $1 million to $3 million. Total employment: 65. Corporate name: The Front Page Eating and Drinking, Inc.

CHATHAMPORT

CHRISTOPHER RYDER HOUSE.... Rte. 28, Chathamport, Mass., 02632. (617) 945-0608. Cuisine: New England/Continental. Credit cards: AE, MC, VISA.

CONCORD

COLONIAL INN....48 Monument St., Concord, Mass., 07142. (617) 369-9200. Cuisine: Continental. Owner: Luther N. Grimes. Open 7 days for breakfast, lunch, and dinner. Credit cards: All major. Private party facilities: Up to 100. Annual sales: $1 million to $3 million. Total employment: 134.

DENNISPORT

JAKE CASSIDY'S....76 Chase Ave., Dennisport, Mass., 02369. (617) 398-0228. Cuisine: Steak & Seafood. Open 7 days. Credit cards: AE, MC, VISA. Annual sales: $250,000 to $500,000. Total employment: 30. Corporate name: Jake Cassidy's of Dennis, Inc.

EDGARTOWN

CHEZ PIERRE.... South Summer St., Edgartown, Martha's Vineyard, Mass., 02539. (617) 627-8947. Cuisine: French. Credit cards: AE, MC, VISA.

FALMOUTH

COONAMESSETT INN.... Jones Rd., Falmouth, Mass., 02541. (617) 548-2300. Cuisine: Seafood. Credit cards: AE, DC, MC, VISA.

FLYING BRIDGE.... Scranton Ave., Falmouth, Mass., 02540. (617) 548-2700. Cuisine: American. Credit cards: AE, DC, MC, VISA.

FOXBORO

LAFAYETTE HOUSE.... Rte. 1, Foxboro, Mass., 02035. (617) 543-5344. Cuisine: American. Credit cards: AE, DC, MC, VISA.

GLOUCESTER

WHITE RAINBOW....65 Main St., Gloucester, Mass., 01930. (617) 281-0017. Cuisine: Continental. Owner: Jeanne M. Dyson. Open 6 days for dinner; Sunday brunch; Closed Monday. Credit cards: All major. Total employment: 12.

HADLEY

CARBURS AT THE ELMWOOD....104 Russel St., Hadley, Mass., 01035. (617) 586-1978. Cuisine: American.

NEW SWORD AND SHIELD OF YORK....554 Main St., Harwich Port, Mass., 02646. (617) 432-9763. Cuisine: American/Seafood. Open 7 days for lunch and dinner; Closed Monday during the winter. Credit cards: AE, MC, VISA. Private party facilities: Up to 60. Annual sales: $1 million to $3 million. Total employment: 50 summer; 25 winter. Corporate name: Sword & Shield of York Restaurant, Inc.

HOLYOKE

THE LOG CABIN.... Easthampton Rd., Holyoke, Mass., 01040. (413) 536-7700. Cuisine: New England/American. Credit cards: All major.

LAWRENCE

BISHOP'S....99 Hampshire at Lowell St., Lawrence, Mass., 01840. (617) 683-7143. Cuisine: Arabic/American. Credit cards: All major. Owner: Constance Bishop.

LENOX

GATEWAYS INN....71 Walker Street, Lenox, Mass., 01240. (413) 637-2532. Cuisine: Continental/Classic American. Owner: Gerhard & Lilliane Schmid. Open 5 days for dinner only; Closed Sunday and Monday. Credit cards: MC, VISA. Private party facilities: Up to 120. Annual sales: $250,000 to $500,000. Total employment: 30.

LYNNFIELD

TOWNE LYNE HOUSE.... Route 1, Lynnfield, Mass., 01940. (617) 592-6400. Cuisine: American. Open 7 days for lunch and dinner. Credit cards: AE, MC, VISA.

MAGNOLIA

THE SURF....56 Raymond St., Magnolia, Mass., 01944. (617) 525-3313. Cuisine: Continental. Credit cards: AE, MC, VISA.

METHUEN

RED TAVERN....5 Pleasant St., Methuen, Mass., 01844. (617) 683-1246. Cuisine: Continental. Credit cards: AE, DC, MC, VISA.

NANTUCKET

THE CLUB CAR....1 Main Street, Nantucket, Mass., 02554. (617) 228-1101. Cuisine: Continental. Credit cards: AE, MC, VISA.

JARED COFFIN HOUSE....29 Broad St., Nantucket, Mass., 02554. (617) 228-0101. Cuisine: Continental. Credit cards: AE, DC, MC, VISA.

NEW BEDFORD

LOUIE'S ON THE WHARF....1776 Homer's Wharf, New Bedford, Mass., 02740. (617) 996-3901. Cuisine: Seafood. Credit cards: AE, MC, VISA.

NEWTON

CAPUCINO'S RESTAURANT....1114 Beacon St., Newton, Mass., 02161. (617) 731-4848. Cuisine: Italian. Owner: Richard S. Kessan. Open 7 days for lunch and dinner. Credit cards: AE, DC, MC, VISA. Private party facilities: 15 to 65. Annual sales: $1 million to $3 million. Total employment: 50. Corporate name: Capucino's Inc.

LEGAL SEA FOODS....43 Boylston St., Chestnut Hill, Newton, Mass., 02167. (617) 277-7300. Cuisine: Seafood. Credit cards: AE.

PILLAR HOUSE....26 Quinobequin Rd., Newton, Mass., 021162. (617) 969-6500. Cuisine: Continental. Credit cards: All major.

NORTH ANDOVER

THOMPSON'S.... Wilson's Corner, 435 Andover St., North Andover, Mass., 01845. (617) 686-4309. Cuisine: American. Credit cards: All major.

NORTHAMPTON

BEARDSLEY'S CAFE-RESTAURANT....140 Main St., Northampton, Mass., 01060. (413) 586-2699. Cuisine: French. Owner: D. Constance. Open 7 days for lunch and dinner. Credit cards: All major. Annual sales: $250,000 to $500,000. Total employment: 25. Corporate name: Beardsley's, Inc.

PIGEON COVE

OLD FARM INN....291 Granite St., Pigeon Cove, Mass., 01966. (617) 546-3237. Cuisine: Continental. Owner: William Balzane.

PLYMOUTH

MCGRATH'S.... Town Wharf, Plymouth, Mass., 02360. (617) 746-3422. Cuisine: Seafood. Credit cards: AE, DC, MC, VISA.

PROVINCETOWN

CAFE AT THE MEWS....359 Commercial St., Provincetown, Mass., 02657. (617) 487-1500. Cuisine: Continental. Credit cards: AE, MC, VISA.

POOR RICHARD'S BUTTERY....432 Commercial St., Provincetown, Mass., 02657. (617) 487-3825. Cuisine: Continental. Credit cards: AE, MC, VISA.

ROCKPORT

PEG LEG....2 King St., Rockport, Mass., 01966. (617) 546-3038. Cuisine: Seafood. Credit cards: MC, VISA.

ROSLINDALE

CASA BEIRUT....4161 Washington St., Roslindale, Mass., 02131. (617) 323-9505. Cuisine: Middle-Eastern. Open 7 days. Credit cards: AE, MC.

SALEM

THE LYCEUM....43 Church St., Salem, Mass., 01970. (617) 745-7665. Cuisine: Continental/American. Owner: Joan Boudreau. Open 7 days for lunch and dinner. Credit cards: All major. Private party facilities: Up to 100. Total employment: 75.

SCITUATE

THE BARKER TAVERN....21 Barker, Scituate, Mass., 02066. (617) 545-6533. Cuisine: Continental. Credit cards: AE, DC, MC, VISA.

SEEKONK

OLD GRIST MILL TAVERN....390 Fall River Ave., Seekonk, Mass., 02771. (401) 336-8460. Cuisine: American. Owner: Edward P. Grace, III. Open 7 days for lunch and dinner. Credit cards: All major. Annual sales: $1 million to $3 million. Total employment: 50.

SIASCONSET

CHANTICLEER.... New St., Siasconset, Mass., 02564. (617) 257-6231. Cuisine: French. Credit cards: AE, MC, VISA.

SOUTH WELLFLEET

YESTERYEARS.... Rte. 6, South Wellfleet, Mass., 02663. (617) 349-9339. Cuisine: Continental. Owner: Allyson Denson. Credit cards: AE, DC, MC, VISA.

SPRINGFIELD

CIRO'S....870 Main St., Springfield, Mass., 01103. (413) 736-9626. Cuisine: Italian/American.

STOCKBRIDGE

RED LION INN.... Main St., Stockbridge, Mass., 01262. (413) 298-5545. Cuisine: Continental. Owner: John Fitzpatrick. Open 7 days. Credit cards: All major. Private party facilities: Up to 100.

STURBRIDGE

PUBLICK HOUSE.... Rte. 131, Sturbridge, Mass., 01566. (617) 347-3313. Cuisine: Continental. Owner: Buddy Adler. Open 7 days. Credit cards: All major. Private party facilities: Up to 200. Annual sales: Over $3 million. Total employment: 250.

SUDBURY CENTER

LONGFELLOW'S WAYSIDE INN.... Wayside Inn Rd., Sudbury Center, Mass., 01776. (617) 443-8846. Cuisine: Continental/American. Credit cards: All major.

WAKEFIELD

PAGE'S AT COLONIAL.... Rte. 128, Wakefield, Mass., 01880. (617) 245-9300. Cuisine: American. Credit cards: All major.

WEST BROOKFIELD

SALEM CROSS INN.... Ware Rd., West Brookfield, Mass., 01585. (617) 867-2345. Cuisine: American. Credit cards: MC, VISA.

WEST DENNIS

THE COLUMNS.... Rte. 28, West Dennis, Mass., 02671. (617) 398-8033. Cuisine: American. Open 7 days for dinner only; Sunday brunch. Credit cards: All major. Private party facilities: Up to 150. Annual sales: $250,000 to $500,000. Total employment: 30.

WEST HARWICH

BISHOP'S TERRACE.... Main St., West Harwich, Mass., 02671. (617) 432-0253. Cuisine: American. Owner: Constance B. McCarthy. Open 6 days for lunch and dinner; Closed Sunday. Credit cards: All major. Private party facilities: Up to 75. Total employment: 35.

CAPE HALF HOUSE.... Rte. 28, West Harwich, Mass., 02671. (617) 432-1964. Cuisine: French. Credit cards: MC, VISA.

WESTMINSTER

OLD MILL.... Rte. 2A, Westminster, Mass., 01473. (617) 874-5941. Cuisine: American. Owner: Don S. Foster. Open 7 days for lunch and dinner. Credit cards: All major. Private party facilities: Up to 150. Annual sales: $1 million to $3 million.

WEST SPRINGFIELD

MONTE CARLO....1020 Memorial Ave., West Springfield, Mass., 01089. (413) 734-6431. Cuisine: Italian/American. Open Monday through Friday for lunch; 7 days for dinner. Credit cards: All major. Private party facilities: Up to 150. Annual sales: $500,000. to $1 million. Total employment: 65.

WEST STOCKBRIDGE

LE PETIT POIS.... Main & Maple Sts., West Stockbridge, Mass., 01266. (413) 232-7770. Cuisine: French. Open 7 days for lunch and dinner; Sunday brunch. Credit cards: AE, MC, VISA. Reservations: Recommended.

WOODS HOLE

LANDFALL.... Water St., Woods Hole, Mass., 02543. (617) 548-1758. Cuisine: Seafood. Credit cards: AE, MC, VISA.

WORCESTER

EL MORROCCO....100 Wall St., Worcester, Mass., 01604. (617) 756-7117. Cuisine: Mid-Eastern. Credit cards: AE, MC, VISA.

NEW HAMPSHIRE

CONCORD

BRICK TOWER....414 South Main St., Concord, N.H., 03301. (603) 224-9565. Cuisine: Continental. Credit cards: All major.

DENAUW'S....161 London Rd., Concord, N.H., 03301. (603) 228-6687. Cuisine: American. Credit cards: AE, MC, VISA.

EXETER

EXETER INN....90 Front St., Exeter, N.H., 03833. (603) 772-5901. Cuisine: Continental/American. Credit cards: All major.

FRANCONIA

FRANCONIA INN.... Route 116, Franconia, N.H., 03580. (603) 823-5542. Cuisine: French. Owner: Richard G. Morris. Open 7 days for dinner. Credit cards: AE, MC, VISA. Private party facilities: Up to 30. Annual sales: $250,000 to $500,000. Total employment: 25.

THE HORSE & HOUND INN.... Wells Rd., Franconia, N.H., 03580. (603) 823-5501. Cuisine: Continental/Innovative. Owner: The Careys. Open for dinner; closed Wednesday; closed April, May, November, and December. Credit cards: None. Total employment: 4-6.

LOVETT'S INN BY LAFAYETTE BROOK.... Franconia, N.H., 03580. (603) 823-7761. Cuisine: Continental. Credit cards: AE, MC, VISA.

GLEN

THE BERNERHOF.... Rte. 302, Glen, N.H., 03838. (603) 383-4414. Cuisine: Continental. Credit cards: MC, VISA.

GORHAM

LITTLE GYPSY....277 Main St., Gorham, N.H., 03581. (603) 466-9484. Cuisine: Continental. Credit cards: AE, DC, MC, VISA.

TOWN & COUNTRY INN.... Rte. 2, Gorham, N.H., 03581. (603) 466-3315. Cuisine: American. Credit cards: AE, DC, MC, VISA.

YOKOHAMA....288 Main St., Gorham, N.H., 03581. (603) 466-2501. Cuisine: Oriental. Credit cards: AE, CB, DC.

HANOVER

HANOVER INN.... Main & Wheelock Sts., Hanover, N.H., 03755. (603) 643-4300. Cuisine: American. Credit cards: AE, DC, MC, VISA.

THE OWL'S NEST....213 Mechanic, Hanover, N.H., 03755. (603) 448-2074. Cuisine: Continental/French. Credit cards: AE, DC, MC, VISA.

INTERVALE

TUCKERMAN'S INN & TAVERN.... Rte. 302, Intervale, N.H., 03845. (603) 356-2752. Cuisine: Italian. Credit cards: MC, VISA.

JACKSON

DANA PLACE.... Rte. 16, Jackson, N.H., 03846. (603) 383-6822. Cuisine: Continental. Owner: M.B. Jennings Open 7 days for dinner. Credit cards: All major. Private party facilities: Up to 30. Total employment: 18.

KEENE

BLACK LANTERN.... Rte. 12, Keene, N.H., 03431. (603) 357-1064. Cuisine: Continental. Open Tuesday-Saturday for dinner; Sunday for lunch and dinner. No credit cards. Private party facilities: Up to 280. Annual sales: $250,000 to $500,000. Total employment: 40. Corporate name: Black Lantern Restaurant, Inc.

KINGSTON

KINGSTON 1686 HOUSE.... Main St., Kingston, N.H., 03848. (603) 642-3637. Cuisine: Continental. Credit cards: AE, DC, MC, VISA.

LACONIA

HICKORY STICK FARM.... Rte. 11, Laconia, N.H., 03246. (603) 524-3333. Cuisine: Continental. Owner: D. Scott & Mary Roeder. Open 7 days seasonally from June til October for dinner; Seasonal Sunday brunch; Closed otherwise. Credit cards: AE, MC, VISA. Private party facilities: 20 to 50. Annual sales: $250,000 to $500,000. Total employment: 20.

MANCHESTER

DAFFODIL'S.... Rte. 101, Manchester, N.H., 03102. (603) 472-5188. Cuisine: Continental. Credit cards: All major

FOUR SEASONS.... Sheraton-Wayfarer Inn, Manchester, N.H., 03102. (603) 622-3766. Cuisine: Continental. Credit cards: All major.

THE RENAISSANCE RESTAURANT....1087 Elm St., Manchester, N.H., 03101. (603) 669-7000. Cuisine: Steak/Italian/Seafood/Greek/American. Owner: Mr. & Mrs. Angelos B. Tsingos. Open 7 days for lunch and dinner. Credit cards: All major. Private party facilities: 18 to 100. Annual sales: $250,000 to $500,000. Total employment: 10. Corporate name: Empire Foods, Inc.

MEREDITH

THE DEPOT.... Box 156, Rte. 3, Meredith, N.H., 03253. (603) 279-7777. Cuisine: Italian. Credit cards: MC, VISA.

HART'S TURKEY FARM.... Box 664, Rte. 3, Meredith, N.H., 03253. (603) 279-6212. Cuisine: American. Credit cards: All major.

MOULTONBORO

COUNTRY FARE INN.... Box 3, Rte. 25 Jct., Moultonboro, N.H., 03254. (603) 476-2300. Cuisine: American. Credit cards: AE, DC, MC, VISA.

MOUNT SUNAPEE

SCHWEITZER'S.... Box 26, NH 103, Mount Sunapee, N.H., 03772. (603) 863-1820. Cuisine: American and German. Owner: John J. Schweitzer. Open 7 days for lunch and dinner. Credit cards: All major. Private party facilities: Up to 150. Annual sales: $250,000 to $500,000. Total employment: 35.

NASHUA

GREEN RIDGE TURKEY FARM.... Daniel Webster Hwy., Nashua, N.H., 03060. (603) 888-2500. Cuisine: Continental. Credit cards: All major.

NEW LONDON

HIDE-AWAY LODGE.... Little Lake Sunapee Rd., New London, N.H., 03257. (603) 526-4861. Cuisine: Continental-American. Owner: Lilli and Wolf Heinberg. Open Mid-May through October; Closed Tuesdays. Credit cards: None. Annual sales: $250,000 to $500,000. Total employment: 18.

NORTH CONWAY

SCOTTISH LION.... Rte. 302 North Conway, N.H., 03860 (603) 356-6381. Cuisine: American/Scottish. Credit cards: AE, DC, MC, VISA.

SNUG HARBOUR INN.... Rte. 16 North Conway, N.H., 03860. (603) 356-3000. Cuisine: Steak/Seafood. Credit Cards: AE, MC, VISA.

PORTSMOUTH

BLUE STRAWBERRY....29 Ceres St., Portsmouth, N.H., 03801.(603) 431-6420. Cuisine: American.

PIER II.... State St., at Memorial Bridge, Portsmouth, N.H., 03801. (603) 436-0669. Cuisine: Seafood/Steak. Owner: Frank Wilson, Pres. Credit cardsL MC, VISA.

YOKEN'S "THAR SHE BLOWS".... Lafayette Rd., Portsmouth, N.H., 03801. (603) 436-8224. Cuisine: Seafood. Credit cards: AE, MC, VISA.

ROCHESTER

LUNEAU.... Box 1707, Rochester, N.H., 03867. (603) 332-6130. Cuisine: Continental. Open for lunch and dinner 7 days. Credit cards: DC, MC, VISA. Private party facilities: 2 rooms—45/125. Annual sales: $500,000 to $1 million. Total employment: 45. Corporate name: Luneau's Restaurant.

RYE

SAUNDERS AT RYE HARBOR.... Rye, N.H., 03870. (603) 964-6466. Cuisine: Seafood. Owner: W. Douglas Zechel. Open 7 days from May to October. Credit cards: AE, MC, VISA. Total employment: 50.

SUNAPEE

WOODBINE COTTAGE.... River Rd., Sunapee, N.H., 03782. (603) 763-2222. Cuisine: American. Owner: Mrs. Eleanor W. Hill. Open 7 days from May to October. Credit cards: MC, VISA. Annual Sales: $250,000 to $500,000. Total employment: 55. Corporate Name Woodbine Cottage, Inc.

WHITEFIELD

MOUNTAIN VIEW HOUSE.... Mountain View Rd., Whitefield, N.H., 03598. (603) 837-2511.

WOLFEBORO

WOLFEBORO INN....44 North Main St., Wolfeboro, N.H., 03894. (603) 569-3016. Credit cards: AE, MC, VISA.

NEW JERSEY

ATLANTIC CITY

RISTORANTE ALBERTO.... Pacific & Mississippi Aves., Atlantic City, N.J., 08401. (609) 344-7000. Cuisine: Italian. Credit cards: All major.

CAPTAIN'S GALLEY....12 South Douglas Ave., Margate, Atlantic City, N.J., 08402. (609) 822-6100. Cuisine: Seafood. Credit cards: None.

DOCK'S OYSTER HOUSE....2405 Atlantic Ave., Atlantic City, N.J. 08401. (609) 345-0092. Cuisine: Seafood. Open Tuesday through Sunday for dinner; Closed Monday. Credit cards: AE, MC, VISA.

FRONT PORCH....132 New York Ave., Atlantic City, N.J., 08401. (609) 345-1917. Cuisine: American/French. Credit cards: AE, DC, MC, VISA.

KNIFE AND FORK INN.... Atlantic & Pacific Aves., Atlantic City, N.J., 08401. (609) 344-1133. Cuisine: Seafood. Credit cards: AE only. Open 7 days for dinner only.

LE GRAND FROMAGE....25 Gordon's Alley, Atlantic City, N.J., 08401. (609) 347-2743. Cuisine: French. Credit cards: MC, VISA.

LE PALAIS.... Resorts International Hotel, Boardwalk at North Carolina Ave., Atlantic City, N.J., 08401. (609) 340-6400. Cuisine: French/Continental. Credit cards: All major.

PEARL GARDEN RESTAURANT....1935 Black Horse Pike, Atlantic City, N.J., 08401. (609) 646-7072. Cuisine: Chinese. Open 7 days for lunch and dinner. Credit cards: All major.

PEKING DUCK HOUSE.... Atlantic and Iowa Aves., Atlantic City, N.J., 08401. (609) 344-9090. Cuisine: Szechuan, Mandarin, and Cantonese Chinese. Open Monday through Saturday for lunch; 7 days for dinner. Credit cards: AE, MC, VISA.

TWELVE SOUTH....12 South Indian Ave., Atlantic City, N.J., 08401. (609) 344-1112. Cuisine: Italian/Seafood/American. Open 24 hours Monday through Friday; Closed noon to 5:00 PM Saturday and Sunday; Otherwise open. Credit cards: All major. Entertainment: Live music and dancing.

ABSECON

RAM'S HEAD INN....1468 White Horse Pike, Absecon, N.J., 08201. (609) 652-1700. Cuisine: American. Owner: Knowles. Credit cards: All major. Private party facilities: 8 to 300. Annual sales: Over $3 million. Total employment: 160.

BELLEVILLE

NANINA'S IN THE PARK....540 Mill St., Belleville, N.J., 07109. (201) 751-1230. Cuisine: Italian. Open Monday through Friday for lunch; 7 days for dinner; Sunday dinner from 1:00 PM. Credit cards: AE, DC, MC, VISA. Reservations: Suggested.

BERNARDSVILLE

OLD MILL INN.... North Maple Ave. & Rte. 202, Bernardsville, N.J., 07924. (201) 221-1100. Cuisine: Continental. Owner's name: Frank Petrozza. Credit cards: AE, MDC, VISA.

BURLINGTON

CAFE GALLERY....219 High St., Burlington, N.J., 08016. (609) 386-6150. Cuisine: International/French. Open Monday through Saturday for lunch; 7 days for dinner; Sunday brunch. Credit cards: AE, MC, VISA. Entertainment: Live music and original art gallery.

CAPE MAY

THE MAD BATTER....19 Jackson St., Cape May, N.J., 08204. (609) 884-5970. Cuisine: French & American Nouvelle Cuisine. Open for breakfast, lunch, and dinner 7 days. Credit cards: MC, VISA. Bring your own wine.

MARQUIS DE LAFAYETTE/THE GOLD WHALE LOUNGE....501 Beach Dr., Cape May, N.J., 08204. (609) 884-3431. Cuisine: Italian/Continental. Open 7 days for breakfast, lunch, and dinner. Credit cards: AE, MC, VISA. Entertainment: Live music and dancing.

TOP OF THE MARQ....501 Beach Dr., Cape May, N.J., 08204. (609) 884-3431. Cuisine: Seafood/Continental. Open 7 nights for dinner only. Credit cards: AE, MC, VISA. Entertainment: Live music and dancing nightly except Monday.

WATSON'S MERION INN....106 Decatur St., Cape May, N.J., 08204. (609) 884-8363. Cuisine: Seafood.

THE WINCHESTER INN....513 Lafayette St., Cape May, N.J., 08204. (609) 883-4358. Cuisine: Seafood. Open Monday through Saturday for lunch; 7 days for dinner. Credit cards: AE, DC, MC, VISA. Entertainment: Live music nightly. Proper attire required.

CEDAR GROVE

VILLA D'ESTE....183 Stevens Ave., Cedar Grove, N.J., 07009. (201) 256-1900. Cuisine: Italian. Credit cards: AE, DC, VISA.

CHATHAM

THE TARRAGON TREE....225 Main St., Chatham, N.J., 07928. (201) 653-7333. Cuisine: French. Open Monday through Friday for lunch; 7 days for dinner. Credit cards: MC, VISA. "Game birds and venison in season."

CHERRY HILL

CASABLANCA RESTAURANT IN THE RICKSHAW HOTEL.... Rte. 70, Cherry Hill, N.J., 08034. (609) 665-6900. Cuisine: American/Continental. Open 7 days for breakfast, lunch, and dinner; Sunday brunch. Credit cards: All major. Private party facilities: Available. Entertainment: Live music and dancing.

CINELLI'S COUNTRY HOUSE....457 Haddonfield Rd., Cherry Hill, N.J., 08002. (609) 662-5050. Cuisine: Italian. Credit cards: All major.

FRANCHIN'S....9 Grove St., (at Rte. 70) Cherry Hill, N.J., 08034. (609) 663-3939. Cuisine: Itaian/Seafood. Open daily for lunch and dinner. No credit cards. Entertainment: Live entertainment nightly.

THE HIDEAWAY....63 Kresson Rd., Cherry Hill, N.J., 08034. (609) 428-7379. Cuisine: Continental/American. Open Monday through Friday for lunch; 7 days for dinner. Credit cards: All major. Private party facilities: Available.

PEKING MANDAEIN INN #2, ROUTE 70....2320 West Marlton Pke., Cherry Hill, N.J., 08002. (609) 665-7559. Cuisine: Mandarin, Hunan, Szechuan, and Cantonese Chinese. Open Monday through Saturday for lunch; 7 days for dinner. Credit cards: MC, VISA. Bring your own wine.

THE SHEPHERD'S INN....1334 Brace Rd., Cherry Hill, N.J., 08034. (609) 795-2228. Cuisine: Italian. Open 6 days for lunch and dinner; Closed Sunday. Credit cards: MC, VISA.

CHESTER

PUBLICK HOUSE....111 Main St., Chester, N.J., 07930. (201) 879-6878. Cuisine: American. Owner's name: Jack Welch and Jeff Beers. Credit cards: AE.

CINNAMINSON

FUJI....404 Rte. 130 North, Cinnaminson, N.J., 08077. (609) 829-5211. Cuisine: Japanese. Open Monday, Wednesday, Thursday, and Friday for lunch; Wednesday through Sunday for dinner. Credit cards: AE, MC, VISA. Bring your own wine.

CLIFFSIDE PARK

BANGKOK THAI CUISINE....783 Pallisades Ave., Cliffside Park, N.J., 07010. (201) 224-7717. Cuisine: Thai. Open Tuesday through Saturday for lunch; Tuesday through Sunday for dinner; Closed Monday. Credit cards: AE, DC, MC, VISA.

CLIFTON

BEL'VEDERE....247 Piaget Ave., Clifton, N.J., 07011. (201). 772-5060. Cuisine: Continental. Open Tuesday through Friday for lunch; Tuesday through Sunday for dinner; Closed Monday. Credit cards: AE, MC, VISA.

CLINTON

BRUNNER'S LANDMARK INN.... Van Sycles Rd., Clinton, N.J., 08809. (201) 638-6585. Cuisine: Swiss. Open 7 days for dinner only. Credit cards: AE, DC, MC, VISA.

COLUMBUS

COLUMBUS INN.... Main St., Columbus, N.J., 08022. (609) 298-4449. Cuisine: Continental. Open Monday through Saturday for lunch; 7 days for dinner. Credit cards: All major.

CONVENT STATION

ROD'S 1890 RANCH HOUSE.... Madison Ave., Convent Station, N.J., 07961. (201) 539-6666. Cuisine: American. Owner: The Keller Family. Open 7 days. Credit cards: All major. Private party facilities: 10 to 400. Annual sales: Over $3 million. Total employment: 180.

CRANBURY

THE CRANBURY INN....21 South Main St., Cranbury, N.J., 08512. (609) 655-5595. Cuisine: American. Open Tuesday through Sunday for lunch and dinner; Closed Monday. Credit cards: AE, DC, MC, VISA. Reservations: Suggested.

CRESSKILL

LA PETITE AUBERGE....44 East Madison Ave., Cresskill, N.J., (07626. (201) 569-2270. Cuisine: French. Jean C. Brecq, Pres. Open Tuesday through Friday for lunch; Tuesday through Sunday for dinner; Closed Monday. Credit cards: All major. Annual sales: $500,000 to $1 million. Total employment: 24.

DOVER

VIENNA.... Rte. 46, Dover, N.J., 07801. (201) 361-6452. Cuisine: Viennese. Open 6 days for dinner only; Closed Monday. Credit cards: AE, DC, MC, VISA.

EAST RUTHERFORD

PEGASUS.... Meadowlands Sports Complex, East Rutherford, N.J., 07073. (201) 935-5650. Cuisine: American/Continental. Open daily for dinner. Credit cards: All major. Reservations: Necessary in both wings of restaurant. "Fine food and lavish decor."

ELBERON

THE SIDE ROOM....1195 Lincoln Sq., Elberon, N.J., 07740. (201) 222-9558. Cuisine: Northern Italian. Open Monday through Friday for lunch; Wednesday through Sunday for dinner. No credit cards. Bring your own wine.

ELIZABETH

DAPHNE'S....901 Spring St., Elizabeth, N.J., 07201. (201) 527-1600. Cuisine: Continental. Credit cards: All major.

EVELYN'S SEAFOOD RESTAURANT....624 Westfield Ave., Elizabeth, N.J., 07208. (201) 352-2022. Cuisine: Seafood. Open daily for lunch; 7 days for dinner. Credit cards: AE, MC, VISA.

ENGLEWOOD CLIFFS

THE OPERA....464 Sylvan Ave., Englewood Cliffs, N.J., 07632. (201) 568-8700. Cuisine: Italian. Credit cards: AE, MC, VISA.

FLORHAM PARK

THE AFTON....2 Hanover Rd., Florham Park, N.J., 07932. (201) 377-1871. Cuisine: American/Continental. Credit cards: AE, DC, MC, VISA.

FORDS

SAHIB....575 New Brunswick Ave., Fords, N.J., 08863. (201) 738-8722. Cuisine: Indian/Pakistani. Open daily for lunch and dinner. Credit cards: AE, MC, VISA.

FORT LEE

CLAM CASINO....66 Main St., Fort Lee, N.J., 07024. (201) 947-0529. Cuisine: Italian/Seafood. Open Monday, Wednesday, Thursday, and Friday for lunch; 6 days for dinner; Closed Tuesday. Credit cards: AE, DC, MC, VISA.

JANICE'S FISH PLACE....2151. Lemoine Ave., Fort Lee, N.J., 07024. (201) 944-8400. Cuisine: Seafood. Open 7 days for lunch and dinner. Credit cards: All major.

KIKU JAPANESE STEAK HOUSE....1616 Palisade Ave., Fort Lee, N.J., 07024. (201) 944-5979. Cuisine: Japanese. Open Monday through Friday for lunch; 7 days for dinner. Credit cards: AE, DC, MC, VISA.

PICCO LISSIMO....1296 Palisades Ave., Fort Lee, N.J., 07024. (201) 944-3812. Cuisine: Italian. Open 7 days for dinner only. Credit cards: Call for cards.

GUTTENBERG

PERIGOURDINE....6717 Bergenline Ave., Guttenberg, N.J., 07093. (201) 869-5021. Cuisine: Continental. Open 6 days for dinner; Closed Tuesday. Credit cards: AE, DC, MC, VISA. Reservations: Suggested.

HACKENSACK

NEW EARTH CONTINENTAL RESTAURANT....414 Hackensack, N.J., 07601. (201) 488-7979. Cuisine: Continental. Open Monday through Friday for lunch; 7 days for dinner. Credit cards: All major. Entertainment: Live entertainment Wednesday through Saturday.

HACKETTSTOWN

CLARENDON....109 Grand Ave., Hackettstown, N.J., 07840. (201) 852-8000. Cuisine: Continental. Credit cards: AE, MC, VISA.

DAVID'S COUNTRY INN....314 Main St., Hackettstown, N.J., 07840. (201) 850-0224. Cuisine: American rustic. Open Tuesday through Saturday for lunch; Tuesday through Sunday for dinner; Closed Monday. Credit cards: AE, MC, VISA.

HADDONFIELD

YANAGI....215 Kings Highway East, Haddonfield, N.J., 08033. (609) 428-0092. Cuisine: Japanese. Open Tuesday through Friday for lunch; Tuesday through Sunday dinner; Closed Monday. Credit cards: All major. Bring your own wine.

HARRISON

LE SAUCIER....600 Cape May Rd., Harrison, N.J., 07029. (201) 485-5072. Cuisine: French. Open Monday through Friday for lunch; Tuesday through Saturday for dinner; Closed Sunday all day and Monday for dinner. Credit cards: AE, DC, MC, VISA. Reservations: Accepted.

HAWTHORNE

LA COURONNE....4 Garfield Ave., Hawthorne, N.J., 07029. (201) 423-0044. Cuisine: Italian. Open Monday through Saturday for lunch and dinner; Closed Sunday. Credit cards: AE, DC, MC, VISA.

HIGHLANDS

DORIS AND ED'S SEAFOOD....36 Shore Dr., Highlands, N.J., 07732. (201) 872-1565. Open 6 days for dinner only; Closed Monday. Credit cards: AE, MC, VISA.

HILLSDALE

CHINA BULL AND BEAR....295 Kindermack Rd., Hillsdale, N.J., 07205. (201) 664-3040. Cuisine: Chinese/ Polynesian. Open Monday through Saturday for lunch; 7 days for dinner. Credit cards: AE, DC, MC, VISA.

HILLSIDE

ALFONSO'S....310 Hillside Ave., Hillside, N.J., 07205. (201) 688-8919. Cuisine: Spanish/Portugese. Open Tuesday through Sunday for lunch and dinner; Closed Monday. Credit cards: AE, MC, VISA.

HOBOKEN

THE BLUEFIN CLUB....The Madison Victorian Saloon, 14th and Washington Sts., Hoboken, N.J., 07030. (201) 420-8422. Cuisine: Sushi. Every other Wednesday from 7:00 PM to 11:00 PM. Credit cards: AE, MC, VISA. Reservations: De riguer.

THE BRASS RAIL....135 Washington St., Hoboken, N.J., 07030. (201) 659-7074. Cuisine: French-style. Open Tuesday through Friday for lunch; Tuesday through Sunday for dinner; Closed Monday. Credit cards: AE, MC, VISA.

CELLAR STEAK HOUSE at UNION CLUB....600 Hudson St., Hoboken, N.J., 07030. (201) 656-0311. Cuisine: Steakhouse. Credit cards: All major.

HOPEWELL

RENAISSANCE RESTAURANT....83 Princeton Ave., Hopewell, N.J., 08525. (609) 466-1700. Cuisine: Continental. Open Tuesday through Friday for lunch; Tuesday through Sunday for dinner; Closed Monday. Credit cards: All major.

JERSEY CITY

SUMMIT HOUSE....510 Summit Ave., Jersey City, N.J., 07306. (201) 963-1010. Cuisine: American/ Continental. Open Monday through Friday for lunch; 7 days for dinner; Sunday dinner from 1:00 PM. Credit cards: AE, CB, MC, VISA.

LAMBERTVILLE

CAFE RENNI....9 Kline's Ct., Lambertville, N.J., 08530. (201) 397-2631. Cuisine: Continental. Open 6 days for dinner only; Closed Monday. Credit cards: MC, VISA.

GERARD'S....8½ Coryell St., Lambertville, N.J., 08530. (609) 397-8035. Cuisine: Continental. Open 6 days for lunch and dinner; Closed Tuesday. Credit cards: AE, MC, VISA. Reservations: Suggested. Bring your own wine.

LITTLE FALLS

SUKEROKU JAPANESE RESTAURANT....68 Rte. 23, Little Falls, N.J., 07424. Cuisine: Japanese. Open 6 days for lunch and dinner; Closed Sunday. Credit cards: All major. Private party facilities: Available tatami rooms.

LIVINGSTON

RUBY'S....550 West Mount Pleasant Ave., Livingston, N.J., 07039. (201) 994-3500. Cuisine: American. Open daily for lunch and dinner; Sunday brunch. Credit cards: AE, DC, MC, VISA. Reservations: Accepted. Entertainment: Live entertainment Monday through Saturday in the lounge.

LONG VALLEY

CAFE PROVENCAL....1 West Mill Rd., Long Valley, N.J., 07853. (201) 876-3400. Cuisine: French. Open Tuesday through Sunday for dinner only; Closed Monday. Credit cards: MC, VISA.

MARGATE

MARGATE FISHERY-CAPTAIN'S GALLEY....12 South Douglas Ave., Margate, N.J., 08402. (609) 822-6100. Cuisine: Seafood. Open Monday through Saturday for lunch; 7 days for dinner .Credit cards: AE, MC, VISA. Bring your own wine.

MARLTON

OLGA'S DINER & BAKERY....Rtes. 70 & 73, Marlton, N.J., 0853. (609) 424-1120. Cuisine: Italian/ American. Owner's name: John Stavros. Credit cards: None. Annual sales: $1 million to $3 million. Total employment: 105.

MEDFORD

BEAU RIVAGE....247 Tauton Blvd., Medford, N.J., 08055. (609) 983-1999. Cuisine: Country French. Open Monday through Friday for lunch; Monday through Saturday for dinner. Credit cards: AE, MC, VISA. Reservations and proper attire a must.

THE HEDGEROW INN....Rte. 541, Medford, N.J., 08055. (609) 654-1600. Cuisine: Continental. Open 6 days for cocktails and dinner; Closed Monday. Credit cards: AE, MC, VISA. Private party facilities: Available.

MENDHAM

BLACK HORSE INN....1 West Main St., Mendham, N.J., 07945. (201) 543-7300; 543-4277. Cuisine: Continental. Owner: Anthony J. Knapp, Jr. Open Tuesday through Sunday. Credit cards: AE, MC, VISA. Private party facilities: Up to 80. Annual sales: $500,000 to $1 million. Total employment: 100. Corporate name: Black Horse Inn of Mendham, Inc.

MIDLAND PARK

STEVE'S WORTENDYKE INN....34 Central Ave., Midland Park, N.J., 07432. (201) 445-4141. Cuisine: French/International. Open Monday through Saturday for lunch and dinner; Closed Sunday. Credit cards: AE, MC, VISA. Reservations: Accepted.

MORRIS PLAINS

LLEWELLYN FARMS....Rtes. 10 & 202, Morris Plains, N.J., 07950. (201) 538-4323. Cuisine: Continental. Credit cards: All major.

MORRISTOWN

THE GRAND CAFE....42 Washington St., Morristown, N.J., 07960. (201) 540-9444. Cuisine: Continental. Open Monday through Friday for lunch; Monday through Saturday for dinner; Closed Sunday. Credit cards: AE, DC, MC, VISA. Reservations: Suggested.

SOCIETY HILL RESTAURANT....217 South St., Morristown, N.J., 07960. (201) 538-4411. Cuisine: Continental/American specialties. Open Monday through Friday for lunch; 7 days for dinner; late supper Monday through Saturday. Credit cards: AE, MC, VISA.

MONCLAIR

JENCARELLI'S....116 Walnut St., Montclair, N.J., 07042. (201) 746-4426. Cuisine: Italian. Open 6 days for lunch and dinner; Closed Tuesday. Credit cards: MC, VISA.

MOUNT LAUREL

THE HIDEOUT....Rte. 38, Mount Laurel, N.J., 08054. (609) 235-8450. Cuisine: Continental/American. Open Monday through Saturday for lunch; 7 days for dinner. Credit cards: AE, MC, VISA. Private party facilities: Available. Entertainment: Live music and dancing.

MOUNTAINSIDE

L'AFFAIRE....1099 Rte. 22 East, Mountainside, N.J., 07092. (201) 232-4454. Cuisine: Continental. Owner: Robert B. Connelly. Open 7 days for lunch and dinner. Private party facilities: Up to 650. Annual sales: Over $3 million. Total employment: 100.

TOWER STEAK HOUSE....Rte. 22, Mountainside, N.J., 07092. (201) 233-5542. Cuisine: Steakhouse. Credit cards: AE, DC, MC, VISA.

NEWARK

CANTANHEDE INTERNATIONAL....195 Ferry St., Newark, N.J., 07105. (201) 344-7016. Cuisine: Portugese. Open daily for breakfast, lunch, and dinner. No credit cards.

MADRID AND LISBON....325 Lafayette, Newark, N.J., 07105. (201) 589-9882. Cuisine: Spanish/Portugese. Open daily for lunch and dinner. Credit cards: AE, DC, MC, VISA.

SEA CREST CLAM BAR....150 Bloomfield Ave., Newark, N.J., 07104. (201) 484-5718. Cuisine: Seafood. Open 6 days for lunch and dinner; Closed Monday. Credit cards: Call for cards.

NEW BRUNSWICK

J. AUGUST'S CAFE....65 Church St., New Brunswick, N.J., 08901. (201) 246-8028. Cuisine: "International and Nouvelle." Open daily for lunch and dinner. Credit cards: MC, VISA. Entertainment: Live entertainment Sunday nights, Jazz Collective Monday nights.

RISTORANTE ALFREDO....276 Hamilton Ave., New Brunswick, N.J., 08901. (201) 247-1174. Cuisine: Italian. Open Monday through Friday for lunch; Monday through Saturday for dinner; Closed Sunday. Credit cards: AE, MC, VISA. Reservations: Essential.

NORTH WILDWOOD

ED ZABERER'S....400 Spruce Ave., North Wildwood, N.J., 08260. (609) 522-1423. Cuisine: Seafood. Credit cards: AE, DC, MC, VISA.

OCEAN CITY

BOOKER'S NEW ENGLAND SEAFOOD HOUSE....9th & Wesley Ave., Ocean City, N.J., 08226. (609) 399-4672. Cuisine: Steak/Seafood. Open 7 days for lunch and dinner. Credit cards: AE, MC, VISA.

THE CULINARY GARDEN....841 Central Ave., Ocean City, N.J., 08226. (609) 399-3713. Cuisine: Northern Italian/Continental. Open Monday through Friday for lunch; Saturday and Sunday for dinner; Sunday brunch. Credit cards: All major.

OLD BRIDGE

CLARE & COBY'S INN-RESTAURANT....Rtes. 9 & 34, Old Bridge, N.J., 08857. (201) 721-4898. Cuisine: American/Continental. Open Tuesday through Saturday for lunch; Tuesday through Sunday for dinner. Credit cards: AE, MC, VISA. Entertainment: Wednesday through Saturday evenings and Sunday afternoons for dancing.

PARAMUS

THE ORCHID GARDEN....108 Rte. 4 East, Paramus, N.J., 07652. (201) 843-6110. Cuisine: Chinese. Open Monday through Friday for lunch; 7 days for dinner. Credit cards: AE, MC, VISA.

PARSIPPANY

THE HARBOR....Rte. 46, Parsippany, N.J., 07054. (201) 334-3232. Cuisine: Seafood. Credit cards: AE, DC, MC, VISA.

PATERSON

CIANCI STREET....26 Cianci St., Paterson, N.J., 07501. (201) 742-8938. Cuisine: Italian/French. Open 5 days for dinner only; Closed Sunday and Monday. Credit cards: MC, VISA. Entertainment: Live entertainment Thursday through Saturday. Reservations: Suggested.

DA TOMASSO....60 Ellison St., Paterson, N.J., 07505. (201) 278-0760. Cuisine: Italian. Open Monday through Friday for lunch; 7 days for dinner; Sunday dinner from 2:00 PM. Credit cards: All major. Reservations: Suggested.

L'OMBRELLO RESTAURANT....10 Marshal St., Paterson, N.J., 07501. (201) 345-1614. Cuisine: Italian. Open Monday through Friday for lunch; 7 days for dinner. Credit cards: All major.

PENNSAUKEN

NERO'S WOODBINE INN....Rte. 73 & Remington Ave., Pennsauken, N.J., 08110. (609) 663-2200. Cuisine: American. Credit cards: All major.

PRINCETON

THE ALCHEMIST & BARRISTER....28 Witherspoon St., Princeton, N.J., 08540. (609) 924-5555. Cuisine: American. Owner: John W. Schmierer, V.P. & Gen. Mgr. Open 7 days for lunch and dinner. Credit cards: AE, MC, VISA. Private party facilities: Up to 40. Annual sales: $1 million to $3 million. Total employment: 78.

CAFE AU LAIT....66 Witherspoon St., Princeton, N.J., 08540. (609) 921-0173. Cuisine: Traditional and Continental. Open Tuesday through Saturday for lunch and dinner; Sunday brunch til 6:00 PM. No credit cards. Bring your own wine.

GREENHOUSE....Nassau Inn, Palmer Sq., Princeton, N.J., 08540. (609) 921-7500. Cuisine: American. Owner: Collins Corp.; Bari Boone, Sales Mgr. for Nassau Inn. Open 7 days for lunch and dinner. Credit cards: All major. Corporate name: Nassau Inn, Inc.

LAHIERE'S....11 Witherspoon St., Princeton, N.J., 08540. (609) 921-2798. Cuisine: French. Open Monday through Saturday for lunch and dinner; Closed Sunday. Credit cards: AE, MC, VISA.

NASSAU INN....Nassau Inn, Palmer Sq., Princeton, N.J., 08540. (609) 921-7500. Cuisine: American. Owner: Collins Corp.; Bari Boone, Sales Mgr. for Nassau Inn. Open 7 days for lunch and dinner. Credit cards: All major. Private party facilities: Available. Corporate name: Nassau Inn, Inc.

THE TAP ROOM AT THE NASSAU INN....Palmer Sq., Princeton, N.J., 08540. (609) 921-7500. Cuisine: American. Owner: Nassau Inn Corporation. Open 7 days for breakfast, lunch, and dinner. Credit cards: All major. Private party facilities: Up to 300. Annual sales: $500,000 to $1 million. Total employment: 190. Corporate name: Collins Development Corporation.

RAMSEY

CASA MARIA....706 Rte. 17, Ramsey, N.J., 07446. (201) 327-5415. Cuisine: Mexican/American. Open Monday through Friday for lunch; 7 days for dinner. Credit cards: AE, MC, VISA.

RED BANK

THE LITTLE KRAUT....115 Oakland St., Red Bank, N.J., 07701. (201) 842-4830. Cuisine: German/Continental. Open Tuesday through Friday for lunch; Tuesday through Sunday for dinner; Closed Monday. Credit cards: AE, CB, MC, VISA. Cocktail lounge.

MOLLY PITCHER INN....Rte. 35, Red Bank, N.J., 07701. (201) 747-2500. Cuisine: American/Continental. Open Monday through Saturday for lunch; 7 days for dinner; Sunday brunch. Credit cards: AE, DC, MC, VISA. Entertainment: Dancing Friday and Saturday evenings.

GABLES....58 Oakland St., Red Bank, N.J., 07701. (201) 842-0300. Cuisine: Continental. Open daily for lunch and dinner. Credit cards: All major.

RIVER EDGE

BOODLES....259 Johnson Ave., River Edge, N.J., 07661. (201) 342-1233. Cuisine: Continental. Open for lunch and dinner daily; Sunday brunch. Credit cards: AE, CB, MC, VISA.

RUMSON

THE PEAR TREE....42 Avenue of Two Rivers, Rumson, N.J., 07760. (201) 842-8747. Cuisine: Continental/American. Open Monday through Friday for lunch; 7 days for dinner; Sunday brunch. Credit cards: All major.

RUNNEMEDE

A.J. MANDELLI'S....101 West Clements Br., Runnemede, N.J., 08078. (609) 939-1588. Cuisine: Italian. Open Monday through Saturday for lunch; Tuesday through Sunday for dinner. Credit cards: AE, MC, VISA. Entertainment: Live music. Proper attire required.

PEKING MANDARIN....Rte. 41 & East Clements Bridge Rd., Runnemede, N.J., 08078. (609) 939-4440. Cuisine: Mandarin, Hunan, Szechun, and Cantonese Chinese. Open Monday through Saturday for lunch; 7 days for dinner. Bring your own wine.

SEA BRIGHT

OLIVIO'S....1072 Ocean Ave., Sea Bright, N.J., 07760. (201) 842-9857. Cuisine: Italian. Open Monday through Saturday for dinner only; Closed Sunday. Credit cards: All major.

THE PENINSULA HOUSE....1049 Ocean Ave., Sea Bright, N.J., 07760. (201) 842-2100. Cuisine: Seafood. Open daily for lunch and dinner. Credit cards: All major.

SECAUCUS

KINGSLEY'S....Meadowland Pkwy., Secaucus, N.J., 07094. (201) 348-6900. Cuisine: French. Open Monday through Friday for lunch; 7 days for dinner. Credit cards: All major. Reservations: Suggested for weekends.

SONNY D'S....1148 Paterson Plank Rd., Secaucus, N.J., 07094. (201) 867-1065. Cuisine: Italian. Open Monday through Friday for lunch; Monday through Saturday for dinner; Closed Sunday. Credit cards: AE, DC, MC, VISA. Reservations: Suggested.

SERGEANTSVILLE

SERGEANTSVILLE INN....Rte. 523, Sergeantsville, N.J., 08557. (609) 397-3700. Cuisine: American. Open Monday through Saturday for lunch; 7 days for dinner; Sunday brunch. Credit cards: MC, VISA. Entertainment: Piano bar nightly.

SHIP BOTTOM

BAYBERRY INN....1302 Long Beach Blvd., Ship Bottom, N.J. 08008. (609) 494-8848. Cuisine: Continental. Owner: Kurica Famiy. Open 7 days. Credit cards: All major. Private party facilities: 10 to 150. Total employment: 60. Corporate name: C.K.-7, Inc.

SHORT HILLS

MERIWETHERS'S....The Mall at Short Hills, Short Hills, N.J., 07078. (201) 467-4199. Cuisine: Steak/Seafood/English Pub. Open 7 days for lunch and dinner; Sunday brunch. Credit cards: AE, MC, VISA.

SHREWSBURY

SHADOWBROOK....Rte. 35, Shrewsbury, N.J., 07701. (201) 747-0200. Cuisine: Continental. Owner: Zweben Family. Open Tuesday through Friday for lunch; Tuesday through Sunday for dinner; Sunday brunch; Closed Monday. Credit cards: All major. Private party facilities: 7 private rooms for up to 400 persons. Annual sales: $1 million to $3 million. Total employment: 170.

SOMERDALE

PEPPINO'S....11 North White Horse Pke., Somerdale, N.J., 08083. (609) 627-7944. Cuisine: Italian. Open 7 days for lunch and dinner. Credit cards: AE, DC, MC, VISA.

O'CONNERS COLONIAL FARMS....1745 Anwell Rd., Somerset, N.J., 08873. (201) 873-3990. Cuisine: American. Owner: M. Taylor. Credit cards: All major.

SPRING LAKE HEIGHTS

OLD MILL INN....Old Mill Rd., Spring Lake Heights, N.J., 07762. (201) 449-5370. Cuisine: American. Credit cards: AE, MC, VISA.

STANHOPE

BLACK FOREST INN....Rte. 206, Stanhope, N.J., 07874. (201) 347-3344. Cuisine: French/German. Open Monday, Wednesday, Thursday, and Friday for lunch; 6 days for dinner; Sunday dinner from 1:00 PM; Closed Tuesday. Credit cards: AE, MC, VISA.

STOCKINGTON

COLLIGAN'S STOCKTON INN....Rte. 29, Stockton, N.J., 08559. (609) 397-1250. Cuisine: American. Open Tuesday through Saturday for lunch; Tuesday through Sunday for dinner; Closed Monday. Credit cards: MC, VISA. Entertainment: Dancing Friday and Saturday nights.

TENAFLY

CLINTON INN....145 Dean Dr., Tenafly, N.J., 07670. (201) 567-4800. Cuisine: Steak/Seafood. Owner: John Rojan. Open 7 days for breakfast, lunch, and dinner. Credit cards: All major. Private party facilities: Up to 400. Annual sales: Over $3 million. Total employment: 200.

LE CHATEAU....115 Country Rd., Tenafly, N.J., 07670. (201) 871-1500. Cuisine: French. Owner: Merry Berger & Jean Claude Estrade. Open Monday through Friday for lunch; Monday through Saturday for dinner; Closed Sunday. Credit cards: AE, MC, VISA. Private party facilities: Up to 100. Annual sales: $250,000 to $500,000. Total employment: 30.

TRENTON

LA GONDOLA....762 Roebling Ave., Trenton, N.J., 08611. (609) 392-0600. Cuisine: Italian. Open Monday through Friday for lunch; 7 days for dinner. Credit cards: AE, DC, MC, VISA.

LANDWEHR'S....River Rd., Trenton, N.J., 08628. (609) 882-0303. Cuisine: American. Owner: C. Eugene Landwehr. Credit cards: AE, MC, VISA. Private party facilities: Up to 350. Annual sales: $250,000 to $500,000. Total employment: 35.

TOTOWA

THE BETHWOOD RESTAURANT....38 Lackawanna Ave., Totowa, N.J., 07512. (201) 256-8316. Cuisine: Italian/Continental. Open Tuesday through Saturday for lunch; Tuesday through Sunday for dinner; Closed Monday. Credit cards: All major. Reservations: Suggested.

UNION CITY

LA GRAND VIA....3905 Bergenline Ave., Union City, N.J., 07087. (201) 864-4835. Cuisine: Cuban. Open 7 days from 8:00 AM for breakfast, lunch, and dinner. Credit cards: AE, DC, VISA.

VOORHEES

CHICAGO PRIME....33 Preston Ave., Voorhees, N.J., 08043. (609) 429-1331. Cuisine: Continental. Open Tuesday through Friday for lunch; Tuesday through Sunday for dinner; Closed Monday. Credit cards: All major. Private party facilities: Available. Proper attire required.

WANAQUE

BERTA'S CHATEAU....7 Grove St., Wanaque, N.J., 07465. (201) 835-0992. Cuisine: Italian. Open 7 days for dinner only. Credit cards: AE, DC, MC, VISA.

WARREN

KING GEORGE INN....181 Mount Bethel Rd., Warren, N.J., 07060. (201) 647-0410. Cuisine: Continental/American. Owner: M. James Hayden, Jr., Pres. Open 6 days for lunch and dinner; Closed Monday. Credit cards: AE, MC. Private party facilities: 3 private rooms (100, 45, and 24 persons). Annual sales: $500,000 to $1 million. Total employment: 40.

WATCHUNG

WERNER'S LAKE EDGE....141 Stirlin Rd., Watchung, N.J. 07060. (201) 755-9344. Cuisine: German/Austrian. Owner's name: Roy and Herma Stamm. Credit cards: AE.

WAYNE

L'AUBERGE DE FRANCE....2320 Hamburg Tpke., Wayne, N.J., 07470. (201) 835-9869, Cuisine: French. Owner: Jean-Louis Todeschini. Open 7 days for lunch and dinner; No lunch Saturday. Credit cards: All major. Private party facilities: 8 to 175. Annual sales: $250,000 to $500,000. Total employment: 30.

WESTFIELD

CHEZ CATHERINE....431 North Ave., Westfield, N.J., 07090. (201) 232-1680, Cuisine: French. Open Monday through Saturday for lunch and dinner; Closed Sunday. Credit cards: AE, MC, VISA. Reservations: Recommended.

WEST LONG BRANCH

KABUTO JAPANESE STEAK HOUSE....Rte. 36, West Long Branch, N.J., 07764. (201) 870-3362. Cuisine: Japanese. Open daily for breakfast, lunch, and dinner. Credit cards: AE, DC, MC, VISA.

WEST NEW YORK

ARMANDO DI VILLA....6319 Bergenline Ave., West New York, N.J. 07093. (201) 861-6212. Cuisine: Italian. Credit cards: All major.

WEST ORANGE

THE MANOR....111 Prospect Ave., West Orange, N.J., 07052. (201) 731-2360. Cuisine: Continental. Owner's name: G. Mang and Mr. Boggier. Credit cards: All major. Annual sales: $500,000 to $1 million.

WHITEHOUSE

RYLAND INN....Rte. 22, Whitehouse, N.J., 08888. (201) 534-4011. Cuisine: American/Continental. Owner W.H. Black. Open 7 days for lunch and dinner. Credit cards: All major. Private party facilities: Up to 125. Annual sales: $1 million to $3 million. Total employment: 85. Corporate name: Ryland Inn, Inc.

WILDWOOD

NEIL'S STEAK AND OYSTER HOUSE....222 East Schellenger Ave., Wildwood, N.J., 08260. (609) 522-6060. Cuisine: Steak/Seafood/Italian. Open 7 days for lunch and dinner. Credit cards: All major. Entertainment: Live entertainment nightly.

UPSTAIRS AT NEIL'S....222 East Schellenger Ave., Wildwood, N.J. 08260. (609) 522-6086. Cuisine: Continental. Open Wednesday through Monday from 6:00 PM for dinner; Closed Tuesday. Credit cards: All major. Entertainment: Live entertainment nightly. Proper attire required.

NEW YORK STATE

ALBANY

JACK'S SEA FOOD & STEAK HOUSE....42 State St., Albany, N.Y., 12207. (518) 465-8854. Cuisine: Seafood/Steak. Credit cards: All major.

L'AUBERGE DES FOUGERES....351 Broadway, Albany, N.Y., 12207. (518) 465-1111. Cuisine: French. Credit cards: AE, MC.

ALEXANDRIA BAY

EDGEWOOD....Rte. 12 & 26, Alexandria Bay, N.Y., 13607. (315) 482-9922. Cuisine: American. Credit cards: All major.

THE SHIP....29 James St., Alexandria Bay, N.Y., 13607. (315) 482-9500. Cuisine: Seafood/American. Credit cards: All major.

AMAGANSETT

GORDON'S....Main St., Amagansett, L.I., N.Y., 11930. (516) 267-2010. Cuisine: American/Continental. Owner: George Polychronopoulos, R. Hans, C. Ankcam. Open for lunch and dinner 7 days; closed Monday during Spring and Fall. Credit cards: AE, MC, VISA. Annual sales: $250,000 to $500,000. Total employment: 20. Corporate name: Varikos Restaurant Corp.

LE COCO BEACH CAFE....Montauk Hwy., Amagansett, L.I., N.Y., 11930. (516) 267-8880. Cuisine: French. Credit cards: All major.

AMITYVILLE

BEACHTREE CAFE....292 Merrick Rd., Amityville, L.I., N.Y., 11701. (516) 691-4423. Cuisine: International. Owner: Richard Freilich and Shohei Yamamoto. Open 7 days for lunch and dinner. Credit cards: All major. Private party facilities: 10 to 120. Annual sales: $1 million to $3 million. Total employment: 60. Corporate name: Beachstreet Cafe Inc.

LA MANSARDE....348 Merrick Rd., Amityville, L.I., N.Y., 11701. (516) 691-6881. Cuisine: French, Northern Italian, Continental. Owner: Rose Albano. Open Sunday through Friday for lunch; 7 days for dinner. Credit cards: All major. Annual sales: $250,000 to $500,000. Total employment: 27.

PIER THREE....35 George Brown Plz., Amityville, L.I., N.Y., 11701. (516) 842-1328. Cuisine: Seafood. Owner's name: Mr. M. Berdebes.

ARDSLEY

CANTINA RESTAURANT....Saw Mill River Rd., Ardsley, N.Y., 10502. (914) 693-6565. Cuisine: Mexican. Credit cards: All major.

THE CHEESE EATERIE....729 Saw Mill River Rd., Ardsley, N.Y., 10502. (914) 693-3233. Cuisine: French. Credit cards: MC, VISA.

COLONIAL COURT.... Village Green, Ardsley, N.Y., 10502. (914) 693-4878. Cuisine: American. Credit cards: All major.

WATER WHEEL....367 Saw Mill River Rd., Ardsley, N.Y., 10502. (914) 693-5522. Cuisine: Italian. Credit cards: All major.

ARMONK

FLOWER DRAGON....85 Old Mt. Kisco Rd., Armonk, N.Y., 10504. (914) 273-3383. Cuisine: Chinese. Credit cards: All major.

OLIVE BRANCH....386 Main St., Armonk, N.Y., 10504. (914) 273-3508. Cuisine: Mediterranean. Credit cards: All major.

WILLOW INN.... Old Rte. 22, Armonk, N.Y., 10504. (914) 273-8117. Cuisine: Seafood. Closed: Monday. Owner: Joyce L. Graefe. Credit cards: DC, MC, VISA. Annual sales; $250,000 to $500,000. Total employment: 40.

ASTORIA

KALYVA....36-15 Ditmars Blvd., Astoria (Queens), N.Y., 11105. (212) 932-9229. Is a large simple restaurant where Greek food is cooked with great care and affection. Prices are low, courtesy abounding. If a few more Greek restaurants could cook such dishes as charcoal broiled quail, *saganaki* and fresh lobster to this standard they would make a fortune. Specialties include shish kebob, pork-peasant style, and roasted leg of lamb. Open 7 days for lunch and dinner. Owner: Gerasimos Moraitis. Credit cards: None. Private party facilities. Reservations: Accepted.

RISTORANTE PICCOLA VENEZIA....42-01 28 Ave., Astoria (Queens), N.Y., 11102. (212) 278-9344. Cuisine: Italian.

SIRENA RISTORANTE....25-71 Steinway St., Astoria (Queens), N.Y., 11102. (212) 545-6186. Cuisine: Italian. Credit cards: All major.

TONY'S....33-12 Ditmars Blvd., Astoria, N.Y., 11105. (212) 278-1505. Tony's is surrounded by neighborhood stores on a crowded street, but don't be put off. The interior is attractive and comfortable, and the food is Northern Italian and excellent. The menu is classic fare—it you'd expect it to be here, it's here: from the *tortellini in brodo* to the chicken cacciatore. And you don't pay an arm and a leg, either. Among the specialties: striped bass *livornese*, veal *sorrentino, scampi alla Tony, calamari* salad. Owner: Frank Lumaj. Open Tuesday through Friday for lunch; Tuesday through Sunday for dinner; closed Monday. Priced moderate to inexpensive. It's not very big, so make reservations. Credit cards: AE, MC, VISA. Private party facilities for between 10 and 30 persons. Annual sales: $500,000 to $1 million. Total employment: 4. Corporate name: Lumaj, Inc.

ATLANTIC PLAZA

DANNY CHANG'S GOURMET RESTAURANT....2 Bridge Plz., Atlantic Plaza, L.I., N.Y., 11509. (516) 239-4800. Cuisine: Chinese/American. Credit cards: All major.

AUBURN

SPRINGSIDE INN....41 West Lake Rd, Auburn, N.Y., 13021. (315) 252-7247. Cuisine: Continental. Owner: Willian G. Dove. Open for lunch and dinner; Closed January. Credit cards: MC, VISA. Private party facilities:. Up to 200. Annual sales: $250,000 to $500,000. Total employment: 30.

BABYLON

EDELWEISS....109 Straight Path Rd., Babylon, L.I., N.Y., 11704. (516) 957-3975. Cuisine: Continental. Owner's name: Angela Rivera. Credit cards: AE, MC, VISA, DC.

THE VILLAGER....345 Deer Park Ave., Babylon, L.I., N.Y., 11702. (516) 587-9070. Cuisine: Continental. Owner's name: Charles A. Pennington. Credit cards: All major.

BALDWIN

LA MERENDA....614 Seaman Ave., Baldwin, L.I., N.Y., 11510. (516) 623-7738

MILBURN INN....2894 Millbum Ave., Baldwin, L.I., N.Y., 11510. (516) 378-3434. Cuisine: American/ Continental. Credit cards: All major.

BAYPORT

LE SOIR....825 Montauk Hwy., Bayport, L.I., N.Y., 11708. (516) 472-9090. Michael Kaziewicz cooks and his wife, Janina, runs the dining room, and they both own it—and it's one of the best values in French dining around. The food is exquisite and the prices are moderate. Specialties include: rack of lamb, salmon (when in season), scampi with garlic butter, *coquilles St. Jacques, escargot de Bourgogne,* duck with orange sauce, and, for dessert, the floating island. French food at moderate prices. Open Tuesday through Sunday for dinner only; Closed Monday. Accepts AE and VISA only. Reservations are required. Annual sales: $250,000 to $500,000. Total employment: 10.

BAY SHORE

CHUAN YANG RESTAURANT....44 East Main St., Bay Shore, L.I., N.Y., 11706. (516) 665-0138. Cuisine: Chinese. Credit cards: All major.

IL GAROFANO RISTORANTE ITALIANO....573 East Main St., Bay Shore, L.I., N.Y., 11706. (516) 665-8080. Cuisine: Italian. Owner: James Karas. Open 7 days. Credit cards: All major. Private party facilities. Up to 50. Annual sales: $250,000 to $500,000. Total employment: 10. Corporate name: J.G. Karas, Inc.

BAYSIDE

HARP & MANDOLIN....219-01 Northern Blvd., Bayside, N.Y., 11361. (212) 224-4300. Cuisine: Italian/American. Credit cards: All major.

JESOMINA....223-20 Union Tpke., Bayside, N.Y., 11361. (212) 465-1791. Cuisine: Italian. Credit cards: All major.

KING'S CHINESE RESTAURANT....220-08 Horace Harding Expy., Bayside, N.Y., 11361. (212) 224-5200. Cuisine: Chinese.

VILLA ARMONDO....222-02 Union Tpke., Bayside, N.Y., 11364. (212) 468-6020. Cuisine: Italian. Owner: Armando Marchione. Open Tuesday through Sunday for lunch and dinner. Credit cards: All major. Private party facilities. Up to 80.

BAYVILLE

REINHARDS.... Reinhard's Park, Bayville, L.I., N.Y., 11709. (516) 628-8766. Cuisine: American.

BEACON

DUTCHESS MANOR.... Rte. 9D, Beacon, N.Y., 12508. (914) 831-3650. Cuisine: Continental. Credit cards: All major.

BEDFORD

BISTRO 22.... Rte. 22, Bedford, N.Y., 10506 (914) 234-7333. Cuisine: French. Credit cards: AE.

CHUCK'S STEAK HOUSE....728 North Bedford Rd., Bedford, N.Y., 10506. (914) 241-1826. Cuisine: Steak. Credit cards: All major.

NINO'S.... Rte. 121, Bedford, N.Y., 10506. (914) 234-3374. Cuisine: Italian. Credit cards: AE, DC.

VILLAGE INN.... Armonk Rd., Bedford, N.Y., 10506. (914) 234-3343. Cuisine: Italian. Credit cards: All major.

BEDFORD HILLS

RAGS.... Rte. 117 & Hill, Bedford Hills, N.Y., 10507. (914) 241-0039. Cuisine: French. Credit cards: AE.

BELLEROSE

ARTURO'S....246-04 Jericho Tpke., Bellerose, L.I., N.Y., 11426. (516) FL2-7418. If your palate is pleading for classy Italian cuisine, place Arturo's at the top of your must visit list. Pastas are one of Arturo's finest things, of course, but the menu has also been filled out by a series of dishes whose cooking, saucing and serving will satisfy the toughest of critics. Specialties include *torta primavera,*seafood salad, and spaghetti *Gismondi.* Lunch and dinner served daily, except Tuesdays. Moderate to expensively priced. Owners: Giuseppe and Vincent Gismondi. Credit cards: All major. Reservations: Necessary. Private party facilities. Annual sales: $500,000 to $1 million.

CHARLEY'S CLAM BAR.... Cross Island Pkwy. & Jericho Tpke., Bellerose, L.I., N.Y., 11426. (516) 354-9808. Cuisine: Seafood. Owner's name: Ivan Kovac. Credit cards: None.

BETHPAGE

FRANCESCO'S RESTAURANT....4119 Hempstead Tpke., Bethpage, L.I., N.Y., 11714. (516) 731-8686. Cuisine: Northern Italian. Owner's name: Frank Assi. Total employment: 18.

MONTEGO BAY....300 Central Ave., Bethpage, L.I., N.Y., 11714. (516) 822-6783. This casual place has bountifully endeared itself to Long Islanders since it opened last year, serving tasty bargains in nourishment up to the limit of seating capacity, which alas, isn't very much. Specialties include: Surf n' Turf, seafood platters and sliced steak on garlic bread. Open for lunch and dinner, 7 days. Prices are inexpensive. Owner: Frank and Richard DiAntonio. Credit cards: All major. Reservations: Accepted. Private party facilities. Entertainment: Bands for Dancing, Friday and Saturday. Annual sales: $500,000. Total employment: 5.

BINGHAMTON

LEFT BANK....4105 Vestal Pky., Binghamton, N.Y., 13903. (607) 723-8277. Cuisine: American. Credit cards: All major.

MOREY'S....1018 Front St., Binghamton, N.Y., 13905. (607) 723-5495. Cuisine: American. Credit cards: All major.

SCOTCH N'SIRLOIN....400 Plaza Dr., Binghamton, N.Y., 13903. (607) 729-6301. Cuisine: American. Credit cards: AE, MC, VISA.

BOHEMIA

BARONS III....3870 Vets. Memorial Hwy., Bohemia, L.I., N.Y., 11716. (516) 981-8181. Cuisine: Continental. Owner's name: Lenny Pfeifer. Credit cards: All major.

BREWSTER

THE ARCH.... Rte. 22, Brewster, N.Y., 10509. (914) 279-5011. Cuisine: French/Continental. Days closed: Monday and Tuesday; No lunch Saturday. Credit cards: All major. Private party facilities: Up to 90. Annual Sales: $500,000 to $1 million. Total employment: 16. Corporate name: Old Arch Inc.

CAPRICCIO RESTAURANT.... Rte. 22, Brewster, N.Y., 10509. (914) 279-2873. Cuisine: Italian.

MIDDLE RANCH.... Carmel Rd., Brewster, N.Y., 10509. (914) 279-9723. Cuisine: Continental. Credit cards: MC, VISA.

BRIARCLIFF MANOR

MAISON LAFITTE.... Rte. 9A, Chappaqua Rd., Briarcliff Manor, N.Y., 10510. (914) 941-5787. Cuisine: French. Credit cards: All major.

SQUIRE'S OF BRIARCLIFF....94 North State Rd., Briarcliff Manor, N.Y., 10510. (914) 941-9568. Cuisine: American. Credit cards: All major.

TORCHIA'S....516 North State Rd., Briarcliff Manor, N.Y., 10510. (914) 941-9559. Cuisine: Italian. Credit cards: None.

VILLA PIETRO.... Rte. 9, Briarcliff Manor, N.Y., 10510. (914) 941-5556. Cuisine: Continental. Credit cards: All major.

BRIDGEHAMPTON

BOBBY VAN'S.... Main St., Bridgehampton, N.Y., 11932. (516) 537-0590. Cuisine: Steak/Seafood. Owner: Robert Charles Van Velson. Open 7 days. Credit cards: None. Annual sales: $500,000 to $1 million. Total employment: 35. Corporate name: VM Restaurants, Inc.

BULLS HEAD INN.... Main St., Bridgehampton, L.I., N.Y., 11932. (516) 537-0011. Cuisine: Continental. Credit cards: MC, VISA.

BRIGHTWATERS

THE JON THOMAS INNE....91 Howells Rd., Brightwaters, L.I., N.Y., (516) 666-2060. You can dine here daily from 11 a.m. to 2 a.m., robustly or lightly depending upon mood or the condition of the days' digestion. Food is mainly American and the standards of preparation are high. Specialties include roast beef melt, veal dishes richly buttered and cheesed, sandwiches and burgers rise well above the corner counter level. Prices are inexpensive to moderate. Owners: Thomas Lally and John Hickey. Credit cards: All major. Reservations: Accepted.

BRONX

ANNA'S HARBOR RESTAURANT....565 City Island Ave., Bronx, N.Y., 10464. (212) 885-1373. Cuisine: Seafood. Credit cards: All major.

DEXTER'S RESTAURANT....5652 Mosholu Ave., Bronx, N.Y., 10471. (212) 548-0440. Cuisine: Continental. Owner's name: Michael Pozit.

DONAGHY'S STEAKHOUSE....5523 Broadway, Bronx, N.Y., 10463. (212) 548-3377. Cuisine: Steak. Credit cards: All major.

EHRING'S....228 West 231 St., Bronx, N.Y., 10463. (212) 549-6750. Cuisine: German. Credit cards: All major.

FAIELLA'S PINE TREE INN....4139 Boston Post Rd., Bronx, N.Y., 10466. (212) 324-1750. Cuisine: Italian.

IL BOSCHETTO'S....1660 East Gun Hill Rd., Bronx, N.Y., 10469. (212) 379-9335. Cuisine: Italian. Credit cards: All major.

SAMMY'S FISH BOX RESTAURANT....41 City Island Ave., Bronx, N.Y., 10464. (212) 885-0920. Cuisine: Seafood.

SEA SHORE RESTAURANT....591 City Island Ave., Bronx, N.Y., 10464. (212) 885-0300. Cuisine: Seafood.

THWAITES INN....536 City Island Ave., Bronx, N.Y., 10464. (212) 885-1023. Cuisine: Seafood.

BRONXVILLE

ALPS....74½ Pondfield Rd., Bronxville, N.Y., 10708. (914) 337-9752. Cuisine: Continental. Credit cards: All major.

LE BISTRO....124 Pondfield Rd., Bronxville, N.Y., 10708. (914) 337-6445. Cuisine: French. Credit cards: All major.

OXFORD TAVERN....131 Parkway Ave., Bronxville, N.Y., 10708. (914) 337-9780. Cuisine: Italian. Credit cards: None.

THE TAP....12 Palmer Ave., Bronxville, N.Y., 10708. (914) 337-1011. Cuisine: American. Credit cards: All major.

TUMBLEDOWN DICK'S....7 Pondfield Rd., Bronxville, N.Y., 10708. (914) 779-6699. Cuisine: English Pub.

BROOKLYN

CASA PEPE....114 Bay Ridge Ave., Brooklyn, N.Y., 11224. (212) 833-8865. Cuisine: Spanish & Mexican. Owner: Jimmy & Victor. Closed Tuesdays. Credit cards: All major.

FOURSOME STEAK PUB....11234. (212) 241-7300. Cuisine: American/Continental. Owner: John Markrinos, Pres. Closed Mondays. Credit cards: All major. Annual sales: $500,000 to $1 million. Total employment: 43.

GAGE & TOLLNER....372 Fulton St., Brooklyn, N.Y., 11201. (212) 875-5181. When you enter these columned portals, you are back in the "elegance" of 1879, gas chandeliers and all. The restaurant delivers a variety of meats, poultry and salads, but it's with seafood that the chef goes to town. Same medium-priced menu for lunch and dinner. Specialties include: crabmeat Virginia, Coho salmon, and lemon sole. Open for lunch and dinner, 7 days. Owner: Edward Dewey and John Simmons. Credit cards: None. Reservations: Accepted. Private party facilities. Entertainment: Piano on weekends. Annual sales: $1 million to $2½ million. Total employment: 40.

GARGIULO....2911 West 15th St., Brooklyn, N.Y., 11224. (212) 266-0906. Cuisine: Italian. Owner's name: Russo Brothers. Total employment: 27. Corporate name: Sirena Restaurant Inc.

GREENHOUSE CAFE....7717 Third Ave., Brooklyn, N.Y., 11209. (212) 833-8200. Cuisine: Continental. Owner: Richard & Fred Abbazio. Open for lunch and dinner 7 days. Credit cards: All major. Private party facilities: Up to 50. Corporate name: JAB Enterprises, Inc.

LE PALAIS....923 Kings Hwy., Brooklyn, N.Y., 11223. (212) 336-2500. Cuisine: Mid-Eastern/Greek.

MONTE'S VENETIAN ROOM....451 Carroll Street, Brooklyn, N.Y., 11215. (212) 264-8984. This restaurant was founded in 1906 and is still operated by the Monte family. You can unquestionably drink some fine wines and eat a great variety of Italian dishes here. Besides a wide assortment of pasta, there are house baked shrimp, crumb-crisped fried zucchini, eggplant *Romana*, chicken *Scarpariello, scungilli fra diavolo*, a selection of veal and beef, a variety of salads, and appetizers. Owner: Nick Monte. Open 7 days for lunch and dinner. Price: Moderate. Reservations: Accepted. Credit cards: VISA only. Private party facilities: Up to 55. Annual sales: $500,000 to $1 million. Total employment: 15. Corporate name: Monte's Venetian Room, Inc.

PETER LUGER STEAK HOUSE....178 Broadway, Brooklyn, N.Y., 11211 (212) 387-7400. Cuisine: Steak. Owner: Marilyn Spencer, Pres. Open daily. Credit cards: House accounts only. Private party facilities. 12 to 45. Total employment: 100. Corporate name: Peter Luger, Inc.

RIVER CAFE....1 Water St., Brooklyn, N.Y., 11201. (212) 522-5200. Cuisine: American. Owner's name: Buzzy O'Keeffe. Credit cards: AE, DC.

SU-SU'S YUM YUM....60 Henry St., Brooklyn, N.Y., 11201. (212) 522-4531. Cuisine: Chinese. Owner's name: Robert Hsu. Total employment: 5 chefs.

TANPOPO JAPANESE RESTAURANT....36 Joralemon St., Brooklyn, N.Y., 11201. (212) 596-2968. Cuisine: Japanese. Owner: James & Helen Power. Credit cards: All major. Open Tuesday through Friday for lunch; Tuesday through Sunday for dinner; Closed Monday. Annual sales: $250,000 to $500,000. Total employment: 8. Corporate name: Tanpopo Restaurant, Inc.

BUFFALO

ACE'S STEAK PIT....166 Franklin St., Buffalo, N.Y., 14202. (716) 842-1549. Credit cards: None.

ANCHOR BAR....1047 Main St., Buffalo, N.Y., 14209. (716) 886-8920. Credit cards: None.

CHEF'S....291 Seneca St., Buffalo, N.Y., 14204. (716) 856-9188. Cuisine: Italian. Credit cards: AE, MC, VISA.

MANNY'S SUPPER CLUB....471 Delaware Ave., Buffalo, N.Y., 14202. (716) 881-3727. Cuisine: Steakhouse. Owner: Besso. Open 7 days for dinner; Monday to Friday for lunch; closed Sunday during July and August. Credit cards: All major. Annual sales: $250,000 to $500,000. Total employment: 30.

THE PARK LANE MANOR HOUSE.... Gates Cir., Buffalo, N.Y., 14209. (716) 885-3250. Cuisine: Continental. Credit cards: All major.

POLONIA....193 Lombard St., Buffalo, N.Y., 14212. (716) 892-4455. Cuisine: Polish. Credit cards: None.

YIANNI'S....581 Delaware Ave., Buffalo, N.Y., 14202. (716) 883-6033. Cuisine: Greek. Credit cards: MC, VISA.

CAMILLUS

TOP O' THE HILL....5633 West Genesee St., Camillus, N.Y., 13031. (315) 673-8148. Cuisine: American. Credit cards: All major.

CANAAN

SHUJI'S....Rte. 22, Canaan, N.Y., 12125. (518) 794-8383. Cuisine: Japanese. Credit cards: AE, MC, VISA.

CARLE PLACE

SASAKI JAPANESE RESTAURANT....540 Westbury Ave., Carle Place, N.Y., 11514. (516) 333-3434. Cuisine: Japanese. Owner: Eiji Sasaki. Closed Monday. Credit cards: AE, MC, VISA. Private party facilities. Up to 20. Annual sales: $250,000 to $500,000. Total employment: 10. Corporate name: Sasaki Restaurant Corp.

CARMEL

DREAMWOLD....Gypsy Trail Rd., Carmel, N.Y., 10512. (914) 225-3500. Cuisine: French. Credit cards: All major.

PETER'S PLUM....Daisy La., Carmel, N.Y., 10512. (914) 277-9580. Cuisine: Italian. Open Monday through Saturday for lunch and dinner. Credit cards: None. Private party facilities. Up to 50. Annual sales: $250,000 to $500,000. Total employment: 13. Corporate name: Peter's Plum Restaurant.

CASTILE

GLEN IRIS....South Park Entrance, Castile, N.Y., 14427. (716) 493-2622. Cuisine: Continental. Credit cards: AE, MC, VISA.

CATSKILL

LA RIVE....Old King's Rd., Catskill, N.Y., 12414. (518) 943-4888. Cuisine: French.

CAZENOVIA

BRAE LOCH INN....5 Albany St., Cazenovia, N.Y., 13035. (315) 655-3431. Cuisine: Scottish/American. Owner: H. Grey Barr. Open 7 days for dinner and Sunday brunch. Credit cards: AE, MC, VISA. Private party facilities. Up to 300. Annual sales: $1 million to $3 million. Total employment: 75.

CEDARHURST

LA VIOLA....571 Chestnut St., Cedarhurst, L.I., N.Y., 1156. (516) 569-6020. Sophisticated and under strong continental influences, but its pasta is really beautiful. Clams and shrimps also emit delicious aromas and tastes. As for service, it's alert, unaffected and considerate. La Viola's facade gives nothing away, nor the location—across from the Cedarhurst railroad tracks. But you will agree that La Viola beongs on anyone's list of "specials." Open for dinner Tuesday through Sunday, closed on Mondays. Moderate to expensive pricing. Owner: Lino Viola. Credit cards: AE, DC. Reservations: Accepted. Private party facilites. Annual sales: $500,000. Total employment: 6.

WERNER BAER....564 Central Ave., Cedarhurst, N.Y., 11516. (516) 374-1999. Cuisine: Continental. Owner: Eva Baer. Open Tuesday to Sunday. Credit cards: All major. Private party facilities. 25 to 125. Annual sales: $1 million to $3 million. Corporate name: 564 Central Ave. Restaurant, Inc.

CENTRAL VALLEY

GASHO OF JAPAN.... Rte. 32, Central Valley, N.Y., 19017. (914) 928-2277. Cuisine: Japanese. Owner: Shiro Aoki. Open 7 days. Credit cards: All major. Private party facilities: 20 to 150. Annual sales: Over $3 million. Total employment: 180. Corporate name: Gasho of Japan, Inc.

CHAPPAQUA

CHAPPAQUA FISH HOUSE....80 South Greeley Ave., Chappaqua, N.Y., 10514. (914) 238-8452. Cuisine: Seafood. Credit cards: None.

NUNZIO'S CHAPPAQUA RESTAURANT....Hunt's La., Chappaqua, N.Y., 10514. (914) 238-8807. Cuisine: Italian/Continental.

THE OCEAN HOUSE....South Greeley Ave., Chappaqua, N.Y., 10514. (914) 238-8452. Cuisine: Seafood. Owner: J. Baker. Credit cards: None.

THE ORDINARY....136 Greeley Ave., Chappaqua, N.Y., 10514. (914) 238-5294. Cuisine: French. Credit cards: All major.

COLD SPRING

BREAK NECK LODGE....Rte. 9D, Cold Spring, N.Y., (914) 265-9669. Cuisine: Continental. Credit cards: All major.

PLUMBUSH....Rte. 9D, Cold Spring, N.Y., 10516. (914) 265-3904. Cuisine: Continental. Credit cards: All major.

COLD SPRING HARBOR

WHALER'S INN....105 Harbor Rd., Cold Spring Harbor, L.I., N.Y., 11724. (516) 367-3166. Cuisine: Seafood. Credit cards: All major.

COMMACK

BON WIT INN....Commack Rd., Commack, L.I., N.Y., 11725. (516) 499-2068. Open 7 days for lunch and dinner. Owners: James and Charles Tunis. Credit cards: All major. Reservations: Accepted. Private Party Facilities. Entertainment: Piano on weekends. Annual sales: $1 million to $3 million. Total employment: 85.

CONGERS

BULLY BOY CHOP HOUSE.... Rte. 303, Congers, N.Y., 10920. (914) 268-6555. Cuisine: English. Credit cards: AE, DC, MC, VISA.

COPIAGUE

ITALIAN LANDMARK....845 Merrick Rd., Copiague, L.I., N.Y., 11726. (516) 842-2210. Cuisine: N. Y., 11726. (516) 842-2210. Cuisine: Italian/Continental. Credit cards: All major.

CORAM

WHITE HOUSE INN....Rte. 25, Coram, L.I., N.Y., 11727. (516) 732-7220. Cuisine: Continental. Credit cards: AE, MC, VISA, DC.

CORNING

GARDEN COURT....Denison Pkwy. East, Corning, N.Y., 14830. (607) 962-5000. Cuisine: Continental. Credit cards: All major.

CROTON FALLS

MONA TRATTORIA.... Rte. 22, Croton Falls, N.Y., 10519. (914) 277-4580. Cuisine: Italian.

CROTON-ON-HUDSON

CROTON COLONIAL RESTAURANT & DINER....221 South Riverside Ave., Croton-On-Hudson, N.Y., 10520. (914) 271-4991. Cuisine: American. Credit cards: All major.

PHIL'S PLACE....120 Grand St., Croton-On-Hudson, N.Y., 10520. (914) 271-5320. Cuisine: Italian.

VILLA MORELLI....352 Riverside Ave., Croton-On-Hudson, N.Y., 10520. (914) 271-8023. Cuisine: Italian. Credit cards: All major.

VIN HOSIER'S....131 East Corning Rd., Corning, N.Y., 14830. (607) 936-3338. Cuisine: French. Owner: Harry Marvin Hosier, Jr. Open Monday through Saturday for dinner only. Credit cards: AE, DC, MC, VISA. Private party facilities: Up to 60. Annual sales: $250,000 to $500,000. Total employment: 17.

DOBBS FERRY

CASA RINA....1 South Field Ave., Dobbs Ferry, N.Y., 10522. (914) 693-6024. Cuisine: Italian. Credit cards: All major.

THE CHART HOUSE....High St., Dobbs Ferry, N.Y., 10522. (914) 693-4130. Cuisine: Seafood. Credit cards: All major.

JIMMIE'S....56 Main St., Dobbs Ferry, N.Y., 10522. (914) 693-9747. Cuisine: Seafood. Credit cards: None.

RUDY'S BEAU RIVAGE RESTAURANT....19 Livingston Ave., Dobbs Ferry, N.Y., 10522. (914) 693-3192. Cuisine: Continental. Owner: Rudy Croese. Closed Monday. Credit cards: AE, MC, VISA. Private party facilities: 10 to 300. Annual sales: $500,000 to $1 million. Total employment: 20. Corporate name: Agcro Restaurant, Inc.

SHAKESPEARE'S....17 Cedar St., Dobbs Ferry, N.Y., 10522. (914) 693-9830. Cuisine: Seafood/Steaks. Owner: Thomas Paul. Open for 7 days for lunch and dinner. Credit cards: AE, MC, VISA. Annual sales: $250,000 to $500,000. Total employment: 6.

SWISS CABIN....92 Main St., Dobbs Ferry, N.Y., 10522. (914) 693-9729. Cuisine: Continental/Swiss. Owner: Dolf & Helene Zueger. Corporate name: Swiss Cabin Restaurant, Inc.

DOUGLASTON

DOUGLASTON MANOR....63-20 Commonwealth Blvd., Douglaston, N.Y. 11005. (212) 224-8787. This is a large, delightful restaurant base on the edge of the golf course. Very tranquil and countrified. Plenty of scope for varying Continental-Italian cuisine. Located in Queens. House specialites include: veal and shrimp francese, softshell crab sauteed with garlic and bouillabaisse. Prices are moderate. Open for lunch, Tuesday through Friday. Dinner: Tuesday through Sunday. Closed Monday. Owner: Robert Santucci. Credit cards: All major. Reservations: Accepted. Private Party Facilities. Ent: Trio for dancing—W,F,Sa. Annual sales: $1 million. Total employment: 35.

DOVER PLAINS

OLD DROVERS INN....Dover Plains, N.Y., 12522. (914) 832-3811. Cuisine: Continental. Credit cards: None.

EAST BLOOMFIELD

HOLLOWAY HOUSE....Rte. 5, East Bloomfield, N.Y., 14443. (716) 657-7120. Cuisine: American. Credit cards: MC, VISA.

EASTCHESTER

ALEX & HENRY'S....680 White Plains Rd., Eastchester, N.Y., 10709. (914) 725-4433. Cuisine: Continental. Owner: The Recines.

CHESTER'S....701 White Plains Rd., Eastchester, N.Y., 10709. (914) 725-0086. Cuisine: American. Credit cards: All major.

EDMONDO'S SEAFOOD RESTAURANT....219 East Main St., Eastchester, N.Y., 10709. (914) 779-7117. Cuisine: Seafood. Credit cards: All major.

SAGANO....480 New Rochelle Rd., Eastchester, N.Y., 10709. (914) 668-3333. Cuisine: Japanese. Credit cards: All major.

EAST FARMINGDALE

THE BLUE DOLPHIN.... Rte. 110 & Conklin St., East Farmingdale, L.I., N.Y., 11735. (516) 420-1950. Cuisine: Continental. Owner: Vincent Schettini.

EAST HAMPTON

HEDGES' HOUSE (EN BROCHETTE)....74 James La., East Hampton, L.I., N.Y., 11937. (516) 324-7100. Cuisine: Continental. Owner: Kenneth J. Baker and Richard C. Spencer. Open Tuesday through Sunday for lunch and dinner. Credit cards: All major. Private party facilities: 50 to 200. Annual sales: $500,000 to $1 million. Total employment: 6 to 30. Corporate name: En Brochette—Beverly Hills/East Hampton.

MICHAEL'S RESTAURANT....28 Maidstone Park Rd., East Hampton, L.I., N.Y., 11937. (516) 324-0725. Cuisine: Continental/Seafood. Owner: Donna & Michael Zingarelli. Open 6 days for dinner; Closed Mondays. Credit cards: All major. Private party facilities: Up to 70. Annual sales: $250,000 to $500,000. Total employment: 9. Corporate name: Miconna Restaurant Corp.

PALM....94 Main Street, (in The Hunting Lodge Inn), East Hampton, L.I., N.Y., 11937. (516) 324-0410. Another less cluttered incarnation of this Manhattan warhorse but don't let the absence of clutter, caricature sketches on the walls, aproned waiters or commotion throw you off track: this is the same Palm and the steaks are just as huge and just as delicious. Owner: Bruce Bozzi and Walter Ganzi. Open Monday through Friday for lunch; Monday through Saturday for dinner; Closed Sunday; Open seasonally (summertime); Call for times and days. Price: moderate to high. Reservations: Suggested. Credit cards: All major. Corporate name: Just One More Restaurant, Inc.—Palm Restaurant, Inc.

THE SEA WOLF.... Box 2024, East Hampton, L.I., N.Y., 11937. (516) 324-1650. Cuisine: Continental/Seafood. Owner: Wolfgang Reiter. Open 7 days May to September. Credit cards: AE, MC, VISA. Private party facilities: 30 to 200 persons. Annual sales: $250,000 to $500,000. Total employment: 20. Corporate name: Wolfsbane Enterprises, Inc.

THE 1770 HOUSE....143 Main St., East Hampton, L.I., N.Y., 11937. (516) 324-1770. Cuisine: International. Owner: Sid and Miriam Perle.

SPRING CLOSE HOUSE.... Montauk Hwy., East Hampton, L.I., N.Y., 11937. (516) 324-0233. Cuisine: Continental.

EAST ISLIP

BEACHTREE CAFE....166 West Main St., East Islip, L.I., N.Y., 11730. (516) 277-4801. Cuisine: International. Owner: Richard Freilich and Shohei Yamamoto. Open 7 days for lunch and dinner. Credit cards: All major. Private party facilities: 10 to 120. Annual sales: $1 million to $3 million. Total employment: 60. Corporate name: Beachtree Cafe, Inc.

EAST MEADOW

MARIO'S....364 Newbridge Ave., East Meadow, L.I., N.Y., 11554. (516) 794-6248. Cuisine: Italian. Owner's name: Mario Saecopus.

THE WINE GALLERY RESTAURANT....2172 Hempstead Pke., East Meadow, N.Y., 11554. (516) 794-8065. Cuisine: Continental. Open 7 days for lunch and dinner. Credit cards: All major. Private party facilities: Up to 100. Annual sales: $1 million to $3 million. Total employment: 42. Corporte name: Notarene Restaurant, Inc.

EAST NORWICH

RISTORANTE ANGELINA....1017 Oyster Bay Rd., East Norwich, L.I., N.Y., 11732. (516) 922-0033. Cuisine: Italian. Credit cards: All major.

EAST PATCHOGUE

PINE GROVE INN.... Chapel Ave.& First St., East Patchogue, L.I., N.Y., 11772. (516) 475-9843. Cuisine: Continental. Owner's name: Ray Hombach.

EAST ROCKAWAY

SHIP'S INN....6 Fifth Ave., East Rockaway, L.I., N.Y., 11518. (516) 593-1440. Cuisine: Seafood. Credit cards: All major.

EAST HILLS

LA PRIMAVERA....148 Glen Cove Ave., East Hills, N.Y., (516) 484-9453. Cuisine: Northern Italian/Continental. Owner: Elio Sobrero. Open Monday through Saturday for lunch and dinner. Credit cards: All major. Annual sales: $250,000 to $500,000. Total employment: 15.

L'ENDROIT....290 Glen Cove Rd., East Hills, L.I., N.Y., (516) 621-6630. Cuisine: Continental. Credit cards: All major.

EAST SETAUKET

DIAMOND'S....40-20 Nesconset Hwy., East Setauket, L.I., N.Y., 11733. (516) 928-4343. Cuisine: Chinese. Credit cards: All major.

RAMANN'S....316 Main St., East Setauket, L.I., N.Y., 11733. (516) 751-2200. Cuisine: Continental/American. Credit cards: All major.

ELMIRA HEIGHTS

PIERCE'S 1894....228 Oakwood Ave., Elmira Heights., N.Y., 14903. (607) 734-2022. Cuisine: Continental/Chinese.

WRIGHT'S BUNN 'N' BRU....118 College Ave., Elmira Heights., N.Y., 14903. (607) 733-6265. Cuisine: American. Credit cards: MC, VISA.

ELMONT

YOUR PLACE...OR MINE....325 Hempstead Tpke., Elmont, L.I., N.Y., 11003. (516) 775-9153. Cuisine: Continental. Credit cards: All major.

ELMSFORD

GAULIN'S RESTAURANT....86 East Main St., Elmsford, N.Y., 10523. (914) 592-4213. Cuisine: French. Credit cards: All major.

TONY'S LA STAZIONE RESTAURANT....15 Saw Mill River Rd., Elmsford, N.Y., 10523. (914) 592-5980. Cuisine: Italian/Seafood. Owner: Mr. & Mrs. Anthony Naro. Open 7 days. Credit cards: All major. Private party facilities: Up to 90. Total employment: 20. Corporate name: Militello Restaurant, Inc.

PIER SIX....210 Saw Mill River Rd., Elmsford, N.Y., 10523. (914) 592-3070. Cuisine: Seafood. Credit cards: All major.

SID ALLEN'S....540 Saw Mill River Rd., Elmsford, N.Y., 10523. (914) 592-2444. Cuisine: American. Credit cards: All major.

WEATHERVANE....45 West Tarrytown Rd., Elmsford, N.Y., 10523. (914) 592-9092. Cuisine: Italian. Credit cards: All major.

FAIRMOUNT CORNERS

WALTER WHITE'S SEA N' SALAD....3700 West Genesee St., Fairmount Corners, N.Y., 13219. (315) 487-5951. Cuisine: American. Credit cards: AE, CB, MC, VISA.

FARMINGDALE

CAPTAIN ANDY'S....196 Main St., Farmingdale, L.I., N.Y., 11735. (516) CH 9-0140. Cuisine: Seafood. Owner's name: Sven Brost.

KIPLING'S....10 Allen Blvd., Farmingdale, L.I., N.Y., 11735. (516) 752-1565. Owner's name: Mr. Allen. Credit cards: All major.

THIRD VOYAGE....711 Main St., Farmingdale, L.I., N.Y., 11735. (516) 694-7766.Cuisine: Seafood. Owner's name: Beverly Scalici. Credit cards: AE, DC, CB, MC, VISA.

FARMINGVILLE

ALGARVE RESTAURANT....800 Horseblock Rd., Farmingville, N.Y., 11738. (516) 732-9438. Cuisine: Portuguese/Continental. Owner: Agostinho Ferradeira. Open Tuesday through Sunday. Credit cards: AE, DC, VISA. Private party facilities: Up to 140. Annual sales: $250,000 to $500,000. Total employment: 6.

FLEETWOOD

TYLOON....545 Gramatan Ave., Fleetwood, N.Y., 10500. (914) 664-5146. Cuisine: Chinese. Credit cards: All major.

FLORAL PARK

ISONO....214 Jericho Tpke., Floral Park, L.I., N.Y., 11001. (516) 437-4552. Cuisine: Japanese. Credit cards: AE, MC, VISA.

THE MERRY PEDLAR....330 Jericho Tpke., Floral Park, L.I., N.Y., 11001. (516) 354-9394. Cuisine: Continental. Owner: Thomas B. J. Moran, Jr. Open 7 days for lunch and dinner. Credit cards: All major. Private party facilities: 15 to 125. Annual sales $250,000 to $500,000. Total employment: 16 Corporate name: The Merry Pedlar Corp.

STELLA'S....152 Jericho Tpke, Floral Park, L.I., N.Y., 11001. (516) 354-9790. Cuisine: Italian. Open 6 days for dinner only; Closed Monday. Owner: Cerrone Family. Credit cards: All major. Reservations: Accepted. Saturdays and parties over 5, a must. Total employment: 40.

VILLA D'ESTE....146 Tulip Ave., Floral Park, L.I., N.Y., 11001. (516) 354-1355. Open Tuesday through Friday for lunch; Tuesday through Sunday for dinner; Closed on Monday. Owner: Nefi Montalti. Credit cards: AE, MC, VISA. Reservations: Accepted. Private party facilities: Total employment: 10.

FLUSHING

LA VENEZIANA....179-22 Union Tpke., Flushing (Queens), N.Y., 11366 (212) 969-0061. Cuisine: Credit cards: AE.

LOBSTER TANK SEAFOOD HOUSE....134-30 Northern Blvd., Flushing (Queens), N.Y., 11354. (212) 359-9220. Cuisine: Seafood. Credit cards: All major.

SEVEN SEAS CHINESE-POLYNESIAN RESTAURANT....167-03 Union Tpke., Flushing, N.Y., 11366. (212) 969-7070. Cuisine: Chinese. Owner: Paul Chow. Open 7 days. Credit cards: All major. Private party facilities: 20 to 65. Annual sales: $500,000 to $1 million. Total employment: 20. Corporate name: East Bamboo Restaurant, Inc.

FOREST HILLS

HESKELS....70-28 Austin St., Forest Hills (Queens), N.Y., 11375. (212) 268-4524. Cuisine: American. Credit cards: All major.

THE STRATTON RESTAURANT....108-36 Queens Blvd., Forest Hills, N.Y., 11375. (212) 263-6100. Cuisine: Continental/American. Owner: Joseph Vogel. Open 7 days. Credit cards: All major. Private party facilities: 40-150. Annual sales: $1 million to $3 million. Total employment: 70. Corporate name: A.S.V. Restaurant, Inc.

TUNG SHING HOUSE....104-70 Queens Blvd., Forest Hills N.Y., 11375. (212) 275-0038. Cuisine: Chinese. Owner: Andrew Han. Open 7 days. Credit cards: AE, DC, MC, VISA. Private party facilities: Yes. Annual sales: $1 million to $3 million. Total employment: 27. Corporate name: Asian Gold Restaurant, Inc.

FREEPORT

DON CICCIO PESCATORE....360 Atlantic Ave., Freeport, L.I., N.Y., 11520. (516) 868-2207. A promising start has been made here by the founder Vincenzo Rossini, who previously established the noted Rossini's on the same site in 1979. He has made don ciccio Pescatore into a solid, reliable, and traditional Italian restaurant. Certain specialties are first-rate; among them veal *illuminati*, layered with Italian ham, mozzarella, and a crown of fresh avacado. Other House specialties: beef and veal combination; chicken Rossini and *Caccioco a la livornese*. Open for dinner only, 7 days. Prices are moderate. Owner: Vincenzo Rossini. Credit cards: All major. Reservations: Accepted. Entertainment: guitar on weekends. Annual sales: $500,000 to 1,000,000. Total employment: 11.

GAETAWAY HARBOUR....500 Atlantic Ave., Freeport, L.I., N.Y., 11520. (516) 546-8500. Cuisine: Continental. Owner's name: Mr. Gaeta. Credit cards: AE, MC, VISA, DC.

MIDSHIP....507 South Guy Lombardo Ave., Freeport, L.I., N.Y., 11520. (516) 378-1300. Cuisine: Seafood. Owner: Robert Porzio. Corporate name: Top Deck, Inc.

MOORINGS....329 South Guy Lombardo Ave., Freeport, L.I., N.Y., 11520. (516) 378-2344. Owner: Bill. Corporate name: TSA-TRAS Rest. Corp.

SALTY BAY YACHT CLUB....180 Westside Ave., Freeport, L.I., N.Y., 11520. (516) 546-4224. Cuisine: Seafood. Credit cards: AE, DC.

TIDES....340 Woodcleft Ave., Freeport, L.I., N.Y., 11520. (516) 868-2331. Cuisine: Seafood. Owner: Robert McDermott. Corporate name: Tides Inn Inc.

VILLA ROSA....244 East Merrick Rd., Freeport, L.I., N.Y., 11520. (516) 378-5435. Cuisine: Italian/Continental. Owner: Michael Carrature. Open 7 days for lunch and dinner. Credit cards: All major. Private party facilities: Up to 150. Annual sales: $250,000 to $500,000. Total employment: 40.

FRESH MEADOWS

VILLA SECONDO....184-22 Horace Harding Expwy., Fresh Meadows, N.Y., 11365. (212) 762-7355. Cuisine: Italian. Credit cards: All major.

GARDEN CITY

McCAULEY'S....660 Franklin Ave., Garden City, L.I., N.Y., 11530. (516) 747-2156. Cuisine: American. Credit cards: All major.

GARRISON

THE BIRD AND BOTTLE INN....Old Albany Post Rd., Rte. 9, Garrison, N.Y., 10524. (914) 424-3000. Cuisine: Continental. Owner: Ira Boyer, Innkeeper. Open 7 days; Closed Monday and Tuesday from November to April. Credit cards: MC, VISA. Private party facilities: 8 to 20. Annual sales: $250,000 to $500,000. Total employment: 12.

GENEVA

BELHURST CASTLE....Lochland Rd., Rte. 145, Geneva, N.Y., 14456. (315) 781-0201. Cuisine: Continental. Owner: Robert J. & Nancy A. Golden. Open 6 days; Closed Monday. Credit cards: All major. Private party facilities: 18 to 225. Annual sales: $500,000 to $1 million. Total employment: 55. Corporate name: Belhurst Castle, Inc.

GLEN COVE

LA BUSSOLA....40 School St., Glen Cove, L.I., N.Y., 11542. (516) 671-2100. Cuisine: Italian. Credit cards: AE, VISA.

LE RESTAURANT....Cedar Swamp Road, Glen Cove, L.I., N.Y., 11542. (516) 671-2890. A most gracious and creative French restaurant. French-Colonial decor gives it a "temple of gastronomy" air, and the taste experiences from the kitchen are authoritative and well-focused. Specialties include: trout radiant with freshness and stuffed with shrimps and mushrooms; rack of lamb for two, parchment crisp outside, tender and moist within; and succulent snapper accompanied by a fascinating lobster sauce. Owners: John Diassinos, Ed Altern, Charles Demirakos. Open Tuesday through Thursday for lunch; Tuesday through Sunday for dinner; Closed Mondays. Price: Expensive. Reservations: Accepted. Credit cards: All major. Private party facilities: 20 to 175. Annual sales: $1 million to $3 million. Total employment: 40. Corporate name: DAD, Ltd.

MY FRIEND'S RESTAURANT....188 Glen Cove Ave., Glen Cove, L.I., N.Y., 11542. (516) 676-9594. Cuisine: Greek/American. Credit cards: All major.

TIFFANY HOUSE....Glen Cove Golf Course, Lattingtown Rd., Glen Cove, L.I., N.Y., 11542. (516) 676-9781. Cuisine: Continental. Owner's name: Charles Santo. Credit cards: MC, VISA.

VERANDA....48 Cedar Swamp Rd., Glen Cove, L.I., N.Y., 11542. (516) 759-0394. Cuisine: Italian/Continental. Credit cards: All major.

ZANGHI....50 Forest Ave., Glen Cove, L.I., N.Y., 11542. (516) 759-0900. Cuisine: French/Italian. Credit cards: All major.

GRANITE SPRINGS

DAMINO'S....Rtes. 118 & 202, Granite Springs, N.Y., 10527. (914) 248-7200. Cuisine: Northern Italian. Closed Mondays. Credit cards: AE, MC, VISA. Private party facilities: Up to 75. Annual sales: $500,000 to $1 million. Total employment: 12. Corporate name: Damiano's Restaurant, Inc.

FISHMARKET INN....Rte. 118, Granite Springs, N.Y. 10527. (914) 245-4388. Cuisine: Seafood. Credit cards: MC, VISA.

GREAT NECK

EPICUREAN FISH HOUSE....218 Middleneck Rd., Great Neck, N.Y., 11021. (516) 487-5603. Cuisine: Seafood. Owner: Fred Izabriskie. Closed Monday. Credit cards: AE, MC, VISA. Private party facilities: Up to 60. Annual sales: $250,000 to $500,000. Total employment: 7. Corporate name: Fanilo Restaurant Corp.

FIORENTINA....4 Welwyn Rd., Great Neck, L.I., N.Y., 11021. (516) 487-1070. Cuisine: Italian. Credit cards: AE, CB, DC.

MAMA LOLA....570 Middle Neck Rd., Great Neck, L.I., N.Y., 11023. (516) 482-1510. Cuisine: Continental. Owner' name: Mario Giacometti. Credit cards: AE, DC, MC, VISA.

PETER LUGER STEAK HOUSE....255 Northern Blvd., Great Neck, L.I., N.Y., 11021. (516) 487-8800. Cuisine: Steak. Owner: Marilyn Spencer, Pres. Open daily. Credit cards: House accounts only. Private party facilities: 12 to 45. Total employment: 100. Corporate name: Peter Luger of Long Island, Inc.

RACHMANINOFF DISRAELI & GLADSTONE....100 Steamboat Rd., Great Neck, L.I., N.Y., 11024. (516) 829-6969. Cuisine: Continental. Credit cards: None.

RENE....158 Middle Neck Rd., Great Neck, L.I., N.Y., 11021. (516) 466-4901. Cuisine: Continental. Credit cards: All major.

SQUIRE RESTAURANT....152 Middle Neck Rd., Great Neck, L.I., N.Y., 11021. (516) HU 7-4032. Cuisine: American. Owner's name: Abe Daniels. Credit cards: AE, MC, DC, VISA.

TAVERN IN THE ALLEY....123 Middle Neck Rd., Great Neck, L.I., N.Y., 11021. (516) 487-4755. Cuisine: American. Credit cards: MC, DC, VISA.

UPSTAIRS....63 Middle Neck Rd., Great Neck, L.I., N.Y., 11021. (516) 466-2260. Cuisine: Continental. Credit cards: AE, DC, MC, VISA.

VILLA PIERRE....158 Middle Neck Rd., Great Neck, L.I., N.Y., 11021. Cuisine: Continental.

VIOLETTE'S....4 South Station Plz., Great Neck, L.I., N.Y., 11021. (516) 466-3881. Cuisine: Italian/French. Credit cards: AE, DC, MC, VISA.

GREENBURG

TYLOON GARDEN....55 Tarrytown Rd., Greenburg, N.Y., (914) 946-2220. Cuisine: Chinese.

GREENPORT

OYSTER FACTORY....160 Fifth St., Greenport, L.I., N.Y., 11944. (516) 477-0100. Cuisine: International/Seafood. Credit cards: MC, VISA.

RHUMB LINE RESTAURANT....36 Front St., Greenport, L.I., N.Y., 11944. (516) 477-9883. Cuisine: Seafood/Steak. Owner: Robert and Carol Copas. Open 7 days. Credit cards: All major. Total employment: 25. Corporate name: Rhumb Line, Inc.

GREENVALE

LA VIGNA....63 Glen Cove Rd., Greenvale, L.I., N.Y., 11548. (518) 621-8440. Cuisine: Italian. Credit cards: All major.

HARRISON

EMILIO RESTAURANT....1 Colonial Pl., Harrison, N.Y., 10528. (914) 835-3100. Cuisine: Italian.

GUSS'S FRANKLIN PARK RESTAURANT....126 Halstead Ave., Harrison, N.Y., 10528. (914) 835-9804. Cuisine: Seafood. Owner: August Kneuer, Pres., Jack Kneuer, V.P., Ernest Kneuer, Secy/Tres. Open 7 days. No credit cards. Annual sales: $250,000 to $500,000. Total employment: 12. Corporate name: Franklin Park Restaurant Corporation, Inc.

HAMPTON BAYS

JUDGE'S RESTAURANT....Hampton Bays, L.I., N.Y., 11946. (516) 728-1717. Cuisine: Americn/Seafood. Owner: Joseph Z. Krajewski. Open 7 days for dinner. Credit cards: All major. Annual sales: $250,000 to $500,000. Total employment: 26.

LAND & SEA....307 Halstead Ave., Harrison, N.Y., 10528. (914) 835-1372. Cuisine: Continental. Credit cards: All major.

RISOLI'S....7 Purdy St., Harrion, N.Y., 10528. (914) 835-1411. Cuisine: Italian. Credit cards: All major.

VIA APPIA....9 East Taylor Sq., Harrison, N.Y., 10528. (914) 949-5810. Cuisine: Italian. Credit cards: None.

HARTSDALE

AUBERGE ARGENTEUIL....42 Healy Ave., Hartsdale, N.Y., 10530. (914) 948-0597. Cuisine: French. Owner: Henri G. Eudes. Open 7 days. Credit cards: All major. Private party facilities: 4 to 50. Corporate name: Auberge Argenteuil.

HUNAN MANOR....149 South Central Ave., Hartsdale, N.Y., 10530. (914) 997-0204. Cuisine: Chinese. Credit cards: All major.

SERGIO'S....18 North Central Ave., Hartsdale, N.Y., 10530. (914) 949-1234. Cuisine: Continental. Credit cards: All major.

TUNG SING....156 Central Ave., Hartsdale, N.Y., 10530. (914) 761-6046. Cuisine: Chinese. Credit cards: All major.

HASTINGS

SAN ROC....Saw Mill River Rd., Hastings, N.Y., 13706. (914) 478-2331. Cuisine: Continental. Credit cards: All major.

HASTINGS-ON-HUDSON

BUFFET DE LA GARE....155 Southside Ave., Hastings-On-Hudson, N.Y., 10706. (914) 478-1661. Cuisine: French. Credit cards: None.

HASTINGS HOUSE....555 Warburton Ave., Hastings-On-Hudson, N.Y., 10706. (914) 478-0410. Cuisine: American. Credit cards: MC, VISA.

MANZI'S....17 Main St., Hastings-On-Hudson, N.Y., 10706. (914) 478-0404. Cuisine: Italian/Seafood. Credit cards: AE, DC, MC, VISA.

THE SWIZZLE....337 South Riverside Ave., Hastings-On-Hudson, N.Y., 10706. (914) 271-8025. Cuisine: American/Continental. Credit cards: All major.

HAUPPAUGE

CELLINI'S....1251 Veterans Memorial Hwy., Hauppauge, L.I., N.Y., 11787. (516) 724-4445. Cuisine: Italian. Credit cards: AE, MC, VISA, DC.

HAWTHORNE

GASHO OF JAPAN....2 Saw Mill River Rd., Hawthorne, N.Y., 10532. (914) 592-5900. Cuisine: Japanese. Owner: Shiro Aoki, Pres. Open 7 days for lunch and dinner; Sunday brunch. Credit cards: All major. Private party facilities: 20 to 130. Annual sales: $1 million to $3 million. Total employment: 46. Corporate name: Gasho of Japan, Inc.

ICHABOD'S INN....27 Saw Mill River Rd., Hawthorne, N.Y., 10532. (914) 592-8452. Cuisine: Continental.

ORIENTAL LOA....500 Commerce St., Hathorne, N.Y., 10532. (914) 769-7555. Cuisine: Chinese. Credit cards: All major.

TACONIC BRAUHAUS.....15 Commerce St., Hawthorne, N.Y., 10532. (914) 769-9842. Cuisine: German. Credit cards: All major.

TINO'S VILLA....Rte. 9A, Hawthorne, N.Y., 10532. (914) 769-7236. Cuisine: Italian/Steakhouse. Open for dinner 7 days. Credit cards: All major. Private party facilities: Up to 90. Annual sales: $500,000 to $1 million. Total employment: 10.

HEWLETT

ARENA RESTAURANT....1270 Peninsula Blvd., Hewlett, L.I., N.Y., 11557. (516) 295-3290. Cuisine: Italian. Credit cards: All major.

SUGGAR'S....1137 Broadway, Hewlett, L.I., N.Y., 11557. (516) 374-1212. A disco and a restaurant all in one with snazzy, jazzy neon lights and signs giving the place a very alive, modern, fun look. It's big and very popular, and deservedly so. The food has a definite American slant, with excellent burgers and sandwiches being supplemented with a few more exotic dishes. Specialties include: Lobster tails, a 16-ounce sirloin, *fettucine primavera* with vegetables and shrimp, veal *marsala*. Owner: William L. Finger. Open Tuesday through Sunday for lunch and dinner; recommend that you go anytime from 11:30 a.m. to 11 p.m. and have a small orgy at ridiculous prices. Open for lunch Tuesday through Friday, dinner, 7 days. Owner: Luigi Dinucci. Credit cards: All major. Reservations: Accepted. Annual sales: $300,000. Total employment: 10.

HICKSVILLE

ALFREDO'S....193 Old Country Rd., Hicksville, L.I., N.Y., 11801. (516) 433-1978. Cuisine: Swiss.

BOCCACCIO....129 North Broadway, Hicksville, N.Y., 11801. (516) 433-0546. Cuisine: Continental. Owner: Frank Antolos. Open Monday to Friday for lunch; Monday to Saturday for dinner. Credit cards: All major. Annual sales: $250,000 to $500,000. Total employment: 10.

LORD STANLEY'S RESTAURANT....275 Old Country Rd., Hicksville, N.Y., 11801. (516) 931-2522-23. Cuisine: American and Elizabethan Feast. Owner: Morris Miller and Leonard Kraft. Open 7 days; weekdays for lunch and dinner; weekends for dinner. Credit cards: AE, MC, VISA. Private party facilities: Up to 200. Annual sales: $250,000 to $500,000. Total employment: 25. Corporate name: Lord Stanley's Restaurant Tavern, Inc.

MILLERIDGE INN....Hicksville Rd. & Jericho Tpke., Hicksville, N.Y., 11803. (516) 931-2201. Cuisine: American. Owner: J.F. Murray. Open 7 days for lunch and dinner. Credit cards: All major. Private party facilities: 10 to 600.

ORIGINAL VILLA PARMA....316 North Broadway, Hicksville, L.I., N.Y., 11801. (516) 938-2050. Cuisine: Italian. Owner's name: Mr. Petrone. Credit cards: AE, MC, VISA.

WICKER'S RESTAURANT....206 Old Country Rd., Hicksville, L.I., N.Y., 11801. (516) 433-6466. Cuisine: American. Credit cards: AE, MC, DC, VISA

HILLSDALE

L'HOSTELLERIE BRESSONE....Rtes. 22 & 23, Hillsdale, N.Y., 12529. (518) 325-3412. Cuisine: French. Open Wednesday through Sunday for dinner only; Closed Monday and Tuesday. No credit cards. Reservations: Recommended.

HOLBROOK

MOMMA LOMBARDS'S....380 Furrows Rd., Holbrook, L.I., N.Y., 11741. (516) 737-0774. Cuisine: Italian. Credit cards: All major.

HOWARD BEACH

HOUSE OF HONG....156-10 Cross Bay Blvd., Howard Beach, N.Y., 11414. (212) 848-5444. Cuisine: Chinese. Owner: Lily Cheung. Open 7 days. Credit cards: All major. Private party facilities: Up to 50. Annual sales: $250,000 to $500,000. Total employment: 14 Corporate name: House of Hong, Inc.

HUNTINGTON

FISH PEDDLER....293 Main St., Huntington, L.I., N.Y., 11743. (516) 423-8620. Cuisine: Seafood. Credit cards: AE, MC, VISA, DC.

GLYNNS INN....182 East Main St., Rte. 25A, Huntington, N.Y., 11743. (516) 421-2646. Cuisine: Continental. Owner: Ronald and Nickelos Mastroianni. Open 7 days for lunch and dinner. Credit cards: All major. Private party facilities: Up to 100. Annual sales: $500,000 to $1 million. Total employment: 42. Corporate name: Glynns Inn Ltd.

IBERIAN....402-404 New York Ave., Huntington, N.Y., 11743. (516) 549-8296. Cuisine: Spanish/Seafood. Owner: Jose L. Estevez. Open Monday through Saturday for lunch; Monday through Sunday for dinner. Credit cards: All major. Private party facilities: Up to 75. Annual Sales: $250,000 to $500,000. Total employment: 15.

KURA BARN....479 New York Ave., Huntington, L.I., N.Y., 11743. (516) 673-0060. Cuisine: Japanese. Credit cards: AE, VISA.

LINDEN TREE....54 New St., Huntington, L.I., N.Y., 549-0360. Cuisine: International. Owner's name: Richard Ley. Credit cards: AE, MC, VISA.

ORLANDO'S RISTORANTE....15 New St., Huntington, N.Y., 11743. (516) 421-0606. Cuisine: Italian. Owner: Michail Loturco, Sr., Pres. Open Monday through Saturday for dinner; Monday through Friday for lunch. Credit cards: AE, MC, VISA. Private party facilities: Up to 110. Annual sales: $250,000 to $500,000. Total employment: 16.

PECHE MIGNON....16 Elm St., Huntington, L.I., N.Y., 11743. (516) 549-8311. Cuisine: French. Credit cards: AE, MC, VISA.

WOK'S....665 West Jericho Tpke., Huntington, L.I., N.Y., 111743. (516) 673-8655. Cuisine: Chinese. Credit cards: All major.

HUNTINGTON STATION

HSU'S DYNASTY....206 East Jericho Tpke., Huntington Station, L.I., N.Y., 11746. (516) 423-6699. Cuisine: Chinese. Owner's name: Edmund Hsu.

HUNAN PALACE....206 East Jericho Tpke., Huntington Station, L.I., N.Y., 11746. (516) 423-6699. Cuisine: Chinese. Credit cards: All major.

LA VIRTU....107 East Jericho Tpke., Huntington Station, L.I., N.Y., 11746. (516) 673-6129. Owner's name: Joseph Lizzul.

ROSE AND THISTLE....47 New St., Huntington Village, L.I., N.Y., 11743. (516) 421-1444. A bit of Great Britain brought across the Atlantic, it serves good, hearty food in a very relaxed pub-ish atmosphere. (And it doesn't cost an arm and a leg either.) The menu, while offering many English dishes, does not exclude the cooking of Scotland, Wales, or Ireland. Specialities include: Trafalger shrimp, Sir Winston's quiche, King Henry's crepe, The Kensington (sliced steak and onion), and the Monte Python. Owner: Kevin Murray, Michael Bernabo, Richard Fish. Open 7 days for lunch and dinner. Prices are moderate. Reservations and all major credit cards accepted. Private party facilities for up to 90 persons.

IRVINGTON

ALIBI INN....5 North Buckhout St., Irvington, N.Y., 10533. (914) 591-9885. Cuisine: Seafood. Credit cards: All major.

BENNY'S IRVINGTON DINER....6 South Broadway, Irvington, N.Y., 10533. (914) 591-9811. Cuisine: Seafood. Credit cards: None.

ISLAND PARK

DAVID JONES....1 Julian Pl., Island Park, L.I., N.Y., 11558. (518) 889-7693. Open for lunch and dinner, 7 days. Owner: John Curtin. Credit cards: All major. Reservations: None. Private party facilities: Entertainment: Combo-Lounge Music. Annual sales: $1 million. Total employment: 70.

ISLIP

CASTLE INN....712 Main St., Islip, L.I., N.Y., 11751. (516) 581-5540. Cuisine: American. Credit cards: AE, MC, VISA, DC.

SEASCAPE RESTAURANT & TAP ROOM....116 Montauk Hwy., Islip, N.Y., 11751. (516) 665-9595. Cuisine: Continental/American. Owner: Frank Gillespie. Open 7 days. Credit cards: All major. Private party facilities: 12 to 75. Annual sales: $1 million to $3 million. Total employment: 40 to 45. Corporate name: Seascape Inn, Inc.

ITHACA

L'AUBERGE DU COCHON ROUGE....1152 Danby Rd., Ithaca, N.Y., 14580. (607) 273-3464. A picturesque little old farmhouse run by chef-proprietor Etienne Merle who is renowned for his French cooking and Friday night lobster festivals. Locals and out-of-towners brave the worst weather to enjoy a dish of veal Oscar and there is much to be said for Mr. Merle's Sunday brunch. Specialties include: terrine Louis Joereau, seafood Newburg crepe, cold cream of spinach soup, chateaubriand periquordine, filet mignon au Rossini, ris de veau au beurre noir, and coquilles St. Jacques provencale. Open 7 days for dinner only; Sunday brunch. Reservations and all major credit cards are accepted. Private party facilities for between 2 and 38 persons. Corporate name: L'Auberge du Cochon Rouge, Inc.

OLDPORT HARBOUR....702 West Buffalo St., Ithaca, N.Y., 14850. (607) 272-6550. Cusine: Continental. Owner: W.A. Dillon, Jr., Commodore. Open 7 days for lunch and dinner. Credit cards: AE, MC, VISA. Private party facilities: Up to 150. Annual sales: $500,000 to $1 million. Total employment: 35 to 65 (varies seasonally).

JACKSON HEIGHTS

EL INCA....85-01 Roosevelt Ave., Jackson Heights., (Queens), N.Y., 11372. (212) 429-9627. Cuisine: Spanish.

JAMESTOWN

HOUSE OF PETILLO....382 Hunt Rd., Jamestown, N.Y., 14701. (716) 664-7457. Cuisine: Continental. Credit cards: MC, VISA.

JAMESVILLE

GLEN LOCH MILL....4626 North St., Jamesville, N.Y., 13078. (315) 469-6969. Cuisine: American. Owner: Tim Ban. Open Sunday to Friday for lunch; open 7 days for dinner. Credit cards: AE, MC, VISA. Private party facilities: Up to 500. Annual sales: $1 million to $3 million. Total employment: Up to 100.

JERICHO

MAINE MAID INN....Rte. 106 & Jericho Tpke., Jericho, L.I., N.Y., 11753. (516) WE 5-6400. Cuisine: American. Owner: Philip G. Munson. Open 7 days for lunch and dinner. Credit cards: AE, DC, VISA. Private party facilities: 10 to 150. Annual sales: $1 million to $3 million. Total employment: 62.

OLD FASHIONED FELLOW....111 Jericho Tpke., Jericho, L.I., N.Y., 11753. (516) 333-6611. Cuisine: American.

THE XII ARCHES RESTAURANT....125 Jericho Tpke., Jericho, N.Y., 11753. (516) 997-8900. Cuisine: Continental. Owner: Seymour Cotten. Open 7 days. Credit cards: AE, MC, VISA. Private party facilities: 25 to 200. Annual sales: $500,000 to $1 million. Total employment: 20. Corporate name: The XII Arches Restaurant Corp.

JONES BEACH

BOARDWALK....Jones Beach State Park, L.I., N.Y., (516) 785-2420. Cuisine: Seafood. Credit cards: MC, VISA.

LAKE GEORGE VILLAGE

DINO'S MONTCALM NORTH....Rte. 9N, Lake George Village, N.Y., 12845. (518) 668-5431. Cuisine: Continental/American. Credit cards: All major.

LAKE PLACID

STEAK & STINGER....15 Cascade Rd., Lake Placid, N.Y., 12946. (518) 523-9927. Cuisine: French. Credit cards: AE, MC, VISA.

LARCHMONT

THE CABBAGE PATCH....1995 Palmer Ave., Larchmont, N.Y., 10538. (914) 834-2999. Cuisine: French. Owner: Chris Wilkinson. Open Tuesday through Sunday. Credit cards: All major. Private party facilities: 15 to 40. Annual sales: $250,000 to $500,000. Total employment: 10 to 15. Corporate name: Le Carre de Choux Ltd.

CARL'S....121 Myrtle Blvd., Larchmont, N.Y., 10538. (914) 834-1244. Cuisine: American.

DONAGHY'S CARRIAGE INN....2071 Boston Post Rd., Larchmont, N.Y., 10538. (914) 834-2577. Cuisine: American. Credit cards: All major.

HARRY'S SAUTEUSE....1885 Palmer Ave., Larchmont, N.Y., 10538. (914) 834-5526. Cuisine: French. Credit cards: AE.

LA COTE D'ARGENT....2047 Boston Post Rd., Larchmont, N.Y., 10538. (914) 834-2310. Cuisine: French. Credit cards: All major.

LARCHMONT TAVERN....104 Chatsworth Ave., Larchmont, N.Y., 10538. (914) 834-9821. Cuisine: American.

LA RISERVA....2382 Boston Post Rd., Larchmont, N.Y., 10538. (914) 834-5584. Cuisine: Northern Italian. Owner's names: Carlo and Michael.

LE CARRE DE CHOUX....1995 Palmer Ave., Larchmont, N.Y., 10538. (914) 834-2999. Cuisine: French. Credit cards: All major.

MARIMO....158 Larchmont Ave., Larchmont, N.Y., 10538. (914) 834-9807. Cuisine: Japanese. Credit cards: All major.

P.K.'S....2094 Boston Post Rd., Larchmont, N.Y., 10538. (914) 834-4955. Cuisine: Italian/American. Owner: Peter F. Kane. Closed Sunday. No credit cards. Annual sales: $250,000 to $500,000. Total employment: 12. Corporate name: P.K.'s Pub, Inc.

TUNG HOY....1294 Boston Post Rd., Larchmont, N.Y., 10538. (914) 834-1934. Cuisine: Chinese. Credit cards: All major.

LEVITTOWN

CARUSO'S....2716 Hempstead Tpke., Levittown, L.I., N.Y., 11756. (516) PE 1-9828. Cuisine: Italian. Owner's name: Martin Harris. Credit cards: AE, MC, VISA, DC.

HUNAN....3112 Hempstead Tpke., Levittown, L.I., N.Y., 11756. (516) 731-3552. Cuisine: Chinese.

LA ZINGARA....2934 Hempstead Tpke., Leavittown, L.I., N.Y., 11756. (516) 579-4566. Cuisine: Italian. Owner: Joe Zingara. Credit cards: MC, VISA.

LEWISTON

DONNA FELICIA'S....490 Center St., Lewiston, N.Y., 14092. (716) 764-7901. Cuisine: Italian. Owner: Samuel J. Shensi, Pres. Open for dinner Wednesday through Sunday. Credit cards: AE, MC, VISA. Annual sales: $250,000 to $500,000. Total employment: 14

LITTLE NECK

ATTILIO'S....59-28 Little Neck Pkwy., Little Neck, L.I., N.Y. 11363. (212) 224-5715. This pleasant place, hosted by owner-chef Attilio Vosilla and his hospitable wife Yolanda, has proven to be a worthwhile addition to the Northern-Italian eat beat, with a country atmosphere favoring leisurely enjoyment. Specialities include: seafood pasta; thin noodles with finely chopped smoked salmon and lumachella boscaiola. Open for lunch and dinner, 6 days. Closed on Sunday. Prices are moderate. Owners: Attilio and Yolanda Vosilla. Credit cards: All major. Reservations: Accepted. Private party facilities. Annual sales: $500,000. Total employment: 9.

LA BARAKA....255-09 Northern Blvd., Little Neck, L.I., N.Y., 11363. (212) 428-1461. Cuisine: Moroccan. Credit cards: AE, MC, VISA.

RAY'S....253-17 Northern Blvd., Little Neck, N.Y., 11636. (212) 225-0336. Cuisine: Italian. Credit cards: All major.

LOCUST VALLEY

CAMINARI'S RESTAURANT....1 Buckram Rd., Locust Valley, N.Y., 11560. (516) 671-2425. Cuisine: Continental. Owner: Franco Vitellozzi. Closed Tuesday; Open for lunch and dinner all other days; Dinners only on Sundays. Credit cards: All major. Annual sales: $500,000 to $1 million. Total employment: 30. Corporate name: Vicaro Foods Corporation.

LOCUST VALLEY INN....225 Birch Hill Rd., Locust Valley, L.I., N.Y., 11560. (516) 676-5377. Cuisine: Continental. Credit cards: All major.

LONG ISLAND CITY

PRUDENTI'S VICIN-O-MARIE....51-02 2 St., Long Island City, N.Y., 11101. (212) 729-7572. Cuisine: Italian. Owner: Anthony Prudenti. Open 7 days. Credit cards: All major. Private party facilities: 30 to 100. Annual sales: $500,000 to $1 million. Total employment: 50. Corporate name: Prudenti's Vicino Mare.

WATER FRONT CRAB HOUSE....2-03 Borden Ave., Long Island City, Queens, N.Y. 11101. Decor is in the old fish-house tradition, with rustic walls of brick and stucco trimmed in seasoned wood, hung with representation of denizens of the deep and an artless confusion of pictures, mock wine barrels, sea nets, and so on. The fish is always fresh—if it's not in season, it's not on the menu. Only the two-pound special lobster tail is the exception, but it's the bigget, most rewarding tail you'll ever encounter. Other tempting creations of brook and ocean include: *Bouillabaise* replete with whole lobster, and the hot seafood antipasto—a large platter of shrimps stuffed with crabmeat, fried fish filets, stuffed clams, calamari, and fried zucchini, covered with a light, flavorsome *marinara* sauce. Owner: Anthony Mazzarella . Open 7 days for lunch and dinner. Prices are moderate. Reservations are necessary on Friday and Saturday. Credit cards: All major. Private party facilities are available. Corporate name: Borden Avenue Restaurant, Inc. Entertainment: Nightly ranging from jazz through opera to dixieland.

LYNBROOK

PAPA NANI'S....161 Union Ave., Lynbrook, L.I., N.Y., 11563. (516) 887-1911. Cuisine: Italian. Owner's name: Gerard P. Nani. Credit cards: AE, MC, VISA, DC.

MAMARONECK

CASA DE NIKOLA....576 Mamaroneck Ave., Mamaroneck, N.Y., 10543. (914) 381-2244. Cuisine: Continental. Credit cards: All major.

CHEF ANTONIO'S....551 Halstead Ave., Mamaroneck, N.Y., 10543. (914) 698-8610. Cuisine: Italian. Credit cards: AE.

CHINA LION....1160 West Boston Post Rd., Mamaroneck, N.Y., 10543. (914) 381-2320. Cuisine: Chinese. Owner's name: Messrs. Poon and Chou. Credit cards: All major.

CRAB SHANTY....1521 East Boston Post Rd., Mamaroneck, N.Y., 10543. (914) 698-1352. Cuisine: Seafood.

JONATHAN SEAGULL....181 East Boston Post Rd., Mamaroneck, N.Y., 10543. (914) 698-6610. Cuisine: American. Credit cards: All major.

LA CANTINA....1137 West Boston Post Rd., Mamaroneck, N.Y., 10543. (914) 698-5584. Cuisine: Italian. Credit cards: All major.

LUM YEN....100 West Boston Post Rd., Mamaroneck, N.Y., 10543. (914) 698-6881. Cuisine: Chinese. Credit cards: All major.

MAGUIRE'S....532 West Boston Post Rd., Mamaroneck, N.Y., 10543. (914) 698-7237. Cuisine: Continental. Open 7 days for lunch and dinner. Credit cards: All major. Annual sales: $500,000 to $1 million. Total employment: 20.

RICH'S PASTA HOUSE....690 Mamaroneck Ave., Mamroneck, N.Y., 10543. (914) 698-4263. Cuisine: Pasta/Seafood/Steak. Open for lunch and dinner 7 days. Credit cards: MC, VISA. Private party facilities: Up to 100. Annual sales: $250,000 to $500,000. Total employment: 7.

TALK OF THE TOWN....1115 Northern Blvd., Manhasset, N.Y., 11030. (516) 627-5415. And rightly named—it is the talk of Manhasset, as restaurants go. That's partly due to the stunning 21st century decor, featuring turrets, skylights, mirrors, and black and plum-colored velvet. And party due to the good food, which may be the definitive ''American Continental.'' Specialities include: coconut fried shrimps, the seafood salad, gazpacho, chicken a la Talk of the Town, baby rack of lamb Persillee (for one), *Jaegerschnitzel*, and red snapper. Owner: John Karayiannis. Open Monday through Friday for lunch; 7 days for dinner. Priced moderate to high. Reservations are suggested. Credit cards: All major. Private party facilities: 50 to 200. Annual sales: $1 million to $3 million. Total employment: 40. Corporate name: 1155 Restaurant, Inc.

MANHATTAN

A BIENVENUE....21 East 36 St., New York, N.Y., 10016. (212) 684-0215.

A BIENTOT BISTRO....9 Barrow St., New York, N.Y., 10014. (212) 924-3583. Cuisine: Bistro French. Open daily for lunch and dinner. Credit cards: Call for cards.

ABRUZZI....37 West 56 St., New York, N.Y., 10019. (212) 489-8110. Cuisine: Abruzzi style Italian. Owner's name: Anthony.

ADAMS RIB....23 East 74 St., New York, N.Y., 10021. (212) 371-8650. Cuisine: American. Owner's name: N.A. Nichols. Annual sales: $500,000 to $1 million. Total employment: 20.

AKBAR RESTAURANT....475 Park Ave., New York, N.Y., 10022. (212) 838-1717. Cuisine: Indian. Owner: A.N. Malhotra. Annual sales: $750,000. Total employment: 20. Corporate name: M.K. Catering Consulting, Inc.

AKITA....12 East 44 St., New York, N.Y., 10017. (212) 697-0342. Owner's name: Eddie Abba.

AVEGERINOS... One Citicorp Cntr., 153 East 53 St., New York, N.Y., 10022. (212) 688-8828. Cuisine: Greek. Owner: Michael Avergrinos. Open 7 days for lunch and dinner. Credit cards: All major. Private party facilities: 6-30. Annual sales: $500,000 to $1 million. Total employment: 18.

A LA FOURCHETTE....342 West 46 St., New York, N.Y., 10036. (212) 245-9744. This long-established brownstone-basement (on the western fringe of theaterdom) is presided over by James Cremonini, noted for his remarkable French-Italian specialties such as duckling *Brigarde*, briny *moules mariniere*, fragrantly delicious seafood *Brecy*, and also for his ability to radiate cheer as well as pour it. Reservations are always in order Pre- and after-theater dinners are popularly priced. Open Monday through Friday for lunch; Monday through Saturday for dinner; Closed Sunday. Credit cards: AE, CB, DC. Private party facilities: 15 to 18. Total employment: 15. Corporte name: Fourchette Restaurant, Inc.

ALFREDO THE ORIGINAL OF ROME...153 East 53 St., New York, N.Y., 10022. (212) 371-3367. A popular Italian restaurant in the base of the Citicorp Center decorated in modern functionality. Where the decor is sharp edges, smooth lines, and primary colors, the cuisine is fresh, knowingly prepared, and lushly eye-appealing. Specialties include: Chicken with lemon and mushroom sauce, veal *milanese*, veal *piccata*, and their famous *fettucine Alfredo*. Owner Guido Bellanca. Open 7 days for lunch and dinner. Priced moderately. Reservations: Accepted. Credit cards: All major. Corporate name: Alfredo the Original of Rome (NY), Inc.

ALGONQUIN....59 West 44 St., New York, N.Y., 10036. (212) 840-6800. Managing Director: Andrew Anspach.

ALLEGRO CAFE.... Avery Fisher Hall, Lincoln Ctr., New York, N.Y., 10023. (212) 874-7400. Cuisine: American/Continental. Credit cards: AE, DC, MC, VISA.

AMERICAN CHARCUTERIE....CBS Bldg., West 52 St. & Ave. of the Americas, New York, N.Y., 10019. (212) 751-5152. Owner's name: Peter Ashkanizy.

ANDREE'S....354 East 74 St.,·New York, N.Y., 10021. (212) 249-6619. Cuisine: Mediterranean. Owner's names: Andree and Charles Abramoff. Total employment: 3.

ANGELINA'S....41 Greenwich Ave., New York, N.Y., 10011. (212) WA 9-1255. Cuisine: Italian. Credit cards: AE, DC.

ANNAPURNA....108 Lexington Ave., New York, N.Y., 10016. (212) 679-1284. Cuisine: Indian. Owner's name: Thomas Thoppil. Total employment: 15.

ANTICA ROMA....40 Mulberry St., New York, N.Y., 10013. (212) 267-2242. Cuisine: Italian. Credit cards: DC, MC.

ANTOLOTTI'S....337 East 49 St., New York, N.Y., 10017. (212) 688-6767. Cuisine: Northern Italian. Owner's name: Mr. Antolotti.

APPLAUSE....360 Lexington Ave., New York, N.Y., 10016. (212) 687-7267. Cuisine: American/Continental.

ARARAT....4 East 36 St., New York, N.Y., 10016. (212) 686-4622. Cuisine: Middle Eastern/American. Owner: Peter Jivekian.

ARIRANG HOUSE....28 West 56 St., New York, N.Y., 10019. (212) 581-9698. Cuisine: Korean. Owner's name: Jung Hoon Cha. Annual sales: $500,000 to $1 million. Total employment: 17.

ARNOLDS TURTLE CAFE....51 Bank St., New York, N.Y., 10012. (212) 242-5623. Cuisine: Vegetarian Gourmet. Owner: Ingrid De Hart and Arthur Fine. Open 7 days for lunch and dinner. Credit cards: MC, VISA. Seats 45. Annual sales: $250,000 to $500,000. Total employment: 30. Corporate name: Arnolds Turtle Cafe, Inc.

THE ASSEMBLY....16 West 51 St., New York, N.Y., 10020. (212) 581-3580. The bill-of-fare is dominated by steak and lobsters, but offers a diversity of poultry, fish and chops within a smartly devised atmosphere. The consequence is a profusion of not only American fare but a parade of savory dishes to please the adventuresome as well as the more timid tastes of diners. Owner: Jerry Ossip, Bal Golden, Brad Ossip. Open Monday through Friday for lunch; Monday through Saturday for dinner; Closed Sunday. Priced moderate to high. Reservations: Suggested. Credit cards: All major. Private party facilities: 20 to 40. Corporte name: Guardian Food Services, Inc.

ASTI....13 East 12 St., New York, N.Y., 10011. (212) 242-9868. Cuisine: Italian. Owner's name: Augusto Mariani. Total employment: 40.

AUBERGE SUISSE....153 East 53 St., (Citicorp Cntr), New York, N.Y., 10022. (212) 421-1420. Cuisine: Swiss. Owner's names: Hans Egg and Robert Keller. Credit cards: All major.

AUCTIONS....1406 Third Ave., New York, N.Y., 10021. (212) 535-2333. Cuisine: Steakhouse. Credit cards: AE, MC, VISA.

AU MANOIR....120 East 56 Street, New York, M.Y., 10022. (212) PL3-1447. Charming, hospitable, sound and long established. The chef cooks French specialties carefully and well. Good value prices prevail for both *a la carte* lunch and *table d'hote* dinner. Owner: Robert Treboux. Open 6 days for lunch and dinner; Closed Sunday. Priced moderate to high. Reservations: Suggested. Credit cards: All major. Private party facilities: 10 to 50. Annual sales: $500,000 to $1 million. Total employment: 15. Corporate name: Le Manoir, Inc.

THE BAILEY SEAFOOD HOUSE....203 East 45 St., New York, N.Y., 10017. (212) 661-3530. Cuisine: Seafood. Owner's name: Joe Benvenuto. Annual sales: $500,000 to $1 million. Total employment: 15. Corporate name: Bailey's Rest Corp.

BALKAN ARMENIAN....129 East 27 St., New York, N.Y., 10016. (212) MU 9-7925. Cuisine: Mid-Eastern/Armenian. Owner: Ervant O. Berberian. Open Monday to Friday for lunch; Monday to Saturday for dinner. Credit cards: AE, CB, DC, VISA. Private party facilities: Available Sunday for 50 to 75. Annual sales: $ 250,000 to $500,000. Total employment: 16.

BALLATO....55 East Houston St., New York, N.Y., 10002. (212) CA 6-9683. Cuisine: Italian. Credit cards: None.

BANGKOK CUISINE....885 Eighth Ave., New York, N.Y., 10019. (212) 581-6370. Cuisine: Thai. Owner: Nrith Kricanakarin.

BANGKOK 54....261 West 54 St., New York, N.Y. 10019. (212) 582-6640. Cuisine: Thai.

BARBETTA....321 West 46 St., New York, N.Y., 10036. (212) 246-9171. One of New York's outstanding Italian institutions , established in 1906 and still run by the founding family. Extremely popular in summer for its stunning outdoor garden dining, and in winter season for its fresh white truffles and piemonte dishes. It is much loved by locals and out-of-towners. Other houses specialties include: bagna cauda, fonduta con tartufi, and bolliti misti. Open for lunch and dinners, 7 days. Owner: Laura Maiglio. Credit cards: All major. Reservations: accepted. Private party facilities. Total employment: 60.

BAR ESPANOL....318 West 23 St., New York, N.Y., 10011. (212) 691-0529. Cuisine: Spanish: Owner: Mr. Prieto.

BEATRICE INN RESTAURANT....285 West 12 St., New York, N.Y., 10014. (212) 929-6165 or (212) 243-9826. In the same spot for some 50 years, Beatrice Inn is an old favorite among devotees of Italian cuisine, where "personal" cooking is stressed by Elsie and Ubaldo Cardia, owners of the amiable Greenwich Village restaurant. Not the least rewarding feature of Beatrice Inn's menu are the prices. They are down to earth. Specialties include: Veal *scallopine piccata,* home made *cannelloi,* shrimps *alla marinara,* broiled sweetbreads with lemon butter sauce. Open Monday through Friday for lunch; Monday through Saturday for dinner; Closed Sunday. Price: Moderate. Reservations: Accepted. Credit cards: All major. Private party facilities: 10 to 50. Annual sales: $250,000 to $500,000. Total employment: 12. Corporate name: Beatrice Inn, Inc.

BEGGAR'S BANQUET....125 West 43 St., New York, N.Y., 10036.(212) 997-0959. Cuisine: American/ Continental. Owner: Gene & Paul Lucarini. Open 6 days for lunch and dinner; Closed Sundays. Credit cards: AE. Private party facilities: Up to 90.

BEIRUT....43 West 32 St., New York, N.Y., 10001. (212) 840-9154.

BELCREP....47 West 44 St., New York, N.Y., 10036. (212) 840-1804. Cuisine: French and Italian. Owner: Donald J. Alonzo. Open for lunch and dinner Monday through Saturday. Credit cards: AE, MC, VISA. Annual sales: $250,000 to $500,000. Total employment: 6.

BEN BENSON'S....123 West 52 St., New York, N.Y., 10019. (212) 581-8888. This is a new West Side steakhouse that for the most part bears the best resemblance to the ideal combination of bar and restaurant in town. Specializing in lots of well-aged over-sized steaks, lobsters, veal and chicken dishes, and some exceedingly good salads. Open 7 days for lunch and dinner. Priced moderate to high. Reservations: Suggested. Credit cards: All major. Corporate name: Bell Restaurateurs.

BENIHANA OF TOKYO, EAST....120 East 56 St., New York, N.Y., 10019. (212) 593-1627. Cuisine: Japanese Steakhouse. Credit cards: AE, CB, DC, MC.

BENIHANA PALACE....15 West 44 St., New York, N.Y., 10036. (212) 682-7120. Cuisine: Japanese Steakhouse. Credit cards: AE, CB, DC, MC.

BENITO II....163 Mulberry St., New York, N.Y., 10013. (212) 226-9012. Cuisine: Italian. Owner: Gina Giacalone. Credit cards: None.

BERNARD'S....218 West 48 St., New York, N.Y., 10036. (212) 560-8058.

BERNSTEIN-ON-ESSEX-STREET....135 Essex St., New York, N.Y., 10002. (212) GR 3-3900. Cuisine: Jewish Deli. Credit cards: None.

BERRYS....180 Spring St., New York, N.Y., 10012. (212) 226-4394. Cuisine: Continental. Owner: Berry Reisdorff. Credit cards: AE, MC, VISA.

BIANCHI & MARGHERITA....186 West Fourth St., New York, N.Y., 10012. (212) 741-9712. Cuisine: Italian. Owner's name: Mr. F. Fagnani.

BILL HONG'S....133 West 52 St., New York, N.Y., 10019. (212) 581-6730. Cuisine: Cantonese.

BIS....1626 York Ave., New York, N.Y., 10028. (212) 737-4211. Cuisine: French. Owner: Suzanne Cadgene. Credit cards: AE, DC, MC, VISA.

BISTRO MONTMARTRE....206 West 79 St., New York, N.Y., 10024. (212) 874-1222. Cuisine: French.

THE BLACK SHEEP....344 West 11 St., New York, N.Y., 10014. (212) 242-1010. Cuisine: French Country cooking. Owner: Michael Safdiah. Open 7 days for dinner. Credit cards: AE, MC, VISA. Annual sales: $500,000 to $1 million. Total employment: 25. Corporate name: The Black Sheep Cafe, Inc.

BLUE FOX....131 Eighth Ave., New York, N.Y., 10011. (212) 929-7183. Cuisine: Continental. Owner: Frank Irizarry. Open Monday through Friday for lunch; 7 days for dinner; Sunday brunch. Credit cards: All major.

BLUE MILL TAVERN....50 Commerce St., New York, N.Y., 10014. (212) 243-7114.

BLUEPRINT 100....100 Park Ave., New York, N.Y., 10017. (212) 684-4500. Cuisine: Continental/Italian. Total employment: 41.

BO BO....20½ Pell St., New York, N.Y., 10013. WO2-9458. Cuisine: Chinese.Credit cards: None.

BOMBAY PALACE....30 West 52 St., New York, N.Y., 10019. (212) 541-7777. Cuisine: Indian. Owner: Sant S. Chatwal. Credit cards: All major.

BONDINI'S....62 West Ninth Street., New York, N.Y., 10011. (212) 777-0670. This is a medium-priced restaurant, cooking definitely well and with a fine cellar which boasts some memorable vintages. The chef cooks with affection and skill, providing a wide range of Northern Italian dishes. And it is a warm, friendly, informal place we have long recommended. House specialties include: Seafood fra diavolo; veal filleto in mustard sauce and veal chops cardinale. Open for lunch and dinner, 6 days. Closed on Sunday. Owner: Anselmo Bondulich. Credit cards: All major. Reservations: Accepted. Private party facilities. Entertainment: Piano. Annual sales: $500,000. Total employment: 10.

BOODLE'S....1478 First Ave., New York, N.Y., 10021. (212) 628-0900.

BOX TREE....250 East 49 St., New York, N.Y., 10017. (212) 758-8320. Cuisine: French/Continental. Owner: Augustin Paege. Open for lunch Monday to Friday; for dinner Monday to Sunday. Credit cards: None. Private party facilities: Up to 16. Total employment: 13.

BRASILIA....7 West 45 St., New York, N.Y., 10036. (212) 869-9200. Owner's name: Frank Yoshioka.

BRASSERIE....100 East 53 St., New York, N.Y., 10022. (212) 751-4840. Cuisine: French. Credit cards: All major.

BRAZILIAN COFFEE....45 West 46 St., New York, N.Y., 10036. (212) 719-2105. Cuisine: Brazilian/Portuguese. Owner: Alfredo Pedro. Credit cards: All major. Total employment: 10. Corporate name: Chateau De Lisboa Ret. Inc.

THE BRAZILIAN PAVILION....316 East 53 St., New York, N.Y., 10022. (212) PL8-8129. Cuisine: Brazilian and Portuguese. Owner: Joaquin Gonzales. Open 6 days for lunch and dinner; Closed Sundays. Credit cards: All major. Private party facilities: Up to 60. Annual sales: $500,000 to $1 million. Total employment: 14.

BRETT'S....304 East 78 St., New York, N.Y., 10021. (212) 628-3725. Is a tiny captivating pink jewelbox, supervised by an English couple who do a remarkable job for particular people. It's noted for fresh filet of sole, escargots, tournado *Antoine*, succulent mushroom caps stuffed with crabmeat, and homemade desserts. Brett's is open for dinner nightly, except Sunday and Monday, at good value prices. Cuisine is Continental and the kitchen closes at 10:30. Owner: Margaret and Andy Cavaciuti. Credit cards: AE, DC, MC, VISA. Reservations: Accepted. Total employment: 6.

BREW'S....156 East 34 St., New York, N.Y., 10016. (212) 889-3369. Cuisine: American. Owner: Richard Brew. Annual sales: $1 million to $3 million. Total employment: 41.

BRIDGE CAFE....279 Water St., New York, N.Y., 10038. (212) 227-3344. Cuisine: American. Open 7 days for lunch and dinner. Credit cards: None. Annual sales: $500,000 to $1 million. Corporate name: Sanwep Restaurant Corporation.

BRISTOL....1632 Second Ave., New York, N.Y., 10028. (212) 988-1424.

BRITTANY DU SOIR....800 Ninth Ave., New York, N.Y., 10019. (212) 265-4820. Cuisine: French. Owner: Gilbert.

BROADWAY BAY....2178 Broadway, New York, N.Y., 10024. (212) 362-5234.

BROADWAY JOE'S STEAK HOUSE....315 West 46 St., New York, N.Y., 10036. (212) 246-6513. Cuisine: Steak House. Owner's name: Sid Zion.

BRUCE HO'S FOUR SEAS....116 East 57 St., N.Y., 10022. (212) 753-2610. Cuisine: Chinese. Owner: Bruce Ho. Credit cards: AE, DC, VISA. Private party facilities: Up to 14. Annual sales: $250,000 to $500,000. Total employment: 28.

BRUNO....240 East 58 St., New York, N.Y., 10022. (212) 688-4190. Cuisine: Northern Italian. Annual sales: $1 million to $3 million. Total employment: 25

BUCHBINDER'S....375 Third Ave., New York, N.Y., 10016. (212) 929-4377. Cuisine: Continental.

CABANA CARIOCA....123 West 45 St., New York, N.Y., 10036. (212) 581-8088. Cuisine: Brazilian. Open daily for lunch and dinner. Credit cards: Call for cards.

CAFE ARGENTEUIL....253 East 52 St., New York, N.Y., 10022. (212) 753-9273. Cuisine: French. Owner's names: Andre Mailhan and Claude Uson. Total employment: 65.

CAFE DE FRANCE....3230 West 46 St., New York, N.Y., 10036. (212) 586-0088. Cuisine: French. Owner's name: Rodger Bonnet. Total employment: 9.

CAFE DES ARTISTES....1 West 67 St., New York, N.Y., 10023. Cuisine: French. Owner's name: George Lang.

CAFE DU SOIR....322 East 86 St., New York, N.Y., 10018. (212) AT 9-9996. Cuisine: French provincial. Owner: Claude Sarfati. Closed Monday; Open for lunch and dinner. Credit cards: AE, DC, MC, VISA. Total employment: 20.

CAFE ESPANOL....172 Bleecker St., New York, N.Y., 10012. (212) 475-9230. Cuisine: Spanish. Credit cards: AE, DC, MC.

CAFE EUROPA....347 East 54 St., New York, N.Y., 10022. (212) PL5-0160. Discloses the welcome of a polished, pretty continental spot, dishing out such memorable meals as beef Wellington, chicken Kiev or stuffed French brioches as big as melons. Cafe Europa, serving lunch, Monday through Friday and dinner Monday through Saturday, is in the moderate price range, meaning the nourishment is of a higher quality than the prices would suggest. Closed on Sunday. Owner Peter Colthup. Credit cards: All major. Reservations: Recommended. Annual sales: $500,000. Total employment: 15.

CAFE 58...232 East 58 St., New York, N.Y., 10022. (212) 758-5665. When funds are running low, this is excellent for a good square French meal with above-average cooking for the prices charged. Renowned locally for its sweetbreads, rabbit with mustard sauce, and tripe. Open for lunch Monday through Saturday, dinner Monday through Sunday. Prices are moderate. Owner: Jacques Pelletier. Credit cards: All major. Reservations: Accepted.

CAFE GEIGER....206 West 86 St., New York, N.Y., 10028. (212) RE4-4428. A find for anyone hungering for Germanic cookery at painless prices. No novelties, just the old favorites. There's lots of non-German dishes, too. It's an age-old place that's changed hands a few times, but it consistently remains true to its origins. Specialties include: *oschen maul, suelze, jaegerschnitzel,* Bavarian *sauerbraten,* broiled salmon, split pea soup—and any one of the sixty desserts which fill the front window and give the place the outward look of a real *konditorei.* Owner: Mihaly Vestergom. Open 7 days for lunch and dinner. Prices are inexpensive. Reservations: Accepted. Credit cards: All major. Private party facilities: 2 to 50. Annual sales: $1 million to $3 million. Total employment: 50. Corporate name: MSV Restaurant, Inc.

CAFE LA FONDUTA....120 East 57 St., New York, N.Y., 10022. (212) 935-5699. Cuisine: Italian.

CAFE REGINETTE....69 East 59 St., New York, N.Y., 10022. (212) 758-0530. Cuisine: French. Owner's name: Regine Zylberberg.

CAFE SAN MARTIN....1458 First Ave., New York, N.Y., 10021. (212) 288-0470. Cuisine: Italian. Owner's name: Francisco San Martin.

CAMELBACK & CENTRAL RESTAURANT....1403 Second Ave., New York, N.Y., 10021. (212) 249-8380. Cuisine: American Continental. Owner: Frank Visakay. Open 7 days for lunch, brunch and dinner.

CANTINA RESTAURANT....221 Columbus Ave., New York, N.Y., 10023. (212) 873-2606. Credit cards: Mexican.

CANTON....45 Division St., New York, N.Y., 10002. (212) 226-9173. Cuisine: Chinese. Open daily for lunch and dinner. Credit cards: Call for cards.

CAPSOUTO FRERES....451 Washington St., New York, N.Y., 10013. (212) 966-4900. Cuisine: French. Credit cards: AE.

CAPT. NEMO....137 West 72 St., New York, N.Y., 10023. (212) 595-5600. Most things about Capt. Nemo are on course, including the "galley." You dine amidst such maritime surroundings as a mock submarine framework fitted with copper and brass riveted walls, portholes, and other sea-going gear. A three-table cocktail area adjoins the bar up-front, in view of the open kitchen and the bubbling lobster-tank. Service is well-timed and you will neither be hurried nor left hunting. Specialties include: rolled oysters broiled in garlic butter, Florida Red Snapper, lobster curry, and crabmeat-stuffed filet of sole. Owner: Vicky Shockey. Open 7 days for lunch and dinner. Priced moderate to inexpensive. Reservations: Accepted. Credit cards: All major. Total employment: 12+. Corporate name: V.S.R. Corporation.

CAPTAIN NEMO....1131 Lexington Avenue, New York, N.Y., 10021. (212) 988-6756. An offshoot of the original Captain Nemo (above). This restaurant continues the sea-related decor theme, the bustling ambience, and the dynamic, especially fresh sea fare. Jules Verne's hero never had it so good. Specialties include: Shrimps stuffed with lobster and crabmeat, lobster curry, Florida Red Snapper, crabmeat-stuffed filet of sole. Owner: Vicky Shockey. Open 7 days for lunch and dinner. Priced moderate to inexpensive. Reservations: Accepted. Credit cards: All major. Corporate name: V.S.R. Corporation.

THE CAPTAIN'S TABLE....860 Second Ave., New York, N.Y., 10016. (212) 697-9538. Cuisine: Seafood. Open daily for lunch and dinner. Credit cards: Call for cards.

CARLOS 1 JAMAICAN SEAFOOD....432 Sixth Ave., New York, N.Y., 10003. (212) 982-3260. Cuisine: Jamaican.

CAROLINE'S....332 Eighth Ave., New York, N.Y., 10001. (212) 924-3499. Owner: Jack Stickney and Carl Christian.

CARROUSEL....1307 Third Ave., New York, N.Y., 10017. (212) 744-4978. Cuisine: French. Owner's name: Sam Arppis.

CASA BELLA....127 Mulberry St., New York, N.Y., 10013. (212) 431-4080. Cuisine: Italian. Owner: Mr. Polizotto.

CASA BRASIL....406 East 85 St., New York, N.Y., 10028. (212) 288-5284. Cuisine: Brazilian/Continental. Owner: Helma Skwarzinski. Closed Sundays. No credit cards. Private party facilities: Up to 24. Annual sales: $250,000. to $500,000. Total employment: 5.

CASTILIAN....303 East 56 St., New York, N.Y., 10022. (212) 688-6435. Cuisine: Spanish: Tony Rodriguez. Open 7 days for lunch and dinner. Credit cards: All major. Private party facilities: Up to 80. Corporate name: Castilian Restaurant, Inc.

THE CATTLEMAN....5 East 45 St., New York, N.Y., 10017. (212) 661-1200. Cuisine: Steakhouse/American.

CEDARS OF LEBANON....39 East 30 St., New York, N.Y., 10016. (212) 725-9251. Cuisine: Middle Eastern. Owner: Francois Hosri. Open 7 days for lunch and dinner. Credit cards: All major. Private party facilities: Up to 125. Annual sales: $250,000 to $500,000. Total employment: 5.

CELESTIAL EMPIRE....144 West 46 St., New York, N.Y., 10036. (212) 869-9183. Cuisine: Szechuan/Mandarin.

CENTRO VASCO....208 West 23 St., New York, N.Y., 10011. (212) 741-1408. Cuisine: Italian. Owner: Louis Ginorio.

CEYLON INDIA INN....148 West 49 St., New York, N.Y., 10019. (212) 730-9293. Cuisine: Indian. Owner: Rustom D. Wadia. Open 7 days for lunch and dinner. Credit cards: AE, DC. Private party facilities: 6 to 60. Annual sales: $150,000. Total employment: 10. Corporate name: Ceylon India Inn, Inc.

CHALET SUISSE....6 East 48 St., New York, N.Y., 10017. (212) 355-0855. Cuisine: Swiss. Owner: Konrad Egli. Open for lunch and dinner; Closed Saturdays, Sundays, and month of August. Credit cards: AE, MC, VISA. Private party facilities: Up to 140. Annual sales: $500,000 to $1 million. Total employment: 27.

CHANTERELLE....59 Grand St. (at Greene St.), New York, N.Y., 10013. (212) 966-6960. Cuisine: French. Open daily for lunch and dinner. Credit cards: Call for cards. Owner's names: David and Karen Waltuck.

CHAP'S....407 Eighth Ave., New York, N.Y., 10001. (212) 594-6305. Cuisine: American/Italian. Owner: Frank Aller.

CHARLEY O'S....33 West 48 St., New York, N.Y., 10036. (212) 582-7141. Cuisine: American. Owner: Peter Ashkanazy.

CHATEAU MADRID....511 Lexington Ave., New York, N.Y., 10017. (212) 752-8080. Cuisine: Spanish/Continental. Open 6 days for dinner; closed Monday. Credit cards: All major.

CHATEAU RUGGERO....461 West 23 St., New York, N.Y., 10011. (212) 242-8641. Cuisine: Italian. Owner's name: Ruggero Garsetti.

CHATFIELD'S....208 East 60 St., New York, N.Y., 10022. (212) 753-5070. Cuisine: Continental. Owner: Kim and Maureen Chatfield.

CHEERS....120 West 41 St., New York, N.Y., 10036. (212) 840-8810. Cuisine: American. Owner: Marty Feurstein.

CHEF HO'S HUNAN MANOR....1464 Second Ave., New York, N.Y., 10021. (212) 570-6700. Cuisine: Chinese. Credit cards: AE, DC, MC, VISA.

CHESHIRE CHEESE....319 West 51 St., New York, N.Y., 10019. (212) 765-0616. Cuisine: English. Credit cards: AE.

CHEZ NAPOLEON....365 West 50 St., New York, N.Y., 10019. (212) CO5-6980. Cuisine: French. Owner: Elyane Vaschetta. Open Monday through Friday for lunch; Monday through Saturday for dinner; Closed Sunday. Credit cards: All major. Annual sales: $250,000 to $500,000. Total employment: 10.

CHEZ VOUS....78 Carmine St., New York, N.Y., 10014. (212) 242-2676. Cuisine: Italian. Owner's name: Joseph Savarose.

CHINA BOWL RESTAURANT....152 West 44 St., New York, N.Y., 10036. (212) 582-3358. Cuisine: Chinese.

CHINA PAVILION....200 West 57 St., New York, N.Y., 10019. 246-6759. Cuisine: Chinese. Owner: Frank Ng.

CHINA ROYAL....17 Division St., New York, N.Y., 10002. (212) 226-0788. Cuisine: Chinese. Credit cards: None.

CHINA SONG....1705 Broadway, New York, N.Y., 10019. 246-6759. Cuisine: Chinese. Owner's name: Fred Ng.

CHIN YA....210 West 55 St., New York, N.Y., 10019. 586-0160. Cuisine: Japanese. Owner: Jim Okayama.

CHRIST CELLA....160 East 46 St., New York, N.Y., 10017. (212) 697-2479. Cuisine: Steakhouse. Owner's name: Mr. Cella.

CHRISTO'S STEAK HOUSE....143 East 49 St., New York, N.Y., 10017. (212) 355-2695. Cuisine: Steakhouse. Owner: Murry Kovant. Credit cards: AE, CB, DC.

CHRISTY'S SKYLIGHT GARDENS....West 11 St., New York, N.Y., 10011. (212) 673-5720. Cuisine: Continental. Owner's name: Mr. Christy.

CHUNG KUO YUAN....1115 Third Ave., New York, N.Y., 10021. (212) 371-9090. Cuisine: Chinese. Owner's name: David Keh. Credit cards: AE.

CIRO'S....1 Lincoln Plz., New York, N.Y., 10023. (212) 799-7722. Open Monday through Friday for lunch; 7 days for dinner. Price structure is expensive. Owner: Tony Cece. Credit cards: AE, DC, MC, VISA. Reservations: Accepted. Private Party Facilities.

CITY LUCK....127 East 54 St., New York, N.Y., 10022. (212) 832-2350. Cuisine: Cantonese/Hunan/Szechuan. Credit cards: All major. Owner: Danny Ceto. Annual sales: $1 million to $3 million. Total employment: 40.

CLAIRE....156 7th Ave., New York, N.Y., 10011. (212) 255-1955. Cuisine: American/Seafood. Owner: Carlos Hunter & Marvin Claire Paige. Open 7 days. Credit cards: AE, MC, VISA. Annual sales: $500,000 to $1 million. Total employment: 20. Corporate name: 7th Avenue Restaurant Corp.

COACH HOUSE....110 Waverly Pl., New York, N.Y., 10011. (212) 777-0303. A distinguished American establishment with a discerning and very constant clientele. Very carefully compiled wine list—elegantly simple service. Specialties include sublime racks of lamb, prime ribs of beef, and lobster. Open for dinner Tuesday through Sunday; Closed Monday. Prices are prix-fixe, avg. $30.00. Owner: Leon Lianides. Credit cards: All major. Reservations: Accepted. Annual sales $1 million to $3 million. Total employment: 33.

CONFETTI....816 Madison Ave., New York, N.Y., 10021. (212) 737-5151. Cuisine: Continental.

CLAUDE'S....205 East 81 St., New York, N.Y., 10028. (212) 472-0487. Cuisine: French. Owner: Claude Baills. Open for dinner, Monday to Saturday. Credit cards: AE, DC, MC, VISA. Annual sales: $500,000 o to $1 million. Total employment: 17.

RESTAURANT CLUB 1407....1407 Broadway, New York, N.Y., 10012. (212) 575-1407. Cuisine: Continental. Owner's names: David and Alan Nussbaum. Credit cards: All major. Total employment: 65.

THE COMMON GOOD....304 East 48 St., New York, N.Y., 10017. (212) 935-9840. A "with-it" place to eat American/Continental, prices reasonable, and quality gamble-proof. The piano bar is a popular rallying spot and a number of celebrated characters prop it up frequently. The menu provides such fare as: Hearty chili, Louisiana shrimp fry, and Deep South Barbequed ribs. Owner: Neal Modglin & Jim Graff. Open 7 days for lunch and dinner; Sunday brunch. Credit cards: AE only. Private party facilities: Up to 250. Annual sales: $500,000 to $1 million. Total employment: 35. Corporate name: 304 East 48 Street Restaurant, Inc.

COMPANY RESTAURANTS....365 Third Ave., New York, N.Y., 10016. (212) 523-5222. Beautifully cooked French/Italian and nouvelle cuisine served here—and naturally rewarding wines and surroundings to support them. Woo a delicate palate with an airy puff-pastry appetizer suspending a cloud of succulent crabmeat in golden parsley-flecked butter-sauce. One of the best main dishes is the duckling, memorable as a presentation platter defining the best of both worlds, nouvelle and traditional. This is also a happy site for the dessert lover. Owner: Carlos Vidal, Thomas Pollara. Open Monday through Friday for lunch; 7 days for dinner; Sunday brunch. Moderately priced. Reservations: Suggested. Credit cards: All major. Private party facilities: 15 to 100. Annual sales: $1 million to $3 million. Total employment: 35. Corporate name: Mathilda, Inc.

COPACABANA....10 East 60 Street, New York, N.Y., 10022. (212) PL5-6010. You'll find something old and something new at this legendary locale that has evolved into our city's unique, all-purpose catering facility accomodating from 75 to 1,000 guests for any type of festivity, party, occasion, or fantasy affair. A savvy local clientele uses this spot for weekday lunches—but this is the only "restaurant" meal offered by the New Copa. Owner: John Juliano, Peter Dorn, Ron Hollick. Open Monday through Saturday for lunch only; Closed Sundays; Private catered parties at other times. Priced moderate for lunch. Reservations are suggested. Credit cards: All major. Private party facilities: 30 to 1000. Annual sales: $1 million to $3 million. Total employment: 50. Corporate name: Dolron Restaurant, Inc.

COPENHAGEN RESTAURANT....68 West 58 St., New York, N.Y., 10019. (212) 688-3690. Cuisine: Scandinavian. Owner: Karen Plume & Sven E. Svenson. Open 6 days for lunch and dinner; Closed Sunday. Credit cards: All major. Annual sales: $500,000 to $1 million. Total employment: 28.

THE COPPER HATCH....247 West 72 St., New York, N.Y., 10023. (212) 799-8377. Cuisine: International. Owner: Michael Danon and Richard Dumas. Annual sales: $750,000. Total employment: 35. Corporate name: Spresso Cafe Inc.

COPPER HATCH II....308 Amsterdam Ave., New York, N.Y., 10024. (212) 724-6897. Cuisine: American/Continental. Owner: Michael Danon and Richard Dumas. Annual sales: $1 million. Total employment: 45. Corporate name: Lemi Inc.

CREPE SUZETTE....313 West 46 St., New York, N.Y., 10036. (212) 974-9002. Cuisine: French. Credit cards: AE, MC, VISA.

CSARDA....1477 Second Ave., New York, N.Y., 10021. (212) 472-2892. Cuisine: Hungarian. Owner: George. Credit cards: AE.

CURTAIN UP....402 West 43 St., New York, N.Y., 10036.(212) 564-7272.

CZECHOSLOVAK RESTAURANT VASATA....339 East 75 St., New York, N.Y., 10021. (212) 988-7166. Cuisine: Czech. Owner: Stan & Linda Petlan. Open 6 days: Closed Monday. Credit cards: All major. Annual sales: $250,000 to $500,000. Total employment: 12. Corporate name: Restaurant Vasata, Inc.

DA SILVANO....260 Sixth Av. New York, N.Y., 10014. (212) 982-0090. Cuisine: Italian. Credit cards: None.

DALLAS COWBOY....60 East 49 St., New York, N.Y., 10019. (212) 697--2500. Cuisine: American.

D'ANGELO'S....242 West 56 St., New York, N.Y., 10019. (212) 247-1070. Cuisine: Italian. Owner: Silvio Vosilla and Benito Latona. Credit cards: All major. Annual sales: $1 million. Total employment: 17.

DANGERFIELDS....1118 First Ave., New York, N.Y., 10021. (212) 593-1650. Cuisine: American. Owner: Rodney Dangerfield, A.R. Bevacqua. Open 7 days for dinner only. Credit cards: All major. Entertainment: Comedy and show acts at 9:15 PM and 11:15 PM; Dinner starts at 8:00 PM.

THE DARDANELLES....86 University Pl., New York, N.Y., 10003. (212) 242-8990. Cuisine: Armenian.

DAVID K'S....1115 Third Ave., New York, N.Y., 10021. (212) 371-9090. Cuisine: Chinese. Owner: David Keh. Open 7 days. Credit cards: AE, DC. Private party facilities: 20 to 100. Annual sales: $1 million to $3 million. Total employment: 34. Corporate name: 1115 Third Avenue Restaurant Inc.

DELEGATE....211 East 43 St., New York, N.Y., 10017. (212) 687-0980. Cuisine: Seafood/Steaks. Owner: Tom Manessis.

DELSOMA....266 West 47 St., New York, N.Y., 10036. (212) 757-9079. Cuisine: Italian. Owner: Frank Cardinale.

DEMARCHELIER...808 Lexington Ave., New York, N.Y., 10021. (212) 223-0047. Cuisine: French. Owner: Eric Demarchelier and Patrick. Credit cards: AE, DC, MC, VISA.

DERBY STEAKHOUSE....109 MacDougal St., New York, N.Y., 10012. (212) GR5-0520. Cuisine: Steak and seafood. Owner: Andrew Scarsi. Open 7 days for dinner. Credit cards: AE, DC, MC, VISA. Annual sales: $250,000 to $500,000. Total employment: 9.

DEVON HOUSE LTD.....1316 Madison Ave., New York, N.Y., 10028. (212) 860-8294. Cuisine: Continental. Open 7 days. Credit cards: AE, DC. Private party facilities: Up to 52. Total employment: 10. Corporate name: Devon House Ltd.

DEWEY WONG....206 East 58 St., New York, N.Y., 10022. (212) 758-6881. Cuisine: Chinese. Owner: Dewey Wong.

DEZALEY....54 East 58 St., New York, N.Y., 10022. (212) 755-8546. Cuisine: Swiss/Continental. Owner: Hans Egg and Robert Keller. Open for lunch Monday through Friday; Open for dinner 7 days. Closed Saturday during July and August. Credit cards: AE, DC, MC, VISA. Annual sales: $250,000 to $500,000. Total employment: 10.

DIMITRI....152 Columbus Ave., New York, N.Y., 10023. (212) 787-7306. Cuisine: Greek. Credit cards: All major.

DINO & HENRY'S....132 West 32 St., New York, N.Y., 10001. (212) 695-7995. Cuisine: Italian. Owner: Dino and Henry.

DI PINTO DI BLU....54 West 45 St., New York, N.Y., 10036. (212) 840-1284. Cuisine: Italian. Credit cards: All major.

DISH OF SALT....1211 Ave. New York, N.Y., 10036. (212) 921-424. This is a congenial restaurant that serves sophisticated Chinese cuisine solicitously in elegant but relaxed surroundings. Undisputed king of the menu is Peking duck, here a daily feature. Other noted specialties are plum squab, orange lamb, lobster cantonese. Lunch is served Monday through Friday, dinner Monday through Sunday. Prices are moderate to expense. Owners: Mary Ann and Kwong Lum. Credit cards: AE, DC. Reservations: Accepted. Private party facilities. Entertainment: Piano Tuesday -Saturday.

DIVINO....1556 Second Ave., New York, N.Y., 10028. (212) 861-1096. Cuisine: Italian.

DONA FLOR....140 West 46 St.,New York, N.Y., 10036. (212) 869-1298. Cuisine: Brazilian. Owner: Carlos Wattino.

DORIENTAL....128 East 56 St., New York, N.Y., 10022. (212) 688-80709. Cuisine: Chinese. Credit cards: AE, DC, MC.

DOWNEY'S....705 Eighth Ave., New York, N.Y., 10036. (212) 758-2272. Cuisine: American. Owner's name: Mr. Wiest.

DOWNING SQUARE....500 Lexington Ave., New York, N.Y., 10017. (212) 826-9730. When you walk in here, your nose tells you that good things are on the fire and your eyes rest on the subdued comfort of England's Regency period. Business booms at lunch; dinner is quieter and less crowded, more relaxing and more gratifying. Specialties include: Prime Chateaubriand for two in *bernaise* sauce, roast prime ribs of beef, broiled lobster tails, and shrimp *Santorini*. Owner: Peter Hagicostas. Open 7 days for lunch and dinner. Price: Moderate to high. Reservations: Suggested. Credit cards: All major. Private party facilities: Available.

DUBROVNIK....88 Madison Ave., New York, N.Y., 10016. (212) 689-7565. Cuisine: Continental-Yugoslavian. Owner: Ziggy. Open Monday to Friday for lunch, Monday to Saturday for dinner. Credit cards: All major.

DUMPLING HOUSE....207 Second Ave., New York, N.Y., 10011. (212) 473-8557. Cuisine: Chinese. Owner: Wilson Chang.

EAMON DORAN....998 Second Ave., New York, N.Y., 10022. (212) 752-8088. Cuisine: Irish. Owner: Eamon Doran.

EARTH ANGEL CAFE....611 Second Ave., New York, N.Y., 10016. (212) 684-9637. Cuisine: Vegetarian. Owner: Danta Bolletino & Haim Hassid. Open 7 days for lunch and dinner. Credit cards: All major. Private party facilities: Up to 42. Annual sales: $250,000 to $500,000. Total employment: 20. Corporate name: Earth Angel Cafe, Inc.

EDDIE ROBERTSON'S HELL'S KITCHEN....598 Ninth Ave., New York, N.Y., 10036. (212) 757-5329. Cuisine: American.

EDUARDO'S...1140 Second Ave., New York, N.Y., 10022. (212) MU8-7390. Cuisine: Italian. Credit cards: None.

ELAINE'S...1703 Second Ave., New York, N.Y., 10028. (212) 534-8103. Cuisine: Italian/American. Owner's name: Elaine Kaufman. Credit cards: AE.

EL CHARRO....4 Charles St., New York, N.Y., 10014. (212) 242-9547. Cuisine: Mexican/Spanish. Credit cards: AE, DC, MC, VISA.

EL COYOTE....774 Broadway, New York, N.Y., 10003. (212) 677-4291. Cuisine: Tex/Mex. Credit cards: VISA, MC, AE.

ELECTRA....949 Second Ave., New York, N.Y., 1002. (212) 421-8425. Cuisine: Greek/American. Owner: Nick Malacos. Open 7 days, 24 hours. No credit cards. Annual sales: $250,000 to $500,000. Total employment: 7.

ELEONORA....117 West 58 St., New York, N.Y., 10019. (212) 765-1427. Cuisine. Italian. Owner: Joe Lyttle. Lyttle.

ELEPHANT & CASTLE....68 Greenwich Ave., New York, N.Y., 10011. (212) 243-1400. Cuisine: American/Continental. Owner: Dr. George Schwartz.

EL CORTIJO....128 Houston St., New York, N.Y., 10012. (212) 674-4080. Cuisine: Spanish. Owner: Luis Trillo. Open 7 days. Credit cards: All major. Private party facilities: 10 to 50. Annual sales: $250,000 to $500,000. Total employment: 9.

ELEPHANT & CASTLE....183 Prince St., New York, N.Y., 10011. (212) 260-8600. Cuisine: American/Continental. Owner: Dr. George Schwartz.

ELIZABETH WHITE....987 First Ave., New York, N.Y., 10022. (212) PL9-7850. Cuisine: American. Owner: Elizabeth White. Credit cards: MC, VISA.

ELMER'S....1034 Second Ave., New York, N.Y., 10022. (212) 751-8020. Cuisine: Steakhouse. Credit cards: All major.

EL JEREZ....34 West 56 St., New York, N.Y., 10019. (212) 765-4535. Cuisine: Spanish. Owner: Mr. Castro.

EMILLO'S...167 East 33 St., New York, N.Y., 10016. (212) 684-3223. Cuisine: Italian. Open daily for lunch and dinner. Credit cards: Call for cards.

THE ENGLISH PUB....900 Seventh Ave., New York, N.Y., 10019. (212) 265-4360. Cuisine: English Pub Owner: Joe Bartolotta. Credit cards: All major.

ENTRE NOUS....396 Third Ave., New York, N.Y., 10016. (212) 679-0828. Cuisine: Continental. Credit cards: All major.

EL PARARDOR CAFE....325 East 34 St., New York, N.Y., 10016. (212) 679-6812. Cuisine: Mexican. Owner's names: Charles Jacott and Odulia Jacott. Corporate name: El Parardor Cafe Inc.

EL POTE ESPANOL....718 Second Ave., New York, N.Y., 10016. (212) 889-6680. Cuisine: Spanish. Owner: Enrico Torres. Open Monday through Friday for lunch; Open 6 days for dinner; Closed Sundays. Credit cards: All major. Total employment: 5. Corporate name: El Pote Espanol, Inc.

EL QUIJOTE....226 West 23 St., New York, N.Y., 10011. (212) 243-9934. Cuisine: Spanish. Owner: Manuel Muino.

EL RINCON DE ESPANA....226 Thompson Street, New York, N.Y., 10013. (212) 371-7777. Like its larger brother in the Wall Street area, the intimate Greenwich Village location serves tasty bargains in Spanish sustenance up to the limit of seating capacity, which, alas, isn't much, but it's comfortable nonetheless. Specialties include: *Paella* (three different versions), *camarones a la Carlos, costillas de cordero a la parrilla, arroz con pollo, filet de cerdo barbacoa con salsa de almendra, natilla, flan, guayaba con queso.* Owner: Julio Rivas, Carlos Ventoso. Open 7 days for dinner; Lunch on Sunday only. Reservations and all major credit cards accepted. Corporate name: Ventoriva, Inc.

EL RINCON DE ESPANA....82 Beaver Street, New York, N.Y., 10005. (212) 344-5228. Large Spanish restaurant. Blithe, colorful atmosphere; well-spaced tables; desire to please. Precisely the dishes you would expect, moderately priced. This location is larger than the intimate Greenwich Village original, but both serve the same quality food. It also has nightly entertainment: A spanish guitarist plays classical as well as modern selections, and on weekends a *Flamenco* group joins him. Specialties include: *paella Valencia, paella Valencia con langosta, paella Marinera, medallones de ternera con salsa de limon, filet de cerdo barbacoa con salsa de almendra, camarones a la Carlos.* Open Monday through Saturday for lunch and dinner; Closed Sunday. Accepting reservations and all major credit cards. Owner: Julio Rivas, Carlos Ventoso. Annual sales: $500,000 to $1 million. Corporate name: Ventoriva, Inc.

ESTIA....308 East 86 St., New York, N.Y., 10028. (212) 628-9100. Cuisine: Greek. Owner's name: Mr. Manza. Total employment: 12.

FACTOR'S FIND CAFE....470 West 23 St., New York, N.Y., 10011. (212) 691-1708. Cuisine: Continental. Credit cards: VISA, MC, AE.

FAREED....1384 First Ave., New York, N.Y., 10021. (212) 535-8598. Cuisine: Lebanese. Credit cards: All major.

FARMFOOD....142 West 49 St., New York, N.Y., 10019. (212) 719-1650. Open 6 days for breakfast, lunch, and dinner; Closed Friday night and Saturday until dusk. No credit cards. Private party facilities: Up to 190. Annual sales: $500,000 to $1 million. Total employment: 24

FASHION PLATE....566 Seventh Ave., New York, N.Y., 10018. (212) 354-0239. Owner: Susan Kate. Susan Kale.

FAYE AND ALLEN'S....1236 Third Ave., New York, N.Y., 10021. (212) 472-9666. Cuisine: Seafood/Steak. Credit cards: AE, DC.

FELIDIA RISTORANTE....243 East 58 St., New York, N.Y., 10022. (212) 758-1479. Cuisine: Northern Italian. Owner: Lidia and Felice Bastianich. Total employment: 16.

FERRARA....195 Grand St., New York, N.Y., 10013. (212) 226-6150. Cuisine: Italian Pastry. Owner: A. Anthony Lepore.

THE FIDDLER....135 West 50 St., New York, N.Y., 100109. (212) 581-7882. Cuisine: Continental.

FINE & SHAPIRO....138 West 72 St., New York, N.Y., 10023. (212) 877-2874. Cuisine: Delecatessen. Owner: Mr. Shapiro.

FIORELLA'S RISTORANTE....1081 Third Ave., New York, N.Y., 10021. (212) 838-7570. Cuisine: Italian. Owner: Mr. Shelly Fireman. Open 7 days for lunch and dinner. Credit cards: AE, MC, VISA. Corporate name: Caffe Concepts, Inc.

FIORELLO ROMAN CAFE....1900 Broadway, New York, N.Y., 10023. (212) 595-5330. Cuisine: Italian.

FISHERMAN'S NET....493 Third Ave., New York, N.Y., 10016. (212) 532-1683. Cuisine: Seafood. Owner's name: Ron Conklin.

FLOWER DRUM....856 Second Ave., New York, N.Y., 10017. (212) 697-4280. Cuisine: Chinese. Owner's name: Peter Lee.

FONDA LA PALOMA....256 East 49 St., New York, N.Y., 10017. (212) 421-5495. It's among our most savory encounters, and appears to be the headquarters of serious culinary values, becoming New York's ranking Mexican restaurant. Another of its triumphs is the intimate and glowing decor which wraps up all the romantic traditions of Mexico. Specialties include camarones a la fonda, chiles rellenos, and platillos combinacion. Prices are moderate. Open for dinner, 7 days. Lunch, Monday through Friday. Owner: Dinna Hernandez. Credit cards: All major. Reservations: Necessary. Entertainment: Strolling guitarists.

FONTANA DI TREVI....151 West 57 St., New York, N.Y., 10019. (212) CI7-5683. Cuisine: Italian. Owner: Armando Mei. Credit cards: AE, DC.

FOO CHOW....1278 Third Ave., New York, N.Y., 10021. (212) UN 1-4350. Cuisine: Chinese. Owner's name: Terry. Credit cards: AE, DC, MC.

FOOD AMONG THE FLOWER'S....18 West 56 St., New York, N.Y., 10019. (212) 541-9030.

FORLINI'S....93 Baxter St., New York, N.Y., 10013. (212) 349-6779. This is a thriving "Little Italy" spot where local judges, attorneys, and businessmen wash down lusty family-style Italian dishes with good Italian wines or beer. The all-red setting is intriguing and the service here is prompt and efficient. Specialties include: *Scaparelli* (for two), rolled shrimp in prosciutto, cheese, and mushrooms in white wine sauce; lobster combination *fra diavolo* (for two); and scampi of veal, chicken and eggplant *Cornuto.* Open 7 days for lunch and dinner except for first two weeks of August. Owner: Frank, Alfredo, and Hugo Forlini. Priced moderately. Priced moderately. Reservations: Suggested. Credit cards: All major. Annual sales: $1 million to $3 million. Total employment: 35. Corporate name: Forlini's Restaurant, Inc.

FORO-ITALICO....455 West 34 St., New York, N.Y., 10001. (212) 564-6619. Cuisine: Italian.

FORTUNE GARDEN....1160 Third Ave., New York, N.Y., 10021. (212) 744-1212. Cuisine: Chinese.

THE FOUR SEASONS....99 East 52 St., New York, N.Y., 10022. (212) 754-9494. The high-ceilinged dining room, with its square, graceful marble pool, is rather like a temple—so leisurely are the movements of the attendants, so ritualistic their performance with chafer and cradle, with corkscrew and coupe. It is of little consequence in terms of quality whether you eat fish or meat, game or poultry, the standards are unvarying. Specialties include: the entire menu. Open for lunch and dinner, 6 days. Also available: theater dinner, prix-fixe. Prices are expensive. Owners: Paul Kovi and Tom Margittai. Credit cards: All major. Reservations: A must. Private party facilities. Annual sales: $5 million plus. Total employment: 165.

FRANKIE & JOHNNIE....269 West 45 St., New York, N.Y., 10036. (212) 664-9566.

FRAUNCES TAVERN RESTAURANT....54 Pearl St., New York, N.Y., 10004. (212) 269-0144. Cuisine: American. Owner: Jackie Norden. Credit cards: AE, CB, DC.

FRENCH SHACK....65 West 55 St., New York, N.Y., 10019. (212) 246-5126. Cuisine: French. Owner: Alain Dupuis. Annual sales: $1 million. Total employment: 32.

FRERE JACQUES....151 West 48 St., New York, N.Y., 10036. (212) 575-1866. Cuisine: French.

FRIAR TUCK....914 Third Ave., New York, N.Y., 10022. (212) 688-4725. Cuisine: English. Credit cards: AE, VISA, CB, DC.

FRIDAY'S....1152 First Ave., New York, N.Y., 10021. (212) 832-8512. Cuisine: American. Owner: Al Stillman.

FUJI....238 West 56 St., New York, N.Y. 10019. (212) 245-8594. Cuisine: Japanese. Owner: Mr. Ohta.

GALLAGHER'S....228 West 52 St., New York, N.Y., 10019. (212) 245-5336. Cuisine: Steakhouse. Owner: Jerry Brody.

GARVIN'S....19 Waverly Pl., New York, N.Y., 10003. (212) 473-5261. A curious blending of charm and scruff. It's without doubt an oasis—not fireworks, but very sound in the moderate price range serving continental cuisine. Specialties include duckling with blueberry sauce, vigorous platters of stuffed trout with jumbo crabmeat, filet of beef *bernaise.* The dessert menu brings rewards of its own. Open 7 days for lunch and dinner; Sunday brunch. Owner: Richard Garvin. Credit cards: All major. Reservations: Requested. Private party facilities. Entertainment: Harp, Piano, Jazz & Vocals. Annual sales: $1½ million. Total employment: 45.

GAYLORD....50 East 58 St., New York, N.Y., 10022. (212) 759-1710. Cuisine: Indian.

GENE'S....73 West 11 St., New York, N.Y., 10011. (212) 675-2048. Cuisine: Continental/Italian. Owner: Albino Ramirez. Open 7 days for lunch and dinner. Credit cards: All major. Total employment: 6.

GENGHIZ KHAN'S BICYCLE....197 Columbus Ave., New York, N.Y., 10023. (212) 595-2138. Cuisine: Turkish.

GENOA RISTORANTE....271 Amsterdam Ave., New York, N.Y., 10023. (212) 787-1094. Cuisine: Italian. Owner: Mr. & Mrs. Robert J. Arena. Open 6 days for lunch and dinner; Closed Monday. Credit cards: AE, MC, VISA. Corporate name: Genoa Restaurant, Inc.

GEORGE MARTIN ...1420 Third Ave., New York, N.Y., 10028. (212) 968-4500. Cuisine: American. Credit cards: AE.

GEORGES REY....60 West 55 St., New York, N.Y., 10019. (212) 245-6764. Cuisine: French. Owner: Mr. & Mrs. Georges Rey. Open 7 days for lunch and dinner. Credit cards: AE, DC, MC, VISA. Private party facilities: Up to 30. Annual sales: $1 million to $3 million. Total employment: 30. Corporate name: Restaurant Francais, Inc.

GEORGIA'S....244 East 51 St., New York, N.Y., 10022. (212) 371-8888. Cuisine: French/Greek. Owner's name: Georgia. Credit cards: AE.

GIAMBELLI RESTAURANT....238 Madison Ave., New York, N.Y., 10016. (212) 685-8727 or (212) 685-8728. Cuisine: Italian. Owner: Rodolfo Cuppi & Mario Boselli. Open Monday through Friday for lunch; Monday through Saturday for dinner; Closed Sunday. Credit cards: All major. Annual sales: $1 million to $3 million. Total employment: 23.

GIAMBELLI 50TH....46 East 50 St., New York, N.Y., 10022. (212) 688-2760. Cuisine: Italian. Owner: Mario.

GIAN MARINO....221 East 58 St., New York, N.Y., 10022. (212) 752-1696. Cuisine: Italian. Owner: Giovanni Di Saverio. Open Tuesday through Sunday for dinner; Tuesday through Friday and Sunday for lunch. Credit cards: All major. Private party facilities: Only on Mondays; Up to 100. Annual sales: $1 million to $3 million. Total employment: 27.

GIBBON....24 East 80 St., New York, N.Y., 10024. (212) 861-4001. Cuisine: Japanese/French. Credit cards: AE, MC, VISA, DC.

GILL'S SEAFOOD....359 East 50 St., New York, N.Y., 10022. (212) 755-3552. Cuisine: Seafood. Owner: Ron Gilbert. Open 7 days for lunch and dinner. Credit cards: All major. Private party facilities: Up to 125. Annual sales: $500,000 to $1 million. Total employment: 15.

THE GINGER MAN....51 West 64 St., New York, N.Y., 10023. (212) 399-2358. This is the best culinary find within walking distance of Lincoln Center, attracting a heavy crowd before curtain time. Looks ordinary enough—like a provincial pub—but it is good. Mike O'Neal maintains a commendable standard and has some excellent American-Continental dishes. Specialties include: shrimp with ginger and scallions; rack of lamb and omelets. Open 7 days for lunch and dinner. Pricing is moderate to expensive. Owner: Mike and Patrick O'Neal. Credit cards: All major. Reservations: Accepted. Private party facilities. Entertainment: Jazz, Thursday, Friday, Saturday.

GINO'S....780 Lexington Ave., New York, N.Y., 10021. (212) 838-9827. Cuisine: Italian. Credit cards: None.

GIN-RAY....148 East 50 St., New York, N.Y., 10022. (212) 759-7454. Cuisine: Japanese. Owner: Hashimoto.

GIORDANO RESTAURANT....409 West 39 St., New York, N.Y., 10018. (212) 947-3883; 947-3884. Cuisine: Italian. owner: Lucio and Bruno Creglia. Open 7 days. Credit cards: All major. Private party facilities: 15 to 50. Annual sales: Over $3 million. Corporate name: Giordano Restaurant, Inc.

GIOVANNI'S ATRIUM....100 Washington St., New York, N.Y., 10006. (212) 344-3777. Cuisine: Italian. Owner: Giovanni Naralucci.

GIRAFE....208 East 58 St., New York, N.Y., 10022. (212) PL 2-3054. Cuisine: Italian. Credit cards: AE, VISA, DC, MC.

G. LOMBARDI....53 Spring St., New York, N.Y., 10012. (212) 226-9866. Cuisine: Italian.

GLOUCESTER HOUSE....37 East 50 St., New York, N.Y., 10022. (212) 755-7394. Cuisine: New England. Owner: Edmund C. Lillys. Open for lunch and dinner for 7 days. Credit cards: All major. Annual sales: $500,000 to $1 million. Total employment: 85.

GOLD COIN....835 Second Ave., New York, N.Y., 10017. (212) 697-1515. Cuisine: Chinese.

GOODALE'S....338 East 49 St., New York, N.Y., 10017. (212) PL5-7317. Cuisine: New England Seafood. Owner: Percy Goodale. Open for lunch and dinner. Closed Saturday and Sunday. Credit cards: AE, DC, MC, VISA. Total employment: 6.

GOOSE & GHERKIN....251 East 50 St., New York, N.Y., 10022. (212) 371-4636. Cuisine: American/Continental. Open 6 days for lunch and dinner; Closed Saturdays. Credit cards: All major. Private party facilities: 10 to 125. Annual sales: $250,000 to $500,000. Corporate name: PRP, INC.

GOTTLIEB'S....243 Bleecker St., New York, N.Y., 10014. (212) 929-7800. Cuisine: American. Owner's name: Mr. Gottlieb.

GRAND CENTRAL OYSTER BAR....Grand Central Station, 42 St., and Vanderbilt, New York, N.Y., 10017. (212) 532-3888. Cuisine: Seafood. Owner: Jerry Brody. Open for lunch and dinner Monday to Friday. Credit cards: All major. Private party facilities: 100-150. Annual sales: Over $3 million. Total employment: 120. Corporate name: Brody Corp.

GRANADOS....125 MacDougal St., New York, N.Y., 10012. (212) OR3-5576. Cuisine: Spanish. Open 7 days for lunch, dinner and weekend brunch. Credit cards: All major. Private party facilities: Monday to Thursday, up to 100.

GREAT AUNT FANNY....340 West 46 St., New York, N.Y., 10036. (212) 765-7374. Cuisine: American. Owner: Ron Pielli.

GREENE STREET....101 Greene Street, New York, N.Y., 10012. (212) 925-2415. A most beguiling architectural marvel, the design of which is highlighted by a soaring two-story mural and a raft of towering palms. It's not only a restaurant, but a supper-club, jazz spot, and art gallery. Then the serious business begins and the cuisine here is quite serious. The extensive menu of superior American *nouvelle* dishes include: a sublime wild mushroom soup, hot ballantine of duck, sauteed slices of Norwegian salmon, tender sauteed veal chop, poached turbot, and a rare breast of duck. Owner: R. Anthony Goldman. Open 7 days for dinner only; Sunday brunch. Priced expensive. Reservations: Suggested. Credit cards: All major. Private party facilities: Available.

GREENER PASTURES....117 East 60 St., New York, N.Y., 10023. (212) 355-3214. Cuisine: Vegetarian. Owner: Jerry. Credit cards: None.

GREGORY'S....1149 First Ave., New York, N.Y., 10021. (212) 371-2220. Cuisine: German snacks and sandwiches. Owner: Norman Silver. Open 7 days for dinner. Credit cards: All major. Annual sales: $250,000 to $500,000. Corporate name: 63rd & First Ave. Corp.

GROTTA AZZURRA....387 Broome St., New York, N.Y., 10013. (212) 226-9283. Cuisine: Italian. Owner: James and John D'Avino.

GUV'NOR....303 Madison Ave., New York, N.Y., 10017. (212) 867-0540. Cuisine: Steakhouse. Credit cards: AE, DC, MC.

HAKUBAI....66 Park Ave., New York, N.Y., 10016. (212) 686-3770. Cuisine: Japanese. Mr. K. Fujimoto, General Manager. Corporate name: Nadaman USA.

HAPPY FAMILY....1619 York Ave., New York, N.Y., 10028. (212) 650-0554. Cuisine: Chinese.

HARBOUR....303 West 48 St., New York, N.Y., 10036. (212) 586-4853. Cuisine: Thai.

HATSUHANA....17 East 48 St., New York, N.Y., 10017. (212) 355-3345. Cuisine: Japanese. Credit cards: All major.

HEE SEUNG FUNG....46 Bowery, New York, N.Y., 10013. (212) 374-1319. Cuisine: Chinese. Open daily for lunch and dinner. Credit cards: Call for cards.

HIME OF JAPAN....1185 Second Ave., New York, N.Y., 10021. (212) 355-4065. Cuisine: Japanese.

HISAE'S....45 East 58 St., New York, N.Y., 10022. (212) 753-6555. Originator of a unique culinary style that combines the exotic flavors of Eastern cookery with sophisticated international accents—plus an eagle-eye for fresh, healthful and vegetarian-oriented components. Specialties include: Sauteed chicken livers with mushrooms and onions, Red Snapper in garlic and butter sauce, *bouillabaise,* and curried shrimp. Owner: Mrs. Hisae Vilca, Herb Wetanson. Open Monday through Friday for lunch; 7 days for dinner. Priced moderately. Reservations are suggested. Accepts all major credit cards. Annual sales: $1 million to $3 million. Total employment: 35. Corporate name: Hgres Gourmet, Inc.

HOEXTER'S MARKET....1442 Third Ave., New York, N.Y., 10028. (212) 472-9322. It caters to the needs of those enamored of agreeably presented and well-prepared dinners, unblemished late suppers and disco dancers, who are permitted to storm the floor after 12:30 a.m. Specialties include: market steak, grilled baby chicken and Hoexter's chocolate cake. Open for dinner, 7 days. Prices are moderate to expensive. Owner: Stuart Lichtenstein, John Uzielli, and Robert Shapiro. Credit cards: All major. Reservations: Accepted.

HO-HO....131 West 50 St., New York, N.Y., 10019. (212) 246-3256. Cuisine: Chinese.

HOME VILLAGE RESTAURANT....20 Mott St., New York, N.Y., 10013. (212) 964-0380. Cuisine: Chinese. Owner: Eddie Chan & S.F. But. Open 7 days. No credit cards. Annual sales: $250,000 to $500,000. Total employment: 25. Corporate name: Home Village Restaurant, Inc.

HORN OF PLENTY....91 Charles St., New York, N.Y., 10014. (212) 242-0636. This combination restaurant, bar and cabaret in the heart of the West Village is a multi-level establishment, cool with large plants and greenery, warm with hospitable staff, and the unofficial headquarters of Southern expatriates at large in the city looking for home cookin'. The menu is an eclectic listing of not only soul, but international cuisine. You'll find ham hocks and pan-fried chicken sharing the page with veal scallopine and beef Stronganoff. Owner: David Williams, Mgr. Open 7 days for dinner only. Priced moderately. Reservations: Accepted. Credit cards: All major. Private party facilities: Available.

HO SHIM....120 West 44 St., New York, N.Y., 10036. (212) 575-9774.

H.S.F.....578 Second Ave., New York, N.Y., 10016. (212) 689-6969. Cuisine: Chinese. Credit cards: AE, MC, VISA.

HUNAM....845 Second Ave., New York, N.Y., 10017. (212) MU7-7471. Cuisine: Chinese. Credit cards: AE, VISA, DC.

HUNAN BALCONY....2596 Broadway, New York, N.Y., 10025. (212) 865-0400. Clean as a new pin and invitingly put together with glistening white stucco walls and green potted plants. Our sample meal of hacked chicken, ham and winter melon soup; whole crisp and golden sea bass; tender, lean roasted duck banana fritters lavishly filled with sweet bean paste and tea was excellent. Bargain prices for Hunan cuisine until you flock there and raise them! House specialties: sliced lamb Hunan-style; shrimp in chili sauce; boned sweet and tender crispy chicken. Open 7 days for lunch and dinner. Owner: David Chan. Credit cards: AE, DC, MC, VISA. Reservations: Accepted. Private party facilities. Total employment: 30.

HUNAN CAFE....214 Columbus Ave., New York, N.Y., 10023. (212) 595-5640. Cuisine: Chinese. Credit cards: AE, VISA, MC.

HURLEY'S STEAK & SEAFOOD....1240 Ave. of the Americas, New York, N.Y., 10020. (212) 765-8981. Cuisine: Steak/Seafood.

HUTTON'S INN....220 Madison Ave., New York, N.Y., 10016. (212) 683-7100. Cuisine: American. Owner: Herb Lipman.

HWA YUAN SZECHWAN INN....40 East Broadway, New York, N.Y., 10002. (212) 966-5534. Cuisine: Chinese. Credit cards: All major.

IL BOCCONICINO....168 Sullivan St., New York, N.Y., 10012. (212) 982-0329. Cuisine: Italian.

IL GALLETTO....120 East 34 St., New York, N.Y., 10016. (212) 889-1990. Cuisine: Italian. Credit cards: AE, VISA, MC.

IL GATTOPARDO....45 West 56 St., New York, N.Y., 10019. (212) 586-3978. Cuisine: Northern Italian. Owner: Mario Gattorna and Peter Chiattella.

IL MENESTRELLO....14 East 52 St., New York, N.Y., 10022. (212) 421-7588. Cuisine: Italian. Owner: Mr. Milan.

IL PESCATORE VENETO....56 West 56 St., New York, N.Y., 10019. (212) 245-9869. Cuisine: Northern Italian. Owner's name: Ferriclaio Hrvatin.

IL RIGOLETTO....232 East 53 St., New York, N.Y., 10022. (212) 759-9384. Cuisine: Italian. Owner's name: Marino.

IL VAGABONDO....351 East 62 St., New York, N.Y., 10021. (212) TE 8-9748. Cuisine: Italian. Credit cards: AE, CB, DC, MC.

INAGIKU....111 East 49 St., New York, N.Y., 10017. (212) 355-0440. Cuisine: Japanese. Credit cards: All major.

INDIAN OVEN....285 Columbus Ave., New York, N.Y., 10023. (212) 362-7567. Cuisine: Northern Indian. Owner: Prem Bhandari, Aman Suri, Betha Sehgal. Open 6 days for lunch and dinner; Closed Monday. Credit cards: All major. Annual sales: $250,000 to $500,000. Total employment: 10. Corporate name: The Indian Oven, Inc.

IPERBOLE....137 East 55 St., New York, N.Y., 10022. (212) 759-9720. Cuisine: Italian. Owner: Armando Mei.

IROHA....731 Seventh Ave., New York, N.Y., 10019. (212) 398-9049. Cuisine: Japanese.

ISLE OF CAPRI....1028 Third Ave., New York, N.Y., 10021. (212) 758-1828. Cuisine: Italian. Owner: Mr. Lamaler.

ITALIAN PAVILION....24 West 55 St., New York, N.Y., 10019. (212) 753-7295. Cuisine: Italian. Owner: Guido.

IZAKAYA....43 West 54 St., New York, N.Y., 10019. (212) 765-4683. Cuisine: Japanese.

JACK'S EPICURE....344 West 46 St., New York, N.Y., 10019. (212) LT1-3449. Cuisine: French/Italian. Open Monday through Friday for lunch; Monday through Saturday for dinner. Closed Sunday. Credit cards: All major. Reservations: Accepted.

JACK'S NEST....310 Third Ave., New York, N.Y., 10010. (212) 260-7110. Cuisine: Southern. Owner: Jack Berkowitz. Open 7 days for lunch and dinner. Credit cards: AE, MC, VISA. Private party facilities: 25 to 150. Annual Sales: $1 million to $3 million. Total employment: 50. Corporate name: Jube Restaurant, Inc.

JACQUELINE'S....132 East 61 St., New York, N.Y., 10021. (212) 838-4559. Cuisine: French *nouvelle*. Open Monday through Saturday for lunch and dinner; closed Sunday. Prices are moderate to expensive. Owner: Jacqueline Ferrero. Credit cards: All major. Reservations: Accepted. Private party facilities.

JANE STREET SEAFOOD CAFE....31 Eighth Ave., New York, N.Y., 10014. (212) 243-9237. Cuisine: Seafood. Owner: Jack. Credit cards: All major.

J. B. TIPTON....932 Second Ave., New York, N.Y., 10022. (212) 759-7800. Cuisine: Continental. Owner: George Malamas. Corporate name: Go-Mac Restaurants Inc.

J.G. MELON....1291 Third Ave., New York, N.Y., 10021. (212) 744-0585. Cuisine: Continental.

J.G. MELON WEST....340 Amsterdame Ave., New York, N.Y., 10024. (212) 874-8291. Cuisine: Continental.

JIM MCMULLEN....1341 Third Ave., New York, N.Y., 10021. (212) 861-4700. Cuisine: American. Owner: Jim McMulen. Credit cards: None.

JIMMY LA GRANGE ROOM....120 East 39 St., New York, N.Y., 10016. (212) 686-4666. Cuisine: American. Owner: Jimmy LaGrange.

JIMMY WESTON'S....131 East 54 St., New York, N.Y., 10022. (212) 838-8384. Cuisine: American. Owner: Mr. Weston.

JOANNA....18 East 18 St., New York, N.Y., 10011. (212) 675-7900. Cuisine: Continental. Credit cards: AE.

JOE ALLEN....326 West 46 St., New York, N.Y., 10036. (212) 581-6464. Cuisine: American. Credit cards: None.

JOE'S CHINATOWN....196 Broadway, New York, N.Y., 10038. (212) 227-2345. Cuisine: Chinese. Owner: Joseph.

JOE'S PIER 52....163 West 52 St., New York, N.Y., 10019. (212) 245-6652. Cuisine: Seafood. Owner: Joe Kipness.

JOE'S RESTAURANT....79 MacDougal St., New York, N.Y., 10012. (212) 473-8834. Cuisine: Italian. Owner: Nick. Credit cards: AE, MC, VISA.

JOE & ROSE RESAURANT....747 Third Ave., New York, N.Y., 10017. (212) 980-3985. Cuisine: Italian/Steak/Seafood. Owner: Rena Resteghini. Open Monday to Saturday for dinner. Credit cards: AE, CB, DC. Annual sales: $500,000 to $1 million. Total employment: 18.

JOHN BARLEYCORN....209 East 45 St., New York, N.Y., 10017. (212) 986-1088. Owner: Jerry Toner.

JOHN CLANCY'S....181 West 10 St., New York, N.Y., 10003. (212) 243-0958. Cuisine: Seafood. Owner: John Clancy and Barry Cullen. Open 6 days for lunch and dinner; Closed Sunday. Credit cards: All major. Private party facilities: Up to 70. Annual sales: $1 million to $3 million. Total employment: 24.

JOHNNIE'S....135 West 45 St., New York, N.Y., 10036. (212) 245-9667. Cuisine: Italian. Owner: John Dilustan.

JOYCE'S....948 Second Ave., New York, N.Y., 10022. (212) PL9-6780. Cuisine: Steak/Seafood. Owner: John Joyce. Corporate name: Joyce's Inc.

KABUKI RESTAURANT....115 Broadway, New York, N.Y., 10012. (212) 962-4654. Cuisine: Japanese. Owner: Arthur Kunimoto. Open Monday to Friday. Credit cards: All major. Annual sales: $1 million to $3 million. Total employment: 30. Corporate name: Kabuki Restaurant, Inc.

KAMEHACHI....14 East 47 St., New York, N.Y., 10017. (212) 765-4737. Kamehachi may not have the maximum ethereal atmosphere, but it's spacious and serene enough with well-positioned tables in the midst of roomy glossy-red half-moon booths, and the kitchen appears to have virtuoso talent that is consistent. The sushi-bar also makes a nice place for meals if you're alone and don't feel like the formality of a table. Owner: Mr. Marubashi. Open Monday through Friday for lunch; Monday through Saturday for dinner; Closed Sundays. Reservations: Accepted. Price: Moderate. Credit cards: All major. Private party facilities: 10 to 60. Annual sales: $500,000 to $1 million. Total employment: 24. Corporate name: Marubashi New York Corporation, Inc.

KAPLAN'S AT THE DELMONICO....59 East 59 St., New York, N.Y., 10022. (212) PL5-5959. Cuisine: Jewish Delicatessen. Owner: Jack Kaplan. Credit cards: All major.

198

JACK KAPLAN'S AT WEST 47 STREET....71 West 47 St., New York, N.Y., 10036. (212) 391-2333. As a Jewish-deli, it's an invigorating assault on your senses—a conflict of lively aromas and tumult, samplings and staccato verbal familiarities from the voluble owner Jack Kaplan (supported by his famous red suspenders) to his customers and the competition as a symbol of New York's distinctive cuisine. Specialties include: Reuben superior sandwich, sautéed chicken livers, lox & cream cheese, ruggelach, coffee cake, and babkas. Owner: Jack & Lee Kaplan. Open Monday through Friday from 6:30 AM to 7:00 PM; Saturday from 9:30 AM to 4:00 PM; Closed Sunday. Moderately priced. No reservations. Credit cards: All major. Private party facilities: 15 to 60. Annual sales: $500,000 to $1 million. Total employment: 25. Corporte name: Cindemar Wholesalers, Inc.

KASHMIR....12 West 46 St., New York, N.Y., 10036. (212) 869-8584. Cuisine: Indian.

KASPER'S....250 West 27 St., New York, N.Y., 10001. Cuisine: Continental. Credit cards: All major.

KATZ'S DELICATESSEN....205 East Houston St., New York, N.Y., 10002. (212) 254-2246. Cuisine: Jewish Style Delicatessen. Owner: Isidor Tarowsky. Leonard Katz, Art Makstein. Open 7 days. Credit cards: None. Annual sales $1 million to $3 million. Total employment: 50. Corporate name: Katz's Delicatessen, Inc.

KEEN'S....72 West 36 St., New York, N.Y., 10018. (212) 947-3636. Cuisine: French/English. Owner: Dr. George Schwarz. Open Monday to Friday for lunch; Monday to Saturday for dinner. Credit cards: All major. Private party facilities: 10 to 300. Annual sales: Over $3 million. Total employment: 54.

KEEWAH YEN....50 West 56 St., New York, N.Y., 10019. (212) 246-0770. In the midst of the skyscrapers, steak houses, and mediocre Italian restaurants of midtown Manhattan sits this change of pace. It's a very sophisticated Chinese restaurant, from the elegant decor (Chinese antiques, original works of art and calligraphy, ivory and jade sculptures, and stunning wooden room dividers) to the subtle, graceful cooking which is mainly Cantonese in outlook. There are some Szechuan and Hunan dishes as well. Specialties include: stuffed crab claws, *dim sum*, veal with snow peas, pine seed chicken, pineapple roast duck, sizzling seafood *wor ba*. Owner: Mr. Wong. Open Monday through Friday for lunch; 7 days for dinner. Priced moderately. Reservations accepted. Credit cards: AE, DC, VISA. Annual sales: $1 million to $3 million. Total employment: 32. Corporate name: Keewah Yen Ltd.

KENERET....296 Bleecker St., New York, N.Y., 10014. (212) OR5-9587. Cuisine: Syrian. Credit cards: All major.

KENNY'S STEAK PUB....565 Lexington Ave., New York, N.Y., 10017. (212) 355-0666. Cuisine: American.

KING DRAGON RESTAURANT....1273 Third Ave., New York, N.Y., 10021. (212) 988-3433. Cuisine: Chinese. Owner: Henry Leung, Scott Chin, Harry Hon, Ching Ng. Open 7 days. Credit cards: All major. Annual sales: $500,000 to $1 million. Total employment: 23. Corporate name: Sing Kwong Ltd.

KIPPY'S PIER 44....271 West 44 St. New York N.Y., 10036. (212) 221-1065. A theatrically-mooded restaurant serving copious portions of continental and seafood items in rustic surroundings located in the very heart of Manhattan's theater district. Specialties include: rich creamy crabmeat and corn soup, poached Boston scrod, tender veal chops, and coconut shrimp. Owner: Milford Plaza. Open 7 days for lunch, dinner, and late supper. Moderately priced. Reservations accepted. Credit cards: All maor. Private party facilities: 10 to 400. Annual sales: $1 million to $3 million. Total employment: 77.

KITCHO....22 West 46 St., New York, N.Y., 10036. (212) 575-8880. Cuisine: Japanese. Owner: Morito. Credit cards: AE, DC.

KITTY HAWK....565 Third Ave., New York, N.Y., 10016. (212) 661-7406. Cuisine: American. Credit cards: AE, CB, DC.

KLEINE KONDITOREI....234 East 86 St., New York, N.Y., 10028. (212) 737-7130. Cuisine: German. Credit cards: AE, DC.

KNICKERBOCKER SALOON....33 University Pl., New York, N.Y., 10003. (212) 228-8490. Cuisine: American.

KNICKER'S....982 Second Ave., New York, N.Y., 10017. (212) 223-8821. Owner: Mike Halbeuion.

LA BANCHINA....200 Grand St., New York, N.Y., 10013. (212) 431-5325. Cuisine: Italian.

LA BIBLIOTHEQUE....341 East 43 St., New York, N.Y., 10017. (212) 661-5757. Cuisine: Continental. Owner: Steve Miesels.

LA BONNE BOUFFE....127 East 34 St., New York, N.Y., 10016. (212) 679-9309. Cuisine: French. Owner: Marcel and Janine Moine. Credit cards: AE.

LA BOURGOGNE EAST....157 East 72 St. New York, N.Y., 10021. (212) UN1-4488. Cuisine: French. Owner: Marcel LeGuellac and Jean Claude Calvez. Credit cards: AE, DC, CB. Reservations: Accepted. Private party facilities. Total employment: 22.

LA CARAVELLE....33 West 55 St., New York, N.Y., 10019. (212) JU6-4252. One of the handful of four-star *haute cuisine* restaurants in New York City, and a must for professional gourmets. La Caravelle is famous for its classic cuisine, ambience, and top-flight table service. One of the finest in New York. Everything is special on La Caravelle's menu. Open Monday through Friday for lunch; Monday through Saturday for dinner; Closed Sunday. Owner: Robert Meyzen, Roger Fessaguet. Priced expensive. Reservations *de rigueur*. Credit cards: All major.

LA CASCADE....645 Fifth Ave., New York, N.Y., 10022. (212) 935-2220. A place to go relax and eat excellent French nouvelle cuisine. A cascading sheet of water takes up one wall of the restaurant, and a mirror reflecting the waterfall—hence the name "La Cascade." The effect is soothing and tranquil. Specialties include: Norwegian smoked salmon, goose liver pate in brioche, Dover sole *meuniere*, veal mignonettes, rack of lamb. There's also a small adjacent place called Le Cafe serving breakfast, sandwiches, and light entrees throughout the day. Owner: Guy Pascal. Open Monday through Friday for lunch and dinner; Closed Saturday and Sunday. Le Cafe is open Monday through Saturday for breakfast, lunch, and dinner; Closed Sunday. Both are priced moderately. Rservations are accepted for La Cascade. All major credit cards are accepted in both establishments. Private party facilities for between 50 and 150 persons. Annual sales: $1 million to $3 million. Total employment: 70. Corporate name: Delices La Cote Basaue, Inc.

LA CAVE HENRI IV....227 East 50 St., New York, N.Y., 10022. (212) 755-6566. Cuisine: French. Owner: Mr. Papayanni.

LA CHAUMIERE....310 West 4 St., New York, N.Y., 10014. 741-3374. Cuisine: French. Credit cards: All major.

LA COCOTTE....147 East 60 St., New York, N.Y., 10022. (212) 832-8972. Cuisine: French. Owner: Ernest.

LA COLOMBE D'OR....134 East 26 St., New York, N.Y., 10010. (212) 689-0666. Cuisine: French. Owner: George Studley.

LA COTE BASQUE....5 East 55 St., New York, N.Y., 10022. (212) 688-6525. One of the great French restaurants in New York. Its handsome setting is for very serious pleasures at the table. Owner-chef Jean Jacques Rachou has devoted experience, taste and talents to his house. Of course, it's costly. Specialties include: *pates* and terrines, veal chop in champagne sauce, chicken breast stuffed with quail *mousse*. Open 6 days for lunch and dinner; Closed Sunday. Lunch and dinner are both prix fixe. Owner: Jean Jacques Rachou. Credit cards: AE, Reservations: Accepted.

LA COUPOLE....2 Park Avenue, New York, N.Y., 10016. (212) 696-0100. The Parisian brasserie La Coupole almost exactly duplicated in New York—and like the Art Deco French original, the American version is equally impressive. The celebrated and beautiful people have discovered this place, so expect to find them tucking in their napkins and tucking in during mealtimes. The food is admirable adn the service solicitous. Specialties include: lentil soup, *L'Americaine*, cassoulet, *bombe pralinee*. Owner:Jean de Noyer, Jean Manuel Rozan. Open 7 days for lunch and dinner. Priced moderate to high. Reservations: Suggested. Accepting all major credit cards.

GEOGRAPHICAL LISTINGS
NEW YORK

WHO'S WHO IN AMERICA'S RESTAURANTS

LA FENICE....242 East 58 St., New York, N.Y., 10022. (212) 759-4660. Cuisine: Northern Italian. Owner: Tony Pino. Total employment: 14. Corporate name: La Fenice, Inc.,

LA FOLIE....21 East 61 St., New York, N.Y., 10021. (212) 765-1400. Now making a fair bid for fresh laurels under the courageous administration of chef Bernard Norget. Memorable prix fixe French meals are impeccably served amidst a stunningly sophisticated decor. House specialties include: *confit* of duck, *la paupiette de sole, chantal,* and at the caviar bar: oysters in champagne. Lunch is served Monday through Friday; Pre-Theatre Monday through Saturday; Dinner, Monday through Saturday; Post Theatre Monday through Saturday; Closed on Sunday. Prices are expensive. Owner: Bernard Norget. Credit cards: All major. Reservations: Accepted. Private party facilities. Entertainment: Dancing on Saturday. Total employment: 45.

LA FONDUE....43 West 55 St., New York, N.Y., 10019. (212) 581-0820. Owner: Herb Jacobson.

LA FORTUNA....16 East 41 St., New York, N.Y., 10017. (212) 685-4890. Cuisine: Italian.

LA GAMELLE....59 Grand St., (off West Broadway), New York, N.Y., 10013. (212) 431-6695. Cuisine: French. Open Monday through Saturday for dinner only. Credit cards: Call for cards.

LA GAULOISE....502 Avenue of the Americas, New York, N.Y., 10011. (212) 691-1363. Cuisine: French. Owner: Camille Dulac and Jacques Alliman. Credit cards: AE, DC, MC, VISA.

LA GOULUE....28 East 70 Street, New York, N.Y., 10021, (212) 988-8169. A polished, stylish restaurant perfectly situated on Manhattan's posh, expensive Upper East Side. Very French in tone, look, and food. The menu is not large, but it is diverse, and the food is good. Specialities include: duck with chestnuts, sole Nantua, *pave d' agneau aux herbes, entrecote au poivre,* mushrooms *a la Greque,* duck pate, bombe praline. Owner: Jean de Noyer. Open Monday through Saturday for lunch and dinner; Closed Sunday. Prices are expensive. Reservations are recommended. Accepting all major credit cards.

LA GRENOUILLE....3 East 52 St., New York, N.Y., 10022 (212) 752-1495. Impressive French cusine and has all the chi-chi imaginable. It is also as costly as any of the very best in New York. There are unquestionably some very beautifully prepared dishes and some very fine wines indeed in the cellars. House specialties include: hot *billi-bi;* frog legs, Dover sole; *quenelles;* lobster Nantua and desserts. Open 6 days for lunch and dinner; Closed Sunday. Owner: Gisele and Charles Masson. Credit cards: AE, DC. Reservations: Necessary.

LA GRILLADE....845 Eighth Ave., New York, N.Y., 10019. (212) 265-1610. Cuisine: French. Credit cards: AE, DC, MC, VISA.

LA GROCERIA....333 Sixth Ave., New York, N.Y., 10014. (212) CH2-3200. Cuisine: Italian. Owner: Gilbert DiLucia. Open 7 days for lunch and dinner. Credit cards: All major. Private party facilities: Up to 85. Annual sales: $250,000 to $500,000. Total employment: 25.

LA LOUISANA....132 Lexington Ave., New York, N.Y., 10016. (212) 686-3959. Cuisine: French. Owner: Abe De La Houssaye. Credit cards: None.

LA MAGANETTE....201 East 50 St., New York, N.Y., 10022. (212) 753-4565. Cuisine: Italian. Credit cards: All major.

LA MAISON JAPONAISE....334 Lexington Ave., New York, N.Y., 10016. (212) 682-7375. Cuisine: Japanese.

LA METAIRIE....189 West 10 St., New York, N.Y., 10014. (212) 989-0343. Cuisine: French. Owner: Roger Delouette. Credit cards: None.

LA MILONGA....742 Ninth Ave., New York, N.Y., 10019. (212) 541-8382. Owner: Jack Dilanga.

LANDMARK TAVERN....11 Ave. & West 46 St., New York, N.Y., 10036. (212) 757-8595. Cuisine: American.

LA PETITE AUBERGE....116 Lexington Ave., New York, N.Y., 10016. (212) 689-5003. Cuisine: French. Owner: Marcel Guelaff and Raymond Auffret. Open 7 days. Credit cards: AE. Private party facilities: 15 to 50.

LA PETITE FERME....973 Lexington Ave., New York, N.Y., 10021. (212) 249-3272. Cuisine: French. Owner: Charles Chevillot. Open 6 days for lunch and dinner; Closed Sunday. Credit cards: All major. Private party facilities: 40 to 55. Annual sales: $250,000 to $500,000. Total employment: 25. Corporate name: La Petite Ferme, Inc.

LA PETITE MARMITE....5 Mitchell Pl., New York, N.Y., 10017. (212) 826-1084. A classy and stylish French restaurant that delivers excellent cookery with just the right dash of nouvelle to keep the menu interesting. The chef achieves good results with appetizers like sauteed prawns, *les haricots verts aux echallotes,* entrees like whitefish filets in Nantua sauce with mushroom puree, sweetbreads with Forestiere sauce, and rare breast of duckling in green peppercorns sauce. Owner: Jacky Ruette, Pierre Derringer. Open Monday through Friday for lunch; Monday through Saturday for dinner; Closed Sunday. Priced expensive. Reservations suggested: All major credit cards accepted. Private party facilities available.

LA POLPETTA....257 West 34 St., New York, N.Y., 10001. (212) 244-2876. Cuisine: Italian. Owner: Stephen and Sandra Turk. Open 7 days for lunch and dinner. Credit cards: AE, DC, MC, VISA. Private party facilities: 10 to 30. Total employment: 20. Corporate name: St. Restaurant Corp.

LA RECOLTE....110 East 49 St., New York, N.Y., 10017. (212) 421-4389. This place strikes us as the most organized and likely to endure of the many expensive French nouvelle cuisine establishments in Manhattan. It is based in a remote corner of the Intercontinental Hotel, but has its own entrance, independent chef and separate kitchen. Definitely good food and service. Restaurant is glossy with polish and bright with flowers. Specialties include: Poached turbot in puff pastry, medallions of veal with leeks and cucumbers, rack of lamb with sage, and braised salmon in lemon butter with endive. Owner: Intercontinental Hotel Corp. Open Monday through Friday for lunch; Monday through Saturday for dinner; Closed Sunday. Priced moderate to high. Reservations: Suggested. Credit cards: All major. Corporate name: Intercontinental Hotel Corp.

LA RIPALLE....605 Hudson St., New York, N.Y., 10014. (212) 255-4406. Cuisine: French. Owner: Patrick and Alain Laurent. Credit cards: MC, VISA.

LARRY'S....886 First Ave., New York, N.Y., 10022. (212) 688-7348.

LA STRADA....134 West 46 St., New York, N.Y., 10036. (212) 245-2660. Cuisine: Italian.

LA STRADA EAST....274 Third Ave., New York, N.Y., 10010. (212) 473-3760. No slick, trendy interior here; instead it's a warm, handsome and restful dining room with a small inviting bar. The staff is courteous and capable, and the Italian dishes are well-presented and consistently good. Personal favorites are: piping hot scampi alla Romana, filled with shrimp in spicy olive oil dotted with fragrant chunks of fresh garlic, and seafood antipasto (a blend of lobster, shrimp, and clams oreganata) in savory garlic sauce. Owner: Louis De Rose. Open 7 days for lunch and dinner. Price: Moderate. Reservations: Accepted. Credit cards: All major. Private party facilities: 12 to 40. Annual sales: $250,000 to $500,000. Total employment: 8. Corporate name: De Paul Gramercy Restaurant, Inc.

LA TABLE DES ROIS....135 East 50 St., New York, N.Y., 10022. (212) 838-7275. Cuisine: French. Owner: Pierrot Amalia. Total employment: 6. Corporate name: Rami Inc.

LA TABLITA....65 West 73 St., New York, N.Y., 10023. (212) 724-9595. Cuisine: Argentine/Italian. Owner: Judy Landers.

LA TRIESTINA....241 Lexington Ave., New York, N.Y., 10016. (212) 532-9256. Cuisine: Italian.

LA TOJA....519 Second Ave., New York, N.Y., 10016. (212) 889-1909. Cuisine: Spanish.

LA TULIPE....104 West 13 St., New York, N.Y., 10011. (212) 691-8860. Cuisine: French.

LAURENT....111 East 56 St., New York, N.Y., 10022. (212) 753-2729. Urbane distinction. One of the venerable eating establishments in New York. Now entering its fourth decade of culinary achievement. Fabulous cellars. No distractions from the serious pleasures of luncheon and dinner. None required. Specialties include: Brochette d'agneau orientale, noisettes de veau aux morilles, red snapper grille au citron vert pointes d'asperges. Owner: Laurent Losa, James Rapacioli, Nat Arrigoni. Cuisine: French. Open Monday through Saturday for lunch; 7 days for dinner. Price: Expensive. Reservations: Suggested. Credit cards: All major. Total employment: 100.

LA VERANDA....60 East 54 St., New York, N.Y., 10022. (212) 758-5560. It's a lively, smoothly run spot, whose culinary vibes reflect a mix of Italian resourcefulness with a touch of French culture. It's a particularly good tack on the map for fettucine Alfredo and the chef also understands what to do with things of the sea. House specialties include: scampi francese, filet mignon burgundy and *agnotti verdi modenesa*. Prices are moderate. Open Monday through Friday for lunch; Monday through Sunday for dinner. Owner: Luigi Badenchini and Tito Lustica. Credit cards: All major. Reservations: Accepted. Private party facilities.

LAVIN'S....23 West 39 St., New York, N.Y., 10018. (212) 921-1288. Cuisine: Continental Owner: Mr. Lavin.

LE ALPI RESTAURANT....234 West 48 St., New York, N.Y., 10036. (212) 582-7792. Cuisine: Italian. Owner: Aquilino Pozzi. Open for lunch and dinner Monday through Saturday. Credit cards: All major. Annual sales: $250,000 to $500,000. Total employment: 12.

LE BIARRITZ....325 West 57 St., New York, N.Y., 10019. (212) 757-2390. Cuisine: French. Owner: Marie Louise.

LE BISTRO....827 Third Ave., New York, N.Y., 10022. (212) 759-5933. Cuisine: French.

LE BON SOIR....240 West 56 St., New York, N.Y., 10019. (212) 755-1795. Cuisine: French. Owner: Dali and Mark.

LE CHAMPIGNON....35 West 56 St., New York, N.Y., 10019. (212) 245-6335. There are few places we would recommend for faithful French cuisine—Le Champignon is a notable exception. The combination of quality, charm, intimacy, and service, with such tastefully flavored dishes as champignon a la Grecque, tender steak au poivre, sauteed filet of sole, and veal sweetbreads with morsels of wild mushrooms is unusual even in New York. In short, there's much to appeal to anyone stopping at this restaurant, which dwarfs in class and cuisine many of its better known neighbors. Owner: Jacqueline Paine. Open 6 days for lunch and dinner; Closed Sunday. Priced moderate to high. Reservations: Suggested. Credit cards: All major. Private party facilities: Up to 100. Total employment: 25. Corporate name: CPC Restaurant, Inc.

LE CHANTILLY....106 East 57 St., New York, N.Y., 10022. (212) 751-2931. As far as we are concerned, chef Roland Chenus's version of classic French cuisine and Paul Dessibourg's direction of the dining room have elevated Le Chantilly to the pinnacle of New York's French establishments. In recognition of this superiority, it is pointless to reproduce the selections of specialties from a menu whereon all is special. Open 6 days for lunch and dinner; Closed Sunday. Price: Expensive (prix-fixe lunch is $21.50; prix-fixe dinner is $36.50). Reservations: Suggested. Credit cards: All major. Private party facilities: 12 to 20. Total employment: 50. Corporate name: Le Chantilly, Inc.

LE CHATEAU RICHELIEU....48 East 52 St., New York, N.Y., 10022. (212) PL1-6565. Cuisine: Continental. Owner: Mr. and Mrs. Peter Robotti. Total employment: 40. Corporate name: Le Chateau Richelieu Inc.

LE CHEVAL BLANC....145 East 45 St., New York, N.Y., 10017. (212) 599-8886. Cuisine: French. Owner: Rene & Roger. Open Monday through Friday for lunch and dinner; Saturday for dinner only; Closed Sunday. Credit cards: All major. Annual sales: $250,000 to $500,000. Total employment: 13. Corporate name: Le Cheval Blanc, Inc.

LE CIRQUE....58 East 65 St., New York, N.Y., 10021. (212) 794-9292. Cuisine: French. Owner: Sirio. Credit cards: AE, CB, DC.

LE CYGNE....55 East 54 St., New York, N.Y., 10022. (212) 759-5941. A distinguished French establishment with high prices to match. Overall atmosphere of urbane serenity. Very much the place for richer tourists and the locals who appreciate fine dining. Scallops *pate* with truffles and the striped bass, baked *en croute* with a nantua sauce are two great features of the menu. There is a sound wine list also. Other specialities include: exceptional soups; *poularde au champagne;* paillard beef; kidneys; Grand Marnier mousse. Open for lunch and dinner, 6 days. Closed Sundays. Owner: Gerrand. Credit cards: All major. Reservations: Required.

LE JACQUES COEUR....448 East 79 St., New York, N.Y., 10021. (212) 249-4920. Cuisine: French. Owner: Mr. & Mrs. Robert Renaud. Open from Tuesday to Sunday. Credit cards: All major. Annual sales: $250,000 to $500,000. Total employment: 5. Corporate name: Le Jacque Coeur, Inc.

LE JARDIN....248 East 49 St., New York, N.Y., 10017. (212) 355-1810. A small townhouse on a quiet street with a petite bar, a narrow stairway leading to private dining quarters, a snug banquette-lined room on the main floor opening onto a softly-lit enclosed country garden, where sensitive French cooking is provided by owner-chef Georges Magerus. Menu items offer a stylish array—from rabbit stew blended with mushrooms, bacon, and onions in red wine sauce and sparkling fresh grilled bass fortified with a mustard and Hollandaise sauce, to a cassoulet brought to the table in a steamy hot crock of beans, sausage, and lamb. Open 6 days for lunch and dinner; Closed Sunday. Price: Moderate. Reservations: Accepted. Credit cards: All major. Private party facilities: 8 to 45. Total employment: 12. Corporate name: Georges Henri Hubert Vent, Inc.

LE JULES VERNE....189 West 10 St., New York, N.Y., 10014. (212) 929-9400. Cuisine: French. Credit cards: AE, MC.

LE LAVANDOU....134 East 61 St., New York, N.Y., 10021. (212) 838-7987. Very special French restaurant and most attractively done up with deep burgundy banquettes and French murals. It's not inexpensive but a value for the money beyond question. Owner-chef Jean Jacques Rachou (he also owns La Cote Basque) really knows what cooking is all about. He knows his wines too and the list is impressive. House specialties include: *cassoulet toulousain, saumon en brioche,* and *coquelet aux ris de veau.* Open for lunch and dinner, 6 days. Closed on Sunday. Prix-fixe for lunch and dinner. Owner: Jean Jacques Rachou. Credit cards: AE. Reservations: Accepted.

LELLO....65 East 54 St., New York, N.Y., 10022. (212) 751-1555. A Northern-Italian restaurant that can stand toe-to-toe with any three-star grading on the grounds of the quality of raw ingredients, the standards of cooking, the range and distinction of wines, the quietly efficient service ad the subdued luxury of its appointments. Lello is noted for its seafood salad, veal chops and classical pasta dishes. Other noted specialities include *scampi ribelli, pollo pappagallo,* and *scalipini St. Elena.* Open for lunch and dinner Monday through Friday; Dinner on Saturday. Closed Sunday. Prices represent quality at prices below average for such standards. Owner: Raffallo Arpaia and Milton Taub. Credit cards: All major. Reservations: Accepted. Private party facilities.

LE MADRIGAL....216 East 53 St., New York, N.Y., 10022. (212) 355-0322. Cuisine: French. Owner: Raymond, Gilbert and Gerard. Closed Sunday. Credit cards: All major. Private party facilities: 16 to 20. Annual sales: $500,000 to $1 million. Total employment: 25. Corporate name: Le Madrigal Restaurant, Inc.

LE MOAL....942 Third Ave., New York, N.Y., 10022. (212) 688-8860. Cuisine: French Provincial. Owner: Andre Le Moal. Open 7 days for lunch and dinner. Credit cards: All major. Annual sales: $1 million to $3 million. Total employment: 26.

THE LEOPARD....253 East 50 St., New York, N.Y., 10022. (212) PL9-3735. A very old town-house in the grand manner, highly fashionable for many years and gradually regaining a fine reputation under the proprietorship of Vincent D'Auria. Of the varied selections available, we especially recommend the roast crisp duckling with plums and plum brandy, filet of salmon baked in a pastry with a lobster cream sauce, and filet mignon sauce Bernaise. On the whole, less expensive than the general run at this level. Meals are *prix-fixe:* Luncheon $25.00 per person including unlimited wine; dinner $32.00 per person including unlimited wine. Reservations are mandatory. Open Monday through Saturday for lunch and dinner; Closed Sunday and major holiday. Credit cards: AE, CB, DC. Private party facilities: 10 to 40. Total employment 16. Corporate name: The Leopard Restaurant, Inc.

LEO'S SALTY SEA....108 East 60 St., New York, N.Y., 10022. (212) 755-9288. Cuisine: Seafood. Owner: Leo.

LE PERIGORD PARK....575 Park Ave., New York, N.Y., 10021. (212) 752-0050. Cuisine: French. Owner: Willy Krouse.

LE PETIT ROBERT....314 West 11 St., New York, N.Y., 10014. (212) 691-5311. Cuisine: French. Owner: Micheal Schaefer and James Peterson. Open Monday to Saturday. Credit cards: AE, DC. Corporate name: 314 West 11th Street Restaurant Corp.

LE PLAISIR....969 Lexington Ave., New York, N.Y., 10021. (212) 734-9430. This is a comfortable yet elegant representative of polished nouvelle cuisine. In internal design and menu construction there is the open discipline of breeding laced with casual charm that characterizes owner Pierre Jourdan. Rather fashionable, so book your table. There are all too few anyway. Prix fixe dinner for $38.00. Specialties include: noisettes of lamb, pigeon breast with green peppercorn sauce, calf's liver, and veal with noodles and foie gras. Open 6 days for dinner only; Closed Sunday. Reservations: Suggested. Credit cards: All major. Corporate name: Bedy Restaurants, Inc.

LE QUERCY....52 West 55 St., New York, N.Y., 10019. (212) 265-8141. Cuisine: French. Credit cards: AE.

LE RELAIS....712 Madison Ave., New York, N.Y., 10021. (212) 751-5108. Cuisine: French. Owner: Francois Marchand. Credit cards: AE.

LE STEAK....1089 Second Ave., New York, N.Y., 10022. (212) 421-9072. Cuisine: French. Owner: Consuelo Almonte.

LE VEAU D'OR....129 East 60 St., New York, N.Y., 10022. (212) 838-8133. Cuisine: French. Owner: Gerrard.

LE VERT-GALANT....109 West 46 St., New York, N.Y., 10036. (212) 382-0022. A fashionable French restaurant with a fine reputation for presenting a varied selection of beautifully cooked lunch and dinner dishes such as rack of lamb, chateaubriand, boneless duckling with wild rice, onion soup crusted over with sardo-cheese, and naturally, outstanding French wines to support them. On the whole, Le Vert-Galant is less expensive than the general run on this level. Moderate to expensive. Open Monday through Saturday for lunch and dinner, closed Sundays. Owner: Maurice Hemery. Credit cards: All major. Reservations: Necessary. Private party facilities. Entertainment: Vocals & Piano.

LES MOUCHES....260 Eleventh Ave., New York, N.Y., 10001. (212) 695-5190. This huge place is a "complex" devoted mainly to nocturnal pleasures and includes a disco, cabaret and posh French dining salon. As a rule, Les Mouches doesn't make it hard for people to get in. Specialties include: pate maison and roast duckling with Cointreau. Open for dinner Wednesday through Saturday. Prices are moderate. Owners: Frank McGourty, John Chambers and Cary Finkelstein. Credit cards: All major. Reservations: Accepted. Private Party Facilities. Entertainment: Cabaret in restaurant. Total employment: 120.

LES PLEIADES....20 East 76 St., New York, N.Y., 10021. (212) 535-7230. Cuisine: French. Credit cards: AE, DC, MC, VISA.

LES PYRENEES....251 West 51 St., New York, N.Y., 10019. (212) 246-0044. Cuisine: French. Owner: Jean Claude Pujol.

LES SANS COLUTTES....1085 Second Ave., New York, N.Y., 10022. (212) 838-6660. Cuisine: French. Owner: John Pierre.

L'HOSTARIA DEL BONGUSTAIO....75 East 55 St., New York, N.Y., 10022. (212) 751-3530. Cuisine: Italian. Owner: Mr. Damiani. Credit cards: AE, MC, VISA.

L'INCONTRO....307 East 45 St., New York, N.Y., 10017. (212) 697-9664. Cuisine: Italian. Owner: Mimmo Gambino. Closed Sundays. Credit cards: All major. Annual sales: $500,000 to $1 million. Total employment: 9. Corporate name: Sardiana, Inc.

LIMERICK'S....573 Second Ave., New York, N.Y., 10016. (212) 683-4686. Cuisine: Irish Pub.

LINO'S....147 West 36 St., New York, N.Y., 10018. (212) 695-6444. Cuisine: Italian. Owner: Lino.

LION'S ROCK RESTAURANT....316 East 77 St., New York, N.Y., 10021. (212) 988-3610. Cuisine: Continental. Owner: William Recht Jr. Open 7 days for dinner and Sunday brunch. Credit cards: All major. Private party facilities: 40 to 100. Annual sales: $1 million to $3 million. Total employment: 30. Corporate name: Rock & Rye Restaurant, Inc.

LITTLE AFGHANISTAN....106 West 43 St., New York, N.Y., 10036. (212) 921-1676. Cuisine: Afghani. Credit cards: AE, DC.

LITTLE SPAIN....232 West 14 St., New York, N.Y., 10011. Cuisine: Spanish.

LONE STAR CAFE....61 Fifth Ave., New York, N.Y., 10003. 242-1664. It's the number-one mecca for authentic country western music, western style settings, and Tex-Mex cooking. The boisterous crowds who come and go on both floors represent steady lines of the world-at-large. House specialties include: Tex-Mex chili—3 degrees, gourmet smoked BBQ ribs and Lone Star beer. Open for lunch and dinner, 7 days. Prices are moderate, plus and added entertainment fee. Catering also available on or off premises. Owners: William Dick and Mort Copperman. Credit cards: All major. Reservations: Accepted. Private party facilities. Entertainment: Nightly—Famous Musical Entertainers & Bands.

LOTUS....228 East 86 St., New York, N.Y., 10028. (212) 535-0099. Cuisine: Chinese. Owner: Raymond Wong.

LOTUS EATERS FIFTH....182 Fifth Ave., New York, N.Y., 10010. (212) 929-4800. Cuisine: Chinese.

LOUISE JUNIOR....317 East 53 St., New York, N.Y., 10022. (212) 752-7832. Cuisine: Northern Italian. Owner: Roschild Paolini. Open for lunch Monday to Friday; Open for dinner Monday to Saturday. Credit cards: AE, CB, DC. Annual sales: $500,000 to $1 million. Total employment: 23.

LUTECE....249 East 50 St., New York, N.Y., 10022. (212) PL2-2225. Up-to-date, well groomed, urbanely run and chef-proprietaire Andre Soltner imparts an air of well-earned grandeur. Cuisine is strictly French. House specialties include: *medallions de veau aux morilles; escalopes de boeuf en croute Lutece.* Also known for *tournedos chasseur,* dessert souffles and pastries. Open for lunch and dinner, 6 days. Closes Sundays. Prices are expensive. Owner: Andre Soltner. Credit cards: AE, DC. Reservations: Required. Private party facilities.

MADAME ROMAINE DE LYON....32 East 61 St., New York, N.Y., 10021. (212) 758-2422. Cuisine: Omlettes. Owner: Romaine Chauepion.

MADRAS WOODLANDS....310 East 44 St., New York, N.Y., 10017. (212) 986-0620. Cuisine: Indian.

MAESTRO CAFE....58 West 65 St., New York, N.Y., 10023. (212) 787-5990. Cuisine: American/Continental. Credit cards: AE, DC, MC, VISA.

MAGIC PAN....149 East 57 St., New York, N.Y., 10022. (212) 371-3266. Cuisine: American/Pancake. Credit cards: AE.

MAHARAJA....2487 Broadway, New York, N.Y., 10025. (212) 362-4554. Cuisine: Indian, Indonesian, and Pakistani. Owner: John Younus, Pres. Open 7 days for dinner. Credit cards: $250,000 to $500,000. Total employment: 6.

MAIN STREET....75 Greenwich Ave., New York, N.Y., 10014. (212) 929-1579. Cuisine: American. Credit cards: AE, DC, MC, VISA.

MALAGA....406 East 73 St., New York, N.Y., 10021. (212) 737-7659. Cuisine: Spanish. Owner: Benny. Credit cards: AE, DC, MC, VISA.

MAMMA LEONE'S....239 West 48 St., New York, N.Y., 10036. (212) JU6-5151. Cuisine: Italian. Credit cards: All major.

MANDARIN INN PELL....34 Pell St., New York, N.Y., 10013. (212) 267-2092. Cuisine: Chinese. Owner: Peter Wong.

MARCHI'S....251 East 31 St., New York, N.Y., 10016. (212) OR9-2494. Cuisine: Italian. Credit cards: AE.

MARMALADE PARK....222 East 39 St., New York, N.Y., 10016. (212) 687-7803-4. Cuisine: Continental. Owner: Micheal Mitchell, Francis Mitchell. Open 7 days for lunch and dinner. Credit cards: AE, DC, MC, VISA. Annual sales: $250,000 to $500,000. Total employment: 20. Corporate name: F.M.M. Restaurant Corp.

MARTELL'S....Third Ave. & 83 St., New York, N.Y., 10028. (212) 861-6110. Owner: Mr. Martell.

MARTY'S....1265 Third Ave., New York, N.Y., 10021. (212) 249-4100. Cuisine: Steak/Seafood. Owner: Marty Ross. Open 7 days for dinner. Credit cards: AE, BA, MC. Private party facilities: Up to 200. Annual sales: $1 million to $3 million. Total employment: 40.

MARVIN GARDENS RESTAURANT....2274 Broadway, New York, N.Y., 10024. (212) 799-0578. Cuisine: Continental. Owner: Marvin Gutin & Michael DiSimone. Open 7 days. Credit cards: AE, MC, VISA. Annual sales: $1 million to $3 million. Corporate name: 2274 Broadway Restaurant Corp.

MARYLOU'S....21 West Ninth St., New York, N.Y., 10011. (212) 533-0012. Cuisine: Seafood. Owner: Marylou Baratta. Credit cards: AE, MC, DC, VISA.

MARY'S....42 Bedford St., New York, N.Y., 10014. (212) 741-3387. Located in a residential building more than a century old, Mary's down and upstairs dining rooms are snug and decorated with simple charm, retaining the character of a modest private home. To some, this appearance may lend a soul-satisfying atmosphere, but it's the homemade Abruzzi-style-Italian cooking at enchantingly reasonable prices that has made meals here an institution for so many years. House specialties include: baked stuffed mushrooms, made-to-order pasta, chicken imperiale (rolled chicken breast filled with cheese, prosciutto and mushrooms) and filet mignon Abruzzi. Open for lunch, Monday through Friday.Open for dinner, 7 days. Owner: Giovanni Celenza. Credit cards: AE, DC, MC. Reservations: Accepted. Private party facilities. Annual sales: Under $500,000. Total employment: 9.

MAXWELL'S PLUM....1181 First Ave., New York, N.Y., 10021. (212) 628-2100. Cuisine: Continental. Owner: Warner LeRoy.

McCARTHY'S FAMOUS STEAK HOUSE....839 Second Ave., New York, N.Y., 10017. (212) MU7-6131. Cuisine: Steakhouse. Credit cards: AE, DC.

McGOWAN'S OFF BROADWAY....57 Greenwich Ave., New York, N.Y., 10006. (212) 929-3340. Cuisine: American.

MCSORLEY'S OLD ALE HOUSE....15 East Seventh St., New York, N.Y., 10003. (212) 473-8800. This unique curio has remained unchanged in operation and appearance since it opened in 1854. Its reputation as a great "gathering place" is obviously secure for some time to come, no matter what transformations Manhattan experiences. It will continue to be a stopping-off point not only for neighboring locals, but tourists from all over the world, merely from the sheer power of its ability to sustain the "status quo" in a relentlessly innovational city. Specializing in their famous ale and a light limited lunch menu. House specialties also include: chili and clam chowder plus sandwiches and burgers. Open 7 days. Owner: Matthew Maher. Credit cards: None. Reservations: Accepted.

MEATBALLS....257 West 34 St., New York, N.Y., 10001. (212) 244-2876. Cuisine: Italian.

MEAT BROKERS STEAK HOUSE....1153 York Ave., New York, N.Y., 10021. (212) 752-0108. Cuisine: Steak/Seafood. Owner: Richad Pucci and Thomas Lucas. Open for dinner 7 days. Credit cards: All major. Private party facilities: 50 to 120. Annual sales: $1 million to $3 million. Total employment: 30. Corporate name: Pucci & Lucas, Inc.

MESON BOTIN....145 West 58 St., New York, N.Y., 10022. (212) 265-4567. Cuisine: Spanish. Owner: Mr. Russo.

MICHAEL PHILLIPS....994 First Ave., New York, N.Y., 10021. (212) 888-0018. Cuisine: Continental. Owner: Mike. Credit cards: All major.

MICKEY'S....44 West 54 St., New York, N.Y., 10019. (212) 247-2979. Cuisine: Cabaret. Owner: Michael Gil.

MILDRED PIERCE....345 West 46 St., New York. N.Y., 10036. (212) 582-4801. Cuisine: American/Continental. Credit cards: AE, DC, MC, VISA.

MILESTONE....75 West 68 St., New York, N.Y., 10021. (212) 874-3679. Cuisine: American. Credit cards: None.

MIMOSA....152 East 33 St., New York, N.Y., 10016. (212) 685-2595. Cuisine: Continental. Credit cards: None.

MIMOSA....232 East 43 St., New York, N.Y., 10017. (212) 697-0049. Cuisine: Continental. Credit cards: None.

MINETTA TAVERN....113 MacDougal St., New York, N.Y., 10012. (212) 475-3850. Cuisine: Italian. Owner: John Bitici. Corporate name: Bitici's Inc.

MIRAKU....129 West 72 St., New York, N.Y., 10023. (212) 874-3575. Cuisine: Japanese/Korean. Credit cards: AE, MC, VISA.

MITALI RESTAURANT....334 East 6 St., New York, N.Y., 10003. (212) 533-2508. Cuisine: Indian. Owner: Abu Sufian Ahmed. Open for lunch and dinner Friday, Saturday, and Sunday; from 3:00 PM Monday through Thursday. Credit cards: AE, MC, VISA. Total employment: 6. Corporate name: Mitali Restaurant, Inc.

MITCHELL'S....122 East 27 St., New York, N.Y., 10016. (212) 689-2058. Cuisine: American. Owner: Michael Mitchell, Francis Mitchell. Open Monday through Friday for lunch and dinner; Closed Saturday and Sunday. Credit cards: AE, DC, MC, VISA. Annual sales: $250,000 to $500,000. Total employment: 10. Corporate name: M.F.M. Restaurant Corp.

MITSUKOSHI....465 Park Ave., New York, N.Y., 10022. (212) 935-6444. Cuisine: Japanese. Credit cards: AE, MC, VISA.

MIYAKO....20 West 56 St., New York, N.Y., 10019. (212) 265-3177. Cuisine: Japanese. Owner: M. Nakajima, C. Okuyama, T. Kinoshita. Open Monday through Saturday. Credit cards: All major. Private party facilities: 10-80. Annual sales: $500,000 to $1 million. Total employment: 25. Corporate name: K.H.I. International, Inc.

MOLFETAS....307 West 47 St., New York, N.Y., 10036. (212) 840-9594. Cuisine: Greek. Owner: Vasilios Triantafillou.

MONA LISA....936 Second Ave., New York, N.Y., 10017. (212) 421-4497. Cuisine: Italian. Owner: Corado Casontine.

MONK INN....35 West 64 St., New York, N.Y., 10023. (212) 874-2710. Cuisine: French.

MON PARIS....111 East 29 St., New York, N.Y., 10016. (212) 683-4255. Cuisine: French. Owner: Rodger Stephen.

MONT D'OR....244 East 46 St., New York, N.Y., 10017. (212) 490-7275. Cuisine: French and Italian. Owner: Richard Bazzalo. Open Monday to Saturday for dinner; open Monday to Friday for lunch. Credit cards: All major. Private party facilities: Up to 20. Annual sales: $250,000 to $500,000. Total employment: 9.

MONTE ROSA....1068 Second Ave., New York, N.Y., 10022. (212) 688-6595. Cuisine: Italian. Owner: Silvano Brencic. Credit cards: All major.

MONTE'S....97 MacDougal St., New York, N.Y., 10012. (212) OR4-9456. Cuisine: Italian. Credit cards: None.

MONT ST. MICHEL....327 West St., New York, N.Y., 10023. (212) 581-1032. Cuisine: French.

MORGEN'S....34 East 52 St., New York, N.Y., 10022. (212) 421-1331. Cuisine: American/Jewish. Owner: Mr. Morgen. Credit cards: AE, CB, DC.

MORMANDO....541 Lexington Ave., New York, N.Y., 10022. (212) 935-9570. Mormando is a pleasant, posh-enough restaurant that features an exemplary French/Italian menu— and chef Anton Varga makes sure the offerings on the menu are well-cooked. Specialties include: linguini with white clam sauce, veal parmagiana, veal chop, clams casino, and tomato and onion salad. Owner: Dusty Mormando. Open 7 days for breakfast, lunch, and dinner. (Mormando is connected with the Dorado Inn Hotel in whose building the restaurant is located, facing out onto Lexington Avenue.) Priced moderate to high. Reservations accepted. Credit cards: All major. Private party facilities: Available.

MORTIMER'S....1057 Lexington Ave., New York, N.Y., 10021. (212) 861-2481. Cuisine: American. Open 7 days for lunch and dinner. Credit cards: AE, MC, VISA. Private party facilities: Up to 60. Annual sales: $1 million to $3 million. Total employment: 57. Corporate name: Tangoringo Corporation.

MOVENPICK RESTAURANT....790 Seventh Ave., New York, N.Y., 10019. (212) 582-0716. Cuisine: Continental. Open 7 days. Credit cards: AE, CB, MC, VISA. Annual sales: Over $3 million. Total employment: 93. Corporate name: Movel Enterprises, Inc.

MR. CHOW'S....324 East 57 St., New York, N.Y., 10022. (212) 751-9030. Cuisine: Chinese.

MR. LEE'S....337 Third Ave., New York, N.Y., 10011. (212) 689-6373. Offers an idyllic unobtrusive setting, family chef-proprietor pattern, and it is imperative to make reservations well in advance, but then this is a New York "original" famous and justly so for its French cuisine. House specialties: banana bass, flambeed to a quintessential glaze; lobster cardinal, and bouillabaisse. Open for lunch Monday through Friday. Dinner, Monday through Saturday. Closed Sunday. Prices are expensive. Owner: Gim and Ruth Lee. Credit cards: All major. Reservations: Necessary. Annual sales: $500,000 to 1,000,000. Total employment: 15.

MRS. J.'S SACRED COW....228 West 72 St., New York, N.Y., 10023. (212) 873-4067. Cuisine: Steak.

MUMTAZ....1493 Third Ave., New York, N.Y., 10028. (212) 879-4797. Cuisine: Northern Indian. Owner: Mr. Choudhury.

MUSEUM CAFE....366 Columbus Ave., New York, N.Y., 10024. (212) 799-0150. Cuisine: Continental.

NADA SUSHI....135 East 50 St., New York, N.Y., 10022. (212) 838-2537. Cuisine: Japanese. Credit cards: AE, MC, DC, VISA.

NADIAS....994 Second Ave., New York, N.Y., 10026. (212) 888-6300. Cuisine: Italian. Open daily for lunch and dinner. Credit cards: Call for cards.

NANNI AL VALETTO....133 East 61 St., New York, N.Y., 10021. (212) 838-3939. Cuisine: Italian. Owner: Luigi Nanni.

NEARY'S PUB....358 East 57 St., New York, N.Y., 10022. (212) 751-1434. Cuisine: Irish/American. Credit cards: All major.

NEW HANKOW....132 West 34 St., New York, N.Y., 10022. (212) 695-4972. Cuisine: Cantonese. Owner: Luke Chong. Total employment: 25.

NEW NILE CAFE....81 Warren St., New York, N.Y., 10007. (212) 732-5402. Cuisine: International. Owner: Grant Stitt. Open Monday through Friday for lunch; Monday through Saturday for dinner; Closed Sunday. No credit cards. Private party facilities: 2 to 200. Annual sales: $250,000 to $500,000. Total employment: 13. Corporate name: Starling Restaurant, Inc.

NEW PORT ALBA....208 Thompson St., New York, N.Y., 10012. (212) 473-9735. Cuisine: Italian. Open Monday through Friday for lunch; Monday through Saturday for dinner; Sunday brunch. Credit cards: Call for cards. Reservations: Suggested.

NICKEL'S STEAK HOUSE....227 East 67 St., New York, N.Y., 10021. (212) 794-2331. Cuisine: Steakhouse. Owner: Mr. Manheimer.

NICOLA PAONE....207 East 34 St., New York, N.Y., 10016. (212) 889-3239. Cuisine: Italian. Owner: Mr. Nicola Paone.

NIPPON....145 East 52 St., New York, N.Y., 10022. (212) 688-5941. Cuisine: Japanese. Owner: Mr. N. Kuraoka. Total employment: 60.

NIRVANA....30 Central Park South, New York, N.Y., 10019. (212) 752-0270. Cuisine: Indian. Owner: Shamsher Wadud.

NO. 1 CHINESE RESTAURANT....202 Canal St., New York, N.Y., 10013. (212) 227-1080. Cuisine: Chinese. Credit cards: MC, VISA (after 6).

NORMA'S RESTAURANT....95 Duane St., New York, N.Y., 10007. (212) 962-8684. Cuisine: Continental/American. Owner: Norma Fontane. Closed Saturday and Sunday. Private party facilities: 20 to 70 persons. Annual sales: $250,000 to $500,000. Total employment: 7.

NUCCIO'S...251 Ave. of the Americas, New York, N.Y., 10014. (212) 620-0545. Cuisine: Italian. Credit cards: AE.

O'CASEY'S....22 East 41 St., New York, N.Y., 10017. (212) 685-6807. Cuisine: American. Credit cards: All major.

OENOPHILIA....473 Columbus Ave., New York, N.Y., 10024. (212) 580-8127. Cuisine: Continental. Open for dinner 7 days and Sunday brunch. Credit cards: All major. Corporate name: 473 Lalieb Food Corp.

OFF B'WAY CO.....141 West 69 St., New York, N.Y., 10023. (212) 496-8002. Cuisine: American.

O'HENRY'S STEAKHOUSE....345 Ave. of the Americas, New York, N.Y., 10011. (212) 242-2000. Cuisine: Steakhouse. Owner: Vincent.

OLD FORGE STEAKHOUSE....200 East 17 St., New York, N.Y., 10003. (212) 473-1767. Cuisine: Seafood/Steak.

OLD HOMESTEAD....56 Ninth Ave., New York, N.Y., 10011. (212) 242-9040. Owner: Mark and Greg.

OLIVER'S....141 East 57 St., New York, N.Y., 10022. (212) 753-9180. A casual, relaxed, and friendly "environment" in which to dine American. The bar is always populated and so is the main floor dining room, as well as the quarters on the second floor. Good quality steak, roast beef, chicken, seafood, properly-cooked burgers, crisp fresh salads, and homemade chili are the kind of fare you will find, and it's all priced for budgets that bruise easily. Owner: Michael Wharton. Open 7 days for lunch and dinner. Price: Inexpensive. Reservations: Unnecessary. Credit cards: All major. Private party facilities: 20 to 80. Annual sales: $500,000 to $1 million. Total employment: 40. Corporate name: Oliver's Restaurant, Inc.

O'LUNNEY'S....915 Second Ave., New York, N.Y., 10017. (212) 751-5470. Owner: Hugh O'Lunney.

O'NEAL'S BALOON....48 West 63 St., New York, N.Y., 10023. (212) 399-2353. Cuisine: Continental/American. Owner: Michael O'Neal, Patrick O'Neal, Ture Tufvesson. Open 7 days for lunch and dinner. Credit cards: All major. Private party facilities: 25 to 50. Annual sales: Over $3 million. Total employment: 75. Corporate name: Patrick O'Neal Enterprises.

O'NEAL'S/43RD....147 West 43 St., New York, N.Y., 10036. (212) 869-4200. Cuisine: Continental. Owner: Michael O'Neal, Patrick O'Neal, Ture Tufvesson. Open 7 days for lunch and dinner. Credit cards: All major. Private party facilities: 15 to 500. Annual sales; $1 million to $3 million. Total employment: 100. Corporate name: 43rd & Broadway Associates, Inc.

O'NEAL'S 57TH STREET....60 West 57 St., New York, N.Y., 10019. (212) 399-2361. Cuisine: Continental/American. Owner: Patrick O'Neal, Michael O'Neal, Ture Tufvesson. Open 7 days for lunch and dinner. Credit cards: All major. Annual sales: Over $3 million. Corporate name: 6th & 57th Street/DBA/O'Neal's.

ONE IF BY LAND, TWO IF BY SEA....17 Barrow St., New York, N.Y., 10014. (212) 255-8649. Cuisine: American. Credit cards: AE, DC, MC.

THE ORCHID RESTAURANT....81 Lexington Ave., New York, N.Y., 10016. (212) 889-0960. Cuisine: Continental/American. Owner: Judith Schiff and Howard Wechsler. Open 7 days for lunch and dinner. Credit cards: All major. Annual sales: $500,000 to $1 million. Total employment: 25. Corporate name: The Orchid Restaurant, Ltd.

ORCHIDIA....145 Second Ave., New York, N.Y., 10003. (212) 473-8784. Cuisine: Italian/Ukranian. Owner: George Pasternok. Open 7 days. Credit cards: MC, VISA. Annual sales: $250,000 to $500,000. Total employment: 8.

O'REILLY'S TOWNHOUSE....21 West 35 St., New York, N.Y., 10001. (212) 244-9418. Owner: Mr. O'Reilly.

OREN & ARETSKY....497 Third Ave., New York, N.Y., 10028. (212) 734-8822. Cuisine: Continental. Open 7 days. Credit cards: AE.

ORIGINAL SAMMY'S EMPORIUM....33 East 32 St., New York, N.Y., 10016. (212) 725-0316. Cuisine: Rumanian/Jewish. Owner: Sammy Friedman. Credit cards: All major.

ORSINI'S....41 West 56 St., New York, N.Y., 10019. (212) 757-1698. New York's most romantic Italian restaurant, crowded daily and sprinkled with some of the most stylish people in town—theatrical celebs, the international set, fashion designers, and models. Owner-host Armando Orsini, a European charmer, blandishes them into a state of palate bliss and general felicity. Northern-Italian cuisine covers the spectrum from arugula salad and pastas with hidden surprises to many delightful varieties of veal. owners: Armando & Elio Orsini. Open 6 days for lunch and dinner; Closed Sunday. Price: Expensive. Reservations: Required. Credit cards: All major. Private party facilities: 30 to 70. total employment: 65. Corporate name: Orsini Cafe, Inc.

OSCAR'S SALT OF THE SEA....1155 Third Ave., New York, N.Y., 10021. (212) 879-1199. An Upper East Side landmark for 36 years, Oscar's Salt of the Sea is a sleekly scandanavian-styled seafood sanctum—from the gleaming glass and panelled interior with its clean geometric lines and no-nonsense polished wood tables, to the vast and moderately priced menu offering only daily-fresh fish and seafoods in many permutations and combinations. Specialties include: "Duo of Sole filets," oysters Rockefeller, clam chowder, fish chowder, crabmeat cocktail, baked crab, lobster. Owner: Tom Lazarakis, Nicholas Panas. Open 7 days for lunch and dinner. Priced moderately. Reservations: Accepted. Credit cards: AE, MC, VISA. Annual sales: $1 million to $3 million. Corporate name: Kohela Corporation.

PADDY'S CLAM HOUSE....215 West 34 St., N.Y., N.Y., 10001. (212) 244-9123. Cuisine: Seafood. Credit cards: AE, CB, DC, MC.

THE PALACE....420 East 59 St., New York, N.Y., 10022. (212) 355-5150. Cuisine: French. Owner: Michael Fitoussi. Open for lunch Monday to Friday. Open for dinner Monday to Saturday. Private party facilities: Up to 130.

PALM....837 Second Ave., New York, N.Y., 10017. (212) MU7-2953. After more than 50 years, this venerable rip-roaring lusty establishment shows no signs of losing its considerable energy, its hordes of customers, its tons of food rolling out of its super-large kitchens. The menu boasts none of the effete fad foods so common nowadays, but hardy meat, Italian and seafood dishes of absolutely gargantuan size. Specialties include: Steaks, lamb or pork chops, shrimp scampi, Italian specialties. Owner: Bruce Bozzi, Walter Ganzi. Open Monday through Friday for lunch; Monday through Saturday for dinner; Closed Sunday. Priced moderate to high. Reservations: Suggested. Credit cards: All major. Corporate name: Just One More Restaurant, Inc.—Palm Restaurant, Inc.

PALM TOO....840 Second Ave., New York, N.Y., 10017. (212) 697-5198. Across the street from the original Palm, Palm Too is a newer anteroom of the place. The food is just as superior in this Palm and the caricatures sketched on the wall will make you feel like you've never left. Arguably the finest steak in Manhattan. Owner: Bruce Bozzi, Walter Ganzi. Open Monday through Friday for lunch; Monday through Saturday for dinner; Closed Sunday. Priced moderate to high. Reservations: Suggested. Credit cards: All major. Corporate name: Just One More Restaurant, Inc.—Palm Restaurant, Inc.

PAMIR....1423 Second Ave., New York, N.Y., 10021. (212) 734-3791. Cuisine: Afghani. Owner: Sultan Bayat. Open 7 days for dinner. Credit cards: MC, VISA.

PAMPLONA....822 Sixth Ave., New York, N.Y., 10001. (212) 683-4242. Cuisine: Spanish. Owner: Valentine Gonzlez and Jose Ibarra.

PANCHO VILLA'S....78 St. & Second Ave., New York, N.Y., 10021. (212) 650-1455. Cuisine: Mexican. Owner: Roman Chappa.

PANTHEON....689 Eighth Ave., New York, N.Y., 10036. (212) 664-8294. Cuisine: Greek. Owner: Theodore Werthmuller. Open Monday through Saturday for lunch and dinner; Closed Sunday. Credit cards: AE, DC, MC, VISA. Annual sales: $250,000 to $500,000. Total employment: 16. Corporate name: The Pantheon Restaurant, Inc.

PAPARAZZI....964 Second Ave., New York, N.Y., 10022. (212) 759-7676. Cuisine: Italian.

PAPRIKA....1529 York Ave., New York, N.Y., 10028. (212) 650-9819.

PARIOLI ROMANISSIMO....1466 First Ave., New York, N.Y., 10021. (212) 288-2391. Cuisine: Northern Italian. Owner: Rubrio Rossi. Open for dinner only. Closed Sunday and Monday. Credit cards: AE, CB, DC.

PARK PLACE....39 East 58 St., New York, N.Y., 10022. (212) 750-9700. Cuisine: Continental. Owner: Nick Pappas, Ray Wolowicz, Harry Haralambopoulos. Open Monday through Friday for lunch; Monday through Saturday for dinner; Closed Sunday. Credit cards: All major. Total employment: 28. Corporate name: 58th Street Park Place Restaurant Corp.

PARMA RESTAURANT....1404 Third Ave., New York, N.Y., 10021. (212) 535-3520. Cuisine: Italian. Owner: Michele D'Acquaviva. and John Piscina. Open 7 days. Credit cards: AE. Corporate name: Piscina Restaurant, Inc.

PATRISSY'S....98 Kenmare St., New York, N.Y., 10012. (212) 226-8509. Cuisine: Italian.

PATSY'S....236 West 56 St., New York, N.Y., 10019. Cuisine: Italian. Open Tuesday through Sunday for lunch and dinner. Credit cards: AE, DC, MC, VISA. Private party facilities: Up to 80. Annual sales: $1 million to $3 million. Total employment: 40. Corporate name: Patsy's Italian Restaurant Inc.

PAUL AND JIMMY'S....54 Irving Pl., New York, N.Y., 10003. (212) 475-9540. Cuisine: Italian. Owner: Cosmo, Louis and Nick Azzollini. Open 7 days. Credit cards: All major. Private party facilities: 15 to 75. Annual sales: $500,000 to $1 million. Total employment: 19. Corporate name: 54 Irving Place Corporation.

PEACHES....353 East 77 St., New York, N.Y., 10021. (212) 249-8511. Cuisine: Continental. Owner: Frank Hausler. Open 7 days for lunch, dinner. Credit cards: AE, CB, DC. Annual sales: $250,000 to $500,000. Total employment: 11.

PEARL'S CHINESE RESTAURANT....38 West 48 St., New York, N.Y., 10036. (212) 586-1060. Cuisine: Chinese. Owner: Pearl. Credit cards: None.

PEGGY'S RESTAURANT....54 Franklin St., New York, N.Y., 10013. (212) 233-1718. Cuisine: French. Owner: Margaret Doyle. Credit cards: All major. Private party facilities: 50 to 250. Total employment: 7. Corporate name: Peggy Doyle, Ltd.

PEKING PARK....100 Park Ave., New York, N.Y., 10017. (212) 725-5570. Cuisine: Chinese. Owner: Wilson Maio.

THE PEN & PENCIL....205 East 45 St., New York, N.Y., 10017. (212) 682-8660. Cuisine: American. Owner: John C. Bruno. Open 7 days for lunch and dinner. Credit cards: All major. Private party facilities: 2 to 136. Annual sales: $1 million to $3 million. Total employment: 62. Corporate name: The Pen & Pencil, Inc.

PENG'S....219 East 44 St., New York, N.Y., 10017. (212) 682-8050. Cuisine: Chinese.

PENG TENG....219 East 44 St., New York, N.Y., 10017. (212) 682-8050. Cuisine: Chinese. Credit cards: AE, CB, DC.

PER BACCO....140 East 27 St., New York, N.Y., 10016. (212) 532-8699. Owner: Gene.

PESCA....23 East 22 St., New York, N.Y., 10010. (212) 533-2293. Cuisine: Seafood. Owner: Eugene Franchia and Michael Barrett. Corporate name: 23 East 22nd St. Corp.

PESTO RISTORANTE....407 East 70 St., New York, N.Y., 10021. (212) 535-2400. Cuisine: Italian.

PETE'S TAVERN....129 East 18 St., New York, N.Y., 10003. (212) 473-7676.

PHEBE'S PLACE....361 Bowery, New York, N.Y., 10003. (212) 473-9008. Cuisine: American.

PHILLIPPINE GARDENS....455 Second Ave., New York, N.Y., 10010. (212) 685-5855. Cuisine: Phillippino. Owner: Sancho Varias.

PICCOLO MONDO....1269 First Ave., New York, N.Y., 10021. (212) 249-3141. Cuisine: Northern Italian. Owner: Gianni Lonza. Open 7 days for lunch and dinner. Credit cards: All major. Private party facilities: 25 to 40. Annual sales: $1 million to $3 million. Total employment: 32.

PIE IN THE SKY....173 Third Ave., New York, N.Y., 10003. (212) 228-2790. A popular spot for lunch or dinner, and even greater for gourmet take-out food. A mother-and-daughter operation, Lynne Bien and Deborah Bien Jensen turn out an impressive array of *pates*, soups, salds, hot and cold sandwiches, hot and cold light entrees, and a slew of delicious desserts. Lynn and Deborah make it all on the premises daily, and "it" ranges from smoked salmon pate to *chili con carne* to *tortellini vinaigrette*. Priced moderately. Open 7 days for lunch and dinner. No reservations. No credit cards. Annual sales: $500,000 to $1 million. Total employment: 35. Corporate name: Lynne Bien, Inc.

PIETRO'S....201 East 45 St., New York, N.Y., 10017. (212) MU2-9760. Owner: Leo.

PIRAEUS, MY LOVE....117 West 57 St., New York, N.Y., 10019. (212) 757-8847. Cuisine: Greek. Owner: Phil D.

PIRANDELLO....7 Washington Pl., New York, N.Y., 10003. (212) 260-3066. Cuisine: Italian. Credit cards: AE.

P.J. CHARLTON....549 Greenwich St., New York, N.Y., 10014. (212) 929-9773. Cuisine: American.

P.J. CLARKE'S....915 Third Ave., New York, N.Y., 10022. (212) PL9-1650. Cuisine: American. Credit cards: None.

P.J. MORIARTY....1034 Third Ave., New York, N.Y., 10021. (212) 838-2438. Owner: Mrs. Moriarty.

PLAZA CAFE....560 Third Ave., New York, N.Y., 10016. (212) 867-7179. Owner: Tom Griffths.

PLAZA ESPANA....130 West 58 St., New York, N.Y., 10019. (212) 757-6434. Cuisine: Spanish. Owner: Joseph Rea.

POLETTI'S....2315 Broadway, New York, N.Y., 10024. (212) 580-1200. Cuisine: Italian. Credit cards: AE, DC, MC, VISA.

POLONEZ PRESS BOX....139 East 45 St., New York, N.Y., 10017. (212) 697-4735. Owner: Vincent Brunhard Jr.

PONGSRI THAILAND RESTAURANT....244 West 48 St., New York, N.Y., 10017. (212) 582-3392. Cuisine: Thai. Owner: Prasit Tang. Open 7 days for lunch and dinner. Credit cards: AE, DC. Annual sales: $250,000 to $500,000. Total employment: 6.

PONTE'S....37 Debrosses St., New York, N.Y., 10013. (212) 226-4621-2-3. A bustling Italian steakhouse filled with apper clientele and strolling musicians. Well-marbled steaks and chops never disappoint, and neither do the sumptuous Italian entrees. Personal favorite: "Hungry Lobster"—a heaping platter of lobster embroidered with jumbo shrimps and meaty clams sauteed in rich olive oil, then baked to a glistening golden-reddish hue. Owners: Joseph, Angelo, Frank, and Tony Ponte. Open Monday through Friday for lunch; Monday through Saturday for dinner; Closed Sundays (except for private parties). Price: Expensive. Reservations: Suggested. Credit cards: All major. Private party facilities: Up to 110. Annual sales: $1 million to $3 million. Total employment: 40. Corporate name: Ponte's Steak House, Inc. Entertainment: Strolling guitar all week; accordian and violins on Fridays and Saturdays.

PORTOROZ....340 Lexington Ave., New York, N.Y., 10017. (212) 687-8195. Though underpriced in our estimation, this place serves excellent Italian/Yugoslavian/ Continental cuisine with style and imagination. Pasta is delicious (try the linguine with resilent rounds of squid), Slavic specialties are succulent, chicken dishes are plump and tender, the fish and seafood are fresh and savory. Specialties include: A pungent and interesting stonefish dish, beef-and-pork Slavic sausage, and stuffed cabbage Macedonian style. Owner: Joseph Lucin. Open Monday through Saturday for lunch; Monday through Friday for dinner; Closed Sunday. Priced moderate. Reservations: Accepted. Credit cards: All major. Annual sales: $500,000 to $1 million. Total employment: 18.

POSSIBLE 20....253 West 55 St., New York, N.Y., 10019. (212) 541-9350. Cuisine: American. Owner: Geoff Lissauer.

POST HOUSE....28 East 63 St., New York, N.Y., 10021. (212) 935-2888. Owner: Al Stillman.

PRIME TIME....355 Amsterdam Ave., New York, N.Y., 10023. (212) 595-0800. Cuisine: American. Owner: Michael Danon and Richard Dumas. Annual sales: $500,000. Total empolyment: 20. Corporate name: Jeni Foods Inc.

PRIMAVERA....1570 First Ave., New York, N.Y., 10028. (212) 8618608. Nicola Civetta serves sophisticated Italian cuisine solicitously in his European-styled, inordinately handsome but relaxed restaurant. Pasta courses and veal entrees are plentiful with first-rate Italian accents built into them, but undisputed king of the house specialties is the tender and sweet *Capratto alla Romano*—succulent baby goat, oven-roasted with the spicy of rosemary. Primavera is very popular, reserve well ahead for a table. Open 7 days for dinner only. Priced moderate to high. Credit cards: All major. Annual sales: $500,000 to $1 million. Total employment: 16. Corporate name: Divetta Enterprises, Inc.

PROMENADE CAFE....Fifth Ave. & Rockefeller Center, New York, N.Y., 10112. (212) PL7-5730. Cuisine: American. Credit cards: MC.

PRONTO....30 East 60 St., New York, N.Y., 10022. (212) 421-8151. The various atmospheres, depending on where you are seated in this dual-levelled restaurant are rather novel, but the most popular seems to be the one suggesting an early 1900's Bologna open kitchen (tended by cooks making pastas that are rolled, cut and hung to dry in full view). Menu highlights cover eggy fettucine with *frutti di mare* seafood sauce, *zuppa di Pesce*, garlic butter scampi, and a full roster of veal scallopines. Salads are good, too, the the vegetables are fresh. Owner: Claudio Bona, Mgr. Open Mondy through Saturday for lunch and dinner; Sunday for dinner only. Price: moderate to expensive. Reservations: Accepted. Credit cards: All major. Corporate name: Pronto Ristorante, Inc.

PULCINELLA....1713 Second Ave., New York, N.Y., 10028. (212) 831-6640. Cuisine: Italian.

QUIET LITTLE TABLE IN THE CORNER....237 Madison Ave., New York, N.Y., 10016. (212) 685-7160. Cuisine: American/Continental. Credit cards: AE, CB, DC, MC.

THE QUILTED GIRAFFE....955 Second Ave. New York, N.Y., 10022. (212) 753-5355. Cuisine: Luxury American. Owner: Susan and Barry Wine. Open Monday to Friday for dinner. Credit cards: AE, DC, MC, VISA. Private party facilities: Up to 20. Annual sales: $1 million to $3 million. Total employment: 20.

QUON LUCK....66 Mott St., New York, N.Y., 10013. (212) 226-4675. Cuisine: Chinese. Credit cards: None.

QUO VADIS....23 East 63 St., New York, N.Y., 10021. (212) 838-0590. This culinary great has recently re-opened after a sorely missed absence and it's very fine to have it back. Quo Vadis specializes in Italian and French *haute cuisine* and has a roster of owners and/or chefs that reads like the best of Escoffier's recent star pupils. Owner: Gino and Bruno (original owners) with Michel Bordeaux, Dieter Schorner, Giorgio Meriggi. Open Monday through Friday for lunch; Monday through Saturday for dinner; Closed Sunday. Prices are expensive. Credit cards: All major. reservations are required.

THE RACING CLUB....206 East 67 St., New York, N.Y., 10021. (212) 650-1675. Cuisine: Italian/Steak.

RADISHES....555 Seventh Ave., New York, N.Y., 10036. (212) LO3-7440. Owner: Irving Reiso.

RAFFAELA'S....134 West Houston St., New York, N.Y., 10012. (212) 475-8675. Cuisine: Italian. Owner: Fred Flengo.

RAGA....57 West 48 St., New York, N.Y., 10036. (212) 757-3450. Virtually a magic-carpet tour of the culture and cuisine of India—muligatawny soup, curry, ginger and herb spices, *tandoori* cooking, lobster Malagar and all that. Tables are formally set, myriad carved wooden pillars and archways prevail; evenings someone starts to play the sinuous music of sitar and tabla. The menu offers certain delicacies unavailable elsewhere: oysters Bombay, delicately handled with minced onion and the tang of ginger; a baked ramekin of spicy shredded crab coa. Chicken *tikke,* giant shrimp, and lamb kabobs are *tandoori* specialties, and the vegetarian cookery of India is well-represented by silky, smoky *baingan bhurta* of seasoned mashed eggplant, aromatic saffron rices and the traditional creamy-chunky lentil *dal.* Owner: Mr. Mahese, Mgr. Open Monday through Friday for lunch; 7 days for dinner. Price: Moderate. Reservations: Accepted. Credit cards: All major. Corporate name: Indian Resorts & Restaurants, Inc.

THE RAINBOW GRILL....30 Rockefeller Plaza, New York, N.Y., 10112. (212) 757-8970. Cuisine: French/Italian. Owner: Brian Daly & Anthony May. Open 6 days for dinner; Closed Sundays. Credit cards: All major. Private party facilities: Up to 400. Annual sales: $7 million. Corporate name: D-M Restaurant Corp.

RAO'S....455 East 114 St., New York, N.Y., 10029. (212) 534-9625. Cuisine: Italian. Owner: Vincent Rao. Credit cards: None.

RAOUL'S....180 Prince St., New York, N.Y., 10012. (212) 966-3518. Cuisine: French. Open 7 days for dinner. Credit cards: AE, MC, VISA. Private party facilities: Up to 80. Annual sales: $500,000 to $1 million. Total employment: 12.

RAPHAEL....33 West 54 St., New York, N.Y., 10019. (212) 582-8993. Owner: Mr. Raphael.

RATNER'S RESTAURANT....138 Delancy St., New York, N.Y., 10002. (212) 677-5588. Cuisine: Fish and Dairy. Owner: Robert Harmatz. Open 7 days for breakfast, lunch and dinner. Credit cards: None. Private party facilities: 20 to 80. Annual sales: Over $3 million. Total employment: 100+. Corporate name: Van Matz Corp.

RAVELLED SLEEVE....1387 Third Ave., New York, N.Y., 10021. (212) 628-8814.

RED TULIP....439 East 75 St., New York, N.Y., 10021. (212) 743-4893. Cuisine: Hungarian. Owner: Kazner Kovacs. Credit cards: AE.

REGINE'S....502 Park Ave., New York, N.Y., 10022. (212) 826-0990. Cuisine: French. Owner: Regine Zylberberg. Credit cards: AE, DC.

REIDY'S....22 East 54 St., New York, N.Y., 10022. (212) 753-2419. Cuisine: Irish/American. Credit cards: None.

RENE PUJOL....321 West 51, New York, N.Y., 10019. (212) 246-3023. A hearteningly traditional French restaurant convenient to the theater district, Rene Pujol boasts an atmosphere reminiscent of a Bordeaux country inn. The bill-of-fare captures all the spirit and flavor of France with such items as *filet de beouf Perigueux,* roast of veal *chasseur, dodines de volaille aux morilles,* soft shell crabs *Meuniere,* and *canard au cassis.* Owner: Rene Pujol. Open Monday through Friday for lunch; Monday through Saturday for dinner; Closed Sunday. Price: Moderate to high. Reservations: Suggested. Credit cards: All major. Private party facilities: 10 to 50. Total employment: 30. Corporate name: Rene Pujol, Inc.

RESTAURANT CLUB 1407....1407 Broadway, New York, N.Y., 10018. (212) 575-1407. Cuisine: American. Owner: David and Alan Nussbaum. Open Monday through Friday. Credit cards: All major. Private party facilities: 4 to 400. Annual sales: $1 million to $3 million. Total employment: 60.

RESTAURANT RAPHAEL....33 West 54 St., New York, N.Y., 10019. (212) 582-8993. Cuisine: French. Owner: Mira & Raphael Edery. Open Monday to Friday for lunch and dinner. Credit cards: AE, CD, DC. Private party facilities: 40 to 46. Annual sales: $500,000 to $1 million. Total employment: 10. Corporate name: Jessica-Oliver Restaurant, Inc.

RICHOUX OF LONDON....153 East 53 St., (Citicorp Bldg.), New York, N.Y., 10022. (212) 753-7721. Cuisine: English.

RINCON DE ESPANA....226 Thompson St., New York, N.Y., 10012. (212) 475-9891. Cuisine: Spanish. Credit cards: All major. Owner: Julio.

RISTORANTE DOMINICO....120 East 40 St., New York, N.Y., 10016. (212) 682-0310. Largely due to new management, this establishment has grown into a really good Italian restaurant. The place is stylish and inviting, with an atmosphere of busy cheerfulness. Its menu has plenty of selections among the pastas, veals, seafoods, steaks, chops and poultry. Specialties include: breast of chicken parmagiana, shrimp oreganata, veal rollatini, and sole meuniere. Owner: Jack O'Brien. Open Monday through Friday for lunch; Monday through Saturday for dinner; Closed Sunday. Priced moderately. Reservations: Accepted. Credit cards: All major. Private party facilities: Up to 200. Total employment: 22. Corporate name: Avenue S Restaurant Corp.

ROBATA....30 East 61 St., New York, N.Y., 10021. (212) 688-8120. Cuisine: Japanese.

ROCK GARDEN OF TOKYO....34 West 56 St., New York, N.Y., 10019. (212) 245-7936. Cuisine: Japanese. Owner: Makoto Kaneda, Shoki Kaneda. Open 6 days for lunch and dinner; Closed Sundays. Credit cards: All major. Annual sales: $250,000 to $500,000. Total employment: 20. Corporate name: Hakim's E.P., Inc.

ROCKING HORSE CAFE....224 Columbus Ave., New York, N.Y., 10023. (212) 724-7816. Cuisine: International.

ROCKY LEE....**987 Second Ave., New York, N.Y., 10022. (212) 753-4858. Cuisine: Italian & thin-crust pizza. Owner: Vinvent Panetta. Credit cards: All major. Private party facilities: Up to 300. Annual sales: $1 million to $3 million. Total employment: 45 Corporate name: Rocky Lee, Inc.**

ROMA DI NOTTE....137 East 55 St., New York, N.Y., 10022. (212) 832-1128. Cuisine: Italian. Owner: Roberto Mei. Open Monday through Saturday. Credit cards: AE, CB, DC. Private party facilities: 20 to 150. Annual sales: $1 million to $3 million. Total employment: 28.

ROMEO SALTA RESTAURANT....30 West 56 St., New York, N.Y., 10019. (212) 246-5772. Cuisine: Italian. Owner: Salvatore & Rosita Salta. Closed Sunday. Credit cards: All major. Private party facilities: 20 to 60. Annual sales: $1 million to $3 million. Total employment: 30. Romeo Salta Restaurant, Inc.

ROSE....41 West 52 St., New York, N.Y., 10019. (212) 974-9004. Owner: Mr. Buzzilino.

ROSEBAY CAFE....#1 Sheridan Sq., New York, N.Y., 10014. (212) 929-0735. Cuisine: French & Continental. Owner: Robert Packer & Danielle Brackett. Open 6 days for dinner; Closed Mondays. Credit cards: All major. Private party facilities: 30 yo 60. Total employment: 5. Corporate name: Auge Restaurant Corporation.

ROSSINI'S....Place Inc., 108 East 38 St., New York, N.Y., 10016. (212) MU3-0135. Cuisine: Northern Italian. Owner: Romano Bemaz. Annual sales: $1,500,000. Total employment: 28.

ROYAL ROOST....154 Wewst 13 St., New York, N.Y., 10011. (212) 255-3619. Cuisine: Continental. Owner: Richard Hendrickson. Open 7 days for dinner; Sunday brunch. Credit cards: AE, MC, VISA. Corporate name: Royal Roost, Inc.

RUC....312 East 72 St., New York, N.Y., 10021. (212) 650-1611. Owner: Jerry Ruc.

RUGGERO'S....**194 Grand St., New York, N.Y., 10013. (212) 925-1340. Our first choice among the restaurants of Little Italy. Ignoring tourist infiltration, it has a vast family clientele. Medium prices, good food, good wines, good service. Special highlights: hot antipasto, veal *zingara,* and Ruggero's own dessert creation of *tortoni,* fresh fruit, lemon liqueur and cognac. Open for lunch and dinner, 7 days. Owner: Joseph Zito. Credit cards: All major. Reservations: Accepted. Private party facilities. Entertainment: Strolling Guitarists. Total employment: 30.**

RUPPERT'S....1662 Third Ave., New York, N.Y., 10028. (212) 831-1900. Cuisine: Continental.

RUSSIAN BEAR....139 East 56 St., New York, N.Y., 10022. (212) 753-0465. Cuisine: Russian. Owner: Mieczslaw Tarwid.

THE RUSSIAN TEA ROOM....150 West 57 St., New York, N.Y., 10019. (212) 265-0947. Cuisine: Classical Russian. Owner: Faith Stewart-Gordon. Open 7 days. Private party facilities: 50 to 110. Annual sales: Over $3 million. Total employment: 170.

RUSTY'S....1271 Third Ave., New York, N.Y., 10021. (212) 861-4518. Cuisine: American/Continental. Owner: Rusty Staub.

SABOR....20 Cornelia St., New York, N.Y., 10014. (212) 243-9579. Cuisine: Cuban. Open daily for lunch and dinner. Credit cards: Call for cards.

SAHIB... 222 East 86 St., New York, N.Y., 10028. (212) 535-6760. Cuisine: North Indian. Owner: Earl Chawla. Open 7 days for lunch and dinner. Credit cards: AE, MC, VISA, Private party facilities: 40 to 50. Annual sales: $250,000 to $500,000. Total employment: 20.

SAITO....305 East 46 St., New York, N.Y., 10017. (212) 759-8897. Cuisine: Japanese. Owner: Mrs. Saito.

SAL ANTHONY'S....55 Irving Pl., New York, N.Y., 10003. (212) 982-9030. Cuisine: Italian. Owner: Anthony Macagnone. Open 7 days for lunch and dinner. Credit cards: AE, DC, MC, VISA. Private party facilities: Up to 100. Annual sales: $1 million to $3 million. Total employment: 45.

THE SALOON....1920 Broadway, New York, N.Y., 10023. (212) 874-1500. Cuisine: Continental. Owner: Stewart Rosen. Credit cards: All major.

SALTA IN BOCCA....179 Madison Ave., New York, N.Y., 10016. (212) 684-1757. Cuisine: Italian. Owner: Fulvio Tramontina. Credit cards: All major.

SAMANTHA....1495 First Ave., New York, N.Y., 10021. (212) 744-9288. Cuisine: Continental. Credit cards: AE, DC, MC, VISA.

SAMMY'S ROUMANIAN....157 Chrystie St., New York, N.Y., 10002. (212) 673-0330. Cuisine: Rumanian Steakhuse. Owner: Stan Zimmerman. Credit cards: None.

SAN MARCO....36 West 52 St., New York, N.Y., 10019. (212) 243-5340. Cuisine: Italian. Owner: Bruno and Peppino.

SAN REMO WEST....393 Eighth Ave., New York, N.Y., 10001. (212) 564-1819. Cuisine: Italian/Continental. Owner: Joe Green.

SAN STEFANO RISTORANTE....322 East 14 St., New York, N.Y., 10011. (212) 473-5953. Cuisine: Italian. Owner: Ray M. Mandich. Open Monday through Saturday for dinner. Credit cards: All major. Annual sales: $250,000 to $500,000. Total employment: 7. Corporate name: 322 East 14th Street Restaurant Corp.

SARDI'S....**234 West 44 St., New York, N.Y., 10036. (212) 221-6440. The name Sardi's automatically summons forth images of the caricatures on the walls, the opening night parties, the glamorous stars stopping in for a drink after a performance, the lookers-on flocking to see the stars—Sardi's is thought to be *the* Broadway restaurant. Specialties include: Canneloni *au gratin,* smoked trout, *minestrone,* crabmeat a la Sardi's, strawberries in *zabaglione.* Owner: Vincent Sardi. Open Monday through Satuirday for lunch; 7 days for dinner; Sunday brunch. Priced moderate to high. Reservations are a must. Credit cards: All major. Private party facilities: Available.**

SAY ENG LOOK....1 East Broadway, New York, N.Y., 10038. (212) 732-0796. Cuisine: Chinese. Manager: Harry Hu. Credit cards: MC.

SAZERAC HOUSE....533 Hudson St., New York, N.Y., 10014. (212) 989-0313. Cuisine: American. Credit cards: None.

SCOOP RESTAURANT....210 Eat 43 St., New York, N.Y., 10017. (212) 682-0483. Cuisine: Italian/American. Owner: Noel Siegel. Open Monday through Friday for lunch; Monday through Saturday for dinner; Closed Sunday. Credit cards: All major. Annual sales: $500,000 to $1 million. Corporate name: N&T Food Services, Inc.

SEA-FARE OF THE AEGEAN....**25 West 56 St., New York, N.Y., 10019. (212) 581-0540. Minute excellence, costly simplicity, reservations imperative and unforgettable gourmet seafoods (embellished with succulent Greek touches) ready for you. Highly cultivated shrimp, Santorini-style; poached red snapper with *avgolemono* sauce and baked stripe bass with clams. The wine list is also impressive. Open 7 days for lunch and dinner. Prices are expensive. Owner: Costas Gounaris, Nick Tsigakos, Joseph A. Milukas. Credit cards: All major. Reservations: Recommended.**

SEASCAPES....**202 East 42 St., New York, N.Y., 10017. (212) 370-0098. One of our favorite new continental-seafood restaurants. It's very engaging and most attractively got up with salmon banquettes and fresh flowers. The repertoire of good dishes reflects the sophistication of the owner Attila Danku, who worked in The Four Seasons for nine years. He knows his wines too. House specialties include: shrimp and *chipolatas;* seafood *fra diavolo* and veal ambrosia. Open for Monday through Friday for lunch; 7 days for dinner. Prices are moderate. Owner: Attila Danku. Credit cards: All major. Reservations: Accepted. Annual sales: $500,000 to $1 million. Total employment: 12.**

SERENDIPITY 3....225 East 60 St., New York, N.Y., 10022. (212) 838-3531. Cuisine: American. Owner: Calvin Holt, Stephen Bruce. Open 7 days for lunch and dinner. Credit cards: AE, DC, MC, VISA. Private party facilities available. Total employment: 60. Corporate name: Serendipity 3, Inc.

SEVEN STEPS DOWN RESTAURANT....231 East 53 St., New York, N.Y., 10022. (212) 750-3256. Cuisine: Continental/Greek. Owner: Alice and Larry Blecker. Open for lunch Monday through Friday; Saturday dinner. Credit cards: CB, DC. Private party facilities: 15 to 35. Annual sales: $250,000 to $500,000. Total employment: 2. Corporate name: 231 Restaurant Corp.

SEVILLA....62 Charles St. New York, N.Y., 10012. (212) 243-9513. Cuisine: Spanish. Owner: Jose Lloves.

SEYMOUR'S PLACE....1162 First Ave.,New York, N.Y., 10021. (212) 355-5577. Cuisine: gourmet-Kosher-Style Delicatessen. Owner: Bernie Ross. Corporate name: Lorbern Entr. Inc.

SHAH JAHAN....980 Ninth Ave., New York, N.Y., 10019. (212) 586-4180. Cuisine: Indian. Owner: Mr. Jahan.

SHALIMAR RESTAURANT....39 East 29 St., New York, N.Y., 10009. (212) 889-1977. Cuisine: Indian. Owner: Lucas Gomes. Open 7 days for lunch and dinner. Credit cards: All major. Private party facilities: Up to 100. Annual sales: $250,00 to $500,000. Total employment. 10. Corporate name: Bombay Calcutta Restaurant, Inc.

SHEBA....151 Hudson St., New York, N.Y., 10013. (212) 925-0885. Cuisine: Ethiopian. Owner: Araya Selassie. Credit cards: None.

SHELTER....540 Second Ave., New York, N.Y., 10003. (212) 362-4360. Cuisine: Continental.

SHEZAN RESTAURANT....8 West 58 St., New York, N.Y., 10019. (212) 371-1414 or 371-1420. Cuisine: Indian. Owner: Mr. Shahnawaz. Open 6 days for lunch and dinner; Closed sunday. Credit cards: All major. Private party facilities: 30 to 100. Annual sales: $500,000 to $1 million. Total employment: 22. Corporate name: Interchez, Inc.

SHINBASHI....280 Park Ave., New York, N.Y., 10017. (212) 661-3915. Cuisine: Japanese. Credit cards: AE, CB, DC, MC.

SHISH MAHAL....161 Madison Ave., New York, N.Y., 10016. (212) 889-3326. Cuisine: Indian. Owner: Kalandar Meah.

SHUN LEE DYNASTY....900 Second Ave., New York, N.Y., 10017. (212) 755-3900. Another offshoot of the Shun Lee series of fine Chinese restaurants. While not as posh or flashy as Shun Lee Palace, this Shun Lee serves the same sort of exemplary food with the emphasis on Hunan, Mandarin, and Cantonese Chinese cookery. Specialties include: Chef Wang's crisp Sea Bass Hunan style, Peking duck, rabbit Szechuan, and the real specialty, Beggar's Chicken (this dish requires a day's advance notice, but it's well worth the effort). Owner: Michael Tong. Open 7 days for lunch and dinner; No dim sum here. Credit cards: AE, DC, CB. Reservations are recommended. Moderate to high prices. Private party facilities for between 10 and 60 persons. Corporate name: Shun Lee Dynasty, Inc.

SHUN LEE PALACE....155 East 55 St., New York, N.Y., 10022. (212) 371-8844. One of New York's flashiest, splashiest, most expensive (if you dine with the whole raft of specialties) and best Chinese restaurants. It's posh and elegant, and you can dine in simple quiet in the front room and exciting, boisterous activity in the back room. You have to give a day's notice for the "Beggar's Chicken," and it's worth it. There's also Peking duck. Head chef and co-owner T.T. Wang prepares all kinds of Chinese cuisines, featuring Cantonese, Szechuan, and Hunan. Owner: Michael Tong, T.T. Wang. Open 7 days for lunch and dinner. Priced moderate to high. Reservations accepted. Credit cards: AE, CB, DC. Total employment: 40. Corporate name: Shun Lee Palace, Inc.

SHUN LEE WEST....43 West 65 St., New York, N.Y., 10023. (212) 595-8895. Started by the same duo that owns Shun Lee Palace (head chef T.T. Wang and Michael Tong), Shun Lee West is by no means a younger brother. Serving a different menu of Cantonese, Szechuan, and Hunan dishes, it matches the prestigious Palace in food and decor. What's more, it serves dim sum dinner late at night and on weekends. Specialties include: Peking duck, crisp sea bass Hunan style, Chef Wang's duckling, vegetable duck pie, and rabbit Szechuan style. Owner: T.T. Wang, Michael Tong. Open Monday through Friday for lunch; dim sum lunch Saturday and Sunday; 7 nights for dinner; dim sum dinner from 10:00 PM to mid-night 7 days. Priced moderate to high. Reservations suggested. Credit cards: AE, CB, DC. Annual sales: $1 million to $3 million. Total employment: 45. Corporate name: T&W Restaurant, Inc.

SIAM INN....916 Eighth Ave., New York, N.Y., 10019. (212) 489-5237. Cuisine: Thai. Owner: Saki. Credit cards: AE, DC.

SICHUAN PAVILION....22 East 44 St., New York, N.Y., 10017. (212) 986-3775. Cuisine: Chinese. Credit cards: All major.

SIMON'S....75 West 68 St., New York, N.Y., 10023. (212) 496-7477. Cuisine: Nouvelle. Owner: John Simon. Credit cards: AE.

SITAR....873 First Avce., New York, N.Y., 10017. (212) 688-7070. Cuisine: Indian. Owner: Senil Puri.

65 IRVING PLACE....65 Irving Place, New York, N.Y., 10003. (212) 673-3939. Cuisine: French/Continental. Owner: Robin and Isabelle Cullinen, Fabrizio and Adriana Bottero. Corporate name: 65 Irving Place Rest. Corp.

THE SKIPPER....47 East 46 St., New York, N.Y., 10017. (212) 688-2365. Cuisine: French.

THE SLATE....852 Tenth Ave., New York, N.Y., 10019. (212) 581-6340. Cuisine: American. Credit cards: AE, DC, MC.

SLOPPIE LOUIE'S....92 South St., New York, N.Y., 10038. (212) 952-9657. Cuisine: Seafood. Owner: Joe. Credit cards: None.

SMITH & WOLLENSKY....201 East 49 St., New York, N.Y., 10017. (212) 753-1530. Owner: Ben Benson.

SOHO CHARCUTERIE....195 Spring St., New York, N.Y., 10013. (212) 226-3545. Cuisine: French. Open daily for lunch and dinner. Credit cards: Call for cards.

THE SOHO WINE BAR....422 West Broadway, New York, N.Y., 10012. (212) 431-4790. Cuisine: Charcuterie. Owner: Alexander Wiener, Mng. Dir. Open 7 days for lunch and dinner. Credit cards: AE only. Private party facilities: 20 to 400. Annual sales: $500,000 to $1 million. Corporate name: R&W Wine Bar, Ltd.

SOOMTHAI....14790 Second Ave., New York, N.Y., 10021. (212) 570-6994. Cuisine: Thai. Credit cards: AE, MC, VISA.

SOUEN....210 Ave. of the Americas, New York, N.Y., 10014. (212) 242-9083. Cuisine: Japanese. Credit cards: AE.

SPAIN....113 West 13 St., New York, N.Y., 10011. (212) 929-9580. Cuisine: Spanish. Owner: Julio Diaz.

SPARKS STEAKHOUSE....210 East 46 St., New York, N.Y., 10017. (212) 687-4855. Cuisine: Steakhouse. Owner: Michael and Pat Cetta.

SPINDLETOP....245 West 47 St., New York, N.Y., 10036. (212) CI5-7455. Cuisine: Continental/American. Owner: Hal Kanter. Open 7 days for lunch and dinner. Credit cards: All major. Private party facilities: Up to 350. Annual sales: $500,000 to $1 million. Total employment: 20.

SPQR....133 Mulberry St., New York, N.Y., 10013. (212) 925-3120. Cuisine: Steakhouse. Open 7 days for lunch and dinner. Credit cards: All major.

STAGE DOOR CANTEEN....270 West 45 St., New York, N.Y., 10036. (212) 221-1065. A lively casual restaurant with the atmosphere of the original Stage Door Canteen recalled by movie out-takes framed on the fabric-covered walls. Enjoy a full meal or light repast. Entertainment nightly from 7:00 PM. Specialties include: Barbequed baby back ribs, Tex-Mex chili, and quiche Lorraine. Owner: Milford Plaza. Open Wednesday and Saturday for lunch; 7 days for dinner and late supper. Priced moderate to inexpensive. Reservations: Accepted. Credit cards: Call for cards. Annual sales: $500,000 to $1 million. Total employment: 25.

STARS DELI....593 Lexington Ave., New York, N.Y., 10022. (212) 935-9480. Cuisine: Delicatessen. Owner: Harold.

STELLA DEL MARE....346 Lexington Ave., New York, N.Y., 10016. (212) 687-4425. Dividied into a downstairs (bar and lounge) and an upstairs (a decorous natural-brick walled main dining room, augmented by a recessed snug glass-ceilinged garden area), the new Stella del Mare is a relaxed place to enjoy Northern-Italian fare—although the rightful centerpiece of this restaurant is seafood. The cooking is not too elaborate but full of ideas. Even the mussels are a special event because of the accompanying sauce mariniere, an especially gentle combination of white wine, garlic, parsley, and fresh tomato. Mako shark steaks (not always available) are remarkable not only for their generous moist boneless cuts, but interesting flavor and texture, and, best of all, simple and immensely tasty butter sauce. Meat selection is limited but prime. Owner: Joseph Lucin. Open Monday through Friday for lunch; Monday through Saturday for dinner; Closed Sunday. Price: Moderate. Reservations: Accepted. Credit cards: All major. Corporate name: Stella del Mare, Inc.

SURF MAID....151 Bleecker St., New York, N.Y., 10012. (212) 473-8845.

SUZANNE....313 East 46 St., New York, N.Y., 10017. (212) 832-2888. Cuisine: Vietnamese. Owner: Huy Ty Pham. Credit cards: All major.

SWEETS....2 Fulton St., New York, N.Y., 10038. (212) 825-9786. Cuisine: Seafood. Open daily for lunch and dinner. Credit cards: Call for cards.

SWEET BASIL....88 Seventh Ave. South, New York, N.Y., 10011. (212) 242-1785.

SWEETWATER'S....170 Amsterdam Ave., New York, N.Y., 10023. (212) 873-4100. Cuisine: Continental/Italian. Credit cards: All major.

SWISS INN....822 First Ave., New York, N.Y., 10017. (212) 758-3258. Cuisine: Swiss. Owner: Willy Zach.

SZECHUAN CUISINE....30 East Broadway, New York, N.Y., 10002. (212) 966-2326. Cuisine: Chinese. Credit cards: None.

SZECHUAN PALACE....1329 Second Ave., New York, N.Y., 10021. (212) 628-8652. Is a solid core of good Szechuan and Cantonese cuisine to which serious eaters without desire for chi-chi gravitate automatically. From the kitchen comes a sensitive assortment of dishes spicy and light, simple and complex. Specialties includes mussels in hot sauce, fried dumplings, shrimp marinated with fresh vegetables, General Chin's chicken (with fancy vegetables in tingling hot sauce), Open for lunch and dinner, 7 days. Moderately priced. Manager: Raymond Kam. Credit cards: All major. Reservations: Accepted.

SZECHUAN TASTE....23 Chatham Square, New York, N.Y., 10038. (212) 267-0672. Szechuan Taste is Chinatown favorite. Chef Lau makes his Szechuan dishes appropriately spicy, but he also gives them a richness and a complexity which raises them above the norm. A glass-enclosed sidewalk dining area allows you to observe Chinatown's hustle and bustle while you eat. Specialties include: hot and sour soup, assorted flavor soup, cold shreds of jellyfish, *young-shun* beef, Imperial shrimp, noodles with sesame paste, noodles with meat sauce. Moderately priced. Owner: Vera Chow. Open 7 days for lunch and dinner. Reservations suggested. Annual sales: $500 Reservations suggested. Annual sales: $500,000 to $1 million. Total employment: 25. Corporate name: Chen & Chow Enterprises, Inc.

TABLE D'HOTE....44 East 92 St., New York, N.Y., 10025. (212) 348-8125. Cuisine: Continental. Owner: Stuart Shultz, Vivek Bandhu and Laurie Gibson. Credit cards: None.

TAJ MAHAL....1154 First Ave., New York, N.Y., 10021. (212) 755-3017. Cuisine: Indian. Owner: Leo Gomes.

TANDOOR....40 East 49 St., New York, N.Y., 10017. (212) 752-3334. Continues to be one of the most awesomely stylish Indian restaurants around, the surroundings with their exotic embellishments are worth viewing. Tandoor's potpourri of succulent dishes from baked Tandoor meats to curries highlight the fanciful menu, and all of the Indian breads are tantalizing and excellent, too. Other specialties include: chicken *tikka masala, kalami kabob,* and lamb *vindaloo.* Open 7 days for lunch and dinner. Prices are moderate. Owner: Victor Khaubani, Credit cards: All major. Reservations: Accepted. Private party facilities.

TANG TANG....1470 First Ave., New York, N.Y., 10021. (212) 744-9320. Cuisine: Chinese. Owner: Mrs. Tang. Credit Cards: AE, MC, DC, VISA.

TANG'S CHARIOT....236 East 53 St., New York, N.Y., 10022. (212) 355-5098. Cuisine: Szechuan. Corporate name: Tang's Third Ave., Palace Inc.

TAVERN ON THE GREEN....Central Park West, New York, N.Y., 10023. (212) 873-3200. Cuisine: American. Owner: Warner LeRoy.

TAVOLA CALDA DA ALFREDO....285 Bleecker St., New York, N.Y., 10014. (212) 924-4789. Cuisine: Italian. Owner: Alfredo Viazzi and Ken Viazzi. Closed Wednesday. Credit cards: None. Annual sales: $250,000 to $500,000. Total employment: 10. Corporate name: Tavola Calda, Inc.

TEDDY'S....219 West Broadway, New York, N.Y., 10013. (212) 226-8131. This is not the same Teddy's that for years was a popular hangout for the big names of the time, but it's in the same building, and the food is excellent. The accent is definitely Italian, and the large menu offers almost all the traditional Italian dishes. Specialties include: lamb chops *Arrabiata,* sole *Savois,* veal *marsala, fettucini ala prosciutto,* and *tortellini ala Bolognese.* Priced moderate to high. Owner: Richard Borsia. Open Monday through Friday for lunch; Monday through Saturday for dinner; Closed Sunday. Reservations and all major credit cards accepted. Private party facilities for between 10 and 100 persons. Corporate name: SalJon Limited, Inc.

TEHERAN....45 West 44 St., New York, N.Y., 10036. (212) 840-1980. Cuisine: Italian. Owner: Hank Mazzuca.

10 PARK AVENUE RESTAURANT....10 Park Ave., New York, N.Y., 10016. (212) 689-6200. Cuisine: Continental.

THE TERRACE....400 West 119 St., New York, N.Y., 10027. (212) 666-9490. Cuisine: Classical French & Nouvelle. Owner: Dusan Bernic. Open for lunch Tuesday to Friday; open to dinner Tuesday to Saturday. Credit cards: All major. Private party facilities: Up to 175. Annual sales: $500,000 to $1 million. Total employment: 30. Corporate name: Butler Hall Terrace Restaurant, Inc.

37TH STREET HIDEAWAY....32 West 37 St., New York, N.Y., 10018. (212) 947-8940. A romantic-mooded restaurant-supper club featuring Italian-Continental cuisine plus dancing and entertainment nightly from 6 p.m. Chef Carlo Mattiello combines classicism, expertise and talent. Complete dinners are moderately priced and on the whole a great deal less expensive than the general run on this level. House specialties include: shrimp scampi, seafood *Marichiare;* veal chop *pepperonato.* Open Monday through Friday for lunch; Monday through Saturday for dinner; Closed on Sunday. Owner: Van and Harry Panopoulos. Credit cards: All major. Reservations: Accepted. Private party facilities. Entertainment: Trio. Annual sales: $500,000 to $1 million. Total employment: 25.

THURSDAYS....57 West 58 St., New York, N.Y., 10019. (212) 371-7777. A popular meeting spot that has attracted a crowd of regulars by offering Continental/American food in an eclectic, comfortably-worn atmosphere. Menu choices range through beef dishes, seafood, fowl, veal, omelettes, and Thursday's celebrated potato skins. The crunchy skins come topped with everything from cheese and bacon to roast beef with Stroganoff sauce and sour cream. Owner: Ben Benson. Open 7 days for lunch and dinner. Credit card: All major. Annual sales: $1 million to $3 million. Corporate name: Thursdays Supper Pub, Inc.

TICKER'S STEAK HOUSE WEST....320 Columbus Ave., New York, N.Y. 10023. (212) 873-4100. Cuisine: AE, DC, MC, VISA.

TINO'S....235 East 58 St., New York, N.Y., 10022. (212) 751-0311. Is Italian Romanticism at its best and frequented by some of the most stylish people in town. Owner Tino Scarpa keeps them coming back with such dishes as pureed broccoli over linguine, steak *pizzaiola* a-sizzle with spicy sauce, and veal shank wih richly cheesed rice. All these give superior Italian wines a fine opportunity to flex themselves. You can not go wrong at Tino's, but prices are fairly high. Open Monday through Friday for lunch; 7 days for dinner. Owner: Tino Scarpa. Credit cards: All major. Reservations: Accepted. Private party facilities. Total employment: 24.

TIO PEPE....168 West 4 St., New York, N.Y., 10014. (212) 242-9338. Spanish and Mexican food in the same place. It's modestly priced, tasty, and there's nightly entertainment. There's a sidewalk cafe, and the back room is almost like dining in a forest. Specialties include: *Paella Valencia, paella Valencia* with lobster, *paella Marinara con langosta, mariscada* in green sauce, *chorizo, orroz con pollo, gazpacho,* and the whole range of Mexican dishes—from *tacos.* to *chile rellenos.* Open 7 days for lunch and dinner. Reservations accepted. Credit cards: All major. Private party facilities: 10 to 75. Annual sales: $1 million to $3 million. Corporate name: Sange Restaurant, Inc.

TORAJI....1590 Second Ave., New York, N.Y., 10028. (212) 650-194. Cuisine: Korean. Credit cards: AE, MC, DC, VISA.

TOSCANA RISTORANTE....246 East 54 St., New York, N.Y., 10022. (212) 371-8144. Cuisine: Italian. Owner: Sergio. Credit cards: AE, MC, DC, VISA.

TOUT VA BIEN....311 West 51 St., New York, N.Y., 10019. (212) 974-9051. Cuisine: French. Credit cards: AE, VISA.

TOVARICH....38 West 62 St., New York, N.Y., 10023. (212) 757-0168. Cuisine: Russian. Owner: Martin Safir & A.H. Weinberger. Open 6 days for lunch and dinner; Closed Sunday. Credit cards: All major. Private party facilities: 20 to 35. Annual sales: $250,000 to $500,000. Total employment: 11. Corporate name: Tovarisch, Inc.

TRADER VIC'S.... Plaza Hotel (Central Park South), New York, N.Y., 10019. (212) PL9-3000. Cuisine: Continental & Polynesian. Owner: Victor J. Bergeron. Open 7 days for dinner, Monday to Thrusday for lunch. Credit cards: All major. Private party facilities available. Annual sales: Over $3 million. Total employment: 100.

TRASTEVERE....309 East 83 St., New York, N.Y., 10028. (212) 734-6343. Cuisine: Italian. Owner: Maurizio and Paul Lattanzi. Credit cards: AE.

TRATTORIA.... Pan Am Building, East 45 St., New York, N.Y., 10017. (212) 661-3090. Cuisine: Italian. Credit cards: AE, CB, DC, MC, VISA.

TRATTORIA DA ALFREDO....90 Bank St., New York, N.Y., 10014. (212) 929-4400. Cuisine: Italian. Owner: Alfred Viazzi. Credit cards: None.

TRATTORIA PINO....981 Third Ave., (58 Street), New York, N.Y., 10022. (212) 688-3817 or 759-1220. Across from a pair of major department stores, Trattoria Pino is the sport to enjoy pizza or light meals between shopping or after a movie. There are twelve varieties of pizza from which to choose, all cooked in a wood-burning oven. The dough is thin and crisp. There is also good *fettucine al pesto*. Desserts are authentic Italian and mesh nicely with available cappucino or espresso. Open 7 days for lunch and dinner. Priced inexpensive to moderate. Reservations accepted. Credit cards: Call for cards. Corporte name: Pronto Ristorante, Inc.

TRE SCALINI....230 East 58 St., New York, N.Y., 10022. (212) 688-6888. Cuisine: Italian. Owner: Giovanni Di Saverio. Open Monday to Saturday. Credit cards: All major. Annual sales: $1 million to $3 million. Total employment: 27. Corporate name: Tre Scalini, Inc.

TRILUSSA RESTAURANT....280 Bleecker St., New York, N.Y., 10012. (212) 929-9104. Cuisine: Italian. Owner: George & Maria Valeri. Open 6 days for dinner; Closed Monday. Credit cards: AE, MC, VISA. Corporate name: Trilussa Corporation.

TRUFFLES RESTAURANT....696 Madison Ave., New York, N.Y., 10021. (212) 838-3725.

TRUMPETS.... Grand Hyatt Hotel, East 42 St., New York, N.Y., 10017. (212) 883-1234. Cuisine: Continental. Credit cards: All major.

TUCANO AT CLUB A....333 East 60 St., New York, N.Y., 10022. (212) 308-2333. A Brazilian wonderland of oversized glass lighting fixtures in assorted fruit shapes, a curved back wall conveying a jungle, and the barbaric splendor of contemporary Brazilian paintings. Here you can order anything from classic French dishes to elements of stylized *nouvelle* cuisine as the chef combines classicism, expertise, and talent. Specialties include: Dover sole *Troisgros*, paillard of beef, *ragout de homard au whiskey*, and quenelles of pike *Nantua*. Owner: Jean Claude Pujol, Richard Amaral. Open Monday through Friday for lunch; Monday through Saturday for dinner; Closed Sunday. Priced expensively. Reservations: Suggested. Credit cards: All major. Private party facilities: 20 to 40. Total employment: 35. Corporate name: Larama Corp.

TUESDAY'S....190 Third Ave., New York, N.Y., 10003. (212) 533-7900. Cuisine: American. Owner: Mel Dansky and Saul Victor. Credit cards: AE, MC, VISA.

21 CLUB....21 West 52 St., New York, N.Y., 10019. (212) 582-7200. Providing you are a really big spender, 21 Club is still one of the world's most exclusive celebrity haunts, operated very much as though it were a private club. It mainly caters to an amalgamated bag of gods and some of the sweetest people in town by virtue of the fact that they got in. The cuisine is American/Continental. Specialties include: game and fish dishes. Open Monday through Saturday for lunch and dinner; Closed Sunday. Owner: Sheldon Tannen and The Kriendlers. Credit cards: All major Reservations: Required. Private party facilities.

UKRAINIAN RESTAURANT....140 Second Ave., New York, N.Y., 10003. (212) 533-6765. Cuisine: Ukrainian.

UNCLE TAI'S HUNAN YUAN....1505 Third Ave., New York, N.Y., 10021. (212) 838-0850. Cuisine: Chinese. Owner: David Keh. Open 7 days. Credit cards: AE, DC. Private party facilities: 10 to 50. Annual Sales: $1 million to $3 million. Corporate name: David Keh Chinese Restaurant Inc.

UPSTREAM....150 East 39 St., New York, N.Y., 10016. (212) 684-1042. Cuisine: Seafood. Owner: Diane B. Silverberg. Open Monday to Saturday. Credit cards: AE, MC, VISA. Private party facilities: 25 to 40; available Sundays. Total employment: 5. Corporate name: Dips Steaks & Seafood.

U.S. STEAKHOUSE....129 West 51 St., (Time Life Bldg.), New York, N.Y., 10019. (212) 757-8800. Cuisine: Steakhouse. Owner: Peter Askanazy. Credit cards: All major.

UZIE'S....1442 Third Ave., New York, N.Y., 10028. (212) 744-8020. Cuisine: Italian. Credit cards: None.

VANESSA....289 Bleecker St., New York, N.Y., 10014. (212) 243-4225. Cuisine: Continental. Credit cards: All major.

VARIATIONS....358 West 23 St., New York, N.Y., 10011. (212) 691-1559. Cuisine: Continental. Credit cards: AE, MC, VISA.

VASATA....339 East 75 St., New York, N.Y., 10021. (212) 650-1686. Cuisine: Czechoslovak. Owner: Stan and Linda Petlan. Closed Monday; Open for dinner and Sunday brunch. Credit cards: All major. Annual sales: $250,000 to $500,000. Total employment: 12.

VIA MARGUTTA....24 Minetta La., New York, N.Y., 10012. (212) 254-7630. Cuisine: Northern Italian. Owner: Bruno Galli. Open for lunch Tuesday to Friday; Open for dinner Tuesday to Sunday. Credit cards: All major. Annual sales: $250,000 to $500,000. Total employment: 8.

VICTOR'S CAFE 52....236 West 52 St., New York, N.Y., 10019. (212) 586-7714. Cuisine: Cuban. Owner: Victor Del Corral. Total employment: 48. Corporate name: Victors Cafe 52, Inc.,

VIENNA PARK....33 East 60 St., New York, N.Y., 10022. (212) 758-1051. Cuisine: Austrian/Viennese. Owner: Peter Brunauer.

VIENNA '79....320 East 79 St., New York, N.Y., 10021. (212) 734-4700. Your dinner here will be faultless—an accolade few restaurants merit. Co-owner Peter Granauer and chef Thomas Frelich have created their own cuisine, *nouvelle Viennese,* which combines the light, delicate techniques and philosophies of *nouvelle cuisine* with the hearty fare of traditional Viennese food to produce a breathtaking new amalgam. Luxuriant desserts provide a lavish climax. Specialties include: *Kalbsmedaillon mit Pfifferlingen* (veal medallions with chantrelles), *Tafelspitz Alt Wien* (Viennese boiled beef with chive and horseradish sauces), *Wiener Schnitzel* (breaded veal cutlet), and Lachsforella mit Dill und Lauchgemuse (salmon/trout in fresh dill sauce). Owner: Karl Zartler, Walter Krainc, Peter Grunnauer. Open 7 days for dinner only. Prices are expensive. Reservations paramount. Accepting all major credit cards. Private party facilities not for more than 10.

VILLA FETTUCINE....974 Second Ave., New York, N.Y., 10022. (212) 759--9820. Cuisine: Italian. Owner: Tony.

VILLA MOSCONI....69 MacDougal St. (Greenwich Village). New York, N.Y., 10012. (212) 673-0390. Is a well-run, attractive, and orderly place for enjoyment of good Italian food. Examples of nourishment offered are distinctly good, particularly the veal kidney with wine and mushrooms, the Panama shrimp in a pungent sauce, and the daily fresh homemade pastas, some served with colossal amounts of fresh clams. Other specialties include chicken Mosconi and chicken livers. Open Monday through Saturday for lunch and dinner; Closed Sunday. Prices are moderate. Owner: Peter Mosconi. Credit cards: AE, DC, VISA. Reservations: Accepted. Private party facilities. Total employment: 15.

VILLAGE GREEN....531 Hudson St., New York, N.Y., 10014. (212) 255-1650. Cuisine: Continental. Owner: Mr. White. Open Tuesday through Saturday for dinner only; Closed Sunday and Monday. Credit cards: AE, MC, VISA. Private party facilities: Up to 40. Annual sales: $250,000 to $500,000.

VINTAGES....216 Columbus Ave., New York, N.Y., 10023. (212) 496-7059.

VIVOLO....140 East 74 St., New York, N.Y., 10021. (212) 628-4671. Cuisine: Italian. Owner: Angelo. Credit cards: AE, MC, VISA.

VOLARE....147 West 4 St., New York, N.Y., 10012. (212) SP7-2849. Cuisine: Italian. Credit cards: All major.

WALLY'S....224 West 49 St., New York, N.Y., 10019. (212) 582-0460. Cuisine: Steakhouse. Owner: Wally.

WASHINGTON STREET CAFE....422 Wshington St., New York, N.Y., 10013. (212) 925-5119. A relatively new wine bar and restaurant in Tribeca, a newly-emerged, quite stylish-in-its-own-funky-way part of town. It serves some dishes you probably won't get anywhere else—gazpacho with a shot of Stolichnaya vodka, for example, and green fettucine sprinkled with prosciutto, covered with melted roquefort cheese, and topped with a cream sauce. It's a very casual, comfortable, pleasant, and pretty restaurant, and there are over forty wines to sample most of which are available by the glass. Other specialties include: veal *marsala*, filet mignon with *bernaise* sauce, the seafood salad. The cuisine is not aligned to any nationality, and it's moderately priced. Open Tuesday through Saturday for dinner only; Closed Sunday and Monday. Owner Jon Blinder, Ronnie Davis. Reservations and major credit cards.

WATER FRONT CRAB HOUSE TOO....325 Bowery, New York, N.Y., 10003. (212) 245-245-0050. An offshoot of the Water Front Crab House in Long Island City, this Crab House is almost identical, though slightly smaller. There are the same rough-hewn walls, unseasoned wood trim, decoration of denizens of the deep, buoys, fish nets, etc. Both Water Front Crab Houses run on this simple motto: If it's not fresh, it's not on the menu. There is *one* frozen entree, though: the South African lobster tails—if unfrozen, they would spoil in transit. Other specialties include: Water Front's famous, and rightly so, *bouillabaisse*, replete with whole lobster, shrimps, clams, mussels, etc., the hot antipasto platter, and the baked crabs. Owner: Anthony Mazerella. Open Tuesday through Sunday for lunch; 7 days for dinner; No lunch on Monday. Priced moderately. Reservations: Imperative on Fridays and Saturdays. Accepting all major credit cards. Private party facilities are available.

WEST 4TH STREET SALOON....174 West 4 St., New York, N.Y., 10014. (212) 255-0518. Cuisine: American/Continental. Open 7 days for lunch and dinner. Credit cards: AE, CB, DC. Private party facilities: Up to 100.

WILDE'S....70 East 56 St., New York, N.Y., 10022. (212) 751-7321.

WINDOWS ON THE WORLD....1 World Trade Center, New York, N.Y., 10048. (212) 938-1111. Splendid view from the 107th floor of this well-furnished Manhattan restaurant. The bar and dining rooms are modern, the city lights, traffic, and rivers flow below, and a procession of fine dishes flow into the establishment. Do not hurry here. Open for lunch and dinner 7 days. Meals are in the moderate to expensive class and there is a *prix fixe* dinner for $19.50. House specialties include: Broiled meats; poached fish; and interesting desserts. Managing Director: Alan Lewis. Credit cards: All major. Reservations: Necessary. Private party facilities.

WINE PRESS....1160 First Ave., New York, N.Y., 10021. (212) 688-4490. This place is a personal salute from radio personality Sally Jessy Raphael to the members of the wine/food establishment who have been her fellow-travellers. Many remain fans of the ebullient blonde who hostesses proceedings on occasional weeknights and always on Saturdays at her very own, whimsically-appointed, wine bar-cum-restaurant. Specialties include: Veal stuffed artichokes, sirloin steak *au poivre*, lamb chops *Dijonaise*, brook trout with mushroom stuffing. Owner: Sally Jessy Raphael, A. Karl Soderlund. Open 7 days for dinner only. Credit cards: All major. Price: Moderate. Reservations: Accepted. Annual sales: $250,000 to $500,000. Total employment: 18. Corporate name: The Wine Press, Inc.

WISE MARIA....210 Spring St., New York, N.Y., 10012. (212) 925-9257. Cuisine: Italian. Owner: Philip Idone. Credit cards: AE.

THE WOK....173 Seventh Ave. South, New York, N.Y., 10011. (212) 243-6046. Cuisine: Chinese. Owner: Kenny.

WONG KEE....117 Mott St., New York, N.Y., 10013. (212) 226-9018. Cuisine: Chinese. Open daily for lunch and dinner. No credit cards.

WOODS.... 718 Madison Ave., New York, N.Y., 10021. (212) 688-1126. Cuisine: Continental. Owner: Zeus. Credit cards: AE, MC, VISA.

WOO LAE OAK OF SEOUL....77 West 46 St., New York, N.Y., 10036. (212) 869-9958. Cuisine: Korean. Credit cards: AE, DC, MC, VISA.

XENIA'S....871 First Ave., New York, N.Y., 10017. (212) 838-1191. Cuisine: Greek/International. Owner: Alex Giannakopoulos.

YANGTZE RIVER....250 West 57 St., New York, N.Y., 100190. (212) 246-3659. A neighborhood place serving dependably good Chinese food (concentrating on Cantonese, Polynesian, and Mandarin). It's bright, bustling, and a bargain. The central location is near Lincoln Center, the Broadway theaters, Carnegie Hall, the best shops, and the midtown business district. Specialties include: boiled and fried dumplings, hot and sour soup, fried shrimp balls, sizzling seafood, crispy whole fish. Inexpensive Chinese food. Open 7 days for lunch and dinner. Accepts all major credit cards and reservations. Private party facilities available.

YE WAVERLY INN....16 Bank St., New York, N.Y., 10014. (212) 929-4377.

YING....220 Columbus Ave., New York, N.Y., 10023. (212) 724-2031. Cuisine: Chinese. Owner: Frank Ying. Credit cards: AE.

YOUNG BIN KWAN....10 East 38 St., New York, N.Y., 10016. (212) 683-9031. Cuisine: Korean. Credit cards: All major.

YUN LUCK RICE SHOPPE....17 Doyers St., New York, N.Y., 10013. (212) 751-1375. Cuisine: Chinese, Credit cards: None.

ZAPATA....330 East 53 St., New York, N.Y., 10022. (212) 223-9408. Cuisine: Mexican. Owner: Frank Ramos.

MANHASSET

LA COQUILLE RESTAURANT....1669 Northern Blvd., Manhasset, L.I., N.Y., 11030. (516) 365-8422. Owner's name: Arturo Guerra.

LAURAINE MURPHY....1445 Northern Blvd., Manhasset, N.Y., 11030. (516) 627-3020. Cuisine: American. Owner: Joachim Jack Terzi. Open 7 days for lunch and dinner. Credit cards: All major. Private party facilities: Up to 200. Annual sales: $1 million to $3 million. Total employment: 150.

SECRET SEA....1191 Northern Blvd., Manhasset, L.I., N.Y., 11030. (516) 869-8422. Cuisine: Chinese Seafood. Credit cards: All major.

VILLAGE BATH HOUSE.... Nordic Leisure Inc., Strathmore Village, Manhasset, L.I., N.Y., 11030. (516) 627-6900. Cuisine: Continental. Owner's name: A. Kenneth Svendsen.

MASSAPEQUA

BAYBERRY HOUSE....5404 Merrick Rd., Massapequa, L.I., N.Y., 11758. (516) 799-0047. Cuisine: Seafood. Owner's name: Gustave Raitz. Credit cards: AE, MC, VISA, DC.

MY PI....333 Sunrise Hwy., Massapequa & Mid-Island Plaza, Hicksville, L.I., N.Y., 11758. (516) 541-4401 and (516) 681-8710. For something new in pizza, try My Pi. It's a deep-dish pizza, laden with heaping helpings of first-rate ingredients. Menus also include salads, garlic bread, sandwiches, chili and a choice of wines, spirits or frosty draft beers. My Pies are contemporary and stylish, proving that a pizza parlor need not be dowdy and mundane. Open 7 days for lunch and dinner. Inexpensive. Owner: Bill Cordo and Leo Waters. Credit cards: None. Private party facilities. Annual sales: $1 million. Total employment: 100.

VILLA MARIA-MASSAPEQUA....746 North Broadway, Massapequa, L.I., N.Y., 11758. (516) 798-9035. We single out this rather modest restaurant-bar-take-out pizzeria for its outstanding Italian cuisine. There are at least three dishes that deserve special attention: linguine with shrimp sauce, seafood marinara and veal sorrentino. We recommend that you go anytime from 11:30 a.m. to 11 p.m. and have a small orgy at ridiculous prices. Open for lunch Tuesday through Friday, dinner, 7 days. Owner: Luigi Dinucci. Credit cards: All major. Reservations: Accepted. Annual sales: $300,000. Total employment: 10.

MASSENA

VILLAGE INN.... Maple Street Rd., Massena, N.Y., 13662. (315) 769-6910. Cuisine: Continental and American. Credit cards: MC, VISA. Private party facilities: Up to 175. Annual sales: $500,000 to $1 million. Total employment: 33. Corporate name: Cecot's Village Inn, Inc. Open for lunch and dinner Wedneday through Monday.

MCGRAW

L'AUBERGE ALPINE....34 Main St., McGraw, N.Y., 13101. (607) 836-8984. Cuisine: French. Credit cards: MC, VISA.

MELVILLE

THE BLACK SHEEP....1197 Walt Whitman Rd., Melville, L.I., N.Y., 11746. (516) 421-3750. Cuisine: Italian/Continental. Credit cards: All major.

CHATEAU RESTAURANT.... Chateau Dr., Melville, L.I., N.Y., 11746. (516) 643-7776. Cuisine: Continental. Owner's name: George Goonan. Credit cards: CB, MC, VISA, DC.

FREDERICK'S....117 Walt Whitman Rd., Melville, L.I., N.Y., 11746. (516) 673-8550. Cuisine: Continental. Credit cards: All major.

SITAR....602 Broadhollow Rd., Melville, L.I., N.Y., 11746. (516) 752-1222. Cuisine: Indian. Credit cards: All major.

MERRICK

NEW HUNAN TASTE....209 West Merrick Rd., Merrick, L.I., N.Y., 11580. (516) 561-9888. Cuisine: Chinese. Owner's name: Tony Eng. Credit cards: AE, MC, VISA.

UMAI JAPNESE RESTAURANT....2057 Merrick Rd., Merrick, N.Y., 11566. (516) 546-3100. Cuisine: Japanese. Owner: Lawrence Kasindorf and Robert Hsieh. Open Tuesday to Sunday for dinner; Tuesday to Friday for lunch. Credit cards: AE, MC, VISA. Private party facilities: Up to 20. Corporate name: Larob Restaurant, In.

MILLERPLACE

SECRET ROAD INN.... North Country Rd., Millerplace, L.I., N.Y., 11764. (516) 473-7565. Cuisine: Seafood/Steak. Owner's name: Mr. Von der Heyden. Credit cards: AE, VISA.

MILLWOOD

TRAVELLERS RESTAURANT.... Rte. 100, Millwood, N.Y., 10546. (914) 941-7744. Cuisine: Continental.

MINEOLA

THE COLONIAL INN....288 Jericho Tpke., Mineola, L.I., N.Y., 11501. (516) 746-9305. Cuisine: American. Owner's names: Artie and Lee McGurk. Credit cards: AE, CB, MC, DC, VISA.

THE ROUND TABLE....39 Mineola Blvd., Mineola, L.I., N.Y., 11501. (516) 248-8933. Cuisine: American. Credit cards: All major.

SAGES....170 Old Country Rd., Mineola, N.Y., 11501. (516) 248-5130. Cuisine: Continental. Open 7 days for lunch and dinner. Credit cards: AE, MC, VISA. Private party facilities: 25-300.

SCALES OF JUSTICE....133 Mineola Blvd., Mineola, L.I., N.Y., 11501. (516) 746-1316. Cuisine: Italian/Continental. Owner's name: Edward. Credit cards: All major.

T.J. POOLE'S....540 Jericho Tpke., Mineola, L.I., N.Y., 11501 (516) 742-0260. Cuisine: American. Owner's name: Robert C. Banks. Credit cards: All major.

WIEGEL'S PLACE....100 Herricks Rd., Mineola, L.I., N.Y., 11501. (516) 746-3713. Cuisine: Pubhouse. Credit cards: All major.

MONTAUK

GOSMAN'S DOCK.... West Lake Dr., Montauk, L.I., N.Y., 11954. (516) 688-9837. Cuisine: Seafood.

MT. KISCO

BROWNSTONE CAFE....213 Main St., Mt. Kisco, N.Y., 10549. (914) 666-4448. Cuisine: Continental. Credit cards: All major.

FIFE & DRUM RESTAURANT....480 Main St., Mt. Kisco, N.Y., 10549. (914) 241-3322. Cuisine: Continental. Owner: Rosemary & Joe Angi. Credit cards: All major. Private party facilities: Up to 65. Annual sales: $500,000 to $1 million. Total employment: 30. Open for lunch and dinner 7 days.

HANKER CHIPS....132 East Main St., Mt. Kisco, N.Y., 10549. (914) 666-9787. Cuisine: Italian. Credit cards: All major.

HO YEN....510 Lexington Ave., Mt. Kisco, N.Y., 10549. (914) 241-1565. Cuisine: Chinese.

KITTLE HOUSE.... Rte. 117, Mt. Kisco, N.Y., 10549. (914) 666-8044. Cuisine: Continental. Credit cards: All major.

MARDINO'S....473 Lexington Ave., Mt. Kisco, N.Y., 10549. (914) 666-9082. Cuisine: Italian. Credit cards: All major.

RED LANTERN INN....568 Lexington Ave., Mt. Kisco, N.Y., 10549. (914) 666-3184. Cuisine: American. Credit cards: All major.

WHITE HORSE TAP ROOM....20 South Moger Ave., Mt. Kisco, N.Y., 10549. (914) 666-9894. Cuisine: American. Credit cards: None.

MT. VERNON

COLOSSEO DI ROMA....41 Gramatan Ave., Mt. Vernon, N.Y., 10550. (914) 668-0187. Cuisine: Continental. Credit cards: All major.

NAPLES

VINEYARD.... Main St., Naples, N.Y., 14512. Cuisine: Continental.

NEW HYDE PARK

LIDO DI ROMA....1635 Hillside Ave., New Hyde Park, L.I., N.Y., 11040. (516) 437-6655. Cuisine: Italian. Credit cards: All major.

STICKS & STONES....265-11 Union Turnpike, New Hyde Park, N.Y., (212) 347-3453. Cuisine: Steak and Seafood. Owner: Sonny, Gus & Dom. Open 7 days. Credit cards: All major. Private party facilities: 15 to 50. Annual sales: $500,000 to $1 million. Total employment: 16 to 20. Corporate name: Gus Do So, Inc.

VILLA MARGHERITA....3338 Hillside Ave., New Hyde Park, L.I., N.Y., 11040. (516) PL 6-9323. Cuisine: Italian. Owner's name: Harold Rashner. Credit cards: AE, DC.

NEW ROCHELLE

DEL PONTE'S....353 North Ave., New Rochelle, N.Y., 108-1. (914) 633-8477. Cuisine: Italian. Credit cards: None.

FRUMPSON'S....72 Quaker Ridge Rd., New Rochelle, N.Y., 10804. (914) 576-1788. Cuisine: Continental. Credit cards: All major.

GIOVANNI'S....700 Main St., New Rochelle, N.Y., 10801. (914) 632-6644. Cuisine: Italian/Continental. Owner: Anthony Corigliano. Open for lunch and dinner Tuesday through Sunday. Credit cards: All major. Private party facilities: Up to 350. Annual sales: $250,000 to $500,000. Total employment: 15.

PEPPINO'S....336 Pelham Rd., New Rochelle, N.Y., 10805. (914) 636-9614. Cuisine: Continental. Credit cards: AE.

SAPARITO'S....1279 North Ave., New Rochelle, N.Y., 10804. (914) 636-7087. Cuisine: Italian. Credit cards: All major.

SZECHUAN EMPIRE....1335 North Ave., New Rochelle, N.Y., 10804. (914) BE 5-6450. Cuisine: Chinese.

TREVI STEAK HOUSE....1 North Ave., New Rochelle, N.Y., 10805. (914) 235-2311. Cuisine: Italian. Credit cards: All major.

UNCLE MEG'S....969 Main St., New Rochelle, N.Y., 10801. (914) 235-6167. Cuisine: American. Credit cards: All major.

VINCENT DIORIO'S....100 Huguenot St., New Rochelle, N.Y., 10801. (914) 636-6000. Cuisine: American/Seafood.

NIAGARA FALLS

JOHN'S FLAMING HEARTH....1965 Military Rd., Niagara Falls, N.Y., 14304. (716) 297-1414. Cuisine: Steak/Seafood. Credit cards: All major.

J.P. MORGAN'S.... Rainbow Mall, Niagara Falls, N.Y., 14303. (716) 285-5555. Cuisine: Continental. Credit cards: AE, MC, VISA.

PEOPLE'S PLUM....102 Lasalle Arterial, Nigara Falls, N.Y., 14303. (716) 285-2000. Cuisine: American/Continental. Credit cards: AE, MC, VISA.

NORTH BELLMORE

SMITHVILLE CAFE RESTAURANT....1759 Bellmore Ave., North Bellmore, L.I., N.Y., 11710. (516) 826-3832. Cuisine: Continental. Owner: Richard Berlinger, Marilyn Gross, Lester Beberman. Open 7 days for lunch and dinner; Sunday brunch. Credit cards: AE, MC, VISA. Annual sales: $250,000 to $500,000. Total employment: 15. Corporate name: M.L.R. Restaurant, Inc.

NORTH CONGERS

BULLY BOY CHOP HOUSE.... Rtes. 117 & 303, North Congers, N.Y., 10902. (914) 268-6555. Cuisine: American. Credit cards: All major except CB.

NORTHPORT

THE AUSTRALIAN COUNTRY INN & GARDENS....1036 Fort Salonga Rd., Northport, L.I., N.Y., 11768. (516) 757-4313. Cuisine: Australian. Credit cards: All major.

GREENSTREET....42 Woodbine Ave., Northport, L.I., N.Y., 11768. (516) 757-8877. Cuisine: French. Credit cards: AE, MC, VISA, DC.

KARL'S MARINERS INN.... Bayview & James St., Northport, L.I., N.Y., 11786. (516) 261-811. Cuisine: Seafood/Continental. Owner's name: R. Karl. Credit cards: AE, MC, VISA, DC.

PANE & PASTA HOUSE....325 Fort Salonga Rd., Northport, L.I., N.Y., 11768. (516) 757-3100. Cuisine: Italian.

WINDJAMMER.... Waterside Ave., Northport, L.I., N.Y., 11768. (516) 261-0677. Cuisine: Seafood. Owner's name: Nick Pappas. Credit cards: All major.

NORTH SALEM

AUBERGE MAXIME.... Rt. 116, North Salem, N.Y., 10560 (914) 669-5450. Cuisine: French. Credit cards: All major.

NORTH TARRYTOWN

PICKWICK'S POST....348 North Broadway, North Tarrytown, N.Y., 10591. (914) 631-3448. Cuisine: Italian. Credit cards: All major.

OAKDALE

COGGS....1575 Montauk Hwy., Oakdale, L.I., N.Y., 11769. (516) 567-9746. Cuisine: Californian. Owner: Mr. Thayer. Credit cards: AE.

SAXON ARMS.... Foot of Consuelo Pl., Oakdale, L.I., N.Y., 11769. (516) 589-2694. Cuisine: Continental. Owner's name: James Finegam. Credit cards: All major

OCEANSIDE

ALIAS SMITH & JONES....2863 Woods Ave., Oceanside, L.I., N.Y., 11572. (516) 766-9553. Cuisine: American. Owner: Don Castronovo. Credit cards: AE, MC, VISA, DC.

OLEAN

CASTLE.... West State Rd., Olean, N.Y., 14760. (716) 372-6022. Cuisine: Continental. Owner: Daniel J. Butchello. Open for lunch and dinner 7 days; Sunday brunch. Credit cards: AE, MC, VISA. Private party facilities: Up to 650. Annual sales: $1 million to $3 million. Total employment: 110.

OSSINING

BRASSERIE SWISS.... Rte. 133, 118 Croton Ave., Ossining, N.Y., 10562. (914) 941-0319. Cuisine: Swiss

DUDLEY'S....6 Rockledge Ave., Ossining, N.Y., 10562. (914) 941-8674. Cuisine: Continental. Credit cards: All major.

HUNAN GOURMET....246 South Highland Ave., Ossining, N.Y., 10562. (914) 762-3888. Cuisine: Chinese. Credit cards: All major.

OSWEGO

VONA'S.... West 10 & Utica St., Oswego, N.Y., 13126. (315) 343-8710. Cuisine: Italian. Credit cards: AE, MC VISA.

OYSTER BAY

MAIN STREET'S 1830 RESTAURANT....41 East Main St., Oyster Bay, L.I., N.Y., 11771. (516) 922-9135. Cuisine: Seafood. Credit cards: AE, MC, VISA.

UWE'S....73 South St., Oyster Bay, L.I., N.Y., 11771. (516) 922-5044. Cuisine: Continental. Credit cards: All major.

PATCHOGUE

PINE GROVE INN.... Chapel Ave., & 1 St., East Patchogue, N.Y., 11772. (516) 475-9843. Cuisine: German/American. Owner: Rainer Hombach & Klaus Haase. Open Wednesday through Monday. Credit cards: All major. Private party facilities: 70. Annual sales: $500,000 to $1 million. Total employment: 50. Corporate name: Pine Grove Inn, Inc.

SOUTH SHORE....388 Medford Ave., Patchogue, L.I., N.Y., 11772. (516) 475-7926. The menu promises Continental cuisine and fine French wines and delivers enough of both to attract a crowd of regulars for lunch and dinner, as well as family trade for Sunday brunch. Specialties include a sensible choice of beef, seafood, veal, poultry and salads. Noteworthy are shrimp, veal, and chicken Francaise, and the seafood special (combination). Open for lunch and dinner, 7 days plus Sunday brunch. Prices are moderate to expensive. Owner: Steve and Peter. Credit cards: All major. Reservations: Accepted. Private party facilities. Entertainment: Piano in Loune. Annual sales: $500,000. Total employment: 25.

PATTERSON

L'AUBERGE BRETONNE.... Rte. 22, Patterson, N.Y., 12563. (914) 878-6782. Cuisine: French. Credit cards: AE, DC, MC, VISA.

MING HOY.... Rte. 22, Patterson, N.Y., 12563. (914) 878-9704. Cuisine: Chinese. Credit cards: All major.

PEEKSKILL

CORTLAND COLONIAL RESTAURANT.... Old Albany Post Rd., Peekskill, N.Y., 10566. (914) 737-5999. Cuisine: Seafood. Credit cards: All major.

RED SCHOOLHOUSE RESTAURANT.... Furnace Woods Rd., Peekskill, N.Y., 10566. (914) 737-8200. Cuisine: Northern Italian and French. Open for lunch and dinner Wednesday through Monday. Credit cards: AE, MC, VISA. Total employment: 10. Corporate name: The Red Schoolhouse Restaurant, Ltd.

REEF 'N' BEEF.... Roa Hook Rd., Peekskill, N.Y., 10566. (914) 737-4959. Cuisine: Seafood. Credit cards: All major.

SORRENTO....307 Railroad Ave., Peekskill, N.Y., 10566. (914) 737-2624. Cuisine: Italian. Credit cards: None.

PEKIN

SCHIMSCHACKS....2943 Upper Mountain Rd., Pekin, N.Y., (716) 731-4111. Cuisine: American. Credit cards: AE, MC, VISA.

PELHAM

EDO PLAZA....4787 Boston Post Rd., Pelham, N.Y., 10803. (914) 738-1413. Cuisine: Japanese. Credit cards: All major.

GIGI'S ITALIAN CONTINENTAL RESTAURANT....146 Fifth Ave., Pelham, N.Y., 10803. (914) 738-1892. Cuisine: Italian/Continental. Credit cards: All major.

JAPANESE STEAKHOUSE....4787 Boston Post Rd., Pelham, N.Y., 10803. (914) 738-1413. Cuisine: Japanese Steakhouse. Credit cards: All major.

VILLA NOVA....6 First St., Pelham, N.Y., 10803. (914) 738-1444. Cuisine: Continental. Credit cards: All major.

PELHAM MANOR

VIVA ZAPATA....105 Wolfs La., Pelham Manor, N.Y., 10803. (914) 738-5881. Cuisine: Mexican. Credit cards: AE.

PLEASANTVILLE

JONATHAN'S....472 Bedford Rd., Pleasantville, N.Y., 10570. (914) 769-8288. Cuisine: American. Credit cards: All major.

THE SAUTE CAFE....75 Cooley, Pleasantville, N.Y., 10570. (914) 769-0500. Cuisine: International. Owner's name: Chaz Yacovelli. Closed Mondays.

VINNY'S....468 Bedford Rd., Pleasantville, N.Y., 10570. (914) 769-9805. Cuisine: Italian. Credit cards: All major.

PORT CHESTER

THE CAPTAIN & THE ADMIRAL....317 Boston Post Rd., Port Chester, N.Y., 10573. (914) 939-8700. Cuisine: Seafood/Italian/Continental.

J. DIROBERTO'S RESTAURANT....179 Rector St., Port Chester, N.Y., 10573. (914) 939-3754. Cuisine: Italian. Owner: Gerard DiRoberto. Closed Mondays. Credit cards: All major. Private party facilities: 30 to 90 persons. Annual sales $250,000 to $500,000. Total employment: 14. Corporate name: J. DiRoberto's Restaurant, Inc.

LITTLE DICK'S.... Irving & Broad St., Port Chester, N.Y., 10573. (914) 937-5740. Cuisine: American. Credit cards: MC, VISA.

MARIANACCI'S....24 Sherman St., Port Chester, N.Y., 10573. (914) 939-3450. Cuisine: Italian. Credit cards: AE.

PEARL OF ATLANTIC RESTAURANT.... Fox Island Rd., Port Chester, N.Y., 10573. (914) 939-4227. Cuisine: Seafood. Owner's name: Salvador Carlos.

PENFIELD ROOM.... Westchester Ave., Port Chester, N.Y., 10573. (914) 939-6300. Cuisine: Continental. Owner: Per Hellman. Open 7 days. Credit cards: All major. Private party facilities: Up to 2000. Annual sales: Over $3 million. Total employment: 300.

SAWPIT....25 South Regent St., Port Chester, N.Y., 10573. (914) 939-1360. Cuisine: Continental. Credit cards: VISA, MC.

TARRY LODGE....18 Mill St., Port Chester, N.Y., 10573. (914) 937-3070. Cuisine: Italian. Credit cards: All major.

PORT JEFFERSON

BAVARO'S....141 West Broadway (25A), Port Jefferson, L.I., N.Y., 11777. (516) 928-2750. Definitely good provincial Italian food, much of it cooked right in the dining room in an open kitchen. Bavaro's is glossy with polish and bright with a skylight, wrap-a-round glass windows, and a roof deck for summer cocktails, or meals-by-request. House specialties include: shrimp in garlic sauce; filet mignon ala conn and chicken Bolognese. Open for lunch Monday through Friday, which is a la carte or prix-fixe—$5.00. Dinner, Monday through Sunday. Brunch on Sunday. Prices are moderate. Owners: Lewis and Thomas Bavaro. Credit cards: All major. Reservations: Accepted. Annual sales: $200,000. Total employment: 5.

THE CARRIAGE POND INNE....326 Wynne La., Port Jefferson, L.I., N.Y., 11777. (516) 331-2200. Cuisine: Continental. Credit cards: All major.

PORT WASHINGTON

DA MARCELLO....175 Manor Haven Blvd., Port Washington, L.I., N.Y., 11050. (516) 683-4660. Cuisine: Italian. Owner's name: Marcello. Credit cards: AE, MC, VISA.

JIMMY'S BACKYARD....415 Main St., Port Washington, L.I., N.Y., 11050. (516) 767-6070. Cuisine: Seafood. Credit cards: All major.

LA GOLETTA....57 Shore Rd., Port Washington, L.I., N.Y., 11050. (516) 883-2111. Cuisine: Continental. Owner's name: Gian Carlo. Credit cards: All major.

RIVIERA RESTAURANT....45 Orchard Beach Blvd., Port Washington, L.I., N.Y., 11050. (516) 883-3766. Cuisine: Italian/Seafood. Credit cards: All major.

STREET BARN....2 Soundview Shopping Ctr., Port Washington, L.I., N.Y., 11050. (516) 883-9527. Cuisine: Steak/Seafood. Credit cards: All major.

WINSTON'S....327 Shore Rd., Port Washington, L.I., N.Y., 11050. (516) 883-7400. Cuisine: French. Credit cards: AE, VISA, MC, DC.

POUGHKEEPSIE

TREASURE CHEST....568 South Rd., Poughkeepsie, N.Y., 12601. (914) 462-4545. Cuisine: Continental/French. Owner: Mrs. Romy Benich. Open for dinner Monday to Saturday; open for lunch Monday to Friday. Credit cards: All major. Private party facilities: Up to 50. Annual sales: $250,000 to $500,000. Total employment: 20.

POUND RIDGE

EMILY SHAW'S INN.... Rte. 137, Pound Ridge, N.Y., 10576. (916) 764-5779. Cuisine: Continental. Open Tuesday through Sunday for lunch and dinner; Closed Monday. Credit cards: All major. Reservations: Required. Proper attire required.

PURDYS

BOX TREE.... Rtes. 22 & 116, Purdys, N.Y., 10576. (914) 277-3677. Cuisine: French. Credit cards: None.

QUEENS VILLAGE

MONTE CARLO.... Monte Carlo Inc., 215-52 Jamaica Ave., Queens Village, N.Y., 11428. (212) 776-4285. Cuisine: Italian. Owner's name: Louis Delpoizzo. Credit cards: AE, DC, VISA. Annual sales: $500,000. Total employment: 16.

REGO PARK

LE CAPON....94-09 63rd Dr., Rego Pk. (Queens), N.Y., 11374. (212) 459-3939. Cuisine: French. Credit cards: All major.

RICHFIELD SPRINGS

LAKE HOUSE.... East Lake Rd., Richfield Springs, N.Y., 13439. (315) 858-9927. Cuisine: Seafood/Steak.

RICHMOND HILL

FOUR BROTHERS TRIANGLE HOFBRAU....117-13 Jamaica, Ave., Richmond Hill (Queens), N.Y., 11418. Cuisine: German/American.

RIDGEWOOD

VILLA MARIA-RIDGEWOOD...805 Cypress Ave., Ridgewood, N.Y., 11385. (212) 456-3230. Introduces palates to the delights of subtly seasoned Italian fare. Examples offered are distinctly good, particularly beef *giardiniera* sighing in a mixture of fresh peas, mushrooms, prosciutto and red peppers. Precincts are embellished in shades of red and walls support an array of oils. Service is brisk and friendly, and meals are inexpensive to moderate. Other house specialties include: *gnocchi* with meat sauce; veal *marsala* and homemade cheese cake. Open for lunch and dinner, 6 days; Closed Tuesdays. Owner: Vincent Reda and Mario Velechic. Credit cards: None. Reservations: Accepted. Private party facilities.

ROCKAWAY

SHIP'S INN....6 Fifth Ave., Rockaway, N.Y., 11518. (516) 593-1440. Cuisine: Seafood. Owner: Jim Weisberg. Open 7 days for dinner; Sundays from noon. Credit cards: All major. Private party facilities: Up to 100. Annual sales: $500,000 to $1 million. Total employment: 30. Corporate name: E. Rockaway Restaurant Corp.

ROCKVILLE CENTER

THE SKIPPER....242 Sunrise Hwy., Rockville Cntr., L.I., N.Y., 11570. (516) 766-3838. Cuisine: Seafood. Owner's name: Frank Scalabrino. Credit cards: AE, MC, VISA, DC.

ROSLYN

CHALET RESTAURANT....1 Railroad Ave., Roslyn, L.I., N.Y., 11576. (516) 621-7975. Cuisine: Continental. Owner's name: Terry Stafford. Credit cards: AE, MC, DC, VISA.

LA SILHOUETTE....1446 Old Northern Blvd., Roslyn, L.I., N.Y., 11576. (516) 484-9550. Cuisine: French/Continental. Credit cards: All major.

OLD TUBBY HOUSE....1401 Old Northern Blvd., Roslyn, L.I., N.Y., 11576. (516) 621-7888. A steadily growing reputation here, and a steady flow of good Continental cuisine supplemented with omelettes, burgers, and "diet-center" specialities, offering low-calorie but not low quality entrees from young Mr. Len de Pas' spotless kitchen to his ever-increasing clientele. Specialities include: chateau briand (for two), avocado and shrimp salad, mussels *marinara*. Moderate to high prices. Lunch Monday-Friday; 7 days; Sunday brunch, Reservations Required in one of dining rooms, suggested in the other.

SPICE CARGO....3 Bryant Ave., Roslyn, L.I., N.Y., 11576. (516) 484-9409. Cuisine: Spice Shop. Owner's name: Helane Flanagan.

TRATTORIA DI MEO....1051 Northern Blvd., Roslyn, L.I., N.Y., 11576. (516) 627-9662. Cuisine: Italian. Credit cards: All major.

VILLA ANTICA....1441 Old Northern Blvd., Roslyn, L.I., N.Y., 11576. (516) 484-2075. Cuisine: Italian. Owner's name: Mario Gattorna. Credit cards: All major.

ROSLYN ESTATES

WEE TAPPEE INN....#1 Intervale Ave., Roslyn Estates, L.I., N.Y., 11576. (516) MA1-2200. Is small, solid, distinguished, extremely comfortable, and obligingly run and supervised by its owner-host Peter. Take counsel with him. He will steer you through the compilation of a delicious Northern-Italian or French meal. Specialties of the house include veal chop Florentine, lobster *fra diavolo*, and duckling and fresh raspberry with orange sauce. Wee Tappee is open for lunch Monday through Friday; Monday through Saturday for dinner; Closed Sunday. It is not bargain priced but in the medium range and certainly worth every penny. Owner: Peter Casuscelli. Credit cards: All major. Reservations: Accepted. Private Party Facilities—Sunday only. Annual sales: $500,000. Total employment: 10.

ROSLYN HEIGHTS

RICKY'S....88 Mineola Ave., Roslyn Hgts., L.I., N.Y., 11577. (516) 484-0555. Although individualistic in its preparations, it's pure Italian, with lots of homemade, cooked-to-order pasta and veal to state its case, and portions are abundant. House specialties: homemade pasta; stuffed veal chop, and veal chicken valentine. Prices are moderate. Open for lunch and dinner, 6 days. Closed on Monday. Owners: Angelo Dundara, Casimiro Runco, and Vittorio Binchi. Credit cards: All major. Reservations: Accepted. Entertainment: Piano on Friday & Saturday. Annual sales: $500,000 to $1, million Total employment: 20.

RYE

THE COACHMAN....667 Forest Ave., Rye, N.Y., 10580. (914) 967-8559. Cuisine: Italian. Credit cards: MC, Visa.

MUG ALE HOUSE....1 Depot Plz., Rye, N.Y., 10580. (914) 967-9807. Cuisine: American. Credit cards: All major.

OLDBODY'S....2 Central Ave., Rye, N.Y., 10580. (914) 967-9896. Cuisine: Continental. Credit cards: All major.

UMBERTO'S....92 Purchase St., Rye, N.Y., 10580. (914) 967-1909. Cuisine: Italian. Credit cards: AE.

WHITE ELEPHANT...530 Milton Rd., Rye, N.Y., 10580. (914) 967-8140. Cuisine: American. Credit cards: All major.

SAG HARBOR

THE AMERICAN HOTEL.... Main St., Sag Harbor, L.I., N.Y., 11963. (516) 725-3535. Cuisine: French. Credit cards: None.

BARON'S COVE INN.... West Water St., Sag Harbor, L.I., N.Y., 11963. (516) 725-3332. A rustic locality and an old-style fishhouse interior are enough to have you enjoying this place before you even look at the menu. Fish and fresh shellfish are this restaurant's specialties, and they're both tasty and well-prepared. While both the broiled and fried fish dishes are very good, your best bet is the *bouillabaise*. This savory seafood stew is bristling with crab claws, chunks of lobster, clams and mussels in their shells, and large succulent shrimp. Desserts are all pleasing with the cheesecake a nice-sized wedge of New York creaminess. Owner: Anthony Mazzerella. Open 7 days for lunch and dinner from April through September; 5 days for lunch and dinner otherwise; Closed Monday and Tuesday. Priced inexpensive to moderate. Reservations and all major credit cards accepted. Private party facilities: 25 to 160. Corporate name: Crab House of Baron's Cove, Inc.

THE FOXES.... Noyac Rd., Sag Harbor, L.I., N.Y., 11963. (516) 725-0810. Cuisine: American. Credit cards: All major.

SAINT JAMES

DA VINCI'S....416 North Country Rd., St. James, L.I., N.Y., 11780. (516) 862-6500. Cuisine: Italian Credit cards: DC, MC, VISA.

THE FROG & THE PEACH....823 Jericho Tpke., St. James, L.I., N.Y., 11780. (516) 265-9865. Cuisine: Continental/Italian. Credit cards: All major.

SAYVILLE

LAMPLIGHTER INN....465 Montauk Hwy., Sayville, L.I., N.Y., 11782. (516) 589-5050. Cuisine: American. Credit cards: All major.

TUDOR ROOM....98 Main St., Sayville, N.Y., 11782. (516) 567-6345. Cuisine: American/Steak/Seafood. Owner: J.S. Moreno. Open Monday through Saturday. Credit cards: All major. Annual sales: $250,000 to $500,000. Total employment: 12.

SCARSDALE

ALBANESE....807 Post Rd., Scarsdale, N.Y., 10583. (914) 723-9607. Cuisine: Italian. Credit cards: None.

BARTHOLOMEW'S....2 Weaver St., Scarsdale, N.Y., 10583. (914) 725-3900. Cuisine: American. Credit cards: All major.

CALEB'S RETREAT....96 Garth Rd., Scarsdale, N.Y., 10583. (914) 723-5525. Cuisine: American. Credit cards: All major.

SOUTH SEAS....835 Central Park Ave., Scarsdale, N.Y., 10583. (914) 472-5610. Cuisine: Chinese. Credit cards: All major, except CB.

SZECHUAN FLOWER....365 Central Park Ave., Scarsdale, N.Y., 10583. (914) 472-1370. Cuisine: Chinese. Credit cards: All major.

SEA CLIFF

SANS SOUCI....395 Prospect Ave., Sea Cliff, L.I., N.Y., 11579. (5126) 671-0200. Cuisine: Italian/Continental. Credit cards: All major.

SEAFORD

BROWN OSPREY....3943 Merrick Rd., Seaford, L.I., N.Y., 11783.(212) 221-9626. Cuisine: American/Continental. Credit cards: All major.

SHANDAKEN

CAFE ST. JACQUES.... Rte. 28, Shandaken, N.Y., 12480. (914) 688-2231. Cuisine: French. Credit cards: AE, MC, VISA.

SHELTER ISLAND HEIGHTS

THE COOK, A RESTAURANT....15 Grand Ave., Shelter Island Heights, N.Y., 11985. (516) 740-2216. Cuisine: Eclectic. Owner: Malcolm R. Willard. Open May through September for dinner and weekend brunch; closed Monday. Credit cards: All major. Annual sales: $250,000 to $500,000. Total employment: 20.

SKANEATELES

THE KREBS....53 W. Genesee St., Skaneateles, N.Y., 13152. (315) 685-5714. Cuisine: American. Owner: Larry N. Loveless. Open 7 days. Credit cards: All major. Private party facilities: Up to 150. Annual sales: $250,000 to $500,000. Total employment: 50.

MANDANA INN.... Rte. 41A, Skaneateles, N.Y., 13152. (315) 685-7798. Cuisine: Seafood. Credit cards: AE.

SHERWOOD INN....26 West Genesee St., Skaneateles, N.Y., 13152. (315) 685-3405. Cuisine: French/American. Credit cards: AE, MC, VISA.

SLATE HILL

LE COQ HARDI.... Rte. 284, Slate Hill, N.Y., 10973. (914) 355-3432. Cuisine: French/Belgian.

SMITHTOWN

JHOOLA....19 East Main St., Smithtown, L.I., N.Y., 11787. (516) 265-9524. Cuisine: Indian. Credit cards: All major.

RANERI'S....519 West Main St., Smithtown, L.I. N.Y., 17350. (516) 265-0505. Cuisine: Italian. Credit cards: AE, MC, VISA, DC.

WATERMILL INN.... Smithtown Bypass, Smithtown, L.I., N.Y., 11787. (516) 724-3242. Cuisine: Continental. Credit cards: All major.

SOMERS

FRITZ'S.... Rtes. 100 & 202, Somers, N.Y., 10589. (914) 277-9537. Cuisine: Italian. Credit cards: None.

SILVANO & EDWARD'S.... Rte. 100, Somers, N.Y., 10589. (914) 232-8080. Cuisine: Italian. Credit cards: All major.

STEER & PIER.... Rtes. 100 & 202, Somers, N.Y., 10589. (914) 277-3000. Cuisine: American. Credit cards: All major.

SOUTHAMPTON

BALZARINI'S RESTAURANT... 210 Hampton Rd., Southampton, L.I., N.Y., 11968. (516) 283-0704. Cuisine: Northern Italian. Owner: Marge & Renato Galante. Serving dinner 7 days for July and August, closed Tuesday other months. Credit cards: All major. Total employment 6 to 16. Corporate name: Gallant Host, Inc.

CAROL'S.... Rte. 27, Southampton, L.I., N.Y. 11968. (516) 283-5001. Cuisine: Continental. Credit cards: All major.

D'ANTONIO'S....1580 North Hwy., Southampton, L.I., N.Y., 11968. (516) 283-3111. Cuisine: Italian. Owner's name: Sal Barone. Credit cards: All major.

HERB McCARTHY'S BOWDEN SQUARE.... Bowden Sq., Southampton, L.I., N.Y., 11968. (516) 283-2800. Owner's name: Herb McCarthy.

SHIPPY'S PUMPERNICKLES EAST....36 Windmill La., Southampton, L.I., N.Y., 11968. (516) 283-0007. Cuisine: German/American. Credit cards: All major.

SILVER'S FAMOUS RESTAURANT....15 Main St., Southampton, L.I., N.Y., (516) 283-6443. Cuisine: Continental/American/Seafood. Owner: Mr. Wellings. Open 7 days. Credit cards: None. Privaty party facilities: 10 to 40. Annual sales: $250,000 to $500,000. Total employment: 10. Corporate name: Silver's Inc.

SOUTHHOLD

ARMANDO'S SEAFOOD BARGE....Main Rd., Southold, L.I., N.Y., 11971. (516) 765-3010. Plain, airy restaurant affording views of Peconic Bay, with a feeling of space and comfort very powerfully diffused. This is an endearing oldtime fishhouse and consequently outstanding for both quality and quantity. There are some unforgettable items on the menu and mamma makes the coleslaw and bakes the pies daily. Most popular preparations are the soft shell crabs, alive and kicking till cooked; four pound steamed lobsters with drawn butter; fried and tender calamari; and New England clam chowder, rich and delicately-flavored, creamed and creamy and filled with tender pieces of clams; as well as hearty and really clammy Manhattan chowder. Owner: Armando Cappa. Open 7 days for lunch and dinner. Price: Moderate. Reservations: Accepted. Credit cards: All major. Private party facilities: 10 to 60. Annual sales: $500,000 to $1 million. Total employment: 40. Corporate name: Ports of Seafood, Inc.

LA GAZELLE.... Main Rd., Southold, L.I., N.Y., 11971. (516) 765-2656. Cuisine: French. Credit cards: All major (gratuities in cash).

MILL CREEK INN.... Main Rd., Southhold, L.I., N.Y., 11971. (516) 765-1010. Cuisine: Seafood/American. Credit cards: All major.

SOUTH SALEM

LE CHATEAU.... Rtes. 35E & 123, South Salem, N.Y., 10590. (914) 533-2122. Cuisine: French.

HORSE & HOUND.... Spring St., South Salem, N.Y., 10590. (914) 763-3108. Cuisine: Continental. Open 7 days for dinner; Sunday brunch. Credit cards: AE, DC, MC, VISA. Reservations: Recommended. Proper attire required.

SPECULATOR

ZEISER'S.... Rte. 30, Speculator, N.Y., 12164. (518) 548-7021. Cuisine: Continental. Credit cards: AE.

SPRING VALLEY

GARTNER'S INN.... Hungry Hollow Rd., Spring Valley, N.Y., 10977. (914) 356-0875. Cuisine: Jewish. Credit cards: All major.

STORMVILLE

HARRALD'S.... Rte. 52, Stormville, N.Y., 12582. (914) 878-6595. Cuisine: International. Owner's name: Eva Durrschmidt.

SYOSSET

ASPARAGII....44 Jericho Tpke., Syosset, L.I., N.Y., 11791. Cuisine: Natural Foods. Owner's name: Mr. Gochman.

BOODLE'S....6800 Jericho Tpke., Syosset, L.I., N.Y., 11791. (516) 496-3525. Cuisine: American. Credit cards: All major.

EL PARRA....8 Berry Hill Rd., Syosset, L.I., N.Y., 11791. (516) 921-2844. Cuisine: Spanish/Italian. Credit cards: AE, DC, MC, VISA.

HEADS & TAILS....33 Berry Hill Rd., Syosset, L.I., N.Y., 11791. (516) 921-3670. Cuisine: American. Owner's name: Arthur Cohen. Credit cards: AE, MC, DC, VISA.

MAGIC WOK....102 W. Jericho Tpke., Syosset, L.I., N.Y., 11791. (516) 364-9330. Cuisine: Chinese. Credit cards: All major.

MAH JONG....140 Jericho Tpke., Syosset, L.I., N.Y., 11791. (516) 921-0500. Cuisine: Chinese. Credit cards: All major.

MIRACLE WOK....102 West Jericho Tpke., Syosset, L.I., N.Y., 11791. (516) 364-9330. Cuisine: Chinese.

VIENNESE COACH... Jericho Tpke., Syosset, L.I., N.Y., 11791. (516) 921-2380. Cuisine: German/Continental. Credit cards: All major.

SYRACUSE

BARBUTO'S....50 Jefferson Towers, Syracuse, N.Y., 13202. (315) 474-3000. Cuisine: Italian. Credit cards: All major.

PHOEBE'S GARDEN CAFE....900 East Genesee St., Syracuse, N.Y., 13210. (315) 475-5154. Cuisine: French/American. Credit cards: AE, CB, MC, VISA.

POSEIDON....770 James St., Syracuse, N.Y., 13203. (315) 472-4474. Cuisine: Continental. Credit cards: All major.

TARRYTOWN

THE PENNYBRIDGE RESTAURANT....455 South Broadway, Tarrytown, N.Y., 10591. (914) 631-5700, Ext. 179.

SHANGHAI INN....350 South Broadway, Tarrytown, N.Y., 10591. (914) 631-2000. Cuisine: Chinese. Credit cards: All major.

TAPPAN HILL.... Benedict Ave., Tarrytown, N.Y., 10591. (914) 631-3030. Cuisine: Continental. Credit cards: All major.

TRUMANSBURG

TAUGHANNOCK FARMS INN.... Rte. 89, Trumansburg, N.Y., 14886. (607) 387-7711, Cuisine: American. Open for lunch Monday through Friday; dinner Monday through Saturday. Owner: C. Keith le Grand. Credit cards: None. Private party facilities: Up to 150. Total employment: 40.

TUCKAHOE

CRABTREE'S PLAZA INN....296 Columbus Ave., Tuckahoe, N.Y., 10707. (914) 779-3200. Cuisine: Continental. Credit cards: All major.

ROBERTO'S....307 Columbus Ave., Tuckahoe, N.Y., 10707. (914) 337-4880. Cuisine: Italian. Open for lunch and dinner 6 days; closed Tuesday. Credit cards: All major. Annual sales $250,000 to $500,000. Total employment: 5. Corporate name: Roberto's Restaurnt.

ROMA RESTAURANT....29 Columbus Ave., Tuckahoe, N.Y., 10707. (914) 961-3175. Cuisine: Italian. Owner: John Tavolilla. Open 6 days; Closed Monday. Credit cards: All major. Private party facilities: 25 to 100. Annual sales: $250,000 to $500,000. Total employment: 37. Corporate name: Roma Restaurant, Inc.

SALERNO'S....100 Main St., Tuckahoe, N.Y., 10707. (914) 793-1557. Cuisine: American. Credit cards: None.

VALHALLA

FRANZL'S....301 Columbus Ave., Valhalla, N.Y., 10595. (914) 946-0308. Cuisine: Continental. Credit cards: All major.

VALHALLA STATION.... Bronx River Pkwy., Valhalla, N.Y., 10595. (914) 949-3386. Cuisine: American. Credit cards: All major.

VESTAL

VESTAL STEAK HOUSE.... Vestal Pkwy., Vestal, N.Y., 13580. (607) 798-7871. Cuisine: Steakhouse. Credit cards: AE, DC, MC, VISA.

WANTAUGH

CAFE DU PARC....3060 Merrick Rd., Wantaugh, L.I., N.Y., 11793. (516) 221-0480. Cuisine: French. Credit cards: All major.

KWONG MING....3342 Jerusalem Ave., Wantaugh, L.I., N.Y., 11793. (516) 221-0408. Cuisine: Chinese. Credit cards: All major.

WAVERLY

O'BRIEN'S.... Atop Waverly Hill, Waverly, N.Y., 14892. (607) 565-2817. Cuisine: American/N.Y. State. Credit cards: All major.

WEST BABYLON

LE PETIT PARIS....767 West Montauk Hwy., West Babylon, L.I., N.Y., 11704. (516) 669-7125. Owner's name: Catherine Sanchez.

WESTBURY

EL MESON....795 Old Country Rd., Westbury, L.I., N.Y., 11590. (516) 997-9018. Cuisine: Spanish. Credit cards: AE, MC, VISA, DC.

ENRICO'S GREENTREE RESTAURANT....199 Post Ave., Westbury, L.I., N.Y., 11590. (516) 997-8111. Cuisine: Italian. Credit cards: All major.

GIULIO CESARE RISTORANTE....18 Ellison Ave., Westbury, L.I., N.Y., 11590. (516) 334-2982. Cuisine: Italian. Credit cards: All major.

THE JOHN PEEL RESTAURANT.... Old Country Rd., Westbury, L.I., N.Y., 11590. (516) 741-3430. Cuisine: Continental/American. Open 7 days. Credit cards: All major. Private party facilities: 35 to 450. Annual sales: Over $3 million. Total employment: 110. Corporate name: Restaurant Associates.

LA GALLERIA....216 Post Ave., Westbury, L.I., N.Y., 11590. (516) 334-1160. Cuisine: Italian. Credit cards: All major.

TESORO....967 Old Country Rd., Westbury, L.I., N.Y., 11590. (516) 334-0022. Cuisine: Italian. Credit cards: AE, DC.

WESTBURY MANOR.... Jericho Tpke., Westbury, L.I., N.Y., 11590. (516) 333-7117. Cuisine: Continental. Credit cards: All major.

WHEATLEY HILLS TAVERN....170 Post Ave., Westbury, L.I., N.Y., 11590. Cuisine: American. Owner's name: Joseph Zaino.

WESTHAMPTON BEACH

CLUB PIERRE.... Beach Rd. & Main St., Westhampton Beach, L.I., N.Y., 11978. (516) 288-4046. Cuisine: French. Owner: Pierre Bovet. Open April through Septmber for dinner only; closed Monday. Credit cards: All major. Private party facilities: 20 to 110. Annual sales: $250,00 to $500,000. Total employment: 21. Corporate name: Bovel Restaurant Corp.

NICOLE'S RESTAURANT....141 Montauk Hwy., Westhampton Beach, L.I., N.Y., 11978. (516) 288-4010. Cuisine: Italian. Owner: Ronald Dionisio. Open Wednesday through Sunday. Credit cards: All major. Private party facilities: 20 to 100. Corporate name: Ron-Mar Trading Corp.

WEST HEMPSTEAD

GUM YING....814 Hempstead Ave., West Hempstead, L.I., N.Y., 11552. (516) 481-3400. Cuisine: Chinese. Owner's name: Eddie Ton.

PORTO BELLO....495 Hempstead Tpke., West Hempstead, L.I., N.Y., 11552. (516) 485-8360. Cuisine: Italian. Owner: Eugene E. Cicanni. Credit cards: All major. Annual sales: $250,000 to $500,000. Total employment: 8.

RED FOX....6 Parlato Dr., Westhampton Beach, L.I., N.Y., 11978. (516) 288-1040. Cuisine: Nouvelle. Owner: Michael James Walsh. Open 7 days for lunch and dinner. Credit cards: MC, VISA. Annual sales: $250,000 to $500,000. Total employment: 30.

WHITE PLAINS

BENGAL TIGER.... 144 East Post Rd., White Plains, N.Y., 10601. (914) 948-5191. Cuisine: Indian.

BROADWAY....811 North Broadway, White Plains, N.Y., 10603. (914) 997-7373. Cuisine: American. Credit cards: All major.

CIRO'S....330 East Post Rd., White Plains, N.Y., 10601. (914) 946-2323. Cuisine: Italian. Credit cards: All major.

DAG'S....200 Hamilton Ave., White Plains, N.Y., 10601. (914) 428-5252. Cuisine: American. Credit cards: All major.

GAMBELLI'S....1 North Broadway, White Plains, N.Y., 10601. (914) 948-8000. Cuisine: Italian. Credit cards: All major.

GISSHA OF TOKYO....200 Hamilton Ave., White Plains, N.Y., 10601. (914) 946-6300. Cuisine: Japanese. Credit cards: All major.

GREGORY....324 Central Ave., White Plains, N.Y., 10606. (914) 428-2455. Cuisine: Italian. Owner: Gregory & William Losapig. Open 7 days. Credit cards: All major. Annual sales: $500,000 to $1 million. Total employment: 20.

JOCKEY CLUB....99 Court St., White Plains, N.Y., 10601. (914) 946-9315. Cuisine: Continental. Credit cards: All major.

LA CREPE....51 Mamaroneck Ave., White Plains, N.Y., 10601. (914) 949-4940. Cuisine: French. Credit cards: All major.

LAMANDA'S....251 Tarrytown Rd., White Plain, N.Y., 10607. (914) 948-9531. Cuisine: Italian. Credit cards: None.

LE GAI PINGUIN....2 Westchester Ave., White Plains, N.Y., 10601. (914) 949-1440. Cuisine: French. Owner: Rita Dix. Open Monday through Saturday. Credit cards: AE, MC, VISA. Private party facilities: 20 to 55. Annual sales: $250,000 to $500,000. Total employment: 11.

THE MAGIC PAN....100 Main St., Galleria, White Plains, N.Y., 10601. (914) 977-8144. Cuisine: Continental. Open 7 days for lunch and dinner. Credit cards: All major. Available for private parties. Annual sales: $500,000 to $1 million. Total employment: 29. Corporate name: Magic Pan, Inc.

MAMMA CARMELA....238 Central Ave., White Plains, N.Y., 10606. (914) 948-9716. Cuisine: Italian. Credit cards: All major.

LE PASTIS...6 Quarropas, White Plains, N.Y., 10601. (914) 949-2311. Cuisine: French. Credit cards: All major.

LE SHACK D'ALSACE....68 Gedney Way, White Plains, N.Y., 10605. (914) 428-1264. Cuisine: French. Credit cards: All major.

MAXL'S RATHSKELLER....736 North Broadway (Rte. 22), White Plains, N.Y., 10603. (914) 949-6111. Cuisine: German. Owner: Mr. Karl M. Lehmann. Open Wednesday through Monday. Credit cards: AE, MC, VISA. Private party facilities: 20 to 200. Annual sales: $500,000 to $1 million. Total employment: 33. Corporate name: Maxl's Rathskeller, Inc.

MESON CASTELLANO....135 East Post Rd., White Plains, N.Y., 10601. (914) 428-8022. Cuisine: Spanish. Credit cards: AE, VISA.

MR. GREENJEANS....100 Main St., Galleria, White Plains, N.Y., 10601. (914) 997-8122. Cuisine: American. Owner: Joseph E. Zuravleff. Open 7 days for lunch and dinner. Credit cards: AE, MC, VISA. Annual sales: $1 million to $3 million. Total employment: 85

OAKLEY'S AMERICAN RESTAURANT....100 Main St., Galleria, White Plains, N.Y., 10601. (914) 949-2100. Cuisine: American. Credit cards: All major.

OLLIVER'S....15 South Broadway, White Plains, N.Y., 10601. (914) 761-6111. Cuisine: Continental. Credit cards: All major.

THE PALM COURT...100 Main St., Galleria, White Plains, N. Y., 10601. (914) 997-8222. Cuisine: American. Credit cards: All major.

PETER PASTOR'S....149 Mamaroneck Ave., White Plains, N.Y., 10601. (914) 761-5160. Cuisine: American. Credit cards: All major.

SAM'S SALOON & DINING EMPORIUM....52 Gedney Way, White Plains, N.Y., 10605. (914) 949-0978. Cuisine: American.

SASSAFRAS....1241 Mamaroneck Ave., White Plains, N.Y., 10605. (914) 761-3660.

SCOTCH N SIRLOIN....White Plains Mall, White Plains, N.Y., 10601. (914) 948-2070. Cuisine: American. Credit cards: All major.

TUTTLES....South Broadway & Lyon Pl., White Plains, N.Y., 10601. (914) 761-8100. Cuisine: American/Continental.

TYLOON IMPERIAL....120 Mamaroneck Ave., White Plains, N.Y., 10601. (914) 948-4844. Cuisine: Chinese. Credit cards: All major.

VICTORIA STATION....15 Water St., White Plains, N.Y., 10601. (914) 948-7652. Cuisine: Continental.

WINGS OF WESTCHESTER....Westchester County Airport, White Plains, N.Y., 10601 (914) 948-5822. Cuisine: Continental. Credit cards: All major.

WHITESBORO

HART'S HILL INN....Clinton St., Whitesboro, N.Y., 13492, (315) 736-3011. Cuisine: American. Credit cards: All major.

WILLISTON PARK

LA MARMITE....234 Hillside Ave., Williston Park, L.I., N.Y., 11596. (516) 746-1243. Cuisine: Italian/French. Credit cards: All major.

MAHONEY'S HILLSIDE RESTAURANT.... 26 Hillside Ave., Williston Park, L.I., N.Y., 11596. (516) 746-9643. Mahoney's is a prize example of a steak and chop house that gives splendid value. Cuisine is mainly American with interesting and often excellent results. Specialties include: an excellent salad bar that includes mussels and shrimp, New York sirloins, fresh catch of the day, and broiled sea scallops. Owner: Robert Gipp. Open 7 days for lunch and dinner. Priced moderate. Reservations: Accepted. Credit cards: All major. Private party facilities: Up to 50. Annual sales: $500,000 to $1 million. Total employment: 23. Corporate name: Mahoney's Hillside Restaurant, Inc.

PAPPAS RESTAURANT....700 Willis Ave., Williston Park, L.I., N.Y., 11596. (516) 742-9191. Cuisine: Seafood. Credit cards: All major.

WOODBURY

HOMER'S SZECHUAN STAR....8285 Jericho Tpke., Woodbury, L.I., N.Y., 11797. (516) 367-9012. Cuisine: Chinese.

WOODMERE

BILLY SHAW'S SAFFRON....730 West Broadway, Woodmere, L.I., N.Y., 11578. (516) 295-0200. A unique menu: Specialties of the house you'll find nowhere else alongside the tried and true—and both are done exceedingly well. The adventurous is what you'd call "American nouvelle." The look is pleasant and relaxed—and pretty, too. Specialties include: veal chop "Saffron," filet of sole caprice, fresh Long Island duck any of the eight ways they serve it, oysters wrapped in bacon *en brochette*. Prices are moderate. Owner: Billy Shaw. Open Tuesday through Sunday for lunch and dinner; Closed Monday. Reservations are suggested. All major credit cards accepted. Private party facilities: 25 to 120. Annual sales: $500,000 to $1 million. Total employment: 25. Corporate name: ABG, Inc.

WOODSIDE

THE MAITRE D'....53-15 Broadway, Woodside (Queens), N.Y., 11377. (212) 274-1300. Cuisine: Italian. Credit cards: All major.

YONKERS

COOKY'S....2601 Central Park Ave., Yonkers, N.Y., 10710. (914) 779-9700. Cuisine: American. Credit cards: All major.

FEDERICO'S....1064 McLean Ave., Yonkers, N.Y. 10704. (914) 237-8823. Cuisine: Italian. Credit cards: VISA.

HOUSE OF LEE....475 South Broadway, Yonkers, N.Y., 10705. (914) 476-1554. Cuisine: Chinese. Credit cards: None.

HUNAN VILLAGE....1828 Central Ave., Yonkers, N.Y., 10710. (914) 779-2272. Cuisine: Chinese. Credit cards: All major.

LA PIETRA'S....623 South Broadway, Yonkers, N.Y., 10705. (914) 969-8738. Cuisine: Italian. Credit cards: All major.

LIGHTHOUSE-ON-THE-HUDSON....55 Alexander St., Yonkers, N.Y., 10701. (914) 969-2600. Cuisine: Seafood. Credit cards: All major.

LOUIE'S....187 South Broadway, Yonkers, N.Y., 10701. (914) 969-8821. Cuisine: Italian/Continental. Credit cards: All major.

LUIGI'S....1920 Central Park Ave., Yonkers, N.Y., 10710. (914) 779-9864. Cuisine: Italian. Credit cards: All major.

RED COACH GRILL....Cross County Shopping Center, Yonkers, N.Y., 10701. (914) 963-4500. Cuisine: American. Credit cards: All major.

RICKY'S CLAM HOUSE....1965 Central Park Ave., Yonkers, N.Y., 10710. (914) 961-8284. Cuisine: Seafood. Credit cards: All major.

7 STARS....1 Fort Hill Rd., Yonkers, N.Y., 10710. (914) 961-4677. Cuisine: Continental. Credit cards: All major.

SIX BROTHERS....2393 Central Park Ave., Yonkers, N.Y. 10710. (914) 779-1005. Cuisine: Italian. Credit cards: All major.

VALLE'S STEAK HOUSE....278 Tuckahoe Rd., Yonkers, N.Y., 10710. (914) 961-4321. Cuisine: Steak/Seafood. Open 7 days for dinner. Credit cards: All major. Private party facilities: Up to 400. Annual sales: $1 million to $3 million.

VENEZIA DI NOTTE....987 Central Park Ave., Yonkers, N.Y., 10704 (914) 969-8856. Cuisine: Continental. Credit cards: All major.

VICTORIA STATION....10 Herman Pl., Yonkers, N.Y., 10710. (914) 779-3900. Cuisine: American.

VIRIATO....285 South Broadway, Yonkers, N.Y., 10705. (914) 963-6212. Cuisine: Portuguese. Credit cards: All major.

YORKTOWN HEIGHTS

HUCKLEBERRY'S....355 Kear St., Yorktown Heights, N.Y., 10598. (914) 245-1984. Cuisine: International. Credit cards: MC, VISA.

LUCY'S....1937 Commerce St., Yorktown Heights, N.Y., 10598. (914) 779-9864. Cuisine: American. Credit cards: All major.

MAY WAH....98 Triangle Shopping Ctr., Yorktown Heights, N.Y., 10598. (914) 245-3311. Cuisine: Szechuan/Cantonese.

SILVER MOON....Rte. 35, Yorktown Heights, N.Y., 10598. (914) 962-4677. Cuisine: Italin. Credit cards: All major.

NORTH CAROLINA

ASHEVILLE

JARED'S....60 Haywood St., Asheville, N.C., 28806. (704) 252-8276. Cuisine: French. Owner: Robert Satz, Pres. Credit cards: MC, VISA. Annual sales: $500,000 to $1 million. Total employment: 30. Open for lunch and dinner Monday through Saturday; Sunday dinner only.

BLOWING ROCK

THE FARMHOUSE....South Main St., Blowing Rock, N.C., 28605. (704) 295-7361. Cuisine: American. Owner: Etson James Blackwell. Open 7 days June through Labor Day. No credit cards. Private party facilities: Up to 500.

BURNSVILLE

NU-WRAY INN....Rte. 19 E, Burnsville, N.C., 28714. (704) 682-2329. Cuisine: American. Open 7 days; Closed December through May. No credit cards. Private party facilities: Up to 65. Annual sales: $250,000 to $500,000. Total employment: 25. Corporate name: Nu-Wray, Inc.

CHAPEL HILL

SLUG'S AT THE PINES.... Raleigh Rd., Chapel Hill, N.C., 27514. (919) 929-0428. Cuisine: American/Continental. Open for dinner 7 days. Credit cards: AE, DC, MC, VISA. Private party facilities: Up to 80. Annual sales: $1 million to $3 million. Total employment: 60. Corporate name: Barclay Enterprises, Inc./Slug Claiborne, CEO.

CHARLOTTE

EPICUREAN.... 1324 East Blvd., Charlotte, N.C., 28203. (704) 377-4529. Cuisine: Continental/American. Credit cards: AE, DC, MC, VISA.

REFLECTIONS.... 2 NCNB Plz., Charlotte, N.C., 28280. (704) 377-0400. Cuisine: Continental. Owner: D.R. Malicki, Rest. Mgr. Open 7 days. Credit cards: All major. Private party facilities: Up to 1000. Annual sales: $1 million to $3 million. Total employment: 100. Corporate name: Radisson Hotel Corp.

DURHAM

SADDLE & THE FOX.... 3211 Hillsborough Rd., Durham, N.C., 27705. (919) 383-5571. Cuisine: Continental. Credit cards: All major.

ALFREDO THE ORIGINAL OF ROME.... Forum VI, Friendly Center, Greensboro, N.C., 27408. (919) 294-5444. Another rendering of the charming New York original. Executive chef Angelo Ceranini plans the menus for all four Alfredo's spread along the East Coast, and nowhere is he better than here. Clean decorative lines, sumptuous well-prepared food, and rapid table turnover is the rule. Specialties include: Chicken with lemon and wild mushroom sauce, veal pizzaiola, and *paglia eh fieno.* Owner: Guido Bellanca. Open 6 days for lunch and dinner; Closed Sunday. Moderately priced. Reservations: Suggested. Credit cards: All major. Corporate name: Alfredo the Original of Rome (NC), Inc.

HATTERAS

CHANNEL BASS.... P.O. Box 147 (Rte. 12), Hatteras (Outer Banks), N.C., 27943. (919) 986-2250. Cuisine: Seafood. Owner: Jackie R. Harrison. Open 7 days for lunch and dinner seasonally (open from April 1 to December 1). Credit cards: MC, VISA. Private party facilities: Up to 40. Annual sales; $250,000 to $500,000. Total employment: 23.

HICKORY

WEDGEWOOD.... 443 Second Ave., Hickory, N.C., 28601. (704) 322-1575. Cuisine: Continental/American. Credit cards: MC, VISA.

HIGHLANDS

LEE'S INN.... Rtes. 64 & 28, Highlands, N.C., 28741. (704) 526-2171. Cuisine: American/Southern. Owner: Richard W. Lee. Open 7 days May to November. Credit cards: AE, MC, VISA. Private party facilities: Up to 175. Annual sales: $500,000 to $1 million. Total employment: 40

KILL DEVIL HILLS

PORT O'CALL.... Rte. 158, Kill Devil Hills (Outer Banks), N.C., 27948. (919) 441-7484. Cuisine: Seafood/Steak. Credit cards: AE, MC, VISA.

MOREHEAD CITY

REX.... Rte. 70, Morehead City, N.C., 28557. (919) 726-5561. Cuisine: Italian/American. Owner: Frank R. Marino, Jr. Open 7 days for dinner; closed Monday from October to May. Credit cards: All major. Annual sales: $500,000 to $1 million. Total employment: 25.

NAGS HEAD

SPENCER'S.... Rte. 64, Nags Head (Outer Banks), N.C., 27959. (919) 441-5633. Cuisine: Seafood. Credit cards: MC, VISA.

NEW BERN

HENDERSON HOUSE.... 216 Pollock St., New Bern, N.C., 28568. (919) 637-4784. Cuisine: Continental. Open 5 days for lunch and dinner; Closed Sunday and Monday. Credit cards: MC, VISA. Private party facilities: 6 to 70. Annual sales: $250,000 to $500,000. Total employment: 6. Corporate name: Henderson House, Inc.

RALEIGH

THE ANGUS BARN.... Durham Hwy., Raleigh, N.C., 27628. (919) 787-3505. Cuisine: American. Owner: Charles Winston & Thad Eure, Jr. Open 7 days for dinner. Credit cards: All major. Private party facilities: Up to 250. Annual sales: Over $3 million. Total employment: 153.

PLANTATION INN.... Rte. 1, Raleigh, N.C., 27604. (919) 876-1411. Cuisine: American. Owner: W.B. Morse. Credit cards: All major. Private party facilities: Up to 128. Annual sales: $250,000 to 500,000. Total employment: 35. Corporate name: Plantation Properties, Inc. Open 7 days for breakfast, lunch and dinner.

WARSAW

COUNTRY SQUIRE.... Rte. 2, Warsaw, N.C., 28398. (919) 296-1727. Cuisine: Steak/Seafood. Credit cards; AE, DC, MC, VISA.

WINSTON-SALEM

OLD SALEM TAVERN.... 736 South Main St., Winston-Salem, N.C., 27101. (919) 748-8585. Cuisine: Continental.

TOWN STEAK HOUSE.... 300 South Strafford Rd., Winston-Salem, N.C., 27103. (919) 722-6307. Cuisine: Continental. Credit cards: AE, MC, VISA.

WRIGHTSVILLE BEACH

GRAY GABLES.... 1209 Airlie Dr., Wrightsville Beach, N.C., 28480. (919) 256-3704. Cuisine: "Early Colonial". Owner: B.C. Hedgpeth. Open for dinner Monday through Saturday. Credit cards: AE, DC, MC, VISA. Private party facilities: Up to 150. Annual sales: $250,000 to $500,000. Total employment: 22

PENNSYLVANIA

ALTOONA

MINUET MANOR DINING ROOM.... Rte. 220, Altoona, Pa., 16601. (814) 742-8441. Cuisine: American. Credit cards: All major.

FLAVIO'S.... 212 Warren Ave., Apollo, Pa., 15613. (413) 478-2961. The food is French and Italian here, and the selection is large enough to accommodate just about everybody. There's eleven versions of veal, six of chicken, nine of beef, and over a dozen pasta offerings—and don't forget the antipasti, soups, and a dozen or so fish and seafood dishes. The house specialties: dry cod cooked in tomato sauce, sauteed boneless chicken breast simmered with chicken livers, veal stuffed with prosciutto and grated parmesan cheese and topped with a tomato sauce, sauteed jumbo shrimp in marinara sauce, and beef Stroganoff. Owner: Flavio O. DiFelippo. Open 7 days.

ARDMORE

THE CHATEAU.... 229 East Lancaster Ave., Ardmore, Pa., 19003. (215) MI 2-1050 or (215) MI 2-9696. Cuisine: Continental/American. Open 7 days for dinner. Credit cards: All major. Private party facilities: Available.

HU-NAN.... 47 East Lancaster Ave., Ardmore, Pa., 19003. (215) 642-3050. Cuisine: Hunan Chinese. Open Monday through Friday for lunch; 7 days for dinner. Credit cards: AE, DC, VISA. Reservations: Suggested. Bring your own wine.

WATSISNAME'S.... 2373 Haverford Rd., Ardmore, Pa., 19003. (215) 896-5106. Cuisine: American. Open Monday through Saturday for lunch; 7 days for dinner. Credit cards: MC, VISA. Private party facilities: 4 to 50.

BALA CYNWYD

EARLENE'S.... 191 Presidential Blvd., Bala Cynwyd, Pa., 19004. (215) MO 7-7777. Cuisine: Continental. Open Monday through Friday for lunch; Tuesday through Sunday for dinner. Credit cards: AE, MC, VISA. Entertainment: Live music. Proper attire required.

MAURICETTE.... 281 Montgomery Ave., Bala Cynwyd, Pa., 19004. (215) 667-1245. Cuisine: French. Open 6 days for dinner only; Closed Sunday. Credit cards: Call for cards. Reservations: Accepted.

SAN MARCO.... 27 City Line Ave., Bala Cynwyd, Pa., 19004. (215) 664-7844. Cuisine: Northern Italian. Open Monday through Friday for lunch; Monday through Saturday for dinner; Closed Sunday. Credit cards: AE, DC, MC, VISA. Private party facilities: Available. Entertainment: Piano bar & live music and dancing available.

THE TAVERN RESTAURANT.... 261 Montgomery Ave., Bala Cynwyd, Pa., 19004. (215) MO 4-3000. Cuisine: Provincial American. Open Monday through Saturday for lunch; 7 days for dinner. Credit cards: AE, DC, MC, VISA. Private party facilities: Private room for up to 75. Reservations: Accepted.

BALLIETSVILLE

BALLIETSVILLE INN.... Cedar Crest Blvd., Ballietsville, Pa., 18037. (215) 799-2435. Cuisine: French/Swiss. Credit cards: AE, DC, MC, VISA.

BEAVER

WOODEN ANGEL.... West Bridgewater St., Beaver, Pa., 15009. (412) 774-7880. Cuisine: American. Credit cards: AE, MC, VISA.

BERWYN

FONZO'S HARBOUR HOUSE....734 Lancaster Ave., Berwyn, Pa., 19312. (215) 644-4691. Cuisine: Italian/Seafood. Open Monday through Saturday for lunch; 7 days for dinner. Credit cards: All major.

BIRD-IN-HAND

AMISH BARN....Rte. 340, Bird-in-Hand, Pa., 17505. (717) 768-8886. Cuisine: Pennsylvania Dutch. Owner: Ted Skiadas, Pano Skiadas, Peter Skiadas, George Skiadas, and Harry Keares. Open 7 days for lunch and dinner; Closed January and February. Credit cards: All major. Private party facilities: Up to 75. Annual sales: $1 million to $3 million. Total employment: 35. Corporate name: Skiadas Brothers Enterprises Inc.

BLUE BELL

BLUE BELL INN.... Skippack & Penlyn Pkes., Blue Bell, Pa., 19422. (215) 646-2010. Cuisine: Continental/American. Credit cards: AE.

BOYERTOWN

THE COLEBROOKDALE INN....Farmingdale Ave. & Colebrookdale Rd., Boyertown, Pa., 19512. (215) 367-2353. Cuisine: French. Open Monday through Saturday for lunch and dinner; Closed Sunday. Credit cards: AE, MC, VISA.

BRYN MAWR

ILLUSIONS....24 Merion Ave., Bryn Mawr, Pa., 19010. (215) 525-3060. Cuisine: International. Open Tuesday through Friday for lunch; Tuesday through Saturday for dinner. Credit cards: AE, MC, VISA. Entertainment: Magic performed nightly at your table.

BUCKINGHAM

BOSWELL'S....Rte. 263, Buckingham, Pa., 18912. (215) 794-7959. Cuisine: "Gourmet" American. Open Tuesday and Wednesday for lunch; 6 days for dinner; Closed Monday; Weekend dinner from 12:00 Noon. Credit cards: AE, DC, MC, VISA. Reservations: Available.

STONE MANOR INN....Bogart's Tavern Rd., Buckingham, Pa., 18912. (215) 794-7883. Cuisine: Continental. Open Tuesday through Saturday for dinner only; Closed Sunday and Monday. Credit cards: AE, DC, MC, VISA. Reservations: Accepted. Entertainment: Music Friday and Saturday evenings.

BUTLER

ERNIE'S ESQUIRE....657 Pittsburgh Rd., Butler, Pa., 16001. (412) 586-7733. Cuisine: Continental. Credit cards: All major

CANADENSIS

PUMP HOUSE INN....Sky Top Rd., Canadensis, Pa., 18325. (717) 595-7501. Cuisine: Continental. Open 6 days for dinner only; Closed Monday. Credit cards: AE, MC, VISA. Reservations: Suggested. Accomodations available.

CEDARS

PFEIFFER'S CEDAR TAVERN....Rte. 73 & Skipjack Pke., Cedars, Pa., 19423. (215) 584-6311. Cuisine: German/American/Continental. Open Tuesday through Saturday for lunch; Tuesday through Sunday for dinner; Closed Monday. Credit cards: AE, MC, VISA. Private party facilities: Available.

CENTER SQUARE

TIFFANY DINING SALOON....799 DeKalb Pke., Center Square, Pa., 19422. (215) 272-1888. Cuisine: Continental/American. Open 7 days for dinner; Sunday dinner from 1:00 PM. Credit cards: AE, MC, VISA. Reservations: Available.

CHAMPION

SEVEN SPRINGS....Country Line Rd., Champion, Pa., 15622. (412) 352-2900. Cuisine: Continental.

COATESVILLE

FAMOUS RESTAURANT....340 East Lincoln Hwy., Coatesville, Pa., 19320. (215) 384-4744. Cuisine: American. Owner: Bill Lazous. Open 6 days for lunch and dinner; Closed Sunday. No credit cards. Annual sales: $250,000 to $500,000. Total employment: 15.

CONSHOHOCKEN

HUNGRY PILGRIM....107 Ridge Pke., Conshohocken, Pa., 19428. (215) 828-7858. Cuisine: American. Open 7 days for lunch and dinner; Sunday dinner from 1:00 PM. Credit cards: AE, MC, VISA. Reservations: Accepted. Entertainment: Piano Friday and Saturday evenings.

SPRING MILL CAFE....164 Barrenhill Rd., Conshohocken, Pa., 19428. (215) 828-1550. Cuisine: Country French. Open Tuesday through Saturday for lunch; Thursday, Friday, and Saturday for dinner; Closed Sunday and Monday. No credit cards. Reservations: Suggested. Bring your own wine.

THE TANKARD INN....Conshohocken Exit off the Schuylkill Expressway., Conshohocken, Pa., 19428. (215) 828-2900. Cuisine: American. Open 7 days for lunch and dinner. Credit cards: MC, VISA. Reservations: Accepted.

CORAPOLIS

HYEHOLDE....190 Hyeholde Dr., Corapolis, Pa., 15108. (412) 264-3116. Cuisine: Continental. Credit cards: MC, VISA.

MYRON'S....Beers School Rd., Corapolis, Pa., 15108. (412) 264-8950. Cuisine: Continental. Credit cards: All major.

COVENTRYVILLE

COVENTRY FORGE INN....Rte. 23, Coventryville, Pa., (215) 469-6222. Cuisine: French. Owner's name: The Callahans. Credit cards: None.

CRABTREE

CARBONE'S....Main St., Crabtree, Pa., 15624. (412) 834-3430. Cuisine: Italian. Owner: Natalie J. Carbone. Open 6 days for dinner only; Closed Sunday. Credit cards: AE only. Private party facilities: Up to 300. Annual sales: $500,000 to $1 million. Total employment: 70.

DEVON

CHINESE DELIGHT....735 Lancaster Ave., Devon, Pa., 19333. (215) 687-1866. Open Monday through Saturday for lunch and dinner; Closed Sunday. No credit cards. No reservations. No liquor. Bring your own wine.

DOYLESTOWN

CONTI CROSS KEYS INN....Rte. 611, Doylestown, Pa., 18901. (215) 348-3539. Cuisine: Continental. Owner: Walter J. Conti. Open Monday through Friday for lunch; Monday through Saturday for dinner ; Closed Sunday. Credit cards: All major. Private party facilities: Up to 100.

DREXEL HILL

DREXELBROOK FINE FOOD & SPIRITS....Drexelbrook Dr. & Valley Rd., Drexel Hill, Pa., 19026. (215) 259-7000. Cuisine: American/Continental. Open Tuesday through Friday for lunch; Tuesday through Sunday for dinner; Sunday brunch; Closed Monday. Credit cards: All major. Entertainment: Live music and dancing.

SZECHUAN ROYAL....3703 Garrett Rd., Drexel Hill, Pa., 19026. (215) 284-4242. Cuisine: Szechuan Chinese. Open 7 days for lunch and dinner. Credit cards: DC, MC, VISA. Bring your own wine.

ELKINS PARK

MING GARDEN....1911 West Cheltenham Ave., Elkins Park, Pa., 19117. (215) 887-7222. Cuisine: Mandarin & Szechuan Chinese. Open Monday through Saturday for lunch; 7 days for dinner. Credit cards: DC, MC, VISA. Private party facilities: Up to 50.

YORKTOWN INN....Old York Rd. & Church Rd., Elkins Park, Pa., 19117. (215) 887-9500. Cuisine: American. Open Monday through Saturday for lunch; 7 days for dinner; Sunday dinner from 1:00 PM. Credit cards: AE, VISA. Reservations: Accepted.

ERWINNA

THE GOLDEN PHEASANT....River Rd., Erwinna, Pa., 18920. (215) 294-9595. Cuisine: Continental. Open 6 days for dinner only; Closed Monday. Credit cards: MC, VISA. Reservations: Accepted.

EXTON

SHIP INN....Rte. 30 & Ship Rd., Exton, Pa., 19341. (215) 363-7200. Cuisine: American. Open Monday through Friday for lunch; 7 days for dinner. Credit cards: All major.

FERNDALE

FERNDALE INN....Rte. 611 and Church Rd., Ferndale, Pa., 18921. (215) 847-2662. Cuisine: Eclectic. Open Tuesday through Saturday for dinner; Sunday brunch; Closed Monday. Credit cards: MC, VISA. Reservations: Required.

FLEETWOOD

MOSELEM SPRINGS INN....U.S. Rtes. 222 and 662, Fleetwood (between Allentown and Reading), Pa., 19522. (215) 944-8213. Cuisine: Pennsylvania Dutch/American. Open 7 days for lunch and dinner. Credit cards: AE, DC, MC, VISA. Reservations: Suggested.

FORT WASHINGTON

THE COACH INN....Commerce Dr., Fort Washington, Pa., 19034. (215) 646-2133. Cuisine: Continental. Open 7 days for dinner; Sunday brunch from 8:00 AM. Credit cards: All major. Reservations: Requested.

FRAZER

BUOY 1....Lancaster Pke. (Rte. 30) at Rte. 401, Frazer, Pa., 19355. (215) 644-0549. Open 7 days for breakfast, lunch, and dinner. No credit cards. No reservations. No alcoholic beverages. Bring your own beer and wine.

GALLITZIN

ERCULIANI'S....Rte. 53, Gallitzin, Pa., 16641. (814) 886-8832. Cuisine: Italian/American.

GETTYSBURG

THE DOBBIN HOUSE....89 Steinwehr Ave., Gettysburg, Pa., 17325. (717) 334-2100. Cuisine: Continental. Credit cards: MC, VISA.

GLENSIDE

LA PETITE FERME....245 South Easton Rd., Glenside, Pa., 19038. (215) 576-5117. Cuisine: French/Continental. Credit cards: None.

RUDY'S....15 Limekiln Pke., Glenside, Pa., 19038. (215) 885-3661. Cuisine: Continental. Open Tuesday through Friday for lunch; Tuesday through Sunday for dinner; Closed Monday. Credit cards: AE, MC, VISA. Entertainment: Piano in lounge Wednesday through Saturday.

HARRISBURG

INN 22....5390 Jonestown Rd., Harrisburg, Pa., 17112. (717) 545-6077. Cuisine: American. Credit cards: All major.

HOLLAND

HOLLAND HOUSE INN....184 Buck Rd., Holland, Pa., 18966. (215) 357-0100. Cuisine: Italian/American. Open Tuesday through Saturday for lunch; Tuesday through Sunday for dinner; Closed Monday. Credit cards: AE, DC, MC, VISA. Reservations: Accepted. Entertainment: Piano Friday and Saturday evenings.

THE MILL RACE....183 Buck Rd., Holland, Pa., 18966. (215) 322-2010. Cuisine: Steaks/Chops/Seafood. Open Monday through Saturday for lunch; 7 days for dinner.Credit cards: AE, CB, MC, VISA. Private party facilities: Available. Entertainment: Live music nightly.

HUNTINGDON VALLEY

THE HUONG RESTAURANT....2651 Huntingdon Pke., Huntingdon Valley, Pa., 19006. (215) 947-6195. Cuisine: French/Chinese/Vietnamese. Open Tuesday through Friday for lunch; Tuesday through Sunday for dinner; Closed Monday. Credit cards: MC, VISA. Bring your own wine.

IRWIN

BEN GROSS....822 Lincoln Hwy., Irwin Pa., 15642. (412) 863-7450. Cuisine: Continental. Credit cards: All major.

JENKINTOWN

COSTA DO SOL....Benson Manor, Township Line Rd. & Washington La., Jenkintown, Pa., 19046. (215) 866-3050. Cuisine: Portuguese. Open Tuesday through Friday for lunch; Tuesday through Sunday for dinner; Closed Monday. Credit cards: AE, MC, VISA.

LA COQUILLE ST. JACQUES....314 Old York Road, Jenkintown, Pa., 19046. (215) 572-5411. Cuisine: French. Owner: Jacques Colmaire. Open Monday through Friday; Monday through Saturday for dinner; Closed Sunday. Credit cards: MC, VISA. Reservations: Suggested.

KENNET SQUARE

LONGWOOD INN....Rte. 1, Kennet Square, Pa., 19348. (215) 444-3515. Cuisine: Continental/American. Owner: Ted Skiadas, Pano Skiadas, Peter Skiadas, George Skiadas, and Harry Keares. Open 7 days for lunch and dinner. Credit cards: All major. Private party facilities: Up to 150. Total employment: 25. Corporate name: Skiadas Brothers Enterprises, Inc.

KING OF PRUSSIA

THE COPPERMILL RESTAURANT....480 North Gulph Rd., King of Prussia, Pa., 19406. (215) 337-1800. Cuisine: American/Continental. Open daily for breakfast, lunch, and dinner. Credit cards: AE, DC, VISA. Entertainment: Live music and dancing.

THE STING....Rte. 363, King of Prussia, Pa., 19406. (215) 265-2550. Cuisine: Steakhouse. Credit cards: None.

VICTORIA STATION....151 North Henderson Rd., King of Prussia, Pa., 19406. (215) 265-6570. Open Monday through Friday for lunch; 7 days for dinner. Credit cards: All major. Private party facilities: Available.

LAFAYETTE HILL

F.G. BRITTINGHAM'S INN....640 Germantown Ave., Lafayette Hill, Pa., 19444. (215) 828-7315. Cuisine: Continental/American. Open 7 days for lunch and dinner. Credit cards: AE, VISA. Reservations: Accepted.

LAHASKA

COCK N' BULL....Rte. 263, Lahaska, Pa., 18931. (215) 794-7051. Cuisine: American. Open 7 days for lunch and dinner. No credit cards. Reservations: Accepted.

THE SOUP TUREEN....Rte. 202, Lahaska, Pa., 18931. (215) 794-7216. Cuisine: Continental/American. Open 7 days for breakfast, lunch, and dinner; Closed Sunday. No credit cards.

LANCASTER

FAMILY STYLE RESTAURANT....Rte. 30, Lancaster, Pa., 17602. (717) 393-2333. Cuisine: American (Amish Family-Style). Owner: Ted Skiadas, Pano Skiadas, Peter Skiadas, George Skiadas, and Harry Keares. Open 7 days for breakfast, lunch, and dinner; Closed January and February. Credit cards: All major. Private party facilities: Up to 300. Annual sales: $1 million to $3 million. Total employment: 100. Corporate name: Skiadas Brother Enterprises, Inc.

JETHRO'S....First and Ruby Sts., Lancaster, Pa., 17603. (717) 299-1700. Cuisine: Continental. Open Tuesday through Saturday for dinner; Sunday dinner from 4:00 PM to 8:00 PM; Sunday brunch; Closed Monday. Credit cards: MC, VISA. Reservations: Suggested.

LEMON TREE....1766 Columbia Ave., Lancaster Pa., 17603. (717) 394-0441. Cuisine: International. Owner: Robert H. Newswanger, Jr. Open 7 days for lunch and dinner. Credit cards: All major. Private party facilities: Up to 50. Total employment: 20.

LANSDALE

HOTEL TREMONT....Main and Broad Sts., Lansdale, Pa., 19446. (215) 855-4266. Cuisine: American/French. Open 6 days for breakfast, lunch, dinner, and late supper; Closed Sunday. Credit cards: MC, VISA. Reservations: Suggested. Entertainment: Pianist Wednesday, Friday, and Saturday evenings.

LEWISBURG

COUNTRY CUPBOARD....Hafer Rd., Lewisburg, Pa., 17837. (717) 524-4475. Cuisine: American. Credit cards: MC, VISA.

LIGONIER

TOWN HOUSE....201 South Fairfield St., Ligonier, Pa., 15658. (412) 238-5451. Cuisine: Continental. Credit cards: MC, VISA.

LIONVILLE

VICKER'S INN....192 Welsh Pool Rd., Lionville, Pa., 19353. (215) 363-6336. Cuisine: Continental. Credit cards: AE, MC, VISA.

LUMBERVILLE

BLACK BASS HOTEL....River Rd., Lumberville, Pa., 18933. (215) 297-5770. Cuisine: American. Open Monday through Saturday for lunch; 7 days for dinner; Sunday brunch. Credit cards: AE, DC, MC. Reservations: Suggested.

MEDIA

D'IGNAZIO'S TOWN HOUSE....117 South Ave., Media, Pa., 19063. (215) 566-6141. Cuisine: Italian/American. Open Monday through Saturday for lunch and dinner; late supper also. Credit cards: All major. Reservations: Suggested. Private party facilities: Available. Children's menu.

WALDO'S....107 West State St., Media, Pa., 19063. (215) 566-5020. Cuisine: Seafood/American. Open Monday through Friday for lunch; Monday through Saturday for dinner; Closed Sunday. Credit cards: AE, MC, VISA. Entertainment: Live music on weekends. Private party facilities: Banquet and party facilities available.

MENDENHALL

MENDENHALL INN....Kennet Pke., Mendenhall, Pa., 19357. (215) 388-1181. Cuisine: American/Continental. Open Tuesday through Saturday for lunch; Tuesday through Sunday for dinner; Sunday dinner from 3:00 PM. Credit cards: AE, DC, MC, VISA. Reservations: Suggested.

MERTZTOWN

BLAIR CREEK INN....Mertztown, Pa., 19539. (215) 682-6700. Cuisine: International/Continental. Open Tuesday through Saturday for dinner; Sunday brunch; Closed Monday. Credit cards: AE, MC, VISA. Reservations: Essential on weekends. Telephone ahead for directions.

MOUNT JOY

GROFF FARM....RD 3, Mount Joy, Pa., 17552. (717) 653-2048. Cuisine: Pennsylvania Dutch. Open Tuesday through Friday for lunch; Tuesday through Saturday for dinner; Closed Sunday and Monday. No credit cards. Reservations: Required. Bring your own wine.

MT. PLEASANT

NINO BARSOTTI'S.... Rte. 31, Mt. Pleasant, Pa., 15666. (412) 547-2900. Cuisine: Continental.

MT. WASHINGTON

LOUIS TAMBELLINI'S....160 Southern Ave., Mt. Washington, Pa., 15211. (412) 481-1118. Cuisine: Seafood/Italian. Credit cards: None.

NEW HOPE

CENTRE BRIDGE INN.... Rtes. 32 & 263, New Hope, Pa., 18938. (215) 862-2048. Cuisine: French/Continental. Open 7 days for lunch and dinner. Credit cards: MC, VISA.

CHEZ ODETTE RESTAURANT.... Rte. 32, New Hope, Pa., 18938. (215) 862-2432. Cuisine: Continental. Open daily for lunch and dinner. Credit cards: AE, DC, MC, VISA. Reservations: Accepted.

THE HACIENDA....36 West Mechanie St., New Hope, Pa., 18938. (215) 862-2078. Cuisine: International. Open Tuesday through Saturday for lunch; 7 days for dinner; Sunday dinner from 1:00 PM. Credit cards: AE, DC, MC, VISA. Reservations: Suggested.

THE INN AT PHILIPS MILL.... North River Rd., New Hope, Pa., 18938. (215) 862-9919. Cuisine: French. Credit cards: None.

THE INTIMATE TOM MOORE'S.... Rte. 202, New Hope, Pa., 18938. (215) 862-5900. Cuisine: Continental. Open Wednesday through Sunday for lunch; 7 days for dinner. Credit cards: AE, MC, VISA.

LA BONNE AUBERGE.... Village 2, New Hope, Pa., 18938. (215) 862-2462. Cuisine: French. Open Wednesday through Sunday for dinner only; Closed Monday and Tuesday. Credit cards: AE only. Proper attire suggested.

LOGAN INN.... Ferry & Main Sts., New Hope, Pa., 18938. (215) 862-5134. Open daily for lunch and dinner through September. After September closed Sunday. Credit cards: MC, VISA. Reservations: Accepted.

NEW WILMINGTON

THE TAVERN....108 New Market St., New Wilmington, Pa., 16142. (412) 946-2020. Cuisine: Continental. Owner: Ernst Durrast. Open 6 days for lunch and dinner; Closed Tuesday. No credit cards. Private party facilities: Available. Total employment: 40.

NORRISTOWN

JEFFERSON HOUSE....2519 DeKalb Pke., Norristown, Pa., 19406. (215) 275-3407. Cuisine: Steaks/Seafood/Continental. Open Monday through Friday for lunch; 7 days for dinner. Credit cards: AE, CB, MC, VISA. Official Bicentennial Culinary Arts Show First Place Award.

MR. RON'S PUBLICK HOUSE....1799 DeKalb Pke., Norristown, Pa., 19406. (215) 277-0590. Cuisine: Italian/American. Open 7 days for lunch and dinner. Credit cards: AE, MC, VISA.

OAKLAND

CORNUCOPIA....328 Atwood St., Oakland, Pa., 15213. (412) 682-7953. Cuisine: Vegetarian. Credit cards: None.

PARK SCHENLEY....3955 Bigelow Blvd., Oakland, Pa., 15213. (412) 681-0800. Cuisine: French/Italian. Credit cards: All major.

SAMRENY'S....4808 Baum Blvd., Oakland, Pa., 15213. (412) 682-1212. Cuisine: Mid-Eastern. Credit cards: None.

OLEY

THE INN AT OLEY.... Main St., Oley, Pa., 19547. (215) 987-3459. Cuisine: French. Open Tuesday through Saturday for dinner only; Closed Sunday and Monday. Credit cards: MC, VISA. Reservations: Strongly suggested.

OVERBROOK

CHUN HING....3901 Conshohocken Ave., Overbrook, Pa., 19131. (215) 879-6270. Cuisine: Chinese. Open 6 days for lunch and dinner; Closed Monday.

PHILADELPHIA

ALFREDO THE ORIGINAL OF ROME....The Bourse Building, 21 South 5th St., Philadelphia, Pa., 19106. (215) 627-4600. This Alfredo's is handsome, eclectic, and subdued—more fitting for a stately dinner feast than the other 3 Alfredo's spread over the U.S. East Coast. In fact, more suited than most other restaurants. Period. Owner: Guido Bellanca. Open 6 days for lunch and dinner; Closed Sunday. Priced moderate to expensive. Reservations: Suggested. Credit cards: All major. Corporate name: Alfredo the Original of Rome (PA), Inc.

ALOUETTE....528 South 5th St., Philadelphia, Pa., 19147. (215) 629-1126. Cuisine: French. Open Wednesday through Monday for dinner; Sunday for brunch; Closed Tuesday. Credit cards: MC, VISA. Bring your own wine.

ARTHUR'S STEAK HOUSE....1512 Walnut St., Philadelphia, Pa., 19102. (215) 735-1590. Cuisine: Steak. Open Monday through Friday for lunch; Monday through Saturday for dinner; Closed Sunday. Credit cards: All major. Private party facilities: Available.

ASTRAL PLANE....1708 Lombard St., Philadelphia, Pa., 19146. (215) 546-6230. Cuisine: International. Open Monday through Friday for lunch; 7 days for dinner; Sunday brunch. Credit cards: AE, DC, MC, VISA. Reservations: Suggested.

BANGKOK HOUSE....117 South St., Philadelphia, Pa., 19147. (215) 925-0655. Cuisine: Thai. Open Monday through Saturday for dinner only. Credit cards: All major. Reservations: Accepted.

THE BARCLAY....18th St. on Rittenhouse Sq., Philadelphia, Pa., 19103. (215) 545-0300. Cuisine: Continental. Open 7 days for breakfast, lunch and dinner. Credit cards: All major. Private party facilities: Available. Annual sales: Over $3 million. Total employment: 75. Corporate name: Hotel Systems International.

BOGARTS.... The Latham Hotel, 17th & Walnut Sts., Philadelphia, Pa., 19103. (215) 563-9444. Cuisine: Steak/Seafood/Continental. Open 7 days for breakfast, lunch, and dinner; Sunday brunch. Credit cards: All major. Reservations: Advised on weekends.

BOOKBINDER'S 15th STREET....215 South 15th St., Philadelphia, Pa., 19102. (215) 545-1137. Open 7 days for lunch and dinner. Credit cards: All major. Reservations: Suggested.

BONJOUR....701 South Fourth St., Philadelphia, Pa., 19147. (215) 592-0800. Cuisine: French. Monday through Friday for lunch; 7 days for dinner; Sunday brunch. Credit cards: AE, MC, VISA. Private party facilities: Available.

THE BRASSERIE.... The Warwick, 17th & Locust Sts., Philadelphia, Pa., 19103. (215) 454-4655. Cuisine: French brasserie. Open 7 days, 24-hours. Credit cards: AE, DC, MC, VISA. Entertainment: Nightly jazz.

BREAD & COMPANY....16th & Walnut Sts., Philadelphia, Pa., 19103. (215) 545-4430. Cuisine: Continental. Open 7 days for breakfast, lunch and dinner. No credit cards.

CAFE LISBOA RESTAURANT.... Newmarket, Second and Pine Sts., Philadelphia, Pa., 19147. (215) 928-0844. Cuisine: Portugese/Continental. Open Tuesday through Sunday for lunch and dinner; Closed Monday. Credit cards: All major. Reservations: Suggested.

CAFE NOLA....328 South St., Philadelphia, Pa., 19147. (215) 627-2590. Cuisine: New Orleans-style cuisine. Open Friday and Saturday for lunch; 7 days for dinner; Sunday brunch. Credit cards: AE, MC, VISA.

CATHAY INN....1004 Race St., Philadelphia, Pa., 19107. (215) 928-1325. Cuisine: Chinese. Open 7 days for lunch and dinner. No credit cards. Private party facilities: Private dining room available.

CAVANAUGH'S....120 South 23rd St., Philadelphia, Pa., 19103. (215) 561-4097. Cuisine: Steak/Seafood. Open Monday through Saturday for lunch and dinner. No credit cards.

CAVANAUGH'S....3121 Market St., Philadelphia, Pa., 19104. (215) 386-4889. Cuisine: Steak/Seafood. Open 6 days for breakfast, lunch, dinner, and late supper; Closed Sunday. Credit cards: AE, MC, VISA. Entertainment: Live music nightly.

CHEF'S....528 South St., Philadelphia, Pa., 19147. (215) 925-4091. Cuisine: Eclectic. Open Saturday only for lunch; 7 days for dinner; Sunday brunch. Credit cards: AE, VISA. Reservations: Suggested. Bring your own wine.

CENT'ANNI....770 South 7th St., Philadelphia, Pa., 19147. (215) 925-5558. Cuisine: Italian. Open 7 days for dinner only; Sunday dinner from 2:00 PM. Credit cards: All major.

CHEZ PATOU....500 South 20th St., Philadelphia, Pa., 19146. (215) 546-3638. Cuisine: French. Open 6 days for dinner; Closed Sunday. Private party facilities: Available for small parties. Credit cards: AE, MC, VISA.

CHIYO....8136 Germantown Ave., Chestnut Hill, Philadelphia, Pa., 19118. (215) 247-8188. Cuisine: Japanese. Owner: Hideko N. Welsh. Open for dinner; Closed Monday and Tuesday. Credit cards: None.

CITY LIGHTS....212 Walnut St., Philadelphia, Pa., 19106. (215) 627-3128. Cuisine: International. Open Tuesday through Friday for lunch; 7 days for dinner. Credit cards: All major. Entertainment: Live entertainment nightly

CITY TAVERN....138 South 2nd St., Philadelphia, Pa., 19106. (215) 923-6059. An early-Americn gem. The settings, food, and service combine to take you back to a different era and help you forget whatever difficulties you may be having in the present one. Glossy, clean, and polished. Prices are moderate, comfort is high. Specialties include: Roast duckling, rack of lamb, baked crab, and "Salmagundy." Owner: Michael J. Nilon, Pres. Open 7 days for lunch and dinner. Moderately priced. Reservations are accepted. Credit cards: AE, MC, VISA. Annual sales: $500,000 to $1 million. Total employment: 40. Corporate name: Nilon, Inc.

CLUB RITTENHOUSE....245 South 20th St., Philadelphia, Pa., 19103. (215) 732-1990. Cuisine: International. Open Tuesday through Friday for lunch; Tuesday through Saturday for dinner; Closed Sunday and Monday. Credit cards: AE, MC, VISA. Reservations: Advised.

THE COMMISSARY....1710 Sansom St., Philadelphia, Pa., 19103. (215) 569-2240. Cuisine: Nouvelle Cuisine/Charcuterie. Open 7 days for lunch and dinner. Credit cards: All major. Private party facilities: Available. Entertainment: Piano bar open 7 days for lunch and dinner.

COUS' LITTLE ITALY....901 South 11 St., Philadelphia, Pa., 19147. (215) 627-9753. Cuisine: Italian. Credit cards: None.

CURLEY'S....1211 South 8th St., Philadelphia, Pa., 19147. (215) 271-1211. Cuisine: Italian/Seafood. Open daily for lunch and dinner. Credit cards: All major.

DANTE'S AND LUIGI'S....762 South 10th St., Philadelphia, Pa., 19147. (215) 922-9501. Cuisine: Italian. Open 7 days for lunch and dinner; Closed Sunday during July and August; Also closed two weeks during July. No credit cards. Reservations: Accepted.

DEJA-VU....1609 Pine St., Philadelphia, Pa., 19103. (215) 546-1190. Cuisine: French. Owner: Salomon Montezinos. Open Tuesday through Saturday for dinner. Private party facilities: Wine cellar dinner or lunch parties available, 8 person minimum. Credit cards: AE, DC, MC, VISA.

DEUX CHIMINEES....251 South Camac St., Philadelphia, Pa., 19107. (215) 985-0367. Open for three seatings of dinner Tuesday through Saturday; one seating on Sunday; Closed Monday. Credit cards: AE, MC, VISA. Reservations: Required.

DICKENS INN....421 South Second St., Philadelphia, Pa., 19106. (215) 928-9307. Cuisine: English/American. Open Monday through Saturday for lunch; Monday through Saturday for dinner; Sunday brunch. Credit cards: All major.

DI NARDO'S....312 Race St., Philadelphia, Pa., 19106. (215) 925-5115. Cuisine: Seafood (Crabs). Monday through Saturday for lunch; 7 days for dinner. Credit cards: AE, MC, VISA.

THE DOCKSIDE FISH COMPANY....815 Locust St., Philadelphia, Pa., 19107. (215) 935-6175. Cuisine: Seafood. Open Monday through Saturday for lunch; 7 days for dinner. Credit cards: AE, MC, VISA.

DOWNEY'S DRINKING AND DINING SALOON....526 South Front St., Philadelphia, Pa., 19147. (215) 629-0526. Cuisine: Irish/Eclectric. Open Monday through Saturday for lunch; 7 days for dinner; Sunday brunch. Credit cards: All major. Reservations: Accepted.

EAST PHILLY CAFE....200 South St., Philadelphia, Pa., 19147. (215) 922-1813. Cuisine: European Provincial. Open Monday through Saturday for lunch; 7 days for dinner; Sunday brunch. Credit cards: All major.

EDEN....1527 Chestnut St., Philadelphia, Pa., 19102. (215) 972-0400. Cuisine: Charcuterie. Open for breakfast Monday through Friday; lunch & dinner Monday through Saturday; Closed Sunday. No credit cards.

elan.... The Warwick, 17th & Locust Sts., Philadelphia, Pa., 19103. (215) 546-8800. Cuisine: Continental. Open 7 days for dinner; Sunday brunch. Credit cards: AE, DC, MC, VISA. Private party facilities: Available.

EL METATE....1511. Locust St., Philadelphia, Pa., 19102. (215) 546-0181. Cuisine: Mexican. Open Monday through Friday for lunch; 7 days for dinner. Credit cards: AE, MC, VISA.

EL TACO GRANDE....1619 Sansom St., Philadelphia, Pa., 19103. (215) 563-1619. Cuisine: Mexican. Open Monday through Saturday for lunch and dinner; Closed Sunday. No credit cards. No reservations. No liquor. Children's specials, if requested.

FAMOUS 4TH STREET DELICATESSEN....700 South 4th St., Philadelphia, Pa., 19147. (215) 922-3274. Cuisine: Jewish Delicatessen. Owner: Samuel Auspitz and David L. Auspitz. Open 7 days. Credit cards: None. Total employment: 32. Corporate name: Society Hill Famous Delicatessen Inc.

THE FIDDLER....1515 Locust St., Philadelphia, Pa., 19102. (215) 546-7373. Cuisine: Continental/Jewish. Open Monday through Friday for breakfast; Sunday through Monday for lunch and dinner; Closed Saturday. Credit cards: All major.

THE FISH MARKET....124 South 18th St., Philadelphia, Pa., 19103. (215) 567-3559. Cuisine: Seafood. Open 6 days for lunch and dinner; Closed Sunday. Credit cards: All major.

FIVE LORDS....613 South 4th St., Philadelphia, Pa., 19147. (215) 592-0866. Cuisine: Chinese. Open 7 days for lunch and dinner. Credit cards: All major.

THE FORTUNE COOKIE....112 Chestnut St., Philadelphia, Pa., 19106. (215) 923-9593. Cuisine: Chinese. Open 6 days for lunch and dinner; Closed Monday. Credit cards: AE, MC, VISA.

FRANKIE BRADLEY'S.... Juniper & Chancellor Sts., Philadelphia, Pa., 19107. (215) 545-4350. Cuisine: Steak/Seafood. Open daily for lunch and dinner. Credit cards: All major.

FRATELLI RAGO....1701 Spruce St., Philadelphia, Pa., 19103. (215) 546-0513. Cuisine: Italian. Open 7 days for dinner; Monday through Friday for lunch. Credit cards: AE, MC, VISA.

FRIDAY, SATURDAY, SUNDAY....261 South 21st St., Philadelphia, Pa., 19103. (215) 546-4232. Cuisine: French. Open Monday through Friday for lunch; 7 days for dinner. Credit cards: AE, DC, MC, VISA.

FROG....1524 Locust St., Philadelphia, Pa., 19102. (215) 735-8882. Cuisine: French/Asian/American. Open Monday through Friday for breakfast and lunch; 7 days for dinner. Credit cards: AE, DC, MC, VISA. Private party facilities: Available. Entertainment. Music nightly in piano bar.

GABRIEL'S HORN AT THE ACADEMY HOUSE....1420 Locust St., Philadelphia, Pa., 19102. (215) 545-1845. Open 7 days for lunch and dinner. Cuisine: Continental. Credit cards: AE, VISA.

THE GARDEN....1617 Spruce St., Philadelphia, Pa., 19103. (215) 546-4455. Cuisine: Award-winning international cuisine. Open Monday through Saturday for lunch and dinner; Closed Sunday. Credit cards: AE, MC, VISA. Reservations: Suggested.

GIOVANNI'S....428 South St., Philadelphia, Pa., 19147. (215) 592-1130. Cuisine: Italian. Open 7 days for dinner only. Credit cards: AE only. Bring your own wine.

THE GOLD STANDARD....1107 South 47th St., Philadelphia, Pa., 19143. (215) 729-6707. Cuisine: Eclectic. Open 6 days for dinner; Closed Monday. No credit cards. Reservations: Suggested. Bring your own wine. Serving imaginative food to a classy clientele.

GOURMET RESTAURANT....3520 Cottman Ave., Philadelphia, Pa., 19149. (215) 331-7174. Cuisine: French. Open Tuesday through Saturday for lunch; Tuesday through Sunday for dinner; Sunday brunch; Closed Monday. Credit cards: AE, VISA. Bring your own wine.

HOFFMANN HOUSE....1214 Sansom St., Philadelphia, Pa., 19107. (215) 925-8778. The dining rooms support carved wooden paneling from a 19th century German schooner, giving the place *Gemutlich* 1923 look which, if absorbent, must by now be saturated with sighs of satisfaction over the provender and quaffstuffs. The German-International cuisine is prepared in bountiful portions by the present owner-chef William Hylan. Specialties include: *ochsenmaulsalat*, black bean soup, *hasenrucken, rehrucken auf Hoffman art, entrecote Strindberg, schnitzel al la Holstein*. Open Tuesday through Friday for lunch; Tuesday through Saturday for dinner; Closed Sunday and Monday. Priced moderate to high. Reservations and all major credit cards accepted. Private party facilities: 20 to 45. Annual sales: $250,000 to $500,000. Total employment: 16. Corporate name: W. Hylan, Inc.

HOLLY MOORE'S UPSTAIRS CAFE....123 South 18th St., Philadelphia, Pa., 19103. (215) 563-9510. Cuisine: American/Continental. Open 7 days for lunch and dinner; Sunday brunch. Credit cards: AE, DC, MC, VISA. Reservations: Accepted.

HORIZON'S.... Franklin Plaza Hotel, 17th and Vine Sts. Philadelphia, Pa., 19103. (215) 448-2901. Cuisine: Eclectic. Open Monday through Saturday for lunch and dinner; Closed Sunday. Credit cards: All major. Reservations: Suggested.

HO SAI GAI....1000 Race St., Philadelphia, Pa., 19107. (215) 922-5883. Cuisine: Chinese (Mandarin/ Szechuan/Cantonese). Open 7 days for lunch and dinner; late, late dinner also available. Credit cards: AE, DC, MC, VISA.

HOUSE OF CHEN....153 North 10th St., Philadelphia, Pa., 19103. (215) 923-9797. Cuisine: Mandarin & Cantonese Chinese. Open for brunch and dinner 7 days from 3:00 PM. Credit cards: All major.

IL GALLO NERO....254 South 15th St., Philadelphia, Pa., 19102. (215) 546-8065. Cuisine: Italian. Credit cards: All major.

IMPERIAL INN....941 Race St., Philadelphia, Pa., 19107. (215) 925-2485. Cuisine: Chinese. Open 7 days for lunch and dinner. Credit cards: All major.

IN SEASON....315 South 13th St., Philadelphia, Pa., 19107. (215) 545-5115. Cuisine: International. Open Monday through Friday for lunch; 7 days for dinner; Sunday brunch. Credit cards: MC, VISA. Reservations: Accepted.

JADE PALACE....2222 Cottman Ave., Philadelphia, Pa., 19149. (215) 342-6800. Cuisine: Chinese (Mandarin/ Szechuan/Peking/Cantonese). Open 7 days for lunch and dinner. Credit cards: AE, MC. Bring your own wine.

JOHN'S VINEYARD-CLASSIC RESTAURANT AND BAR....9355 Old Bustleton Ave., Philadelphia, Pa., 19115. (215) HO 4-3195. Cuisine: French. Open Tuesday through Sunday for dinner only; Closed Monday. Credit cards: AE, CB. Entertainment: Live entertainment.

JUDY'S CAFE.... Third and Bainbridge Sts., Philadelphia, Pa., 19147. (215) 928-1969. Cuisine: International. Open Monday through Saturday for lunch; 7 days for dinner. Credit cards: AE, MC, VISA. No reservations.

KANPAI.... NewMarket at Head House Sq., Philadelphia, Pa., 19147. (215) 925-1532. Cuisine: Japanese. Open Tuesday through Friday for lunch; 7 days for dinner. Credit cards: All major. Entertainment: Available.

KNAVE OF HEARTS....230 South St., Philadelphia, Pa., 19147. (215) 922-3956. Cuisine: International. Open Saturday only for lunch; 7 days for dinner; Sunday brunch. Credit cards: AE, DC. No reservations.

KONA-KAI....Marriot Hotel, City Line Ave. & Schuylkill Expwy., Philadelphia, Pa., 19131. (215) 667-0200. Cuisine: Polynesian/American. Open 7 days for dinner only. Credit cards: All major.

LA CAMARGUE....1115 Walnut St., Philadelphia, Pa., 19107. (215) 322-3148. Rustic and timbered with pink tablecloths and a delightful fireplace. But rustic is not say unrefined, and there's an understated elegance present, too. The *pates* are, from the coarse tangy country version to the delicate goose liver version. Try the fish soup, which is flavored with a fragrant garlic-pepper paste they add just before serving. Don't miss: the calf's liver, the fish in parchment, the scallops with fettucine. Owner: Marcel and Dorie Brossette. French cuisine. Open Monday through Friday for lunch; Monday through Saturday for dinner; Closed Sunday. Price moderate to high. Reservations and all major credit cards accepted. Private party facilities for between 10 and 30 persons. Annual sales: $500,000 to $1 million. Total employment: 22. Corporate name: La Camargue, Inc.

LA CHAUMIERE....2040 Sansom St., Philadelphia, Pa., 19103. (215) 567-8455. Cuisine: French. Owner: William Zimmerman. Open Tuesday through Saturday for dinner. Credit cards: AE, DC, MC, VISA. Private party facilities: Available.

LA CUCINA....117 South St., Philadelphia, Pa., 19147. (215) 325-3042. Cuisine: Northern Italian. Open 7 days for dinner only. Credit cards: AE, MC, VISA.

LA FAMIGLIA....8 South Front St., Philadelphia, Pa., 19106. (215) 922-2803. Cuisine: Italian. Open Tuesday through Saturday for lunch; Tuesday through Sunday for dinner; Closed Monday. Credit cards: AE, DC, MC, VISA.

LA GROLLA....782 South Second St., Philadelphia, Pa., 19147. (215) 627-7701. Cuisine: Northern Italian/French. Owner: Giovanni Massaglia. Open 7 days for dinner; Sunday brunch 12:00 to 3:00 PM. Credit cards: All major. Valet parking available.

LA PAELLA TIO PEPE RESTAURANT....12012 Bustleton Ave., Philadelphia, Pa., 19126. (215) 677-8016. Cuisine: Spanish/Portugese. Open 5 days for dinner only; Closed Monday and Tuesday.

LA PANETIERE....1602 Locust St., Philadelphia, Pa., 19103. (215) 546-5452. Cuisine: French. Owner: Peter von Starck. Open Monday through Friday for lunch; Monday through Saturday for dinner; Closed Sunday. Credit cards: AE, CB, DC. Private party facilities: Up to 60. Annual sales: $500,000 to $1 million. Total employment: 28.

LA TERRASSE....3432 Sansom St., Philadelphia, Pa., 19104. (215) 387-3778. Cuisine: Classic and nouvelle French cuisines. Open Monday through Friday for lunch; 7 days for dinner; Sunday brunch. Credit cards: All major. Private party facilities: Available. Entertainment: Live classical piano music.

THE LATEST DISH....613 South Fourth St., Philadelphia, Pa., 19147. (215) 925-1680. Cuisine: "Cosmopolitan." Open 7 days for dinner and late supper; Sunday brunch. Credit cards: AE, MC, VISA. Reservations: Accepted.

LAUTREC....408 South 2nd St., Philadelphia, Pa., 19147. (215) 923-6660. Cuisine: French. Open Tuesday through Sunday for dinner; Sunday brunch; Closed Monday. Credit cards: AE, DC, MC, VISA. Entertainment: Live jazz in the Borgia Cafe.

LA TRUFFE....10 South Front St., Philadelphia, Pa., 19106. (215) 627-8630. One of the best in Philadelphia, tucked away near the waterfront. This is a costly little place, as you might expect from the quality of the French cuisine and the striking setting to match. The tremendous expertise of the management in that impression of leisured assurance which inspires confidence in the most diffident diner. Specialties include: duck done with olives, veal kidney with mustard saucing, veal with morel mushrooms, Beluga caviar, Maine lobster with caviar, and saffron-touched salmon filets. Owner: Jeannine Mermet, Leslie Smith. Open Tuesday through friday for lunch; Monday through Saturday for dinner; Closed Sunday. Reservations strongly suggested. Credit cards: All major. Private party facilities: for between 10 and 50 persons. Corporate name: Jeannine et Jeannine, Inc.

LE BEAU LIEU....The Barclay, 18th St. & Rittenhouse Sq., Philadelphia, Pa., 19103. (215) 545-0300. Cuisine: Continental. Open 7 days for breakfast, lunch, and dinner. Credit cards: All major. Private party facilities: Available. Entertainment: Piano nightly; harp on Sundays.

LE BEC FIN....1312 Spruce St., Philadelphia, Pa., 19107. (215) 732-3000. Cuisine: French. Owner: George Perrier. Open Monday through Saturday for two seatings of dinner at 6 PM and 9:00 PM; Closed Sunday. No credit cards. Private party facilities: 30 to 36.

LE BISTRO....757 South Front St., Philadelphia, Pa., 19147. (215) 389-3855. Cuisine: French. Credit cards: AE, MC, VISA.

LE CHAMPIGNON....122 Lombard St., Philadelphia, Pa., 19147. (215) 925-1106. Cuisine: French. Open Monday through Friday for lunch; 7 days for dinner; call for times. Credit cards: AE, VISA. Reservations: Suggested.

LISBON MADRID....609-611 East Passyunk Ave., Philadelphia, Pa., 19147. (215) 922-3959. Cuisine: Portugese/Spanish. Open 7 days for dinner only; Sunday dinner from 1:00 PM. Credit cards: AE, DC, MC, VISA. Reservations: Accepted.

LONDON....2301 Fairmont Ave., Philadelphia, Pa., 19130. (215) 978-4545. Cuisine: British/American. Open Monday through Friday for lunch; Monday through Saturday for dinner; Closed Sunday. Credit cards: All major. Private party facilities: Available. Entertainment: Nightly.

LONDON RESTAURANT AND BAR....114 South 12th St., Philadelphia, Pa., 19147. (215) 569-1050. Cuisine: British/American. Open Monday through Friday for lunch; Monday through Saturday for dinner; Closed Sunday. Credit cards: All major. Private party facilities: Available. Entertainment: Wednesday, Friday, and Saturday nights.

LOS AMIGOS....50 South Second St., Philadelphia, Pa., 19106. (215) 922-7061. Cuisine: Mexican. Open Monday through Friday for lunch; 7 days for dinner. Credit cards: All major. Entertainment: Live Mexican music on weekends.

MAIKO-HAN....1918 Chestnut St., Philadelphia, Pa., 19103. (215) 564-6565. 564-6565. Cuisine: Japanese. Open Monday through Friday for lunch; Monday through Saturday for dinner; Closed Sunday. Credit cards: AE, DC, MC, VISA. Reservations: Accepted.

MANDALAY INN RESTAURANT....214-215 North Tenth St., Philadelphia, Pa., 191070. (215) MA 7-3834. Cuisine: Chinese-Burmese. Owner: Ah Chan Chin & Mary Ann Lee. Open 7 days. Credit cards: All major. Annual sales: $250,000 to $500,000. Total employment: 7.

MANDANA....18 South 20th St., Philadelphia, Pa., 19103. (215) 569-4050. Cuisine: International. Open Monday through Friday for lunch; Monday through Saturday for dinner; Closed Sunday. Credit cards: AE, DC, MC, VISA. Private party facilities: Available.

MARRA'S....1734 East Passyunk Ave., Philadelphia, Pa., 19148. (215) 463-9249. Cuisine: Italian (Oldest in Philadelphia). Open 6 days for lunch and dinner; Closed Monday.

MARRAKESH....517 South Leithgow St., Philadelphia, Pa., 19147. (215) 925-5929. Cuisine: Morrocan. Open nightly for dinner. No credit cards. Reservations: Essential.

MAUREEN....11 South 21 St., Philadelphia, Pa., 19103. (215) 567-9895. Cuisine: French. Owner's names: Steve and Maureen Horn. Credit cards: AE, MC, VISA.

MAXWELL'S PRIME....623 South St., Philadelphia, Pa., 19147. (215) 923-6363. Cuisine: Steakhouse. Credit cards: AE, DC, MC, VISA.

MAYFAIR DINER AND DINING ROOM....7343-73 Frankford Ave., Philadelphia, Pa., 19136. (215) German/American. Open 24 hours, 7 days weekly. No credit cards.

MAYFLOWER...1010 Cherry St., Philadelphia, Pa., 19107. (215) 923-4202. Cuisine: Szechuan Chinese. Open 7 days for lunch and dinner. Credit cards: AE, DC, MC, VISA. Private party facilities: Available.

MESON DON QUIJOTE....110 Chestnut St., Philadelphia, Pa., 19106. (215) 925-1889. Cuisine: Spanish. Credit cards: All major.

THE MIDDLE EAST....126 Chestnut St., Philadelphia, Pa., 19106. (215) 922-1003. Cuisine: Middle Eastern. Open Monday through Saturday for lunch; 7 days for dinner. Credit cards: All major. Entertainment: Live Arabic music and Oriental belly dancing.

MISS HEADLY'S WINE BAR....54 South 2nd St., Philadelphia, Pa., 19106. (215) 627-6482. Cuisine: American. Open Tuesday through Sunday for dinner; Sunday brunch; Closed Monday. Credit cards: All major.

MITCHEL'S....207 South Juniper St., Philadelphia, Pa., 19107. (215) 735-1299. Cuisine: American. Credit cards: All major.

THE MONTE CARLO LIVING ROOM....Second & South Sts., Philadelphia, Pa., 19147. (215) 925-2220. Cuisine: Northern Italian. Open 7 days for dinner. Credit cards: AE, MC, VISA. Private party facilities: Available.

MONTSERRAT....Penn's Landing at Chestnut St., Philadelphia, Pa., 19106. (215) 627-4224. Cuisine: American/International. Open Monday through Saturday for lunch; 7 days for dinner. Credit cards: All major.

MORGAN'S....24th & Sansom Sts., Philadelphia, Pa., 19103. (215) 567-6066. Cuisine: French/Italian. Open Monday through Friday for lunch; Monday through Saturday for dinner; Closed Sunday. Credit cards: AE, DC, MC, VISA.

MUSHULU.... Penn's Landing at Chestnut St., Philadelphia, Pa., 19106. (215) 925-3237. Cuisine: Steak/Seafood. Open Monday through Friday for lunch; 7 days for dinner. Credit cards: AE, DC, MC, VISA.

THE NEW LEAF.... Sheraton Airport Hotel, Philadelphia, Pa., 19153. (215) 365-4150. Cuisine: Continental. Owner: John Canas. Open Monday to Saturday for dinner. Credit cards: All major. Private party facilities: 800 to 1,000. Annual sales: $250,000 to $500,000. Total employment: 125.

NEW SHIPPENS.... 701 South Fourth St., Philadelphia, Pa., 19147. (215) 923-1111. Cuisine: American. Open 6 days for dinner only; Closed Sunday. Credit cards: AE, MC, VISA. Reservations: Suggested. Entertainment: Live entertainment on weekends. Outdoor dining in favorable weather.

94TH AERO SQUADON.... 2750 Red Lion Rd., Philadelphia, Pa., 19115. (215) 671-9400. Cuisine: Continental. Open Monday through Saturday for lunch; 7 days for dinner. Credit cards: All major. Entertainment: Old movies before 8:00 PM and dancing.

NORTH STAR BAR.... 27th & Poplar Sts., Philadelphia, Pa., 19130. (215) 235-7827. Cuisine: American. Open Monday through Friday for lunch; 7 days for dinner; Sunday brunch. Private party facilities: Available. Entertainment: Live music nightly.

NOVEK'S SEAFOOD.... 9857 Bustleton Ave., Philadelphia, Pa., 19115. (215) 673-6650. Cuisine: Seafood. Open 6 days for dinner only; Closed Monday. Bring your own wine.

OCTOBER.... 26 South Front St., Philadelphia, Pa., 19106. (215) 925-4447. Cuisine: Regional American. Open Monday through Friday for lunch; 7 days for dinner. Credit cards: AE, DC, MC, VISA. Reservations: Suggested. Entertainment: Piano bar on Thursday, Friday, and Saturday.

OLD BRAUHAUS RESTAURANT.... 9111. (215) 728-9440. Cuisine: German. Open 5 days for lunch and dinner; Closed Monday and Tuesday. Credit cards: MC, VISA.

OLD ORIGINAL BOOKBINDER'S.... 125 Walnut St., Philadelphia, Pa., 19106. (215) 925-7027. Oldest fish and seafood house in Philadelphia (1865) and closest to source of supply. It is also within sight of all the revered landmarks of Independence National Park, leading right into Ben Franklin's and Betsy Ross's section, and where the Declaration of Independence was unveiled and where the Liberty Bell rang its sweet song, then became silent forever. Expect to see large crowds eating stolidly for a minimum of 1½ hours. Specialties include: Baked imperial crab, jumbo steamed shrimp, provino veal, and U.S. Prime Kansas Sirloin. Open 7 days for lunch and dinner. Price: Moderate. Reservations: Suggested. Credit cards: All major. Private party facilities: 50 to 250. Annual sales: Over $3 million. Total employment: 35.

ONASSIS.... 1735 Sansom St., Philadelphia, Pa., 19103. (215) 568-6960. Cuisine: Greek. Open Monday through Saturday for lunch; 7 days for dinner and late supper. Credit cards: AE, MC, VISA. Reservations: Accepted. Entertainment: Live Greek music Tuesday through Sunday.

ONCE UPON A PORCH.... 414 South Second St., Philadelphia, Pa., 19147. (215) 923-3525. Cuisine: American. Open 7 days for lunch and dinner. Bring you own wine.

OSTERIA ROMANA.... 935 Ellsworth St., Philadelphia, Pa., 19147. (215) 271-9191. Cuisine: Roman Italian. Open 6 days for dinner; Closed Monday. Credit cards: All major.

PEKING DUCK RESTAURANT.... 907 Race St., Philadelphia, Pa., 19107. (215) 923-2635. Cuisine: All Chinese cuisines. Open Monday through Saturday for lunch; 7 days for dinner; Late supper every night. Credit cards: MC, VISA.

PHILIP'S.... 1145 South Broad St., Philadelphia, Pa., 19147. (215) 334-0882. Cuisine: Italian. Open Tuesday through Sunday for lunch and dinner; Closed Monday. Credit cards: AE, DC, MC (no gratuities on credit cards). Reservations: Accepted.

PICCOLO PADRE.... 303 South 11th St., Philadelphia, Pa., 19107. (215) 925-8192. Cuisine: Italian. Open Tuesday through Saturday for dinner only; Closed Sunday and Monday. Credit cards: AE, DC, MC, VISA. Reservations: Suggested.

PIPPO'S.... 5718 Rising Sun Ave., Philadelphia, Pa., 19120. (215) 722-1434. Cuisine: Northern Italian. Open Tuesday through Saturday for lunch; Tuesday through Sunday for dinner; Closed Monday. Credit cards: MC, VISA.

PYRENEES.... Second and Bainbridge Sts., Philadelphia, Pa., 19147. (215) 925-9117. This is a Franco-Spanish establishment with a charming Mediterranean setting and some excellent nourishment. No fastidious diner could turn up his nose at the dishes which come from owner-chef Tony Sanchez, which include such specialties as mussels *costa brava*, *soupe a la Mariscada* (zesty Spanish seafood soup), steak with *Bordelaise* sauce, *ciopinno*, roast pork and clams (or veal and clams) in tomato and wine sauce, and rack of lamb. Excellent desserts. Open 7 days for dinner only. Priced moderate.

RASCAL'S ROOST.... 207 Chestnut St., Philadelphia, Pa., 19106. (215) 627-2540. Cuisine: American. Open 7 days for lunch and dinner. Credit cards: AE, DC, MC, VISA.

THE RESTAURANT.... 2129 Walnut St., Philadelphia, Pa., 19103. (215) 561-3649. Cuisine: International. Open Tuesday through Saturday for dinner only; Closed Sunday and Monday. Credit cards: AE, DC, MC, VISA. Reservations: Suggested.

RESTAURANT MAUREEN.... 11 South 21st St., Philadelphia, Pa., 19103. (215) 561-3542. Cuisine: French. Open Tuesday through Friday for lunch; Tuesday through Saturday for dinner; Closed Sunday and Monday. Credit cards: AE, MC, VISA. Reservations: Suggested.

RICK'S CABARET AT LE BISTRO.... 757 South Front St., Philadelphia, Pa., 19147. (215) 389-3855. Cuisine: International. Open 7 days for dinner; Monday through Friday for lunch. Credit cards: All major. Private party facilities: Available. Entertainment: "Best live entertainment in Philadelphia."... Philadelphia Magazine.

RIPLEMYER'S CAFE VIENNA.... 1300 Pine St., Philadelphia, Pa., 19102. (215) 546-0777. Cuisine: Austrian/Greek/Italian. Open Tuesday through Sunday for dinner; Sunday brunch; Closed Monday. No credit cards. Reservations: Suggested.

RISTORANTE DILULLO.... 7955 Oxford Ave., Philadelphia, Pa., 19111. (215) 725-6000. Cuisine: Italian. Owner: Joseph V. DiLullo. Open 7 days for lunch and dinner. Credit cards: All major. Private party facilities: 15 to 200. Total employment: 75. Corporate name: Joseph V. DiLullo & Co., Inc.

RISTORANTE IL GALLO NERO.... 254 South 15th St., Philadelphia, Pa., 19102. (215) 546-8065. Cuisine: Italian. Open Monday through Friday for lunch; Monday through Saturday for dinner; Closed Sunday. Credit cards: AE, DC, MC, VISA. Reservations: Suggested.

RISTORANTE LA BUCA.... 711 Locust St., Philadelphia, Pa., 19106. (215) 928-0556. Cuisine: Italian. Open 7 days for lunch and dinner. Credit cards: All major. Entertainment: Live music and half-price cocktails 4:30 to 7:00 PM daily.

RIVERFRONT RESTAURANT.... North Delaware Ave. & Poplar St., Philadelphia, Pa., 19123. (212) 925-7000. Cuisine: Continental. Open Tuesday through Saturday for lunch; Tuesday through Sunday for dinner; Closed Monday. Credit cards: AE, DC, MC, VISA. Private party facilities: Available. Entrtainment: Live music.

RIVERSIDE CHINESE RESTAURANT.... 234 North Ninth St., Philadelphia, Pa., 19107. (215) 923-4410. Cuisine: Chinese. Open 7 days for lunch and dinner; Dim Sum from 11:30 AM to 3:00 PM. Credit cards: MC, VISA. No reservations.

RIVERFRONT RESTAURANT AND DINNER THEATRE.... On the Delaware River north of Spring Garden St. at Poplar St., Philadelphia, Pa., 19130. (215) 925-7000. Cuisine: International. Open Tuesday through Saturday for lunch; Tuesday through Sunday for dinner; Closed Monday. Credit cards: AE, DC, MC, VISA. Reservations: Suggested. Entertainment: Dinner theater nightly.

ROBERT'S.... Front & Lombard Sts., Philadelphia, Pa., 19147. (215) 923-4343. Cuisine: American/Continental. Open 7 days for lunch and dinner. Credit cards: All major. Entertainment: Piano bar.

THE ROYAL THAI BARGE.... 23rd & Sansom Sts., Philadelphia, Pa., 19103. (215) 567-2542. Cuisine: Thai. Open 7 days for dinner only. Credit cards: AE, CB, MC, VISA.

RUSSELL'S.... 1700 Lombard St., Philadelphia, Pa., 19146. (215) 735-8070. Cuisine: International. Open Monday through Friday for lunch; 7 days for dinner; Sunday brunch. Credit cards: All major. Reservations: Suggested.

THE RUSTY SCUPPER.... Box 34, New Market Sq., (Front St. between Pine & Lombard Sts.) Philadelphia, Pa., 19147. (215) 923-0291. Cuisine: Steak/Seafood. Owner: Steven Zimmer, Gen. Mgr. Open 7 days for lunch & dinner. Credit cards: All major. Private party facilities: Up to 100. Annual sales $1 million to $3 million. Total emloyment: 92. Corporate name: Borel Restaurant Corp.

SAIGON RESTAURANT.... 935 Washington Ave., Philadelphia, Pa., 19147. (215) 925-9656. Cuisine: Vietnamese. Open 7 days for lunch and dinner. No credit cards. no reservations. Bring your own wine or beer.

SALADALLEY.... 1720 Sansom St., Philadelphia, Pa., 19103. (215) 564-0767. Cuisine: International (Nouvelle). Open Monday through Saturday for lunch; 7 days for dinner; Sunday brunch. No credit cards.

SALADALLEY.... The Warehouse, 4040 Locust St., Philadelphia, Pa., 19104. (215) 349-7644. Cuisine: Homemade soups, salads, and desserts. Open 7 days for lunch and dinner; Sunday brunch. No credit cards. Bring your own wine. Entertainment: Live classical music and jazz piano during lunch and dinner hours.

SALOON.... 750 South 7th St., Philadelphia, Pa., 19147. Cuisine: Steaks/Italian. Open Monday through Friday for lunch; Monday through Saturday for dinner; Closed Sunday. No credit cards. Entertainment: Nightly.

SANNA'S.... 239 Chestnut St., Philadelphia, Pa., 19106. (215) 925-4240. Cuisine: "Gourmet eclectic." Open Monday through Friday for lunch; Tuesday through Saturday for dinner; Closed Sunday. Credit cards: AE, MC, VISA. Entertainment: Live jazz on Sundays.

SAMSOM STREET OYSTER BAR.... 1516 Sansom St., Philadelphia, Pa., 19102. (215) 567-7683. Cuisine: Seafood. Open Monday through Saturday for lunch and dinner. Credit cards: MC,VISA.

SCHWABEN STUBLE AT OLD BRAUHAUS.... 7980 Oxford Ave., Philadelphia, Pa., 19111. (215) 728-9440. Cuisine: Greman Black Forest five course *prix-fixe* dinners. Open Friday and Saturday evenings for dinner only; two seatings for dinner—6:00 PM & 9:00 PM. Credit cards: MC,VISA.

SECHUAN GARDEN.... 1322 Walnut St., Philadelphia, Pa., 19107. (215) 735-3334. Cuisine: Chinese. Open Monday through Saturday for lunch; 7 days for dinner. Credit cards: AE, DC, MC, VISA. Reservations: Accepted.

SHANGHAI GARDEN.... 919-921 Race St., Philadelphia, Pa., 19107. (215) 925-3535. Cuisine: Cantonese Chinese. Open Monday through Saturday for lunch; 7 days for dinner. Credit cards: All major.

THE SHERWOOD INN.... 1913 Welsh Rd., Philadelphia, Pa., 19115. (215) 464-9200. Cuisine: Continental. Open 7 days for lunch & dinner; breakfast Sundays only from 9:00 AM. Credit cards: AE, MC, VISA. Private party facilities: Available. Proper attire suggested.

SIVA'S.... 34 South Front Street, Philadelphia, Pa., 19106. (215) 925-2700. Siva's serves the food of Northern India, yet it makes each dish its own by using a blend of over a dozen different spices. They also have a *tandoor*—a special clay oven using charcoal—and from it come many of the specialties: *tandoori* chicken, *reshami kebab, tandoori* prawns, and others. They also serve many vegetarian offerings: *mattar paneer,* saag paneer, sabzi kofta, and *dahi bhalia* being among the better. Owner: Amar D. Bhalla. Open Tuesday through Friday for lunch; Tuesday through Sunday for dinner; Sunday brunch; Closed Monday. Accepting reservations and all major credit cards. Corporate name: B.K.S. Enterprises, Inc.

STROLLI RESTAURANT.... 1528 Dickinson St., Philadelphia, Pa., 19146. (215) 336-3390. Cuisine: Italian. Open Monday through Saturday for lunch and dinner; Closed Sunday. No credit cards. Reservations: Accepted.

TANG'S.... 429 South St., Philadelphia, Pa., 19147. (215) 928-0188. Cuisine: Chinese. Open 7 days for dinner only. Credit cards: All major.

TELL ERHARDT'S CHESTNUT HILL HOTEL.... 8229 Germantown, Ave., Philadelphia, Pa., 19118. (215) 247-2100. Cuisine: International. Open 5 days for dinner; Sunday brunch; Closed Monday and Tuesday. Credit cards: AE, DC, MC. VISA. Reservations: Suggested.

THA HUONG II.... 7559 Haverford Ave. Philadelphia, Pa., 19151. (215) 877-8181. Cuisine: French/Chinese. Open 6 days for lunch and dinner; Closed Monday. Credit cards: MC, VISA.

THAI ROYAL BARGE.... 23rd & Sansom Sts., Philadelphia, Pa., 19103. (215) 567-2542. Cuisine: Thai. Open 7 days for dinner only. Credit cards: AE, CB, MC, VISA. Reservations: Suggested. No liquor served; bring your own wine.

TOP OF CENTER SQUARE.... First Pennsylvania Tower, 15th & Market Sts., Philadelphia, Pa., 19102. (215) 563-9494. Cuisine: Seafood. Open Monday through Friday for lunch; Monday through Saturday for dinner; Closed Sunday. Credit cards: All major. Entertainment: Tuesday through Friday from 8:00 PM; Saturdays from 9:00 PM.

TRIPP'S.... Lewis Tower Bldg., 15 & Lewis Sts., Philadelphia, Pa., 19130. (215) 735-1118. Trip the light fantastic high above Center City at Tripp's. Around the corner from the Academy of Music, Tripp's offers sumptuous fare, elegant atmosphere and a view guaranteed to take your breath away. By day the ambience is open and airy. A diversified lunch menu features salads, quiches, sandwiches and omelets. But as night descends, Tripp's is transformed. The atmosphere becomes relaxed, elegant—perfect for intimate dining. A varied menu features exciting continental cuisine. Specialties: steaks. Open for lunch, Monday through Friday. Open for dinner, Monday through Saturday. Closed on Sunday. Owner: Kirk Richey. Credit cards: All major. Reservations: Requested. Private Party Facilities.

TRUDIE BALL'S EMPRESS.... 1711 Walnut St., Philadelphia, Pa., 19103. (215) 665-0390. Solid, comfortable Chinese restaurant, urbanely-run and supervised by Andrew and Hannah Ball. A contemporary bar greets you as you enter, with a huge baker's rack behind used for bottles and glassware. The spacious earthtone dining room is highlighted by some interesting examples of Chinese art. Specialties include: Peking duck, lobster cantonese, *Kung Pau* beef. Open Monday through Saturday for lunch; 7 days for dinner. Price moderate to high. Reservations: Suggested. Credit cards: All major. Private party facilities: 8 to 25. Annual sales: $250,000 to $500,000. Total employment: 15. Corporate name: Trudie Ball's Empress Restaurant, Inc.

20TH STREET CAFE.... 261 South 20th St., Philadelphia, Pa., 19103. (215) 546-6867. Open Monday through Friday for lunch; Monday through Saturday for dinner; Sunday bunch only. Credit cards: AE, MC, VISA. No reservations.

ULANA'S.... 205 Bainbridge St., Philadelphia, Pa., 19147. (215) 922-4152. Cuisine: Continental/Chinese. Open 6 days for dinner and dancing; Closed Monday. Credit cards: AE, DC, MC, VISA. Private party facilities: 50 to 150. Annual sales: $250,000 to $500,000. Total employment: 12. Corporate name: Ulana's, Ltd. Entertainment: Multi-level disco upstairs.

UNDER THE BLUE MOON.... 8042 Germantown Ave., Philadelphia, Pa., 19118. (215) 247-1100. Cuisine: International/Continental. Open Tuesday through Saturday for dinner only; Closed Sunday and Monday. No credit cards. Reservations: Suggested.

VERSAILLES.... Broad & Walnut Sts., Philadelphia, Pa., 19102. (215) 893-1776. Cuisine: Classical French, nouvelle. Open Monday to Friday for lunch; Monday to Saturday for dinner. Credit cards: All major. Annual sales: $500,000 to $1 million. Total employment: 18.

VILLA ANNA.... 7900 Frankford Ave., Philadelphia, Pa., 19136. (215) 332-1921. Cuisine: Italian. Open Monday through Friday for lunch; 7 days for dinner. Credit cards: AE, MC, VISA.

VILLA DI RIETI.... 1919 East. Passyunk Ave., Philadelphia, Pa., 19148. (215) 462-4255. Cuisine: Italian. Open 7 days for lunch and dinner; brunch served daily. Credit cards: AE, DC, CB. Entertainment: Live music and dancing nightly.

THE VINEYARD.... 32 South 22nd St., Philadelphia, Pa., 19103. (215) 972-0482. Cuisine: Northern Italian. Open Monday through Friday for lunch; Monday through Saturday for dinner; Closed Sunday. Credit cards: AE, MC, VISA.

VITALES RESTAURANT.... 2100 St. Vincent St., Philadelphia, Pa., 19149. (215) 624-5015. Cuisine: Italian. Open Monday through Saturday for lunch; 7 days for dinner. No credit cards. Live music for comfortable dining nightly.

WALT'S "KING OF CRABS".... 804-6 South 2nd St., Philadelphia, Pa., 19147. (215) 339-9124. Cuisine: Seafood. Open 7 days for lunch and dinner.

WARSAW CAFE.... 306 South 16th St., Philadelphia, Pa., 19102. (215) 546-0204. Cuisine: Eastern European. Open Monday through Saturday for lunch and dinner; Closed Sunday. Credit cards: AE only. Reservations: Suggested on weekends. Bring your own wine.

THE WAY WE WERE.... 20th & Lombard Sts., Philadelphia, Pa., 19146. (215) 735-2450. Cuisine: Continental. Open Wednesday through Saturday for dinner only; Closed Sunday, Monday and Tuesday. Credit cards: MC, VISA. Reservations: Almost essential. Private party facilities: Restaurant is composed of only eight tables and entirely available for parties. Bring your own wine.

WILDFLOWERS.... 514 South Fifth St., Philadelphia, Pa., 19106. (215) 923-6708. Cuisine: International. Open Monday through Saturday for lunch; 7 days for dinner; Sunday brunch. Credit cards: AE, MC, VISA. Reservations: Strongly suggested. Entertainment: Jazz piano nightly.

YI HO GARDEN CHINESE RESTAURANT.... 622 South Second St., Philadelphia, Pa., 19147. Cuisine: Chinese (Szechuan & Peking-style). Open 6 days for lunch and dinner; Closed Mondays. Credit cards: MC, VISA. Bring your own wine.

PHOENIXVILLE

COLUMBIA HOTEL..... 148 Bridge St., Phoenixville, Pa., 19460. (215) 933-9973. Cuisine: American. Open Monday through Saturday for lunch; 7 days for dinner. Credit cards: AE, DC, MC, VISA. Reservations: Suggested on weekends.

KIMBERTON INN AND COUNTRY HOUSE.... just off Rte. 113, near Phoenixville, Pa., (215) 935-8148. Cuisine: International. Open Tuesday through Friday for lunch; 7 days for dinner; Sunday dinner from 2:00 PM. Credit cards: All major. Entertainment: Piano bar Friday and Saturday; Dancing Saturday.

SEVEN STARS INN.... Ridge Rd., Rte. 23, Phoenixville, Pa., 19460. (215) 495-5205. Cuisine: American. Open Tuesday through Saturday for dinner only; Closed Sunday and Monday. No credit cards. Reservations: Required on Saturday.

PITTSBURGH

ALEX TAMBELLINI'S WOOD STREET.... 213 Wood St., Pittsburgh, Pa., 15222. (412) 281-9956. Cuisine: Seafood/Italian. Credit cards: None.

CHRISTOPHER'S.... 1411 Grandview Ave., Mt. Washington, Pittsburgh, Pa., 15211. (412) 381-4500. Cuisine: American. Credit cards: All major.

THE COMMON PLEA.... 308 Ross St., Pittsburgh, Pa., 15219. (412) 281-5140. Cuisine: Continental. Owner: John C. Barsotti. Open Monday through Friday for lunch; Monday through Saturday for dinner; Closed Sunday. Credit cards: AE only. Private party facilities: Up to 40. Annual sales: $500,000 to $1 million. Total employment: 40.

DE FORO'S.... Forbes Ave., Lawyers Bldg., Pittsburgh, Pa., 15222. (412) 391-8873. Cuisine: Italian/French. Credit cards: AE, MC, VISA.

HUGO'S ROTISSERIE.... Pittsburgh Hyatt House, Chatham Ctr., Pittsburgh, Pa., 15219. (412) 391-5000. Cuisine: Continental. Credit cards: AE, DC, MC, VISA.

LA NORMADE.... 5030 Central Ave., Pittsburgh, Pa., 15202. (412) 621-0744. Cuisine: French. Owner: Reuben Jacob Katz. Credit cards: All major. Private party facilities: Up to 125. Annual sales: $1 million to $3 million. Total employment: 50.

MAX'S ALLEGHENY TAVERN.... Middle & Suisman Sts., Northside, Pittsburgh, Pa., 15212. (412) 231-1899. Cuisine: German. Jeffrey L. Bodner, Gen. Mgr., Open 7 days for lunch, dinner and Sunday brunch. Credit cards: All major. Total employment: 65. Corporate name: Speciality Restaurants, Inc.

RICHEST'S DOWNTOWN.... 140 Sixth St., Pittsburgh, Pa., 15222. (412) 471-7799. Cuisine: Kosher Delicatessen. Credit cards: None.

SARAH'S ETHNIC.... 52 South 10th St., Pittsburgh, Pa., 15203. (412) 431-9307. Cuisine: Balkan. Owner's name: Sara. Credit cards: None.

PLUMBSTEADVILLE

PLUMBSTEADVILLE INN.... Rte. 611, Plumbsteadville, Pa., 18949. (215) 766-7500. Cuisine: American/Continental. Open Tuesday through Saturday for lunch; Tuesday through Sunday for dinner; Sunday brunch; Closed Monday. Credit cards: AE, MC, VISA. Entertainment: Live music and dancing

POTTSTOWN

COVENTRY FORGE INN.... Rte. 100, Pottstown, Pa., 19464. (215) 469-6222. Cuisine: French.

CUTILLO'S RESTAURANT.... 2688 East High St., Pottstown, Pa., 19464. (215) 327-2910. Cuisine: "American/Cosmopolitan." Open Monday through Friday for lunch; 7 days for dinner; Sunday brunch. Credit cards: AE, DC, MC, VISA. Entertainment: Live music and dancing.

QUAKERTOWN

BENETZ.... Rte. 309, Quakertown, Pa., 18591. (215) 536-6315. Cuisine: American. Open Monday through Saturday for lunch; 7 days for dinner; Sunday dinner from 1:00 PM. Credit cards: All major. Reservations: Suggested.

SIGN OF THE SORREL HOUSE.... Old Bethlehem Rd., Quakertown, Pa., 18951. (215) 536-4651. Open Wednesday through Sunday for dinner; Sunday brunch; Closed Monday and Tuesday. Credit cards: MC VISA. Reservatios: Suggested.

RADNOR

THE GREENHOUSE.... King of Prussia Rd. and Belrose La., Radnor, Pa., 19087. (215) 687-2801. Open Monday through Friday for lunch; 7 days for dinner; Sunday brunch. Credit cards: AE, DC. Reservations: Advised. Entertainment: Music Friday and Saturday evenings, Greenhouse patio.

THE UPPER CRUST CAFE.... 175 King of Prussia Rd., Radnor, Pa., 19087. (215) 964-9040. Cuisine: Continental/French. Open Monday through Friday for lunch; Wednesday through Saturday for dinner; Closed Sunday. Credit cards: AE, MC, VISA. Bring your own wine.

READING

GREEN HILLS INN.... Rte. 10, Reading, Pa., 19603. (215) 777-9611. Open Tuesday through Friday for lunch; Monday through Saturday for dinner; Closed Sunday. Credit cards: MC, VISA. Personal checks accepted. Reservations: Suggested. Fine wine cellar.

GREEN HILLS INN.... Rte. 1, Reading, Pa., 19607. (215) 777-9611. Cuisine: French.

JOE'S.... 450 South Seventh St., Reading. Pa., 19602. (215) 373-6794. Cuisine: Continental. Owner's name: Jack Czarnecki. Credit cards: AE, DC, MC, VISA.

SCENERY HILL

CENTURY INN.... Rte. 40, Scenery Hill, Pa., 15360. (412) 945-5180. Cuisine: American.

SHADYSIDE

ENCORE I.... 5505 Walnut St., Shadyside, Pa., 15232. (412) 683-5656. Cuisine: Steakhouse. Credit cards: AE, CB, MC, VISA.

SHOHOLA

VINTON'S COUNTRY HOUSE.... Off Rte. 434, Shohola, Pa., 18458. (717) 559-7644. Cuisine: French Gourmet. Owner: John & Patricia Pavy. Open for dinner April to October; Closed Thursday. No credit cards. Private party facilities: Up to 60. Annual sales: $250,000 to $500,000. Total employment: 12.

SOMERSET

OAKHURST TEA ROOM.... Rte. 31, Somerset, Pa., 15501. (814) 445-5762. Cuisine: Pennsylvania Dutch and Smorgasbord. Open for lunch and dinner; closed Monday. Credit cards: MC, VISA. Private party facilities: 40 to 400. Annual sales: $500,000 to $1 million. Total employment: 50. Corporate name: Oakhurst Tea Room, Inc.

SOUDERTON

YE OLDE RELIANCE.... 103 East Reliance Rd., Souderton, Pa., 18946. (215) 723-7230. Cuisine: Continental/American. Dinner served 4:30 PM to 6:00 PM daily. Credit cards: Call for cards.

SPRINGFIELD

VILLAGE PORCH.... Olde Sproul Village, Springfield, Pa., 19064. (215) 544-3220. Cuisine: American. Open 7 days for lunch and dinner. No credit cards.

SPRING HOUSE

SPRING HOUSE TAVERN.... Bethlehem Pike, Spring House, Pa., 19477. (215) 646-1788. Cuisine: American. Open Tuesday through Sunday for dinner only; Closed Monday. Credit cards: Call for cards. Reservations: Accepted.

STARFORD

HELEN SIGEL WILSON'S L'AUBERGE.... Spread Eagle Village, Starford, Pa., 15770. (215) 687-2840. Cuisine: French. Owner: Charles E. Wilson. Open Tuesday through Saturday for lunch and dinner; Closed Sunday and Monday. Credit cards: AE only. Private party facilities: Up to 100. Annual sales: $500,000 to $1 million. Total employment: 55.

SCOTTS TOWNSHIP

THE COLONY.... Greentree & Cochran Rds., Scotts Township, Pa., (412) 561-2060. Cuisine: American. Credit cards: All major.

SOUTHAMPTON

HAMPTON HOUSE RESTAURANT.... 762 2nd St. Park, Southampton, Pa., 18966. (215) 357-1444. Cuisine: Continental (Over 40 entrees). Open Monday through Friday for lunch; 7 days for dinner. Credit cards: AE, DC, MC, VISA. Entertainment: Live entertainment and dancing.

UNIONTOWN

THE COAL BARON.... Rte. 40, Uniontown, Pa., 18920. (412) 439-1111. Cuisine: Continental. Credit cards: AE, DC, MC, VISA.

UPPER BLACK EDDY

INDIAN ROCK INN.... Rte. 32, Upper Black Eddy, Pa., 18972. (215) 982-5300. Cuisine: Continental. Open 6 days for dinner only; Closed Monday. Credit cards: AE, MC, VISA.

UPPER BLACK EDDY INN.... River Rd., (Rte. 32) Upper Black Eddy, Pa., 18972. (215) 982-5554. Cuisine: Continental. Open daily for dinner only. Credit cards: AE only. Reservations: Accepted. Entertainment: Piano Friday, Saturday, and Monday.

WARMINSTER

TOY SUN RESTAURANT.... 993 West County Line Rd., Warminster, Pa., 18974. (215) 672-6699. Cuisine: Chinese. Open Monday through Friday for lunch; 7 days for dinner; Saturday dinner starts at 2:00 PM; Sunday dinner starts at 3:00 PM. No credit cards. Reservations: Accepted. Bring your own wine.

WEISEL PERKASKIE

LAKE HOUSE INN.... 1100 Old Bethlehem Pke., Weisel Perkaskie, Pa., 19844. (215) 257-5351. Cuisine: Seafood. Open daily for lunch and dinner. Credit cards: AE, MC, VISA.

WELLSBORO

PENN-WELLS.... 62 Main St., Wellsboro, Pa., 16901. (717) 724-2111. Cuisine: Continental/French. Open 7 days for breakfast, lunch, and dinner. Credit cards: AE, MC, VISA. Private party facilities: Up to 250. Annual sales: $500,000 to $1 million. Total employment: Corporate name: Wellsboro Hotel Corp.

WEST CHESTER

DILWORTHTOWN INN.... Old Wilmington Pke. & Brinton Bridge Rd., West Chester, Pa., 19380. (215) 399-1390 Cuisine: French/Continental. Open 7 days for dinner only. Credit cards: All major.

LA COCOTTE....24 West Gay St., West Chester, Pa., 19380. (215) 436-6722. Cuisine: French. Open Monday through Friday for lunch; Monday through Saturday for dinner; Closed Sunday. Credit cards: AE, MC, VISA. Reservations: Suggested.

WEST POINT

MACPHEE'S.... West Point Pike & Garfield Ave., West Point, Pa., 19486. (215) 699-3585. Cuisine: French/American. Open Monday through Friday for lunch; 7 days for dinner. Credit cards: AE, MC, VISA. Reservations: Suggested.

WRIGHTSTOWN

THE ANCHOR INN.... Crossroads of Rtes. 413 & 232, Wrightstown, Pa., 18940. (215) 598-7469. Cuisine: Continental. Open daily for lunch and dinner. Credit cards: All major. Reservations: Accepted. Private party facilities: Available.

WRIGHTSVILLE

ACCOMAC INN.... Accomac Rd., Wrightsville, Pa., 17368. (717) 252-1521. Cuisine: Continental. Credit cards: AE, DC, MC, VISA.

WYNNEWOOD

STOUFFER'S....339 East Lancaster Ave., Wynnewood, Pa., 19096. (215) 649-1560. Cuisine: American/Steak/Seafood. Open Monday through Saturday for lunch; 7 days for dinner; Sunday brunch. Credit cards: AE, DC, MC, VISA. Private party facilities: Available.

YARDLEY

YARDLEY INN.... Delaware & Afton Aves., Yardley, Pa., 19067. (215) 493-3800. Cuisine: American. Open daily for lunch and dinner. Credit cards: AE, MC, VISA. Reservations: Suggested.

RHODE ISLAND

CHARLESTOWN

WINDSWEPT FARM.... Rte. 1, Charlestown, R.I., 02813. (401) 364-3333. Cuisine: American. Credit cards: AE, MC, VISA.

JAMESTOWN

THE FERRY BOAT.... Jamestown Harbor at Ferry Wharf, Jamestown, R.I., 02835. (401) 423-0101. Cuisine: Seafood.

NEWPORT

BLACK PEARL.... Banister's Wharf & West Pelham St., Newport, R.I., 02840. (401) 846-5264. Cuisine: French. Credit cards: All major.

THE CLARKE COOKE HOUSE.... Bannister's Wharf, Newport, R.I., 02840. (401) 849-2900. Cuisine: French. Owner: David Warren Ray. Open 7 days for lunch and dinner. Credit cards: All major. Private party facilities: Up to 100. Annual sales: $1 million to $3 million. Total employment: 150.

LA PETITE AUBERGE....19 Charles St., Newport, R.I., 02840. (401) 849-6669. Cuisine: French. Open 7 days for dinner. Credit cards: All major. Annual sales: $250,000 to $500,000. Total employment: 15. Corporate name: La Petite Auberge.

THE PIER RESTAURANT....P.O. Box #480, Howard Wharf, Newport, R.I., 02840. (401) 847-3645 and (401) 849-3100. Cuisine: Steak/Seafood. Owner: Leonard Ossick, Fred Bucci, Enid Bucci. Open 7 days for lunch and dinner. Credit cards: AE, MC, VISA. Private party faciities: 25 to 100. Annual sales: $1 million to $3 million. Total employment: 100. Corporate name: Howard Wharf Corp.

WHITE HORSE TAVERN.... Marlborough St. & Farewell, Newport, R.I., 02840. (401) 849-3600. Cuisine: French/Continental. Credit cards: AE, CB, DC, MC, VISA.

NORTH KINGSTOWN

RED ROOSTER TAVERN....7385 Post Rd., North Kingstown, R.I., 02852. (401) 295-8804. Cuisine: Continental. Open 6 days for dinner; Closed Monday. Credit cards: All major. Private party facilities: Up to 30. Annual sales: $500,000 to $1 million. Total employment: 52. Corporate name: Red Rooster Tavern, Inc.

PROVIDENCE

CAMILLE'S ROMAN GARDENS....71 Bradford St., Providence, R.I., 02903. (401) 751-4812. Cuisine: Italian. Credit cards: All major.

THE LEFT BANK....220 South Water St., Providence, R.I., 02906. (401) 421-2828. Cuisine: Continental. Credit cards: AE, MC, VISA.

PROVIDENCE PROVISIONS COMPANY.... Charles & Orms Sts., Providence, R.I., 02904. (401) 272-2400. Cuisine: Seafood. Credit cards: All major.

WARREN

FORE 'N AFT....1070 Main St., Warren, R.I., 02885. (401) 245-1900. Cuisine: Seafood. Credit cards: All major.

WARWICK

GREAT HOUSE....2245 Post Rd., Warwick, R.I., 02886. (401) 739-8600. Cuisine: Chinese/New England. Open Tuesday through Saturday for dinner; Sunday for brunch and dinner; Closed Monday. Credit cards: All major. Private party facilities: Up to 115. Total employment: Over 25.

PLANTATION'S ROOM....2081 Post Rd., Warwick, R.I., 02886. (401) 738-0023. Cuisine: Continental/American. Owner: J & W College. Credit cards: All major. Private party facilities: 25 to 300. Annual sales: $1 million to $3 million. Total employment: 72. Corporate name: R.I. Inn & J & W College, Inc.

WESTERLY

SWISS CHALET.... Box 632, RFD. 1, Rte. 1, Westerly, R.I., 02891. (401) 322-0314. Cuisine: French. Credit cards: AE, DC, MC, VISA.

SOUTH CAROLINA

CHARLESTON

BARBADOES ROOM....115 Meeting St., Charleston, S.C., 29401. (803) 577-2400. Cuisine: Seafood/Southern. Credit cards: All major.

CHAPEL MARKETPLACE RESTAURANT.... 32 Market St., Charleston, S.C., 29401. (803) 577-4095 or 577-4883. Cuisine: French/Continental. Owner: Wilbur Burbage. Open 5 days for lunch and dinner; Closed Sunday and Monday. Credit cards: All major. Private party facilities: Up to 100. Annual sales: $500,000 to $1 million. Total employment: 30. Corporate name: The Market Place, Inc.

THE COLONY HOUSE....35 Prioleau St., Charleston, S.C., 29401. (803) 723-3424. Cuisine: Steak/Seafood/Japanese/German. Owners: Franz X. Meier & Christof M. Weihs. Open Monday through Saturday for lunch; 7 days for dinner. Credit cards: All major. Private party facilities: 20 to 300. Annual sales: $1 million to $3 million. Total employment: 120. Corporate name: Trigon, Inc.

THE WINE CELLAR....35 Prioleau St., Charleston, S.C., 29401. (803) 723-9463. Cuisine: Continental. Owner: Franz W. Meier. Credit cards: All major.

COLUMBIA

MARKET....1205 Assembly St., Columbia, S.C., 29201. (803) 799-5010. Cuisine: Seafood. Credit cards: All major.

GREENVILLE

COLONIAL.... Rte. 29, Greenville, S.C., 29602. (803) 233-5393. Cuisine: American. Credit cards: AE, MC, DC, VISA.

MURRELLS INLET

PLANTER'S BACK PORCH RESTAURANT.... Hwy. 17 at Wachasaw Rd., Murrells Inlet, S.C., 29576. (803) 651-5263. Cuisine: American. Owner: David L. Gilbert, Pres. Open 7 days for dinner. Credit cards: AE, MC, VISA. Private party facilities: Up to 150. Annual sales: $1 million to $3 million. Total employment: 75.

SEA CAPTAIN'S HOUSE.... Rte. 17, Murrells Inlet, S.C., 29576. (803) 651-2416. Cuisine: Seafood. Credit cards: AE, MC, VISA.

MYRTLE BEACH

CAGNEY'S OLD PLACE.... Hwy. 17, Myrtle Beach, S.C., 29577. (803) 449-3824. Cuisine: Seafood & Beef. Open 6 days for dinner; Closed Sundays. Credit cards: AE, MC, VISA. Total employees: 70. Corporate name: Cagneys, Inc.

CHRISTY'S.... Rte. 17, Myrtle, Beach, S.C.29582. (803) 272-5107. Cuisine: Seafood. Credit cards: All major.

THE LIBRARY....1212 North King's Hwy., Myrtle Beach, S.C., 29582. (803) 488-4527. Cuisine: French. Credit cards: AE, MC, VISA.

THE RICE PLANTER'S RESTAURANT....6707 King's Hwy. North, Myrtle Beach, S.C., 29577. (803) 449-3456. Cuisine: American. Owner: David L. Gilbert, Pres. Open 7 days for dinner. Credit cards: AE, MC, VISA. Private party facilities: Up to 150. Annual sales: $1 million to $3 million. Total employment: 75.

VERMONT

BARRE

COUNTRY HOUSE....276 North Main St., Barre, Vt., 05641. (802) 476-4282. Cuisine: Italian/American Credit cards: All major.

BENNINGTON

BRASSERIE....324 Country St., Bennington, Vt., 05201. (802) 447-7531. Cuisine: Continental/French. Credit cards: MC, VISA.

HERITAGE HOUSE....218 Northside Dr., Bennington, Vt., 05201. (802) 447-0000. Cuisine: Steak/Seafood. Open 7 days for breakfast, lunch and dinner. Owners: Bruce E. Shotland & David W. Cook. Credit cards: AE, MC, VISA. Total employment: 35.

BRATTLEBORO

THE COUNTRY KITCHEN.... Rte. 9, Brattleboro, Vt., 05301. (802) 257-0338. Cuisine: Continental. Credit cards: AE, MC, VISA.

BURLINGTON

ICE HOUSE....171 Battery St., Burlington, Vt., 05401. (802) 862-9339. Cuisine: American. Owner: James Lampman. Open 7 days for lunch and dinner. Credit cards: AE, MC, VISA. Private party facilities: 40 to 100. Annual sales: $1 million to $3 million. Total employment: 75.

SIRLOIN SALOON.... Shelburne Rd., Burlington, Vt., 05401. (802) 985-2200. Cuisine: Steak/Seafood. Credit cards: AE, MC, VISA.

WHAT'S YOUR BEEF....152 St. Paul St., Burlington, Vt., 05401. (802) 862-0326. Cuisine: American. Credit cards: MC, VISA.

COLCHESTER

PIERRE.... Rte. 2, Colchester, Vt., 05446. (802) 878-3377. Cuisine: French. Credit cards: AE, MC, VISA.

EAST DORSET

CHANTECLEER.... Rte. 7, East Dorset, Vt., 05255. (802) 362-1616. Cuisine: Continental/French. Credit cards: MC, VISA.

JEFFERSONVILLE

WINDRIDGE INN.... Main St., Jefferson, Vt., 05464. (802) 644-8281. Cuisine: French/American.

KILLINGTON

GREY BONNET INN.... Rte. 100, Killington, Vt., 05751. (802) 775-2537. Cuisine: French. Credit cards: AE, MC, VISA.

LAURENS.... Rte. 4, Killington, Vt., 05751. (802) 422-3886. Cuisine: French. Credit cards: AE, MC, VISA.

VERMONT INN.... Rte. 4, Killington, Vt., 05751. (802) 773-9847. Cuisine: Continental and New England. Open Tuesday through Sunday for dinner. Owner: Alan Carmasin. Credit cards: All major. Annual sales: $250,000 to $500,000. Total employment: 15.

LYNDONVILLE

THE OLD CUTTLER INN.... East Burke Rd., Lyndonville, Vt., 05851. (802) 626-5152. Cuisine: Continental. Credit cards: MC, VISA.

TOWN & COUNTRY.... Rte. 114, Lyndonville, Vt., 05851. (802) 626-9713. Cuisine: American.

MANCHESTER

JIMMY'S .... Rte 7, Manchester, Vt., 05254. (802) 362-3807. Cuisine: French. Credit cards: MC, VISA.

RELUCTANT PANTHER INN.... Manchester, Vt., 05255. (802) 362-2568. Cuisine: Continental. Credit cards: AE.

SIRLOIN SALOON.... Rte. 11, Manchester, Vt., 05255. (802) 362-2600. Cuisine: American. Credit cards: AE, MC, VISA.

TOLL GATE LODGE.... Rte. 11, Manchester, Vt., 05255. (802) 362-1779. Cuisine: Continental. Owner: John Donahue. Credit cards: AE.

MARLBORO

SKYLINE.... Rte. 9, Marlboro, Vt., 05344. (802) 464-5335. Cuisine: American. Open 7 days for breakfast, lunch and dinner. Owner: Richard H. Hamilton, Pres. Credit cards: All major. Private party facilities: Up to 135. Annual sales: $250,000 to $500,000. Total employment: 20.

MENDON

GILLIAM'S ON THE MOUNTAIN.... Rte. 4, Mendon, Vt., 05701. (802) 773-6424. Cuisine: Continental. Credit cards: All major.

MONTGOMERY CENTER

ON THE ROCKS.... Hazen's Notch, Montgomery Center, Vt., 05471. (802) 326-4500. Cuisine: French. Open daily for dinner; Closed Monday. Owner: Jon P. Zachadnyk. Credit cards: MC, VISA. Private party facilities: Up to 38. Total employment: 5.

MONTPELIER

LOBSTER POT....118 Main St., Montpelier, Vt., 05602. (802) 223-3961. Cuisine: Seafood/Steak. Credit cards: All major.

STOCKYARD INN....3 Bailey Ave., Montpelier, Vt., 05602. (802) 223-7811. Cuisine: American. Owner: Alan McCarthy. Open 7 days. Credit cards: All major. Private party facilities: Up to 60. Annual sales: $500,000 to $1 million. Total employment: 35.

NEWFANE

FOUR COLUMNS.... Village Green, Newfane, Vt., 05345. (802) 365-7713. Cuisine: Traditional and Nouvelle French. Owner: Sandra and Jacques Allembert. Open for dinner, open for lunch during the summer; Closed Tuesday. Credit cards: MC, VISA. Private party facilities: Up to 70. Annual sales: $250,000 to $500,000. Total employment: 16.

OLD NEWFANE.... Rte. 30, Newfane, Vt., 05345. (802) 365-4427. Cuisine: Continental.

NEWPORT

FRANK & PIERRE'S STEAK HOUSE....45 Main St., Newport, Vt., 05855. (802) 334-7765. Cuisine: American/Italian/Chinese. Owner: Frank Tochance. Open 7 days for lunch and dinner. Credit cards: All major. Annual sales: $250,000 to $500,000. Total employment: 12. Corporate name: Frank Steak House, Inc.

QUECHEE

PARKER HOUSE....16 Main St., Quechee, Vt., 05059. (802) 295-6077. Cuisine: Continental and American. Owner: John Blizzard. Open for dinner: Closed Wednesdays after Labor Day. Credit cards: MC, VISA. Private party facilities: Up to 80. Annual sales: $250,000 to $500,000. Total employment: 20.

RUTLAND

121 WEST....121 West St., Rutland, Vt., 05701. (802) 773-7148. Cuisine: Continental. Open for lunch and dinner; closed Sunday. Owner: Frank Czachor. Credit cards: All major. Private party facilities: none. Annual sales: $250,000 to $500,000. Total employment: 19.

ROYAL'S HEARTHSIDE....37 North Main St., Rutland, Vt., 05701. (802) 775-0756. Cuisine: New England. Credit cards: All major. Annual sales: $500,000 to $1 million. Total employment: 40. Corporate name: Royal's Hearthside Restaurant. Open 7 days for lunch, dinner and Sunday brunch.

SHELBURNE

THE SIRLOIN SALOON.... Rte. 7 (RD #2, Box 2700), Shelburne, Vt., 05482. (802) 985-3226. Cuisine: Steak/Seafood. Open 7 days for lunch and dinner. Credit cards: AE, MC, VISA. Private party facilities: 12 to 65. Annual sales: $1 million to $3 million. Total employment: 115. Corporate name: The Sirloin Saloon, Inc.

SOUTH BURLINGTON

CRIMSON HEARTH....1068 Williston Rd., South Burlington, Vt., 05401. (802) 863-6361. Cuisine: American. Credit cards: AE, DC, MC, VISA.

SOUTH LONDONDERRY

FUNDADOR.... Rtes. 30 & 100, S. Londonderry, Vt., 05155. (802) 297-1700. Cuisine: Continental/French. Credit cards: AE, MC, VISA.

SPRINGFIELD

THE PADDOCK.... Paddock Rd., Springfield, Vt., 05156. (802) 885-2720. Cuisine: Continental. Open for dinner and Sunday brunch; closed Monday. Owner: Mary La Fountain. Credit cards: MC, VISA. Private party facilities: Up to 125. Annual sales: $500,000 to $1 million. Total employment: 25.

STOWE

CHARDA.... Rte. 100, Stowe, Vt., 05672. (802) 253-4598. Cuisine: Hungarian/Austrian.

GREEN MOUNTAIN INN.... Main St., Stowe, Vt., 05672. (802) 253-7301. Cuisine: Continental. Credit cards: AE, MC, VISA.

THE INN AT THE MOUNTAIN.... Mountain Rd., Stowe, Vt., 05672. (802) 253-7311. Cuisine: Continental. Credit cards: AE, CB, MC, VISA.

TEN ACRES LODGE.... Ballows Rd., Stowe, Vt., 05672. (802) 253-7638. Cuisine: Continental. Credit cards: AE, CB, MC, VISA.

VERGENNES

BASIN HARBOR CLUB.... Rte. 22 A, Vergennes, Vt., 05491. (802) 475-2311. Cuisine: New England/Continental. Credit cards: MC, VISA.

PAINTER'S TAVERN....5 North Green St., Vergennes, Vt., 05491. (802) 877-3413. Cuisine: French/American. Credit cards: AE, DC, MC, VISA.

WARREN

COMMON MAN....German Flats Rd., Warren, Vt., 05674. (802) 583-2800. Cuisine: European. Open 7 days for dinner in winter; closed Monday other seasons. Owner: Michael C.G. Ware. Credit cards: MC, VISA. Annual sales: $250,000 to $500,000. Total employment: 20.

SUGARBUSH INN....Sugarbush Access Rd., Warren, Vt., 05674. (802) 683-2301. Cuisine: Continental. Credit cards: AE, MC, VISA.

WATERBURY

THE GOLDEN HORN EAST....Kneeland Flat Rd., Waterbury, Vt., 05676. (802) 244-7855. Cuisine: Central European/Continental. Owners: Hubert & Trude Erhard. Open for dinner only; Closed Sundays, May, and November. Credit cards: All major. Private party facilities: Up to 25. Annual sales: $250,000 to $500,000. Total employment: 14.

WEST BRATTLEBORO

JOLLY BUTCHER'S....Rte. 9, West Brattleboro, Vt., 05301. (802) 254-6043. Cuisine: Continental. Owner: W.C. Skilling, Jr., V.P. Open 7 days for lunch and dinner. Credit cards: AE, MC, VISA. Private party facilities: Up to 60. Annual sales: $500,000 to $1 million. Total employment: 25.

WHITE RIVER JUNCTION

KELTIES BUM STEER....Sykes Ave., White River Junction, Vt., 05001. (802) 295-3071. Cuisine: Steak/Seafood. Credit cards: AE, MC, VISA.

WILMINGTON

THE HERMITAGE....Coldbrook Rd., Wilmington, Vt. 05363. (802) 464-3759. Cuisine: Continental. Credit cards: AE, DC, MC, VISA.

WOODSTOCK

THE PRINCE & THE PAUPER....24 Elm St., Woodstock, Vt., 05091. (802) 457-1100. Cuisine: Continental and French Nouvelle. Open 7 days for dinner. Credit cards: MC, VISA. Annual sales: $250,000 to $500,000. Total employment: 18. Corporate name: The Prince and the Pauper, Inc.

VIRGINIA

ALEXANDRIA

BAMIYAN....300 King St., Old Town, Alexandria, Va., 22314. (703) 548-9006. Cuisine: Afghani. Open 7 days for lunch and dinner. Reservations: Suggested.

CEDAR KNOLL INN....Mount Vernon Hwy., Alexandria, Va., 22313. (703) 360-7880. Cuisine: Regional American. Open 7 days for lunch and dinner. Reservations: Required.

EAST WIND....809 King St., Alexandria, Va., 22314. (703) 360-7880. Cuisine: Vietnamese. Open Monday through Friday for lunch; 7 days for dinner. Reservations: Preferred.

THE FISH MARKET....105 King St., Alexandria, Va., 22314. (703) 836-5676. Cuisine: Seafood. Open daily for lunch, dinner, and late supper. Credit cards: AE, MC, VISA. Reservations: Suggested.

GERANIO....724 King St., Alexandria, Va., 22314. (703) 548-0088. Cuisine: Italian. Open Monday through Friday for lunch; Monday through Saturday for dinner; Closed Sunday. Credit cards: AE, MC, VISA. Reservations: Required.

HENRY AFRICA RESTAURANT....607 King St., Alexandria, Va., 22314. (703) 549-4010. Cuisine: French. Owner: Theodore Manousakis. Open Tuesday through Sunday. Credit cards: All major. Private party facilities: 4 to 150. Annual sales: $1 million to $3 million. Total employment: 65.

KING'S LANDING....121 South Union St., Alexandria, Va., 22314. (703) 836-7010. A large, popular restaurant serving good food with a French accent—although there's quite a few "American" seafood dishes as well. The atmosphere is friendly and relaxed, and the building is of historical interest: in the 19th century it was an active wharfside loading dock. The bar upstairs may be the longest you've seen. Specialties include: St. Germain soup, grilled salmon, pompano with tomatoes and anchovies, veal saute *chasseur, entrecote* Alexandria. Owner: Brian M. McMahon, Jacques F. Duplaa. Open 7 days for lunch and dinner; Closed major holidays. Priced moderate to high. Reservations suggested. Accepting all major credit cards. Private party facilities: 8 to 100. Annual sales: $1 million to $3 million. Total employment: 50. Corporate name: John Mac Brian, Inc.

LA BERGERIE....220 North Lee St., Alexandria, Va., 22314. (703) 683-1007. Cuisine: French. Open Monday through Saturday for lunch; 7 days for dinner. Credit cards: AE, MC, VISA. Reservations: Required. Free parking over dinner.

SEAPORT INN....6 King St., Alexandria, Va., 22314. (703) 549-2341. Cuisine: Steak/Seafood. Owner: Paul A. Bynum, Pres., Open 7 days for lunch and dinner. Credit cards: All major. Private party facilities: 15 to 50. Annual sales: $500,000 to $1 million. Total employment: 45. Corporate name: Old Town Seaport Corporation.

TAVERNA CRETEKOU....818 King St., Alexandria, Va., 22314. (703) 548-8688. Cuisine: Middle Eastern (Greek). Open Tuesday through Saturday for lunch; Tuesday through Sunday for dinner; Sunday brunch; Closed Monday. Credit cards: AE, MC, VISA. Reservations: Suggested; Required on weekends. Free parking.

219....219 King St., Alexandria, Va., 22314. (703) 549-1141. Cuisine: American regional/Southern. Open Monday through Friday for lunch; 7 days for dinner; Saturday and Sunday brunch. Credit cards: AE, MC, VISA. Reservations: Required.

THE WAYFARERS....110 South Pitt St., Alexandria, Va., 22314. (703) 836-2749. Cuisine: English. Open Tuesday through Saturday for lunch; Monday through Saturday for dinner; Closed Sunday. Credit cards: AE, MC, VISA. Reservations: Suggested.

YENCHING PALACE OF ALEXANDRIA....905 North Washington St., Alexandria, Va., 22314. (703) 836-3200. Cuisine: Chinese. Open 7 days for lunch and dinner; Sunday brunch. Credit cards: All major. Reservations: Accepted.

ANNANDALE

DUCK CHANG'S....4427 John Marr Dr., Annandale, Va., 22003. (703) 941-9400. Cuisine: Chinese. Open 7 days for lunch and dinner; Sunday brunch. Credit cards: AE, MC, VISA. Reservations: Some restrictions on party size.

ARLINGTON

CAPRICCIO....1999 Jefferson Davis Hwy., Arlington, Va., 22202. (703) 521-5500. Cuisine: Italian. Credit cards: All major.

CHALET DE LA PAIX....4506 Lee Hwy., Arlington, Va., 22212. (703) 522-6777. Cuisine: French. Credit cards: AE, CB, MC, VISA.

CHARDA'S....523 South 23rd St., Arlington, Va., 22209. (703) 920-7892. Cuisine: Hungarian. Open Monday through Saturday for dinner only; Closed Sunday. Credit cards: All major. Reservations: Suggested.

CHEZ FROGGY....409 South 23rd St., Arlington, Va., 22202. (703) 979-7676. Cuisine: French. Open for lunch weekdays; for dinner Monday through Saturday. Credit cards: MC, VISA. Annual sales: $500,000 to $1 million. Total employment: 9. Corporate name: Cam Inc.

CHEZ FROGGY....509 South 23rd St., Arlington, Va., 22202. (703) 979-7676. Cuisine: French. Open Monday through Friday for lunch; Monday through Saturday for dinner; Closed Sunday. Credit cards: MC, VISA. Reservations.

THE COMPANY INKWELL....4109 Wilson Blvd., Arlington, Va., 22203. (703) 525-4243. Cuisine: French. Open Monday through Friday for lunch; Monday through Saturday for dinner; Closed Sunday. Credit cards: All major. Reservations: Required on weekends.

L'ALOUETTE....2045 Wilson Blvd., Arlington, Va., 22201. (703) 525-1750. Cuisine: French. Open Monday through Friday for lunch; Monday through Saturday for dinner; Closed Sunday. Credit cards: AE, MC, VISA. Reservations: Suggested. Free parking.

LEBANESE TAVERNA....5900 North Washington Blvd., Arlington, Va., 22205. (703) 241-9301. Cuisine: Lebanese/Middle Eastern. Owner: Tanios, Marie, Dory and Dany Abi-Najem. Open 7 days for dinner; Monday to Saturday for lunch. Annual sales: $250,000 to $500,000. Total employment: 10. Corporate name: Lebanese Taverna, Inc.

LIDO DI VENEZIA....200 North Glebe Rd., Arlington, Va., 22203. (703) 525-8770. Cuisine: Italian. Open Monday through Friday for lunch; daily for dinner. Reservations: Suggested.

MATUBA....2915 Columbia Pike, Arlington, Va., 22204. (703) 521-2811. Cuisine: Japanese. Open Monday, Wednesday, Friday, Saturday, and Sunday for dinner; Closed Tuesday. Credit cards: DC, MC, VISA. Reservations: Accepted; Required on weekends. Beer and wine only.

QUINCY'S RESTAURANT....5444 Columbia Pike, Arlington, Va., 22204. (703) 671-2774 or (703) 237-9422. Cuisine: Steak/Seafood/American. Owner: Michael Slade, Robert Slade. Open 7 days for lunch and dinner. Credit cards: AE, MC, VISA. Private party facilities: 8 to 150. Annual sales: $1 million to $3 million. Total employment: 60. Corporate name: H.F.S. Corporation.

VIETNAM INN....1345 North Courthouse Rd., Arlington, Va., 22201. (703) 525-7796. Cuisine: Vietnamese. Open Monday through Saturday for dinner; Closed Sunday. Credit cards: MC, VISA. Reservations: Accepted only on weekends.

BAILEYS CROSSROAD

EL BANDITO....5825 Seminary Rd., Baileys Crossroad, Va., 22041. (703) 820-5775. Cuisine: Mexican. Open Monday through Saturday for lunch and dinner; Closed Sunday. Credit cards: All major. No reservations.

BEDFORD

PEAKS OF OTTER.... Blue Ridge Pkwy., Bedford, Va., 24523. (703) 586-1081. Cuisine: American. Credit cards: MC, VISA.

BLACKSBURG

JACOB'S LADDER....900 Prices Fork Rd., Blacksburg, Va., 24060. (703) 552-7001. Cuisine: Continental. Gerald Carter, Gen. Mgr. Open 7 days for breakfast, lunch and dinner. Credit cards: All major. Private party facilities: Up to 300. Annual sales: $1 million to $3 million. Total employment: 80.

BRIDGEWATER

CANDELIGHT INN....312 North Main St., Bridgewater, Va., 22812. (703) 828-6776. Cuisine: Regional American. Open 6 days for lunch and dinner; Closed Monday. Reservations: Suggested.

CHARLOTTESVILLE

C & O RESTAURANT....515 East Water St., Charlottesville, Va., 22901. (804) 971-7044. Cuisine: Continental. Owner: Sandy McAdams. Open Monday through Friday for lunch; Monday through Saturday for dinner; Closed Sunday. Reservations: Suggested.

FELLINI'S....200 West Market St., Charlottesville, Va., 22901. (804) 295-8003. Cuisine: Northern Italian. Open 5 days for dinner only. Reservations: Suggested.

LE SNAIL RESTAURANT....320 West Main St., Charlottesville, Va., 22901. (804) 295-4456. Cuisine: French/Viennese. Open 7 days for dinner only. Reservations: Advised on weeknights; essential on weekends. Proper attire required.

CHINCOTEAGUE

CHANNEL BASS....100 Church St., Chincoteague, Va., 23336. (804) 336-6148. Cuisine: Continental. Credit cards: AE, DC, MC, VISA.

DOSWELL

JARRELL TRUCK PLAZA....Doswell exit of Interstate 95, Doswell, Va., 23047. (804) 876-3361. "Everything that a hungry driver might have a handering for after a long stint at the wheel.—Famed for its Southern fried chicken, country-style steak, hamburger steak with onions and gravy, and homemade bisquits and rolls—New York Times." Owner: O.V. Jarrell and family, Gordon Taylor, Food Service Mngr. Open 7 days, 24 hrs. daily. Cuisine: "The best American truck-stop cooking." Credit cards: AE, DC, MC, VISA. Priced inexpensive to moderate. Total employment: 240. On 16 acres of beautiful Virginia countryside.

FAIRFAX

CHINA GOURMET....9444 Arlington Blvd., Fairfax Va., 22031. (703) 591-8380. Cuisine: Chinese. Open Monday through Saturday for lunch; 7 days for dinner. Credit cards: AE, MC, VISA. Reservations: Suggested on weekends.

J.R.'S STEAKHOUSE....9401 Lee Hwy., Fairfax, Va., 22031. (703) 591-8448. Cuisine: Steak/Seafood. Owner: J.M. Wordworth, Pres. Open 6 days for dinner; Closed Monday. Credit cards: AE, MC, VISA. Private party facilities: 6 to 110. Annual sales: $1 million to $3 million. Total employment: 60. Corporate name: J.R.'s Good Times, Inc.

FALLS CHURCH

GENJI....2816 Graham Rd., Falls Church, Va., 22042. (703) 573-0112. Cuisine: Japanese. Open Tuesday through Friday for lunch; Tuesday through Sunday for dinner; Closed Monday. Credit cards: MC, VISA. Reservations: Suggested.

LA GUINGUETTE....811 Lee Hwy., Falls Church, Va., 22042. (703) 560-3220. Cuisine: French. Open for lunch and dinner 7 days. Credit cards: All major. Private party facilities: Up to 400. Annual sales $1 million to $3 million. Total employment: 50. Corporate name: R & W Music Enterprises.

PEKING GOURMET INN....6029 Leesburg Pike, Falls Church, Va., 22041. (703) 671-8088. Cuisine: Chinese. Open 7 days for lunch and dinner. Credit cards: MC, VISA. Reservations: Suggested on weekends and for parties of seven or more.

FRONT ROYAL

CONSTANT SPRING INN....413 South Royal Ave., Front Royal, Va., 22630. (804) 635-7010. Cuisine: American regional. Open 7 days weekly for lunch and dinner. Reservations: Accepted. Lodging also available.

GREAT FALLS

L'AUBERGE CHEZ FRANCOIS....332 Springvale Rd., Great Falls, Va., 22066. (703) 759-3800. Cuisine: French/Alsatian. Owner: Francois R. Haeringer. Open Tuesday through Saturday for dinner; Sunday dinner begins at 2:30 p.m.; Closed Monday. Credit cards: AE, MC, VISA. Reservations: Suggested. Free parking. Annual sales: $250,000 to $500,000. Total employment: 31.

SERBIAN CROWN II....1141 Walker Rd., Great Falls, Va., 22066. (703) 759-4150. Cuisine: Slavic. Open Tuesday through Saturday for lunch; Tuesday through Sunday for dinner; Closed Monday. Credit cards: AE, MC, VISA. Reservations: Required.

IRVINGTON

CAP'N B'S.... Rte. 3, Irvington, Va., 22480. (804) 438-5500. Cuisine: American. Credit cards: MC, VISA.

HOT SPRINGS

SAM SNEAD'S TAVERN.... Rte. 220, Hot Springs, Va., 24445. (703) 839-2828. Cuisine: Regional American.

MANASSAS

BRADY'S....9412 Main St., Manassas, Va., 22110. (703) 369-1469. Cuisine: Continental/American. Open 7 days for dinner; Sunday brunch. Reservations: Suggested.

MARSHALL

JOHN MARSHALL RESTAURANT.... Main St., Marshall, Va., 22115. Cuisine: Steak/American. Open 6 days for dinner only; Closed Monday. Reservations: Accepted.

McLEAN

CAFE TATTI....6627 Old Dominion Dr., (McLean Mall), McLean, Va., 22101. (703) 790-5164. Open Monday through Saturday for lunch; Monday through Saturday for dinner. Credit cards: AE, DC, MC, VISA. Reservations: Suggested.

EVANS FARM INN....1696 Chain Bridge Rd., McLean, Va., 22030. (703) 356-8000. Cuisine: American. Main dining room hours: Open Monday through Saturday for lunch; 7 days for dinner. Pub hours: Open Monday through Friday for lunch; Monday through Saturday for dinner; Closed Sunday. Credit cards: AE, DC, MC, VISA. Reservations: Accepted in pub, but not in main dining room

J.R.'S STOCKYARDS INN....8130 Watson St., McLean, Va., 22102. (703) 893-3390. Cuisine: Steak/Seafood. Owner: J.M. Wordsworth, Pres. Open Monday through Friday for lunch; 7 days for dinner; Sunday brunch. Credit cards: AE, MC, VISA. Private party facilities: 6 to 110. Annual sales: $1 million to $3 million. Total employment: 60.

ZACHARY'S....6238 Old Dominion Dr., Mclean, Va., 22101. (703) 821-1976. Open Monday through Saturday for lunch; 7 days for dinner. Credit cards: AE, DC, MC, VISA. Reservations: Suggested.

MIDDLEBURG

RED FOX TAVERN....2 East Washington St., Middleburg, Va., 22117. (703) 687-6301. Cuisine: American. Open 7 days for lunch and dinner. Reservations: Accepted. "America's oldest original inn" from 1728.

WINDSOR HOUSE ENGLISH RESTAURANT AND PUB.... Two West Washington St., Middleburg, Va., 22117. (703) 687-6800. Cuisine: English-style. Open 6 days for lunch, cocktails, and dinner; Closed Monday. Reservations: Unnecessary.

MIDDLETOWN

WAYSIDE INN SINCE 1797....7783 Main St., Middletown, Va., 22645. (703) 869-1797. Cuisine: American. Owner: Marjorie Alcarese, Gen. Mgr. & Sr. V.P. Open 7 days, year round. Credit cards: AE, MC, VISA. Private party facilities: 10 to 30. Annual sales: $1 million to $3 million. Total employment: 100. Corporate name: Wayside World Corp.....see above

MONTEREY

HIGHLAND INN.... Main St., Monterey, Va., 24465. (703) 468-2143. Cuisine: Regional American/Continental. Open 7 days for dinner. Reservations: Accepted.

MONTROSS

INN AT MONTROSS.... Rte. 622, Montross, Va., 22520. (703) 493-9097. Cuisine: Regional American. Open 7 days for lunch and dinner. Reservations: Suggested. An historic landmark whose basement was started in 1684.

NORFOLK

ESPLANADE....777 Waterfront Dr., Norfolk, Va., 23510. (804) 622-6664 ext. 7147. Cuisine: Continental. Credit cards: All major.

LOCKHART'S OF NORFOLK....8440 Tidewater Dr., Norfolk, Va., 23518. (804) 588-0405. Cuisine: Continental/Seafood. Owner: John A. Lockhart. Open 7 days for dinner. Credit cards: All major. Private party facilities: Up to 50. Annual sales: $250,000 to $500,000. Total employment: 20.

RICHMOND

CAPRI....1 East Grace St., Richmond, Va., 23219. (804) 644-5813, Cuisine: Italian. Credit cards: MC, VISA.

HUGO'S ROTISSERIE.... Hyatt Richmond, 6624 West Broad St., Richmond, Va., 23230. (804) 285-8666. Cuisine: Continental. Open 7 days for lunch and dinner. Credit cards: All major. Annual sales: $500,000 to $1 million. Total employment: 30-40. Corporate name: Hyatt Hotels Corporation.

LA PETITE FRANCE....2912 Maywill St., Richmond, Va., 23230. (804) 353-8729. Cuisine: French. Owner: Paul U. Elbling. Open for lunch and dinner Tuesday through Saturday. Credit cards: AE, MC, VISA. Private party facilities: Up to 34. Annual sales: $500,000 to $1 million. Total employment: 22.

TONY'S SUPPER CLUB....3309 West Broad St., Richmond, Va., 23230. (804) 355-5463. Cuisine: American. Credit cards: AE, MC, VISA.

ROANOKE

ALEXANDER'S....125 East Campbell Ave., (at Market Sq.), Roanoke, Va., 24011. (703) 982-6983. Cuisine: New Orleans-style American. Open Monday through Friday for lunch; Friday and Saturday for dinner only. Credit cards: MC, VISA.

BILLY'S RITZ....102 Salem Ave., Roanoke, Va., 24011. (703) 343-6992. Cuisine: Tex-Mex/American. Open daily for-dinner.

THE LIBRARY....3117 Franklin Rd., SW, Roanoke, Va., 24014. (703) 985-0811. Cuisine: Continental. Open Monday through Saturday for dinner only; Closed Sunday. Call for credit cards. Reservations: Suggested.

REGENCY ROOM....19 North Jefferson St., Roanoke, Va., 24026. (703) 343-6992. Cuisine: Continental/American. Open 7 days. Credit cards: All major. Private party facilities: Up to 1000. Annual sales: $1 million to $3 million. Total employment: 350. Corporate name: Norfolk Southern, Inc.

ROSSLYN

ALEXANDER'S....1500 Wilson Blvd., Rosslyn, Va., 22209. (703) 527-0100. Cuisine: Continental. Open Monday through Friday for lunch; Monday through Saturday for dinner; Closed Sunday. Credit cards: All major. Reservations: Suggested. Free parking over dinner.

STAUNTON

DIFFERENT DRUMMER....24 North Central Ave., Staunton, Va., 24401. (703) 886-9440. Cuisine: Continental/American. Call for times and credit cards. Reservations: Suggested.

MCCORMICK'S PUB AND RESTAURANT....41 North Augusta St., Staunton, Va., 24401. (703) 885-3111. Cuisine: American. Open daily for lunch and dinner. Call for credit cards. Reservations: Suggested.

VIRGINIA BEACH

THE IRONGATE HOUSE....36 St., at Atlantic Ave., Virginia Beach, Va., 23451. (804) 422-5748. Cuisine: Continental. Owner: Michael C. Peel. Open for dinner Tuesday through Saturday. Credit cards: MC, VISA. Annual sales: $250,000 to $500,000. Total employment: 20.

WARM SPRINGS

THE WATERWHEEL....Box 359, Gristmill Sq., Warm Springs, Va., 24484. (703) 839-2311. Cuisine: Continental/American. Credit cards: AE, MC, VISA.

WARRENTON

SIXTY-SEVEN WATERLOO....67 Waterloo, Warrenton, Va., 22186. (703) 347-1200. Cuisine: French. Owner Philip A. Harway. Open for lunch and dinner Tuesday through Sunday. Credit cards: AE, MC, VISA. Private party facilites: Up to 75. Annual sales: $250,000 to $500,000. Total employment: 26.

WILLIAMSBURG

CHRISTIANA CAMPBELL'S TAVERN....Waller St., Williamsburg, Va. 23815. (804) 229-2141. Cuisine: American.

LAFAYETTE....1203 Richmond Rd., Williamsburg, Va., 23815. (804) 229-3811. Cuisine: Continental. Credit cards: AE, MC, VISA.

REGENCY ROOM....Francis St., Williamsburg, Va., 23815. (804) 229-2141. Cuisine: Continental.

WILLIAMSBURG LODGE....South England St., Williamsburg, Va., 23815. (804) 229-1600. Cuisine: Continental.

WINCHESTER

MICHEL'S....Rte. 522 North, Winchester, Va., 22601. (703) 667-9797. Cuisine: French. Open daily for dinner. Call for credit cards. Reservations: Suggested.

YORKTOWN

SEAWELL'S ORDINARY....Rte. 17, Yorktown, Va., 23690. (804) 642-2102. Cuisine: American. Credit cards: MC, VISA.

WASHINGTON, D.C.

THE AMERICAN CAFE....1211 Wisconsin Ave., NW, Washington, D.C., 20007. (202) 337-3600. Cuisine: American. Owner: Christine Britton, Gen. Mgr. Open 7 days for lunch and dinner. Credit cards: AE, MC, VISA. Annual sales: Over $3 million. Total employment: 425 (corp.). Corporate name: Monolith Enterprises, Inc. Other locations in Georgetown, Chevy Chase, Capitol Hill, and Harborplace, Baltimore.

AMERICAN CAFE....227 Massachusetts Ave., NE, Washington, D.C. 20002. (202) 547-8200. Cuisine: American. Open 7 days for lunch, dinner, and late supper; Weekend brunch. Credit cards: MC, VISA. Private party facilities: Available. Reservations: Accepted all times except for parties of five or more between 11:45 AM and 1:45 PM weekdays.

ANNA MARIA'S....1737 Connecticut Ave., NW, Washington, D.C., 20009. (202) 667-1444. Cuisine: Italian. Open Monday through Saturday for lunch; 7 days for dinner. Credit cards: All major. Reservations: Suggested.

APANA....3066 M St., NW, Washington, D.C., 20007. (202) 965-3040. Cuisine: Indian. Open 7 days for dinner only. Credit cards: All major. Reservations: Required.

ARABIAN NIGHTS....2915 Connecticut Ave., NW, Washington, D.C., 20008. (202) 232-6684. Cuisine: Middle Eastern. Open 6 days for lunch and dinner; Closed Tuesday. Credit cards: AE, MC, VISA. Reservations: Accepted.

ASTOR....1813 M St., NW, Washington, D.C., 20036. (202) 331-7994. Cuisine: Middle Eastern (Greek). Open 7 days for lunch and dinner. Credit cards: AE, DC, MC, VISA. Reservations: Accepted.

AU PIED DE COCHON....1335 Wisconsin Ave., NW, Washington, D.C., 20007. (202) 333-5440. Cuisine: French. Open 7 days for lunch and dinner. No credit cards. No reservations.

AUX BEAUX CHAMPS....The Four Seasons Hotel, 2800 Pennsylvania Ave., Washington, D. C. 20007. (202) 342-0444. One of the most distinguished hotel-restaurants in walnut, crystal and velvet drenched setting; drawing a steady stream of passing trade, which is more than can be said for the average "grand hotel" restaurant. Costly certainly. Fastidious attention to smallest details. Specialties include: Mignonettes of beef, lamb, and veal with three different kinds of mustard; paillard of veal with lemon bernaise sauce; and supreme of salmon grilled with fennel. Seamus McManus, Gen. Mgr., Four Seasons Washington. Open 7 days for breakfast, lunch, dinner, and late supper. Price: Expensive. Reservations: Suggested. Credit cards: All major. Private party facilities: Available. Corporate name: Four Seasons Hotels, Inc.

AUX FRUITS DE MER....1329 Wisconsin Ave., NW, Washington, D.C., 20007. (202) 965-2377. Open 7 days for lunch, dinner, and late supper. No credit cards. No reservations.

A.V. RISTORANTE....607 New York Ave., NW, Washington, D.C., 20001. (202) 737-0550. Cuisine: Italian. Credit cards: AE, CB, DC.

BACCHUS....1827 Jefferson Pl., NW, Washington, D.C., 20036. (202) 965-2377. Cuisine: Middle Eastern. Open Monday through Friday for lunch; Monday through Saturday for dinner; Closed Sunday. Credit cards: AE, MC, VISA. Reservations: Suggested.

BAMIYAN RESTAURANT....3320 M. St., NW, Washington, D.C. 20007. (202) 338-1896. Cuisine: Afghani. Credit cards: MC, VISA.

BAOBAB....2106 18th St., NW, Washington, D.C., 20009. (202) 265-2540. Cuisine: West African. Open 7 days for dinner only. Credit cards: MC, VISA. Reservations: Suggested, especially on weekends.

THE BIG CHEESE....3139 M St., NW, Washington, D.C., 20007. (202) 338-3314. Cuisine: American. Open 7 days for lunch and dinner. Credit cards: MC, VISA. Reservations: Suggested.

BISTRO FRANCAIS....3128 M St., NW, Washington, D.C., 20007. (202) 338-3830. Cuisine: French. Open 7 days for lunch and dinner; Saturday and Sunday brunch. Credit cards: AE, DC, MC, VISA. Reservations: Suggested.

BLUE NILE....1701 16th St., NW, (in the rear of the Chastelton Apartments), Washington, D.C., 20009. (202) 232-8400. Cuisine: Ethiopian. Open 6 days for lunch; 7 days for dinner; No lunch on Monday. Credit cards: AE, MC, VISA. Reservations: Suggested, required Friday and Saturday nights.

BLUES ALLEY....1073 Wisconsin Ave., NW, Washington, D.C., 20007. (202) 337-4141. Cuisine: American. Credit cards: AE, DC, MC, VISA.

THE BREAD OVEN....1220 19th St., NW, Washington, D.C., 20036. (202) 466-4264. Cuisine: French. Open Monday through Saturday for breakfast, lunch, and dinner; Closed Sunday. Credit cards: MC, VISA. Reservations: Suggested, required on weekends.

THE BROKER....713 8th St., SE, Washington, D.C., 20003. (202) 546-8300. Cuisine: Swiss. Open Monday through Friday for lunch, 7 days for dinner; Sunday brunch. Credit cards: AE, MC, VISA. Reservations: Suggested.

CAFE DE ARTISTAS....3065 M St., NW, Washington, D.C., 20007. (202) 338-0417. Cuisine: Latin American. Open for 7 days for lunch and dinner; Sunday brunch. Credit cards: AE, MC, VISA. Reservations: Suggested on weekends.

CAFE DE PARIS....3056 M St., NW, Washington, D.C., 20007. (202) 965-2920. Cuisine: French. Open Tuesday through Thursday for lunch and dinner; open continuously from 10:00 AM Friday until 3:30 AM Monday. No credit cards. No reservations.

CAFE RONDO....Adriatic Inc., 1900 Q St., NW, Washington, D.C., 20009. (202) 232-1885. Cuisine: International. Owner's name: Willy Kmetowich. Credit cards: MC, VISA. Annual sales: $500,000 to $1 million. Total employment: 23.

CAFE SORBET....1810 K St., NW, Washington, D.C., 20006. (202) 293-3000. Cuisine: French. Open Monday through Friday for lunch and dinner; Closed Saturday and Sunday. Credit cards: AE, MC, VISA. Reservations: Accepted for dinner only.

CAFFE ITALIANO....3516 Connecticut Ave., NW, Washington, D.C., 20008. (202) 966-2172. Cuisine: Italian. Open Monday through Friday for lunch; 7 days for dinner. Credit cards: AE, MC, VISA. Reservations: Suggested, required for dinner between 7:30 PM and 9:30 PM.

CALVERT CAFE....1967 Calvert St., NW, Washington, D.C., 20009. (202) 232-5431. Cuisine: Middle Eastern. Credit cards: None.

CANTINA D'ITALIA....1214-A 18 St., NW, Washington, D.C., 20036. (202) 659-1830. Cuisine: Italian. Owner: Joseph and Jeanne de Assereto. Open Monday to Friday. Credit cards: All major. Annual sales: $1 million to $3 million. Total employment: 34. Corporate name: Tres Bon, Inc.

CHAMPAGNE/BEAUJOLAIS....1 Washington Cl., NW, Washington, D.C., 20037. (202) 293-5390. Cuisine: Continental. Champagne hours: Open Monday through Friday for lunch; Tuesday through Saturday for dinner; Sunday brunch. Beaujolais hours: Open 7 days for breakfast; Monday through Friday for lunch and dinner. Credit cards: All major. Reservations: Accepted.

CHARING CROSS....3027 M St., NW, Washington, D.C., 20007. (202) 338-2141. Cuisine: Italian. Open Monday through Friday for lunch; 7 days for dinner. Credit cards: All major. Reservations: Accepted only for parties over five.

CHEZ CAMILLE....1737 DeSales St., NW, Washington, D.C., 20036. (202) 393-3330. Cuisine: French. Open Monday through Saturday for lunch and dinner; Closed Sunday. Credit cards: All major. Reservations: Suggested.

CHEZ GRAND' MERE....3057 M St., NW, Washington, D.C., 20007. (202) 337-2436. Cuisine: French. Open Tuesday through Friday for lunch; Tuesday through Sunday for dinner; Closed Monday. Credit cards: All major. Reservations: Accepted.

CHEZ MARIA....3338 M St., NW, Washington, D.C., 20007. (202) 337-4283. Cuisine: Vietnamese. Open Monday through Saturday for lunch; Sunday for dinner only. Credit cards: All major. Reservations: Suggested.

CHINA INN....631 H St., NW, Washington, D.C., 20001. (202) 628-9282. Cuisine: Chinese. Credit cards: AE, MC, VISA.

CHURRERIA MADRID....2505 Champlain St., NW, Washington, D.C., 20009. (202) 483-4441. Cuisine: Spanish. Open Tuesday through Sunday for lunch and dinner; Closed Monday. Credit cards: CB, MC, VISA. Reservations: Weekdays only.

CLYDE'S....3236 M St., NW, Washington, D.C., 20007. (202) 333-0294. Cuisine: American. Open 7 days for breakfast, lunch, dinner and late supper; Saturday and Sunday brunch. Credit cards: AE, MC, VISA. No reservations.

COURT OF THE MANDARINS....1824 M St., NW, Washington, D.C., 20036. (202) 223-6666. Cuisine: Mandarin Chinese. Open Monday through Friday for lunch; Monday through Saturday for dinner; Closed Sunday. Credit cards: MC, VISA. No reservations.

CSIKO'S....3601 Connecticut Ave., NW, (in the Broadmoor Apartments), Washington, D.C., 20008. (202) 362-5624. Open 6 days for dinner only; Closed Sunday. Credit cards: All major. Reservations: Required.

DANCING CRAB....4611 Wisconsin Ave., NW, Washington, D.C., 20016. (202) 244-1882. Cuisine: Seafood. Open 7 days for lunch and dinner. Credit cards: AE, MC, VISA. No reservations.

DANKER'S....1209 E St., N.W., Washington, D.C., 20004. (202) 628-2330. This is a large masculine-type (stucco and wood) steak and seafood house in the heart of the theatre district, serving first-rate tender and juicy steaks, chops and fresh seafood in substantial portions, at moderate prices. Warm friendly and inviting, Danker's offers lunch, dinner and after-theatre menus. You will also find the casual staff to be gracious and efficient. House specialties: blue ribbon sirloin; Danker's flanker and Luau. Open for lunch and dinner, 6 days. Closed Sundays. Owner Richard Danker. Credit cards: All major. Reservations: Accepted. Private party facilities. Annual sales: $1.2 million. Total employment: 30.

DANKER'S....525 School St., SW, Washington, D.C. 20024. (202) 554-7854. An offshoot of Danker's in Washington's NW neighborhood, this Danker's is in the Jim Thorpe Foundation ARTBA Building and is, thus, the place to stop into after viewing exhibits about "the world's greatest athlete." The menu is very much the same as that in the NW Danker's—steak and seafood in an unaffected decor and atmosphere—with the prices moderate and the serving staff warm, friendly, and inviting. Specialties include: blue ribbon sirloin, Danker's flanker and Luau, Alaskan king crab, jumbo shrimp, and barbequed Western-style spareribs. Owner: Richard Danker. Open 6 days for lunch and dinner; Closed Sunday. Reservations, AE, MC, and VISA accepted. Private party facilities 20 to 150. Total employment: 25. Corporate name: Horse Parlor, Inc.

DA VINCI....2514 L St., NW, Washington, D.C., 20037. (202) 965-2209. Cuisine: Italian. Open Monday through Friday for lunch; 7 days for dinner; Closed Sunday during the summer. Credit cards: AE, CB, DC, MC. Reservations: Required.

DOMINIQUE'S....1900 Pennsylvania Ave., NW, Washington, D.C., 20006. (202) 452-1126. Cuisine: French. Open Monday through Friday for lunch; Monday through Saturday for dinner; After-theatre menu from 10:30 to midnight Monday through Saturday; Closed Sunday. Credit cards: All major. Reservations: Required.

DUPONT GARDEN RESTAURANT....1333 New Hampshire Ave., NW, Washington, D.C., 20036. (202) 296-6500. Cuisine: Chinese. Owner: Raymond Wong, Toleung Pon, and Tommy K. Liu. Open 7 days for lunch and dinner. Credit cards: AE, MC, VISA. Private party facilities: Up to 200. Annual sales: $500,000 to $1 million. Total employment: 30. Corporate name: 888, Inc.

EL BODEGON SPANISH RESTAURANT....1637 R St., NW, Washington, D.C., 20009. (202) 667-1710. Cuisine: Spanish. Owner: Jose Lopez-Guerra, Ebe Martinez-Vidal, Malisa Tripodi. Open for lunch Monday to Friday; for dinner Monday to Saturday. Credit cards: All major. Private party facilities: 20 to 40. Annual sales: $250,000 to $500,000. Total employment: 20. Corporate name: El Bodegon, Inc.

EL CARIBE....3288 M St., NW, Washington, D.C., 20007. (202) 338-3121. Cuisine: Latin American. Open 7 days for lunch and dinner. Credit cards: All major. Reservations: Suggested.

EL CARIBE....1828 Columbia Rd., NW, Washington, D.C., 20009. (202) 234-6969. Cuisine: Latin American. Open 7 days for lunch and dinner. Credit cards: All major. Reservations: Suggested.

EL DORADO....1832 Columbia Rd., NW, Washington, D.C., 20009. (202) 232-0333. Cuisine: Latin American. Open 7 days for lunch and dinner. Credit cards: All major. Reservations: Suggested, required on weekends.

EL TIO PEPE....2809 M St., NW, Washington, D.C., 20007. (202) 337-0730. Cuisine: Spanish. Open Monday through Friday for lunch; Monday through Saturday for dinner; Closed Sunday. Credit cards: AE, DC, MC, VISA. Reservations: Suggested, required on weekends.

ENRIQUETA'S....2811 M St., NW, Washington, D.C., 20007. (202) 338-7772. Open 7 days for lunch and dinner; Sunday brunch. Credit cards: AE, DC, MC, VISA. Reservations: Suggested for parties of four or more.

F. SCOTT'S....1232 36th St., NW, Washington, D.C., 20007. (202) 965-1789. Cuisine: Continental. Owner: Peter J. McCooey. Credit cards: All major. Corporate name: 1789, Inc.

FIO'S RESTAURANT....3636 16 St., NW, Washington, D.C., 20010. (202) 667-3040. Cuisine: Italian. Owner: Fiorenzo E. Vasaio. Open Tuesday through Sunday. Credit cards: All major. Private party facilities: 10 to 40.

THE FISHERY....5511 Connecticut Ave.,NW, Washington, D.C., 20015. (202) 363-2144. Cuisine: Seafood. Open Monday through Saturday for lunch; 7 days for dinner. Credit cards: AE, MC, VISA. No reservations.

FLORIDA AVENUE GRILL....1100 Florida Ave., NW, Washington, D.C., 20009. (202) 265-1586. Cuisine: American/Southern. Open Monday through Saturday for breakfast, lunch, and dinner. No credit cards. No reservations. No alcoholic beverages.

FOGGY BOTTOM CAFE....924 25th St., NW, Washington, D.C., 20037 (202) 338-8707. Cuisine: American. Open 7 days for breakfast and dinner; Monday through Friday for lunch. Credit cards: All major. Reservations: Required pre-theater, suggested at other times.

GANGPLANK RESTAURANT....600 Water St., SW, Washington, D.C., 10014. (202) 554-5000. Cuisine: Seafood. Owner: Thomas C. Rowan & Patricia Y. Byrne. Open 7 days. Credit cards: AE, MC, VISA. Private party facilities: 30 to 100 persons. Annual sales: $1 million to $3 million. Total employment: 75. Corporate name: Gangplank, Inc.

GARDEN TERACE.... Four Seasons Hotel, 2800 Pennsylvania Ave., NW, Washington, D.C., 20007. (202) 342-0444. Cuisine: French. Open 7 days for lunch and dinner. Credit cards: All major. No reservations.

GEPPETTO....2917 M St., NW, Washington, D.C., 20007. (202) 333-2602. Cuisine: Italian. Owner: Charles M. Lenkin. Open 7 days for lunch and dinner. Credit cards: All major. Annual sales: $500,000 to $1 million. Total employment: 27. Corporate name: Number One Son, Inc.

GERMAINE'S ASIAN CUISINE....2400 Wisconsin Ave., NW, Washington, D.C., 20007. (202) 965-1185. Cuisine: Pan-Asian. Owner: Dick & Germaine Swanson. Open 7 days for dinner, Monday to Friday for lunch. Credit cards: All major. Total employment: 35. Corporate name: Germaine Inc.

THE GOLDEN OX....1615 L St., NW, Washington, D.C., 20036. (202) 347-0010. Cuisine: Steak. Credit cards: AE, DC, MC, VISA.

GOLDEN PALACE....726 7th St., NW, Washington, D.C., 20001. (202) 783-1225. Cuisine: Chinese. Open 7 days for lunch and dinner; Saturday and Sunday brunch. Credit cards: AE, DC, MC, VISA. Reservations: Suggested for parties of four or more.

HARVEY'S....1001 18th St., NW, Washington, D.C., 20036. (202) 833-1858. Cuisine: Seafood. Open Monday through Friday for lunch; 7 days for dinner; Closed Sunday during the summer. Credit cards: All major. Reservations: Required for seatings at noon and 1:30 PM; suggested otherwise.

IL GIARDINO....1110 21st St., NW, Washington, D.C.,20036. (202) 223-4555. Cuisine: Italian. Open Monday through Friday for lunch; Monday through Saturday for dinner; Closed Sunday. Credit cards: All major. Reservations: Required. Free parking.

IL NIDO....4712 Wisconsin Ave., NW, Washington, D.C., 20016. (202) 363-2672. Cuisine: Italian. Open Monday through Friday for lunch; 7 days for dinner. Credit cards: AE, CB, MC, VISA. Reservations: Suggested.

INTRIGUE....824 New Hampshire Ave., NW, Washington, D.C., 20037. (202) 333-2266. Cuisine: Continental. Open Monday through Friday for lunch; Monday through Saturday for dinner; Closed Sunday. Credit cards: AE, DC, MC, VISA. Reservations: Suggestd. Free valet parking.

IRON GATE INN....1734 N St., NW, Washington, D.C., 20036. (202) 737-1370. Cuisine: Middle Eastern. Open 7 days for lunch and dinner Credit cards: AE, DC, MC, VISA. Reservations: Required for dinner.

"JACQUELINE'S RESTAURANT"....1990 M St., NW, Washington, D.C., 20006. (202) 785-8877. Cuisine: French. Owner: Ms. Jacqueline Rodier. Open Monday through Friday for lunch; Monday through Saturday for dinner; Closed Sunday. Credit cards: All major. Private party facilities: Up to 55. Total employment: 35. Corporate name: Bonfood's, Inc.

JAPAN INN....1715 Wisconsin Ave., NW, Washington, D.C., 20007. (202) 337-3400. Cuisine: Japanese. Owner: Mr. Kokei Yoshimoto. Open Monday through Friday for lunch; Monday through Saturday for dinner; Closed Sunday.Credit cards: All major. Private party facilities: 8 to 60. Annual sales: $500,000 to $1 million. Total employment: 25. Corporate name: Japan Inn, Inc.

JEAN-LOUIS....2626 Virginia Ave., NW, Washington, D.C., 20037. (202) 337-7750. Cuisine: French. Open Monday through Saturday for dinner only; Closed Sunday. Credit cards: All major. Reservations: Required.

JEAN-PIERRE RESTAURANT....1835 K St. NW, Washington, D.C., 20006. (202) 466-2022. Worth saving up to go here for a memorable French meal. Service irreproachable; setting attractive; food and wine delicious. A conference with owner Jean-Michel Farret is essential if you are to experience the full range of kitchen talents. Specialties include: Chateaubriand with Roquefort sauce, sole *Meuniere,* veal kidneys *bernaise.* Open 6 days for lunch and dinner; Closed Sunday. Priced expensive. Reservations are a must. Accepting all major credit cards. Annual sales: $1 million to $3 million. Total employment: 32. Corporate name: Jean's Inc.

JOCKEY CLUB....2100 Massachusetts Ave., NW, Washington, D.C., 20008. (202) 659-8000. Cuisine: French. Open daily for lunch and dinner. Credit cards: All major. Reservations: Required. Free valet parking.

JOE AND MO'S....1211 Connecticut Ave., NW, Washington, D.C., 20036. (202) 659-1211. Cuisine: Steakhouse. Open Monday through Friday for lunch; Monday through Saturday for dinner; Closed Sunday. Credit cards: All major. Reservations: Suggested. Free valet parking for dinner.

KHYBER PASS AFGHAN RESTAURANT....2309 Calvert St., NW, Washington, D.C., 20008. (202) 234-4632. Cuisine: Afghani. Owner: Tabibi. Credit cards: AE, MC, VISA. Annual sales: $250,000 to $500,000.

KNICKERBOCKER GRILL....539 Eighth St., SE, Washington, D.C., 20003. (202) 546-7766. Cuisine: American/Greek. Owner: George Eliades; Geo Hindall; Dan O'Leary. Open Sunday through Friday for lunch; 7 days for dinner; Saturday, dinner only. Credit cards: All major. Private party facilities: 6 to 66. Annual sales: $500,000 to $1 million. Total employment: 18. Corporate name: Ciz, Inc.

KRAMERBOOKS & AFTERWORDS....1517 Connecticut Ave., NW, Washington, D.C., 20036. (202) 387-1462. Cuisine: American. Open 7 days for breakfast, lunch, and dinner. No credit cards. No reservations.

KRAMERBOOKS & AFTERWORDS....1912 I St., NW, Washington, D.C., 20006. (202) 466-3111. Cuisine: American. Open 7 days for breakfast, lunch, and dinner. Credit cards: AE, MC, VISA. No reservations.

LA BRASSERIE....239 Massachusetts Ave., NE, Washington, D.C., 20002. (202) 546-9154. Cuisine: French. Open 7 days for lunch and dinner. Reservations: Accepted, suggested on weekends.

LA CASITA....723 8th St., SE, Washington, D.C., 20003. (202) 543-9022. Cuisine: Mexican. Open Monday through Friday for lunch; 7 days for dinner; Saturday and Sunday brunch. Credit cards: AE, MC, VISA. Reservations: Accepted.

LA CHAUMIERE....2813 M St., NW, Washington, D.C., 20007 (202) 338-1784. Cuisine: French. Open Monday through Friday for lunch; Monday through Saturday for dinner; Closed Sunday. Credit cards: AE, DC, VISA. Reservations: Suggested.

LA FONDA....1639 R St., NW, Washington, D.C., 20009. (202) 232-6965. Cuisine: Mexican. Open Monday through Friday for lunch; Monday through Saturday for dinner; Closed Sunday. Credit cards: AE, MC, VISA. Reservations: Accepted. Free Parking.

LA FOURCHETTE....2429 18 St., NW, Washington, D.C., 20009. (202) 332-3077. Cuisine: French. Open Monday through Friday for lunch; Monday through Saturday for dinner; Closed Sunday. Credit cards: AE, DC, MC, VISA. Reservations: Suggested on weekends.

LA MAREE....1919 I St., NW, Washington, D.C., 20006. (202) 659-4447. Cuisine: French. Open Monday through Friday for lunch; Monday through Saturday for dinner; Closed Sunday. Credit cards: AE, MC, VISA. Reservations: Suggested.

LA RUCHE....1039 31st St.,NW, Washington, D.C., 20007. (202) 965-2684. Cuisine: French. Open Monday through Saturday for lunch; 7 days for dinner. Credit cards: MC, VISA. No reservations. Beer and wine only.

LE BAGATELLE....2000 K St., NW, Washington, D.C., 20006. (202) 872-8677. Cuisine: French. Owner: Paul Zucconi, Jacques Scarella, Robert Greault. Open Monday to Friday for lunch; Monday to Saturday for dinner. Credit cards: All major. Annual sales: $1 million to $3 million. Total employment: 40. Corporate name: Le Bagatelle, Inc.

LE CELLIER DES MOINES....3107 M St., NW, Washington, D.C., 20007. (202) 338-9225. Open Monday through Friday for lunch; 7 days for dinner; Monday through Saturday for late supper. Credit cards: AE, DC, MC, VISA. Reservations: Accepted.

LE GAULOIS....2133 Pennsylvania Ave., NW, Washington, D.C., 20037. (202) 466-3232. Cuisine: French. Open Monday through Friday for lunch; Monday through Saturday for dinner; Closed Sunday. Credit cards: AE, MC, VISA. Reservations: Required two weeks in advance.

LE LION D'OR....1150 Connecticut Ave., NW, Washington, D.C., 20036. (202) 296-7972. Cuisine: French. Open Monday through Friday for lunch; Monday through Saturday for dinner; Closed Sunday. Credit cards: All major. Reservations: Required. Free parking in garage next door.

LE MANOUCHE....1724 Connecticut Ave., NW, Washington, D.C., 20009. (202) 462-8771. Cuisine: Slavic. Open Monday through Satuday for dinner; Closed Sunday. Credit cards: All major. Reservations: Suggested.

LE PAVILLON....1820 K St., NW, Washington, D.C., 20006. (202) 833-3846. Cuisine: French. Open Monday through Friday for lunch; Monday through Saturday for dinner; Closed Sunday. Credit cards: AE, CB, MC, VISA. Reservations: Suggested. Free valet parking for dinner.

LE PROVENCAL....1234 20th St., NW, Washington, D.C., 20036. (202) 223-2420. Cuisine: French. Open Monday through Saturday for lunch and dinner; Closed Sunday. Credit cards: All major. Reservations: Suggested. Free parking after 6:00 PM.

L'ESCARGOT....3309 Connecticut Ave., NW, Washington, D.C., 20008. (202) 966-7510. Cuisine: French. Open Monday through Saturday for lunch and dinner; Closed Sunday. Credit cards: AE, DC, MC, VISA. Reservations: Suggested.

GEOGRAPHICAL LISTINGS
WASHINGTON, D.C.

WHO'S WHO IN AMERICA'S RESTAURANTS

LE STEAK....3060 M St., NW, Washington, D.C., 20007. (202) 965-1627. Cuisine: French. Open daily for dinner only. Credit cards: AE, DC, MC, VISA. Reservations: Accepted.

MAISON BLANCHE....1725 F St., NW, Washington, D.C., 20006. (202) 842-0070. Cuisine: French. Owner: Tony Greco. Open Monday to Friday for lunch; Monday to Saturday for dinner. Credit cards: All major. Annual sales: $1 million to $3 million. Total employment: 50. Corporate name: 1725 F Street, Inc.

MALABAR....4934 Wisconsin Ave., NW, Washington, D.C., 20016. (202) 363-8900. Cuisine: Indian. Open Monday through Friday for lunch; 7 days for dinner. Credit cards: All major. Reservations: Accepted.

MAMA AYESHA'S CALVERT CAFE....1967 Calvert St., NW, Washington, D.C., 20009. (202) 232-5431. Open daily for lunch and dinner. No credit cards. Reservations: Suggested.

MAMMA DESTA....4840 Georgia Ave., NW, Washington, D.C., 20011. (202) 882-2955. Cuisine: Ethiopian. Open noon til midnight daily. No credit cards. Reservations: Accepted, required for parties over four.

THE MAN IN THE GREEN HAT....301 Massachusetts Ave., NE, Washington, D.C., 20002. (202) 546-5900. Cuisine: American. Open Monday through Friday for lunch; 7 days for dinner; Saturday and Sunday brunch. Credit cards: All major. Reservations: Accepted.

MARKET INN....200 E St., NW, Washington, D.C., 20001. (202) 554-2100. Cuisine: Seafood. Open for lunch, dinner, and late supper 7 days. Credit cards: All major. Reservations: Suggested.

MARSHALL'S WEST END....2525 Pennsylvania Ave., NW, Washington, D.C., 20037. (202) 659-6886. Cuisine: Italian. Open Monday through Saturday for lunch; 7 days for dinner; Sunday brunch. Credit cards: AE, MC, VISA. Reservations: Accepted.

MAXIME....5300 Wisconsin Ave., NW, (in the Mazza Gallery), Washington, D.C., 20015. (202) 244-7666. Cuisine: French. Open Monday through Saturday for lunch and dinner; Sunday brunch only. Credit cards: MC, VISA. Reservations: Suggested. Free parking.

MIKADO....4707 Wisconsin Ave., NW, Washington, D.C., 20016. (202) 244-1740. Cuisine: Japanese. Open Tuesday through Friday for lunch; Tuesday through Sunday for dinner; Closed Monday. No credit cards. Reservations: Accepted on same day only.

MIKE PALM'S....231 Pennsylvania Ave., SE, Washington, D.C., 20003. (202) 543-8337. Cuisine: American. Open 7 days for lunch, dinner, and late supper; Saturday and Sunday brunch. Credit cards: AE, MC, VISA. No reservations.

MONPELIER ROOM....15 & M Sts., NW, Washington, D.C., 20005. (202) 862-1712. Cuisine: Continental. Open Monday through Friday for lunch; 7 days for dinner. Credit cards: AE, CB, MC, VISA. Reservations: Required. Free valet parking.

NAPOLEON'S....2649 Connecticut Ave., NW, Washington, D.C., 20008. (202) 265-8955. Cuisine: French. Open daily for dinner only. Credit cards: All major. Reservations: Suggested, required on weekends.

NATHAN'S....3150 M St., NW, Washington, D.C., 20007. (202) 338-2000. Cuisine: Italian. Open Monday through Saturday for lunch; 7 days for dinner; Sunday brunch. Credit cards: All major. Reservations: Suggested.

NINO'S....1204 20th St., NW, Washington, D.C., 20036. (202) 659-8024. Cuisine: Italian. Open Monday through Friday for lunch; 7 days for dinner. Credit cards: AE, DC, MC, VISA. Reservations: Accepted for parties over eight only.

NORA'S....2132 Florida Ave., NW, Washington, D.C., 20008. (202) 462-5143. Cuisine: American. Open Monday through Friday for lunch; Monday through Saturday for dinner; Closed Sunday. No credit cards. Reservations: Suggested.

OLD EBBITT GRILL....1427 F St., NW, Washington, D.C., 20004. (202) 347-5560. Cuisine: American. Credit cards: AE, MC, VISA.

OLD EUROPE....2434 Wisconsin Ave., NW, Washington, D.C., 20007. (202) 333-7600. Cuisine: German. Open Monday through Saturday for lunch; 7 days for dinner; Sunday dinner from 1:00 PM. Credit cards: All major. Reservations: Suggested. Free valet parking.

OMEGA....1858 Columbia Rd., NW, Washington, D.C., 20009. (202) 462-1732. Cuisine: Latin American. Open 6 days for lunch and dinner; Closed Monday. Credit cards: All major. No reservations.

PALM....1225 19th St. NW, Washington, D.C., 20036. (202) 293-9091. This is the Palm's Washington incarnation and, save for the trendy NW location, it could be the same Palm they have in New York. Authentic down to the caricatures on the wall and the tender delicious aged sirloins on the plate. Make reservations, though, Palm has taken D.C. by storm. Owner: Bruce Bozzi, Walter Ganzi. Open Monday through Friday for lunch; Monday through Saturday for dinner; Closed Sunday. Priced moderate to high. Credit cards: All major. Private party facilities: Available. Corporate name: Just One More Restaurant, Inc.—Palm Restaurant, Inc.

PARU'S INDIAN VEGETARIAN RESTAURANT....2010 S St., NW, Washington, D.C., 20009. (202) 483-5133. Cuisine: Indian. Open Monday through Saturday for lunch and dinner; Closed Sunday. No credit cards. No reservations. No alcoholic beverages.

PAUL YOUNG'S....1120 Connecticut Ave., NW, Washington, D.C., 20036. (202) 331-7000. Cuisine: American/Continental. Credit cards: All major.

PETITTO'S....2653 Connecticut Ave., NW, Washington, D.C., 20008. (202) 667-5350. Cuisine: Italian. Open Monday through Friday for lunch; Monday through Saturday for dinner; Closed Sunday. Credit cards: All major. Reservations: Suggested.

PONTE VECCHIO....2555 M St., NW, Washington, D.C., 20037. (202) 466-3883. Cuisine: Italian. Open Monday through Friday for lunch; Monday through Saturday for dinner; Closed Sunday. Credit cards: All major. Reservations: Suggested. Free valet parking for dinner only.

THE PRIME RIB....2020 K St., NW., Washington, D.C., 20006. (202) 466-8811. Cuisine: American. Credit cards: AE, MC, VISA.

PUBLICK HOUSE....3218 M St., NW, Washington, D.C., 20007. (202) 333-6605. Cuisine: Steakhouse. Open Monday through Saturday for dinner; Sunday for brunch and dinner. Credit cards: AE, MC, VISA. Reservations: Suggested. Free two-hour parking for dinner.

RIVE GAUCHE RESTAURANT....1312 Wisconsin Ave., NW, Washington, D.C. 20007. (202) 333-6440. All the appurtenances of the well-run deluxe French establishment. Founded in the early 1950's, it's a godsend in a confoundedly lean area. Chef-proprietaire Michel Laudier cooks with affection and skill. His rabbit pate with the hazelnuts, baked lobster souffle, are certainly not easily forgotten. Prices are not low, but it is not to be expected. Wine cellar is exceptional. Open 6 days for breakfast, lunch, and dinner; Sunday for brunch and dinner. Reservations are de rigueur. Credit cards: All major. Private party facilities for between 20 and 120. Annual sales: $1 million to $3 million. Total employment: 50. Corporate name: M.L., Inc., T/A Rive Gauche.

ROMEO AND JULIET....2020 K St., NW, Washington, D.C., 20006. (202) 296-7112. Cuisine: Italian. Open Monday through Friday for lunch; Monday through Saturday for dinner; Closed Sunday. Credit cards: AE, DC, MC, VISA. Reservations: Suggested.

ROOF TERRACE....2700 F St., NW, (In the Kennedy Center), Washington, D.C., 20037. (202) 833-8870. Cuisine: Continental. Open daily for lunch and dinner; also daily after-theater menu. Credit cards: AE, DC, MC, VISA. Reservations: Suggested.

SAMURAI SUSHIKO....2309 Wisconsin Ave., NW, Washington, D.C., 20007. (202) 333-4187. Cuisine: Japanese. Open Tuesday through Friday for lunch; Tuesday through Sunday for dinner; Closed Monday. No credit cards. Reservations: Suggested.

SANS SOUCI....726 17th St., NW, Washington, D.C., 20006. (202) 298-7424. Cuisine: French. Open Monday through Friday for lunch; Monday through Saturday for dinner; Closed Sunday. Credit cards: All major. Reservations: Required. Free parking lot.

SERBIAN CROWN....4529 Wisconsin Ave., NW, Washington, D.C., 20016. (202) 966-6787. Cuisine: Slavic. Open 7 days for dinner only. Credit cards: All major. Reservations: Suggested. Free parking.

1789....1226 36th St., NW, Washington, D.C., 20007. (202) 965-1789. Cuisine: Continental. Open Monday through Saturday for dinner and after-theater supper; Closed Sunday. Credit cards: All major. Reservations: Suggested. Free valet parking.

STAR OF INDIA....2100 Connecticut Ave., NW, Washington, D.C., 20008. (202) 232-7130. Cuisine: Indian. Open Monday through Friday for lunch; 7 days for dinner. Credit cards: All major. Reservations: Suggested.

SZECHUAN....615 I St., NW, Washington, D.C., 20001. (202) 393-0131. Cuisine: Chinese. Open Monday through Friday for lunch; 7 days for dinner; Saturday and Sunday brunch. Credit cards: AE, VISA. Reservations: Accepted for parties of four or more only.

SZECHUAN EAST....1805 H St., NW, Washington, D.C., 20006. (202) 396-3588. Cuisine: Chinese. Open Monday through Saturday for lunch and dinner; Closed Sunday. Credit cards: AE, DC, MC, VISA. Reservations: Suggested.

234

TANDOOR....3316 M St. NW, Washington, D.C., 20007. (202) 333-3376. This is a tastefully decorated authentic Norther-Indian place which has been currying along since 1975. Meals can be a mild Tandoor dish or a fleet of them. If you're out to gather "memories that bless and burn," try the chicken Anarkali (curried chicken, full strength). As fire extinguishers there are home made ice cream desserts with almonds and pistachio, Indian tea and beer, or cocktails. Specialties include: Filet of lamb tandoor, shrimp *biriani, gosht vindalu* (spicy curried lamb stew). Owner: Jagdish (Jack) Katyal. Open 7 days for lunch and dinner. Moderately priced. Reservations: Accepted. Credit cards: All major. Annual sales: $250,000 to $500,000. Total employment: 9. Corporate name: Tandoor, Inc.

TAVERNA THE GREEK ISLANDS....307 Pennsylvania Ave., SE, Washington, D.C., 20003. (202) 547-8360. Cuisine: Middle Eastern (Greek). Open Monday through Saturday for lunch; 7 days for dinner. Credit cards: AE, VISA. Reservations: Suggested.

TED LIU'S RESTAURANT....1120 20th St. NW, Washington, D.C., 20036. (301) 223-5160. Highlighting Szechuan and Hunan cuisine, Ted Lui's is a thing of beauty—serene, harmonious, breathtaking in its decor and design. Attentive service combined with the atmosphere free the mind and taste buds, that they may fully appreciate the culinary artistry of the chef's celestial mixture of lobster, beef, chicken, duck, almonds, chestnuts, pork, mushrooms, and pea pods. Specialties include: Hunan beef, *Yuan Yang* lobster, Szechuan shredded chicken, and shredded pork with Nanking sauce. Owner: Ted Liu, Hung Kai Liu. Open 7 days for lunch and dinner. Price: Moderate. Reservations: Accepted. Credit cards: All major. Private party facilities: Up to 50. Annual sales: $250,000 to $500,000. Total employment: 20. Corporate name: Ted Liu's Szechuan Garden, Inc.

THAI ROOM....5037 Connecticut Ave., NW, Washington, D.C., 20008. (202) 244-5933. Cuisine: Thai. Credit cards: DC, MC, VISA.

THAI ROOM....527 13th St., NW, Washington, D.C., 20004. (202) 638-2444. Cuisine: Thai. Open Monday through Friday for lunch; Monday through Saturday for dinner; Closed Sunday. Credit cards: AE, DC, MC, VISA. Reservations: Suggested.

TIBERIO....1915 K St., NE, Washington, D.C., 20006. (202) 542-1915. Cuisine: Italian. Open Monday through Friday for lunch; Monday through Saturday for dinner; Closed Sunday. Credit cards: All major. Reservations: Suggested. Free valet parking for dinner.

TIMBERLAKES....1726 Connecticut Ave., NW, Washington, D.C., 20009. (202) 483-2266. Cuisine American. Open Monday through Friday for lunch; 7 days for dinner; Saturday and Sunday brunch. Credit cards: AE, MC, VISA. No reservations.

THE TOMBS....1226 36th St., NW, Washington, D.C., 20007. (202) 965-1789. Cuisine: Continental. Owner: Richard J. McCooey. Open every day. Credit cards: All major. Corporate name: 1789, Inc.

TORREMOLINOS....2014 P St., NW, Washington, D.C., 20036. (202) 659-4382. Cuisine: Spanish. Open Monday through Friday for lunch; Monday through Saturday for dinner; Closed Sunday. Credit cards: AE, MC, VISA. Reservations: Suggested.

TRADER VIC'S....16th & K Sts., NW, (In the Capitol Hilton), Washington, D.C., 20006. (202) 347-7100. Open Monday through Friday for lunch; 7 days for dinner. Credit cards: All major. Reservations: Suggested.

TRATTU....1823 Jefferson Pl., NW, Washington, D.C., 20036. (202) 466-4570. Cuisine: Italian. Open Monday through Friday for lunch; Monday through Saturday for dinner; Closed Sunday. Credit cards: All major. Reservations: Suggested for dinner.

TRUDIE BALL'S EMPRESS RESTAURANT....1018 Vermont Ave., NW, Washington, D.C., 20005. (202) 737-2324. A congenial restaurant which serves Chinese dishes solicitously and tucks up its contented clientele in relaxed surroundings. While owner Peter Ball would be the last person on earth to frustrate your desire for Hunan chicken in hot sauce or any combination of the chef's many Oriental specialties, he will nonetheless encourage you to try his tender beef with steamed crunchy broccoli. Other specialties include: Peking duck, General Tso's hot and spicy chicken, and Peking pork with plum sauce. Open 7 days for lunch and dinner. Moderately priced. Reservations: Accepted. Credit cards: All major. Annual sales: $1 million to $3 million. Total employment: 75. Corporate name: Empress, Inc.

TWIGS....16th & K Sts., NW, (In the Capitol Hilton), Washington, D.C., 20006. (202) 393-1000, Ext. 1621. Cuisine: American. Open 7 days for breakfast, lunch, and dinner; Sunday brunch. Credit cards: All major. Reservations: Accepted.

209½....209½ Pennsylvania Ave., SE, Washington, D.C., 20003. (202) 544-6352. Cuisine: American. Open Monday through Friday for lunch; Monday through Saturday for dinner; Closed Sunday. Credit cards: All major. Reservations: Suggested.

VIETNAM GEORGETOWN....2934 M St., NW, Washington, D.C., 20007. (202) 337-4536. Cuisine: Vietnamese. Credit cards: None.

W.H. BONE....401 M St., SW, Washington, D.C., 20024. (202) 488-7859. Cuisine: American (Southern). Open Monday through Friday for lunch; 7 days for dinner. Credit cards: All major. Reservations: Suggested.

YENCHING PALACE....3524 Connecticut Ave., NW, Washington, D.C., 20008. (202) 362-8200. Open Monday through Saturday for lunch; 7 days for dinner; Sunday brunch. Credit cards: AE, CB, DC, VISA. Reservations: Accepted. Free parking.

Alphabetical Index

*Cross-referencing by name every
restaurant that appears in this publication*

Index

BOBBY RUBINO'S PLACE FOR RIBS, Pompano Beach, FL, American (Ribs), 165
BOBBY'S SEAFOOD AND SPIRITS, Tampa, FL, Creole/Seafood, 166
BOBBY VAN'S, Bridgehampton, NY, Steak/Seafood, 184
BO BO, New York, NY, Chinese, 191
BOCCACCIO, Hicksville, NY, Continental, 188
BODEGA, Miami, FL, American, 161
BOGARTS, Philadelphia, PA, Steak/Seafood/Continental, 220
BOGEY'S WATERFRONT, Miami Beach, FL, American, 163
BOMBAY CUISINE, Hartford, CT, Indian, 148
BOMBAY INDIAN, Ft. Lauderdale, FL, Indian, 157
BOMBAY PALACE, New York, NY, Indian, 191
BON APPETIT, Dunedin, FL, Continental, 157
BON APPETIT, Westport, CT, French, 153
BONDINI'S, New York, NY, Northern-Italian, 191
BONG HWANG CHINESE RESTAURANT Tampa, FL, Chinese, 166
BONJOUR, Philadelphia, PA, French, 220
BON WIT INN, Commack, LI, NY, Seafood/Continental/American, 185
BOODLES, River Edge, NJ, Continental, 181
BOODLE'S, New York, NY, American/Continental, 191
BOODLE'S, Syosset, LI, NY, American, 214
BOODLE'S, Greenwich, CT, American, 147
BOOKBINDER'S 15TH STREET, Philadelphia, PA, American/Seafood, 220
BOOKER'S NEW ENGLAND SEAFOOD HOUSE, Ocean City, NJ, Steak/Seafood, 181
BOOK TEA NOOK, Camden, ME, American, 170
BOONE'S, Portland, ME, Seafood/Steak, 171
BOOTH HOUSE, New Milford, CT, French, 150
BOOTLEGGER, Groton, CT, American, 147
BO SHING, Brookline, MA, Chinese, 176
BOSWELL'S, Buckingham, PA, Gourmet American, 218
BOULDERS, New Preston, CT, Continental, 150
BOURBON STREET, New Haven, CT, American, 150
BOUY 1, Frazer, PA, American, 219
THE BOWDOIN STEAK HOUSE, Brunswick, ME, Steak/Seafood, 169
BOX TREE, New York, NY, French/Continental, 191
BOX TREE, New York, NY, Nouvelle French
BOX TREE, Purdys, NY, French, 213
BRADY'S, Manassas, VA, Continental/American, 229
BRAE LOCH INN, Cazenovia, NY, Scottish-American, 185
BRANDING IRON RESTAURANT, Winthrop, ME, Steak/Seafood, 172
BRASILIA, New York, NY, Brazilian, 191
BRASSERIE, New York, NY, French, 191
THE BRASSERIE, Philadelphia, PA, French brasserie, 220
BRASSERIE, Bennington, VT, Continental/French, 227
BRASSERIE DE PARIS, Miami, FL, French, 161
BRASSERIE SWISS, Ossining, NY, Swiss, 212
THE BRASS RAIL, Stamford, CT, Italian, 152

THE BRASS RAIL, Hoboken, NJ, French-style, 180
BRAUHAUS, Ft. Lauderdale, FL, German, 157
BRAZILIAN COFFEE, New York, NY, Brazilian/Portuguese, 192
THE BRAZILIAN PAVILION, New York, NY, Brazilian and Portuguese, 192
BREAD & COMPANY, Philadelphia, PA Continental, 220
THE BREAD OVEN, Washington, DC, French, 231
BREAKAWAY, Fairfield, CT, American, 146
BREAK NECK LODGE, Cold Spring, NY, Continental, 185
THE BREAKWATER RESTAURANT AND INN, Kennebunkport, ME, American, 170
BRENTWOOD INN, Baltimore, MD, American, 172
BRETT'S, New York, NY, Continental, 192
BREW'S, New York, NY, American, 192
THE BRICK OVEN, Bar Harbor, ME, Continental, 169
BRICK TOWER, Concord, NH, Continental, 177
BRICKYARD, Ft. Lauderdale, FL, American, 157
BRIDGE CAFE, New York, NY, American, 192
BRIGHAM'S OF CHINATOWN, Boston, MA, Ice cream & sandwiches, 174
BRISTOL, New York, NY, American, 192
BRITANNIA SPOON, Yalesville, Ct, American, 154
BRITTANY DU SOIR, New York, NY, French, 192
BROADWAY, White Plains, NY, American, 215
BROADWAY BAY, New York, NY, American/Seafood, 192
BROADWAY JOE'S STEAK HOUSE, New York, NY, Steak House, 192
BROCK'S, New Canaan, CT, American, 149
BROCK'S, West Hartford, CT, American, 153
THE BROKER, Washington, DC, Swiss, 231
BROOK'S, Deerfield Beach, FL, French/Continental, 157
BROTHERS TWO, Miami, FL, American, 161
BROWN BROS, WHARF, Boothbay Harbor, ME, Seafood, 169
BROWN OSPREY, Seaford, LI, NY, American/Continental, 214
BROWN THOMPSON & CO., Hartford, CT, International, 148
THE BROWNSTONE, Hartford, CT, American, 148
BROWNSTONE CAFE, Kisco, NY, continental, 211
BRUCE HO'S FOUR SEAS, New York, NY, Chinese, 192
BRUNNER'S LANDMARK INN, Clinton, NJ, Swiss, 179
BRUNO, New York, NY, Northern Italian, 192
BUBBA'S JAZZ RESTAURANT, Ft. Lauderdale, FL, American, 157
THE BUCCANEER, Sarasota, FL, Seafood/Steak, 166
BUCCIONE'S, Coconut Grove, FL, Italian, 156
BUCHBINDER'S, New York, NY, Continental, 192
BUCHBOARD, Farmington, CT, American, 147
THE BUCKBOARD RESTAURANT, New Milford, CT, Continental, 150

BUFFET DE LA GARE, Hastings-On-Hudson, NY, French, 188
BUGATTI, Atlanta, GA, Italian, 168
BULLY BOY CHOP HOUSE, Congers, NY, English/American, 211
BULL'S BRIDGE INN, Kent, CT, Continental, 149
BULLS HEAD INN, Bridgehampton, LI, NY, Continental, 184
BURLINGTON INN, Burlington, CT, Continental, 145
BUSCH'S CHESAPEAKE INN, Annapolis, MD, Steak/Seafood, 172
BUSCH'S SEAFOOD RESTAURANT, Ocean Ridge, FL, Seafood, 165
BUSHWACKER, Ft. Lauderdale, FL, American, 157

CABANA CARIOCA, New York, NY, Brazilian, 192
THE CABBAGE PATCH, Larchmont, NY, French, 189
CAFE ARGENTEUIL, New York, NY, French, 192
CAFE AT THE MEWS, Provincetown, MA, Continental, 177
CAFE AU LAIT, Princeton, NJ, Traditional and Continental, 181
CAFE BAGATELLE, Greenwich, CT, French, 147
CAFE BUDAPEST, Boston, MA, Hungarian, 174
CAFE CHAUVERON, Miami Beach, FL, French, 163
CAFE DE ARTISTAS, Washington, DC, Latin American, 231
CAFE DE FRANCE, New York, NY, French, 192
CAFE DE GENEVE, Ft. Lauderdale, FL, Swiss, 157
CAFE DE LA PLAGE, Westport, CT, Continental/Seafood, 153
CAFE DE PARIS, Washington, DC, French, 231
CAFE DE PARIS, Tampa, FL, French, 166
CAFE DE PARIS, Baltimore, MD, Mediterranean, 172
CAFE DES ARTISTES, New York, NY, French, 192
CAFE DES ARTISTES, Baltimore, MD, French, 172
CAFE DU BEAUJOLAIS, Ft. Lauderdale, FL, French, 157
CAFE DU BEC FIN, French, 151
CAFE DU PARC, Wantaugh, LI, NY, French, 215
CAFE DU SOIR, New York, NY, French Provincial, 192
CAFE ESPANOL, New York, NY, Spanish, 192
CAFE EUROPA, New York, NY, Continental, 192
CAFE EUROPA, Coconut Grove, FL, French, 156
CAFE 58, New York, NY, French, 192
CAFE FLORIAN, Boston, MA, Continental, 175
CAFE GALLERY, Burlington, NJ, International/French, 179
CAFE GEIGER, New York, NY, German, 16, 192
CAFE GENEVA, Tampa, FL, Swiss, 166
CAFE LAFAYETTE, Madison, CT, French, 149
CAFE LA FONDUTA, New York, NY, Italian, 192

C'EST SI BON RESTAURANT, Boston, MA, Continental, 174

CEYLON INDIA INN, New York, NY, Indian, 193

CHADWICK PARK, Boston, MA, American, 174

CHALET DE LA PAIX, Arlington, VA, French, 228

CHALET GOURMET, Miami, FL, American, 161

CHALET RESTAURANT, Roslyn, LI, NY, Continental, 213

CHALET SUISSE, New York, NY, Swiss, 193

THE CHAMBERS, Westport, CT, Continental, 153

CHAMPAGNE/BEAUJOLAIS, Washington, DC, Continental, 231

CHANNEL BASS, Chincoteague, VA, Continental, 229

CHANNEL BASS, Hatteras, NC, Seafood, 217

CHANTECLEER, East Dorset, VT, French, 227

CHANTERELLE, New York, NY, French, 193

CHANTICLEER, Siasconset, MA, French, 177

CHAPEL MARKETPLACE RESTAURANT, Charleston, SC, French/Continental, 226

CHAPPAQUA FISH HOUSE, Chappaqua, NY, Seafood, 185

CHAR'S, New York, NY, American/Italian, 193

CHARADE, Coral Gables, FL, Continental, 156

CHARDA, Stowe, VT, Hungarian/Austrian, 227

CHARDA, Miami, FL, Hungarian, 161

CHARDAS, Brookline, MA, Hungarian & International, 176

CHARDA'S, Arlington, VA, Hungarian, 228

CHARING CROSS, Washington, DC, Italian, 231

THE CHARLES ON BEACON HILL, Boston, MA, Northern Italian, 174

CHARLES STREET WHARF, Boston, MA, Seafood, 174

CHARLEY O'S, New York, NY, American, 193

CHARLEY'S CLAM BAR, Bellerose, LI, NY, Seafood, 183

CHARLEY'S CRAB, Palm Beach, FL, Seafood, 165

CHARLEY'S EATING & DRINKING SALOON, Braintree, MA, American, 176

CHARLIE'S EATING & DRINKING SALOON, Boston, MA, American, 174

CHART HOUSE, Chester, CT, Continental, 145

CHART HOUSE, New Haven, CT, American, 150

THE CHART HOUSE, Savannah, GA, Steak/Seafood, 169

CHART HOUSE, Boston, MA, American, 174

THE CHART HOUSE, Dobbs Ferry, NY, Seafood, 185

CHATEAU BIANCA, Meriden, CT, Continental, 149

THE CHATEAU, Ardmore, PA, Continental/American, 217

CHATEAU MADRID, New York, NY, Spanish/Continental, 193

CHATEAU PARISIEN, FRENCH GOURMET RESTAURANT, Tampa, FL, French, 166

CHATEAU RESTAURANT, Melville, LI, NY, Continental, 211

CHATEAU RUGGERO, New York, NY, Italian, 193

CHATFIELD'S, New York, NY, Continental, 193

CHAVEZ AT THE ROYAL, Tampa, FL, Continental, 166

THE CHEECHAKO, Damariscotta, ME, Seafood, 170

CHEERS, New York, NY, American, 193

THE CHEESE EATERIE, Ardsley, NY, French, 182

CHEF ANTONIO'S, Mamaroneck, NY, Italian, 190

CHEF HO'S HUNAN MANOR, New York, NY, Chinese, 193

CHEF'S, Buffalo, NY, Italian, 184

CHEF'S, Philadelphia, PA, Eclectic, 220

CHELLO OYSTER HOUSE, Guilford, CT, Seafood, 148

THE CHESAPEAKE, Baltimore, MD, Seafood, 172

CHESAPEAKE CRAB HOUSE, Silver Spring, MD, Seafood, 174

CHESHIRE CHEESE, New York, NY, English, 193

CHESTER'S, Eastchester, NY, American, 186

CHEZ BACH, Branford, CT, Vietnamese, 145

CHEZ BRUCHEZ, Daytona Beach, FL, French, 157

CHEZ CAMILLE, Washington, DC, French, 231

CHEZ GRAND MERE, Washington, DC, French

CHEZ CATHERINE, Westfield, NJ, French, 182

CHEZ EMILE, Key West, FL, Continental, 160

CHEZ FROGGY, Arlington, VA, French, 228

CHEZ MARCEL, Boca Raton, FL, French, 155

CHEZ MARIA, Washington, DC, Vietnamese, 231

CHEZ MAURICE, Coral Gables, FL, French, 156

CHEZ NANCY, Key West, FL, French, 160

CHEZ NAPOLEON, New York, NY, French, 193

CHEZ ODETTE RESTAURANT, New Hope, PA, Continental, 220

CHEZ PATOU, Philadelphia, PA, French, 220

CHEZ PIERRE, Stafford Springs, CT, French, 152

CHEZ PIERRE, Westport, CT, French, 153

CHEZ PIERRE, Edgartown, MA, French, 176

CHEZ RAINER, Brookline, MA, French, 176

CHEZ SERGE, Avon, CT, French, 145

CHEZ VENDOME, Coral Gables, FL, French, 156

CHEZ VOUS, New York, NY, Italian, 193

CHIAPPARELLI'S, Baltimore, MD, Italian, 172

CHICAGO PRIME, Voorhees, NJ, Continental, 182

CHI CHIS, Clearwater, FL, Mexican, 155

CHI CHI'S, Ft. Lauderdale, FL, Continental, 157

CHILLINGSWORTH, Brewster, MA, French

CHINA BOWL RESTAURANT, New York, NY, Chinese, 193

CHINA BULL AND BEAR, Hillsdale, NJ, Chinese/Polynesian, 180

CHINA GARDEN, Bethesda, MD, Cantonese, 173

CHINA GOURMET, Fairfax, VA, Chinese, 229

CHINA INN, Washington, DC, Chinese, 231

CHINA LION, Mamaroneck, NY, Chinese, 190

CHINA MAID, Miami, FL, Cantonese Chinese, 161

CHINA PAVILION, New York, NY, Chinese, 193

CHINA ROYAL, New York, NY, Chinese, 193

CHINA SONG, New York, NY, Chinese, 193

CHINATOWN MONGOLIAN BARBEQUE, Tampa, FL, Mongolian Barbeque, 166

CHINATOWN MONGOLIAN BARBEQUE, Tampa, FL, Mongolian Barbeque, 166

CHINESE DELIGHT, Devon, PA, Chinese, 218

CHINESE PAVILLION, Tampa, FL, Chinese, 166

CHIN YA, New York, NY, Japanese, 193

CHIYO, Philadelphia, PA, Japanese, 220

THE CHOPPING BLOCK, East Lyme, CT, American, 146

CHOPPING BLOCK, Greenwich, CT, American, 147

CHOWDER POT III, Branford, CT, Seafood/American, 145

CHRIST CELLA, New York, NY, Steakhouse, 193

CHRISTIANA CAMPELL'S TAVERN, Williamsburg, VA, American, 230

CHRISTINE LEE'S GASLIGHT, Miami Beach, FL; Szechuan Chinese, 164

CHRISTINE LEE'S NORTHGATE, Ft. Lauderdale, FL, Chinese, 157

CHRISTOPHER RYDER HOUSE, Chathamport, MA, New England/Continental, 176

CHRISTOPHER'S, Pittsburgh, PA, American, 225

CHRISTOPHER'S, Brookfield, CT, American, 145

CHRISTO'S STEAK HOUSE, New York, NY, Steakhouse, 193

CHRISTY'S, Coral Gables, FL, Steakhouse, 156

CHRISTY'S, Myrtle Beach, SC, Seafood, 226

CHRISTY'S SKYLIGHT GARDENS, New York, NY, Continental, 193

CHUAN YANG RESTAURANT, Bay Shore, LI, NY, Chinese, 183

CHUCK'S STEAK HOUSE, Danbury, CT, Steak/Seafood/American, 146

CHUCK'S STEAK HOUSE, Darien, CT, American, 146

CHUCK'S STEAK HOUSE, East Haven, CT, Steak/Seafood/American, 146

CHUCK'S STEAK HOUSE, Farmington, CT, Steak/Seafood/American, 147

CHUCK'S STEAK HOUSE, Mystic, CT, Steak/Seafood/American, 149

CHUCK'S STEAK HOUSE, New London, CT, Steak/Seafood/American, 150

CHUCK'S STEAK HOUSE, Putnam, CT, Steak/Seafood/American, 151

CHUCK'S STEAK HOUSE, Rocky Hill, CT, Steak/Seafood/American, 151

CHUCK'S STEAK HOUSE, Westport, CT, American, 153

CHUCK'S STEAK HOUSE, Ft. Lauderdale, FL, Steak/Seafood/American, 157

CHUCK'S STEAK HOUSE, Tampa, FL, American, 167

CHUCK'S STEAK HOUSE, Bedford, NY, Steakhouse, 183

CHUNG KUO YUAN, New York, NY, Chinese, 193

CHUN HING, Overbrook, PA, Chinese, 220

MARTHA'S, Key West, FL,
Steak/Lobster, 160
MARTY'S, New York, NY,
Steak/Seafood, 201
MARVIN GARDENS RESTAURANT,
Continental, 201
MARYLOU'S, New York, NY, Seafood, 201
MARY'S, New York, NY,
Abruzzi Style Italian, 202
**MARY MAC'S TEA ROOM, Atlanta, GA,
Southern Regional/American, 168**
MASA-SAN, Miami Beach, FL,
Japanese, 164
THE MAST AND RUDDER,
Northeast Harbor, ME,
Continental/"Down East," 171
MASTHEAD, Miami, FL, American, 162
MATTHEW'S, Westport, CT, American, 154
MAUREEN, Philadelphia, PA, French, 222
MAURICE, South Paris, ME, French, 171
MAURICETTE, Bala Cynwyd, PA,
French, 217
MAX'S ALLEGHENY TAVERN,
Pittsburgh, PA, German, 225
MAXIME, Washington, DC, French, 233
MAXL'S RATHSKELLER, White Plains,
NY, German, 216
MAXWELL'S PLUM, New York, NY,
Continental, 201
MAXWELL'S PRIME, Philadelphia, PA,
Steakhouse, 222
MAYA OF JAPAN, Greenwich, CT,
Japanese, 147
MAYFAIR DINER AND DINING ROOM,
Philadelphia, PA, German/American, 222
MAYFLOWER, Philadelphia, PA,
Szechuan Chinese, 222
MAYFLOWER INN, Washington, CT,
American, 152
MAY WAH, Yorktown Heights, NY,
Szechuan/Cantonese, 216
McCARTHY'S FAMOUS STEAK HOUSE,
New York, NY, Steakhouse, 202
McCAULEY'S, Garden City, LI, NY,
American, 187
McCORMICK'S PUB AND RESTAURANT,
Staunton, VA, American, 230
McGOWAN'S OFF BROADWAY,
New York, NY, American, 202
McGRATH'S, Plymouth, MA, Seafood, 177
McKEEN'S RESTAURANT & LOUNGE,
Bethel, ME, American/Italian, 1699
McKINNON'S LOUISIANE, Atlanta, GA,
Creole, 168
McLELLAN'S, North Edgecomb, ME,
Seafood/American, 171
McSORLEY'S OLD ALE HOUSE,
New York, NY, American Rustic, 82, 202
MEATBALLS, New York, NY, Italian, 202
MEAT BROKERS STEAK HOUSE,
New York, NY, Steak/Seafood, 202
MELODY INN, Coral Gables, FL,
Swiss/French, 156
MELTING POT, Tampa, FL, Fondue, 167
MENAGE, Miami, FL,
Continental/American, 162
MENDENHALL INN, Mendenhall, PA,
American/Continental, 219
MERIWETHER'S, Short Hills, NJ,
Steak/Seafood/English Pub, 181
THE MERRY PEDLAR, Floral Park, NY,
Continental, 186
MESON BOTIN, New York, NY,
Spanish, 202
MESON CASTELLANO, White Plains, NY,
Spanish, 216
MESON DON QUIJOTE, Philadelphia, PA,
Spanish, 222

MIAMI RIVER RAW BAR, Miami, FL,
Seafood, 162
MICHAEL'S BACKYARD, Ft. Lauderdale,
FL, Continental, 158
MICHAEL PHILLIPS, New York, NY,
Continental, 202
MICHAEL'S RESTAURANT,
East Hampton, NY,
Continental/Seafood, 186
MICHEL'S, Winchester, VA, French, 230
**MICHAEL'S WATERFRONT
RESTAURANT,** Boston, MA,
Continental/Steak/Seafood, 175
MICKEY'S, New York, NY, Cabaret, 202
THE MIDDLE EAST, Philadelphia, PA,
Middle Eastern, 222
MIDDLE EAST RESTAURANT,
Miami, FL, Arabic, 162
MIDDLE RANCH, Brewster, NY,
Continental, 184
MIDNIGHT SUN, Atlanta, GA,
European, 168
MIDSHIP, Freeport, LI, NY, Seafood, 187
MIKADO, Washington, DC, Japanese, 233
**MIKE GORDON'S SEAFOOD
RESTAURANT,** Miami, FL, Seafood, 162
MIKE PALM'S, Washington, DC,
American, 233
MILDRED PIERCE, New York, NY,
American/Continental, 202
MILESTONE, New York, NY,
American, 202
MILLER'S RED LION, Bangor, ME,
american, 169
MILLERIDGE INN, Hicksville, NY,
American, 188
MILLER'S SEA FOOD CENTER,
Tampa, FL, Seafood, 167
MILLPOND TAVERNE, Northford, CT,
American, 151
THE MILL RACE, Holland, PA,
Steaks/Chops/Seafood, 219
MIMOSA, New York, NY, Continental, 202
MIMOSA, New York, NY, Continental, 202
MINETTA TAVERN, New York, NY,
Italian, 202
MING GARDEN, Elkins Park, PA,
Mandarin/Szechuan Chinese, 218
MING HOY, Patterson, NY, Chinese, 212
MINUET MANOR DINING ROOM,
Altoona, PA, American, 217
MY PI, Hicksville, LI, NY,
Pizza & More, 87, 210
MIRABELLA'S, Tampa, FL, Seafood, 167
MIRACLE WOK, Syosset, LI, NY,
Chinese, 214
MIRAKU, New York, NY, Japanese/
Korean, 202
MISS HEADLY'S WINE BAR,
Philadelphia, PA, American, 222
MITALI RESTAURANT, New York, NY,
Indian, 202
MITCH'S STEAK RANCH, Miami Beach,
FL, American, 164
MITCHEL'S, Philadelphia, PA,
American, 222
MITCHELL'S, New York, NY,
American, 202
MITSUKOSHI, New York, NY,
Japanese, 202
MIYAKO, New York, NY, Japanese, 202
MODERN TIMES CAFE, Cambridge, MA,
American, 176
MOLFETAS, New York, NY, Greek, 201
MOLLY PITCHER INN, Red Bank, NJ,
American/Continental, 181
MOMMA LOMBARDS'S, Holbrook, LI,
NY, Italian, 188
MONA LISA, New York, NY, Italian, 202

MONA TRATTORIA, Croton Falls, NY,
Italian, 185
MONK INN, New York, NY, French, 202
MON PARIS, New York, NY, French, 202
MONPELIER ROOM, Washington, DC,
Continental, 233
MONT D'OR, New York, NY,
French/Italian, 202
MONTE CARLO, Queens Village, NY,
Italian, 213
MONTE CARLO, West Springfield, MA,
Italian/American, 177
MONTE CARLO, Tampa, FL,
Continental, 167
THE MONTE CARLO LIVING ROOM,
Philadelphia, PA, Northern Italian, 222
MONTE ROSA, New York, NY, Italian, 202
MONTEGO BAY, Bethpage, LI, NY,
Italian, 85, 183
MONTE'S, New York, NY, Italian, 202
MONTE'S VENETIAN ROOM,
Brooklyn, NY, Italian, 84, 184
MONTSERRAT, Philadelphia, PA,
American/International, 222
MONT ST. MICHEL, New York, NY,
French, 202
MONTSWEAG FARM, Woolwich, ME,
Steak/Seafood, 172
MONTY TRAINER'S BAYSHORE,
Coconut Grove, FL, Seafood, 156
THE MOORING, Westport, CT,
Seafood, 153
MOORINGS, Freeport, LI, NY,
American/Continental, 187
MOREY'S, Binghamton, NY, American, 184
MOREY'S MARKET, Homestead, FL,
American, 160
MORGAN, Glenville, CT, American, 147
MORGAN'S, Philadelphia, PA,
French/Italian, 222
MORGEN'S, New York, NY,
American/Jewish, 202
MORMANDO, New York, NY,
French/Italian, 85, 202
MORTIMER'S, New York, NY,
American, 202
MOSELEM SPRINGS INN, Fleetwood, PA,
Pennsylvania Dutch/American, 218
MOSHULU, Philadelphia, PA,
Steak/Seafood, 223
MOTHER RHINE, Plantation, FL,
German, 165
THE MOUNTAIN LAUREL, Enfield, CT,
American/Seafood, 146
MOUNTAIN VIEW HOUSE,
Whitefield, NH, American, 178
MOUNTAIN VIEW INN, Norfolk, CT,
Continental, 150
MOVENPICK RESTAURANT,
New York, NY, Continental, 202
MR. CHOW'S, New York, NY, Chinese, 202
MR. FISHBONE'S, Pompano Beach, FL,
Seafood, 165
MR. GREENJEANS, White Plains, NY,
American, 216
MR. GUMPS, Sunrise, FL, American, 166
MR. LAFF'S, Ft. Lauderdale, FL,
American, 158
MR. LEE'S, New York, NY, French, 86, 202
MR. RON'S PUBLICK HOUSE,
Norristown, PA, Italian/American, 220
MRS. J.'s SACRED COW, New York, NY,
Steak, 202
MRS. K'S TOLL HOUSE, Silver Spring,
MD, 174
MUCHMORE'S RESTAURANT,
Bernardston, MA, American, 174
MUG ALE HOUSE, Rye, NY,
American, 213

PEPPINO'S, New Rochelle, NY,
Continental, 211
PEPPINO'S, Somerdale, NJ, Italian, 182
PER BACCO, New York, NY, Italian, 205
PERIGOURDINE, Guttenberg, NJ,
Continental, 180
PESCA, New York, NY, Seafood, 205
PESTO RISTORANTE, New York, NY,
Italian, 205
PETER LUGER STEAK HOUSE,
Brooklyn, NY, Steakhouse, 184
PETER LUGER STEAK HOUSE,
Great Neck, NY, Steakhouse, 187
PETER OTT'S TAVERN & STEAKHOUSE,
Camden, ME, Steak/Seafood, 170
PETER PASTOR'S, White Plains, NY,
American, 216
PETER'S PLUM, Carmel, NY, Italian, 185
PETE'S TAVERN, New York, NY,
American, 205
PETITE AUBERGE, Atlanta, GA,
French, 168
PETITE FLEUR INTERNATIONAL
RESTAURANT, Tampa, FL,
French/Continental, 167
PETITE MARMITE, Palm Beach, FL,
French, 165
PETITTO'S, Washington, DC, Italian, 233
PEWTER MUG, Atlanta, GA,
American, 168
PFEIFFER'S CEDAR TAVERN, Cedars,
PA, German/American/Continental, 218
PHEBE'S PLACE, New York, NY,
American, 205
PHILIP'S, Philadelphia, PA, Italian, 223
PHILIPS CRAB HOUSE, Ocean City, MD,
Seafood, 173
PHILLIPPINE GARDENS, New York, NY,
Phillippino, 205
PHIL'S PLACE, Croton-On-Hudson, NY,
Italian, 185
PHOEBE'S GARDEN CAFE, Syracuse, NY,
French/American, 215
PICCADILLY HEARTH, Miami, FL,
Continental, 163
PICCIOLO'S, Miami Beach, FL, Italian, 164
PICCO LISSIMO, Ft. Lee, NJ, Italian, 180
PICCOLO MONDO, New York, NY,
Northern Italian, 205
PICCOLO PADRE, Philadelphia, PA,
Italian, 223
PICKFORD'S, Coral Gables, FL,
American, 156
PICKWICK'S POST, North Tarrytown,
NY, Italian, 212
PIE IN THE SKY, New York, NY,
French/Charcuterie, 94, 205
THE PIER, South Norwalk, CT,
Seafood, 152
PIERCE'S, 1894, Elmira Heights, NY,
Continental/Chinese, 186
PIER HOUSE, Key West, FL, American, 160
PIERRE, Colchester, VT, French, 227
THE PIER RESTAURANT, Newport, RI,
Steak/Seafood, 226
PIER SIX, Elmsford, NY, Seafood, 186
PIER THREE, Amityville, LI, NY,
Seafood, 182
PIER II, Portsmouth, NH,
Seafood/Steak, 178
PIETRO'S, New York, NY, Italian, 205
PIETRO'S, Miami Beach, FL, Italian, 164
PILLAR HOUSE, Newton, MA,
Continental, 177
PILOT'S GRILL, Bangor, ME,
Steak/Seafood, 169
PIMLICO HOTEL, Baho, MD,
Continental/Chinese, 172

PINE AND BAMBOO, Rockville, MD,
Chinese, 174
PINE GROVE INN, East Patchogue, NY,
German/American, 212
PINES OF ROME, Bethesda, MD,
Italian, 173
PIPPIE'S, Hartford, CT, Italian, 148
PIPPO'S, Philadelphia, PA,
Northern Italian, 223
PIRAEUS, MY LOVE, New York, NY,
Greek, 205
PIRANDELLO, New York, NY, Italian, 205
PIRATE'S HOUSE, Savannah, GA,
Southern/Regional, 169
PITTYPAT'S PORCH, Atlanta, GA,
Southern, 168
P.J. CHARLTON, New York, NY,
American, 205
P.J. CLARKE'S, New York, NY,
American, 205
P.J. MORIARTY, New York, NY,
American, 205
P.K.'S, Larchmont, NY, Italian, 189
THE PLACE FOR STEAK,
North Bay Village, FL,
Steak/American, 164
THE PLANKHOUSE, Orange, CT,
Steak/Seafood, 151
THE PLANKHOUSE, Darien, CT,
Steaks, 146
THE PLANKHOUSE, Danbury, CT,
Steaks, 146
PLANTATION HOUSE, Charlemont, MA,
American/Continental, 176
PLANTATION INN, Raleigh, NC,
American, 217
PLANTATION'S ROOM, Warwick, RI,
Continental/American, 226
PLANTER'S BACK PORCH
RESTAURANT, Murrells Inlet, SC,
American, 226
PLATIA, Stamford, CT, Greek, 152
PLAZA CAFE, New York, NY,
American, 205
PLAZA ESPANA, New York, NY,
Spanish, 205
PLUMBLEY'S OFF THE COMMON,
Amherst, MA, American, 174
PLUMBUSH, Cold Spring, NY,
Continental, 185
THE PLUM ROOM, Ft. Lauderdale, FL,
Continental, 158
PLUMSTEADVILLE INN, Plumsteadville,
PA, American/Continental, 225
POCO LOCO, New Haven, CT,
Mexican, 150
POLETTI'S, New York, NY, Italian, 205
POLONEZ PRESS BOX, New York, NY,
Italian, 205
POLONIA, Buffalo, NY, Polish, 189
POMPOUS BULL, Bridgeport, CT,
Steak/Seafood, 145
PONGSRI THAILAND RESTAURANT,
New York, NY, Thai, 205
PONTE'S, New York, NY,
Italian/Steakhouse, 95, 204
PONTE VECCHIO, Washington, DC,
Italian, 233
POOR RICHARD'S, Waterford, CT,
Continental, 153
POOR RICHARD'S BUTTERY,
Provincetown, MA, Continental, 177
THE PORCH, Miami Beach, FL,
American, 164
PORTAGE, Ft. Lauderdale, FL,
Continental, 158
PORT GALLEY, Portland, ME,
"Maine Seafood," 171

PORTO BELLO, Hempstead, NY,
Italian, 215
PORT O'CALL, Kill Devil Hills, NC
Seafood/Steak, 217
PORT OF CALL, Key West, FL,
Continental, 160
PORT OF CALL, Ft. Lauderdale, FL,
Seafood, 158
PORTOFINO, Greenwich, CT, Italian, 147
PORTOFINO RESTAURANT,
Ft. Lauderdale, Continental, 158
PORTOROZ, New York, NY,
Italian/Yugoslavian/Continental, 96, 204

POSEIDON, Syracuse, NY, Continental, 214
POSSIBLE 20, New York, NY,
American, 205
POST HOUSE, New York, NY,
American, 205
PRIMAVERA, New York, NY,
Italian, 97, 205
PRIME RIB, Baltimore, MD, American, 173
THE PRIME RIB, Washington, DC,
American, 233
PRIME STEAK HOUSE, North Miami, FL,
Steaks, 164
PRIME TIME, New York, NY,
American, 205
PRINCE HAMLET, Miami, FL,
Scandanavian, 163
THE PRINCE & THE PAUPER,
Woodstock, VT, Continental/
French Nouvelle, 228
PROMENADE CAFE, New York, NY,
American, 205
PRONTO, New York, NY, Italian, 98, 205
PRONTO RISTORANTE,
Coconut Grove, FL, Italian, 156
PROVIDENCE PROVISIONS COMPANY,
Providence, RI, Seafood, 226
PRUDENTI'S VICIN-O-MARE,
Long Island City, LI, NY, Italian, 190
PUBLICK HOUSE, Chester, NJ,
American, 179
PUBLICK HOUSE, Washington, DC,
Steakhouse, 233
PUBLICK HOUSE, STURBRIDGE, MA,
Continental, 177
PULCINELLA, New York, NY, Italian, 205
PUMPERNIK'S, Miami, FL,
Deli Specials, 163
PUMPERNIK'S, Miami, FL,
Deli Specials, 163
PUMPERNIK'S, Miami Beach, FL,
Deli Specials, 164*
PUMP HOUSE INN, Canadensis, PA,
Continental, 218
PYRENEES, Philadelphia, PA,
French/Spanish, 99, 223

THE QUEEN'S TABLE, American, 160
QUIET LITTLE TABLE IN THE CORNER,
American/Continental, 205
THE QUILTED GIRAFFE, New York, NY,
Luxurious American, 205
QUINCY'S RESTAURANT, Arlington, VA,
Steak/Seafood/American, 228
QUINTESSENES, Continental, 160
QUON LUCK, New York, NY, Chinese, 205
QUO VADIS, New York, NY,
Italian/French, 205
QUO VADIS, New York, NY,
Italian/French, 205

RACHMANINOFF DISRAELI &
  GLADSTONE, Great Neck, LI, NY,
  Continental, 187
THE RACING CLUB, New York, NY,
  Italian/Steak, 205
RADISHES, New York, NY,
  American/Continental, 205
RAFFAELA'S, New York, NY, Italian, 205
RAGA, New York, NY, Indian, 100, 205
RAFFA'S, Glastonbury, CT, Italian, 147
RAGAMONT INN, Salisbury, CT,
  Swiss/German, 152
RAGS, Bedford Hills, NY, French
RAIMONDO'S RESTAURANT, Coral
  Gables, Northern Italian, 101, 156
THE RAINBOW GRILL, New York, NY,
  French/Italian, 204
RAINBOWS, South Miami, FL,
  French/Seafood, 102, 166
RAINDANCER, Ft. Lauderdale, FL,
  Steakhouse, 158
RAINTREE, Ft. Lauderdale, FL,
  American, 165
RALPH'S AMERICAN CAFE, Coral
  Gables, FL, American, 156
RAMANN'S, East Setauket, LI, NY,
  Continental/American, 186
RAM'S HEAD INN, Absecon, NJ,
  American, 179
RANERI'S, Smithtown, LI, NY, Italian, 214
RAO'S, New York, NY, Italian, 205
RAOUL's, New York, NY, French, 205
RASCAL HOUSE RESTAURANT,
  American/Delicatessen, 164
RASCAL'S ROOST, Philadelphia, PA,
  American, 223
RATHSKELLER, Ft. Lauderdale, FL,
  German, 158
RATNER'S RESTAURANT, New York,
  NY, Fish/Dairy, 205
RAVELLED SLEEVE, New York, NY,
  Continental, 205
RAY'S, Little Neck, NY, Italian, 189
THE READING ROOM, Farmington, CT,
  "Eclectic", 147
RED BARN, Westport, CT, American, 154
RED CABOOSE EAST RESTAURANT,
  Hauppauge, LI, NY, Italian, 188
RED COACH GRILL, Darien, CT,
  American, 146
RED COACH GRILL, West Haven, CT,
  American, 153
RED COACH GRILL, Yonkers, NY,
  American, 216
THE RED DERBY, Ft. Lauderdale, FL,
  Steak, 158
RED FOX, Westhampton Beach, NY,
  Nouvelle, 215
RED HORSE STEAK HOUSE, Hagerstown,
  MD, Steak/Seafood, 173
RED LANTERN INN, Mt. Kisco, NY,
  American, 211
RED LION INN, Stockbridge, MA,
  Continental, 177
RED ROOSTER TAVERN, North Kingston,
  RI, Continental, 226
RED SCHOOLHOUSE RESTAURANT,
  Peekskill, NY, Northern
  Italian/French, 212
RED TAVERN, St. Methuen, MA,
  Continental, 177
RED TULIP, New York, NY,
  Hungarian, 205
THE REEF, Ft. Lauderdale, FL,
  American/Seafood, 158
REEF 'N' BEEF, Peekskill, NY,
  Seafood, 212
REFLECTIONS, Charlotte, NC,
  Continental, 217

REFLECTIONS AT MIAMARINA, Miami,
  FL, Continental, 163
REGENCY ROOM, Williamsburg, VA,
  Continental, 230
REGENCY ROOM, Roanoke, VA,
  Continental/American, 230
REGINE'S, New York, NY, French, 205
REIDY'S, New York, NY,
  Irish/American, 205
REINHARDS, Bayville, LI, NY,
  American, 183
RELUCTANT PANTHER INN, Manchester,
  VT, Continental, 227
RENAISSANCE RESTAURANT, Hopewell,
  NJ, Continental, 180
THE RENAISSANCE RESTAURANT
  Manchester, NH, Steak/Italian/Seafood
  Greek/American, 178
RENE, Great Neck, LI, NY,
  Continental, 187
RENE PUJOL, New York, NY,
  French, 103, 205
THE RESTAURANT, Philadelphia, PA,
  International, 223
RESTAURANT CLUB, New York, NY,
  American, 193
RESTAURANT DU VILLAGE, Chester,
  CT, French, 145
RESTAURANT MAUREEN, Philadelphia,
  PA, French, 223
RESTAURANT RAPHAEL, New York, NY,
  French, 205
RESTAURANT ST. MICHEL, Coral
  Gables, FL, French, 156
REUBEN'S RESTAURANT, East Hartford,
  CT, American, 146
REX, Morehead City, NC,
  Italian/American, 217
RHUMB LINE RESTAURANT, Greenport,
  NY, Seafood/Steak, 187
THE RIB ROOM, Cambridge, MA,
  Continental, 176
RIB ROOM, Hartford, CT, American, 148
RIB ROOM, Key Biscayne, FL,
  American, 160
THE RICE PLANTER'S RESTAURANT,
  Myrtle Beach, SC, American, 227
RICHOUX OF LONDON, New York, NY,
  English, 205
RICHEST'S DOWNTOWN, Pittsburgh, PA,
  Kosher Delicatessen, 225
RICH'S PASTA HOUSE, Mamaroneck, NY,
  Pasta/Steak/Seafood, 190
RICH'S PLACE, Chevy Chase, MD,
  Continental, 173
RICK'S CABARET AT LE BISTRO,
  Philadelphia, PA, International, 223
RICKY'S, Roslyn Heights, LI, NY,
  Italian, 213
RICKY'S CLAM HOUSE, Yonkers, NY,
  Seafood, 216
RIPLEMYER'S CAFE VIENNA,
  Philadelphia, PA,
  Austrian/Greek/Italian, 223
RISING SUN RESTAURANT, Hartford,
  CT, Japanese, 148
RISOLI'S, Harrison, NY, Italian, 187
RISTORANTE ALFREDO, New Brunswick,
  NJ, Italian, 181
RISTORANTE ANGELINA, East Norwich,
  LI, NY, Italian, 186
RISTORANTE DILULLO, Philadelphia,
  PA, Italian, 223
RISTORANTE DOMENICO, New York,
  NY, Italian, 205
RISTORANTE GIAN CARLO, Ft.
  Lauderdale, FL, Italian, 158
RISTORANTE IL GALLO NERO,
  Philadelphia, PA, Italian, 223

RISTORANTE LA BUCA, Philadelphia,
  PA, Italian, 223
RISTORANTE PICCOLA VENEZIA,
  Astoria (Queens), NY, Italian, 183
RISTORANTE ZI'TERESA, Ft. Lauderdale,
  FL, Italian, 158
THE RITZ DINING ROOM, Boston, MA,
  French, 175
RIVE GAUCHE RESTAURANT,
  Washington, DC, French, 104, 233
RIVER CAFE, Brooklyn, NY,
  American, 184
RIVERFRONT RESTAURANT AND
  DINNER THEATRE, Philadelphia, PA,
  International, 223
RIVERSIDE CHINESE RESTAURANT,
  Philadelphia, PA, Chinese, 223
THE RIVERVIEW ROULETTE, Deerfield
  Beach, FL, Regional Plus Western
  Beef, 157
RIVIERA RESTAURANT, Port
  Washington, LI, NY, Italian/Seafood, 213
RIZZO'S, Boca Raton, FL, Italian, 155
ROBATA, New York, NY, Japanese, 206
ROBERT'S, Philadelphia, PA,
  American/Continental, 223
ROBERTO'S, Tuckahoe, NY, Italian, 215
ROCCO'S, Westport, CT, Italian, 154
ROCK GARDEN OF TOKYO, New York,
  NY, Japanese, 206
ROCKING HORSE CAFE, New York, NY,
  International, 206
ROCKY LEE, New York, NY, Italian, 206
ROCK OVENS, Bailey Island, ME,
  Steak/Seafood, 169
RODEO STEAKHOUSE, Miami, FL, South
  American "Churrascaria Gaucho", 163
ROD'S 1890 RANCH HOUSE, Convent
  Station, NJ, American, 179
ROGER SHERMAN INN, New Canaan, CT,
  Continental, 149
ROGER'S ON THE GREEN, Key Biscayne,
  FL, Continental, 160
ROLLANDE ET PIERRE, St. Petersburg,
  FL, French, 166
THE ROMA, Portland, ME, Italian, 171
ROMA RESTAURANT, Tuckahoe, NY,
  Italian, 215
ROMEO AND JULIET, Washington, DC,
  Italian, 233
ROMEO SALTA RESTAURANT, New
  York, NY, Italian, 206
ROOF TERRACE, Washington, DC,
  Continental, 233
ROOFTOP CAFE, Key West, FL,
  American, 160
RORY'S, Darien, CT, American, 146
ROSE, New York, NY, Italian, 206
ROSE AND THISTLE, Huntington Village,
  LI, NY, British, 105, 189
ROSEBAY CAFE, New York, NY,
  French/Continental, 206
ROSSINI'S, New York, NY, Northern
  Italian, 206
ROTISSERIE NORMANDIE, New Haven,
  CT, French, 150
ROUGH RIDERS RESTAURANT, Tampa,
  FL, American/Steak/Seafood, 167
ROUND TABLE, Coral Gables, FL,
  American, 156
ROUND TABLE, Miami, FL,
  American, 163
THE ROUND TABLE, Mineola, LI, NY,
  American, 211
ROYAL'S HEARTHSIDE, Rutland, VT,
  New England, 227
ROYAL ROOST, New York, NY,
  Continental, 206